Canaanite in the Amarna Tablets

Volume 2

Handbook of Oriental Studies
Handbuch der Orientalistik

The Near and Middle East
Der Nahe Und Mittlere Osten

Consulting editor for this volume

T. Muraoka

CANAANITE IN THE AMARNA TABLETS
A Linguistic Analysis of the Mixed Dialect Used
by the Scribes from Canaan

Volume 2

Canaanite in the Amarna Tablets

A Linguistic Analysis of the Mixed Dialect Used by the Scribes from Canaan

Volume 2
Morphosyntactic Analysis of the Verbal System

By
Anson F. Rainey

SBL
Society of Biblical Literature
Atlanta

This edition published under license from Koninklijke Brill NV, Leiden, The Netherlands by the Society of Biblical Literature.

Library of Congress Cataloging-in-Publication Data

Rainey, Anson F., 1930–

Canaanite in the Amarna tablets : a linguistic analysis of the mixed dialect used by scribes from Canaan / by Anson F. Rainey.
v. cm. — (Handbook of Oriental studies ; v. 1)
Originally published: Leiden ; New York : E. J. Brill, 1996.
Includes bibliographical references and index.
Contents: v. 1. Orthography, phonology, morphosyntactic analysis of the pronouns. nouns, numerals — v. 2. Morphosyntactic analysis of the verbal system — v. 3. Morphosyntactic analysis of the particles and adverbs — v. 4. references and index of texts cited.
ISBN 978-1-58983-471-2 (v. 1 : pbk. : alk. paper) — ISBN 978-1-58983-472-9 (v. 2 : pbk. : alk. paper) — ISBN 978-1-58983-473-6 (v. 3 : pbk. : alk. paper) — ISBN 978-1-58983-474-3 (v. 4 : pbk. : alk. paper)
1. Tell el-Amarna tablets. 2 Canaanite language. I. Title.
PJ3887.R35 2010
492'.6—dc22 2010002175

This volume is respectfully dedicated to

Professor W.L. Moran

CONTENTS

Introduction xix

In Search of the Canaanite Verb 1
Pioneer Studies (Pre-WW I) 2
The Interim (Between the Wars) 4
The Breakthrough (Post WW II) 5
Suffix Conjugation 5
Prefix Conjugation 6
Infinitive 8
Recent Developments 8
Modes and Tenses 9
Barth-Ginsberg Law 10
Jerusalem Scribe 10
D Stem Forms 11
Hybrid Forms 13
Concluding Remarks 15

The Akkadian Base Language 17
Mimation 18
Initial Vowels in I[st] Weak Verbs 19
Initial *W* 19
Radical I[st] *W* 19
A › *E* Before *I* 20
Nasalization of Geminated Consonants 21
Š › *L* Before a Dental 21
With The *Š*- of Accusative and Dative Suffixes 23
Assyrianisms 24
3rd Masculine Plural 26
Old Babylonian in Canaan 28
The Late Bronze Jargon in Canaan 31

Prefix Conjugation — Person and Number 33
y- for 3rd Masculine Singular 34
t- for 3rd Feminine Singular 37
t- for 2nd Masculine Singular 39
Ø- for 1st Common Singular 40
t- . . . -*ū*/-*ūna* for 3rd Masculine Plural 43
t- . . . -*ū*/-*ūna* for 2nd Masculine Plural 45
n- for 1st Common Plural 46
Concluding Remarks 47

Prefix Conjugation — G & Gp Stems 49
The Active G Stem 50
Akkadian Forms 50
(w)abālu 50
akālu 51
alāku 51
amāru 51
(w)aṣû 51
dabābu 52
dagālu 52
dâku 52
epēšu 52
ezēbu 52
ḫadû 53
ḫalāqu 53
idû 53
izzuzu 53
kalû 53
kapālu 54
kašādu 54
leqû 54
lamādu 55
leʾû 55
magāru 55
maḫaṣu 55
malāku 55

maqātu 56
mâtu 56
nadānu 56
namāšu 57
naṣāru 57
qabû 58
qâlu 59
qerēbu 59
raʾāmu 59
ṣabātu 59
šaʾālu 59
šakānu 59
šapāru 60
šemû 60
tarāṣu 61
târu 61
The Barth-Ginsberg Law 61
The Ancient Semitic Pattern 62
Hebrew 63
Ugaritic 64
The Amarna Evidence 65
yaqtul 65
yaqtil 67
yiqtal 69
Summary and Conclusions 73
Gp — The Passive of the Basic Stem 75
Attestation 76
(w)arû 76
dâku 76
epēšu 77
leqû 77
maḫāṣu 78
nasāḫu 78
qabû 78
šapāru 78
šemû 79

Diachronic Significance 80
Prefix Conjugation — Gt & Gtn Stems 81
The Scribal Conventions 81
Lexical Gt's from Akkadian 82
Verbs of Motion 82
(w)aṣû 82
elu 83
erēbu 86
ezēbu 87
kašādu 88
Verbs of Repetition 89
qabû 89
šanû 90
Verbs of Reflexive Action 92
šaʾālu 92
šakānu 92
West Semitic Lexical Gt's 93
amāru 93
naṣābu 94
šemû 95
Verbs with no Lexical Gt 98
leqû 98
riāḫu 101
šapāru 101
**šḫḫn* 109
epēšu 111
The Gtn Stem 113
alāku 113
šemû 114

Prefix Conjugation — N Stem 117
Passive of Transitive Verbs 117
apālu 117
kašāšu 117
mašāʾu 118
maḫāṣu 118

paṭāru 119
šaḫāṭu 119
šakānu 119
šemû 120
Reflexive Actions 121
abātu / naʾbutu 121
epēšu / nenpušu 123
malāku 126
naʾarruru 127
nabalkutu 129
namāru 129
našû 130
paṭāru 131
šaqû 132

Prefix Conjugation — D, Dt, Dp 133
Morphological Problems 133
Contamination of G and D Stem Forms 133
G Present-Futures as D Stem 133
Prefix *i*- on D Stem Forms 135
Ambiguous Orthography 136
Geminated Radicals 136
Prefix Vowels 136
Thematic Vowel 137
D Stem Verbs 138
Factitive Verbs 138
bulluṭu 138
buʾʾû 140
dubbubu 146
dubburu 146
**qubbulu* 148
urrudu 148
Causative Verbs 149
ḫulluqu 149
ḫummuṭu 150
kubbudu 150

kullu 151
lamādu, lummudu 151
magāru, mugguru 152
muššuru 152
puḫḫuru 153
ṣeḫēru, ṣuḫḫuru 153
turru 154
wuššuru 157
"Intensive" Verbs 168
kalû, kullû 168
kašādu / kuššudu 168
maḫāṣu, muḫḫuṣu 169
maqātu 169
naʾāṣu 170
naṣāru, nuṣṣuru 171
palāḫu, pulluḫu 172
**raǵāṣu (raḫāṣu)* 173
šaʾālu 174
šâṭu, šuṭṭu 175
ṭarādu, ṭurrudu 176
The Dt Stem 176
The Dp Stem 179

Prefix Conjugation — Š & H Stems 181
Š Stem Causatives 181
erēbu/šūrubu 181
*târu/*šutūru* 182
(w)abālu šūbulu 182
(w)aṣû/šūṣu 183
Š Stem Factitives 183
balāṭu/šubulṭu 183
ḫalāqu/šuḫluqu 184
pašāḫu/šupšuḫu 184
**šḫḫn* 185
Special Lexical Meanings 186
ešēru/šūšuru/šutēšuru 186

ezēbu/šūzubu 188
Canaanite H Stem Forms 190
ḫlq 190
**mwt* 190
**qll* 191
**rym* 192
**yṣʾ* 192
Concluding Remarks 193

Prefix Conjugation — Modes and Tenses 195
The so-called "Subjunctive" 195
Peripheral Dialects 196
The Texts from Canaan 197
The Akkadian Ventive 202
Stock Expressions 202
With Accusative Suffix 203
šapāru 203
wuššuru/muššuru 204
leqû 205
izuzzu 206
turru 210
(w)aṣû 208
Conclusion 211
The Precative 211
Morphology 212
Syntax 214
Conclusion 219

West Semitic Modes and Tenses 221
The Basic Patterns 221
The Indicative Mode 222
Preterite 222
In Main Clauses 222
In Subordinate Clauses 223
Akkadian *iparras* as Ws Preterite 225
Contrast with Imperfect 225

Imperfect ... 227
Terminology ... 227
Present ... 228
Future ... 230
Past Continuous ... 232
Circumstantial ... 234
Energic ... 234
Interrogative Sentences ... 236
Associated with Questions ... 239
Conditional Sentences ... 239
Asseverations ... 241
Argumentative ... 243
Subordinate Clauses ... 244
The Injunctive ... 244
Jussive ... 245
Morphology ... 245
Wish, Request, Command ... 246
Purpose Clauses ... 249
Conditional Sentences ... 252
Complex Sentences ... 254
Volitive ... 254
Terminology ... 254
Morphology ... 255
Wish, Request, Command ... 256
Purpose Clauses ... 257
After a Verb of Fearing ... 260
Conditional Sentences ... 260
Complex Sentences ... 261
Evaluation ... 262
Energic ... 263

The Imperative ... 265
Morphology ... 265
Canaanite ... 265
Akkadian ... 266
Anomalous Forms ... 269

Plural 270
With Pronominal Suffixes 272
Syntagmas 273
Introductory Formulae 273
Blessing 274
Presentation Particle 274
Exhortation 276
Commands 277
Requests 278
Advice 278
Adjurations 278
Apodoses 278
Purpose Clauses 279

Suffix Conjugation — Morphology 281
Person Markers 283
Akkadian First Common Singular 283
Canaanite First Common Singular 284
Second Masculine Singular 287
Third Masculine Singular 287
Third Feminine Singular 288
First Common Plural 289
Second Masculine Plural 290
Third Masculine Plural 290
Third Feminine Plural? 293
Thematic Forms 295
qatal 296
qatil 301
qitil/qetil 306
qatul 306
qittul = *pitrus* 306
naqtal 307
quttul 309
quttil 310
qattul 312
quttal 312

šuqtil 312
hiqtil 315
Summary 316

Suffix Conjugation — Special Hybrids 317
The Preformative Statives 317
išû 317
ibašši 319
izuzzu 321
idû 323
leʾû 328
Other Suffix Conjugation Hybrids 333
Reflexive Stems 333
nenpušu 333
etpušu 338
ḫatû 338
riāḫu 338
Verbs of Motion 339
(w)aṣû 339
elû 339
erēbu 341
Other Verbs 342
epēšu 342
ezēbu 342
raʾāmu 343
Concluding Observations 346

Suffix Conjugation — Syntax 347
Past Tense 348
Transitives 348
Verbs of Motion 349
Statives 350
Present Tense 352
Future Tense 355

Protases 355
Apodoses 358
Purpose Clauses 363
Optative 364
Summary 366

The Infinitive — Morphology 367
Theme Forms 367
G Stem 367
qatāl 367
qitīl/qitāl 375
N Stem 376
D Stem 377
quttul 377
quttal/quttāl 378
qattil 379
Š Stem 380
Št Stem 381
Inflection 381
Dependent 381
Accusative 382
Finite 382

The Infinitive — Morphosyntax 383
As a Finite Verb 383
Past Narrative 384
"As Soon As" 385
Conditional Sentences 386
Paranomastic Usage 389
Direct Object of Another Verb 390
buʾʾû 391
leʾû 393
amāru "to See" 396
ḫummuṭu 396
magāru 397
namguru 397
malāku 397

nadānu 398
qâlu "to Keep Silent" 398
*qu*ʾʾ*û* 398
ṣabû "to Desire" 398
uḫḫuru "to Be Late, to Delay" 399
Attributive 399
The Infinitive — Morphosyntax (Cont.) 401
Expressions of Purpose 401
ana 401
aššum 406
ina 407
ištu 407
Circumstantial 408
Concurrent 408
Prospective 410
ana ūmi/ina ūmi 410
adi 411
Retrospective 412
adi 412
ištu 412
Correspondent 413

INTRODUCTION

The history of research leading up to the present monograph is outlined in Chapter I. It remains to explain something of the logic behind the organization of this volume. In the companion study on the Particles and Adverbs, justification was given for the practice of making extensive quotations from complete contexts in order to illustrate the various usages discussed. The reasons given back in 1984 have not lost their validity. The absence of a comprehensive transcription of all the EA texts means that the reader must still refer to the splendid but outdated edition of Knudtzon (1915) and the small (also obsolete) text collection published by the present author (Rainey 1978b).

Critical evaluations of the project by various scholars led me to the recognition that the linguistic features of the parent language, which was originally a conservative form of Old Babylonian, would have to be isolated and clarified before trying to analyze the peripheral and the specifically Canaanite features. Therefore, Chapter II is devoted to the Akkadian dialect adopted by the Canaanite scribes as their base language. The ensuing chapters then deal with the verbal system of the EA texts from Canaan under four categories: (1) the prefix conjugation (Chapters III - X); (2) the imperative (Chapter XI); (3) the suffix conjugation (Chapters XII - XIV); and (4) the infinitive (Chapters XV - XVII). It was deemed necessary to devote a chapter to each aspect of the respective conjugation pattern and, as could be expected, eight chapters deal with various facets of the prefix conjugation. The suffix conjugation was surveyed in only three chapters and surprisingly, there were enough interesting traits of the use of the infinitive to warrant three chapters as well. The reader will not find the customary numbering of paragraphs so much in vogue today. On the other hand, there are ample cross references between the chapters and subdivisions. Furthermore, vol. 4 contains a separate list of references with all the bibliographical entries and a text index that facilitates comparison between the treatments of individual texts in all the parts of this three volume work.

CHAPTER I

IN SEARCH OF THE CANAANITE VERB

The centennial of the el-Amarna discoveries was celebrated in 1987. At a symposium commemorating the end of the first century of Amarna studies, the course of scholarly progress towards an understanding of the verbal system in these cuneiform documents was reviewed (Rainey 1987c). From the standpoint of language, there is no more distinctive feature of the Amarna letters than their verb forms. It is no wonder that Assyriologists found the texts difficult and frustrating; they represent such a radical departure from the Akkadian norm that many were disposed to call them "barbaric." Today that charge can no longer be sustained, especially for the letters written from the land of Canaan, that is, the Levant south of the Nahr el-Kebîr and ancient Kedesh on the Orontes.

North of that border, it was obvious almost from the beginning that the epistles were composed in a dialect having features not known elsewhere. Later discoveries, such as the Boghazköi, Nuzi and Alalakh archives, demonstrated that northern Mesopotamia, northern Syria and Anatolia had witnessed the development of an Akkadian strongly flavored by the Hurrian language spoken by large segments of the mid-second millennium population there. This Hurrianized Akkadian enjoyed considrable prestige in that area due to the flowering of Hurrian society and the rise of the political state (or empire) of Mitanni. Reference will be made to studies in that dialect below. The present monograph will touch on it only when it is necessary to elucidate some particular synchronic point. Instead, the emphasis here will be on those letters written in the special hybrid dialect, a sort of pidgin, or jargon, or more appropriately, the "interlanguage" (Gianto 1990:11), used by the "school" of scribes who belonged to the geographical (and socio-political) entity known as Canaan.

One of the surprising facts of the Amarna archive is that the dialect in question is limited to a particular geographical area, one that corresponds amazingly with the "Land of Canaan" as defined in the Bible (Num. 34:1-12; Ezek. 47:13-48:29). It is the same geographical area encompassed by the topographical list from Thutmose III's first military campaign (Rainey 1982:336-337).

The most significant contribution of Amarna studies to West Semitic linguistics has been delineation of the verbal system in the texts from Canaan. Since those epistles are written in Akkadian, it has not been easy to discern the exact measure of Canaanite influence. Only a small number of real Canaanite verb forms appear (cf. *infra,* pp. 65-73, concerning the Barth-Ginsberg Law). Nevertheless, there is enough Canaanite "interference" in the Akkadian morphology to reveal a few salient features of the local paradigms and the syntax was markedly un-Akkadian.

One must recognize, however, that when the Amarna letters were first discovered, even the knowledge of standard Akkadian grammar was still at an elementary level among western scholars. Furthermore, the refinements of West Semitic grammar and syntax were still being elucidated by the pillars of our profession, men such as Nöldeke, Barth and others. Therefore, it was difficult to separate the West Semitic factors from true Akkadian in the Amarna letters. It was also easy to confuse the evidence from texts representing various dialects in the Amarna corpus; no one had as yet heard of Hurrian, and its influence on the texts not from Canaan was not properly understood. Therefore, in the Canaanized texts, there were too many opportunities for superficial comparisons with Hebrew.

PIONEER STUDIES (PRE-WW I)

In spite of several useful studies contributed during the last decade of the nineteenth century (e.g. Zimmern 1890a, Knudtzon 1899a, 1899b, 1899c), the fundamental study of the Canaanite verb can be said to begin with the essays of Böhl (1909) and Ebeling (1910). Both these men had had access to the new edition being prepared by J. A. Knudtzon (1915) and for which Ebeling was making the glossary. Subsequently, they were followed by Dhorme (1913, 1914), whose work surpassed them only by its naïve assumptions of Hebrew prototypes in the Amarna letters. But before touching on some of the West Semitic morphology that they emphasized, notice must be taken of a brilliant but neglected essay by D. H. Müller (1906), in which the clausal syntax was shown to be strikingly similar to that of biblical Hebrew. Müller demonstrated, with numerous examples, that the coordinating conjunction, *u*, was functioning in the Amarna letters from Canaan like the Hebrew *wə*-. Only one of his passages will be cited here; it illustrates the coordinating conjunction marking a logical connection between clauses, the second deriving from the first:

> *mi-ia-mi* / ^{LÚ}UR.GI$_{12}$ *u la-a* / *yi-iš-te-mu a-wa-ta*$_5$ / LUGAL EN-*ia*,
> "Who is the dog *that* he would not heed the word of the king, my lord?" (EA 323:17-20; Müller 1906:3-7).

The salient features of the Canaanite verb which Böhl (1909:42-48) and Ebeling (1910:56-58) demonstrated extensively were generally morphological departures from the Akkadian norm. Above all, there were abundant examples of the Suffix Conjugation functioning as in ancient Hebrew but in a manner unlike what was known of Akkadian (cf. *infra*, pp. 347-366). There were many examples of *qatal* in transitive temporal usage, such as *ša-pár*, "he sent" (EA 126:4). The first person forms usually are marked by the *-ti* suffix known from Hebrew rather than the *-āku* of Akkadian, for example, *ša-pár-ti*, "I sent" (EA 126:34). Everyone was struck by the special treatment given to the Prefix Conjugation. Third person forms were characterized by the affixing of consonantal *y*- plus vowel. Scholars recognized that the PI-sign, which served in the older Akkadian dialects for *wa, we, wi, wu,* was used by the Amarna scribes to write *ya, ye, yi, yu* (cf. Gelb 1970:537, 539-540). They also noted that forms having the *i*- prefix, representing 3rd person in Akkadian, served to express 1st singular in these letters. By the same token, they observed that the *t*- prefix frequently occurred with an *i*- vowel rather than the customary *a*- vowel of Akkadian. Unfortunately, they misinterpreted the significance of the *i*- vowel in these instances. It was assumed that the vowel was representative of Canaanite verbal forms and comparisons were made with the biblical *yiqṭōl* / *ʾeqṭōl* pattern (cf. Böhl 1909:54; Ebeling 1910:46-47; also Dhorme 1913:377-381). Only decades later did progress in the study of Hebrew morphology in its historical perspective make it clear that this direct comparison with Hebrew was out of order (for details, cf. below regarding the Barth-Ginsberg Law). For the time being, the works of Böhl and Ebeling remained the standard references for Hebrew scholars seeking illustrations of fourteenth century B.C.E. verbal forms. This led to some serious misconceptions regarding the diachronic development of verbal morphology within the Canaanite family.

THE INTERIM (Between the Wars)

The discovery of ancient Ugaritic with its cuneiform alphabetic texts tended to overshadow the West Semitized Amarna tablets; the decipherment and subsequent analysis of the Ugaritic language engaged the talents of the leading Hebrew scholars. Only rarely was reference made to the Amarna texts for illustrative material. A notable exception to this neglect was the recognition by Herdner (1938) that both Ugaritic and Canaanite had a 3rd m.pl. built on the *taqtulû* /*taqtulûna* pattern. One scholar who was deeply involved in the study of Ugaritic also had the wisdom to take a new look at the Amarna letters from Canaan, viz. W. F. Albright. The fruit of his labors found expression in a series of articles (Albright 1937, 1942a, 1942b, 1943a, 1943b) devoted to individual texts. Albright's notes to these text studies were full of important observations on West Semitic linguistics, some of which are still valid today. His most famous commentary pertained to a "proverbial saying". This "proverb," supposedly almost "pure Canaanite," has only four words that are properly West Semitic: *kî, namlu, tumḫaṣu, tanšuku.*

> . . . *ki-i na-am-lu / tu-um-ḫa-ṣú la-a / ti-ka-pí-lu ù ta-an-šu-ku / qà-ti* LÚ-*lì ša yi-ma-ḫa-aš-ši* ". . . when ants are smitten, they do not just curl up but they bite the hand of the man who has smitten them" (EA 252:16-19; Albright 1943b:3l; cf. *infra*, pp. 65, 78, 148-149).

Albright's own reconstruction of the Canaanite proverb reveals that he assumed a *yiqátal* pattern for Canaanite (Albright 1943b:29, also n. 18 on p. 31). In spite of his many brilliant insights, Albright was far from unlocking the secrets of the verbal system.

THE BREAKTHROUGH (Post WW II)

One of Albright's own students, G. E. Mendenhall (1947b:5-7), took up the question of *yiqátal* in Northwest Semitic and demonstrated that no such verbal form was functioning in either Ugaritic or the Canaanite of the Amarna letters. Mendenhall thus acknowledged that he was confirming the opinion of Ebeling (1910:52) that the Canaanite scribes really did not have a *yiqátal* in their native tongue and often used the Akkadian *iparras* forms as if they were Canaanite D stem. Unfortunately, this doctoral thesis remained unpublished and its conclusions ignored.

It was another student of Albright's who finally solved the real mystery of the Canaanite verbal system. W. L. Moran (1950a) made a syntactical analysis of the Amarna letters from Byblos, choosing that corpus because it consisted of nearly seventy texts, all from one city. The approach was properly syntactic but by that means the functions of the principle morphemes of the verbal system were defined. Moran can truly be credited with discovering the Canaanite verbal system.

SUFFIX CONJUGATION. During the course of his research, Moran found that he had arrived independently at a conclusion reached many decades earlier by J. A. Knudtzon, namely that the suffix conjugation had been developed in Semitic from the non-verbal clause (Knudtzon 1892; Moran 1950a:34-39 and n. 87 on p. 121). Both transitive and stative forms could serve to express past, present or future meaning. The suffix conjugation did not, therefore, express completed action or state as taught by S. R. Driver (1892:13-26; Moran 1950a:34). The full range of tense functions fulfilled by the suffix conjugation was amply illustrated by Moran from the Byblos letters.

Such a wide spectrum of tense functions proves that the suffix conjugation was originally tenseless but that it was adopted to express temporal nuances in accordance with (1) the nature of the respective verb and (2) the syntagma. With stative verbs Moran found a predominance of present tense usages; with transitive verbs there were more past tense examples. Because the latter usage was so standard in the Byblos letters, Moran could rightfully assume that the suffix conjugation had virtually taken over the entire preterite function (Moran 1950a:51). As for the future tense function, nearly all of Moran's examples have the suffix conjugation form in clauses introduced by the conjunction, *u*, being dependent on a preceding clause, either as an apodosis of a conditional sentence or as the consequence of an injunctive. In a later essay (Moran 1961:65) he recognized that this function of the suffix conjugation was a development of its optative nuance as noted earlier in some Ugaritic passages by H. L. Ginsberg (1936:177).

Concerning the morphology of the Suffix Conjugation, Moran noted that in the G stem, there was a tendency to use *qatal* for the transitive verbs and *qatil* for the statives, but this was fairly well understood already. On the other hand, Moran noted carefully the distinction between active and passive with transitive verbs. This was a distinct *qatal* /*qatil* contrast. There is no evidence of a *qutil* passive as in Arabic (Moran 1950a:116-117 n. 70).

PREFIX CONJUGATION. Moran's contributions to the study of the Prefix Conjugation were no less spectacular than for the suffix forms. They placed the entire system of West Semitic verbal nuances on a new footing.

The presence of an imperfect *yaqtulu* (3rd m.pl. *taqtulûna*), which Moran called "the indicative" in accordance with Arabic grammars, confirmed Mendenhall's thesis that there never was a *yiqátal* pattern in West Semitic. The Canaanite *yaqtulu* fulfilled all the functions of the Akkadian *iparras* (Moran 1950a:39-49; 1951). Above all, *yaqtulu* is the standard form for present-future. But it also became clear that *yaqtulu* could express continuous or repeated action in the past. Usually a temporal adverb was employed, thus confirming the past time of the clause and its verbal action.

Although translators had long recognized that many *yaqtul* forms had to be rendered as jussives, they did not try to describe the jussive as a modal conjugation pattern. It was Moran who carefully assembled the evidence to prove that *yaqtul* was clearly distinct from *yaqtulu,* and that it was primarily a jussive in function.

The role of *yaqtul* as preterite was of little consequence in the Byblos letters, though not entirely absent. Moran was led to suspect that those preterites were simply due to Akkadian influence; it remained for subsequent studies to confirm *yaqtul* as an effective tense in Canaanite of this period (cf. below). Alongside the jussive, Moran discovered the volitive *yaqtula,* which functioned like the jussive and may have originally been a more emphatic form (Moran 1950a:89-104; 1960). The Akkadian precative is relatively rare in the Byblos letters but now and then it serves to open a chain of injunctives. In line with his usual practice of following the accepted terminology of Arabic grammar, Moran called the *yaqtula* "subjunctive". He nevertheless classed it as a volitive along with the jussive. He admitted that the formal correspondence with the Akkadian ventive made some examples doubtful.

The energic in these letters had been noted already by Ebeling (1910:69-73). However, he had included all the Imperfect plurals in *-ûna,* not realizing that they represented the West Semitic *yaqtulu* mode. Neither did he draw any comparative conclusions from the observable differences between the Arabic and the EA energics. Moran clarified the distinction between energics and true WS imperfects (1950a:53-56), and identified the one almost certain instance of an injunctive (*yaqtulan*[*n*]*a*) energic:

> *pal-ḫa-ti* LÚ.MEŠ *ḫu-u*[*p-ši-ia*] / *ul ti-ma-ḫa-ṣa-na-*[*ni*], "I fear [my] yeoman [farmers], lest they smite [me]" (EA 77:36-37; Moran 1950a:86, 100-101).

Consequently, Moran had thus far accounted for five prefix patterns: *yaqtulu* "indicative," *yaqtulun*(*n*)*a* "indicative" energic, *yaqtul* jussive, *yaqtula* "subjunctive," and *yaqtulan*(*n*)*a* "subjunctive" energic. He was not yet willing to concede the existence of a West Semitic *yaqtul* preterite because the past tense function was normally filled by the suffix forms. The fact that the suffix forms expressed the past tense (especially single instance) in Phoenician (Segert 1976:191-195, §64.4), as against the prefix forms for future and for continuous past, supported Moran's view. In this respect, Byblos Akkadian was diachronically the precursor of later Phoenician.

INFINITIVE. Of special interest is Moran's identification of the infinitive used as a finite verb (Moran 1950a:57-59; 1950b; 1952; *infra*, pp. 383-388). Its subject may be expressed by a noun or a nominative pronoun. It might indicate a past event but frequently stands in the protasis of a conditional sentence without a conditional particle.

RECENT DEVELOPMENTS

A detailed commentary on the Byblos letters EA 68-96 was written by R. F. Youngblood under the guidance of Moshe Held (Youngblood 1961). It was replete with valuable linguistic observations. However, it remained an unpublished dissertation and, for those few who obtained copies, it did not have an index. Youngblood was aware of Moran's work and utilized it to some extent, but seems not to have realized the far-reaching importance of Moran's conclusions. In any case, Youngblood scored an important "first" in recognizing the Amarna scribes' knowledge of *ibašši* as a stative (von Soden 1952a:102, §78b), so that they conjugated it like the suffix conjugation: *i-ba-ša-ti,* (also *i-ba-aš-ša-ku*), *i-ba-ša-ta, i-ba-ša-at, i-ba-ša-tu-nu, et al.* (Youngblood 1961:120-121, 343; Rainey 1973c:242-261; cf. *infra,* pp. 319-321).

MODES AND TENSES. Böhl and Ebeling wrote their studies long before Assyriologists came to the realization that there was a real tense form in Akkadian marked by the infixed *-t-*. Therefore, the past tense forms with the infix were all classed as Gt. Even after the *iptaras* tense was identified, it did not occur to scholars interested in the Amarna texts to ask themselves how the Canaanite scribes utilized the *t-* forms. As it turns out, they usually employ a form with infixed *-t-* only when there is a particular lexical nuance for the Gt stem, such as with verbs of motion. But on occasion they may simply choose the *-t-* form of a weak verb as their theme form upon which to build their West Semitic conjugation. In such cases there is no special nuance to the infix; the scribes were simply aware that, in the peripheral dialects of the Middle Babylonian/Assyrian period, the *-t-* forms served exactly as their simple preterite counterparts, without any difference in function. The Canaanite scribes also knew the significance of the *-tan-* forms, which they inserted now and then as Akkadianisms in their West Semitized texts (Rainey 1971c). The search for these infixed forms led to an unexpected by-product, namely the proof that outside of Byblos the *yaqtul* preterite was still an active tense conjugation.

Further studies revealed more examples of the *yaqtul* preterite (Rainey 1975a:401-403, 410-411) and, even at Byblos, one could find valid examples. The existence of the *yaqtul* preterite was also accepted by Moran (1975a:149 n. 2). It has now become possible to define the modes and tenses of the Canaanite Prefix Conjugation; there are six patterns in the Prefix Conjugation, divided into two modes with three conjugations in each mode. The patterns of the indicative can legitimately be called "Tenses" (Rainey 1985). The system as a whole and in its constituent parts will be discussed in detail later on (cf. *infra,* pp. 221-264). With the Canaanite pattern thus established, it has also become possible to define its survivals in biblical Hebrew (Rainey 1986, 1988c) and in Ugaritic (Rainey 1987a:397-398). This is the major by-product of research in the Amarna letters from Canaan.

BARTH-GINSBERG LAW. It was after H. L. Ginsberg had demonstrated that Barth's law of thematic vowels in the Hebrew G stem prefix and suffix conjugations was also functional in Ugaritic (Ginsberg 1932-33:382-383; 1939:318-322), that Albright also looked for it in the el-ᶜAmârnah tablets (Albright 1943a:17 n. 60) albeit in his presumed *yiqátal.* So a thorough study of the phenomenon was still needed (Rainey 1978a; cf. *infra,* pp. 61-75).

The forms attested in the syllabic spellings of proper nouns as well as all the glosses and other West Semitic vocables from Ugarit, Alalakh and Amarna have been brought together in a glossary and analyzed grammatically by D. Sivan (1984). In fact his discussion of the verbal forms makes possible a synchronic comparison of the Ugarit and Alalakh materials with the Canaanite evidence from Amarna.

Once the Barth-Ginsberg Law is recognized as valid for Canaanite, it becomes obvious that the forms which so impressed Böhl and Ebeling and the other pioneer students, namely *yi-iš-pu-ur,* are nothing but hybrids. The Akkadian *išpur* has been furnished with a Canaanite consonantal prefix. The *tišpur* forms and the 1st person *Øišpur* are built in the same manner, an Akkadian *išpur* with a Canaanite prefix. There can be no question of comparing these hybrids with the late Hebrew *yišmōr* forms, which have undergone attenuation of the prefix vowel, not in the Amarna period but sometime in the Byzantine age (Rainey 1978:12*-13*). Therefore, we are in a better position to understand the linguistic history of Massoretic Hebrew.

JERUSALEM SCRIBE. It was always obvious that the scribe of the Jerusalem correspondence stood somewhat apart from the authors of the other epistles from Canaan. An analysis of the verbal forms in terms of their semantic function was made by Sh. Nitzan (1973:53-64, 96-98). He noted that the Jerusalem letters use the Prefix Conjugation for past tense but for the present-future they employ the Akkadian *iparras* forms. Only in some direct quotations does the scribe adopt the West Semitic *yaqtulu,* as in the following example where the quotation is introduced by Akkadian *aqabbi* in its function as an expression of repeated action in the past, while the verbs within the direct quote are West Semitic *yaqtulu*'s to express present action:

> *a-qa-bi a-na* LÚMAŠKÍM LUGAL E[N-*ia*] / *am-mi-nim-mi ta-ra-ia-m*[*u*] / LÚ*ḫa-pí-ri ù* LÚ.MEŠ*ḫa-zi*[*-a-nu-ti*] / *ta-za-ia-ru ù ki-na-an-na* / *ú-ša-à-ru i-na pa-ni* LUGAL EN-*ia,* "I repeatedly said to the commissioner of the king, [my l] ord, 'Why do you favor the ᶜ*Apîrû* and hate the city [rulers] so that thus I am being slandered before the king, my lord?'" (EA 286:17-21).

Shortly afterwards, Moran entered the lists again with a masterful analysis of the Jerusalem letters, particularly from the standpoint of the strong Assyrian influence evident in verbal morphology. There is a mixture in these letters of Babylonian and Assyrian forms unknown in the other texts from Canaan (Moran 1975b:153-154). A particularly striking case of Assyrian morphology, lack of contraction and lack of harmonious vowel coloring, is applied to a verb form with the Canaanite Imperfect suffix, *-u:*

> *a-qa-bi ḫal-qa-at-mi* KUR.ḪÁ LUGAL-*r*[*i*] / *la ta-ša-mé-ú a-na ia-a-ši,* "I repeatedly said 'The king's lands are lost (but) you do not listen to me'" (EA 286:49-50).

D STEM FORMS. The publication of an Amarna-type letter from Kâmed el-Lôz provided the correct vocalization of the Prefix Conjugation in the D Passive. In the following excerpts, the first has a seldom recognized D Passive and the second has a typical G Passive:

> *qí-bi ù lu-ú* / *tu-wa-aš-ša-ru-na* / *ú-nu-tu*MEŠ*-šu . . . ù* / *qí-bi ù lu-ú* / *tu-ud-da-nu-n*[*a*], "Speak that his implements may be sent . . .

so speak that they may be given" (KL 72:600:11-13, 20-21; Rainey 1976; Wilhelm 1982:126).

Now it is clear that the old Canaanite D Passive was vocalized like the Arabic, *viz. yuqattal,* rather than like the Hebrew *yᵊquṭṭal,* which is evidently secondary.

In his study of the Gezer Amarna letters, Sh. Izre'el devoted his attention to the form of the active D stem Suffix Conjugation (and also to the Š stem). He demonstrates that it was *quttil,* which almost seems to be a hybrid between Akkadian D Stative, *purrus,* and Hebrew Piel, *qiṭṭēl* (Izre'el 1976:60-64; 1978b:74-78). Besides the ubiquitous *uš-ši-ir-ti, uš-ši-ir-ta, uš-ši-ir, uš-ši-ra-at* forms of *wuššuru,* he could also point to some real Canaanite verb forms, e.g. 3 ms *ḫu-lí-iq* (EA 250:8, 39) and 3 cpl *du-bi-ru* (EA 104:27).

Izre'el's case is considerably strengthened by the documentation of forms for the D stem infinitive. That the usual infinitival form of *wuššuru* in the Byblos letters was *uš-ša-ar* (EA 82:22) had been observed by Youngblood (1961:231), who noted that the theme vowel should be short *ă* because otherwise a Byblian scribe would have written *uš-šu-ur,* which would resemble the later, mainly Assyrian, form of this verb's infinitive (*GAG*:141, §103q; *AHw*:1485).

The proof of the true West Semitic nature of these *quttalu* infinitives was furnished by the multilingual dictionary from Ugarit. There one finds *ḫu-wa-ú* for **ḥuwwayu,* "to give life" (*Ug* 5, 137:II, 17') and *pu-la-ṭu* for **pullaṭu,* "to rescue, deliver" (*Ug* 5, 137:II, 20'; Rainey 1969:108).

Incidentally, Izre'el also concluded that the *šu-ši-ir-ti* type Š forms of the Prefix Conjugation are an indication that the causative stem in Canaanite may have had an original **huqtil* pattern in spite of the one example of *ḫi-iḫ-bi-e* (EA 256:7), which seems to stand for **hiḥbiʾ* or **hiḥbîʾ* (Izre'el 1978b:77 n. 245). One wonders if the theme vowel may not have been lengthened in this latter form because of quiescent aleph, which then might have led to vowel harmony affecting the vowel of first syllable, thus **huḥbiʾ › *huḥbî › *hiḥbî.*

HYBRID FORMS. Today it is possible to define more clearly the process whereby the Canaanite scribes built their pseudo-Akkadian verb forms in conformity with the Canaanite conjugation patterns and syntactic functions. A primary aim of our research has been to isolate those elements which are truly Canaanite from those which are merely "pidgin Akkadian." All told, three linguistic strands have been found woven together in the language of the Amarna texts from Canaan. First of all, there is the Old Babylonian dialect that serves as the stock language. The scribes of Canaan had learned this dialect, probably late in the Middle Bronze Age, and preferred to use it as their Akkadian basis instead of the contemporary Middle Babylonian, which formed the base for the peripheral dialects present in other archives from this period. The scribes from Canaan do know and understand Middle Babylonian and its peripheral extensions, and on occasion they even insert a Middle Babylonian verb form as a sort of gloss, an Akkadianism (e.g. the Gtn *eltenemme,* EA 300:23 and EA 378:26), but they prefer their more archaic brand of Old Babylonian, e.g. with the 3 m.s. independent pronoun *šūt* and verb forms without the *št* › *lt* shift (cf. *eštemû* in EA 300:25). However, their Akkadian base language has undergone some independent developments of its own and the resultant forms are without parallels in either West Semitic or other contemporary peripheral dialects, e.g. the infinitives of I[st] Aleph verbs, *i-pé-šu* (EA 82:46) instead of *e-pé-šu* (EA 179:17) and *i-re-ba* (EA 114:37) instead of *e-re-ba* (EA 98:20). This second linguistic strand can perhaps be defined as "colloquialism." Finally, there is the direct influence of the native West Semitic language(s) spoken by the scribes. Considering the geographical distribution of the West Semitized texts, it is not inappropriate to assume that that West Semitic language was Canaanite. The Canaanite Amarna scribes seldom utilized a purely West Semitic verbal form. There are, of course, many purely West Semitic verb forms in the proper names (cf. Sivan 1978, 1984; Hess 1984, 1993a), but by and large, the scribes preferred hybrid formations. It was their general custom to pick out one Akkadian form from the paradigm of each verb and to ring the changes on it according to the Canaanite modes and tenses. As a result, we have an almost complete set of West Semitic conjugation morphemes attached to Akkadian verb forms. This process was discussed in detail by Izre'el (1978b:78-79) in conjunction with his study of the Gezer letters (also Izre'el 1976:65-67); these verbal base forms will be referred to herein as themes (actually logograms). Those in the Megiddo and Shechem letters and their Canaanite inflections have been tabulated by Rabiner (1981:67-81); the Tyrian forms were analyzed by Finkle (1977:88-110).

Often the scribes would take the present-future Akkadian 3 m.sg. as their theme, e.g. they usually chose *illak* from *alāku* and *ubbal* from *wabālu* even though it seems certain that their native tongue had a thematic *-i-*, **yalik* and **yabil*. Why they did not choose to use *illik* and *ubil* is a mystery. They also preferred the present-future *idaggal* from *dagālu* even though there may have been a real West Semitic verb with a thematic *-u-*. The prefix stative of *bašû*, the present-future *ibašši*, was their theme for the suffix conjugation of the verb, "to be," e.g. *ibaššâti*, "I am," so they also used the present-future as the suffix conjugation theme for some other verbs, viz. *ippušti* from *epēšu* (EA 280:12) and *irrubāti* from *erēbu* (EA 253:21) and the like. (Rainey 1973c:249-250, 258-260). For the verb *leqû*, they normally used the preterite *ilqe* but now and again they followed the practice of other peripheral dialects and borrowed the Past with infixed *-t-*, that is, *ilteqe*. With *šemû*, "to hear," they used the present-future *išemme* now and then, but for the most part they took the preterite *išme*.

In order to give an idea of how the system worked, the following table records selected forms from *šemû*; the theme is in bold type; although references are not furnished, all the forms are documented in the texts (cf. Ebeling 1915:1511-1513; Rainey 1978b:94):

Pret. 1st c.s. *iš-me* = Ø + **išme** + Ø

Imperf. 1st c.s. *iš-mu* = Ø + **išm** + u

Pret./Juss. 3rd m.s. *yi-iš-me* = y + **išme** + Ø

Imperf. 3rd m.s. *yi-iš-mu* = y + **išm** + u

Imperf. 3rd m.pl. *ti-iš-mu-na* = t + **išm** + ûna

Imperf. Pass. 3rd m.pl. *tu-uš-mu-na* = tu + **šm** + ûna

Pret. (sic!) 3rd m.s. *yi-še*$_{20}$*-mé* = y + **išemme** + Ø

Pret. (sic!) 1st c.s. *i-še*$_{20}$*-me* = Ø + **išemme** + Ø

Besides the West Semitic inflectional morphemes applied to many Akkadian verbs, there is also the matter of syntax. It is here that the strongest West Semitic influence is felt. Not only are the hybrids markedly different in outward shape from standard Akkadian forms, but they also appear in non-typical word order and often express semantic nuances which, while corresponding to the standard Akkadian categories, are usually realized in Akkadian by other forms and combinations.

CONCLUDING REMARKS

It should be obvious now that none of the old reference tools for the Amarna letters is an adequate guide for the student today. But thanks to the patient labors of many scholars, especially in the light of Ugaritic, there is a better understanding of West Semitic morphology and syntax. The nature of Akkadian in its relevant dialects (Old Babylonian, Middle Babylonian and Middle Assyrian) is also more clearly defined. It is easier today to sort out the different factors at play in the peculiar "dialect" of the Amarna letters from Canaan. Their unique "encoding" of Canaanite thoughts in Akkadian dress becomes a fascinating object of research. When and where the scribes came to a mutual agreement to write in that particular manner is still a mystery; that they did establish such a consensus, apparently as early as the fifteenth century B.C.E. (Rainey 1977), is a matter of wonder and admiration. The study of how their method was applied is a gold mine for the history of the West Semitic verb. It is also the proper backdrop for a synchronic study of neighboring text groups such as those from Amurru (Izre'el 1985, 1991a) and Egypt (Cochavi-Rainey 1988).

A summary of all the evidence, systematically organized and thoroughly documented, is the object of this present monograph.

The vast majority of verbal forms in the Amarna texts from Canaan are in the prefix conjugation pattern. For that reason, the prefixed verbal forms will receive considerably more attention. First, Chapter III is devoted to the peculiar characteristics of the person, gender, number and modal / tense morphs in this corpus of texts. Because of the special nature of the evidence, it was deemed advisable to treat the prefix forms of the various stems (G, D, Š, N, etc.) in Chapters IV-VIII. The morphosyntactic system for expressing tense and mode, undoubtedly the most important aspects of the entire Canaanized verbal system in these texts, is the subject of Chapters XI-XII. The suffix conjugation, including its morphology (inflection and stems) and syntax, is brought together in Chapters XIII-XIV. The infinitival forms are treated in Chapters XV-XVII.

CHAPTER II

THE AKKADIAN BASE LANGUAGE

Any effort to search out the West Semitic elements in the Amarna letters from Canaan must first attempt to identify and distinguish both the original features of the Akkadian base language and the colloquialisms that developed in the jargon used by the Canaanite scribes. The verbal themes, or stem forms, that they used as the base for building their hybrid verb forms were generally those of the standard Akkadian stems: G, Gt, N, D, Dt, Š. The instances of confusion between G and D stem morphology will be discussed under the latter. But before dealing with the actual hybrid forms, it is necessary to delineate the kind of Akkadian being used. It will be seen that most of the scribes have drawn on a particular linguistic stock of forms representing a dialect of Old Babylonian that, while preserving what appear to be some archaic features, nevertheless, exhibits traits that developed in the later stages of OB (Moran 1987b:27; 1992:xxi-xxii). Distinctive Middle Babylonian developments are surprisingly rare, especially in view of the fact that these scribes were receiving communications from Egypt and elsewhere that were couched in fairly good MB style Akkadian. Assyrian forms are typical of only two sources, Jerusalem and Tyre.

The paleography of the Amarna letters is an important element in the determination of the scribal traditions. The table by Schroeder (1915j:73-94; Moran 1975b:146-150), though based on the Berlin tablets only, gives a fairly clear picture. There is a recognizable script which can be called "southern" and another which can be called "northern." The Jerusalem letters are written in the latter (Moran *loc. cit.*). Knudtzon personally collated nearly all the texts as did Moran and the late Edmund Gordon. A comprehensive work on palaeography alone would require a separate volume, especially if it did justice to the comparative materials from other archives (cf. Moran 1987b:24-26 and especially n. 48; 1992:xix-xxii, n. 49). The raw material for such a study may be available in the notes left by E. Gordon.

Orthographic practices and the syllabary will be dealt with throughout this present volume, but only as they arise in connection with specific verbal forms and spellings. The phonetic features of the peripheral dialects in the MB period, as they are reflected in the cuneiform syllabary, have been treated in depth and breadth by Jucquois (1966). His work has provided the data base for all subsequent studies, such as the present one. The emphasis in this and the subsequent chapters will be on linguistic features, morphological and syntactical.

MIMATION

As in all the post classical dialects (and already in late OB, including Mari, Jucquois 1966:260), mimation was disappearing in the Amarna letters. However, the scribes from Canaan were still aware of it and sporadic instances occur, e.g. *i-ka-ša-da-am* (EA 362:34), *yu-ṣa-am* (EA 362:60). Such ventives will be discussed more thoroughly in the chapter on the modes and tenses (cf. *infra*, pp. 202-211). On occasion, the true 1st c.s. dative pronominal suffix is intended: *li-di-nam-mi* (EA 244:34) but usually the ventive lacks mimation and dative force, as seen in this fifteenth century example from Taanach:

> *at-ta ta-⌜aš⌝-pu-⌜ra⌝ /a-na ia-ši* "You have written to me" (TT:1:8-9; Rainey 1977:43)

The infinitive generally lacks mimation, the exception being *i-re-ši-im* (EA 74:19). The dative pronominal suffixes are also without it: *li-di-na-ku* (EA 87:12). The syllabic signs for closed syllables with final *-m* that served so often to represent the final syllable of forms with mimation, such as *lim, tam* and *tum,* can usually be transcribed without the *-m* (for detailed discussion, cf. Jucquois 1966:260-262). One obvious example is *ni-mu-tu*$_4$ (EA 288:61), where there is no grammatical justification whatever for a final *-m* (Nitzan 1973:62; Moran 1975b:166 n. 78).

INITIAL VOWELS IN Ist WEAK VERBS

While some of the non-WS texts (i.e.. from Mitanni, N. Syria or Amurru) still display the plene writing of initial vowels in finite forms of the IIIrd weak verbs (*GAG*:126, §97c), such spellings are absent from the Canaanized epistles. One may compare Mitannian 3rd m.s. *i-il-la-ak* (EA 19:57) and Amurru *i-il-la-ká-am* (EA 166:30) with *il-la-*⌈*ak*⌉ (EA 230:12); 1st c.s. *e-ep-pu-uš* (EA 19:45) with 1st c.s. *ep-pu-šu* (EA 254:46), 3rd m.pl. *ú-ub-ba-lu* (EA 20:25, 28) with 1st c.s. *ub-ba-lu-šu* (EA 296:39), or 3rd pl. *ú-uṣ-ṣa-ni* (EA 55:13) with 1st c.s. *uṣ-ṣa-am* (EA 88:51). So while that distinctive feature of OB spelling survived in the peripheral dialects of N. Syria, it was rejected by the scribes of Canaan.

INITIAL *W*

Although the initial *w-* of the D imperative and the substantival forms is usually preserved in OB (*GAG*:140, §103i), it was dropped in MB and this is the case in the EA texts from Canaan. Thus, one finds *a-ṣí* (EA 70:23; 71:26; *et passim*), *a-na a-ša-bi* (EA 138:41), and the infinitive (as d.o.) *uš-ša-ar* (on the WS vocalic pattern; EA 82:22; 113:29; 117:44, 59), etc.

RADICAL 1st *W*

The OB verb *wuššuru* is treated in MB as *muššuru* but the Canaanite scribes continue to use the OB forms, thus preserving the intervocalic *-w-*. One glaring exception is the scribe from Jerusalem, who knows the MB paradigm (which is also generally common to the N. Syrian peripheral dialects; Böhl 1909:47 n. 1; Moran 1975b:151). By way of example, one may note the following 1st c.s. forms — from a Canaanite scribe: *ú-wa-še-ru* (EA 255:13); from Mitanni: *ú-maš-šer* (EA 29:150); from Jerusalem: *ú-ma-še-er* (EA 289:35). The Taanach texts contain the more conservative forms, e.g. *tu-wa-še-ru-na* (TT 6:11), putting the date of their use in Canaan back in the fifteenth century B.C.E. Here it would seem that we have a genuine survival of an OB trait. On the other hand, there are a few shortened forms without the first radical: 3rd m.s. *yu-uš-ši-ra* (EA 180:6; 182:8; 269:11, 14; 270:24; 271:18; 279:14); *yu-uš-ši-ir-mi* (EA 280:9); also: 3rd m.s. *yu-ša-ru* (EA 362:10), *yu-ši-ru* (EA 126:22; 131:15; *yu-ši-ra* (EA 104:14; 131:12; 216:15; 281:11, 27; 366:30). Only four Byblos tablets employ the shortened forms. One Rib-Haddi letter written in Beirut has the 3rd m.s. hybrids *yi-iš-ši-ru* (EA 139:34, 36, 38), *yi-iš-ši-ra* (EA 139:30-31). Outside of the verbal forms, note that intervocalic *-w-* appears in WS texts, e.g. *a-wa-tu* (EA 81:23), etc., while the N. Syrian, Mitannian, Tyrian and Jerusalem letters use *a-ma-tu*$_4$ (EA 29:13, 47, 153), etc. The MA spelling, *a-ba-at* (EA 211:10, 19) is a rare exception in a WS text.

A › *E* BEFORE *I*

In MB there is a tendency for short *a* vowels to shift to short *e* when followed by an *i* in the next syllable (Aro 1955:40-49). But the shift is not always carried through, especially in the letters. From the EA archive itself, Aro (1955:41, 43) cites *ú-na-ak-ki-su* (EA 8:36) in contrast to *tu-bi-ʾi-i-ma* (EA 4:15), both from Babylon. In the Mitanni letters, the shift is more prevalent than in the MB letters known to us (Adler 1976:23-24 with many examples), but this is hardly a phenomenon derived from Hurrian as suggested by Adler. With the lone exception of *tu-⸢bi⸣-⸢ʾu*$_5$*⸣-na* (EA 250:10), the shift *a* › *e* before *i* does not occur in the Amarna texts from Canaan. Even the Jerusalem letters, which show so much influence from N. Syria, do not have it; compare the Mitannian *ú-me-eš-še-ru* (EA 29:69), *up-te-eḫ-ḫé-er* (EA 20:47) and *li-me-eš-šir-šu-nu* (EA 17:48) with Jerusalem *ú-ma-še-er* (EA 289:35) and *lu-ma-še-er* (EA 288:58; 289:42) and *i-ḫal-li-iq* (EA 286:37). Mitannian *uk-te-eb-bi-du-ši* (EA 23:21) can be compared with Megiddo *yu-ka-bi-id* (EA 145:39; which, as a gloss, could be a purely Canaanite form). Alashia has *ia-qá-ar-ri-ib* (EA 39:19) without the shift, and examples from all over Canaan may be cited: *ú-da-mì-iq* (EA 120:44; most likely 1st c.s.!), *tu-ga-me-ru-nu* (EA 299:25), *yu-la-mi-dá* (EA 272:23), *yi-ma-lik* (EA 94:12; *et al.*), *i-na-ṣí-ru* (EA 119:15; *et al.*), *ti-⸢pa⸣-⸢ṭì⸣-⸢ir⸣* (EA 299:25). The absence of this typical MB and peripheral shift marks another conservative trait in the Akkadian used by the Canaanite scribes.

NASALIZATION OF GEMINATED CONSONANTS

This shift occurs frequently in MB and throughout the peripheral area, especially with geminated dentals and the verb *nadānu* in particular (*GAG*:32-33, §32; Aro 1955:36; Adler 1976:19; Huehnergard 1979:29-190; Berkooz 1937:45; Wilhelm 1970:24-25). The Egyptian Amarna letters generally have the nasalization; for example: *i-na-an-di-nu-na-ši* (EA 1:68), *a-na-an-din-šu-nu* (EA 1:76), *a-na-an-din-šu-nu-ti* (KL 69:277:8) and also *ú-ma-an-de-*$\check{s}i_x$(ŠE) (EA 1:17), while the Egyptian letters from Hattusas vary from *ta-na-an-di-i[n]* (*KBo* 1 15 + 19: r.15; also *KUB* 3, 27: r.8; 67:11') to *ta-na-ad-di-in* (NBC 3934: 3.1) and *tá-na-di-in* (*KBo* 1 15 +19: r.17). The only Canaanite town where this phenomenon occurs is Tyre (Finkle 1977:94): *i-na-an-din-ni* (EA 154:13), *i-na-an-din-*ni_7 (EA 155:13); and *i-na-an-ṣár* (EA 150:9), *a-na-an-ṣár* (EA 147:61; 151:6; 153:15). On the other hand, from Taanach comes: *a-na-*⸢*din*⸣ (TT 1:10), and from Beirut: *a-na-din-mi* (EA 137:55). A Nuǵassi letter has 3rd m.s. *i-ma-an-gur* (EA 51: r. 13), but from Acco we find 1st c.s. *i-ma-gur* (EA 234:27). By and large, the Canaanite scribes have not acquired this phonetic shift so common to MB and the other peripheral dialects. The Tyrian scribe either learned it from North Syria or perhaps from a N. Syrian teacher with whom he studied in Egypt. The Jerusalem letters have no examples of the present future from *nadānu, naṣāru* or *magāru,* so there is no way to ascertain whether this trait was present in that scribe's dialect or not. Again, the Akkadian used by the scribes of Canaan reflects an older dialect than the contemporary peripheral.

Š › *L* BEFORE A DENTAL

This is, perhaps, the most striking phonetic development from the OB to the MB period (*GAG*:31, §30g). The shift is not uniformly carried out in the MB letters (Aro 1955:37-38). In Nuzi it is still only partially used (Wilhelm 1970:19-21), while at Alalakh it is nearly absent (Giacumakis 1970:29). In Mitanni it is practically universal (Adler 1976:20-22) and in Carchemish and Ugarit it also predominates in the verbal forms (cf. Huehnergard:1979:28, 188-189). The Amarna letters from Egypt reveal a mixture of old and late forms, e.g. *uš-te-bi-la-ku* (EA 367:3) alongside *ul-te-bi-la-ak-ku* (EA 162:61; 369:3). However, in the Amarna letters from Canaan, the (almost) universal rejection of this shift is one of the principal signs of the archaic nature of the Akkadian base language. One may compare the MB imperative, *kul-da* (PBS 1/II, 24:9), with the Byblos *ku-uš-da* (EA 82:52), the MB *-t-* preterite, *ik-ta-al-d*[*a*] (EA 10:37), with Byblos *yi-*[*ik-t*]*a-aš-du-na* (EA 85:61), or Mitannian *el-te-me* (EA 20:10) with Byblos *eš-te-me* (EA 108:24). Other forms in the Canaanite texts where the shift might have been expected are: *yi-iš-ta-al* (EA 280:25), *yi-iš-ta-ka-nu-ni* (EA 125:31), *iš-ta-ni* (EA 125:21; *et al.*), or the many variants of *iš-ta-ḫa-ḫi-in* (EA 298:12) and others. The putative *ú-ul-ta-ša-aš* of EA 82:50 (supported by *CAD* A/2:424b) has been duly discredited by Moran (1987b:264 n. 6; 1992:152-153 n. 6); the other two possible cases which he cites there, viz. EA 92:39 and EA 130:41 are to be read [*iš*]-*t*[*a-p*]*a-ru* and *ul-ta-ma!-*[*n*]*a* "I will antagonize," respectively. Especially noteworthy is the rare Gtn (with WS imperfect suffix), 1st c.s. *iš-te-nem-mu* (EA 261:10), which fills the semantic slot where most Canaanite letters have the West Semitized Gt imperfect, *iš-te-mu* (EA 212:14; *et passim;* Rainey 1971:96-101). Of course, the Gtn is quite foreign to the West Semitic languages (cf. *infra*, pp. 113-116); therefore, none can doubt the intrusiveness of two examples from the common MB/peripheral paradigm of present tense Gtn's with the *št* › *lt* shift: *él-te*$_9$*-né-em-mé* (EA 378:26) and ⸢*él*⸣-⸢*te*$_9$⸣-⸢*né*⸣-*mé* (EA 300:23), especially since the latter form is paralleled by *iš-*[*t*]*e*$_9$*-mu* (EA 300:25) in the same context! The scribes who wrote EA 261, EA 300 and EA 378 all wanted to impress pharaoh with the continuous faithful obedience of the city rulers for whom they were writing. So they chose a universally acknowledged Akkadian stem, the iterative Gtn, to express their meaning. The latter two scribes even went so far as to use the *koine* form from the MB and peripheral dialects which they knew was employed by the Egyptian scribes. Thus, they injected these two Akkadianisms with the *št* › *lt* shift! That these two examples are unique in the corpus of texts from Canaan should be sufficient proof that the basic Akkadian dialect adopted by the Canaanite scribes did not have the *št* › *lt* phenomenon. We see, therefore, another important feature in which the Akkadian of Canaan resembles OB rather than the contemporary "peripheral" dialects being used throughout the Levant and Mesopotamia during the Late Bronze Age (Middle Babylonian period). On the other hand, it is obvious that the Canaanite scribes were aware of this phonetic development in the international correspondence of their age.

WITH THE *Š*- OF ACCUSATIVE AND DATIVE SUFFIXES

The peripheral dialects have usually lost the consonantal assimilation or partial assimilation found in the last radical of Babylonian verb forms in juncture with pronominal suffixes beginning with *š* (*GAG*:30, §30f).

A sibilant or dental + *š* › *ss* in OB and in literary texts. The Amarna archive contained evidence for such shifts in the literary texts found there: *iṣ-ba-si* (= *iṣbassi* ‹ *iṣbat* + *ši;* EA 357:86) and *ú-še-eṣ-bi-is-su* (*ušeṣbissu* ‹ *ušeṣbit* + *šu;* EA 356:37) and *ni-ip-pu-us-su* (= *nippussu* ‹ *nippuš* + *šu* EA 356:60). In MB one finds ⸢*iṣ*⸣-*ṣa-bat-si* (BE 17/I 33:11), evidently for *iṣbassi,* while the shift is entirely ignored at Megiddo, *yi-iṣ-bat-ši* (EA 244:28, 37; Rabiner 1981:55) and at Byblos, *ṣa-bat-ši* (EA 106:12). As for sibilants, the Mitanni texts have numerous examples like *e-ep-pu-us-sú-nu* (EA 29:147; Adler 1976:19), *i-te-ri-is-sí* (EA 29:17) and *i-na-aḫ-ḫi-is-sú-nu* (EA 29:152). But at Tunip, the scribe ignores the shift, *i-te-pu-uš-šu-nu* (EA 59:35), *ni-ir-ri-iš-šu-ni*$_7$ (EA 59:16). At Ugarit (Huehnergard 1989:102-104) one text has *i-ḫu-uz-ši* (RS 16.144:8; Nougayrol 1955:76) and *li-ra-ḫi-iṣ-šu* (*ibid,* lines 9, 13), while another (possibly older?) has [. . *i*]*r-ku-us-sú* (Ug 5, No. 2:5; Nougayrol 1968:3). The only example documented from the Canaanite Amarna letters reveals a different situation altogether: *yi-ma-ḫa-aš-ši* (EA 252:19; Albright 1943b:31 n. 17; Rabiner

1981:55); the *ṣ* has assimilated to the *š*. When the final consonant is *n*, mainly with the verb *nadānu*, OB often showed assimilation to the *š* of the suffix pronoun, e.g. *inaddišši* (CH §146). In MB and the peripheral dialects such an assimilation is virtually unknown: Babylon, [*i*]*d-di-in-ši-na-*⌜*ti*⌝ (EA 2:11); Mitanni, *at-ta-din-ši* (EA 29:23, 28), but note a unique form, *na-dá-a-an-sú-nu-ma* (EA 27:21); Egypt *a-na-an-din-šu-nu* (EA 1:76), Tunip, *li-id-din-šu* (EA 59:17), Alashia *i-din-šu* (EA 35:34), Ugarit *id-din-šu* (RS 15.89:7; Nougayrol 1955:53) and *ta-na-din-šu* (*ibid*, lines 13, 15, 16; Huehnergard 1989:101). So it is not surprising that the texts from Canaan also do not have it: *ya-di-in*$_4$*-ši* (EA 197:29, 30), *ya-di-in*$_4$*-šu-ni* (EA 197:11, 12). This does not mean that their dialect is just another branch of peripheral Akkadian. But it does indicate the distance between this dialect and the Babylonian homeland from which it had migrated westwards. What the Canaanite scribes are using is an attenuated form of Old Babylonian.

ASSYRIANISMS

The two main focal points for Assyrianisms in the texts from Canaan are Jerusalem and Tyre. The Assyrian traits in the Jerusalem letters were analyzed in detail by Moran (1975b:152-154). Moran brings numerous other Assyrian features besides verb forms but only the latter will be discussed here. Moran enumerates the following:

(1) The precative takes the Assyrian form wherever it differs from the Babylonian (10x): 1st c.s. *la-mur-mi* (EA 286:40), *la-mur* (EA 286:46), *le-lu-ub* (EA 286:46; an obvious error for *lērub*, Moran 1975b:164 n. 59; Rainey 1978c:144-145), 3rd m.s. *lu-ṣi-mi* (EA 286:56), *lu-ma-še-er* (EA 288:58; 289:42), *lu-ma-šir*$_9$ (EA 290:20), *lu-ma-še-ra* (EA 285:28; 287:18), *lu-ti-ra* (EA 290:21).

(2) Verbs Ist aleph$_{3-5}$ are consistently Assyrian in form (13x), G present, *te*$_9$*-ep-pa-ša* (EA 287:71), *e-pa-aš* (EA 289:9) and probably *ep-pu-šu* (EA 287:19; with vowel harmony, *eppušū* ‹ *eppašū*, though the script would permit the Babylonian reading, *ip-pu-šu* = *ippušū*), G preterite, *e-pu-šu* (EA 289:12), *e-pu-šu-né*

(EA 290:5), G infinitive, *e-ra-ba* (EA 286:43), *e-za-bi-ša* (EA 287:20), Gt present *e-tel-li* (EA 287:45), Š present, *ú-še-ru-bu* (EA 287:11, vowel harmony), Š imperative, *še-ri-ib* (EA 286:62; 287:67; 288:64).

(3) The Jerusalem scribe apparently uses the Assyrian stative form from *dâku* as the theme for his suffix conjugation forms, namely *d*[*e*$_4$-*k*]*a* (EA 288:41), *de*$_4$-*k*[*a*] (EA 288:45), and *de*$_4$-*ka-ti* (EA 287:73). The use of TE for a syllable with *d* goes back to an ancient syllabary, at least as old as the Isin-Larsa period, that distinguished /di/ from /de/ (Moran 1975b:161 n. 34). Thus the value *de*$_4$ for TE is not a Hurrianism (*contra* Artzi 1968:167).

(4) Third weak verbs have uncontracted forms characteristic of Assyrian, viz. *ta-ša-mé-ú* (EA 286:50), *te-le-qé-ú* (EA 288:38, but with Babylonian vowel harmony!), *li-il-qé-a-ni* (EA 288:59), *ig-ge-ú* (EA 288:44).

The Tyrian letters, which have many features in common with the Jerusalem texts, also present some Assyrian verbal formations (Finkle 1977:88 ff.). The most striking examples are:

(1) I[st] aleph, G present-future, *i-ra-ab* (EA 150:11), and *i-ra-bu* (EA 151:13); the prefix follows the colloquial pattern with *i-*, though the thematic vowel is according to the Assyrian model. Note the colloquial infinitive (with *i-*) in Babylonian style, *i-re-bi* (EA 149:28).

(2) I[st] aleph, G preterite, *ta-aš-me* (EA 151:36). Note the Babylonian form, *iš-me* (EA 147:17, 30, 34, 41; 151:2).

(3) I[st] aleph, G *-t-* preterite, *aš-te-me* (EA 154:5), *aš-te-mu* (EA 149:42), *ta-aš-te-me* (EA 149:56; Finkle 1977:91). Note the Babylonian form, *iš-te-me* (EA 147:45; 153:12)

(4) I[st] aleph, G precative *le-ru-ub* (EA 149:19, 78). Note that *li-ru-ub* with colloquial use of 3rd m.s. for 1st c.s. is also possible—the next clause has *li-mur* (EA 149:20, 78).

(5) I[st] aleph, Gtn preterite (?), *i-ta-zi-ib* (EA 149:50). The context calls for past tense, with an emphasis on the long term (Abimilki has had to stay away from his seaboard town of Usu for an extended period of time). The Assyrian *t-* preterite of the G stem or the preterite of the Gt would be *ētizib* (cf. Hecker 1968:149, §90a) or *ētezib* (Mayer 1971:68). If the spelling *i-ta-zi-ib* reflects the scribe's knowledge of the paradigm, then the *a* vowel

would only be preserved before geminated *z;* thus, *ītazzib* (‹ **ītanzib*).

Moran (1975b:164 n. 58) has noted the Assyrian Š imperatives, namely *še-zi-ba-an-[ni]* (EA 381:14) and also *še-zi-bá-an-na-ši-mi* (EA 62:30), but with the reservation that they may be merely the result of misunderstanding the Babylonian form. The scribes may have thought that one could form the imperative simply by removing the prefix from *tušēzib.* Another superficially Assyrian form, *i-pa-aš* (EA 196:32, 41) is certainly a Canaanite adaptation to represent the WS transitive suffix conjugation 3rd m.s. The Assyrian form would have to be *eppaš,* 3rd m.s. present future. But the contexts in EA 196 make it clear that a past tense is required and a punctiliar one at that. Therefore, *i-pa-aš* most likely represents a past tense verb on the *qatal* pattern (Rainey 1973c:239). As Moran has remarked, some of these sporadic "Assyrianisms" might be due to a simple lack of understanding regarding proper Babylonian (Moran 1975b:164 n. 58). Others may be due to some WS morphological feature.

3rd MASCULINE PLURAL

Some very archaic texts from Mari, dating to approximately the Isin-Larsa period, have produced a few examples of 3rd m.pl. verb forms with preformative *ti-* (*ARM* 19, 41:3; 42:3; 43:3; 44:3; 45:3; 382:10; M 10556, Durand 1982). All but two of these are administrative dockets employing an as yet unidentified verb, *mazāʾu.* In similar contexts, when the subject is in the singular, the formulation with that verb is:

> 1 guruš / *ru-si* / *im-za-ʾà* (*ARM* 19, 46:1-3).

But when the subject is plural the formula is

> 5 guruš / *ru-si* / *tim-za-u* (*ARM* 19, 42:1-3).

Both the singular and plural forms have been recognized as preterites, which is not only commensurate with the morphology, but also is what one would expect from administrative documents ("descriptive texts"; Levine 1963). One text has an entry of commodities followed by a plural subject and the verb form *ti-ku-lu* "(They) have consumed" (*ARM* 19, 382:10). A legal document recording the sale of real estate concludes as follows:

> ÉŠ-GID *šu sí-kà-ti /tim-ḫa-ṣú* / NINDA *ti-ku-lu* /kaš *ti-iš-tá-u* /*ù* Ì *ti-il-tap-tu* "The surveyors who drove in the stakes; bread they have eaten, beer they have drunk and with oil they have anointed themselves" (M 10556: Durand 1982:81-83).

The distinction between the singular and plural forms of these verbs has been the subject of much discussion (Limet 1975:48; Westenholz 1978:165b; Gelb 1981:64; Edzard 1985:85-86; Izreᵓel 1987:87-88). Although it has been suggested that the 3rd m.pl. with *ti-* may have been common Semitic (Ezdard *loc. cit.*) or at least part of the western dialect of Old Akkadian, it seems more likely that the true source is West Semitic. The archaic tablets in question derive, after all, from Mari. Obviously, during the "Mari Age" under Zimri-Lim and under the intruder, Yasmaḫ-Addu, a form of northern Old Babylonian was adopted by the scribes. The prestige of this Babylonian was so great as to suppress the local "Amurrite" language except in proper nouns and in a few syntactic features. The process that led to the archaic plurals , *timzaᵓū, tīkulū, timḫaṣū, tištaᵓū* and *tiltapatū,* was probably identical with that at work in Ugaritic and Canaanite. The use of the 3rd f.s. (with *t-* prefix) with collective nouns would have led to the adoption of forms with the *ti* prefix for plurals while preserving the *-ū* suffix. The modal and tense distinctions of the plural, viz. the addition of the *-na* suffix for indicative imperfect and its absence (-Ø) for indicative preterite, jussive and volitive (cf. *supra,* pp. 9-10; *infra,* pp. 221-234) were perpetuated, as least in Ugaritic and Canaanite, on the newly developing *t-* forms.

Incidentally, one might have even ventured to suggest that *timzaᵓu, timḫaṣū* and *tištaᵓū* reflect the Barth-Ginsberg law, something not present in the later Amurrite names from Mari (Rainey 1978a:*8-*9). However, the other G stem verb, *tīkulū,* would have had to be **tākulū*, so the Barth-Ginsberg law is out of the question here. In any case, the *ti-* prefix in the Canaanized plurals from the Amarna archive is nothing but the result of carrying over the initial vowel of the theme from a 3rd m.s. Akkadian form, usually *iparras* or *iprus*, to the other persons (cf. *infra*, pp. 73-75, concerning the implications of the Barth-Ginsberg law). Therefore, one can find no justification for seeking some proto-Semitic or proto-West Semitic plural form with the *ti-* prefix (Edzard 1985:85-86).

On the other hand, Izreʾel (1987:88-89) has observed that there are enough plural forms in the Amarna texts from Canaan that have neither a *y-* nor a *t-* prefix, to preclude any suggestion that the basic Akkadian utilized by the scribes had had a *t-* prefix for masculine plurals in its paradigm. Note, for example, *i-du-ku-šu* (EA 75:26; Moran 1987b:254 n. 4; 1992:146 n. 4), *i-pu-šu* (EA 83:9; *et al.*), *iz-zi-bu-ni* (EA 366:18), *i-zi-bu* (EA 73:13), *i-ti-zi-bu* (EA 93:22), *ip-ḫu-ru-ni*$_7$ (EA 149:61), ⸢*ip*⸣*-pa-ṭá-r* (EA 292:50), and also *i-qa-bi-ú* (EA 288:54).

Therefore, the possibility that the Canaanite of the Amarna scribes might have an ancient ancestor or relative spoken at Mari prior to the Amurrite dominance is tantalizing. It can only be hoped that further documentation of that dialect will shed more light on the problem. On the other hand, it is obvious that the world of the Mari letters, from the reign of Zimri-Lim and his contemporaries, was the time when Old Babylonian became the international language of diplomacy and commerce (the Old Assyrian in Anatolia was a more parochial matter). The question remains as to just what brand of Old Babylonian formed the basis for the language adopted by the authors of the EA letters from Canaan.

OLD BABYLONIAN IN CANAAN

The question arises as to when and from where this brand of Akkadian came to the land of Canaan. There are known at present seven cuneiform texts dating to the Old Babylonian

(Middle Bronze) period discovered in Canaan itself (Anbar and Naʾaman 1986-87:7-11).

The oldest may be the legal text found out of context at Hazor (Hallo and Tadmor 1977). None of its forms reflect the West Semitized verbal system known from the Amarna letters but some peripheral features are in evidence: *ig-ru-ú* (line 4), G preterite 3rd m.pl. of *gerû*, appears in a standard legal idiom attested in Babylonian and peripheral dialects (*CAD* G:62; Hallo and Tadmor 1977:6); *⸢i⸣-re-bu* (line 7), G preterite 3rd m. pl. of *erēbu*, a peripheral form with thematic *-e-* or *-i-*, known not only from Alalakh, *i-re-bu* (AT 12:7; Hallo and Tadmor 1977:9 n. 49; suggested to Tadmor by A. Shafer), but also from Beirut, where Canaanite pidgin forms are attested, viz. 1st c.s. *i-re-bu* (EA 137:34), and 3rd c. pl. *ti-re-bu* (EA 137:42; 138:134), from Byblos, 3rd m.pl. with ventive, *i-re-bu-ni*$_7$ (EA 127:19) and from Ḫasi in the Beqa^c Valley, 3rd m.pl. *i-re-bu-mi* (EA 186:50), *i-re-bu-ni* (with ventive, EA 185:20), *i-re-bu-nu* (EA 185:36, 40). Mimation in the Hazor legal text appears on some independent nouns but has been dropped from a noun in construct even though the case ending is still preserved (Hallo and Tadmor 1977:9). Its grammar and style may seem provincial compared with the contemporary documents of Mari and southern Babylonia, but its verbal modes and tenses are basically OB.

The same may be said, more or less, of the Shechem letter (Shechem 1378:5; Böhl 1926, 1974), which Landsberger judged to be "in gutem Altbabylonisch geschreiben" (Landsberger 1954:59 n. 121); its principal verb forms are: *tu-uš-pí-la-an-ni* (Shechem 1378:5), 2nd m.s. preterite plus ventive and 1st c.s. accusative suffix from the quadriliteral, *šupēlu*, *tu-ša-ab-ba-lu-[ni-ni]*, 2nd m.s. present subjunctive with 1st c.s. dative suffix (*ibid.*, line 7) from *šūbulu*, *ta-pa-ul-[an-ni]* (*ibid.*, line 9), 2nd preterite (for *tāpulanni*) or present (for *tappalanni*) from *apālu*, *il-ta-na-pá-tù* (*ibid.*, line 11), 3rd m.pl. Gtn present subjunctive from *lapātu* (Landsberger *loc. cit.*; *contra* Albright 1942a:31 nn. 28, 29), *ar-tu-ú-[ub]* (*ibid.*, line 15), 1st c.s. indicative past tense with infixed *-t-*, from *raʾābu* *li-ša-ḫi-⸢za-an-ni⸣* (*ibid.*, line 20), 3rd m.s. Š precative of *aḫāzu* with ventive and 1st c.s. dative suffix. The verbs all come at the end of their respective clauses as in good Akkadian, especially OB, and in contrast to the Amarna texts from Canaan. But in spite of Landsberger's dictum about the OB character of this text, even he had to admit that several points of syntax, viz. *ul . . . ša* (lines 6-7), the use of *inūma* to introduce a "that" clause (line 9) and the conjunction *u* to express consequence ("so that"), are "provinziell" (*loc. cit.*). We might add the use of *ana muḫḫiya* (instead of *ana yāši* or *ana ṣēriya*), which is typical of MB and its contemporary peripheral dialects (*CAD* M/2:175b). That is to say, though the letter seems to be OB in script and verbal usage, it reflects some syntactic phenomena that later become standard in the periphery, especially in Canaan.

Anbar's administrative fragment from Hebron (Anbar and Naʾaman 1986-87:3-12) seems to be good OB as far as script is concerned. There is, however, the loss of mimation typical of late OB and there is the *-t-* preterite form, *ir-te-ḫu,* which could represent the peripheral preference for *-t-* forms in weak verbs (Anbar and Naʾaman 1986-87:6). It might also reflect the predilection evidenced in the Byblos Amarna texts to use such forms of *riʾāḫu* as the equivalent of WS statives (Rainey 1971b:93-94; 1973c:255-256).

The Hazor liver model fragments (Landsberger and Tadmor 1964), found in an LB I archaeological context, within a temple, have inscriptions that can be classified as OB but with some hints at a provincial origin. The verbal system of tenses and moods is definitely Akkadian: 3rd m.s. D stem future of *kanāšu, ú-ka-na-aš* (Frag. A, text a); 3rd m.s. G stem future, *i-ba-ar* (*ibid.*, text e); 3rd m.s. G stem future, *i-ka-al* (Frag. B, text f:2; with possible 3rd f.s. subject, Landsberger and Tadmor 1964:210 n. 22); 3rd m.pl. G stem present with ventive, from *târu, i-tu-ru-ni* (Frag. B, text g). On the latter form, the clear absence of mimation for the plural dative is noteworthy.

The recently discovered fragments from Hazor, though found in Iron Age contexts, show affinities with the cuneiform horizon of Mari. The first (Hazor M/5142/31050) is a roster containing PN's of typical Mari types, most of them built on well known WS patterns, all of which could be considered "Amurrite" but not necessarily "Canaanite" (Horowitz and Shafer 1992a:21-33). The second text, a fragmentary letter, has the uncontracted ventive form *iq-bi-am* (Hazor A2/3423/92/17-23086: line 8).

THE LATE BRONZE JARGON IN CANAAN

The Taanach letters, dating from LB I, i.e. the mid-fifteenth century B.C.E. (Glock 1983:58-59), share the same OB traits and lack of MB traits as the Amarna letters from Canaan. They also have a strong West Semitic flavor, especially in the verbal usages (Rainey 1977). The various forms will be cited and analyzed under their respective categories. Therefore, only a general summary need be given here. The two texts that probably were sent from Gaza (TT 5, 6) have clear Canaanisms; their ductus is almost identical with that of the Megiddo Amarna texts. The remaining two (TT 1, 2) present a mixture of standard OB style and usage with some other, more Canaanized features; their ductus is similar to certain Amarna letters, e.g. EA 63 and EA 64 (probably from southern Canaan; Naᵓaman 1979:676-677), EA 235 from Acco and EA 228 from Hazor (Glock 1983:59). Therefore, we have in the Taanach epistles our earliest testimony for the use of the system of verbal morphosyntax discovered in the Amarna letters from Canaan.

The political, social and cultural factors that led to the establishment of a "school" of scribes, all following these agreed conventions, can only be guessed at. If, as Moran suggested, this was a real spoken pidgin, how did these bureaucratic practitioners come to speak it? The proper nouns, both personal and geographic names, show no reflection of such a pidgin — they are purely West Semitic (cf. Sivan 1984).

One thing does seem clear: those who elected to use such a jargon had inherited an Old Babylonian dialect having some archaic but also some late OB features. They held that dialect in such veneration that they kept it alive in opposition to the almost world-wide trend to adopt the Middle Babylonian dialect at the expense of the classical tongue.

It has been suggested that the hybrid language of the EA texts from Canaan was actually used in the courts and schools of the Late Bronze Age. Technially, it seems more correct to call it an "interlanguage" (Gianto 1990:10-11; Rainey 1992b:330b-331a) rather than a pidgin (Moran 1992:xxi). Moran has most recently defined this hybrid in a most appropriate manner:

> The language can only be described as an entirely new code, only vaguely intelligible (if at all) to the West Semite because of the lexicon, and to the Babylonian because of the grammar (Moran 1992:xxii)

In fact, the idea of a "code" had occurred to this writer many years before. The practice was imagined in which a messenger used the Akkadian text, with its West Semitic verbal system and word order, as a kind of "pony" from which he sight-translated into Canaanite for the benefit of the recipient or the recipient's representative (such as an official at the Pharaonic court or at the headquartes in Gaza). The message might, in turn, be translated into Egyptian for Pharaoh's ears. This hypothetical usage may be compared with what appears to have been the practice at Ugarit, where translations into Ugaritic were prepared from what may have been Akkadian originals. At least the Ugaritic epistles show strong Akkadian influence in the word order.

To what degree the scribes and officials of Canaan actually spoke this "interlanguage" is impossible to ascertain. If they did, then they must have been at varying degrees of proficiency in attaining the target language. The result must be reflected in the many variations in verbal morphology. The syntax, however, certainly reflects their native West Semitic mother tongue(s).

CHAPTER III

PREFIX CONJUGATION — PERSON AND NUMBER

The principle of word building adopted by the Canaanite scribes for their verb forms was described in the first chapter (cf. *supra*, pp. 14-15). A glance at the glossary developed by Ebeling (1915) will reveal the scribal preferences for any particular verb. Sometimes they used only one form, either the Akkadian present-future or the preterite as their base, "theme," but sometimes they varied their selections between the two. In the case of some weak verbs, they even adopted the Akkadian past form with the *-t-* infix (wrongly called the perfect) as was frequently done by other peripheral scribes (cf. the remarks of Gordon 1938:215-219). There are very few purely Canaanite verb forms apart from those in personal or geographic names. Identification of the theme is the first step in analyzing any Canaanized hybrid.

Assyriologists were immediately struck by the pattern of person markers in the Amarna texts from Canaan. The obvious departures from the standard Akkadian patterns, which had been painstakingly established during the latter decades of the nineteenth century, were the subject of considerable discussion (Böhl 1909:48-51; Ebeling 1910:46-50, 51-52; Dhorme 1913:377-383). Understandably, it was something of a sensation to find, in the Amarna correspondence, West Semitic morphs and patterns, some of which were foreign to Akkadian.

Before reviewing the WS elements, however, it must be noted that some scribes used them only sparingly, giving preference to standard Akkadian forms. Such would appear to be the case with the scribe of EA 127, a letter from Byblos. Two of the earlier letters from Amurru, from ᶜAbdi-Ashirta (EA 60, 371), do exhibit most of the WS features for the prefix conjugation, but another letter (EA 62) avoids the *y-* prefix; in fact, the Amurru Amarna letters have a unique morphological mix of their own (Izreᵓel 1985:134-136; 1991a:131-142, §2.4.1.1). The Tyrian letters also use many purely Akkadian prefix verb forms and only occasionally a WS hybrid; even so, the WS modal and tense system (discussed *infra*, pp. 221-264) does seem to be recognized (Finkle 1977:88-98). The penchant of the Jerusalem scribe for Akkadian forms of the present-future, with WS forms restricted almost entirely to direct quotations, is well known (Nitzan 1973:57-59; Moran 1975b:153-154). The two lengthy epistles from Mayarzana of Ḫasi, in the Lebanese Beqaᶜ Valley, also eschew the *y-* prefix though some acquaintance with the WS modal and tense system seems evident (EA 185; 186). Furthermore, throughout the correspondence exhibiting strong WS influence, there is a scattering of Akkadian forms without a consonantal prefix, mainly 3rd person, but not exclusively, from Ist aleph and Ist waw roots. There are compelling reasons to assume that the Canaanite scribes were using such forms as themes for the WS suffix conjugation. The arguments in support of that interpretation will be presented under the discussion of the suffix conjugation pattern (*infra*, pp. 342-345).

There are no documented verb forms in the West Semitized texts for the 2nd f.s., the 2nd f.pl. or the 3rd f.pl. This is an accidental happenstance, as least for the 2nd person forms. For the persons that are represented, only a selection of typical forms are cited below. Nevertheless, it was felt that a generous sampling was necessary because of the unique nature of the texts involved.

y- FOR 3rd MASCULINE SINGULAR

Scholars were astonished to find so many finite forms beginning with the Akkadian PI sign. It was recognized, however, that this sign, which also had the values *wa, we, wi, wu,* was being used here for the values *ya, ye, yi, yu.* These values will be transcribed thus throughout this work following the lead of Gelb (1970:537; also adopted by Borger 1978:156, No. 383), *contra* the values adopted by von Soden and Röllig (1976:43), viz. *ia*$_8$, *ji, iú*. Malbran-Labat (1976:177) has adopted a compromise, giving *ia*$_8$ as well as *ju*^{i,a}.

The vowel accompanying this consonantal prefix can be either *-a-*, *-i-*, or *-u-*. The *-u* is confined to the Gp, D and Š stems, and G stem verbs Ist *waw*. The *-a-* is relatively rare and this was the cause of much misunderstanding about the diachronic development of the WS prefix patterns of the G stem (cf. *infra*, pp. 61-75, on the Barth-Ginsberg law). The overwhelming majority of forms have the *-i-* vowel, simply because the theme chosen from the Akkadian paradigm was the 3rd m.s. on the *iprus* pattern. The three syllabic prefix alternatives, *ya-*, *yi-*, and *yu-* can be illustrated by unequivocal orthographies as follows:

Those forms with *ia-* are the easiest to identify, namely, *ia-ta-mar* (EA 74:52), *ia-ak-šu-du-na* (EA 130:2), *ia-mu-tu* (EA 138:27); *ia-di-in*$_4$ (EA 116:46), *ia-di-na* (EA 74:54; 85:19, 76; 100:33; 117:78; 118:11, 16; 137:39), *ia-di-nu* (EA 105:85; 110:50; 116:34; 119:51; 125:16; 126:14, 18), *ia-di-nu-šu-nu* (EA 114:58); *ia-aq-bi* (EA 83:34; 101:32; 116:32), *ia-aq-bu* (EA 101:19; 105:88; 117:7; also EA 119:36); *ia-qú-ul* (EA 132:44; 137:25, 94), *ia-qú-ul*$_{11}$ (EA 137:59), *ia-qá-ar-ri-ib* (EA 39:19), *ia-aš-al* (EA 224:10), *ia-aš-ku-un* (EA 108:59; 139:33); *ia-aš-ku-n*[*u*] (EA 113:6), *ia-aš-pu-ur* (EA 117:60; probably also EA 247:9), *ia-aš-pur* (EA 250:23), *ia-aš-pu-ru* (EA 89:36; 138:123), *ia-aš-pu-ra* (EA 234:23; 250:28; possibly also EA 138:67), *ia-aš-ta-pár* (EA 233:16), *ia-tu-ru-na* (126:54), *ia-az-ku-ur-mi* (EA 228:19). Except for about five instances , all of the examples are from Byblos texts (or Rib-Haddi's correspondence while he was a political exile residing at Beirut).

Forms in which the PI sign must be read *ya-* are *ya-am-li-ik* (EA 105:6), *ya-am-lik* (EA 114:20), *ya-ar-ḫi-ša* (EA 137:97), and in the PN, ^{I}*Ya-an-ḫa-mu* (EA 270:4). These are the only forms in which the second sign, completing the first syllable, assures that the vowel is *-a-* . Knudtzon's transcriptions would add a few more examples, but without confirmation by an immediately following aC sign: *ya-di-*⸢*in*⸣ (EA 337:13), *ya-di-na* (EA 93:11), *ya-di-nu* (EA 117:42; 225:10), *ya-qú-lu* (EA 140:5), *ya-qí-ìl-li-ni* (EA 245:38). The latter are possible but unprovable. Given the dozens and dozens of other forms in which the PI sign must be read *yi-*, it would seem that these *ya-* spellings are mere exceptions to the general rule. For one thing, *yarḫiša* is nothing but a pseudo-verb developed from the adverb *arḫiš* (pointed out to me by Sh. Izreʾel) Yanḥamu is a personal name of unusual vocalic pattern (Amorite?). True Canaanite verbs might be represented in *yamlik* (Rainey 1987a:10*) and also *yaqūlu* and *yaqillini* (or: *yiqillini*). The case for reading *ya-di-nu*, etc. is considerably weaker; though *yaddin-* could be a way of echoing Canaanite **yatin-* /**yattin-*, *yiddin-* is just as likely a normalization.

For the reading *yi-*, confirmation by a following syllable is much more plentiful: *yi-in*$_4$*-na-pí-iš* (EA 250:33), *yi-iz-zi-iz* (EA 250:42), *yi-iḫ-di* (EA 142:9; 144:16), *yi-i-de*$_9$ (EA 267:15), *yi-ik-šu-du* (EA 227:15), *yi-il*$_5$*-ma-ad* (EA 64:8; 142:18; *et al.*), *yi-ìl-ma-ad* (EA 264:23; 337:17; 366:17), *yi-il*$_5$*-qé* (EA 197:10; 245:25), *yi-ìl-qé* (EA 116:36; *et al.*), *yi-il*$_5$*-qé-ni* (EA 284:12), *yi-ìl-qé-šu* (EA 119:47; 245:30), *yi-ìl-qé-ši* (EA 90:12; 95:33), *yi-il*$_5$*-qe-šu-nu* (EA 281:14, 29), *yi-ìl-qé-šu-nu* (EA 129:79), *yi-il*$_5$*-qa* (EA 197:27), *yi-ìl-qa* (EA 71:30; 91:6), *yi-ìl-qa-ni* (EA 81:32), *yi-ìl-qa-nu* (EA 138:68), *yi-ìl-qa-šu-nu* (EA 118:33), *yi-ìl-qú* (EA 71:18; *et al.*), *yi-ìl-qú-ši*$_x$(ŠE) (EA 124:15), *yi-im-qú-ut* (EA 295:17), *yi-id-din* (EA 248:11), *yi-ip-ṭú-ra* (EA 234:21), *yi-iṣ-bat* (EA 138:28; 250:46), *yi-iṣ-bat-ši* (EA 244:28, 38), *yi-iš-al-šu* (EA 60:21), *yi-iš-me* (EA 119:26; *et al.*), *yi-iš-mé* (EA 94:4; *et al.*), *yi-ìš-me* (EA 78:17; *et al.*), *yi-ìš-mé* (EA 85:16, 75; *et al.*), *yi-iš-ma* (EA 82:23), *yi-iš-mu* (EA 109:16, 18; *et al.*), *yi-ìš-mu* (EA118:54), *yi-ìš-mu-na* (EA 85:7), *yi-iš-te-mé* (EA 211:13), *yi-iš-te-mu* (EA 323:19; *et al.*), *yi-iš-te*$_9$*-mu* (EA 233:18), *yi-iš-pu-ra-am* (EA 362:22), *yi-ìš-ta-pár* (EA 73:26), *yi-ìš-ta-pa-ru* (EA 103:20; 112:7, 119:8), *yi-iš-tap-ru* (EA 106:14), *yi-ìš-ta-pa-ra* (EA 130:15), *yi-iš-tap-pa-ra* (EA 130:9), *yi-ìš-tap-ru-na* (EA 121:7), *yi-it-ru-uṣ* (EA 103:40; 250:22).

Readings with *yu-* followed by a uC sign are rare indeed, but by their nature, they confirm the necessity to read *yu-* in many other instances, purely on semantic grounds. The attested forms which have syllabic confirmation are: *yu-ú-ul-qú* (EA 117:33), *yu-ú-ul-qú-na* (EA 117:68), *yu-up-pa-šu* (EA 232:20), *yu-uq-ba* (EA 83:16), *yu-uq-bu* (EA 83:19), *yu-uš-ši-ra* (EA 182:8; *et al.*). These demonstrate that PI must be read *yu-* in forms of the G passive, and the D active stems. To these can be added the Š stem and undoubtedly the 1st waw verbs in the G stem. If further proof were needed, one may also compare the spellings for the persons other than 3rd person, which usually have *tu-* or *ú-* as the first sign (cf. discussion below).

t- FOR 3rd FEMININE SINGULAR

As is well known, one of the fundamental distinctions between the Babylonian and the Assyrian dialects is that the former generally used the 3rd m.s. prefix form for the 3rd f.s. (*GAG*:99, §75h). However, OB does have some archaic examples as does the poetic OB (hymnisch-epische). Therefore, it is possible that the Old Babylonian dialect which is the basis for the Canaanite pidgin Akkadian also had preserved the distinct forms for 3rd f.s. with the *t-* prefix. The other peripheral dialects vary in their adherence to the Babylonian pattern. The Mitanni letters almost never use a separate form for 3rd f.s. (Adler 1976:41) and the Hattusas dialect avoids a *t-* form altogether (Labat 1932:64). Only one text has *t-* 3rd f.s. forms at Carchemish (Huehnergard 1979:52-53). But at Ugarit, where a WS language was the native tongue, *t-* forms are plentiful (Huehnergard 1989:158-159).

One can hardly avoid the conclusion that the forms used in the Canaanized Amarna texts were in accordance with WS practice, viz. the distinguishing of 3rd f.s. verbs with *t-* from 3rd m.s. with *y-*.

The Akkadian paradigm would call for *-a-* as the prefix vowel with the *t-* prefix in the G stem. But for the 3rd f.s., such forms are practically non-existent. An epistle from Egypt has two: *ta-mu-ur* (EA 1:90), and *ta-ka-ša-ad* (EA 1:60); but the same text also has *ti-na-din* (EA 1:24; Cochavi-Rainey 1988:141, 144) and may even have a good Babylonian form, viz. *ip-t*[*i-i*] (EA 1:41). From Byblos come two others: *ta-ša-aš* (EA 82:50; Moran 1987b:264 n. 6; 1992:152 n. 6; *contra CAD* A/2:424b) and *ta-ap-šu-uḫ* (EA 107:31), while a Rib-Haddi letter written in Beirut has *ta-aq-bi* (EA 138:111) alongside *ti-iq-bi* (EA 138:44), which latter represents the standard practice of the scribe throughout the remainder of that particular epistle.

As with the 3rd m.s., prefixes with an *-i-* vowel are the rule. The forms come not only from Byblos but from other places located throughout Canaan. The G stem examples are: *ti-mu-ru* (EA 138:61), *ti-pu-uš* (EA 122:47), *ti-ša-šu* (EA 122:39), *ti*$_7$*-iḫ-la-aq* (EA 274:14), *ti-zi-za* (EA 107:33), *ti-ik-šu-du* (EA 221:14), *ti-le-eq-qé* (EA 228:35), *ti-id-di-in*$_4$ (EA 68:5), *ti-di-in* (EA 74:3), *ti-di-in*$_4$ (EA 76:4; *et al.*), *ti-din* (EA 73:4; *et al.*), *ti-na-mu-uš* (EA 100:37), *ti-na-mu-šu* (EA 296:17), *ti*$_7$*-na-mu-šu* (EA 292:13), *ti-na-ma-šu* (EA 266:19), *ti-iq-bi* (EA 138:44), *ti-ra-ḫa-aṣ* (EA 141:31), *ti-ra-am* (EA 323:22). From the N stem we have: *ti-né-pu-uš* (EA 74:35; 117:94; 129:80) and *ti*$_7$*-né-pu-*⌜*uš*⌝ (EA 87:19); and from what might be meant for a Gt: *ti-ir-ti-ḫu* (EA 103:54), or a G stem from the standpoint of WS, but built on the Akkadian *-t-* past. Peripheral forms with *ti*-prefix are found at Emar (Ikeda 1995:73).

The prefix *-u-* vowel appears where it would be expected, for example, in verbs with Ist waw: *tu-uṣ-sa* (EA 234:7) and *tu-ṣa-na* (EA 86:14). The G passive stem, which is foreign to standard Akkadian, is also well represented: *tu-pu-uš* (EA 281:13), *tu-ra* (EA 245:8), *tu-ul-qé* (EA 91:8), *tu-ul-qú* (83:15; 132:15), *tu-um-ḫa-ṣú* (EA 252:17), *tu-sà-aḫ-mì* (EA 245:8), *tu-uš-mu* (EA 138:96). For the D stem, one also finds: *tu-da-bi-ir* (EA 76:39) and most probably *tu-b*[*a-ú*] (EA 100:18) and *tu-ba-‹ú›* (EA 70:26; or 3rd c. pl. *tu-ba-‹ú-na›*), *tu-ra-du* (EA 257:20).

So the situation is parallel to that of the 3rd m.s., viz. very few *ta-* prefixes (even though they would be the normal Akkadian forms, unlike the situation in 3rd m.s.), some *tu-* prefixes where semantic or phonetic factors would be expected to require them, and many, many *ti-* prefixes in spite of the fact that they have no real precedent in the standard Akkadian paradigm.

The fact that 3rd f.s. is distinguished from 3rd m.s. is most reasonably explained as due to the influence of the WS language of the scribes, just as was the case in the Akkadian texts from Ugarit. It is not necessary to posit some Assyrian influence here. On the other hand, the preference for the *ti-* prefix instead of the correct Akkadian *ta-* has nothing to do with the original Canaanite morphology, as will be demonstrated further on (cf. *supra*, pp. 14-15, *infra*, pp. 73-75).

t- FOR 2nd MASCULINE SINGULAR

No examples are recorded of the 2nd f.s. in verbs since none of the texts are addressed to women. The 2nd m.s. forms show the same general pattern of variation in the prefix vowel as do the 3rd f.s.

A few specific verbs seem to have been employed in the standard Akkadian form, with the *ta*- prefix. For *nadānu* the Byblos scribes have *[t]a-di-in*$_4$ (EA 91:17) and *[t]a-din-ni* (EA 83:30; Moran 1950a:93, 96, 106; Youngblood 1960:246). A Tyrian letter has *[t]a-din* (EA 150:35). Byblos occasionally uses the *ta*- prefix for *qabû: ta-aq-[bi]* (EA 77:21), *táq-bi* (EA 86:15), *táq-bu* (EA 73:7; also Tyre, EA 145:23) and *táq-bu-ú* (EA 96:7), but see the many examples of the *ti*- prefix below. A letter from Alashia has *ta-qáb-bi* (EA 38:8, 13). For *palāḫu* one example comes from Byblos: *ta-pa-la[-aḫ]* (EA 82:26). From *šakānu* the Alashia letters have both *ta-ša-kà-an* (EA 38:30) and *ti-˹ša˺-kán* (EA 34:12) in the G stem and also *ta-ša-ki-in* (EA 35:50) in the N stem, alongside *ti-na-qú* (EA 34:12). Twice a Byblos letter has Gt (or Gtn?) forms from *šanû* with *ta-: ta-aš-ta-na* (EA 82:14) and *ta-aš-ta-ni* (EA 82:27). The forms of *šapāru* all have the Akkadian prefix: *ta-aš-pur* (EA 38:24), *ta-aš-pu-ra* (EA 77:7; 95:7; TT 1:8), *ta-aš-tap-ra* (EA 34:8; 102:14), perhaps because these forms were part of the traditionally fixed phraseology of the scribal craft. A Jerusalem letter uses two 2nd m.s forms with *ta*-, viz. *ta-ra-ia-mu* (EA 286:18) and *ta-za-ia-ru* (EA 286:20).

It seems proper to list as correct Babylonian forms the handful of examples where vowel coloring seems certain: *te-ep-pu-šu* (EA 96:26), *te-ri-šu* (EA 34:49), *te-ri-iš-šu* (EA 35:17, 22, 23), and the Gtn *te-eš-te-nem-me* (EA 62:41, 44). The Tyrian scribe adopts an Assyrian form, *ta-aš-te-me* (EA 149:56; Finkle 1977:109-110). On the other hand, one must prefer *ti-ìš-me* to *te*$_9$*-eš-me* (EA 90:13), *ti-iš-mé* to *te*$_9$*-eš-mé* (EA 86:17), and *ti-ìš-mu-na* to *te*$_9$*-eš-mu-na* (EA 74:50); the *eš* sign appears too often in places where the reading *ìš* must be expected. Furthermore, a Taanach text has *ti-iš-mé* (TT 1:16) and from Sidon comes *ti-iš-te*$_9$*-mé* (EA 145:25).

Of course, the forms from the irregular verb *idû* have *ti-* in Akkadian, so it is no surprise to find *ti-de* (EA 69:5; *et al.* including EA 102:21), *ti*$_7$*-de* (EA 230:20) and *ti-i-de* (EA 73:15; *et al.*).

There still remain over a dozen forms that violate the Akkadian paradigm by clearly adopting the *ti-* prefix: *ti-il*$_5$*-la-ku-un!*(EN)*-na* (TT 6:9), ⸢*ti*⸣-⸢*il*$_5$⸣*-la-ku-*⸢*na*⸣ (TT 6:14), *til-la-ku-na-mí* (EA 250:26), *ti-ta-ṣa-am* (EA 97:7), *ti-it-*[*ta-ṣ*]*ú-na* (EA 244:19; Moran 1987b:469 n. 2; 1992:299 n. 2; citing E. Gordon), *ti*$_7$*-du-ku-nu* (EA 138:40 f.), *ti-pu-šu* (EA 250:18), *ti-zi-ib-ši* (EA 287:50), *ti-zi-ib-ši*$_x$(ŠE) (EA 129:48), *ti-le-ú* (EA 83:20; *et al.*), *ti-ma-ḫa-aṣ* (EA 77:12), *ti-ma-qú-tu* (EA 73:10), *ti-iq-bi* (EA 83:45), *ti-iq-bu* (EA 71:12), *ti-qa-bu* (EA 117:30; 124:35; 252:23), *ti-*⸢*pa*⸣*-*⸢*ṭe*$_6$⸣*-*⸢*er*⸣ (EA 138:11), *ti-ša-i-lu* (EA 89:40).

The *tu-* prefix appears where expected: in the G stem of verbs I[st] waw, *tu-ṣa-na* (EA 73:9), *tu-ša-ab* (EA 34:52, actually in an Alashia text where the forms are not necessarily WS); in the D stem, *tu-ḫal-li-iq-mi* (EA 97:9), and the many forms of *wuššuru*, *tu-wa-še-ru* (TT 6:5), *tu-wa-še-ru-na* (TT 6:11), *tu-wa-ši-ra* (EA 34:9), *tu-wa-ši-ru* (EA 90:50), *tu-wa-ši-ru-ni* (EA 34:48), *tu-wa-‹ši›-ru-na* (EA 103:53); and the Š stem, *tu-še-zi-ba-an-ni* (EA 318:20), *tu-šu-ru-ba-ni* (EA 300:18).

Ø- FOR 1st COMMON SINGULAR

The prefix for 1st c.s. in Akkadian is *Øv-*. This can be seen by comparing *taprus* with *aprus*, *taparras* with *aparras*, *tērub* with *ērub*, *tuparras* with *uparras*, etc. The second person prefix is, of course, *tv-*; to form a first person form from second person, one just drops the *t*. The same holds true for the language of the Amarna letters from Canaan but the variation in prefix vowels does not always comply with the Akkadian paradigm, particularly in the G, Gt and N stems. Only a representative selection of examples will be cited.

To be sure, there are abundant cases of proper forms, with *Øa-* as the prefix. The conventional formula of obeisance in most peripheral archives ends with *amqut*, "I have fallen (prostrated)." In the EA letters it is usually written *am-qú-ut* (EA *passim*), or in a variant such as *am-qut* (EA *passim*). Nevertheless, three texts have *im-qú-ut* (EA 260:5; 317:6; 318:7). Good spellings such as *al-la-ak-mì* (EA 189: r. 6) and *a-al-la-ak-mì* (EA 191:16) are matched by *i-la-ak* (EA 155:69), *ìl-la-ku* (EA 201:16; 202:14), *il*$_5$*-la-ka* (EA 294:32), and *il*$_5$*-la-lu-mì* (EA 193:16). For *a-qa-bi* (EA 92:30; 286:17, 39, 49), *a-qa-bu-na* (EA 85:11; 119:53) and the most unusual Jerusalem spelling, *à-qa-bi* (EA 286:22; Moran 1975b:151), there are also *i-qa-bi* (EA 106:46), *i-qa-bu* (EA 127:30), and *i*$_{15}$*-qa-bi* (EA 180:16). One finds *aš-pu-ur* (EA 138:31,42; 362:18) and *aš-pu-ru* (EA 362:52 *et passim*) but once the Tyre scribe uses *iš-pu-ur* (EA 147:70). A high frequency verb is *naṣāru*, represented by *a-na-ša-ar* (EA 60:22; 127:37; 138:29; 231:16), *a-na-ṣa-ru* (EA 221:12; *et passim*) and other similar variants. But there are also forms such as *i-na-ṣa-ru* (EA 65:10; *et passim*), *i-na-ṣa-ru-na* (EA 112:10; 125:12), not to mention *i-na-ṣí-ru* (EA 119:15; 130:49), *i-na-ṣí-ru-na* (EA 123:32), and *i-na-ṣí-ra* (EA 123:27) as well as *i*$_{15}$*-na-ṣa-ar* (EA 179:26) and *i*$_{15}$*-na-ṣa-ru* (EA 187:20; 220:25). Furthermore, one also finds *iṣ-ṣú-ru* (EA 220:15; 292:23; 293:12; 294:12) and even (Rainey 1975b:408, 413, 417; 1978b:84) *ú-ṣur-ru* (EA 337:28), $^{\ulcorner}$*uṣ*$^{\urcorner}$*-ṣúr-*$^{\ulcorner}$*šu*$^{\urcorner}$ (EA 230:13), *ú-ṣur-ru-na* (EA 252:28), *ú-ṣur-ru-šu-nu* (EA 252:31), *uṣ-ṣú-ru* (EA 141:41; 142:12), and *uṣ-ṣur-ru-na* (EA 252:8)! Clearly, the prefix *Øa-* can be replaced by *Øi* or even *Øu-* without any change in meaning.

The alteration between *Øa-* and *Øi-* is not confined to G present and preterite; for Gt (Gtn) note the ubiquitous *aš-ta-pa-ar, aš-tap-pár, aš-ta-pa-ru* (*passim*) alongside *iš-ta-pár* (EA 90:14), *iš-tap-ru* (EA 85:6; 106:18; 114:21), *íš-tap-pa-ar* (EA 134:31) and *íš-tap-ru* (EA 85:55). A possible N stem form is *i-ma-la-ku* (EA 191:9; *contra* *CAD* B:71b; M/1:155b and Moran 1987b:430; 1992:271).

On occasion, the typical Akkadian vowel coloring (*a/ā › e/ē*) is expressed correctly, but this is almost never uniform for any particular verb. For example, for *epēšu*, from Tyre comes *e-te-pu-uš* (EA 153:5; 154:9) while Beirut gives us *i-te*$_9$*-pu-šu* (EA 138:46); there are also *i-pu-uš* (EA 38:9; 317:18), *i-pu-šu* (EA 114:26; 125:39; 328:26), *i-pu-ša* (EA 83:24), *i-pu-šu-na* (EA 74:63; *et passim*) and *i-pu-ša!*(MA)*-am* (EA 136:28). One may compare the following, all from *erēbu: e-ru-ub-mi* (EA 286:39) with *i-ru-ub* (EA 102:31), *e-ri-ub* (EA 180:14) with *i-re-ba* (EA 137:34), not to mention *i-ra-ab* (EA 150:11) and *i-ra-bu* (EA 151:13), as well as *i-te-ru-ub* (EA 155:31) and *i-te₉-ru-ub* (EA 104:44).

A purist would prefer to read *ep-pu-šu* (EA 254:46; 280:38) and *ep-pu-šu-mì* (EA 378:17), *ep-pu-šu-na* (EA 92:15; 249:10), but in view of the spellings beginning with *i-* listed above, the question seems purely academic. Knudtzon's *ip-pu-šu*, etc. are just as plausible. Likewise, one might insist on reading *ez-zi-ib* (EA 88:20) and *ez-zi-ba* (EA 294:31) but they exist alongside *i-zi-bu* (EA 138:47), *i-zi-ba-ši* (EA 126:45) and even *i-te₉-zi-ib* (EA 82:43; 83:46, 49; 103:16). From *šemû*, the few cases like *eš-me* (EA 105:40), *eš-mé* (EA 91:26), *eš-mu* (EA 116:16), *eš-te-me* (EA 108:24) and *eš-te₉-mé* (EA 82:35), are overshadowed by the forms like *iš-me* (EA 136:15; 147:17, 30, 34; 260:8), *iš-mé* (EA 34:11; 39:12; 317:12, 22, 24), *iš-mu* (EA 251:15), and the ubiquitous *iš-te-me, iš-te-mé, iš-te-mu, iš-te₉-mu* etc. that are documented plentifully throughout the corpus. For *leʾû* we have an isolated Babylonian form, *e-le-éʾ-e* (EA 238:8) and an Assyrian (from Jerusalem), *a-la-áʾ-e* (EA 286:42; 287:58; Moran 1975b:154), but the dominant spellings are *i-le-ú* (EA 82:22; *et al.*), *i-le-e* (EA 81:21), *i-lé-e* (EA 151:10), *i-le-i* (EA 144:32), *i-le-ʾì* (EA 102:19) and *i-la-ú-mi* (EA 137:27; probably not an Assyrianism, Moran 1975b:164 n. 67).

Of course, for *idû* there is nothing surprising in finding forms like *i-de* (EA 83:9; *et passim*), and *i₁₅-de* (EA 254:28, 32). This "prefix-stative" takes *īde* for 1st c.s. in Akkadian (*GAG*:102, §78b, 152, §106q; cf. Rainey 1973c:244-247)

On the whole, the *Øu-* prefix appears where it would be expected. In verbs Ist waw, the G stem forms are usually correct, e.g. *ub-ba-lu* (EA 365:19, 25), *uṣ-ṣú-na* (EA 333:16), *ú-ša-ab* (EA 260:14), *et al.*, but there is also *i-ba-lu* (EA 326:19), where the *Øi-* prefix has intruded. Most of the D stem forms are normal, e.g. *ú-ba-ú* (EA 74:64; 109:55), *ú-ba-ú-na-ši* (EA 143:15), *ú-da-bi-ra* (EA 85:68), *ú-ka-li* (EA 108:48), *ú-wa-še-er* (EA 255:13), *ú-wa-ši-ir* (EA 333:24), *uš-ši-ru-na-ši* (EA 142:16), but again, one finds *i-wa-ši-ir* (EA 137:8; Rainey 1975b:419). In the Š stem, note *ú-še-ez-zi-bá-šu-nu* (EA 62:31).

The denominative D stem *urrudu* (from [*w*]*ardu*), shows *ur-ra-ad* (EA 84:30), *ur-ra-da* (EA 294:33), *ur-ra-du* (EA 189: r. 24; *et al.*), and *ú-ra-du-šu* (EA 257:18). On the other hand, one also finds *i-ru-du* (EA 250:51, 59), *i-ru-da-am* (EA 300:20), and *i-r*[*i*]*-du* (EA 186:7).

The quadriliteral verb, developed from *šuka*ʾʾ*unu, šukênu* (*GAG*:158, §109m; *AHw*:1263), exhibits *Øu-* in the G preterite, *uš-ḫé-ḫi-in* (EA 221:7; *et al.*), *uš-ḫé-ḫi-in*$_4$ (EA 223:6; 242:8), *uš-ḫe-ḫi-in*$_4$ (EA 222:6; certainly also EA 214:6 according to Moran's collation), but with infixed *-ti-* we find, *iš-ta-ḫa-ḫi-in* (EA 298:12), *iš-ti-ḫa-ḫi-in* (EA 301:10), *iš-tu-ḫa-ḫi-in* (EA 331:10-11) and *iš-tu-ḫu-ḫi-in* (EA 325:8).

Therefore, the mass of evidence indicates that, for the 1st c.s. of the prefix conjugations, the prefix vowel of the G stem 3rd m.s. often intruded, so that we find *Øi-* in place of either *Øa-*, *Øe-* or *Øu-*. In other words, it is mainly the absence of a consonantal prefix, that is, the presence of a Ø - prefix, that indicates 1st c.s.

t- . . . -ū /*-ūna* FOR 3rd MASCULINE PLURAL

One of the most interesting morphological features of the prefix conjugation in the Amarna texts from Canaan is the predominance of the prefix *tv-* for the 3rd m.pl. (Böhl 1909:52-53; Ebeling 1910:48-50). The same construction was found in Ugaritic and the isogloss with the EA texts was duly observed (Herdner 1938). Albright, followed by Moran (Albright and Moran 1948:243-244), had thought that these forms were 3rd f.s. forms but later Moran (1951) demonstrated that the syntactic alternations between forms with *-ū* and forms with *-ūna* was modally conditioned (parallel to 3rd f.s. with *-Ø* /*-a* and *-u*, respectively) and therefore represented true plural forms. Nevertheless, the fact that 3rd f.s. forms can take a feminine collective (e.g. EA 252:16-19; Albright 1943b:31 n. 15), or even a plural subject (EA 77:37; 103:22), strongly suggests that this was the source of the analogical replacement of an original *y-* by the *t-* prefix in the plural forms (Moran 1951:35b).

It has been argued that there are also 3rd m.s. forms in these texts with the *y-* prefix, and various examples were listed in Ebeling 1915 (*passim*). Izreʾel (1987) has collected the suggested examples, sixteen in number, and analyzed them. All but two could be explained as singulars. The two forms in question are both from *namāšu;* their respective contexts are:

> *ù la-a yi-na-mu-šu-n[a]* /*[a-]bu-tu-ka iš-tu a-[b]u-[ti-ia*] "but your fathers never did desert [my] father[s]" (EA 109:7-8); *ya-di-in*$_4$ ᵈUTU TE[Š-*ia* !] /*i-na pa-ni-ka ù šu-up-ši-i[ḫ* ÌR.MEŠ-*ka* !] /*ù la-a yi-na-mu-šu* /*iš-tu mu-ḫi-ka* "May the sun-god grant [me!] digni[ty] in your presence and (you) bring tranquili[ty to your servants!] and they will never defect from you" (EA 113:32-35).

As Izreʾel points out (1987:86-87), the rule of modal congruence (Moran 1950a:81-88; 1951:33; 1960:9-11) should require that in the latter context the final vowel be the injunctive plural (jussive or volitive). The first example is even more obvious; the subject is masculine plural and there is no apparent reason for the singular energic (with *-una*). So we must posit *yinammušūna* and *yinạmmušū*. The new translation by Moran (1987b:314; 1992:187) assumes [ÌR-*ka*] at the end of line 33. In that case, he must also assume a violation of the modal congruence. Thus, we have suggested [ÌR.MEŠ-*ka*]. However, Moran may be right and that would eliminate one of the anomalous forms. In EA 109:7, one may conjecture that the scribe changed his mind in mid-stream, switching from singular to plural in his thinking and thus producing a singular form with the plural ending. At any rate, *yinammušūna* may be a *hapax*.

Turning to the 150 or so documented forms of 3rd m.pl. with *t-*, one is struck by the paucity of forms with *ta-*. Quite a few of those recorded by Ebeling (1915: *passim*) can be demonstrated to be 3rd f.s., often with *ālu* "city" as the subject. There remain: *ta-di-nu-ni* (EA 126:64, 66), *tal-qú-ni* (EA 70:16, in a broken context), *ta-ša-mé-ú* (EA 286:50; note Assyrianizing vocalization and lack of contraction, Moran 1975b:153, 164 n. 63) and *ta-aš-pu-ru-na* (EA 138:122). The latter appears in a text which also uses *ti-iš-pu-ru-na* (EA 138:137). But to this handful of *ta-* forms, one may add a few with characteristic vowel coloring: *te-lé-ú-na* (EA 249:3), *te-èl-qú-ni* (EA 180:22), *te-èl-qú-na* (EA 126:13), *te-pa-šu* (EA 197:14), *te-né-pu-šu-na* (EA 138:93) and *te*$_9$*-e-te-pu-šu* (EA 129:88).

The mass of examples from the G and related stems have *ti-*. The predominance of the TI sign in these spellings assures that the occasional TE sign must be read *ti*$_7$, for example, *ti-la-ku* (EA 101:34) alongside *ti*$_7$*-la-ku* (EA 203:19), *ti-la-ku-na* (EA 73:16; 109:35; 126:12) and *ti*$_7$*-la-ku-na* (EA 249:5), or *ti-iq-bu-na* (EA 73:29; 129:32; 250:15, 40) and *ti*$_7$*-iq-bu-*⸢*na*⸣ (EA 94:14; also 136:10; 197:16; 362:21), *ti-ma-ḫa-ṣú-ka* (EA 252:27) and *ti*$_7$*-ma-ḫa-ṣú-nu* (EA 271:21), *ti-na-ṣa-ru* (EA 85:22; *et passim*) and *ti*$_7$*-na-ṣa-ru* (EA 180:8). The theme chosen from the Akkadian paradigm may be the present, e.g. *ti-da-ga-lu* (EA 197:41), *ti-ma-ga-ru* (EA 138:62), or the preterite, *ti-ìl-qú* (EA 84:32; *et passim*), *ti-iṣ-ba-tu* (EA 137:40); note also the Gt, *ti-iš-te*$_9$*-mu-na* (EA 216:18; 250:52).

The prefix *tu-* is represented in the usual categories — Ist waw G stem: *tu-ub-ba-lu-na* (EA 224:14), *tu-ba-lu-na* (EA 101:22; 108:39, 53; 117:18; 126:58-59); G passive: *tù-da-ku-na* (EA 132:50), *tu-ul-qú-na* (EA 108:58), *tu-da-nu* (EA 137:6; 138:43), *tu-da-nu-na* (EA 83:23; TT 2:20), and also *tu-ud-da-nu-n*[*a*] (KL 72:6000:21), *tu-uš-mu-na* (EA 89:10; *et al.*). But especially the D stem: *tu-ba-ú-ni* (EA 60:15), *tu-ba-ú-na* (EA 73:24; *et al.*), *tu-ba-ú-na-nu* (EA 100:17), also *tu-*⸢*bé*⸣*-*⸢*ʾu*$_5$⸣*-na* (EA 250:10), and *tu-wa-ši-ru-na* (EA 125:44). Of special note, however, are the D stem forms showing intrusion of the *ti-* prefix: *ti-ba-ú-na* (EA 129:29), *ti*$_7$*-ba-ú-na* (EA 362:24), *ti-ba-ú-na-ši* (EA 129:19), *ti-dáb-bi-bu* (EA 138:49), *ti-dáb-bi-ru* (EA 138:69), *ti-pa-li-ḫu-na* (EA 105:22), and *ti*$_7$*-pa-ṭe*$_4$*-ru-na* (362:35).

t- . . . -ū /*-ūna* FOR 2nd MASCULINE PLURAL

Due to the accident of discovery, the 2nd m.pl. in prefix forms of the verb is attested in only one certain context (for the 2nd m.pl. imperative, also with the *-ū* suffix, cf. discussion *infra*, pp. 270-272):

> *at-tu-nu tu-ša-ab-li-ṭú-na-nu* / *ù at-tu-nu* /\ *ti-mi-tu-na-nu* "You give us life and you put us to death" (EA 238:31-33; Moran 1987b:464 n. 2; 1992:295 n. 2).

The first verb is a hybrid built on the Akkadian preterite *tušabliṭ-* plus the WS imperfect plural suffix *-ūna*. The second verb is marked by the gloss sign and is evidently a WS H(?) causative; its prefix vowel probably represents regressive assimilation due to the long *ī* vowel of this middle weak root. Thus, **timītūnani* ‹ **tumītūnani*. That the suffix is from the WS repertoire is confirmed by the plural imperatives (cf. *infra*, pp. 270-272), which almost without exception (EA 147:36; 280:19) have *-ū* or the energic *-ūna*.

One Amurru letter (EA 170) has two 2nd m.pl. forms side by side, one with the *-ūni* suffix typical of the Amurru corpus (Izreʾel 1985:142; 1991a:136, §2.1.1.1) and the other with a unique example of a "literary" Akkadian form with the proper suffix,*-āni:*

> ŠÀ-*bá-ku-nu la tù-uš-ma-ra-ṣa-ni*$_7$ /*ù mi-im-ma i-na* ŠÀ-*ku-nu la ta-šak-kán-:nu-ni*$_7$ "Do not trouble your heart and do not take anything to heart!" (EA 170:40-41).

It can hardly be doubted that the 2nd m. pl. suffix in *-ū* reflects true WS morphology. It occurs in an Akkadian text from Ugarit, *ta-al-ta-qu-mì* (RS 8.279:8'; Nougayrol 1955:170; Huehnergard 1979:229-230 and n. 238; 1989:159-160) but is not typical of the other peripheral dialects.

n- FOR 1st COMMON PLURAL

The normal Akkadian prefix in the G, Gt, Gtn and N stems for 1st c.pl. is *ni-*, taken from the first syllable of the 1st c.pl. pronoun, *nīnu* (*GAG*:98, §75e). Only two examples have been suggested as West Semitized forms with *na-*, namely a G stem volitive *na-*⌜*ad*⌝*-na pa-ni-nu* "we will devote ourselves" (EA 89:16; Albright and Moran 1950:166; but cf. *infra*, pp. 295, 405); and an N stem imperfect *ni-‹nu› na-lá-qú* "w‹e› are being taken over" (EA 131:22; Moran 1987b:350 n. 6; 1992:213 n. 6). On the other hand, the substitution of *na-* for correct Akkadian *ni-* is known at Ugarit (Huehnergard 1979:229; 1989:159) and in treaties and legal texts from Carchemish (Huehnergard 1979:53). In three instances, *nu-* was substituted for *ni-*: *nu-du-uk* (EA 197:17), *nu-ú-du-lu* (EA 100:39), *nu-˹uš˺-pu-ru* (EA 85:84; not passive! Moran 1987b:270; 1992:157). As with the other persons, the 1st c.pl. is documented with G present and preterite as themes for the hybrid forms, e.g. *ni-da-gal* (EA 74:57), *ni-ma-qú-[ut]* (EA 74:32), *ni-na-ṣa-ar* (EA 181:9), *ni-na-ṣa-ru* (EA 100:9, 30), *˹ni˺-˹re˺-bu-ka* (EA 138:12) and *ni-di-nu* (EA 112:52), *ni-ìl-qú* (EA 103:57), *ni-iṣ-bat* (EA 138:101), *ni-iš-mu-ú* (EA 200:7), *ni-iš-pu-ru* (EA 112:53) as respective examples. Note also the reflexive Gt's, *ni-tel-lí* (EA 264:15), but *né-e-ta-lí* (EA 178:4; or: *ni-i*$_{15}$*-ta-lí*?), *ni-te-pu-uš-mi* (EA 138:45), *ni-te*$_{9}$*-pu-uš* (EA 73:22; 105:33). Note the aberrations: *ni-am-qú-ut* (EA 100:6), *ni-[u]m?-˹qu˺-ut* (EA 200:5). The prefix statives may also appear in 1st c.pl., usually with the expected forms: *ni-de* (EA 108:43), *ni-le-ú* (EA 88:20; *et al.*), *ni-la-ú* (EA 211:18), *ni-zi-iz* (EA 279:18).

Besides four cases cited above where *nu-* has usurped the place of *ni*, the *nu-* prefix is documented for the usual classes of verbs, e.g. Ist waw, *nu-ub-ba-lu-uš-šu* (EA 245:7) and the D stem, *nu-ba-li-iṭ* (EA 85:38), *nu-bal-li-iṭ* (EA 68:28), and *nu-da-bir*$_{5}$ (EA 74:34). But in two instances, the *ni-* has usurped the place of *nu-*: *ni-du-bu-ur* (sic! EA 279:20) and *ni-wa-aš-ši-ru-šu* (EA 197:18).

CONCLUDING REMARKS

The most important contribution of the evidence cited above to the understanding of the West Semitic verbal morphology is the deviation from standard Akkadian prefixes. The *y-* for 3rd m.s. and the *t-* for 3rd m.pl. are the most striking examples. The 2nd m.pl. *-ū(na)* suffix instead of the Akkadian *-ā* is also worthy of note. This latter contrast with Akkadian was not so strongly felt by the earlier grammarians of EA, perhaps because it was not yet clear that Akkadian did not use *-ū*.

As will be seen in the next chapter, the choice of Ø- prefix for the 1st c.s. and the concomitant disregard, in most cases, for the proper vowel for 1st c.s. in Akkadian was the cause for considerable misunderstanding of the paradigm and its systematic application. Too often, superficial similarities with Massoretic vocalizations led to false conclusions concerning the diachronic significance of the evidence from the Canaanite EA letters. Comprehension of the table presented above (pp. 14-15) would prevent many misapprehensions in the comparative value of the EA data. The ensuing discussions will strive to distinguish between the true Canaanite elements and the features deriving from a practical development of peripheral forms.

CHAPTER IV

PREFIX CONJUGATION — G AND Gp STEMS

The Akkadian of the Canaanite scribes had the usual repertoire of verbal stems: G, Gt, N, D, Dt and Š. There are some rare and unusual instances of Gtn and Št forms, the implications of which will be discussed under the appropriate heading. The occasional use of *i* vowel prefixes instead of prefixes with *u* in the D and Š stems will be dealt with under the respective headings; they are colloquial features, analogic developments from the G stem prefixes, and not Canaanisms. True West Semitic features exist in the Gp and the Dp and also the very rare examples of H causatives, all of which are totally foreign to Akkadian. This present chapter will concentrate on the basic G and Gp stems; those are the stems built primarily on the Akkadian G stem themes.

As with the person markers treated in the previous chapter, only the prefix conjugation will be studied here. The reason for this departure from the customary practice is that the syntactical categories of the prefix conjugation are considerably different from those of the suffix conjugation, even though the latter was in the process of usurping some functions of the former. The morphosyntactical approach adopted in this work focuses on the morphological realization of intended semantic (syntactic) nuances. Therefore, the suffix conjugation, with its different morphological system, will be treated as a separate entity, including all the stem forms.

Though the tense and modal system will be treated in a subsequent chapter, it will be necessary here to remark on the use of the Akkadian present-future, preterite and preterite with infixed *-t-* (the so-called "perfect") forms as such, especially since they seem to have been chosen by the Canaanite scribes somewhat arbitrarily for each particular verb, without necessarily intending to imply their tense function in Akkadian. Spelling out the details of this practice on their part is one of the chief objectives of this work. Note that many of the "present" forms cited in this chapter actually express jussive/volitive or preterite in their respective contexts while the "preterites" and so-called "perfects" (with *-t-*) may express present, future or past continuous as well as preterite and jussive/volitive. In this chapter, the emphasis is on form rather than the WS modal/tense function.

THE ACTIVE G STEM

AKKADIAN FORMS.

It is remarkable that the Canaanite scribes usually chose one particular form from the Akkadian paradigm to serve in all the tense and modal functions of their own system (Rainey cited by Izreʾel 1978b:79 and n. 257). It should be noted that in Ebeling's day, Assyriologists had not all come to the realization that the G present-future was characterized by gemination of the second radical. The Akkadian scribes, especially those of the Assyrian tradition, but also the Babylonians, did not feel obligated to express the gemination orthographically. The peripheral scribes had learned the same orthographic principle. Therefore, a perusal of the glossary will reveal many instances where only the thematic vowel identifies the original Akkadian tense form. A review of the principal high-frequency verbs in the corpus is most revealing. Both weak and strong verbs are lumped together here, otherwise, the picture would be distorted. It should be remembered that the Jerusalem letters generally use the true Akkadian verbal system for present-future while the Tyre letters often use the Akkadian present-future and preterite in their proper tense functions. The order followed is that of the *CAD* whereby I[st] waw verbs come under A (similar to Ebeling 1915).

(w)abālu . The unanimous preference is for *ubbal* as the theme. There are no examples in the WS texts of *ubil*

(Huehnergard 1987:191-193; Gelb 1961:126; Reiner 1966:93). The gemination is often not expressed orthographically, e.g. 3rd m.s. *yu-ba-lu* (EA 113:41; et al.), 1st c.s. *ú-ba-al* (EA 327:9), 3rd m.pl. *tu-ba-lu-na* (EA 108:39; et al.), but it can be, 1st c.s. *ub-ba-lu* (EA 365:14, 25), 3rd m.pl. *tu-ub-ba-lu-na* (EA 224:14; 365:22)

akālu. Of the few forms documented, *ikkal* is the theme for Byblos, *ti-ka-lu* (EA 100:36), Shechem, 3rd m.s. *yi-ka-lu* (EA 254:16; Izreʾel 1987:83), and Jerusalem (where the Akkadian present-future is used instead of the WS imperfect; Nitzan 1973:57-59), 3rd m.pl. *i-ka-lu* (EA 286:6). But *īkul* is employed in a text from Tyre: 3rd m.s. *i-ku-ul* (EA 151:56), *i-kúl* (EA 151:57).

alāku. Here again we see a verb for which the WS texts have no example of the Akkadian preterite form. The present-future, *illak*, is the theme for nearly all conjugated forms from WS texts: 3rd m.s. *⸢ìl⸣-la-ku* (EA 92:39), *yi-la-ak* (EA 144:27; 197:26), *yi-la-ku* (EA 179:16; 365:27), 2nd m.s. energic *til-la-ku-na-mì* (EA 250:26), 1st c.s. *i-la-ak* (EA 155:69), *ìl-la-ku* (EA 201:16; 202:14), *il*$_{5}$*-la-ka* (EA 294:32), *ìl-la-ku-mì* (EA 193:16), 3rd m.pl. *ti-la-ku* (EA 101:34), *ti-la-ku-na* (EA 73:16; *et al.*). There are some isolated cases of 1st c.s. *al-la-ak-mì* (EA 189: r. 6; 191:16). Nevertheless, the documented imperative singulars (EA 102:15; 136:11, 27) are *alik* with the *i* thematic vowel.

amāru. By contrast, the WS texts use only the preterite, *īmur*, as the theme, with one possible exception. In EA 364:21, *⸢a⸣-⸢ma⸣-ru* might be either a finite form, perhaps even a Canaanism, "I continually ordered," but it is more likely an infinitive (Moran 1987b:560 n. 3; 1992:362 n. 3). The principal forms are: 3rd m.s. *yi-mur* (EA 138:61; *et al.*), 3rd f.s. *ti-mu-ru* (EA 138:61), 1st c.s. *i-mur* (EA 147:45; 155:35), *i-mu-ru* (EA 141:45; Moran 1987b:371 and n.7; 1992:227, 228 n. 6), 3rd c.pl. *ti-mu-ru* (EA 137:11; 138:36; 141:34).

(w)aṣû. The evidence is ambiguous. One finds, e.g. 3rd m.s. *yu-uṣ-ṣí* (EA 232:16), 3rd f.s. *tu-uṣ-ṣa* (EA 234:17), 1st c.s. *uṣ-ṣa-am*

(EA 88:51) and *uṣ-ṣú-na* (EA 333:16) but there are also forms like 3rd m.s. *yu-ṣa-na* (EA 74:39; 77:27), 3rd f.s. *tu-ṣa-na* (EA 76:31; *et al.*), 2nd m.s. *tu-ṣa-na* (EA 73:9), *tu-ṣú* (EA 362:62), where the scribe may or may not have intended gemination.

dabābu. The only two examples from WS texts use the present-future theme: 1st c.s. *a-da-bu-ba* (EA 119:23), 3rd m.pl. *ti-dáb-bi-bu* (EA 138:49), the latter of which is certainly for the D stem (Rainey 1973c:254 and n. 96).

dagālu. The WS texts know only the *idaggal* form as their theme, e.g. *i-da-gal* (EA 75:19; *et al.*), *yi-da-ga-lu* (EA 85:62), 3rd m.pl. *ti-da-ga-lu* (EA 101:34; 120:34!), 1st c.pl. *ni-da-gal* (EA 93:12).

dâku. Only the preterite, *idūk,* seems to have been used, e.g. 2nd m.s. *ti$_7$-du-ku-nu* (EA 138:40, 41), 1st c.s. *a-du-uk-šu-nu* (EA 138:29), 3rd m.pl. *ti-du-ku* (EA 75:33), *ti-du-ku-na* (EA 104:34; *et al.*), and note *nu-du-uk* (EA 197:17).

epēšu. Although a few forms show gemination; most of the time the scribe uses a theme that is probably based on the preterite, *īpuš,* though the script is naturally ambiguous, cf. e.g. 1st c.s. *ip-pu-šu-na* (EA 249:10) and *i-pu-šu-na* (EA 74:63; *et al.*) in identical contexts. Note two transitive instances of the theme taken from the preterite with infixed *-t-*: 3rd m.s. *yi-te-pu-uš* (EA 258:7), 1st c.pl. *ni-te$_9$-pu*[*-u*]*š* (EA 105:33).

ezēbu. The only three examples with a consonantal personal prefix lack the gemination, namely 3rd m.s. *yi-zi-ib* (EA 197:40), 3rd f.s. *ti-zi-ib-ši* (EA 287:50), *ti-zi-ib-ši$_x$*(ŠE) (EA 129:48). Of the 1st c.s. forms, two lack gemination: *i-zi-bu* (EA 138:47), *i-zi-ba-ši* (EA 126:45); but two have it: *iz-zi-ib* (EA 88:29), *iz-zi-ba* (EA 294:31). An imperative even takes the geminated form as its base: *iz-zi-ib-mi* (EA 294:29). There are two 3rd m.pl. forms, one with and one without gemination: *i-zi-bu* (EA 73:13), iz-zi-bu-ni$_7$ (EA 366:18); these will be treated as reflecting the pidgin suffix conjugation (cf. *infra,* pp. 342-343).

ḫadû. Only one suffix form is documented; it occurs in letters from Beirut, 3rd m.s. *yi-iḫ-di* (EA 142:9; 144:15); less likely is the alternate transcription is *ya-aḫ-di* (note the *i* theme characteristic of western peripheral).

ḫalāqu. The Jerusalem letters use the Akkadian present-future; thus, 3rd m.s. *i-ḫal-li-iq* (EA 286:37) used transitively as if D (Ebeling 1915:1413 n. 1); elsewhere, the preterite is the base: 3rd m.s: *iḫ-li-iq* (EA 186:66, 68), 3rd f.s. *ti₇-iḫ-la-aq* (EA 274:14), 1st c.s. *iḫ-la-aq* (EA 270:29). Note the 3rd m.s. transitive form *ya-aḫ-li-qú* (EA 254:9), which might represent a causative stem (cf. *infra*, p. 190).

idû. Naturally, this verb has only the preterite, *īde*, which serves for 3rd m.s. and 1st c.s. Since it was recognized by the Amarna scribes as a stative (Rainey 1973c:244-247; cf. *infra*, pp. 323-328), there are many forms without a consonantal suffix. However, there are also numerous examples of this verb functioning within the WS modal system. Therefore, there is a considerable number of forms (and variants) such as 3rd m.s. *yi-de* (EA 70:24; *et passim*) and 2nd m.s. *ti-de* (EA 100:23; *et passim*), as well as one 3rd m.pl. *ti-du* (EA 105:36) and one 1st c.pl. *ni-de* (EA 108:43).

izzuzu. Apart from three examples of the present-future theme without prefixed *y*-, which are most likely to be reckoned as suffix conjugation forms (cf. Rainey 1973c:248-249; cf. *supra*, pp. 322-323), the prefix conjugation forms prefer the preterite theme, e.g. 3rd m.s. *yi-iz-zi-iz* (EA 250:42), *yi-zi-iz* (EA 74:61; *et passim*), *yi-zi-za* (EA 132:48), *yi-zi-zu* (EA 362:65), 1st c.s.*iz-zi-iz* (EA 197:20), *iz-zi-iz-mì* (EA 245:9), *i-zi-za* (EA 71:25), *i-zi-zu-na* (EA 124:16), 1st c.pl. *ni-zi-iz* (EA 279:18).

kalû. Only two forms are attested in the WS texts, both with the Akkadian present-future gemination but in one case with the thematic vowel of the D preterite (Rabiner 1981:79): 1st c.s. *a-kal-li* (EA 254:13, 14), *a-kal-lu-ši* (EA 254:40).

kapālu. An Akkadian G present, with intranisitive meaning (*CAD* K:174-175), is used in the proverb about the ants:

> . . . *ki-i na-am-lu / tu-um-ḫa-ṣú la-a / ti-ka-pí-lu ù ta-an-šu-ku / qà-ti* LÚ-*lì ša yu-ma-ḫa-aš-ši* ". . . when ants are smitten, they do not just curl up, but they bite the hand of the man who has smitten them" (EA 252:16-19; Albright 1943b:31; Rainey 1989-90:68b-69a; cf, *infra*, pp. 148-149).

kašādu. The WS texts have the preterite theme: 3rd m.s. *ia-ak-šu-du-na* (EA 130:12; possibly reflecting Barth's law), *yi-ik-šu-du* (EA 227:15), and present-future 1st c.s. *i-ka-ša-da-am* (EA 362:34).

leqû. From this high-frequency verb, only two Akkadian present-futures are attested in the WS texts and they are both from Jerusalem: 3rd f.s. *ti-le-eq-qé* (EA 288:35), 3rd m.pl. *ti-le-qé-ú* (EA 288:38). The latter form, as Moran (1975b:164 n. 63) has noted, is evidently comprised of three morphological components, the WS *t*- prefix for 3rd m.pl., Babylonian vowel coloring, and Assyrian lack of final vowel contraction (cf. also Izreʾel 1987:89-90).

Throughout the rest of the WS corpus, the preference is for the preterite theme, or occasionally for the preterite with -*t*- infix. Here is a representative selection of the many preterite themes: 3rd m.s. *yi-ìl-qé* (EA 116:36; *et passim*), *yi-ìl-qú* (EA 71:18; *et passim*), 3rd f.s. *ti*$_7$*-ìl-qé* (EA 362:20), 2nd m.s. *ti-ìl-qú* (EA 138:41), 3rd m.pl. *ti-ìl-qú* (EA 84:32; *et passim*), *ti-ìl-qú-na* (EA 104:22, 25, 32), *et al.*

Of the forms based on the -*t*- preterite, many lack any consonantal prefix and one must suspect that, in the mind of the Canaanite scribe, they were to be reckoned syntactically with the suffix conjugation (cf. *infra*, pp. 339-341). There are still a few, nevertheless, that do have WS suffixes: 3rd m.s. *yi-il-te-qú* (EA 254:25), *yi-ìl-te*$_9$*-qú* (EA 109:17, 19; Moran 1950b:167-168), *yi-ìl-te-qé-ni* (EA 270:27), *yi-il*$_5$*-te-qé* (EA 239:13), *yi-il*$_5$*-te-qú* (EA 280:31), 3rd m.pl. *ti-ìl-te*$_9$*-qú-na* (EA 71:15).

lamādu. This verb is used frequently in the WS letters, usually in the jussive; all prefix forms have the preterite as their theme: 3rd m.s. *yi-ìl-ma-ad* (EA 264:23; 337:17; 366:17), *yi-il₅-ma-ad* (EA 64:8; *et passim*), *yi-ìl-ma-du* (EA 251:9).

leʾû. In spite of its Akkadian role as a preformative stative, this verb is usually conjugated in the WS texts (Rainey 1973c:247-248). The theme is the present-future: 3rd m.s. *yi-la-ú* (EA 326:15), *yi-le-ú* (EA 114:36; 124:53, Izreʾel 1987:81), 2nd m.s. *ti-le-ú* (EA 83:20; *et passim*), *ti-le-ú-na* (EA 82:6), 1st c.s. *i-le-ú* (EA 82:22; *et passim*), *i-le-e* (EA 81:21), *i-lé-e* (EA 151:10), *i-le-i* (EA 144:32), *i-le-ʾì* (EA 102:9), *i-le-éʾ-e* (EA 238:8), *e-la-ú-mi* (EA 137:27), and the Assyrianizing Jerusalem forms (Moran 1975b:154) *a-la-ʾe-e* (EA 286:42; 287:58), 3rd m.pl. *te-le-ú-na* (EA 249:13), 1st c.pl. *ni-le-ú* (EA 88:20; *et passim*), *ni-la-ú* (EA 211:18).

Three examples without consonantal prefixes are to be taken as statives: 3rd m.s. *i-le-e* (EA 79:39) and 3rd m.pl. *i-le-ú* (EA 106:12, 13).

magāru. Only two examples in the WS texts, perhaps to be considered as D (cf. EA 283:10): 3rd f.s. *ti-ma-ga-ru* (EA 138:62), 1st c.s. *i-ma-gur* (EA 234:27), unless they are N.

maḫāṣu. All documented forms have the present-future theme, perhaps to represent D: 3rd m.s. *yi-ma-ḫa-aš-ši* (EA 252:19), 3rd f.s. *ti-ma-ḫa-ṣa-na-*[*ni*] (EA 77:39; Moran 1950b:60, 86, 100-101, 128 n. 118), 3rd m.pl. *ti-ma-ḫa-ṣú-ka* (EA 252:27), *ti₇-ma-ḫa-ṣú-nu* (EA 271:21).

malāku. The scribes vary between the present-future theme: 3rd m.s. *yi-ma-lik* (EA 94:12), *yi-ma-li-ku* (EA 104:16; 114:12), which was probably meant for D or N stem in the light of the precative 3rd m.s. ⌜*li*⌝-⌜*ma*⌝-*lik* (EA 94:72; a likely reading in spite of Youngblood's objections, 1961:386). On the other hand, there are preterite themes, mainly for WS jussives, some with the normal Akkadian *i* theme, but with the WS prefix vowel, viz. 3rd m.s. *ya-am-li-ik* (EA 105:6), *ya-am-lik* (EA 114:20), while others (all but one from Beirut) have a *u* theme but an *i* prefix vowel: 3rd m.s. *yi-im-lu-uk* (EA 136:40), *yi-im-lu-ku* (EA 142:17; 216:20), 1st c.s. *im-lu-uk* (EA 136:26).

maqātu. In the epistolary introduction, nearly all Canaanite scribes use the preterite, *amqut*, or some spelling variant for the plural, *nimqut* (cf. EA 100:6; 200:5). However, this is a learned formula, standard in epistles from all over the Levant (Salonen 1967:6-70, 74-76; *CAD* M/1:242b-243a). Only one clear example has the preterite in the message of a letter, 3rd m.s. *yi-im-qú-ut* (EA 295:17). The other passages all use the present-future theme, probably to represent a D stem nuance (unattested for good Akkadian): 3rd m.s. or 1st c.s. *i-ma-qú-*⸢*ut*⸣ (EA 173:2), 3rd m.s. *yi-ma-qú-ta* (EA 81:31; 83:43), 2nd m.s. *ti-ma-qú-tu* (EA 73:10), 1st c.s. *ni-ma-qú-*⸢*ut*⸣ (EA 74:32).

mâtu. It is most difficult to determine which Akkadian tense form is being preferred. One ideographic spelling is BA.UG$_7$-*at* (EA 87:31) for *amât*. All the other instances in WS texts have vocalic endings which, in Babylonian, would require gemination of the last radical and a return of the root vowel, *u*, as the theme, i.e. *amuttu* (*GAG:*143, §104f). The 3rd m.s. *ia-mu-tu* (EA 138:27) looks purely WS, as does the 3rd m.pl. *ta-mu-tu-na* (EA 362:44). The 1st c.s. *a-mu-tu* (EA 137:52; 285:30) and *a-mu-*⸢*ta*⸣ (EA 114:68; 130:51) could be either for *amuttu* and *amutta* or *amūtu* and *amūta* respectively. The latter is more likely in view of the 1st c.s. BA.UG$_7$.MEŠ$^{ni\text{-}mu\text{-}ut}$ (EA 362:11); so one may also posit a preterite theme for the Jerusalem spelling BA.UG$_7$$^{ni\text{-}mu\text{-}tu_4}$ (EA 288:60-61).

nadānu. There are only two examples of the present-future form, one from Beirut and one from Taanach (Rainey 1975b:397-404): 1st c.s. *a-na-din-mi* (EA 137:55), *a-na-*⸢*din*⸣ (TT 1:10); it is not certain whether the latter form is functioning in an Akkadian or a WS syntagma (Rainey 1977:55-56). Nearly all the other instances of this verb in the WS texts from Amarna use the preterite theme with a few examples of the preterite with infixed -*t*-. Byblos shows a preference for forms such as 3rd m.s. *ia-di-in*$_4$ (EA 116:46), *ia-di-nu* (EA 105:85; *et passim*), and *ia-di-na* (EA 74:54; *et passim*), which might imply that 3rd m.s. forms with initial PI are to be read: *ya-di-in*$_4$ (EA 113:32), *ya-di-nu* (EA 225:10), *ya-di-na* (EA 93:11), *ya-di-na*$_7$ (EA 127:27) *et al.* However, the 3rd f.s. forms, *ti-di-in* (EA 74:3), *ti-din* (EA 73:4; *et passim*), *ti-id-di-in*$_4$ (EA 68:5), *ti-di-in*$_4$ (EA 76:4; *et passim*), and the 3rd m.pl. *ti-di-nu* (EA 71:5; 86:4; 87:6; 95:5; Moran 1950b:62-63), suggest that some Byblos scribes used the PI sign rather than the *ia* precisely because they intended *yi-di-in*$_4$ etc.! Nevertheless, *ya-ti-na* (EA 83:31) might represent the true Canaanite (Phoenician, also Ugaritic) form, viz. **yatin* (Youngblood, 1961:248). The Tyrian scribe has 1st c.s. *id-din* (EA 155:27; Finkle 1977:89, 90). For 1st c.pl., in addition to the Akkadian forms, *ni-din-mì* (EA 191:20) and *ni-di-nu* (EA 112:52), Albright and Moran (1950:166) pointed to *na-ad-na* (EA 89:16) as 1st c.pl. Hence, we may posit a Canaanite prefix *na-*.

One Egyptian letter uses 3rd m.s. *yi-ta-din* (EA 369:28; Cochavi-Rainey 1988:143-144). The Tyrian scribe had a penchant for 3rd m.s. *it-ta-din* (EA 149:39; 155:24) and 1st c.s. *at-ta-din* (EA 148:6; *et passim*).

namāšu. This verb always appears in the present-future theme, usually with the *u* thematic vowel, e.g. 3rd m.s. *yi-na-mu-šu* (EA 250:53) *et al.*, but there are two instances of an *a* theme: 3rd m.s. *yi-na-ma-aš* (EA 196:42) and 3rd f.s. *ti-na-ma-šu* (EA 266:19).

naṣāru. In the majority of cases, this verb appears in the present-future theme (Rainey 1975b:404-419), e.g. 3rd m.s. *yi-na-ṣa-ra-ni* (EA 119:10), *yi-na-ṣa-ru-ni* (EA 112:17) and other variants, 1st c.s. *a-na-ṣa-ru* (EA 221:12; *et passim*) and other variants, 3rd m.pl. *ti-na-ṣa-ru* (EA 85:22; *et passim*), *ti*$_7$*-na-ṣa-ru* (EA 180:8), 1st c.pl. *ni-na-ṣa-ar* (EA 181:9), *ni-na-ṣa-ru* (EA 100:9, 30). There are many 1st c.s. forms based on the Akkadian present-future 3rd m.s. theme + Ø preformative: *i-na-ṣa-ru* (EA 65:10; *et passim*) with other variants. But the most significant variation is in the numerous forms with *i* thematic vowel: 3rd m.s. *yi-na-ṣí-ru* (EA 112:14), *yi-na-ṣí-ru-ni* (EA 112:18), *yi-na-ṣí-ra-an-ni* (EA 112:13;

121:10), *yi-na-ṣí-ra-ni* (EA 130:20), 1st c.s. *i-na-ṣí-ru* (EA 119:15); 130:49), *i-na-ṣí-ru-na* (EA 123:32), *i-na-ṣí-ra* (EA 123:27), 3rd m.pl. *ti-na-ṣí-ru* (EA 130:48). It has long been recognized that these *i* theme forms reflect the scribes' feeling that the themes with geminated second radical must be equated with D stem (Ebeling 1910:52; Albright and Moran 1950:165-166; Youngblood 1961:151-152; Rainey 1975b:417-419; cf *infra,* pp. 171-172). Further confirmation derives from 1st c.s. *ú-na-ṣár* (EA 327:5).

On the other hand, there is an appreciable number of epistles which use the preterite theme. Apart from 3rd m.pl. *ti-ṣú-ru* (EA 88:41, also line 25; Youngblood 1961:316-317), all the examples are 1st c.s., *aṣ-ṣur-*⸢*mi*⸣ (EA 364:14), *i-ṣú-ru* (EA 220:15; 292:23; 293:12; 294:12). A special group of forms seem to take the 2nd m.s. imperative as their theme (Rainey 1974:306; 404-417 passim; 1978b:84)! All of them are, in fact, 1st c.s., *uṣ-ṣú-ru* (EA 141:41; 142:12), ⸢*uṣ*⸣*-ṣur-*⸢*šu*⸣ (EA 230:13), *uṣ-ṣur-ru-na* (EA 252:8), *ú-ṣur-ru* (EA 337:28), *ú-ṣur-ru-šu-nu* (EA 252:31), *ú-ṣur-ru-na* (EA 252:28).

qabû. There are a number of forms with the present-future theme, e.g. 3rd m.s. *yi-qa-bi* (EA 234:16), *yi-qa-bu* (EA 117:83; *et passim*), and *i-qa-bu* (EA 106:30), 2nd m.s. *ti-qa-bu* (EA 117:30; 124:35; 253:23), 1st c.s. *a-qa-bi* (EA 92:30; and Jerusalem EA 286:17, 39, 49), *a-qa-bu-na* (EA 85:11; 119:53), *i-qa-bi* (EA 106:46), i_{15}*-qa-bi* (EA 180:16), 3rd m.pl. *yi-qa-bu* (EA 124:17; 131:41), *yi-qa-bu-na* (EA 116:8), *i-qa-bu-*ni_7 (EA 127:10).

However, there is very extensive use of the preterite theme, for example: 3rd m.s. *iq-bi* (EA 68:2; *et passim*), *yi-iq-bi* (EA 85:23; *et passim*), *yi-iq-bu* (EA 129:84; *et passim*), *ia-aq-bi* (EA 83:84; *et passim*), *ia-aq-bu* (EA 101:19; *et passim*), 3rd f.s. *ta-aq-bi* (EA 138:11), *ti-iq-bi* (EA 138:44), *ta-aq-bu* (EA 89:40; 122:41), *ti-iq-bu* (EA 138:90), 2nd m.s. *taq-bi* (EA 86:15), *ti-iq-bi* (EA 83:45), *taq-bu* (EA 73:7), *taq-bu-ú* (EA 96:7), *ti-iq-bu* (EA 71:12), 1st c.s. *aq-bi* (EA 75:28; *et passim*), *aq-ba* (EA 121:25), *aq-bu* (EA 107:10; 109:15), *aq-bu-na* (EA 138:82), 3rd m.pl. *ti-iq-bu* (EA 138:40; 185:55; 186:58), ti_7*-iq-bu-*ni_7 (EA 362:17, 25), ti_7*-iq-bu-na* (EA 94:14; 137:10; 197:16; 362:21).

qâlu. Usually this verb appears in the suffix form. The examples of the prefix conjugation can have either the present-future theme, e.g. 3rd m.s. *i-qa-al* (EA 185:67), 2nd m.s. *ta-qa-al-mi* (EA 74:13, 48; 76:45; 90:57), or the preterite theme: *i-qú-ul* (EA 149:41, from Tyre), *ia-qú-ul* (EA 132:44; *et passim*), *ya-qú-lu* (EA 140:5), 2nd m.s. *ta-qú-ul* (EA 139:5).

qerēbu. Note *ia-qá-ar-ri-ib* (EA 39:19; from Alashia).

raʾāmu. Of all the attested examples of this verb, only two have a consonantal suffix. The rest are probably to be considered as "preformative statives" or suffix conjugation (cf. *infra*, pp. 343-345). The two forms in question represent both the present-future theme, 2nd m.s. *ta-ra-ia-mu* (EA 286:18; hybrid with WS tense function in direct discourse, Nitzan 1973:41, 61), and the preterite, 3rd f.s. ⌈*ša*⌉ *ti-ra-am* / dUTU, where the verb must represent a translation of the Egyptian perfective passive participle, *mry*.

ṣabātu. The few attested forms in WS texts use the preterite theme, e.g. 3rd m.s. *yi-iṣ-bat* (EA 138:28), *yi-iṣ-ba-tu-ši* (EA 137:62; Moran 1987b:361 n.12; 1992:220 n. 12; Izreʾel 1987:81-82), 3rd m.pl. *ti-iṣ-ba-tu* (EA 137:98), *ti₇-iṣ-ba-tu* (EA 137:40), 1st c.pl. *ni-iṣ-bat* (EA 138:101).

šaʾālu. There seems to be a decided preference for the preterite theme, viz. *ia-aš-al-mì* (EA 224:10), *yi-iš-al-šu* (EA 60:21), and *yi-ša-al* (EA 124:23; *et passim*),. Three forms, viz. 3rd m.s. *yi-ša-i-lu* (EA 89:15, 34, 45), *yi-ša-a-lu* (EA 89:12, 13) and 2nd m.s. *ti-ša-i-lu* (EA 89:40), have the present-future theme but appear to be intended to function as D stem (Albright and Moran 1950:165-166).

šakānu. The few attested forms are not only preterite, but they look like pure WS verb forms: 3rd m.s. *ia-aš-ku-un* (EA 108:59), *ia-aš-ku-nu* (EA 113:6), with the exception of 1st c.s. *ni-iš-kán* (EA 149:52), which, being from Tyre, is probably an error for the present-future *ni-ša!-kán*.

šapāru. There are three or four problematic cases of the present-future theme, 3rd m.s. *i-ša-pa-ru* (EA 123:29), 2nd m.s. *ti-ša-pa-ru* (EA 93:8), *ta-šap-pár* (EA 102:38; for the suffix conjugation form, *ta-šap-pár-ta*, line 10, cf. *infra*, pp. 338, 345-346). The first two express repeated action in the past, not because they are Akkadian present forms, but because of the WS imperfect suffix, *-u* (cf. *infra*, pp. 232-233).

There are numerous forms built on the preterite theme plus the various Canaanite tense and modal suffixes, for example: 3rd m.s. *ia-aš-pu-ur* (EA 117:60; 247:9), *yi-iš-pur-mì* (EA 250:23), *ia-aš-pu-ru* (EA 89:36; 138:23), *ia-aš-pu-ra* (EA 234:23; *et al.*), *yi-iš-pu-ra-am* (EA 362:22), 2nd m.s. *ta-aš-pu-ra* (EA 77:7; 95:7; TT 1:8). 1st c.s. *aš-pu-ur* (EA 138:31, 42; 362:18), *aš-pu-ru* (EA 83:44; *et passim*), 3rd m.pl. *ta-aš-pu-ru-na* (EA 138:122), *ti-iš-pu-ru-na* (EA 138:137), *ti-ìš-pu-ru-na* (EA 118:47), 1st c.pl. *ni-iš-pu-ru* (EA 112:53).

šemû. There are only a handful of forms based on the present-future theme; all of them have -Ø suffix. Two of them are definitely past tense (Rainey 1975b:424-426; Moran 1987b:273 n.1; 1992:159 n. 1), viz. 3rd m.s. *i-še*$_{20}$*-me* (EA 87:18), and 1st c.s. *i-še*$_{20}$*-me* (EA 87:15); and one other probably is, viz. 3rd m.s. *i-še*$_{20}$*-mé* (EA 92:21; cf. Moran 1987b:283; 1992:166). Another could be simple past, i.e. an error for *yišme* or *yišteme*, but it could also be expressing past continuous like the Akkadian present-future, in spite of the WS consonantal prefix: 3rd m.s. *yi-še*$_{20}$*-mé* (EA 92:15; Rainey 1975b:420-421; cf. Moran 1987b:282; 1992:166). The last one, 1st c.s. *i-še*$_{20}$*-mé* (EA 106:39), could be present (Moran 1950b:67) or past (Moran 1987b:303; 1992:179). Note that these are all spellings in which the *ši* sign could simply be an error for *iš*.

One form listed by Ebeling as G present, viz. *yi-ša-ma* (EA 227:10), is actually N stem (Rainey 1975b:421-422; cf. *infra*, p. 120).

There is an abundance of forms using the preterite theme; a selection of some of the most frequent will suffice: 3rd m.s. *yi-iš-me* (EA 119:26;*et passim*), *yi-iš-mé* (EA 94:4; *et passim*), *yi-ìš-me* (EA 78:17; *et passim*), *yi-ìš-mé* (EA 85:16; *et passim*), *yi-iš-mu*

(EA 109:16, 18; *et passim*), 2nd m.s. *ti-ìš-me* (EA 90:13; 109:14), *ti-ìš-mé* (EA 86:17), 1st c.s. *eš-me* (EA 105:40), *eš-mé* (EA 91:23), *iš-me* (EA 136:15; *et al.*), *iš-mé* (EA 317:12, 22; *et al.*), *iš-mu* (EA 251:15), 3rd m.pl. *ti-ìš-mu-na* (EA 82:11; 108:51), 1st c.pl. *ni-iš-mé* (EA 185:50; 186:52), *ni-iš-mu-mi* (EA 185:75), *ni-ìš-mu* (EA 211:14). Note that the 2nd m.s. forms could be transcribed *te₉-eš-me* and *te₉-eš-mé* respectively, but nothing would be gained thereby.

tarāṣu. All the G stem examples of this verb are precative except for two jussives based on the preterite theme: 3rd m.s. *yi-it-ru-uš* (EA 103:40; 250:22).

târu. The three attested forms are probably all on the preterite theme, though two of them, with vocalic suffixes might be on the Babylonian present-future base: 3rd m.s. *ia-tu-ru-na* (EA 126:54), 1st c.s. *a-tu-ur* (EA 136:33), 3rd m.pl. *ti-tu-ru-na* (EA 134:14).

When one realizes that for most verbs, only one theme or the other is used, it becomes evident that the indicators of tense and mode must be other than the standard Akkadian distinction between the *iparras* and the *iprus* patterns. The actual WS system of tense and modal expression will be dealt with in chapter 10 (cf. *infra*, pp. 221-264).

THE BARTH-GINSBERG LAW.

Meanwhile, it remains to treat another important feature of the G stem verbs used in these texts, viz. the distinction between the colloquial use of prefix vowels, as outlined in the preceding chapter, and the actual Canaanite patterns of vocalization that existed in the scribes' mother tongue. It is important for the diachronic study of the North West Semitic dialects that the true linguistic situation in the Amarna texts from Canaan be clearly delineated. Much confusion generated by the older interpretations of the Amarna dialect evidence can thereby be dispelled.

The original pattern of the G stem morphology for ancient Hebrew was discovered by J. Barth (1889, 1894). The vocalic system that he delineated will be discussed below. An important milestone in the study of Northwest Semitic was H. L. Ginsberg's discovery that Ugaritic possessed the same system of vocalization that Barth had found in Hebrew (Ginsberg 1932-33:38-838; 1939:318-322). Albright (1943a:17 n. 60; 1943b:31 nn. 17, 20) was quick to grasp the implications of Ginsberg's discovery for the Amarna texts from Canaan although he tried to apply it to a presumed *yaqatal* pattern which does not actually exist in Northwest Semitic. The discovery and publication of a large selection from the Mari tablets gave new impetus to the study of the so-called Amurrite personal names in the Middle Bronze Age (Huffmon 1965; Buccellati 1966; Gelb 1968,1980; Sasson 1972). It soon became clear that Amurrite, as reflected in these PN's, was thoroughly West Semitic but lacked the typical Barth-Ginsberg developments. At that time, no one thought to examine the evidence from the Amarna letters written in Canaan (Rainey 1978a). Ebeling (1910:45-50), Böhl (1909:48-58) and Dhorme (1913:376-382; 1914:49-59; 1951:412-419, 445-456) dealt with problems of the prefix vowels in the EA verbs, but only Ebeling (1910:47) made reference to Barth's work, and then just to his discovery that the *i* thematic vowel had originally been more prevalent in ancient Hebrew than was reflected in the Tiberian tradition (Barth 1889). Ebeling and the others were so impressed by the ubiquity of verbal forms in the Canaanized texts that had *yi-*, *ti-*, and *Øi-* prefixes, that they jumped to the superficial conclusion that EA forms such as *yi-ik-šu-du* (EA 227:15), *yi-im-qú-ut* (EA 295:17), *yi-ip-ṭú-ra* (EA 234:21), *yi-iš-pu-ra-am* (EA 362:22) and *yi-it-ru-uṣ* (EA 103:40; 250:22) were the equivalent of Hebrew *yišmōr.* Their view was passed on to some of the leading grammars of biblical Hebrew (Bauer and Leander 1922:194, §14x; Bergsträsser 1929:78, §14f[1]).

THE ANCIENT SEMITIC PATTERN. The evidence now at hand suggests the following patterns for Semitic languages in general. The most ancient witness is Akkadian. The Akkadian 3rd m.s. is of no value here, of course, because the ancient prefix *ya-* became *i-* in all G stem verb classes of Akkadian; neither is there any relevance in the *iparras* forms since their choice of thematic vowel is conditioned by factors other than the Barth-Ginsberg law (*GAG*:113, §87c; 135, §101b; 137, §102f; 138, §103b; 139, §103f). The original prefix vowel is found in the 2nd singular and plural and 1st singular forms of the preterite, e.g. *taprus / aprus, tapqid / apqid, taṣbat / aṣbat.* So it is clear that the ancient pattern of vocalization goes back to proto-Semitic *yaqtul, yaqtil, yaqtal* (*GAG*:98, §75e).

The same patterns are discernible in the Amurrite PN's, especially from Mari. Representative examples are: *Yagmur-Ilu, Yantin-Ilu,* and *Yasmaᶜ-Ilu,* all of them written syllabically; *Ia-ag-mu-ur*-DINGIR (*ARM* 7, 169:12), *Ia-an-ti-in*-DINGIR (*ARM* 5, 35:27), and *Ia-ás-ma-aḫ*-DINGIR (*ARM* 6, 22:16), respectively (Huffmon 1965:63-78, especially p. 64). Names like these, with the simple prefix conjugation form plus -Ø suffix, could be either jussive or preterite. Corresponding Akkadian names from Mari such as *Iddin-Sîn* (*ARM* 5, 47:5) and *Išme-Dagan* (*ARM et passim*) suggest that they are preterites. The corresponding Amurrite jussive/optative PN's seem to have a *la-* proclitic particle (Huffmon 1965:78-81).

Now it is well known that the testimony of Akkadian and Amurrite corresponds to the patterns in use in Arabic, e.g. *yaktub, yaḍrib,* and *yamraḍ* (Fischer 1972:105, §216). So the oldest documented Semitic language, Akkadian, and the oldest documented West Semitic language, Amurrite (the evidence from Eblaite has still to be evaluated), and the most conservative living Semitic language, classical Arabic, all point to an original set of patterns for the prefixes of the finite verbs: *yaqtul, yaqtil, yaqtal.*

HEBREW. It was Barth's discovery that Hebrew had originally employed the first two of those ancient patterns, viz. *yaqtul, yaqtil,* but that the third was not *yaqtal,* but rather *yiqtal,* which he thought was the original (Barth 1894:4-5). The situation in Tiberian Hebrew has been obscured by a much later phenomenon, viz. the attenuation of short *a* vowels in closed, unaccented syllables to short *i* /*e* (cf. *infra,* pp. 73-75). Thus, ancient

**yašmur* eventually became *yišmōr* and **yattin* became *yittēn*. However, there are verbal roots, the morphology of which prohibits the closing of the first syllable, and they reveal the system of forms delineated by Barth. Among roots with a reduplicated second radical, one finds *yāsōḇ* (1 Ki. 7:15), *yāḡēn* (Isa. 31:5; originally G but later understood as H stem; Barth 1889:175; Bergsträsser 1929:135, §27d), but *yēraḵ* (Isa. 7:4), which derive from the *yaqtul, yaqtil* and *yiqtal* patterns respectively. The hollow roots (those with IInd *w* /*ū* or *y* /*ī*) also show the same three basic forms: *yāqûm* (Ex. 21:19), *yāśîm* (Gen. 30:42), and *yēḇôš* (Isa. 29:22) respectively (Bergsträsser 1929:142-145, §§28a-d). It was Barth's contention that many *yaqtil* verbs had become either *u* theme or *a* theme during the course of time (Barth 1889:42). As is well recognized, the *yiqtal* verbs either have their a theme either semantically, because they are stative in meaning, or phonetically, because there is a guttural consonant in the second or third root position, or both due to conditions being present (at least some IIIrd yod verbs must have originally had the *yiqtal* pattern; Joüon and Muraoka 1991:205, §79*e*-).

UGARITIC. As mentioned above, Ginsberg (1932-33:382-383; 1939:318-322) discovered that Ugaritic displayed the same patterns as did biblical Hebrew. The almost strictly consonantal Ugaritic script limited his examples to 1st c.s. of the prefix conjugation where the aleph signs varied according to the prefix vowel. Thus, one could surmise that Barth's law was at work on the basis of forms such as: *amlk* = **ʾamluk-*, *amt* = **ʾamût-*, *atn* = **ʾatin-*, *ašr* = **ʾašîr*, and finally *ilak* = **ʾilʾak-*, *išal* = **ʾišʾal-* (for references and other examples, cf. Gordon 1965:71, §9.9).

Ginsberg's analysis of finite verb forms in the alphabetic texts has been confirmed by Ugaritic PN's preserved in syllabic transcription (Gröndahl 1967:57-59; cf, also Sivan 1984:147-158 *et passim*), as illustrated by the following examples with the corresponding alphabetic spellings: [I]*Ia-ku-un*-DINGIR = *yknil* = **Yakun-ʾIlu* (for the references, cf. Sivan 1984:239; Gordon 1965:410b); [I]*Ia-šu-ub*-DINGIR = **Yaṯub-ʾIlu* (Sivan 1984:282); [I]*Ia-ti*$_7$*-nu* (cf. *ytn*, finite verb) = **Yatinu* (Sivan 1984:292; Gordon

1965:415b-416a); and finally ^{I}*Ig-ma-ra-*^{d}IŠKUR (cf. *ygmr*, PN) = *(*Y*)*igmar-Haddu* (Sivan 1984:220; Gordon 1965:380).

THE AMARNA EVIDENCE. With this picture in mind, viz. the patterns *yaqtul, yaqtil* and *yiqtal,* it is necessary to examine the evidence from the Canaanized Amarna letters to see if traces of the Barth-Ginsberg law may be found (Rainey 1978a:9*-13*).

yaqtul. As noted already by Ebeling (1910:46) and Dhorme (1913:377 = 1951:416), the original Canaanite pattern is reflected in a gloss from Hazor:

> [*ù*] *li-iḫ-šu-uš-mi* / \ *ia-az-ku-ur-mi* / ^{I}*šàr-ri* EN-*ia* / *mi-im-ma ša* / *in*$_4$*-né-pu-uš-mi* / UGU ^{URU}*Ḫa-ṣú-ra*^{KI} / URU.KI-*ka ù* / UGU ÌR-*ka* "May the king, my lord, be mindful (gloss: take thought) of all that has been done against Hazor, your city, and against your servant" (EA 228:18-24; *CAD* Ḫ:123b; Z:22b.

The form, *ya-az-ku-ur* = **yazkur,* 3rd m.s. jussive, clearly signifies the Canaanite translation of Akkadian *liḫsus.* The jussive modal conjugation pattern will be discussed in a subsequent chapter (cf. *infra,* pp. 245-254). So this gloss reveals that the true WS pattern is *yaqtul,* with an *a* vowel in the prefix. (Barker 1969:33-34)

A 3rd f.s. Canaanite form with a singular collective subject was noted by Albright (1943b:31 n. 17):

> . . . *ki-i na-am-lu* / *tu-um-ḫa-ṣú la-a* / *ti-ka-pí-lu ù ta-an-šu-ku* / *qà-ti* LÚ-*lì ša yi-ma-ḫa-aš-ši*". . . when ants are smitten, they do not just curl up but they bite the hand of the man who has smitten them" (EA 252:16-19; Albright 1943b:31; cf. Rainey 1989-90:68b-69a; *supra,* pp. 4-5, *infra,* p. 78).

Although a form like **tanšuku,* with the *ta-* prefix, could be good 3rd f.s. in Assyrian and occasionally in poetic or late Babylonian (cf. *supra,* pp. 37-38), the syntactic environment in this context shows that the form is most likely Canaanite.

Other instances of Canaanite, neither hybrid nor Akkadian, forms include the following:

> *i-ia-nu* LÚ.MEŠ*ḫa-za-na* LU[GAL] *k[i-ma i]a-ši* / *a-na* LUGAL *ša-a ia-mu-tu* [UGU *be-l*]*i-ia* "The king does not have a ro[yal] city-ruler l[ike m]e, who would die [for] my [lor]d" (EA 138:26-27).

The prefix indicates that the Beirutian scribe intended WS **yamûtu,* certainly not Akkadian *imuttu* . Even more certain is the purely Canaanite for in this next passage, where the verb can only be Canaanite **tamûtûna,* 3rd m.pl. imperfect:

> *ù i-du i-nu-ma ta-mu-tu-na* "and they know that they will die" (EA 362:44),

To these may be added two examples of *šakānu,* since this verb can have the meaning, "place, put, impose," etc. in WS (for Ugaritic, cf. Gordon 1965:490a) as well as in Akkadian:

> [*ú*]-*u*[*l i*]*a-aš-ku-un* / *lum-ni*[-*ia i*]-*na lìb-bi*-⸢*ka*⸣ "[Do]n't think bad of me" (EA 108:59-60; *contra* Moran 1987b:307 n. 9; 1992:182 n. 10); *‹l›a ia-aš-ku-un* [L]UGAL ŠÀ-*šu* / *i-na mi-im-mi ša yi-iš-ši-ru* / I*A-zi-ru a-na ša-šu* "May the king [no]t pay attention to the things that Aziru is sending to him" (EA 139:33-35; Moran 1987b:368 n. 7; 1992:226 n. 8); *ù ú-ul y*[*i-pu-šu*] / *ar-na ù ia-aš-ku*[-*n*]*u* / *i-na lìb-bi-šu* "that is not co[mmitting] a crime or harbori[n]g, in his heart" (EA 113:5-6; with Moran 1987b:315 n. 3; 1992:188 n. 3).

The forms **yaškun* and **yaškunu,* all in WS idioms, are the only G stem 3rd m.s. prefix forms of this verb in the texts from Canaan (EA 119:58 has an N form, not a G present; Rainey 1975b:422; cf. *infra*, pp. 119-120). It stands to reason that they should reflect true Canaanite verb forms.

Sivan (1984:148) includes the somewhat enigmatic form introduced by the gloss sign: *ia-ak-wu-un-*⸢*ka*⸣ (EA 145:28), which he renders "He will be honest with you" (more likely jussive or preterite). His derivation is from *kânu,* and he presupposes a scribal error for **yakûn* (probably **yakun*).

There should be no doubt that the real Canaanite forms reflect *yaqtul.* This would justifiably lead one to suspect that the non-WS verb, *šapāru,* which is so ubiquitous in the Gt (Gtn?), may have been intentionally dressed in Canaanite vocalization when appearing in the G stem, viz. *ia-aš-pur* (EA 250:23), *ia-aš-pu-ur* (EA 117:60), *ia-aš-pu-ru* (EA 89:36; 138:123), *[ia-a]š-pu-ra* (EA 138:67)

yaqtil. This vocalization is documented by a Canaanite gloss which not only shows the contrast between the Akkadian and the WS forms, but also demonstrates the absence of a *yaqattal* verb form in the WS G stem (Rainey 1975b:423):

> *a-nu-um-ma a-na-ku-ma / er-ri-šu \ aḫ-ri-šu / i-na* ^{URU}*Šu-na-ma*^{KI} "Now, (it is) I (who) am cultivating (gloss: am cultivating) in Shunem" (EA 362:10-12; *CAD* Ḫ:96; Barker 1969:45).

The gloss, *aḫ-ri-šu,* was given to clarify the hybrid, *er-ri-šu,* which is Akkadian 1st c.s. present-future plus the WS *-u* imperfect suffix. The Canaanite form was 1st c.s. **ʾaḥriṯu,* "I am cultivating." In the original publication of this text, Thureau-Dangin (1922a:97) transcribed *iḫ-ri-šu,* simply because he was unaware of the WS linguistic rule. The first cuneiform sign is v+*ḫ,* which would leave the question open. Thureau-Dangin should have followed Knudtzon's example in transcribing the other instance of the same verb form. Although the signs are partially effaced, the reading is certain; Knudtzon correctly rendered the passage as follows:

> *a-nu-ma / ⸢i⸣-ri-šu \ aḫ-r[i-šu]* "Now, I am cultivating (gloss: am cult[ivating])" (EA 226:10-11).

Knudtzon was evidently more aware of the requirements of WS linguistics. In any case, he was correct in assuming the presence of an *a* vowel in the 1st c.s. prefix. From these two examples, the Canaanite thematic vowel is seen to be *i* rather than the *u* of

Hebrew, e.g *yaḥ^{a}rōš* (Isa. 28:24). Classical Arabic has both *ʾaḥriṯu* and *ʾaḥruṯu* (colloquial Palestinian is *aḥrot*). Akkadian has an *i* theme in the principal dialects but OAkk has one documented instance of 1st c.s. *à-ru-uš* (Smith 1932:296, line 9) and an *a-u* pattern existed in later Assyrian (for references, cf. *CAD* E:285-289). The verb, *yḥrṯ*, is documented in Ugaritic (Rainey 1971b:164-165) but the vocalic pattern is unknown.

Further examples of *yaqtil* may be adduced from the exclusively EA usage of *malāku* in the meaning, "to care for, to show concern" (*CAD* M/1:156b). Hybrids based on the Akkadian verb are often used to express this nuance, e.g. the G precative, *li-im-li-ik* (EA 149:8, 54; *et al.*) and the D or N precative, *li-ma-lik* (EA 94:72). The latter suggests that 3rd m.s. *yi-ma-lik* (EA 94:12) and *yi-ma-li-ku* (EA 104:16; 114:48) are also meant to be D or N. The Beirut letters show a *u* thematic vowel in hybrid forms: 1st c.s. *im-lu-uk* (EA 136:26), 3rd m.s. *yi-im-lu-uk* (EA 136:36, 40) and *yi-im-lu-ku* (EA 142:17; also EA 216:20). However, two jussives in the Byblos letters seem to reflect the real Canaanite vocalization:

> *ya-am-li-ik šàr-ru* / *a-na* URU*Ṣu-mu-ra* "May the king show concern for Ṣumur" (EA 105:6-7); *ù ya-am-lik* LUGAL / *a-na* URU-*šu ù* ÌR-*šu* "And may the king show concern for his city and his servant" (EA 114:20-21).

The antiquity of the *i* theme for this verb is attested in both Akkadian and Arabic; the Hebrew *yimlōḵ* with its *u* theme (which also pops up in the Beirut references cited above), like *yaḥ^{a}rōš* (cited above), illustrate the process posited by Barth (1889:185), by which many *i* theme verbs either had two themes, *i* or *u*, or else shifted to another pattern, frequently to the *u* theme but sometimes to the *a* theme (when there was a guttural in the second or third position of the root).

It has long been noted that *ia-ti-na* (EA 83:31) probably represents the true Canaanite form of the verb, "to give," documented as *ytn* in both Phoenician and Ugaritic (Böhl 1909:21, §9d, 50 §28f; Dhorme 1914:50-51; 1951:447; Youngblood 1961:248). By the same token, there are numerous Byblos spellings like 3rd m.s. *ia-di-in*$_4$ (EA 116:46), *ia-di-nu* (EA 105:85; *et passim*), and *ia-di-na* (EA 74:54; *et passim*), which surely reflect the WS vocalization even though they preserve the Akkadian second radical.

There are some PN's which also reflect the *yaqtil* pattern. One clear example is ^{I}*Ia-ab-ni*-DINGIR = *Yabni-ʾilu* (EA 328:4), also known from Ugarit (alphabetic *ybnil*, syllabic as in EA; Gordon 1965:373b; Gröndahl 1967:335b, 390b; Sivan 1984:212). Another, ^{I}*Ia-*⌜*aḫ*⌝*-ṭì-ri* (EA 296:4), is evidently from the root *^{c}ṭr;* thus, *Ya^{c}ṭiri* (*contra* Hess 1993a:79-80; the final vowel is a dependent case ending, as proven by *ep-ri* in line 5; cf. Albright 1942b:33 n. 7; Marcus 1948:223-224). Two other PN's that might be G stem *yaqtil* could also be H causatives; for example, ^{I}*Ia-aḫ-zi-ba-da* (EA 275:4; 276:4) = *Ya^{c}zib-Hadda;* though Arabic has both *i* and *u* thematic vowels for this root, the Akkadian semantic parallels to this PN are Š stem (Stamm 1939:170) and Hebrew has *u* as the thematic vowel of G. Note also ^{I}*Ia-ap-ti-iḫ*-^{d}IŠKUR (EA 288:45) and ^{I}*Ia-ap-ti-ḫa-da* (EA 335:9), which represent *Yaptiḫ-Hadda* (Hess 1993a:86). The Hebrew G has an *a* theme; cf. the PN *Yip̄tāḥ* and Ugaritic *ypt*ḥ (Gröndahl 1967:58).

The apparent *yaqtil* verbal form, *ya-ar-ḫi-ša* (EA 137:97), is actually a denominative from the adverb *arḫiš* (personal observation by S. Izreʾel)!

yiqtal. While the 3rd m.s. forms with unambiguous cuneiform signs are crucial for establishing the *yaqtul* and *yaqtil* patterns, it is the 3rd f.s. that provides the crucial documentation for *yiqtal*. Albright (1943a:17 n. 60) recognized the true Canaanite nature of the negative jussive in the following context:

> *yi-ki-im* LUGAL / *be-li* KUR-*šu* / *iš-tu qa-te* / LÚ.MEŠ SA.GAZ.MEŠ / *la-a te-eḫ-la-aq* "May the king deliver his land from the grasp of the *^{c}apīrū* men lest it be lost!" (EA 274:10-14).

The verbal root, *ḫlq*, with the meaning, "lost," is known from Ugaritic (Gordon 1965:402b) as well as Akkadian. Albright was aware that Akkadian *ḫalāqu* was an *i* theme verb and that the proper Babylonian form for this nuance would be *lā iḫalliq* (e.g. *ARM* 5, 87:23). It was also obvious to him that the form of the verb in this passage, whether it be transcribed *te-eḫ-la-aq* or *ti₇-iḫ-la-aq*, corresponded to the known Hebrew and Ugaritic pattern for stative verbs in the prefix conjugation, viz. an *a* theme with an *i/e* prefix vowel. So everything points to **tiḫlaq /teḫlaq* as a true Canaanite verbal form in spite of the absence of a gloss sign or other indicator. By the same token, there is every justification for rejecting Knudtzon's transcription *aḫ-la-aq* in the following :

> *ù lu-ú yu-uš-ši-ra* / LUGAL *be-li* / GIŠGIGIR.MEŠ *ù lu-ú* / *yi-il-te-qé-ni* / *a-na mu-ḫi-šu la-a* / *iḫ-la-aq* "And may the king, my lord, send chariots and may he take me to him, lest I be lost!" (EA 270:24-29; Izreᶜel 1978b:73)

The verb in the negative final clause is surely Canaanite **ʾiḫlaq*, which, once again, is the proper vocalization for a stative verb.

In the following example of 3rd m.s., the first two signs are admittedly ambiguous, but this time Knudtzon transcribed them correctly. He may have reasoned, quite logically, that the scribe used the PI sign instead of the *ia* sign precisely because he intended to write an *i* prefix vowel:

> *šum-ma* LUGAL *be-li yi-iḫ-na-nu-ni ù* / *yu-te-ru-ni a-na* URU.KI *ù a-na-ṣár-š*[*i*] "If the king, my lord, will be gracious to me and return me to the city, then I will guard i[t]" (EA 137:81-82).

Ebeling (1910:46-47) had noted the exact Hebrew parallel, *yeḥᵉnan* (Amos 5:15). The Akkadian cognate, *enēnu*, evidently had a *u* theme (*AHw*:217b; *CAD* E:164b where the entry *enēnu* C is probably the G stem of *enēnu* A on pp. 162-164), and the same was usually true for biblical Hebrew, as demonstrated by the predominance of forms such as *yāḥōn* (Dt. 28:50), *tāḥōn* (Ps. 59:6) and *ʾāḥōn* (Ex. 33:19).

Although the following form could correspond to the true Canaanite vocalization purely as the result of coincidence, one may cite the 1st c.s. form in a letter from Megiddo:

> *ù ir-ka-ab-mi* / *it-ti* [I]*Ya-aš-da-ta* "So I mounted up with Yashdata" (EA 245:11-12).

The theme of *rakābu* in Akkadian is *a* (*AHw*:944b) and the proper form would have been *arkab*. The prefix vowel *i* in this passage could be due simply to the process of using the Akkadian 3rd m.s. as the theme with Ø- prefix for 1st c.s. Nevertheless, it is worthy of note that the Hebrew form is *ᵓerkab̲* (2 Sam. 19:27), so the Megiddo scribe could have intended to represent Canaanite **ᵓirkab*.

Another verb common both to Akkadian and to the WS dialects is *lamādu*. In both language families, this verb has an *a* thematic vowel; note, for instance, biblical *yilmad̲* (Dt. 17:19); that *a* theme undoubtedly expresses the idea that learning is primarily a subjective thing (thus the stative pattern) even though the verb may take a direct object. Unfortunately, no 1st c.s. examples are documented in the EA texts, so there is no way of knowing whether the scribe would have used the proper Akkadian, *almad*, or a Canaanized *ilmad*. However, there are numerous 3rd m.s. forms, all of them functioning within the framework of Canaanite syntax, viz. *yi-ìl-ma-ad* (EA 264:23; *et al.*), *yi-il₅-ma-ad* (EA 64:8; *et passim*) and *yi-ìl-ma-du* (EA 251:9). These, too, may simply be combinations of the Akkadian 3rd m.s. *ilmad* as theme, plus the *y*- prefix, but it may not be pure coincidence that the resultant form corresponds to the **yilmad*- that we would expect in Canaanite.

By the same line of reasoning, an example from *šaᵓālu*, "to ask," from an Amurru letter may be included, in spite of the Akkadian accusative suffix:

> [*a-mur*] / [[I]*Pa*]-*ḫa-na-*⌈*te*⌉ L[Ú]M[AŠKIM-*ia*] / *yi-iš-al-šu* LUGAL [d][UT]U / *šum-ma la a-na-ṣa-ar* / [URU]*Ṣu-mu-ri* [URU]*Ul-la-sà* / *i-nu-ma* [LÚ]MAŠKÍM-ia / *i-na ši-pir₆-ti* LUGAL [d]UTU "[Behold,] [Pa]ḫanate, [my] co[missioner], may the king, the sun god, ask him whether I guard(ed) the city of Ṣumur (and) the city of Ullasa while my commissioner is(was) on a mission of the king, the sun god" (EA 60:19-25; Rainey 1975b:410-411; Moran 1987b:234 n. 6; 1992:132 n. 6).

The jussive function of this verb is according to WS syntax (Izreʾel 1985:251). Therefore, it is not amiss to observe that **yišʾal* would be the expected WS jussive form; cf. Hebrew (indicative) *yišʾal* (Ex. 22:13).

On the other hand, there are two examples of verb forms that violate Barth's law whereby *yaqtal* › *yiqtal*, and one of them is from *šaʾālu*, viz. 3rd m.s. jussive *ia-aš-al-mì* "May the king ask" (EA 224:10). The other is 3rd m.s. preterite from *naʾāṣu*, that is, *ia-an-aṣ-ni* "he despised me" (EA 137:23); contrast Hebrew *yinʾaṣ* (Prov. 15:5). These are just the opposite of Akkadianisms; the Amurrite PN's with their preservation of *yaqtal* immediately come to mind. Could these forms reflect a contemporary Amurrite dialect, or are they simply scribal aberrations?

Finally, it remains to deal with a PN that also defies Barth's law, namely that of the renowned commissioner, Yanḥamu. His name is documented in all the nominal cases: ᴵ*Ia-an-ḫa-mu* (EA 85:23; *et al.*), nominative; ᴵ*Ia-an-ḫa-mi* (EA 83:81; et al.) and ᴵ*Ia-an-ḫa-mì* (EA 117:61; *et al.*), dependent; ᴵ*Ia-an-ḫa-ma* (EA 106:36; *et al.*), accusative. The same name with the same vocalization appears a century later at Ugarit (Sivan 1984:253); in fact, it seems to have been quite popular there (Gröndahl 1967:58, 336). But even more remarkable is the total absence of this ostensibly "Amurrite" PN from any of the Middle Bronze Age sources available (Gelb 1980)! It does not appear in any of the "Amurrite" PN's of the Ur III period (Buccellati 1966:210-211) or from Mari (Huffmon 1965:237-239; Birot, Kupper and Rouault 1979:221). The earliest attestation of the name *Yanḥamu* appears to be AT 189:2 from Alalakh Stratum IV, fifteenth century B.C.E. (Wiseman 1953:136; Dietrich and Loretz 1970:93). So if *Yanḥamu* is supposed to be "Amurrite," it is strangely absent from the known Amurrite societies.

Now there is no known cognate for this root (*nḥm*) in Akkadian and the G stem is missing in Hebrew and the Aramaic dialects, but it is present in Arabic, albeit with an *i* thematic vowel! One possibility that ought to be considered is an original G stem preterite/jussive in which the *i* thematic vowel shifted to *a*. The conditions for such a vowel shift may have been as follows:

(1) the name is obviously a sentence name shortened by the dropping of the theophoric element (Albright 1943a:10 n. 15). In such a combination, viz. **Yanḫim-ʾilu,* the last syllable of the verb would have received at least a secondary accent, as in biblical *ḥᵃṣár šûʿāl* (Josh. 15:28; *et al.*). This accent, on an originally closed syllable, would have permitted the operation of Philippi's law (Philippi 1878:42; Bergsträsser 1918:149), that is, the shift of *ĭ* to *ă*, **Yanḫim* › **Yanḫam.* The hypocoristic PN, frozen in its vocalic shape, was nominalized by the addition of the case endings, which did nothing to change the fixed vocalization. If this should prove to be the correct explanation of the name *Yanḫamu,* it still remains a mystery why a similar process did not affect the other known PN's with a *yaqtil* vocalic shape, such as *Yaʿṭir-* and *Yatin-*.

The Jerusalem scribe, however, provides us with two very weird spellings of this PN, viz. ᴵ*E-en-ḫa-mu* (EA 286:28; probably also to be supplied in EA 285:10) and ᴵ*Ye-éʾ-en-ḫa-mu* (EA 289:45), which could also be transcribed ᴵi_{15}-*in*$_4$-*ḫa-mu* and ᴵ*Yi-íʾ-in*$_4$-*ḫa-mu* respectively. The scribe seems to be trying to spell this PN in accordance with the Barth-Ginsberg law, i.e. *Yenḫamu /Yinḫamu.* This is the same scribe who demonstrates a tendency to get mixed up, to turn things around (Rainey:1978c). A scribe who could write ᴵ*I-li-mil-ki* (EA 286:36) when he really meant ᴵ*Mil-ki-lì* (EA 289:5) or ᴵ*Mil-ki-ili* (DINGIR) would not be beyond trying to write *Yinḫamu* for *Yanḫamu.*

SUMMARY AND CONCLUSIONS. The examples assembled above show that the Barth-Ginsberg law was functioning in all Canaanite glosses and all *yqtl* PN's. This confirms the synchronic relationship with Ugaritic and the diachronic relationship with Hebrew. The Barth-Ginsberg law must have been operative in the mother tongue of the WS scribes who wrote the Amarna letters sent from Canaan.

The resultant conclusion has far reaching consequences for the evaluation of most verb forms in the Amarna letters from Canaan, a fact that has been stressed elsewhere (Rainey 1971b:164; 1978a:12*-13*). Ebeling (1910:46), Böhl (1909:56, §8t) and Dhorme (1913:37-381 = 1952:413-418) all assumed that the verbs in this corpus built on the *yikšud* pattern were somehow related to the shape of the biblical Hebrew verbs with the *yišmōr* pattern. Their assumption was taken up and cited in most of the standard grammars of biblical Hebrew; it was viewed as a diachronic fact. However, the *yišmōr-yittēn* verb forms actually reflect the shift of *ă* to *ĭ* known as attenuation. The evidence for that shift, especially as it pertains to nominal forms, is that it began to operate in the very late Roman period. An important line of evidence is the vocalization of the Babylonian as against the Tiberian system (Bergsträsser 1918:146-147). The witness of Jerome's transcriptions, albeit mainly from nominal forms (Siegfried 1884:77), strongly suggests that attenuation of *ă* › *ĭ* in closed, unaccented syllables had not generally taken place. Jerome represents *ā* by *a*, e.g. *yāšûḇ* = *jasub*, while both *ă* and *ĭ* appear as *e* when in combination with *y-*, viz. *yaḥᵃrōš* = *jeros, yaśpîqû* = *jesphicu*, and *yišʾaḡ* = *jesag, yiṯmāhû* = *jethmau*, but also MT *yizbᵊlēnî* = *iezbulen* (Siegfried 1884:48). Analysis within Tiberian Hebrew of comparable verb and noun forms makes it clear that an original *ă* generally behaves the same in the verb as in the noun; cf. e.g. *mišmōr* — *yišmōr, māqôm* — *yāqûm, maʿamāḏ, yaʿamōḏ*, though some contrasts also occur, e.g. *meḥqār* — *yaḥqōr, mattān* — *yittēn*. However, the behavior of middle weak verbs such as *yāšûḇ* and *yāšîṯ* vs *yēḇôš* and Ist guttural verbs like *yaḥgōr* vs *yeḥzaq* prove that the Barth-Ginsberg shift of *yaqtal* › *yiqtal* is a phenomenon distinct from the attenuation that led to *yaqtul* › *yiqtōl* and *yaqtil* › *yiqtēl*. The Amarna Canaanite and Ugaritic evidence treated herein shows that the shift of *yaqtal* › *yiqtal* must go back to at least as early as the second millennium B.C.E., at least for those two languages.

So why does one find numerous forms in the Amarna texts from Canaan such as 1st c.s. on the *Øiprus* pattern, 2nd m.s. on the *tiprus* pattern and 3rd m.s. (only a dozen or so G stem!) on the *yiprus* pattern? This is hardly representative of a vocalic shift in the Canaanite mother tongue of the scribes; the glosses and the PN's are all against such a view. Internal analysis of Tiberian Hebrew and comparison with other systems of vocalization (Babylonian, LXX, Jerome) contradict an early date for the shift of *yaqtul* › *yiqtōl*. The conclusion seems inescapable that the prefix *i* vowel in so many Canaanite Amarna verb forms (*yi-*, *ti-*, *Øi-*) is a colloquialism confined to the Akkadian interlanguage being used by scribes whose mother tongue was Canaanite. This interlanguage phenomenon derives (as indicated *supra*, pp. 14-15) from the adoption of Akkadian themes, either of the *iparras* or *iprus* type, to which the Canaanite consonantal person morphemes, *y-*, *t-* and *Ø-*, were applied. Personal names and the occasional gloss of a purely Canaanite verb form reveal that in the mother tongue, the Barth-Ginsberg law was operative. In other cases, where the same verbal root serves both Akkadian and Canaanite, the forms written by the scribes seem to reflect their native vocabulary, e.g. *ia-aš-ku-un*, *yi-ìl-ma-ad*, and similar forms mentioned above. Cases like *ia-aš-al-mì* and *ia-an-aṣ-ni* may perhaps be viewed as hypercorrections on the part of scribes who took Akkadian 1st c.s. *aṣbat*, *amḫaṣ*, and 2nd m.s. *taṣbat*, *tamḫaṣ*, as their theme. There is always the outside chance, of course, that they derive from some dialect in which *yaqtal* had not shifted to *yiqtal*, but that is not very likely (cf. the discussion of Yanḥamu, *supra*, pp. 72-73).

Gp — THE PASSIVE OF THE BASIC STEM

By the end of the nineteenth century, it was reasonably clear to Assyriologists that there was no G passive for the true Akkadian G stem. Therefore, the presence of just such passive forms in the Amarna letters from Canaan was already noted as a purely West Semitic phenomenon (Böhl 1909:60-63; Ebeling 1910:59-60). The basic pattern is *yuqtal-*, as one might have expected from Arabic. A few examples have the Akkadian present as theme; 3rd f.s. *tu-ṣa-bat* (EA 85:46), might be a simple error for *tu-uṣ-bat*, as noted long ago (Ebeling 1910:60; Youngblood 1961:278). It has long been recognized that G passives existed in Ugaritic (Gordon 1965:80-81, §9.31), but in the absence of any 1st c.s. forms the prefix vowel remains unattested in the Ugaritic consonantal texts; that the thematic vowel was *a* (as was to be expected) is seen in examples such as:

ktlakn /*ǵlmm* = **kî tul*ʾ*akâni ǵalmâmi* "When the (two) lads were sent" (*KTU* 1.4: r. V, 42-43).

ATTESTATION. The earliest attestation of the G passive comes from the fifteenth century Taanach letters:

ša-ni-tam šum-ma GIGAG!.[NI].Ú.TAG.GA URUDU.ḪÁ / *i-ba-aš-šu ù* ⌜*lu*⌝*-ú tu-da-nu-na* "Furthermore, if there are copper arrows (Sachs 1939:373-373), then let them be given" (TT 2:19-20; Rainey 1977:37-38; Glock 1983:60).

The other documented forms will be presented according to the respective verbs:

(*w*)*arû* (WS **yrw* ‹ **wrw*). Ebeling had not recognized the nature of the Canaanite gloss in the following passage; he had suggested that it might be a Sumerian gloss on an Egyptian word, *aḫ-me*, with the meaning of "stall" (Ebeling 1915:1601). The correct understanding of the passage is reflected in the translation by Albright, Mendenhall and Moran (1955:485a) but the interpretation was first explained in detail by Campbell (1965:198 n. 11).

ù tu-sà-aḫ-mì \ *tu-ra* / MÍ.ANŠE.KUR.RA-*ia* "But my mare was shot (gloss: shot)" (EA 245:8-9; Rabiner 1981:11).

The gloss is the Gp preterite 3rd f.s. (Rabiner 1981:98, §5.2.2.2; 101, §5.2.3). It translates the hybrid Gp 3rd f.s. from *nasāḫu* (cf. *infra*, p. 78).

dâku. Two examples of the passive from this verb are attested. Although the first in a somewhat broken context, its content is reasonably certain:

ù pa[*l-ḫ*]*a-ti a-n*[*a-k*]*u* / *la-a-mi ú-da-a-k*[*a* . . .] "And I am af[ra]id lest I be kille[d]"(EA 131:27-28; Moran 1960:14; 1987b:349, 351 n. 7; 1992:212, 213 n. 7).

The form *ú-da-a-k*[*a*] is Gp volitive 1st c.s. in a negative result clause after a verb of fearing (Moran 1960:14). The second form is in a letter closely associated with EA 131; this time in the apodosis of a conditional sentence:

> *šum-ma i-na-na* / *qa-la-ta ù* ^{I}*Pi-ḫu-ra* / *la-a yi-zi-za i-na* / ^{URU}*Ku-mì-di u ka-li* LÚ.MEŠ / [*ḫ*]*a-za-ni-ka tù-da-ku*[*-n*]*a* "If now you keep silent and Piḫura does not make a stand in Kumidi, then all your city rulers will be killed" (EA 132:46-50).

The form *tù-da-ku*[*-n*]*a* is Gp imperfect 3rd m.pl. These same two epistles happen to have three examples of the Gp suffix forms (EA 131:9, 22; 13:45) and perhaps one of the Gp participle (EA 131:20).

epēšu. One of the examples from this verb shows gemination of the second radical, i.e. the form has the Akkadian present-future as its theme:

> *ki-ma ša yu-uṣ-ṣí* / *iš-tu pí-i* / ^{d}UTU *iš-tu* / *sa-me-e ki-na-an-na* / *yu-up-pa-*⸢*šu*⸣*-mi* "According to what is issued from the mouth of the sun god from heaven, thus it shall be done" (EA 232:16-20; Moran 1987b:459; 1992:291).

The other forms do not show gemination, viz. 3rd m.s. preterite *yu-pa-aš-mi* (EA 137:96) and 3rd m.s. imperfect *yu-pa-šu* (EA 114:42; 138:74, 75, 135; 271:26; 272:21). The spelling *tu-pu-uš* (EA 281:13) is an error for an active form, evidently 3rd f.s. *ti-pu-uš* or something similar (cf. translation by Moran 1987b:503; 1992:322).

leqû. It happens that all of the documented examples come from the Byblos correspondence. In a few cases, the scribe has written AN as the second sign, which is read *ìl* in active forms; here it is to be transcribed *ul*$_{11}$. The Forms with modal -Ø suffix (preterite and jussive) show vowel coloring in the thematic vowel: 3rd m.s. jussive *yu-ul-qé* (EA 105:82), 3rd f.s. preterite ⸢*tu*⸣*-ul-qé* (EA 91:8, note 3rd m.s. active preterite *yi-ìl-qa* in line 6!). The 1st c.pl. *nu-ul*$_{11}$*-qa-am-mi* (EA 362:23) may be parsed as volitive or as ventive by modus attraction from the preceding *yi-iš-pu-ra-am* (EA 362:22). The remaining forms have other suffixes which preempt the thematic vowel: 3rd m.s. imperfect *yu-ul-qú* (EA 86:11), *yu-ú-ul-qú* (EA 117:33), and imperfect energic *yu-ú-ul-qú-na* (EA 117:68), 3rd f.s. imperfect *tu-ul-qú* (EA 83:15), 3rd m.pl. jussive/volitive *tu-ul-qú* (EA 132:15), 3rd m.pl. imperfect *tu-ul-qú-na* (EA 90:18; 108:58), *tu-ul*$_{11}$*-qú-na* (EA 126:6; Moran 1987b:341 n. 2; 1992:206 n. 2).

maḫāṣu. There is one attested form, 3rd f.s. (with feminine collective subject) *tu-um-ḫa-ṣú* (EA 252:17; Albright 1943b:31 n. 15).

nasāḫu. One example is documented; it is explained by a WS gloss (cf. *supra*, p. 76):

> *ù tu-sà-aḫ-mì* \ *tu-ra* / MÍ.ANŠE.KUR.RA-*ia* "But my mare was shot (gloss: shot)" (EA 245:8-9; Rabiner 1981:11).

qabû. Two forms that appear to be built on the Akkadian present-future theme: 3rd m.s. *yu-qa-bu* (EA 108:20; with pl. subj.! Moran 1987b:305-306), [*yu*]-*qa-bu* (EA 85:65); but they could also be N stem, viz. *yi-qa-bu* = **yiqqabu* (cf. *CAD* Q:41b-42b). The other two examples are contrasting 3rd m.s. preterite and imperfect forms:

> *ú-ul yu-uq-ba i-na* / UD.KAM.MEŠ LÚ.MEŠ MAŠKÍM *la-qú* LÚ.MEŠ GAZ.MEŠ / *ka-li* KUR.MEŠ *ú-ul ka-a-ma* / *yu-uq-bu i-na* UD.KAM.MEŠ-‹*ka*› / *ù la-a ti-te-ú la-qa-ši* "Was it not said in the days of the commissioners, 'The *ᶜapîrû* men have taken all the territories'? Let it not be said in ‹your› days, 'And you are unable to take them'" (EA 83:16-20; *contra* Moran 1950a:142 n. 252; 1960:4; 1987b:265 n. 1; 1992:154 n. 1; Youngblood 1961:243)

šapāru. The supposed passive forms from this verb are illusory. The first, in EA 94:1, is to be read [*i*]*š*-[*t*]*a-pár* (Youngblood 1961:381; Moran 1987b:286 n. 1). The second, *nu-u*[*š*]*-pu-ru* (EA 85:84) is an erroneous spelling for an active form, **nišpuru*.

šemû. The Rib-Haddi correspondence provides all the examples. Unlike *leqû*, no examples are documented with -Ø tense/modal suffix, so there is no way of knowing whether such forms would have had vowel coloring or not. One construction is rather unusual, representing an impersonal statement:

> [*a-*]*nu-ma ki-a-ma ‹aš-›pu-ru a-na* ⸢É⸣.⸢GAL⸣ / [*ù*] *la-a yu-uš-mu* / [*a-n*]*a ia-ši* "[N]ow, thus [I] was writing to the ⸢palace⸣ [but] no one was listening [t]o me" (EA 132:51-52; cf. Moran 1987b:352; 1992:214).

In another context (from Beirut), the 3rd f.s. appears:

> *la-a tu-uš-mu / a-wa-ti* "My word is not heeded" (EA 138:96-97).

Elsewhere, the form is always 3rd m.pl. with *awātū* "words" as subject, evidently construed as a calque on a Canaanite masculine (cf. Hebrew *dᵊḇārîm*). A typical context is:

> *ù ú-ul tu-uš-mu-n*[*a*] / *a-wa-tu-ia* "But my words are not heeded" (EA 91:29-30; similarly EA 89:10, 37; 90:17;122:55).

On occasion, the scribe confused the active and passive constructions:

> *ù ú-ul ti-iš-mu-na a-wa-tu-ia* (EA 74:50); *šum-ma a-wa-te-ia tu-uš-mu-*[*na*] (EA 117:32).

In the first instance, the verb is active 3rd m.pl. with an apparent accusative with nominative case ending. The verb was probably meant to be passive, *tušmûna* (cf. Youngblood 1961:149) though Moran (1987b:250; 1992:143) takes the verb as 2nd m.s. (or 2nd m.pl. of respect?) and considers the direct object to be an error for *awātēya*. The second example has the proper passive form for the verb but its subject has the oblique case ending, which is probably an error for *awātūya.* As Youngblood surmised (*loc. cit.*), the scribes may have tended to confuse the two means of expressing the central idea. One may wonder if the cause for this confusion might have been the interference of other impersonal constructions such as the singular passive cited above, or the widely known use of 3rd m.pl. verbs in impersonal expressions, thus the confusion between *tišmûna* and *tušmûna.* The absence of the thematic vowel in this IIIrd weak verb may have contributed to the tendency to confuse the active and passive forms.

DIACHRONIC SIGNIFICANCE. The presence of the finite G passive in the EA texts from Canaan is of special importance for the diachronic study of the West Semitic languages. Only survivals of the Gp exist in Hebrew and most of them have been obscured in the Massoretic vocalization (Joüon and Muraoka 1991:166-168 §58). Gp is present in Ugarit (cf. *supra,* pp. 75-76), Aramaic (Degen 1969:66) and of course in Classical Arabic. It does not appear in any native dialect of Akkadian. The Ugaritic and Aramaic evidence and the EA testimony from Canaan do strengthen the argument for the Gp in ancient Hebrew. However, it seems obvious that Gp has almost disappeared during the Israelite monarchial period. Phoenician and Moabite show no traces of it, either.

CHAPTER V

PREFIX CONJUGATION — Gt & Gtn STEMS

This chapter is devoted to two stems, one of which is common to Akkadian and to WS, and another which is totally foreign to the latter.

THE SCRIBAL CONVENTIONS

In Chapter IV, several cases were noted in which the scribes chose an *iptaras* form from the Akkadian paradigm to serve as the theme for a particular verb. There was evidently no intention on their part of implying that the infixed *-t-* had any special semantic force. On the other hand, the ensuing discussion will indicate that the Canaanite scribes seem to have known about certain verbs with lexical Gt's in Akkadian (Rainey 1971b).

As mentioned in previous chapters, the existence of a tense form with infixed *-t-* in the Akkadian system was not yet known to scholars such as Böhl and Ebeling when they were working on the Amarna corpus. Therefore, numerous G preterites with infixed *-t-* (wrongly denoted the perfect by Assyriologists today) were classified as Gt in their respective studies of the verb and in the glossary to Knudtzon's edition (Ebeling 1915). For the dialects outside of Canaan, more recent studies have carried out the proper classification, e.g for the Mitanni letters, Adler's (1976:255-344) and for the MB letters, Aro's glossary (Aro 1957).

It remains to sort out the various forms with infixed *-t-* in the Amarna letters from Canaan so as to distinguish between those G preterites with infixed *-t-* that are simply serving as themes for the WS G stem, without any special significance being assigned to the infixed *-t-*, and those for which the Canaanite scribe really intended to express some semantic nuance by means of the infix.

LEXICAL GT'S FROM AKKADIAN

Since the semantic force expressed by the Gt stem of certain verbs in Akkadian was evidently known to the Canaanite scribes, they occasionally used such Gt's whenever that special nuance was appropriate to the context of their message.

VERBS OF MOTION.

The stem with infixed *-t-* can express a partitive or separative idea with verbs of motion (*GAG*:121, §92e). The Gt forms conjugated as suffix verbs will be dealt with in a subsequent chapter (cf. *infra*, pp. 339-341).

(w)aṣû. Only three forms with consonantal person prefixes are documented. The first is 3rd m.s. with either a volitive or a ventive suffix:

> *yi-di-i*[*n*] / [DING]IR *ša* LUGAL ⸢EN⸣-*ia* /.*ú yi-ta-ṣa* / ᴵLUGAL EN-*ia qa-du* / ERÍN.MEŠ.GAL-*šu* "May [the go]d of the king, my lord, grant that the king, my lord, come forth with his army" (EA 337:13-17).

So the idea of coming forth *from* Egypt is expressed by the infixed *-t-*, while the apparent ventive gives the nuance of coming *hither*. The second example is 2nd m.s. with ventive suffix:

> [*i*]-*de*₉ *ki-i-ma* / ⸢*la*⸣-*mi-in šum-ka* / *a-na pa-ni* LUGAL *ù* / ⸢*la*⸣-*a ti-ta-ṣa-am* / [*i*]*š-tu* ᴷᵁᴿ*Mi-iṣ-ri* "[I] know that your name is slandered before the king so that you cannot come forth from Egypt" (EA 97:4-8; Moran 1987b:289; 1992:170).

The third example is a corrected reading by Moran (1984:299):

> *i-nu-ma la-ma-ad-mì* / *ù l*[*a*]-*a-mì ti-it-*[*ta-ṣ*]*ú-na* / ERÍN.MEŠ *pí-ṭá-tu*₄ "when he learned that the regular troops are not [coming]forth" (EA 244:18-20).

Several other instances of this verb in the Gt (or G preterite with -*t*-), are either in the Tyre letters, e.g. 3rd m.s. *it-ta-ṣí* (EA 147:6 *et passim*) or other borderline contexts like 3rd m.pl. [*it-t*]*a-ṣú-ni*$_{7}$ (EA 67:10) or from Jerusalem, *it-ta-ṣú-ú* (EA 286:48). The 3rd m.s. *it-ta-ṣí* (EA 279:11) and *it-ta-ṣi* (EA 239:11; 326:20) may have been meant for suffix conjugation forms like the 3rd f.s. hybrid *it-ta-ṣa-at* (EA 297:19; Rainey 1971b:90; 1973c:256; cf. *infra*, p. 339).

elû. The Canaanite scribes' recognition of a lexical Gt for this verb is demonstrated by three examples of the Akkadian present-future. The first is in an epistle that has some WS features, but the WS tense nuance, whether volition or past indicative, is hard to establish in this context:

> *ù a-nu-ma ni-i*$_{15}$*-ta-lí i-na* KUR.MEŠ / [x] *ye-ta-lí* / [*ù*] *i*$_{15}$*-na-ṣa-ar-šu* / [*a*]-*d*[*i*] *ka*$_{4}$*-ša-du*(sic!) / ^{LÚ}GAL EN-*ia* "And now, we have ascended(?) into the mountains (!); [*x*] has ascended [and] I will/am guard(ing) him [u]nt[il] the arrival of the official, my lord" (EA 178:4-8; Rainey 1989-90:66a).

The 1st c.pl. *nītalli* and the theme of 3rd m.s. *yētalli* appear to be Assyrianisms. The anaptyctic vowel with the -*t*- infix would be -*e*- in Babylonian or it would become -*i*- in Assyrian if the second radical, *l*, were not geminated. The second verb form, incidentally, was taken by Knudtzon and by Moran (1987b:417; 1992:262) as a GN, *Yi-ta-ni*. But there is no justification for reading an otherwise unknown GN when the form has the same sequence, -*ta-ni*(=*lí*), as the verb in the previous line. In view of the 3rd m.s. imperfect *yi-qa-bu* in line 21, it is obvious that the scribe knows and uses the WS modal system. Therefore, in the narrative report of an epistle such as this, one may justifiably conjecture that the -Ø suffix on the forms *nītalli* and *yētalli* can also indicate *past* tense while the -Ø suffix on *ninaṣṣaršu* could reflect the jussive.

The second instance of the Gt present-future is in a Jerusalem letter. In the Jerusalem letters the narrative present-futures of all verbal stems are nearly always strictly Akkadian in form.

> *li-iš-al-mi šàr-ri a-na ša-šu-[nu]* / *ma-ad* NIG.ḪÁ *ma-ad* Ì.ḪÁ *ma-ad* TÚG.ḪÁ-⸢*ti*⸣ / *a-di e-tel-li* ^{I}*Pa-ú-ru* ^{LÚ}MAŠKÍM *šàr-ri* / *a-na* KUR ^{URU}*Ú-ru-ša*$_{10}$*-lim*^{KI} "May my king requisition for the[m] much food, much oil and much clothing until Pawuru, the king's commissioner, ascends to Jerusalem" (EA 287:43-46).

The verb form, *ētelli,* is an Assyrianism (Moran 1975b:153), typical of the Jerusalem letters.

The third context is highly poetical. It has been taken in the past to reflect Canaanite poetry (Weber 1915:1324; Böhl 1914:337 = 1953:375; Jirku 1933:116), but note has not been taken of the Akkadian morphosyntax. That the text has Canaanite glosses might reflect the existence of a Canaanite original, but then again, it might mean just the opposite! In any case, the verbs are 1st c.pl. Akkadian present-future, including the Gt of *elû,* and reveal that the scribe was striving to compose a poetic passage in good, standard Akkadian:

> *a-mur ni-nu a-na mu-ḫi-ka*$_4$ / 2 IGI-*ia šum-ma ni-tel-lí* / *a-na* AN \ *ša-me-ma šum-ma* /*nu-ra-ad i-na er-ṣé-ti*$_7$ / *ù* SAG.DU-*nu* \ *ru-šu-nu* / *i-na qa-te-ka* "Behold, as for us, my (sic!) two eyes are on you; if we should ascend to heaven (= heavens), if we should descend to hell, then our head (= our head) is in your hands" (EA 264:14-19).

Even though the narrative context of this epistle is strongly WS and pidgin, it would be stretching credulity to make the two verbs, *nītelli* and *nurrad,* into WS preterites with -Ø suffix. The implications of the fact that the scribe felt it necessary to use good Akkadian forms in a poetic passage is worthy of consideration for the light it sheds on their attitude to high literary language. After all, literary compositions were present in their local libraries.

On the other hand, there are two passages where the theme form might be the G stem *iptaras* of *elû*. However, the sense of each context suggests that there is here an intentional use of the Gt nuance. In both cases, the forms clearly reflect the WS imperfect modal nuance of repeated action in the past and they bear the proper WS *-u* suffix. The first example has the 3rd m.s. consonantal prefix:

> *ù an-nu-ú i-na-na* / *nu*-KÚR ^{I}*Ia-pa*-^{d}IŠKUR *it-ti* ^{I}*A-zi-ri* / *a-na ia-ši ù al-lu-ú ṣa-bat* ^{GIŠ}MÁ-*ia* / *ù al-lu-ú ki-na-na-ma yi-te*$_{9}$*-lu* / *i-na* ⸢*lìb*⸣*-bi a-ia-ba aš-šum ṣa-ba-at* / ^{GIŠ}MÁ.MEŠ-*ia* "And behold, now Yapaᶜ-Haddi is hostile along with Aziru against me, and behold, he has seized my ship, and behold, thus he is going out on the high seas in order to seize my ships" (EA 114:15-20).

The second example has the modal suffix but lacks the consonantal prefix; it happens to be in a letter which avoids the *y*-prefix throughout:

> *ù an-nu-ú i-qa-bu* BE-*ia* / *ki-ma pa-na-nu-um i-te*$_{9}$*-lu* ^{I}ÌR-*Aš-ra-tu*$_{4}$ / *a-na ṣé-ri-ia* ⸢*da*⸣-⸢*na*⸣-⸢*ku*⸣ "And behold, I am/have been saying, 'My lord, when formerly ᶜAbdi-Ashirta was attacking me, I was strong'" (EA 127:30-32; Moran 1950a:124a n. 104; 1987b:342; 1992:207; Rainey 1971b:88).

Moran has discovered that, in a similar passage, where Knudtzon had read an impossible form, *i-ti-ì*[*l-*]*l*[*i*]*k*, the correct reading had to be the Gt of *elû*,

> *ù a-nu-ú i-te*$_{9}$-⸢*èl*⸣*-lu*! / [*i-*]*na-an-na a-na ṣe-ri-ia* "And behold he is attacking me now" (EA 92:23; cf. Moran 1987b:283: n.3; 1992:166 n. 3).

This leads to another instance in which the *lu* sign was confused with the *lik* sign, perhaps because of sloppy writing on the part of the scribe:

> *a-nu-ma* / *ki-ma iš-*[*tap-*]*ru a-na ka-ta*$_{5}$ UGU / ^{URU}*Ṣu-mu-ra a-nu-ma i-te*$_{9}$*-lu*! / *ù a*[*ḫ-*]*ta-ni* ERÍN.M[EŠ] *a-na* / [*na-ṣa-ri-*]*ši ù a-nu-‹ma› i-te*$_{9}$*-zi-ib-ši* / [*ù pa-aṭ-ru* LÚ.MEŠ] UN-*tù ù* / / [*ki-na-na iš-tap-*]*ru* "Now, as (*contra* Moran 1987b:317 n. 4; 1992:189-190 n. 5) I was wr[iti]ng to you concerning Ṣumur, now I was going

> up (there) and I ex[ho]rted the troops to [guard i]t, but now I have abandoned it [and] the garrison [troops have departed (Moran 1987b:318 n. 6; 1992:190 n. 7)] and [thus I have been writ]ing (Moran 1987b:318 n. 7; 1992:190 n. 8)" (EA 114:26-32).

Knudtzon's *i-ti-lik* is an impossible form for *alāku,* for which we would have to have *ittalak.* Therefore, reading the last sign as *lu* seems to be the only reasonable solution. Incidentally, all of the above forms, with *-u* suffix, show that the use of the TI sign need not be taken as an Assyrianism (the Assyrian form would have to be *ētiliu*). The transcriptions adopted here assume a Babylonian form; the resultant verb, *i-te₉-lu,* is here taken as Gt imperfect 1st c.s. like the preceding *iš-*[*tap-*]*ru.* The next 1st c.s. form, *i-te₉-zi-ib-ši,* is understood as a Babylonian form serving as Gt preterite with -Ø suffix.

Finally, there are three passages, all from Byblos, where forms with infixed *-t-* have either the Akkadian ventive or a -Ø modal suffix but no consonantal person marker. In every context the verb expresses the idea of mounting an attack, possibly reinforced by the ventive in two cases, but probably also reflected in the infixed *-t-*. One of them (EA 88:17) is expressing past action; another (EA 124:12) is in the protasis of a conditional sentence while the other (EA 81:46) is in the apodosis. All three are fulfilling syntactic roles where the WS suffix conjugation is frequently used by the Byblos scribes. The theme involved may be simply the G preterite with *-t-*, or the Gt preterite or even the Gt present or Gtn preterite, i.e. *īteli* / *ītelâ*(*m*) or *ītelli* /*ītellâ*(*m*) . The most likely explanation is that these forms are employed here as intentional Akkadianisms standing syntactically for the 3rd m.s. suffix conjugation. For that reason, their respective contexts are dealt with among the true suffix conjugation verbs in Chapter 13, *infra,* pp. 339-341).

erēbu. The Gt of this verb means "to enter for an extended period" (*AHw*:460b). There are two examples of WS imperfect, 3rd m.s. *yi-te-r*[*u-bu!*] (EA 117:39) and 1st c.s. *i-te₉-ru-bu* (EA 104:44) and one 1st c.s. preterite *i-te-ru-ub* (EA 155:31). One preterite will be discussed as a possible calque on the WS suffix conjugation (*infra*, p. 342).

ezēbu. This verb has a Gt recognized by the dictionaries (*AHw*:268b; *CAD* E:416a). In the EA correspondence, it seems to express the transitive idea of "abandoning" (*CAD* E:417a). There are six instances of 1st c.s. forms spelled *i-ti-zi-ib*, which cannot be classed as Assyrianisms since that would call for *ētizib*. Instead, the forms in question probably represent an orthographic peculiarity in which TI is to be read te_9. Two 3rd m.s. examples have the obvious Babylonian spelling *i-te-zi-ib* (EA 74:9; 148:42); in both cases they express past time and, at least in the Byblos passage (EA 74:9), may be reckoned as a theme for the suffix conjugation (cf. *infra*, pp. 342-343). The Tyrian context (EA 148:42) probably reflects Akkadian morphosyntax, i.e. the G preterite with infixed *-t-* or the Gt preterite. The one documented 3rd m.pl. form is *i*-TI-*zi-bu* (EA 93:22), for which the correct orthography would have been *i*-te_9-*ez-bu* for *ītezbū*. So the scribe may have been thinking of Gt present-future or the Gtn preterite, with geminated second radical, thus *ītezzibū* (cf. Youngblood 1961:376). In either case, the demands of grammar require that one transcribe the second sign as te_9.

One 1st c.s. example from Tyre appears to be a partly Assyrianized form, but if so, it has to be reckoned as a Gtn preterite with geminated second radical; the spelling is *i-ta-zi-ib-šu* (EA 149:50). A Gt present form seems unlikely but not impossible even though the context appears to require the past tense:

> *il-qè* [I]*Zi-im-re-da* [URU]*Ú-sú* / *iš-tu* *ÌR-dì‹-ka›* *i-ta-zi-ib-šu* / *ù ia-nu* A.MEŠ *ia-nu* GIŠ.MEŠ *a-na ia-ši-nu* "Zimredda has taken Usu from ‹your› servant; I have abandoned (or: am abandoning) it and there is no water or wood for us" (EA 149:49-51; Moran 1987b:383; 1992:1992:236).

The six other 1st c.s. forms with the TI sign can, with reasonable certainty, be transcribed *i*-te_9-*zi-ib*. Two of them are past tense; one of them *i-te$_9$-zi-ib-ši*, is cited *supra*, pp. 85-86; the other is:

> *ù a-nu-ma i-na* / ^{URU}*Ṣu-mu-ra i-zi-za-ti* / *i-nu-ma ma-ri-iṣ* ^{LÚ}GAL / UGU *nu-kúr-ti i-te$_9$-zi-ib* / ^{URU}*Gub-la ù ia*[*-nu*] / ^{I}*Zi-im-re-da* [*ù*] / ^{I}*Ia-pa-*^{d}IŠKUR [*it*]*-ti-ia* "And now I have taken up position in Ṣumur because the officer is in distress (or: sick) over the hostility; I have abandoned Byblos [but] Zimredda and Yapa^{c}-Haddi are[n't wi]th me" (EA 103:13-19; cf. Moran 1987b:297; 1992; 176; *contra* Moran 1987b:298 n. 1; 1992:176 n. 1).

Four other examples of the same spelling all appear in a syntagma where the jussive is required:

> *šum-ma* / 2 ITU *ia-nu* ERÍN.MEŠ *pí-ṭá-ti* / *ù i-te$_9$-zi-ib* URU.KI / *ù pa-aṭ-ra-ti ù* / *bal-ṭá-at* ZI-*ia a-di* / *i-pé-šu i-pí-iš lìb-bi-ia* "If in two months there are no regular troops, then I will abandon the city and I will depart and my life will be saved, while I do whatever I desire" (EA 82:41-46); *šum-ma ki-a-ma la-a ti-iq-b*[*u?*] *a-na ša-šu* / *ù i-te$_9$-zi-ib* UR[U] *ù pa-aṭ-ra-ti ša-ni-tam šum-ma la-a* / *tu-te-ru-na a-wa-ta$_5$ a-na ia-ši* / *ù i-te$_9$-zi-ib* URU / *ù pa-aṭ-ra-ti qa-du* LÚ.MEŠ / *ša i-ra-a-mu-ni* "If thus you do not spea[k] to him, then I will abandon the city and I will depart; furthermore, if you do not send back word to me, then I will abandon the city and I will depart with the men who are loyal to me" (EA 83:45-51; Moran 1987b:266 n. 7; 1992:154 n. 7); *uš-si-ra* / ^{LÚ}MAŠKÍM *yi-ìl-qa-šu-nu* / *ú-ul* ›DIŠ‹ *i-te$_9$-zi-ib* UR[U]*-lì* / *ù i-pa-ṭá-ra* / *a-na mu-ḫi-ka* "Send a commissioner; let him seize them, lest I abandon my city and go off to you" (EA 118:32-36).

kašādu. There is one isolated form of this verb with infixed *-t-* which might be just the G *iptaras* theme, but which could also express the separative idea:

> [*a*]*-di yi*[*-ik-t*]*a-aš-du-na šàr-ru* / *ù yi-*[*d*]*a-ga-lu šàr-ru* / ÌR *ki-ti-šu* "[Un]til the king should come [fo]rth and see to his loyal servant" (EA 85:61-62).

VERBS OF REPETITION.

There are a number of verb forms with the infixed *-t-* that clearly indicate repeated action, often in the past. The "habitative" and "durative" nuances of some lexical Gt's in Akkadian (*GAG*:121, §92f) relfect an overlapping in Akkadian between the Gt and the Gtn stems. The WS dialects, which did not develop forms with the infixed *-tan-*, may have expressed the iterative function by means of the stem with infixed *-t-*. In the Amarna texts from Canaan, there are certain verbs with the *-t-* infix that often seem to express the repetitive, habitative or iterative nuance.

qabû. There are four examples of this verb with infixed *-t-*. One of them, with a scribal error, *iq-ta!*(BA)*-bi* (EA 275:9), is probably just the Akkadian G past with *-t-* infix. The second, [*ti-i*]*q-ta-bu* (EA 86:10), has the WS imperfect suffix or else is a preterite plural, but the context is unclear. However, the remaining two instances clearly have to do with repetition. Note the pairing with a *-t-* form of a second verb, *šanû*, which is the explicit vehicle for expressing repeated action (cf. discussion *infra*, p. 90).

> *aq-ta-bi ù aš-ta-ni* "I said and said again" or "I said over and over again" (EA 82:10).

One may argue with some degree of plausibility that the first verb form has resulted from analogy with the second. Or it could be said that both these forms are actually Gtn preterites. There is a final example in which only the context makes it clear that the repetition of several acts in the past is intended; again, the form might be Gtn (Rainey 1976b:338):

> *šap-ra-ti*$_7$*-mì* / *2-šu 3-šu* UGU *ú-nu-te* / ^{I}*Bi-ri-di-ya* / *a-na ka-ta*$_5$ *ù* / *ti*$_7$*-iq-ta-bi* "I have written to you twice or three times, concerning the implements of Biridiya and (each time) you have said . . . " (KL 72:600:1-5).

Note, incidentally, that the prefix *ti-* indicates a hybrid, interlanguage form (not something from West Semitic! *contra* Wilhelm 1982:124 n. 5).

šanû. This denominative verb from the numeral for "two" (*AHw*: 1165b) means "to do something a second time," "to do again." It happens that all attested forms in the WS texts from Canaan have infixed *-t-*. The 3rd m.s. forms do not have a prefixed *y-* and all but one have -*Ø* modal suffix.

The iterative force of these forms is clearly seen in EA 82 (cf. the translations by Albright and Moran 1948:241-242; *contra* Youngblood 1961:229). First, Rib-Haddi says to Aman-appa: *aq-ta-bi ù aš-ta-ni / a-na ka-ta*$_5$ "I said to you time and again . . . " (EA 82:5-6) and then quotes his message about his need for deliverance; then he says *ù / ta-aš-ta-na a-wa-ta*$_5$ *a-na ia-ši* "and you repeatedly replied to me . . ." (EA 82:13-14). The latter verb form evidently has the ventive unless the *-na* is due to dittography from the preceding line (cf. Youngblood, *loc. cit.*). The same repetitive nuance is probably to be understood in line 25 where *ta-a[q-ta-bi]* is the most likely form to be restored. Then later on, Rib-Haddi once again reminds Aman-appa of his reply: *ù ta-aš-ta-ni a-wa-ta*$_5$ *a-na ia-ši* (EA 82:27).

With only those two exceptions (EA 82:13-14, 27), these *-t-* forms of *šanû* follow a preceding verb, as with *aq-ta-bi* (EA 82:5-6) cited above. It was noted in the discussion of that same passage that the infixed *-t-* in *aq-ta-bi* could be by attraction from the following *aš-ta-ni* (*supra*, p. *113*). The same might be said for the first verb form in the next example:

> *an-nu-ú i-na-na / iš-ta-ḫa-aṭ-ni* ᴵ*A-zi-ru / ù iš-ta-ni* "Now, Aziru has repeatedly attacked me" (EA 125:19-21).

However, it is by no means certain that any of the above would have been iterative without the helping verb. In fact, there are several places where the verb being augmented clearly has no iterative morpheme of its own. The repeated action in these latter contexts is expressed solely by the helping verb:

> *aq-bi aš-ta-ni a-na* ^{I}*Pa-ḫa-na-te* / ^{LÚ}MAŠKÍM-*ia le-qa-mi* / ERÍN.MEŠ *til-ta-tì a-na na-ṣa-ri* / KUR.⸢ḪÁ⸣ LUGAL "I said repeatedly to Paḫanate, my commissioner, 'Take auxiliary troops to guard the territories of the king'" (EA 60:10-13; Izreʾel 1985:251, 262; 1991a:261, §3.7); *ša-ni-tam šap-ra-ti a-na* LUGAL EN-*ia ù iš-ta-ni* "Furthermore, I wrote repeatedly to the king, my lord" (EA 136:17); *a-nu-ma* [PN?] DUMU *ši-ip-ri-[ia]* / *[uš]-ši-ir-ti-šu ù aš-ta-ni* / *[m]a-ni* UD.KAM.MEŠ *ú-wa-ši-ru-šu* / *ù la-a yi-le-ú* / *i-re-ba a-na* ^{URU}*Ṣu-mu-ra* "Now, as for [PN?], my emissary, I repeatedly [se]nt him; [h]ow many days did I send him and he was unable to enter into Ṣumur?" (EA 114:32-37; Moran 1987b:316; 1992:198).

In the last quotation, the ensuing rhetorical question was cited to emphasize how the context stresses the repeated action in the past, viz. by the use of the adverbial expression, *ma-ni* UD.KAM.MEŠ, along with the WS imperfect verb forms, *ú-wa-ši-ru-šu, yi-le-ú*.

Finally, a letter from Tyre employs a 3rd m.s. form after a 3rd m.pl. verb form. Both are Akkadian forms (without WS prefixes), a practice typical of the Tyrian correspondence on the whole:

> ^{I}*Zi-im-re-da* ^{URU}*Ṣí-du-na* / *ù* ^{I}*A-zi-ra* LÚ *ar-ni* LUGAL / *ù* LÚ.MEŠ ^{URU}*Ar-wa-da it-mu-ni* / *ù iš-ta-ni ma-mi-ta i-na be-ri-šu-nu* / *ù ip-ḫu-ru-ni*$_7$ ^{GIŠ}MÁ.MEŠ GÌR.MEŠ-*šu-nu* / *a-na ṣa-ba-ti* ^{URU}*Ṣur-ri* GEMÉ LUGAL "Zimredda (of) Sidon and Aziru, the king's rebel, and the men of Arvad have sworn and repeated the oath between themselves and their ships and troops have assembled in order to seize Tyre, the king's handmaiden" (EA 149:57-63).

On the other hand, when the main verb is *aš-tap-pár*, then one might suspect that it, too, was intentionally expressing the repetition (EA 126:53-55; cf. also EA 75:17-18; 88:4-5). The relevant passages will be treated along with all the occurrences of -*t*- forms from *šapāru* (cf. *infra*, pp. 101-109).

VERBS OF REFLEXIVE ACTION.

The Canaanite scribes were also aware of certain other Akkadian verbs with lexical Gt stems that expressed a particular kind of action, in some sense reflexive or reciprocal.

šaʾālu. The Gt of this verb has the meaning, "to consult, to investigate" (*GAG*:121, §92*d*; 130-131, §92*g-h*). The action is transitive, as illustrated by the imperative *ši-ta-a-al-ši* "consult her" (EA 29:46, from Mitanni). Shuwardata, a ruler in S. Canaan (possibly Gath; Naʾaman 1979:682-684), urged Pharaoh to investigate certain allegations that had been made against him:

> *ša-ni-tam* / *yi-iš-ta-al* LUGAL *be-li* / *šum-ma el-te₉-qé* LÚ / *ù šum-ma* I-*en* ⌜GUD⌝ / *ù šum-ma* ANŠE *iš-tu* / *mu-ḫi-šu* "Furthermore, may the king, my lord, inquire whether I have taken a man or whether one ox or whether an ass away from him" (EA 280:24-29; Rainey 1971b:89.

šakānu. There is one passage where the Gt of this verb, complemented by the preposition *kīma*, means "to compare" (Liverani 1967:8 n. 1; 1971:264 n. 6 = 1979:83; Moran 1987b:339 n. 3; 1992:205 n. 3; not discussed in either *CAD* Š/1:151b-151b or *AHW*:1137b):

> *ša-ni-tam a-‹na› mi-ni yi-ìš-ta-ka-nu-ni* / *šàr-ru ki-ma* LÚ.MEŠ *ḫa-za-nu-ti* / LÚ.MEŠ *ḫa-za-nu-tu* URU.MEŠ-*šu-nu* / *a-na ša-šu-nu* LÚ.MEŠ / *ḫu!-‹up›-šu-šu-nu i-na* / *šap-li-šu-nu ù* / *a-na-ku* URU.MEŠ-*ia a-na* ᴵ*A-zi-ri* / *ù ia-ti yu-ba-ú* "Furthermore, [w]hy does the king compare me with the city rulers? As for the city rulers, their towns belong to them, their yeoman farmers are subservient to them; but as for me, my towns belong to Aziru and he is seeking (to get) me" (EA 125:31-38).

The context makes it clear that a comparison is meant. Rib-Haddi makes his own unfavorable comparison to show Pharaoh how different his own situation is.

WEST SEMITIC LEXICAL Gt's

In three instances, there may be evidence for WS Gt in verbs that normally to not have a lexical Gt in Akkadian. If that assumption should be correct, then the Canaanite scribes would seem to have chosen Akkadian forms corresponding to the *-t-* forms in their mother tongue.

amāru. This verb has no Gt in Akkadian. It was surprising to find that the same root, *ʾmr*, with the meaning "to see" as in Akkadian, appears in Ugaritic with an infixed *-t-* although it has transitive force, thus probably meaning "to look, gaze":

> *ytmr . bᶜl / bnth* (= *yittamiru Baᶜlu binātihu*) "Baal looks at his daughters" (*KTU* 1.3:I, 22-23); *išt . ištm . yitmr .ḥrb . lṭšt* (= *ʾišātu, ʾišātuma! yiʾtamiru ḥarba laṭūšata!*) "Fire, Fire! He sees a burnished sword" (*KTU* 1.2:I, 32).

The following example from the Rib-Haddi correspondence might be just an adoption of the G preterite with *-t-* infix as the theme. The prefix *ia-* is unusual, and comparison with the Ugaritic evidence would suggest that the vocalic pattern for Canaanite Gt's ought to have been **yiqtatil-*. The past tense of the Byblos example is guaranteed by the -Ø suffix (Rainey 1990b:409-412; 1975b:422-426):

> *a-nu-ma* ^{I}*A-ma-an!-ap-pa it-ti-ka ša-al-šu / šu-ut yi-de ù ia-ta-mar pu-uš-[qa] / ša* UGU-*ia* "Now Aman-ʾappa is (there) with you. Ask him. He knows and he has seen the difficu[lty] that besets me" (EA 74:51-53).

The following 1st c.s. example is in a broken context and thus somewhat ambiguous as to the time factor:

> [*ù*] URU.KI *ša* i_{15}*-ba-as-š[a-]ti / [i-n]a lìb-bi-ši a-nu-um-ma / [n]a-aṣ-ra-ti-ši / a-di a-ta-mar* ^{UZU}2.IGI.⸢MEŠ⸣ / ^{LÚ}*ḫa-za-an ša* ^{I}*šàr-ri* / EN-*ia* "[But] as for the city in which I am, now I

guarded (or: am guarding) it until I saw (or: shall see) the eyes of the king's city ruler" (EA 237:13-16).

The problem stems from [*n*]*a-aṣ-ra-ti-ši*, which could be present or past tense. As a transitive, one might expect past tense but this is not a hard and fast rule. Then we have *a-ta-mar*, which would normally be future after *adi*. However, WS usage would call for the imperfect suffix *-u*. In any event, Akkadian would not use the form with *-t-* infix for the future. So there is some cause for suspicion that behind this form stands an original Canaanite Gt from the root *ʾmr*. The other context with *a-ta-mar* is on a broken last line of a difficult tablet (EA 197:43); no conclusions can be drawn from it.

naṣābu. A putative WS verb from this root is recognized by *CAD* N/2:33b and *AHw*:755a. All of the examples come from the Tyre letters (Finkle:1977:101). The common WS verbal root, **nṣb*, means "to be erect," or in causative stems, "to erect" (Jean and Hoftijzer 1965:184). The Tyrian forms with infixed *-t-* immediately bring to mind the Hebrew tD from the cognate root **yṣb*, *hiṯyaṣṣēḇ* "to take a stand, to take up a position" (Ex. 34:5, etc.). Two of the passages in question present little problem in interpretation:

> *šàr* URU*Ḫa-ṣú-ra* / *i-te-zi-ib* É*-šu ù it-ta-ṣa-*⸢*ab*⸣ / *it-ti* LÚSA.GAZ "The king of Hazor has abandoned his house and has taken up a position with the *ʿapîru*" (EA 148:41-43); *i-de*$_4$ LUGAL *be-li e-nu-*⸢*ma*⸣ / *i-na* ŠÀ! d*ab-ba ni-ta-ṣ*[*a-a*]*b* / *ia-nu* A.MEŠ *ù ia-nu* GIŠ.MEŠ / *a-na ia-ši-nu* "The king, my lord, knows that we are situated in the midst(!) of the sea; we have no water or wood" (EA 151:41-44).

The third context has been partly misunderstood by the commentators. Albright (1937:198 n.9) thought that the verb was being wrongly used in an active (i.e. transitive) sense. This same understanding has also been followed by Moran (1987b:378; 1992:233).

> *ša it-ta-ṣa-ab gáb-bi* KUR-*ti* / *i-na pa-ša-ḫi i-na du-ni* ZAG \ *ḫa-ap-ši‹-šu›* "Who the whole land is stabilized in peace by the might of ‹his› arm" (EA 147:12), i.e. "by whose arm . . . ."

The solution lies in the recognition that this passage, an Egyptianizing eulogy on pharaoh, reflects the Egyptian use of both participles and relative forms as epithets. The participial clause, e.g. "who gave forth his voice in heaven like the storm god while all the land was in fear through his voice" (EA 147:12-13) has the antecedent as the subject of the main verbal action. It is pharaoh who gives his voice. But the clause in which the verb is an Egyptian relative form has a subject other than the antecedent (Polotsky 1976:7-13). The antecedent is represented by some other element in the subordinate clause; in this case it should have been the pronominal suffix on the word *ḫa-ap-ši* "arm." The scribe simply forgot to add it. Note that Albright, in his attempted translation of the passage into classical Egyptian, supplied the suffix, i.e. he read *ḫpš.f* (Albright 1937:198 n. 12). Moran also supplies the suffix in his translation without noting that it is missing in the original cuneiform text (Moran 1987b:378, "de son bras"; 1992:233, "of his arm").

šemû. A verb of very high frequency in the Amarna texts is *šemû* "to hear" (Rainey 1971b:96-101). In Akkadian there seems to be only a very limited use of Gt with this verb, mainly in late texts (*AHw:*1213a). The two MB examples cited by Aro (1957:102) are precatives and probably represent the usurpation of preterite functions by the preterite with *-t-* infix (Rainey 1971b:96 n. 65). On the other hand, the Gt stem of this verb is documented in WS. In Ugaritic we find the imperative: *ištmᶜ . wtqǵ udn* (= *ʾištamiᶜ wattaqiǵ ʾudna*) "give heed and be attentive of ear" (*KTU* 1.16:VI, 42, also 29-30). A biblical Hebrew toponym is the Gt infinitive, *ʾeštᵊmôᵃᶜ*, Eshtemoa (Josh. 21:14; 1 Sam. 30:28; 1 Chron. 4:17, 19; 6:42; = *eštᵊmōʰ*, Josh. 15:20).

To be sure, there are some contexts in the Canaanite Amarna letters where the form with infixed *-t-* is probably nothing more than the G stem *-t-* preterite as theme, e.g. 1st c.s.

eš-te-me (EA 108:24); *eš-te₉-mé* (EA 82:35). However, the frequent occurrences of the *-t-* forms from this verb in the Amarna letters consist mainly of replies to instructions received by local rulers from the king of Egypt. A good example is the following:

> *iš-te-mé / a-wa-te* MEŠ *ša iš-pu-ur* / LUGAL EN-*ia a-na* ÌR-*šu* / *ú-ṣur-mi* LÚMAŠKÍM-*ka* / *ù ú-ṣur* URU.DIDLI.ḪÁ *ša* / LUGAL EN-*ka a-nu-ma* / ⌈*iṣ*⌉-*ṣú-ru ù a-nu-ma* / ⌈*iš*⌉-*te-mu* UD.KAM-*ma* / *ù mu-ša a-wa-te*MEŠ *ša* / LUGAL EN-*ia* "I have listened to the words which the king, my lord, sent to his servant, 'Protect your commissioner and protect the cities of the king, your lord.' Now I am protecting and now I am obeying day and night the words of the king, my lord" (EA 292:17-26).

One could simply assume that this scribe has used the G preterite with *-t-* infix as his theme. That is certainly possible, but the widespread use of forms with infix *-t-* in contexts where "heeding, obeying," is so appropriate strongly suggests that the infix was meant to carry the same nuance as in the Ugaritic imperative cited above. A clear-cut distinction between *išme* "he listened," and *išteme* "he heeded," can be seen in a poetic passage from Tyre, which, while Egyptian in idiom and flavor (Albright 1937:199), reveals a brilliant use of the Akkadian interlanguage in rendering the flowery style of the original Egyptian poetic composition(s) that must have stood behind the Akkadian composition as we have it:

> *ša iš-me a-na* LUGAL *be-li-šu ù* / *ú-ra-ad-šu i-na aš-ra-ni-šu* / *ù it-‹ta›-ṣí* dUTU *i-na muḫ-ḫi-šu* / *ù i-sà-ḫír še-ḫu* DÙG.GA *iš-tu* UZU*pí be-li-šu* / "He who listened to his lord and serves him in his place(s), then the sun god comes forth to him and the sweet breath from the mouth of his lord restores (him)" (EA 147:41-44); *ù la-a iš-te-mé a-ma-ta₅* LUGAL *be-li-šu* / *ḫal-qá-at* URU-⌈*šu*⌉ *ḫa-li-iq* É-*šu* / *ia-nu šu-um-šu i-na gáb-bi* / KUR-*ti i-na da-ri-ti* "But (as for) he (who) heeded/heeds not the word of the king, his lord, his city is lost, his house is lost, his name shall not exist in the whole land forever" (EA 147:45-48); *a-mur* / ÌR-*da ša*

> *iš-me a-na ›a-na‹ be-li-šu / šul-mu* URU-*šu šul-mu* É-*šu / šum-šu a-na da-ri-ti* "Behold the servant who listens/listened to his lord, his city is at peace, his house is at peace, his name endures forever" (EA 147:48-51).

The *išme* forms have an adverbial complement, *ana* (*šarri*) *bēlišu*, while *išteme* governs a direct accusative, *amāta*. The use of the prefixed tense forms in the Tyrian letters does not conform to the pattern typical of most other letters from Canaan. Therefore, these Tyrian anomalies make it necessary to look elsewhere for more conclusive proof of the relationship between forms with infixed -*t*- and those without.

Such a contrast is observable in the so called "dog formula," several variations of which are documented among the epistles in the Ashkelon correspondence, e.g. one context has infixed -*t*-:

> *mi-ia-mi* / ^{LÚ}UR.GI$_{12}$ *u la-a* / *yi-iš-te-mu a-wa-ta*$_5$ / LUGAL EN-*ia* "Who is the dog that he should not heed the word of the king, my lord" (EA 323:17-20; also EA 324:16-18; 325:12-14);

while a parallel passage uses the Akkadian preterite form as its model,

> *mi-ia-mi* ^{LÚ}*kal-bu* / *u la-a yi-iš-mu* / *a-na a-wa-te* LUGAL EN-*šu* "Who is the dog that he should not listen to the words of the king, his lord" (EA 320:22-24; also EA 322:17-19).

Both verbs have the WS imperfect suffix -*u*. The form with infixed -*t*- might be construed as *yištemmû*, Gt present future, but the form without the infix is based on the Akkadian G preterite theme. The proverbial nature of this saying assures that the tense is present-future, that is, the original tense of the Akkadian theme is irrelevant! The WS prefix and suffix determine the tense and mode, viz. indicative imperfect. The form with the infix takes a direct object in the accusative, *a-wa-ta*$_5$, the form without the infix takes an indirect object in the form of an adverbial complement.

The many replies to pharaoh's communications mentioned above reflect the desire on the part of local rulers to impress their master with how attentive they had been in listening to a message from the king. Therefore, they used the forms with infixed *-t-* in the "reflexive" sense. Note that the first example cited above (EA 292:17-26) begins with *iš-te-mé* without the presentation particle *anumma*. Further on, *anumma* serves to introduce the affirmation that pharaoh's orders are being carried out, *a-nu-ma* / ⌜*iṣ*⌝*-ṣú-ru ù a-nu-ma* / [*i*]*š-te-mu*. The form from *naṣāru* has no infixed *-t-*, only that from *šemû*. The reason is that the scribe wants to stress the "heeding" in the sense of the WS Gt. This point must be emphasized so as to avoid the superficial assumption that, in other contexts, where *išteme* or *ištemû* do follow *anumma*, the resemblance to the well known Akkadian syntagma of *anumma* plus a *-t-* preterite (*GAG*:104, §80c; Heimpel and Guidi 1969:148-152) is only coincidental.

Therefore, it would appear that the scribes of Canaan frequently used forms with infixed *-t-* from the verb *šemû* because they had a Gt stem in their mother tongue.

VERBS WITH NO LEXICAL Gt

Finally, there are some verbs for which forms having infixed *-t-* are fairly prevalent but for which one is hard pressed to find a satisfactory explanation. They are grouped together here, not because there is any solid reason to posit a functioning Gt, but simply for easy reference. At least, most of them add further proof that the Akkadian preterite with infixed *-t-* was not a vital, functioning tense form in this dialect or in the mother tongue of the scribes. The few examples that do occur can be reckoned as Akkadianisms.

leqû. The dictionaries either do not have a Gt for this verb (*AHw*:544b-546a) or, if recognizing Gt forms (*CAD* L:131a), do not assign them any special semantic category. *CAD* (L:131a, 135a) cites the following forms from an Akkadian epistle, evidently written to a queen of Ugarit, as examples of Gt:

> *na-mu-ur-te-e* / *ša* ^{I}*Ur-tá-ni* / *il-ta-qa-a* / *e-ni-in*$_4$*-na a-nu-ma* / 1 GAL GUŠKIN 1 ^{SÍG}GADA / 1 *me-at* ^{SÍG}*ḫu-uṣ-ma-ni* / 1 *me-at* ^{SÍG}*ta-kíl-ta* / *a-na* ^{I}*A-bi-ma-ni* / *at-ta-din il-te-qa-ki* "He has taken the audience gifts of Urtana (CAD N:254b); now then, one gold cup, one wool garment, one hundred (shekels of) blue-green wool, one hundred (shekels of) blue-purple wool, to Abimānu I have given (and) he has taken for you" (RS 12.33:r. 1'-9'; Nougayrol 1955:14-15; Virolleaud 1951:54-55).

Huehnergard (1979:244, 259-261; 1989:171-172) does not deal with these particular forms at all. It is hard to see why *CAD* saw them as Gt unless they took the final verb as a future. All of them are most likely G preterites with *-t-* infix.

There are not very many forms with infixed *-t-* from this verb in the Canaanite Amarna texts, as against the plethora of G stem examples. Some of the *-t-* forms, viz. those without a consonantal suffix, can be taken as Akkadian G preterites with *-t-* infix: 3rd m.s. *ìl-te*$_9$*-qé* (EA 74:23; 81:8, 47), *il*$_5$*-te-qé* (EA 280:22), 1st c.s. *el-te*$_9$*-qé* (EA 280:26), 3rd m.pl. *ìl-te*$_9$*-qú-mi* (EA 69:10), *il*$_5$*-te*$_9$*-qú* (EA 237:5), *il*$_5$*-te*$_9$*-qú-ú* (EA 237:2, 11; 238:6, 25, 27). But two of the forms lacking consonantal suffix serve functions other than that of a preterite or any other normal function in the Akkadian dialects. One of the examples in question expresses the future!

> *la-a* / *i-le-ú uš-ša-ar-*[*šu*] / *ú-ul yi-iš-ma* ^{I}ÌR-*A-ši-i*[*r-ta*] / *ù ma-an-nu ìl-te*$_9$*-qa-n*[*i*] / *i*[*š-*]*tu qa-ti-šu* "I am unable to send [him] lest ᶜAbdi-Ashirta should hear, and who would rescue m[e fr]om his hand?" (EA 82:21-25).

The other is a volitive:

> *ù ú-ul ìl-te*$_9$*-qa mi-im-ma*^{MEŠ} / *ša* DINGER.MEŠ-*ka* ^{LÚ}UR.GI$_7$ *šu-ut* "But let not that dog seize the property of your god(s)!" (EA 84:34-35).

The forms with WS consonantal prefix generally conform to the Canaanite modal/tense system, with one glaring exception:

> *gáb-bi a-wa-te* MEŠ / *šàr-ri* EN-*ia* / *i-ba-aš-ši* / *a-di it-ta-ṣi* / LÚGAL *ù* / *ye-el-te-qé* / *mi-im-ma* / *ša iq-bi* / I*šàr-ru* / *be-li-ia* "All the things (*awātē*) of (= for) the king, my lord, are on hand (*contra* Moran 1987b:464 n. 1; 1992:296 n. 1) for the coming forth of the officer that he may take the supplies of which the king, my lord, spoke" (EA 239:8-17).

One would have expected *yittaṣ*(*ṣ*)*û* and *yelteqû*, 3rd m.s. imperfects. In this case, the form with infixed *-t-* may have been due to "modus attraction" with the preceding verb which itself is probably a pseudo-infinitive, cf. *adi ētelli* (EA 287:45). The "proper" hybrid imperfect form does occur, e.g. as a future:

> *a-na-ku aq-bu* / [*šum-ma* UD.K]ÁM.MEŠ *yi-iš-mu šàr-ru* / [*ù* UD].KÁM.MEŠ *yi-ìl-te*9*-qú-šu-nu* / [*ù šum*]*-ma mu-ša yi-iš-mu ù* / [*mu-š*]*a yi-ìl-te*9*-qú-šu-nu* "I say (or: have been saying), '[If one (sic! Moran 1987b:309 n. 2; 1992:184 n. 2) da]y the king should hear, [then in one da]y he could seize them, [and i]f one night he should hear, then [one nigh]t he could catch them" (EA 109:15-19).

Also as a present:

> *pu-uḫ-ri-iš-mi* / *yi-il-te-qú šàr-ru* / *mim-mi-ia* "The king is taking over my property completely" (EA 254:24-26);

alongside a past continuous:

> *ša-ni-tam* I*La-ab-a-yu* / BA.UG7 *ša ye-el-te-qú* / URU.DIDLI.ḪÁ-*ni-nu ù* / *a-nu-ma* I*La-ab-a-yu* / ⌈*ša*⌉-⌈*nu*⌉ IÌR-*ḫe-ba ù* / [›*ù*‹] *ye-el-te-*⌈*qú*⌉ URU.DIDLI.ḪÁ-*nu* "Furthermore, Labʾayu is dead, who used to take over our cities, but now ʿAbdi-Kheba is another Labʾayu and he is taking over our cities" (EA 280:30-35).

And finally, there is a clear-cut example of the very non-Akkadian jussive:

ù lu-ú yu-uš-ši-ra / LUGAL *be-li* / ^{GIŠ}GIGIR.MEŠ *ù lu-ú* / *yi-ìl-te-qé-ni* / *a-na mu-ḫi-šu la-a* / *iḫ-la-aq* "Thus may the king, my lord, send chariots and may he take me unto himself lest I perish" (EA 270:24-29; Izreʾel 1978b:61-61).

In short, all the forms of *leqû* with infixed *-t-* may simply represent the use of the G *t*-preterite as theme. Rarely, the bare form, *ilteqe,* may stand alone, probably as a calque for WS **laqaḥ(a)*. Otherwise, the tense and modal nuances are generally expressed by WS prefixes and suffixes.

riāḫu. With one exception, the forms of this verb in the Canaanite Amarna texts are hybrids of the suffix conjugation (Rainey 1971b:93-94; 1973c:255-256; cf. *infra,* pp. 338-339). It may be that the G preterite with infixed *-t-* was chosen as the theme for all forms in accordance with a known tendency among peripheral scribes to prefer *-t-* augmented forms for weak verbs (cf. Gordon 1938:215). Nevertheless, one cannot escape the impression that the scribes associated some reflexive nuance with the stative concept, "to remain, to be left over." The one prefix form is 3rd f.s. imperfect with "city" as subject (feminine in accordance with Canaanite, not Akkadian usage, *CAD* A/1:379a):

šum-ma / *la-a* ERÍN.MEŠ *pí-ṭá-‹ta›* *la-a* / *tu-wa-‹ši›-ru-na ù* / *ia-nu* URU *ša-a ti-ir-ti-ḫu* / *a-na ka-ta*$_5$ "If you do not se‹n›d the army, then there is no town that will remain to you: (EA 103:51-55).

šapāru. The most complex situation pertains to the forms of *šapāru* with infixed *-t-* . Some of them have orthographic gemination of the second radical, e.g. 3rd m.s. *iš-tap-pa-ar* (EA 74:30), *ìš-tap-pa-ar* (EA 121:1), *iš-tap-pa-ra-ni* (EA 305:17), *ia-aš-tap-pár* (EA 233:16), *yi-iš-tap-pa-ra* (EA 130:9), and 1st c.s. *aš-tap-pár* (EA 88:13; *et passim*), *ìš-tap-pa-ar* (EA 134:31); morphologically, they can be based on the present-future of the Akkadian Gt or on the preterite of the Akkadian Gtn. Other forms have no express gemination, but they have vocalic suffixes without eliding the thematic vowel, which implies gemination of the second radical: 3rd m.s. *yi-ìš-ta-pa-ru* (EA 112:7), *yi-ìš-⸢ta⸣-pa-ru* (EA 103:20), *yi-ìš-ta-pa-ra* (EA 130:15), 2nd m.s. *ti-ìš-ta-pa-ru* (EA 117:31), 1st c.s. *aš-ta-pà-ru* (EA 89:7; *et passim*), 3rd m.pl. *ti-iš-ta-pa-ru-na* (EA 124:38; Moran 1987b:336; 1992:203). One can hardly doubt that gemination is intended; note, for example, that *yi-iš-tap-pa-ra* (EA 130:9) and *yi-ìš-ta-pa-ra* (EA 130:15) appear in parallel clauses in the same letter. On the other hand, it will become clear in the ensuing discussion that the gemination in these forms has become little more than an orthographic convention (cf. the discussion of this phenomenon by Youngblood 1961:140).

There are also forms with vocalic suffixes that elide the thematic vowel, thus precluding gemination of the second radical: 3rd m.s. *iš-tap-ra-am* (EA 321:17), *iš-tap-ru* (EA 92:35; 106:30), *iš-tap-ra-an-ni* (EA 253:10; *et al.*), *yi-iš-tap-ru* (EA 106:14), *yi-ìš-tap-ru-na* (EA 121:7), 2nd m.s. *ta-aš-tap-ra* (EA 34:8; 102:14), *ti-ìš-tap-ru* (EA 124:36), *ti-ìš-tap-ru-na* (EA 117:8), 1st c.s. *iš-tap-ru* (EA 85:6; *et al.*), *ìš-tap-ru* (EA 85:55; 133:15). Such examples as these can only be based on the G preterite with infixed *-t-* or on the Gt preterite. They certainly cannot be derived from the Akkadian Gtn stem.

Finally, there are many forms without a vocalic suffix that do not show gemination of the second radical orthographically, but which could be interpreted either way because the scribe was not obligated to express a double consonant in the spelling: 3rd m.s. *iš-ta-pár* (EA 108:1; *et passim*), *iš-ta-pár-ka* (EA 71:9), *yi-ìš-ta-pár* (EA 73:26), 1st c.s. *aš-ta-pa-ar* (EA 74:49;*et passim*), *aš-ta-pár* (EA 81:22; *et passim*); these latter forms are by far the most numerous.

Semantic analysis reveals that gemination or lack of it does not seem to be a factor in determining the verbal nuance. A single action in the past is expressed in the opening clause in many of Rib-Haddi's letters:

> ^{I}*Ri-ib-*^{d}IŠKUR *iš-ta-pár* / *a-na* ^{I}EN-*šu* . . . "Rib-Haddi has written to his lord . . . " (EA 108:1; 116:1; 119:1; 123:1; 124:6-7; also EA 94:1, Moran 1987b:286 n. 1; 1992:168 n. 1).

Another version proves the simple past tense of the verb in this formula:

> [I]*Ri-ib-ad-da iq-bi a-na* EN-*l*[*i-šu*] "Rib-Hadda said to [his] lor[d]" (EA 74:1; also EA 68:1-2; 75:1-2; 76:1-2; 78:1-2; 79:1-2; 81:1; 83:1-2; 88:1; 89:1-2; 92:1-2; 105:1; 106:1; 107:1-2; 109:1; Salonen 1967:62-63).

The reference in both cases is, of course, to the letter in hand, a single instance. At least once, and perhaps twice (EA 121:1-2), a scribe used a form with geminated second radical in this syntagma:

> [[I]]*Ri-ib-*[d]IŠKUR *iš-tap-pár* / [*a*]-*na* EN-*šu* "Rib-Haddi has written [t]o his lord" (EA 122:1).

So all of these may be reckoned as Akkadianisms, i.e. standing for the G preterite with infix *-t-*. Note, however, that there is no distinctive function for the infix; it has lost the special force that it carried in OB and now expresses the same simple past tense like the plain preterite. It is used in this manner in the letters from Tyre (EA 148:4; 149:24, 55; 151:49; 154:6).

But the fact is that forms with clear gemination also serve to express single instances in the past, precluding any possibility of their having iterative force, for example:

> *a-wa-at iš-tap-pár* / LUGAL EN-*ia* DINGIR.MEŠ-*ia* / [[d]]UTU-*ia* *a-na ia-ši* / [*a-nu*]-*ma i-šu-ši-ru-šu* / [*a-n*]*a* LUGAL EN-*ia* "As for the word which the king, my lord, my god(s), my sun-[god] has sent to me, [no]w I am preparing it [fo]r the king my lord" (EA 276:9-13).

The "word" sent by the king is singular (construct without final vowel) and, like most replies to royal commands, this epistle undoubtedly refers to a specific message recently received from the court. The reference may also be to a particular emissary who had just brought a message. Note this example with gemination:

> ^{LÚ}DUMU *ši-ip-ri* / *ša iš-tap-pár šàr-ri* EN-*ia* / *a-na ia-a-ši* / *iš-te-me a-wa-te* ^{MEŠ}-*šu* / [*m*]*a-gal ma-gal* "As for the emissary whom my king, my lord, has sent unto me, I heeded his words very diligently" (EA 302:11-15).

This may be compared with an almost identical context where the verb lacks gemination (the thematic vowel being elided) but has the ventive suffix:

> ^{LÚ}MAŠKÍM \ *ra-bi-iṣ* / *ša* LUGAL EN-*ia* / *ša iš-tap-ra-am* / LUGAL EN-*ia* ^{d}UTU / *iš-tu* AN$^{\textit{sa-me}}$ / *a-na ia-a-ši* / *iš-te*$_9$*-me* / *a-wa-›wa‹-te*^{MEŠ}-*šu* / [*ma*]-*gal ma-gal* "As for the commissioner of the king, my lord, whom the king, my lord, the sun-god from heaven, has sent to me, I have heeded his words very diligently" (EA 321:15-23; similarly EA 145:11-13; 253:7-10; 254:6-7; 305:17; 329:15).

In another passage, a form with gemination appears in context with a real Akkadianized Gtn, but still it is in a relative clause which has as its antecedent a single "word" (construct without final vowel), and therefore, it must be referring to a single instance in the past.

> *iš-te*$_9$*-né-me* / *a-wa-at* LUGAL EN-*ia* / *ša iš-tap-pa-ra-an-ni* "I am heeding the word of the king, my lord, which he sent to me" (EA 305:15-17).

It would be easy to write off all the forms discussed above as simple confusion between the Akkadian G preterite with infix -*t*- and the Gtn preterite. They lack the typical WS *y*- prefix and have either -Ø suffix or the ventive. Note, incidentally, how many of the examples cited are in subordinate clauses *without* any trace of the Akkadian subjunctive marker!

Examination of the examples with WS consonantal *y*- as prefix reveals that the infixed -*t*- and the gemination (or lack of it) play little, if any, role in determining the tense and mode of the respective forms. It is evidently the -Ø suffix that serves to mark the following verbs as past tense within the syntactic framework of these letters:

> *i-nu-ma yi-iš-ta-pár a-na* LÚ.MEŠ / URU*Am-mi-ia* "Because he wrote to the men of Ammiya" (EA 73:26-27); *ša ya-aš-tap-pár* / *be-lí-ia a-na* ÌR-*šu* / *yi-iš-te₉-mu* "What my lord has written to his servant, he will heed" (EA 233:16-18).

In both cases, one might take the forms as Gtn preterites signifying that the subject has written more than once (thus Rabiner 1981:4, 75). However, EA 73 is dealing with a specific instance and quotes that message, while the second text must be seen in the context of the orders issued by pharaoh to each key city ruler to get ready for a military campaign. The message is undoubtedly the response to a particular communication from pharaoh.

Two other instances of this verb have the ventive suffix; they appear in parallel passages from the same letter, each dealing with a specific message sent by the king. Both passages reflect gemination of the second radical although only the first expresses it orthographically:

> *i-nu-ma yi-iš-tap-pa-ra* / *šàr-ru a-na ia-ši a-nu-ma* / I*I-ri-ma-ia-aš-ša* / *ia-ak-šu-du-na a-na mu-ḫi-ka ú-ul ka-ši-id* / *a-na mu-ḫi-ia i-nu-ma* / *yi-iš-ta-pa-ra šàr-ru* / *a-na ia-ši ú-ṣur-mì* / *ra-ma-an-ka ù* / *ú-ṣur* URU *šàr-ri ša-a* / *it-ti-ka ma-an-nu* / *yi-na-ṣí-ra-ni* "Inasmuch as the king has written to me, 'Now Irimayassa is coming to you,' he has not arrived; inasmuch as the king has written to me, 'Protect yourself and protect the king's city that is in your charge,' who will protect me?" (EA 130:9-20).

In the latter instance, one might assume that numerous messages had been sent out admonishing the local rulers to see to the safety of their respective towns, but in the first case, there was a message about the arrival of a single emissary. Can one believe that said emissary was preceded by a series of letters announcing his coming? A similar context has a 2nd m.s. verb:

> *i-nu-ma ta-aš-tap-ra a-na ia-ši* / *a-lik-mi i-zi-iz a-na* URU*Ṣu-mu-ur* / *a-di ka-ša-di-ia* / [*t*]*i-de i-nu-ma nu-kúr-tu*$_4$MEŠ / KAL.GA *ma-gal* UGU-*ia* / *ù ú-ul i-le-ú! a-la*[*-ka*]*m* "Inasmuch as you have written to me, 'Go, take up a position at Ṣumur until I arrive,' [k]now that hostilities are very strong against me and I am unable to g[o]" (EA 102:14-19).

Examples of 1st c.s. with -Ø suffix also serve to express single instances in the past. Despite the badly broken context, EA 92:12, 16, 38, 44) uses *aš-tap-pár* four times, each concerning a different message sent by Rib-Haddi to the king. The Tyrian letters employ the spelling, *aš-ta-pár,* when dealing with specific instances in the past (EA 148:23; 149:11, 70; also from Byblos, EA 91:7). Quite a few of the documented forms refer to Rib-Haddi's earlier correspondence with Amenhotep III and his ministers about the misdeeds of ᶜAbdi-Ashirta. Most of the contexts seem to call for a simple preterite meaning, and in fact, parallel contexts use the G preterite, *aš-pu-ur* (EA-138:31; 362:18-20). A typical example with the infixed *-t-* is the following:

> *ù aš-ta-pa-ar a-na* / *a-bi-ka uš-ši-ra-mi* / ERÍN.MEŠ *pí-ṭá-ti šàr-ri* / *ù tu-ul-qú ka-l*[*i*] / KUR *i-na* UD.KÁM.MEŠ "So I wrote to your father, 'Send forth regular army troops and all the land will be captured in a day'" (EA 132:12-16; cf. EA 117:63 for the ideogram without MEŠ; Moran 1987b:309 n. 2, 352 n. 1; 1992:184 n. 2, 214 n. 1).

Similar statements reiterate this identical theme with slight variations (EA 108:28; 117:24; 121:41).

One also finds certain contexts in which the form itself is evidently past tense, but nevertheless, it is followed in the next clause by an imperfect verb, e.g.

> *a-nu-ma ki-a-ma aš-ta-pa-ar a-na* É.GAL / *ù ú-ul ti-iš-mu-na a-wa-tu-ia* "Now, thus did I write to the palace, but my words are not heeded(sic!)" (EA 74:49-50; for the misspelled passive verb form, cf. Ebeling 1915:1370 n. 1; Youngblood 1961:149);

> *ša-ni-tam aš-ta-pár a-na* LÚ.MEŠ *ma-ṣa-ar-ti* / *ù a-na* ANŠE. KUR.RA.MEŠ *ù la-a* / *tu-da-nu-na* "Furthermore, I wrote for garrison troops and for horses (cavalry) but they were/are not given" (EA 83:21-23; also EA 81:22).

Still, a specific request made at a certain time seems to be indicated in each of these instances. The fact that the ensuing imperfect verbs are all passives (correct or misspelled) may have a bearing on these contexts (cf. *infra*, p. 234). With regard to EA 74:49, it should be noted that this is the only time a verb with -Ø follows *anūma kīamma,* the other instances having a form with *-u*, e.g. 3rd m.s. *yi-ìš-˹ta˺-pa-ru* (EA 103:20), 1st c.s. *aš-ta-pa-ru* (EA 89:7), and 1st c.s. *iš-tap-ru* (EA 85:6-7); in all three cases the ensuing clause has an imperfect verb.

By contrast, there are three times when Rib-Haddi wanted to stress that he had had to write repeatedly to the palace. In such cases, the scribe might have been thinking of the Gtn preterite; two of the pertinent examples have orthographic gemination. But to render Rib-Haddi's complaint unmistakably clear, he reinforced the first verb with a form of *šanû* having infixed-*t-*:

> *aš-tap-pár aš-ta-ni la-a* / *ia-tu-ru-na a-wa-tu* / *a-na ia-a-ši* "I wrote repeatedly (but) no word came back to me" (EA 126:53-55; cf. EA 75:17-18).

One final passage of this type contrasts earlier multiple communications with the sending of a subsequent single embassage:

> *aš-tap-pár aš-ta-ni a-n*[*a* ERÍN.MEŠ *ma-ṣa-ar-ti*] / *ù la-a tu-da-nu-na* [*ù la-a*] / *yi-iš-mé* LUGAL *be-li a-wa-t*[*e* ÌR-*šu*] / *ù i-wa-ši-ir* LÚDUMU *š*[*ìp-ri-ia*] / *a-na* É-*ti* É.GAL *ù i*[*a?-tu-ur*] / *ri-qú-tam i-ia-nu* ERÍN.MEŠ *ma-ṣa-a*[*r-ta*$_5$] / *a-na ša-a-šu* "I wrote repeatedly f[or garrison troops], but they were not given [and] the king, my lord, did [not] listen to the word[s of his servant]; so I sent [my] ambas[sado]r to the palace but he re[turned]

> empty-handed, no garrison troops being with him" (EA 137:5-11).

The question remains as to whether the repetition of the earlier messages could have been stated without the helping verb, *aš-ta-ni*.

When we come to examine all the forms of *šapāru* with infixed *-t-* on which the WS imperfect suffix is appended, the contrast with the examples discussed above proves most interesting. There are two cases where the absence of a WS consonantal prefix did not prevent the scribe from using the WS imperfect suffix, *-u*. The forms in question, both from Gulba letters, do not show gemination of their second radical (their thematic vowel is elided) and they are not in subordinate clauses where the Akkadian subjunctive suffix might be conjectured:

> *[al]-⌜lu⌝-⌜mi⌝ ⌜iš⌝-tap-ru* / ^{I}*Ri-ib-ad-d[a]* / *a[-n]a ka-tu-nu a-na ti-la-ti* "[Be]hold (Moran 1950a:161), Rib-Hadda is (has been) writing t[o] you(pl.) for auxiliary troops (Youngblood 1961:361)" (EA 92:35-36); *a-na* $mi\text{-}ni_7$ *iš-tap-r[u]* / ^{I}*Ri-ib-*^{d}IŠKUR *ṭup-pa a-na ma-ḫar be-li-š[u]* "Why does Rib-Haddi send a tablet to hi[s] lord?" (EA 106:30-31).

Quite a number of the relevant instances pertain to the "dialogue" between Rib-Haddi and Pharaoh during the former's troubles with the sons of ᶜAbdi-Ashirta. That corresondence has been given considerable attention by scholars (cf. for example Liverani 1971). The extraordinary number of letters sent by Rib-Haddi to the Egyptian king stirred up considerable irritation on the part of Pharaoh and this finds expression in the responses from Egypt (e.g. EA-106:13-15; EA 117:6-9). Those responses are known mainly from allusions in Rib-Haddi's own letters. Apparently, the king had replied more than once to the effect that Rib-Haddi should "be on guard" and look out for himself (rather than always pestering the imperial authorities for support and protection) as indicated by several allusions in the Byblos texts. Rib-Haddi responds:

> *a-na mi-ni yi-iš-ta-pa-ru* / *šàr-ru* EN-*li a-na ia-ši* / *ú-ṣur-mi lu-ú na-ṣir-ta* "Why does the king, my lord, write to me, 'Guard! May you be watchful'" (EA 112:7-9; likewise EA 119:8-9; 121:7-8).

And Pharaoh's letters must have charged, or implied, that Rib-Haddi was not telling the truth:

> *a-wa-te ša-ru-ta aš-ta-pa-ru* / *a-na* EN-*ia ù ti-qa-bu a-na mi-ni* / *ti-iš-ta-pa-ru a-wa-te ša-ru-ta* "(Is it) false words (that) I am writing to my lord? that you should say, 'Why do you write false words?'" (EA 117:29-31); cf. *ù be-li i-de i-nu-ma* / *la-a aš-pu-ru a-wa-at* / *ka-az-bu-te a-na be-li-ia* "And my lord knows that I do not write lies to my lord" (EA 362:51-53).

Rib-Haddi's exasperation with Pharaoh's impatience provides us with two more examples of these *-t-* forms in the imperfect mode:

> [*k*]*i-a-ma ti-qa-bu at-‹ta›-m*[*a*] / [*t*]*i-iš-tap-ru a-na ia-ši iš-t*[*u*] / [*k*]*a-li* LÚ.MEŠ *ḫa-za-nu-ti a-*[*na*] / [*m*]*i-ni ti-iš-ta-pa-ru-na š*[*u-nu*] / [*a-n*]*a ka-ta*₅ URU.MEŠ-*nu a-na š*[*a-šu-nu*] / [URU].MEŠ-*ni-ia la-qa* ᴵ*A-z*[*i-ru*] "Thus yo‹u› are saying, 'You write to me mor[e] than [a]ll the (other) city-rulers!' Why should they write to you! (Their) cities belong to th[em]. My [citi]es, Aziru has taken!" (EA 124:35-40).

Whatever the original motive for choosing themes with infixed *-t-* and frequent gemination of the second radical, the forms discussed here find their usual tense and modal expression in the WS suffixes, either *-Ø* or *-u*. The *-t-* forms are generally optional; there are often close parallels with G stem preterite themes lacking the infix.

**š̮ḫ̮ḫ̮n*. The verb forms appearing to have this root were evidently generated in Hurrian speaking areas from *šukēnu*, "to prostrate oneself" (*GAG*:158, §109m; *AHw*:1263). The phenomenon appears, for example, at Nuzi. Although there is no lexical Gt in Akkadian for this quadrilateral verb, the examples with infixed *-t-* are discussed here because of the possibility that there may have been some feeling of reflexiveness on the part of the scribes, i.e. "to prostrate oneself." It is worth noting that all the forms in question (with and without *-t-*) are known in the Amarna archive only from texts written in Canaan. In addition, there are a few examples from Ugarit and Hattusas (*AHw:*1293). The Assyrian form of *šukēnu* appears a few times in epistolary greeting formulas, e.g.

> *ul-ta-ka-in* / *a-na di-na-an* EN-*ia at-ta-lak* "I have prostrated myself; as a substitute for my lord I have gone (agreed to go)" (Finkelstein 1953:13X, No. 62:3-4; 63:3-4).

The verb form, *ul-ta-ka-in* (= *ultakaʾʾin*) appears to be G past with infixed *-t-* but the question has been raised whether it is not iterative (*AHw:*1263a).

Though there are many examples of the simple preterite in the Amarna letters (e.g. *uš-ḫé-ḫi-in* EA 221:7; *et al*; *uš-ḫé-ḫi-in*$_4$ EA 223:6; 242:8), the majority have an infixed *-t-* (*iš-ta-ḫa-ḫi-in* EA 298:12; *et passim*; *iš-ti-ḫa-ḫi-in* EA 301:10; *et al.*; *iš-tu-ḫa-ḫi-in* EA 331:10-11). Most of these latter are preceded by the emphatic particle, *lū*. The suggestion that these are iterative forms is tempting, especially because of the usual prostration formula as exemplified in the following:

> *7-šu ù 7-ta-a-an* / *lu-ú iš-ta-ḫa-ḫi-in* / ^{UZU}*ka-bat-tum-ma* / *ù* ^{UZU}*ṣe-ru-ma* "Seven times and seven times I have verily prostrated, on the stomach and on the back" (EA 305:11-14).

Interestingly enough, the ensuing line in the same letter begins with a Gtn present-future, *iš-te*$_9$*-né-me* (EA 305:15), which can only be viewed as an Akkadianism!

Nevertheless, it is impossible to refute the accepted view that these are merely G preterites with infixed *-t-* from the "Hurrianized" root of *šukēnu*. Their appearance in the obeisance formulas, where the usual verb is the Akkadian G preterite *amqut*, is a curiosity.

epēšu. Neither does Akkadian have a documented lexical Gt for this verb. The unique Amarna usage of the N stem from *epēšu* will be discussed in the next chapter. But because there are about half a dozen cases of forms with infixed *-t-* that have the same idiomatic nuance as the Amarna N stem, they must be Gt stem forms since the G stem would hardly have served the same purpose (Rainey 1971b:91-93; 1973c:254-255).

To be sure, there are three passages where the transitive nature of the construction indicates that the scribes have used the G preterite with infix *-t-* as the theme for simple past tense. In an earlier study they had been interpreted as possible reflexive Gt's with the force of suffix conjugation verbs taking adverbial accusatives (Rainey 1973c:255). Although they may in some sense represent a calque on WS suffix verbs, the assumption that they carried a reflexive nuance was undoubtedly wrong and is refuted by those contexts in which the identical meaning is expressed by purely G stem forms. The three particular passages in question are as follows:

> *ki*[*-n*]*a-na i-te*$_9$*-p*[*u-u*]*š* / ⌈*nu*⌉-KÚR *a-na ia-ši* "Th[u]s, he has ma[d]e war against me" (EA 105:39-40); *al-lu-mi* / [I]*Ia-pa-*[d]IŠKUR *i-t*[*e*$_9$*-p*]*u-*[*uš*] / *ar-na* "Behold, Yapaᶜ-Haddi has committed a crime" (EA 113:7-9); *iš-tu i-re-bi* ERÍN.MEŠ *pí-ṭá-ti* / *i-te*$_9$*-pu-uš-mì* [I]*La-ab-a-yu* / *nu-kúr-ta*$_5$ *i-na mu-uḫ-ḫi-ia* "Since the return (home) of the standing army, Labʾayu has made war on me" (EA 244:9-12).

Another purely transitive example has the WS prefix *y-* showing that the *-t-* form is simply a theme:

> *gáb-bi mi-im-mì* / *ša yi-te-pu-uš* / LUGAL EN-*ia!*(EN) *a-na* KUR-*šu* / SIG$_5$.GA *ma-gal* "Everything that the king my(!) lord has done for his land is very good" (EA 258:6-9).

The reflexive nuance of the other passages is best demonstrated by the ensuing context where Gt's alternate with N stem forms:

> [*ù*] *tu-*⸢*ba*⸣!*-ú-na ur-ra* / [*ù*] *mu-ša-am a-ṣé* ERÍN.MEŠ / *pí-ṭá-ti ù ni-te*$_9$*-pu-uš* / *a-na ša-a-ši*$_x$(ŠE) *ù ka-li* / $^{\text{LÚ.MEŠ}}$*ḫa-za-nu-te tu-ba-ú-na* / *i-pé-eš an-nu-tu*$_4$(sic!) *a-na* ^{I}ÌR-*A-ši-ir-ta* / *i-nu-ma yi-iš-ta-pár a-na* LÚ.MEŠ / ^{URU}*Am-mi-ia du-ku-mi* EN-*ku-nu* / *ù in-né-ep-šu a-na* / LÚ.MEŠ GAZ *ki-na-na ti-iq-bu-na* / $^{\text{LÚ.MEŠ}}$*ḫa-za-nu-tu*$_4$ *ki-na-na* / *yi-pu-šu a-na ia-ši-nu* / *ù ti-né-pu-šu ka-li* KUR.MEŠ / *a-na* LÚ.MEŠ GAZ "[And] they are seeking day and night the coming forth of the army that we may join ourselves to it and all the city rulers are seeking to do this to ᶜAbdi-Ashirta because he wrote to the men of Ammiya, 'Slay your master and join the *ᶜapîru* men.' Thus the city rulers are saying, 'Thus will he do to us and all the lands will go over to the *apîru* men.'" (EA 73:20-33).

Both the Gt and N forms express the meaning "to join, to side with" (Moran 1987a):

> *ù ti-iq-bi* URU.KI *i-*⸢*zi*⸣*-bu-šu* / *ni-te-pu-uš-mi a-na* ^{I}*A-zi-ri ù* / *aq-bi ki-i i-te*$_9$*-pu-šu a-na ša-šu* / *ù i-zi-bu* LUGAL *be-li ù yi-iq-bu* / ŠEŠ-*ia ù* [*yi*]-⸢*it*⸣*-mi a-na* URU.KI / *ù ti-dáb-bi-bu ù!* LÚ.MEŠ BE URU.KI / [*ti-t*]*e-pu-šu-mi a-na* DUMU.MEŠ ^{I}ÌR-*Aš-ra-*⸢*ti*⸣ "And the city said, 'Abandon(pl.) him! Let us side with Aziru!' But I said, 'How can I side with him and abandon the king, my lord?' And my brother spoke and [sw]ore to the city and they conspired together and the nobles of the city went over to the sons of ᶜAbdi-Ashirta" (EA 138:44-50; Rainey 1973c:254; also Moran 1987b:363, 365 n. 10, 366 nn. 11, 12; 1992:222, 224 nn. 10, 11, 12).

Two other examples complete the list:

> *te*$_9$*-e-te-pu-š*[*u*] / [KUR.MEŠ] *a-na* LÚ.MEŠ ⸢SA⸣.G[AZ.MEŠ] "[The lands] have gone over to the *ᶜap*[*îrû*] men" (EA 129:88-89); *qa-*⸢*bu*⸣ DUMU.MEŠ / [^{I}ÌR-]*A-ši-ir-ta a-na* / [LÚ.MEŠ] GAZ.MEŠ *ù* LÚ.MEŠ / [*ša i-*]*te*$_9$*-ep-šu* "The sons of [ᶜAbdi-]Ashirta spoke to the *ᶜapîrû* [men] and to the men [who have] gone over (to them)" (EA 121:19-22; Moran 1987b:332; 1992:200).

The latter form might be restored [*ti-*]*te*$_9$-*ep-šu*, 3rd m.pl. Gt preterite with WS *t-* prefix. This is the only example of this syntagma where the verb does not have an adverbial complement signifying to whom the people involved have become aligned.

One is reminded of Hebrew *bəhillāḥᵃmô* (2 Ki. 8:29; 9:15; 2 Chron. 22:6) versus Moabite *bhltḥmh* (= **behiltaḥimô?* Mesha Stele, *KAI* 181:19). Cf. also *wənib̲rək̲û* (Gen. 18:18) and *wəhit̲bārᵃk̲û* (Gen. 22:18) in identical contexts. It may be significant that these Amarna Gt's come from Byblos and Beirut where 10th century Phoenician had the Gt. In any case, these few examples of Gt instead of N stem in this particular semantic function are an important witness to the nature of the two verbal stems.

THE Gtn STEM

Some of the Gt verbs discussed above may have had iterative force. The possibility was explored as to whether some of the apparent Gt present-futures (with geminated middle radical) might actually be Gtn preterites (e.g., concerning *šapāru*, cf. *supra*, pp. 101-110). It was seen that even geminated forms could refer to a single instance in the past (cf. EA 305:15-20, *supra*, pp. 102-106). The only clearly recognizable Gtn forms are, in fact, those with an unassimilated *-tan-* infix. However, there is no basis for assuming that West Semitic had ever had a *-tan-* infix like Akkadian (*contra* Speiser 1955a). Perusal of the glossaries to the Amarna tablets (Ebeling 1915; Rainey 1978b:61-99) reveals that the epistles from Canaan seldom utilize the Akkadian Gtn and there are no Dtn or Štn forms. When the Canaanite scribes did employ such an iterative construction, it is worthy of special note. One noteworthy feature is the use of the Gtn present-future form to refer to iterative action that has already taken place. With two exceptions, such constructions do not have any WS modal suffixes; they stand as Akkadianisms replacing the WS imperfect of the G and/or Gt stems.

alāku. One time a Gtn is attested; it is in a letter from Labᵓayu, ruler of Shechem, and the context suggests that the form was a response to a charge made by pharaoh. However, the Amarna letters from Egypt do not attest to any Gtn's though the stem is found in the Egyptian texts found at Boghazköi (Cochavi-Rainey 1988:174). In any event, it is remarkable that Labʾayu's scribe employs a Gtn, augmented by the WS imperfect *-u* suffix, to describe the customary behavior of Labʾayu's son. That son has, in the meantime, been remanded into custody. So the customary behavior being discussed is now terminated; it is a thing of the past!

> *ša-ni-tam* / *a-na* ᴵDUMU.MU-*ia ša-pár šàr-ru* / *ú-ul* i_{15}*-de i-nu-ma* / ᴵDUMU.MU-*ia it-ti* / LÚ.MEŠ SA.GAZ / *it-ta-na-la-ku* / *ù al-lu-ú na-ad-na-*ti_7*-šu* / *i-na* ŠU ᴵ*Ad-da*[*-i*]*a* "Furthermore, the king has written concerning my son; I did not know that my son was consorting (running around) with the ᶜ*apîrû* men! But, behold, I have turned him over to (the commissioner) Adda[y]a" (EA 254:30-37; Moran 1975a:149).

šemû. Counting two examples in an Amurru letter that is generally not WS in style (Izreʾel 1991a:381,§6.3), there are six Gtn forms of this verb. The Amurru passage clearly uses the Gtn present-future to express present iterative, customary action (Izreʾel 1991:156,§2.4.2.3.1):

> [*i-nu-m*]*a* ⌜*i*⌝-[*k*]*a*-[*a*]*z-zi-bu-*ni_7 / [LÚ.MEŠ] *ḫa-za-nu-te*ᴹᴱŠ *a-na pa-ni-ka* / [*ù t*]*e-eš-te-nem-me a-na ša-šu-nu* / [*ù* ᴵ*I*]*a-ma-ia i-nu-ma i-šap-pár* / [*a-na mu*]*ḫ-ḫi-*⌜*ka*⌝ *ù i-ka-az-zi-ib* / [*a-na pa-n*]*i-ka ù te-eš-te-nem-me* / [*a-na a-wa-*]*te*ᴹᴱŠ*-šu* "[Whe]n the city-rulers lie to you [and y]ou listen to them! [And Y]amaya, when he writes [t]o you and lies [t]o you and you listen to his [wor]ds!" (EA 62:39-45; Izreʾel 1985:*8; 1991a:13; Moran 1987b:237 nn. 9, 10; 1992:134 nn. 9, 10).

Only one of the attestations in a Canaanite letter has a WS imperfect suffix. The form in question stands in a context where many other letters have a Gt with the WS imperfect (cf. *supra*, pp. 78-80):

> *gáb-bi mi-im-me* / *ša yi-iq-bu* / LUGAL EN-ia / *iš-te-nem-mu* "I am heeding everything that the King, my lord, says" (EA 261:7-10).

The subordinated verb, *yi-iq-bu,* has the form of a WS imperfect. On the other hand, it is tempting to see here an Akkadian subjunctive since similar contexts usually pertain to some specific instruction received from pharaoh. But there are so many other relative clauses without the Akkadian subjunctive that one must resist the temptation. On the contrary, the phrase, "every thing," probably assures us that the reference is to every communication that pharaoh *has been sending,* i.e. to all of the king's recent instructions. The Gtn form, *iš-te-nem-mu,* is present iterative on two counts: the theme is Akkadian Gtn present-future, and the modal suffix in WS imperfect.

The next example uses the Gtn present-future theme with -Ø suffix in a context where other letters have the Gt with -Ø suffix (cf. e.g. EA 292:17-26; 328:17-26; Rainey 1975b:96-101):

> *iš-te*$_9$*-né-me* / *a-wa-at* LUGAL EN-*ia* / *ša iš-tap-pa-ra-ni* / *ù a-nu-ma a-na-ṣa-ru* / *a-šar* ⸢LUGAL⸣ *ša* / *it-t*[*i-*]*ia* "I have heeded the word of the king, my lord, which he sent to me and now I am guarding the place of the king which is assigned to me" (EA 305:15-20).

Cf. the discussion of *iš-tap-pa-ra-ni,* which could itself be a Gtn preterite (*supra,* p. 104).

Finally, there are two examples that even have the MB shift, *št* › *lt.* One of them is in a context similar to the passage just cited:

> *u a-nu-ma* [*é*]*l-t*[*e*$_9$*-n*]*é-mé* / *a-na a-w*[*a-*]*t*[*e*^{ME}]^{Š} L[UGA]L EN-ia / ⸢*u*⸣ *iš-*[*t*]*e*$_9$*-mu* [*a-n*]*a a-wa-te*^{MEŠ} / ^{I}*Ma-i*[*a* ^{LÚ}M]AŠ[KÍ]M [LU]GAL / EN-*ia* ⸢^{d}⸣[UTU] *iš-tu* / AN$^{sa\text{-}ma}$ D[UMU] ⸢^{d}⸣UTU "And now [I] a[m] heeding the words of the ki[ng], my lord, and I am heeding the words of Maya, [the co]mm[issio]ner of the [ki]ng, my lord, the [sun god] from heaven, the s[on of] the sun god" (EA 300:23-28; *infra,* p. 278).

The other is a variation on the "dog formula" used by vassals in expressing their subordination and obedience to their lord:

> [*u m*]*a-an-nu-mì a-na-ku* UR.GI$_7$ / [*u ma*]*-an-nu* ⸢É⸣*-ia* / ⸢*u*⸣ ⸢*ma*⸣*-an-nu* x[. . .]-⸢*ia*⸣ / *u* ⸢*ma*⸣*-an-nu gáb-ba* / *mi-im-me ša* ⸢*i*⸣-⸢*ba*⸣*-aš-ši* / ⸢*a*⸣*-na ia-si u a-wa-te*^{MEŠ} / LUGAL EN-*ia* ^{d}UTU ⸢*iš*⸣*-tu* / AN$^{\textit{sa-mì-i}}$ *ú-*⸢*ul*⸣ / *él-te*$_9$*-né-em-me* "[And w]ho am I, a dog, [and w]ho are my household and who are my [. . .] and who are all that I have that the words of the king, my lord, the sun god from heaven, I should not heed?" (EA 378:19-26).

Other formulations of this type use forms such as *yi-iš-mu* (EA 320:22-24; 322:17-19) or *yi-iš-te-mu* (EA 323:17-20; also EA 324:16-18; 325:12-14), i.e. the WS imperfect of the G or the Gt stem. In fact, the parallels between those forms and this Akkadian Gtn present-future confirmed the semantic nature of the WS imperfect (Rainey 1971b:96-101).

CHAPTER VI

PREFIX CONJUGATION — N STEM

There are relatively few N stem verb forms in the Amarna letters from Canaan. Nevertheless, those that we do find are often of special interest. Furthermore, a couple of forms originally taken to be G present-future have been re-evaluated and shown to be better understood if taken as N stem. It should also be noted that in such cases, the gemination of the first radical due to assimilation of the *-n-* stem morpheme was not expressed orthographically. Other hints, such as thematic vowel and context, were the only indicators of N stem.

PASSIVE OF TRANSITIVE VERBS

The existence of the Gp stem (cf. *supra*, pp. 75-80) meant that there was a morphological vehicle ready at hand for expressing the passive of transitive verbs. Nevertheless, the N stem does fulfill a similar function on occasion and since the Gp stem does not exist in Akkadian, it is not surprising that some N forms are utilized, even when other scribes may have used the Gp for the same verb.

apālu. The corrected reading of one cuneiform sign by Gordon and Moran has led to the following example of an N stem preterite 3rd m.s. (Moran 1987b:476 n. 4; 1992:476 n. 4):

> *yi-in$_4$-⸢na⸣-⸢pí⸣-⸢il⸣!/ [šu-ul]-⸢ma⸣!-⸢nu⸣-um i-⸢na⸣ lìb-bi-šu-ni* "A [treaty] gift was paid between the two of them" (EA 250:33-34).

kašāšu. The two examples of this normally *a-u* verb (*CAD* K:286) both have an *-i-* theme vowel. The best solution seems to be to take them as N stem forms, even though the first radical is not geminated orthographically (Rainey 1974:304; 1978b:76):

> *šu-ut i-de* ⸢*i*⸣[*-nu-ma ia-nu* L]Ú *ša-na* / *ù* A*mé-e* *i-*[*n*]*a-š*[*a*]*-šu-nu-ma* / *šu-ut yu-*TIL.LA*-aṭ-šu-nu* / *i-nu-ma i-ka-ši-iš a-na-ku* / LÚ.MEŠ GAZ! *nu-kùr-tu i-na ia-ši* / *ù šu-ut* TE.LA*-aṭ-šu-nu-ma* "He knows t[hat there is no] other [ma]n and (that) I am/was bringing them water; he must supply them because I am being improverished, the *ᶜapîru* men are at war with me so he must supply them" (EA 94:64-69; cf. Youngblood 1961:385; Moran 1987b:285; 1992:168).

The financial connotation of this verb, concerning the exaction of services or payments of debts (*CAD* K:286; *AHw*:462) seems appropriate for these contexts where the ability to furnish supplies is in question. The Gublites can then be understood as complaining about the economic burden of Aziru's aggression:

> *ù a*[*nu-m*]*a i-na-na* / *l*[*a-qa*/*qi* U]R[UṢ]*u-m*[*u-ri* I]*A-zi-ru* / *ù ti-mu-*[*r*]*u* ⸢LÚ⸣.⸢MEŠ⸣ ⸢URU⸣[*G*]*ub*⸢*ub*⸣-⸢*li*⸣ / *a-di ma-ti ni-ka-ši-šu* DUMU IÌR-[*A-ši-ir-ti*] "And n[ow] then Aziru has t[aken] ⸢Ṣumur⸣ and the ⸢men⸣ of Byblos saw it (and said), 'How long will we be impoverished by the son of ᶜAbdi-[Ashirta]?,'' (EA 138:34-37; cf. Moran 1987b:362, 365 n. 7; 1992:221, 223 n. 7).

mašāʾu. The N stem of this verb appears three times in the Rib-Haddi letters. Originally, it was thought to be *mašāḫu* (Ebeling 1910:65; 1915:1466). One of the contexts is clear; the others are virtually identical but broken:

> *ù* 2 MU *am-ma-ša-ʾu₅* / ŠE*im*ḪÁ*-ia* "And for two years I have been plundered of my grain" (EA 85:9-10; cf. also EA 90:63; 91:61; Youngblood 1961:272-273, 358; *AHw*:625a; *CAD* M/1:362b; Moran 1987b:269, 279, 281; 1992:156, 164, 165).

maḫāṣu. The scribes are aware, of course, that the first radical on an N stem prefix form was geminated. This is seen in two cases dealing with the same incident that have an N preterite 1st c.s. form of this verb. In one place at least (EA 82:38), the scribe has added the accusative suffix *-ni* as if the form were G stem 3rd m.s. *imḫaṣni* (Albright and Moran 1948:248 n. 25). It would appear that the scribe got somewhat confused when he switched from the active to the passive, especially when the active clause contained a special idiom with a stative verb plus an adverbial accusative. The first passage (EA 81:24) is in such a broken context that little can be gained from citing it (cf. Youngblood 1961:220). The second context is as follows:

> *ù iq-bi a-na* LÚ *ù iz-zi-iz* / GÍR ZABAR UGU-*ia ù am-ma-ḫa-aṣ-ni* / 9-*ta-an* "So he spoke to a man and he rose up against me (with) a bronze dagger and I was smitten nine times" (EA 82:37-39; Moran 1987b:263, cf. 264 n. 5; 1992;152 n. 5).

paṭāru. Of the two occurrences of this verb where the N stem is involved, one is treated below in the next section because it seems to express a reflexive action (cf. *infra,* pp. 131-132). The true passive example, 3rd m.pl. *ip-pa-ṭá-ru* (EA 292:50), appears alongside 3rd f.s. *in*$_4$*-né-ep-ša-at* (EA 292:46), which is conjugated as a suffixed verb form.

The normal 3rd m.pl. forms of the prefix conjugation have *t- -u(-na).* It is likely that the form in question here is an Akkadianism; the preserved theme vowel suggests present-future *ippaṭṭarū.*

šaḫāṭu. Ebeling (1915:1508) was correct (*contra* Albright 1943b:31 n. 20 and Moran 1987b:479; 1992:305, 306 n. 4; also *CAD* Š/1:87b) that, in *ki-i a-na-ku i-ša-ḫa-ṭú* (EA 252:20), the verb is from *šaḫāṭu.* It is either *šaḫāṭu* A, "to atack" (*CAD* Š/1:88-92a) or *šaḫāṭu* B, "to strip off" (*CAD* Š/1:92b-95a). If from A, then the passage means "How I am being attacked!" (EA 252:20; cf. *CAD* Š/1:92b). But if it is from B, then one could translate "How I am being stripped!", which would suit the context since Labʾayu is complaining about the loss of two of his towns and of his patrimony and family cult statue (Rainey 1989-90:69a).

šakānu. That N stem forms of this verb may occur in the Amarna corpus without orthographic gemination of the first radical is demonstrated by an MB royal letter, *i*[*t-t*]*i-ka i ni-ša-ki-in* "that we may side [wit]h you" (EA 9:22; cf. *infra*, p. 128). Two examples are attested in a letter from Alashia; the first is paralleled by the stative, *la-a ša-ki-in* (EA 35:15).

> *a-ḫi ki-i* ⸢*ṣe*⸣-*ḫé-er* URUDU *i-na lìb-bi-ka la-a i-ša-ki-in* "My brother, that the copper is a small amount, let it not be put in your heart (i.e. "may it not be taken to heart")" (EA 35:12); *it-ti šàr Ḫa-at-ti*$_7$ *ù it-ti šàr Ša-an-ḫa-ar* / *it-ti-šu-nu la ta-ša-ki-in* "With the king of Hatti and with the king of Shanghar, with them you are not ranked" (EA 35:49-50; Moran 1987b:202, 203 n. 10; 1992:108, 109 n. 10; Vincentelli 1973:143-144).

Therefore, in the following passage from Byblos, an N stem form has been proposed (Rainey 1975b:422; 1989-90:61a; *contra* Moran 1987b:329; 1992:197). The passage pertains to another tablet (undoubtedly EA 120; Moran 1987b:330 n. 1; 1992:199 n. 1) listing the disputed items in a lawsuit:

> *a-nu-ma ṭup-pí ša-nu* / *ù ka-li ú-nu-tu-ia* / *ša it-ti* ^{I}*Ia-pa-*^{d}IŠKUR / *šu-ut yi-ša-kan* / *i-na pa-ni šàr-ri* "Now, as for my other tablet having all my implements that are with Yapa^{c}-Haddi, may it be placed before the king" (EA 119:55-59).

This removes an anomaly; all WS texts use the G preterite theme.

šemû. The N stem provides a similar solution to another anomalous form in the following:

> *u i*$_{15}$*-nu-ma iš-te-me a-wa-ti*$_7$^{MEŠ}*-ka* / *an-tu-ta*$_5$ *u a-ṣí* TI ^{d}UTU *ána* (AN) *ia-ši* / *u ki yi-ša-ma aḫ!-dì-am ri*[*-iš-ta*$_5$!] / *u il*$_5$*-la-ti-ya ia-ṣa-at ša-li-*⸢*mu*⸣(?) "And when I heard these words of yours and the coming forth of the life force of the sun god to me, I rejoiced joy[fully(?)] and my exultation sprang forth altogether" (EA 227:8-13; Rainey 1975b:421-422; Moran 1987b:456 n. 3; 1992:289 n. 3).

REFLEXIVE ACTIONS

Apart from the passives of transitive verbs discussed above in the previous section, there are a number of N stem verb forms that express some kind of reflexive nuance; that is, the subject of the verb is in some way being committed or has some kind of self-involvement in the action. In most cases, there is an Akkadian precedent, but not always.

abātu / *naʾbutu*. The G stem of this verb is only attested for OA (*CAD* A/1:45). Elsewhere, it is the N stem that carries the meaning "to run away, to flee." Thus, in the Amarna letters from Canaan, there are seven (possibly eight) instances of this verb. None of them have a consonantal prefix; only one seems to have the imperfect *-u* suffix. There is, therefore, the possibility that the WS scribes thought of these forms as calques on their own suffix conjugation.

The initial syllable sign alternates between IN and EN (= in_4), which is surely only an orthographic variation. However, the second syllable of the singular regularly has the NI sign. This could be taken as case of Assyrian vowel harmony, but in MA, that same vowel remains unassimilated to the following: 3rd m.s. preterite *in-na-bi-it* (Mayer 1971:67 for references). Therefore, it has been assumed here that some vowel coloring has occurred in the peripheral jargon; the second sign is transcribed *né*. Perhaps some analogy has developed from *innepuš* (see below). Goetze (1956:85 n. 1) had noted that the thematic vowel in *innabitu* etc. does not elide in OB. Such is generally the case in the Amarna examples except for two plurals. For one example of *-a-* theme, cf. EA 318:21 below.

One of the 3rd m.s. forms occurs in a text that may not reflect WS morphosyntax:

> *ù* [*i*]*-ma-*⌜*gar*⌝ *na-da-an* / LÚSA.GAZ.MEŠ *ù ìl-qé-šu-nu-mi a-na mu-ši* / *ù in-na-bi-*⌜*it*⌝*-mi a-na* LÚSA.GAZ.MEŠ "So [he] agreed to hand over the *ʿapîrû* men, but he took them by night and he fled to the *ʿapîrû* men" (EA 185:61-63).

The two other singulars are in the same context:

> *ki-i qa-bi-mì / i-na pa-ni-ka* ^IMu-ut-^dIŠKUR*-mì / in-né-bi-it* ^IA-ia-ab / \ *ḫi-iḫ-bé-e ki-i in₄-né-bi-tu / šàr* ^URU*Pí-ḫi-lì iš-tu / pa-ni* LÚ.MEŠ *ra-bi-ṣí* \ *sú-ki-ni / šàr-ri* EN-*šu li-ib-lu-uṭ / šàr-ru* EN-*ia li-ib-lu-uṭ / šàr-ru* EN-*ia šum-ma i₁₅-ba-ši /* ^IA*-ia-ab i-na* ^URU*Pí-ḫi-lì* "How is it said in your presence, 'Mut-Baᶜlu has deserted; he has hidden Ayyāb.'? How could the king of Peḥel desert from the commissioners (overseers) of the king, his lord? May the king, my lord, live! May the king, my lord live! If Ayyāb is in Peḥel!" (EA-256:4-13).

It is hard to believe that *kī innebitu* reflects the Akkadian subjunctive; the preceding *kī* does not govern a subjunctive. So the *-u* on *innebitu* is apparently the WS imperfect suffix. Since *naᵓbutu* is not transitive, the gloss sign in line 7 can hardly signify anything other than that a Canaanite word follows,viz. *ḫi-iḫ-bé-e* (**hiḥbêᵓ*) "he has hidden."

There is, however, one instance where the 3rd m.pl. seems not to elide the thematic vowel, but the crucial sign in question is broken:

> *ù uš-ši-‹ra›* LÚ.MEŠ *ma-ṣa-ar-ta / a-na* ^URU*Ṣu-mu-ra ù / a-na* ^URU*[I]r-qa-ta šum-ma / in₄-na-b[i-]tu ka-li /* LÚ.MEŠ *ma[-ṣa-]ar-ti iš-tu /* ^URU*Ṣu-mu[-ra]* "and sen‹d› garrison troops to Ṣumur and to ᶜIrqat in case all the garrison troops have fled from Ṣumur" (EA 103:34-39; cf. Moran 1950a:11; 1987b:298; 1992:176).

Two wedges are seen as the beginning of the third sign in *in₄-na-b*[*i-*]*tu*. In Schroeder's copy they do resemble the beginning of BI; however, there is still the possibility that they represent the beginning of AB. In the other two plural examples, the thematic vowel is definitely elided, e.g.

> *a-nu-ma* LÚ.MEŠ *ša na-ad-na-ti / a-na ia-si in₄-na-ab-tu gáb-bu* "Now the men that you assigned to me have all fled" (EA 82:32).

The last plural form also seems to have suffered a misspelling, the second sign being omitted; otherwise, we would have to posit an unlikely form such as **inʾabtū:*

> *pa-na-nu da-ga-li-ma* / ⸢LÚ⸣ ^{KUR}*Mi-iṣ-ri ù in*$_4$*-‹na›-ab-tu* / ⸢LUGAL⸣.MEŠ ^{KUR}*Ki-na-aḫ-ni iš-tu pa-n*[*i-šu*] "Formerly, seeing a man of Egypt, then the kings of Canaan fled bef[ore him]" (EA 109:44-46).

One possible *-a-* theme form is the following 1st c.s. present-future:

> *ù at-*⸢*ta*⸣ LUGAL GAL / *be-li-ia* / *tu-še-zi-ba-an-ni* / *ù i-na-ba-a-a*[*t*](?) / *a-na* LUGAL GAL *be-li-*[*ia*] "So may you, great king, my lord, deliver me that I may escape to the great king, my lord" (EA 318:18-22; Artzi 1968:170; in contrast to the interpretation by Moran 1987b:542 n. 4; 1992:350 n. 4).

epēšu / *nenpušu*. The most striking use of the N stem in the entire Amarna corpus is the idiomatic expression meaning "to join, become aligned with" (Moran 1987a; *CAD* E:235). The most attention has been directed to the hybrid suffix conjugation forms (Rainey 1973c:250-254; cf. *infra*, pp. 333-337), but there are several prefix conjugation forms. In the following transcriptions, note that the NI sign has been consistently transcribed *né* in the verb forms as befitting the normal Akkadian pattern; the sign NE (Labat No. 173) is never used in the EA texts with the value *ne* (it often does appear with the old value *bí*), so there is no sound reason not to transcribe NI by *né* when grammar is in favor of it. The TI signs serving to represent the prefix have not, however, been rendered *te*$_9$ because one cannot be sure whether the scribe intended to employ the correct vocalization or whether (more likely) he was simply using a pidgin prefix based on the theme of the 3rd m.s.

A volitive 3rd m.s. example happens to represent the same reflexive nuance as the others, but with a different twist, having a prepositional phrase with UGU as its complement; here the meaning is "to turn against." Since a ventive is not typical of this verb, it is possible to understand the form as a WS volitive in a result clause after another volitive:

> *ù la-a* / [*yi-i*]*š*-⸢*te*$_9$⸣-*ma šàr-ru* / [EN-*ia*] *ù yi-né-pu*-⸢*ša*⸣ / [^{I}*Šu-t*]*a* UGU-*ia* "But if the king, [my lord, does] not give heed, then [Shut]a will turn against me!" (EA 234:30-33; cf. Moran 1987b:460; 1992:293).

There are two partly broken 3rd m.s. forms with *i-* prefix in a text which avoids the *y-* ; the first is probably preterite, the second imperfect:

> *ù ki-i i-qa-bu* LUGAL *a-na mi-ni*$_7$ *iš-tap-r*[*u*] / ^{I}*Ri-ib*-^{d}IŠKUR *ṭup-pa a-na ma-ḫar be-li-š*[*u*] / UGU *lu-um-ni ša pa-na-nu-um i-né-p*[*u-uš*] / *ù a-nu-ma i-na-an-na la i-né-pu*-[*šu*] / *ki-šu-ma i-na-an-na a-na ia-a-ši* "But how can the king say, 'Why does Rib-Haddi keep sending a tablet to his lord concerning an evil which was do[ne] formerly?' But right now, is not the same thing being do[ne], even now, unto me?" (EA 106:30-34; cf. Moran 1987b:303 n. 7; 1992:180 n.8; Rainey 1989-90:60a).

The imperfect 3rd f.s. based on the N preterite theme, with elision of the thematic vowel, illustrates this special nuance of *nenpušu*:

> *ù šu*[*m-ma la-a yi-iš-mu!*] / [L]UGAL BE-*ia a-na a-wa-te* Ì[R-*šu*] / *ù in*$_4$*-né-ep-ša‹-at›* ^{URU}*Gub*[*-la*] / *a-na ša-šu ù gáb-bi* KUR.ḪÁ L[UGAL] / *a-di* ^{KUR}*Mi-iṣ-ri ti-né-ep-šu* / *a-na* LÚ.MEŠ SA.GAZ.MEŠ "But i[f] the [k]ing, my lord, does not heed the words of [his] ser[vant], then Byblos will go over to him (ᶜAbdi-Ashirta) and all the territories of the k[ing] as far as Egypt will go over to the *ᶜapîrû* men" (EA 88:29-34; Moran 1950a:62, 74; Greenberg 1955:37; Rainey 1973c:252).

Note that, after *šumma,* the imperfect is called for. Therefore, the verb, *tinnepšu,* cannot be 3rd m.pl. (*contra* Ebeling 1915:1404).

Another 3rd f.s. example, this time with preservation of the thematic vowel, has been interpreted by scholars in the past as the 3rd m.pl.:

> *ki-na-na ti-iq-bu-na* / LÚ.MEŠ*ḫa-za-nu-tu*$_4$ *ki-na-na* / *yi-pu-šu a-na ia-ši-nu* / *ù ti-né-pu-šu ka-li* KUR.MEŠ / *a-na* LÚ.MEŠ GAZ "Thus the city rulers are saying, 'Thus he will do to us and all the territories will go over to the *ᶜapîrû* men'" (EA 73:29-33; Moran 1950a:62; 1987a; 1987b:248, 249 n. 4; 1992:141, 142 n. 4; Rainey 1973c:251).

The N preterite 3rd f.s. appears in a Byblos text, once for certain and possibly a second time (but in the passive sense) providing that the emendation proposed by Mendenhall can be accepted:

> *ù an-nu-uš i-na-an-na* / *iš-tap-pa-ar* ᴵÌR-*A-ši-ir-ta a-na* ERÍN.MEŠ / AŠ É.NINIB *pu-ḫu-ru-nim-mi ù* / *ni-ma-qú-ut* UGU URU*Gub-la šum-ma ia-*[*nu*] / LÚ-*lì ša ú-še*$_{20}$*-ze-bu-*⸢*ši*$_x$⸣(⸢ŠE⸣) *iš-tu qa-ti-n*[*u*] / *ù nu-da-bir*$_5$ LÚ.MEŠ*ḫa-za-nu-ta iš-tu* / *lìb-bi* KUR.KUR.KI *ù ti-né-pu-uš ka-li* KUR.KUR.MEŠ.KI / *a-na* LÚ.MEŠ ⸢GAZ⸣ *ù* [*k*]*i-t*[*u*] *ti-in‹-né-pu-uš›-ma* / *a-na ka-li* KUR.KUR.KI *ù pa-aš-ḫu* DUMU.MEŠ / *ù* DUMU.MÍ.MEŠ *a-‹na› da-ri-ti* UD.KAM.MEŠ "And now ᶜAbdi-Ashirta has written to the troops, 'Assemble in Bīt-Ḥôrôn(?) and let us pounce upon Byblos; because there is no man who who can rescue it from our grasp, and we will exterminate the city rulers from within the territories and all of the territories will go over to the *ᶜapîrû* men and a ⸢treaty⸣ will be ‹made› for all the territories and the sons and daughters will be at peace forever more'" (EA 74:29-38; Mendenhall 1947a; Rainey 1989-90:58b *contra* Moran 1953:78 n. 4; 1987b:252 n. 7; 1992:144 n. 7).

In the same letter we also find a 3rd m.pl. form built on the Akkadian N stem preterite theme. The form in question has elision of the thematic vowel, but it has the *t-* prefix typical 3rd c.pl. in the WS texts:

> *ù iq-bi a-na* LÚ.MEŠ ^{URU}*Am-mi-ia du-ku-mi* / [E]N-*la-ku-nu ù i-ba-ša-tu-nu ki-ma ia-ti-nu* / *ù pa-aš-ḫa-tu-nu ù ti-né-ep-šu ki-ma* / [*a-w*]*a-te*^{MEŠ}*-šu ù i-ba-aš-šu ki-ma* / LÚ.MEŠ GAZ "And he spoke to the men of Ammiya, 'Slay your [l]ord so that you become like us and so that you will be at peace,' and they went over in accordance with his words and they became like the *ᶜapîrû* men" (EA 74:25-29; Moran 1950a:31; 1961:64-65; 1987b:250, 252 nn. 7, 8; 1992:143, 144 nn. 7, 8; also Greenberg 1955:34; Rainey 1973c:250).

The N stem imperfect 3rd m.pl., built on the preterite theme, without eliding the thematic vowel, occurs in a Rib-Haddi' letter from Beirut:

> *ù ti-iq-bu* URU.KI *al-lu-mi* ^{I}[*Ri-ib-ad-di*] / *a-ši-ib a-na* ^{URU}A.PÚ *a-ya-mi* LÚ-*lu* / *ša a-lik iš-tu* KUR.MEŠ *Mi-iṣ-ri a-na maḫ-‹ri›-šu* / *ù te-né-pu-šu-na a-na* ^{I}*A-zi-ri* "And the city is saying, 'Behold. [Rib-Haddi] is in Beirut; where is the man who came from Egypt to him?' So they are joining Aziru" (EA 138:90-93; cf. Moran 1987b:366:n. 19; 1992:224 n. 19).

The last form is a 3rd m.pl. jussive/volitive built on the N preterite theme. It concludes a chain of volitional clauses that begins with an imperative:

> *uš-ši-ra* ERÍN.MEŠ *pí-ṭá-ti* / *ra-ba ù tu-da-bi-ir* / *a-ia-bi* LUGAL *iš-tu* / *lìb-bi* KUR-*šu ù* / *ti-né-ep-šu ka-li* / KUR.KUR.MEŠ *a-na šàr-ri* "Send a great army and you will exterminate the enemies of the king from within his land and all the territories will go over to the king" (EA 76:38-42; Moran 1950a:62; especially Moran 1987a:210).

malāku. There is one occurrence of this verb where the N stem is possible. The form has been taken to be 3rd m.pl. G (*CAD* B:71b; M/1:155b) but it seems to make better sense as 1st c.s. Furthermore, the N stem of this verb, expressing "to take counsel, to consider," is more suitable to the context:

> *ù i-ma-la-ku ba-li-mì / ur-ru-ud* LUGAL EN-*ia* "But would I consider not serving the king, my lord?" (EA 191:9-10).

Moran (1987b:430; 1992:271) seems to have taken the form as 3rd m.pl. impersonal. Admittedly, the interpretation proposed here assumes a 1st c.s. N stem with WS imperfect suffix (Rainey 1989-90:66; Moran 1992:271). The text as a whole does not have any unequivocal traits of a Canaanized epistle. Nevertheless, the 1st c.s. prefix *i-* is a common feature of the interlanguage and it should not be surprising if it occurs in a letter such as this.

naʾarruru. This quadrilateral verb was evidently first discerned by Albright (1934:105; 1943a:12 n. 34). Outside of EA, the verb has subsequently been identified in OB and especially in Mari. The Mari and EA contexts are all military in nature (*CAD* N/1:7; *AHw*:694a). Unlike the OB/Mari forms, those from EA show gemination of the *-n-* due to assimilation of the ʾ. The initial vocalic prefix is written either *in-* or *en-*, so the prefix vowel cannot be strictly defined. They will all be represented here as if it were uniformly *i-*.

Of the six examples documented in the Amarna archive, all of them seem to derive from Canaan, though two of the epistles are from ᶜAbdi-Ashirta, whose dialect is not strictly that of the other WS texts (cf. Izreʾel 1985:380-381) and a third text is so broken as to preclude exact dialectical definition (EA 173). Two letters (EA 256 and EA 366) are WS in their general morphosyntax.

Five of the forms are either certainly or probably 1st c.s. The other is 3rd m.pl. The most broken text has a spelling error, *in-né-ri-ri* (EA 173:3); the context seems to suggest that the form is 1st c.s. (Moran 1987b:413; 1992:259) and the thematic vowel, *-i-* indicates that the theme is preterite. One of ᶜAbdi-Ashirta's letters is also badly broken: the form, *in₄-né-ri-ir* (EA 371:25), is presumably also 1st c.s. preterite (Moran 1987b:566; 1992:367). The two examples from the other ᶜAbdi-Ashirta letter both refer to the same event. The 1st c.s. independent pronoun assures that both of the verb forms are also 1st c.s.:

> [*ù in-n*]*é-ri-ir a-na-ku iš-tu* ^{URU}*Ir-*[*qat* ^{K}]^{I} "[so] I, myself, [went] to help from ᶜIr[qat]" (EA 62:13); *ù i-nu-ma in-né-ri-ir a-na-*[*k*]*u* / *iš-tu* ^{URU}*Ir-qat* ^{KI} *ù ak-*[*š*]*u-ud-m*[*i a*]*-na-ku* / *i-na* ^{URU}*Ṣu-mu-ri* ^{KI} *ù ia-nu* LÚ.MEŠ / *ša aš-bu i-na* É.GAL-*ši* "but when I rushed to help from ᶜIrqat and I ar[r]ived in Ṣumur, then there were no men located in its palace" (EA 62:21-24; Izreʾel 1985:7*).

One of the apparent 1st c.s. examples was formerly taken as 3rd m.s. (Albright 1943a:35). This context is not particularly easy to interprete. It is obscured by the use of Sumerian logograms in the preceding line. Nevertheless, it is possible to arrive at a satisfactory rendering:

> *a-di iš-tu* / GÁN.BA ^{I}DI.^{d}AMAR.UTU / ^{URU}*Aš-tar-ti in*$_4$*-né-ri-ir* / *i-nu-ma na-ak-ru gáb-bi* / URU.DIDLI.ḪÁ ^{KUR}*Ga-ri* "Still, from the market place(?) of Silim-Marduk(?) I rushed to the help of Ashtaroth because all the towns of Garu were hostile" (EA 256:19-23; cf. Moran 1987b:484 n. 4; 1992:309-310 n. 3).

The one certain 3rd m.pl. form is written without a consonantal *-y-* prefix and was evidently considered by the scribe to be an Akkadianism. Therefore, he seems to have deemed it necessary to clarify his meaning by adding a pure Canaanite gloss:

> *ù* ^{I}*Sú-ra-ta* LÚ ^{URU}*Akka* ^{KI} / *ù* ^{I}*In*$_4$*-da!-*⸢*ru*⸣*?-ta* LÚ ^{URU}*Ak-ša-pa* / *šu-ni-ma in*$_4$*-né-ri-ru* \ *na-az-a-qú* / *i-na* 50 ^{GIŠ}GIGIR.ḪÁ / *a-na mu-ḫi-ia* "But Surata, the ruler of Acco and Indaruta, the ruler of Achshaph, they (two) hastened to help me (were called out) with fifty chariots" (EA 366:22-26; Moran 1973:51; 1987b:562; 1992:364; Finklestein 1969:33).

The gloss, representing WS *nazᶜaqū* (Finklestein 1969:33), is itself WS N stem 3rd m.pl. of the suffix conjugation. It is likely, therefore, that the scribe of this letter was using *innerrirū,* without prefixed *-y-*, as if it were a suffix conjugation verb. Note that there is a similar use of *izzibūni,* an Akkadian present serving syntactically as a prefix conjugation verb, in the same text (EA 366:18).

nabalkutu. This quadriliteral verb appears but once in the WS texts. The form is WS jussive/volitive 3rd m.pl. and refers to a local population that might abandon their allegiance to pharaoh if their town is occupied by the Amurru forces (*CAD* N/1:17a):

> *ù* [*y*]*i*-[*din* LUGAL ERÍN].MEŠ *ù* / *ni-iṣ-bat* UR[U.K]I *l*[*a-a ti-ìl-qé-ši*] / ERÍN.MEŠ DUMU.MEŠ ᴵÌR-*Aš-ra-ti a-na* [*ša-šu-nu*] / *ù ti-bal-ki-*⸢*tu*⸣ LÚ.MEŠ-*ši* "So may [the king g]i[ve troop]s that we may take the ci[ty] l[est] the troops of the sons of ᶜAbdi-Ashirta [take it] for [themselves] and its people change allegiance" (EA 138:100-103; Moran 1987b:367 n. 23; 1992:224 n. 23).

This same idiom is attested in the MB royal correspondence:

> *a-na qa-an-ni* KUR / ⸢*ku*⸣-⸢*uš*⸣-*da-am-ma i ni-ba-al-ki-ta-am-ma* / [*it-t*]*i-ka i ni-ša-ki-in* "Come to the border of the land that we may change our allegiance and side [wit]h you" (EA 9:20-22; *CAD* N/1:17a; Moran 1987b:81-82 nn. 3-4; 1992:18-19 nn. 4-5; von Soden 1952b:431).

namāru. The letters from Beirut and Sidon happen to use the N stem from this verb in a particular idiom. One example is based on the present-future theme and the other employs the preterite theme (with elision of the thematic vowel). Both forms have to be 3rd m.pl. even though the subject is feminine dual (the eyes) and neither form has a consonantal prefix. Therefore, it is quite possible that these particular verb forms were considered to represent the suffix conjugation pattern. The two passages in question are:

> *ù en-du-um* / [*iš*]-*te-me a-wa-te*ᴹᴱŠ DUB LUGAL EN-*ia* / *ù yi-iḫ-di* ŠÀ-*ia ù* / [*i*]*n₄-nam-mu-ru* 2 IGI.MEŠ-*ia ma-gal* "And when [I] heard the words of the tablet of the king, my lord, then my heart rejoiced and my two eyes brightened" (EA 142:7-10); *ù*

> *i-nu-ma iš-te-mé a-wa-at* / LUGAL EN-*ia i-nu-ma iš-tap-pár a-na* ÌR-*šu* / *ù yi-iḫ-di lìb-bi-ia ù* / *yi-*[*š*]*a-qí* SAG-*ia ù* in_4*-nam-ru* / 2 IGI-*ia* \ *ḫi-na-ia i-na ša-me* /` *a-wa-at* LUGAL EN-*ia* "And when I heard the word of the king, my lord, that he wrote to his servant, then my heart rejoiced and my head was raised and my two eyes brightened upon hearing the word of the king, my lord" (EA 144:13-17)

It should be noted that the G stative of this verb is used in another poetic idiom attested in three of the epistles from southern Canaan (EA 266:12, 15; 292:10, 12; 296:14, 16).

našû. The same text mentioned with the N stem gloss, **nazᶜaqū* (cf. *supra*, p. 128), has another enigmatic gloss that might also be interpreted as an example of the N stem.

> *li-il-ma-ad šàr-ru* EN-*ia* / *i-nu-ma* LÚ SA.GAZ ⌜*ša*⌝ / *yi-na-aš-ši* \ *na-aš-ša-a* / *i-na* KUR.KI.ḪÁ *na-da-an* / DINGIR-lu_4 *ša šàr-ri* EN-*ia a-na ia-ši* / *ù i-du-uk-šu* "May the king, my lord, be apprised that, as for the *ᶜapîru* who rose up (has risen up) in the territories, the god of the king, my lord, has delivered to me and I have smitten him" (EA 366:11-16; Naʾaman 1975:120; Rainey 1978b:32-33; Moran 1987b:561-562 and n. 1; 1992:366 and n. 1).

It is possible, of course, that the gemination of the *š* in both or either of these forms is purely graphic. However, there is a good possibility that the scribe intended as the gloss, **naśśaʾa* ‹ **nanśaʾa*, 3rd m.s. N stem suffix conjugation. If that be the case, then perhaps the verb form being glossed might also be intended for N stem, **yinnašši* 3rd m.s. based on the Akkadian N present-future theme with WS *y*- and -*Ø* for the past tense. Such a meaning as required by this context is compatible with the N stem of **nśʾ* in Hebrew. That verb, in both Akkadian and WS, is transitive in the G stem. Although *CAD* (N/2:103a) places this passage under the intransitive G, they also record an instance of the meaning "to rise up against" for the N stem (*CAD* N/2:112a).

The closest attested Hebrew parallel is with the tD stem:

> *waʾ ᵃḏôniyyāʰ ḇen-Ḥaggîṯ miṯnaśśēʾ lē(ʾ)mōr ʾ ᵃnî ʾemlōḵ wayyaᶜaś lô reḵeḇ upārāšîm waḥᵃmiššîm ʾîš râṣîm lᵉpānā(y)w* "And Adonijah the son of Haggith has exalted himself, saying 'I will reign,' and he made for himself a chariot and fifty riders to go before him" (1 Ki. 1:5).

One is also reminded of the Akkadian verb *tebû* and its semantic nuances, "to rise up," and "to rebel" (*AHw:*1342-1343), especially the participle, *tēbû*, which can designate an "insurgent" (*AHw:*343b).

paṭāru. Two prefix forms of this verb have an *-i/e-* theme vowel which suggests that they are N stem. Although the G stem is the standard in these texts for expressing the idea of "departing," there are also good Akkadian examples of the N stem carrying this same meaning (*AHw:*851a-b).

The first relevant Amarna context is this negative admonition:

> *ù a-[nu-m]a i-na-an-na ša-ap-ru-mi* / LÚ.ME[Š] ⌜*ša*⌝ URU*Gub*[*ub*]*-la a-na ia-ši* / *la-a-mi ti-*⌜*pa*⌝*-*⌜*ṭe*₆⌝*-*⌜*er*⌝ *iš-tu* URUA.PÚ.KI.MEŠ "And n[ow] then men of Byblos have written to me, 'Don't leave Beirut!'" (EA 138:9-11; Moran 1987b:362; 1992:221; cf. Rainey 1975b:419).

The example in the second passage is a WS 3rd m.pl. imperfect in the apodosis of a conditional sentence introduced by *inūma* (Rainey 1992a:181):

> *i-nu-m*[*a*] / *i-ka-ša-da-am* KUR.KUR.MEŠ.KI / *ù ti*₇*-pa-ṭe*₄*-ru-*⌜*na*⌝ LÚ.MEŠ-*tu* / *a-na la-qé* KUR.KUR.MEŠ-*i-mi* / *a-na ša-a-šu-nu ù ia-nu-*AM / LÚ.MEŠ-*li a-na na-ṣa-ar* URU.KI*Gub-li* / URU.KI LUGAL EN-*ia* "If I conquer the territories, then the men will desert to take territories for themselves, and there will be no men to guard Byblos, the city of the king, my lord"

(EA 362:33-37; Rainey 1978b:20-21; Moran 1987b:558 n. 4; 1992:361 n. 4; 1960:pp. 4, 15).

šaqû. It happens that a form from this verb cited above in connection with *namāru* (cf. *supra*, pp. 129-130) is also recognized by *AHw:*1181a as a unique instance of the N stem. The idiom is reminiscent of the similar use of *našû* discussed above. The clause in question, *yi*-[*š*]*a-qí* SAG-*ia* "My head was raised up/elevated" (EA 144:16), deals with a series of past actions. Therefore, this form cannot be Akkadian G present-future.

CHAPTER VII

PREFIX CONJUGATION — D, Dt, Dp

The factitive, or causative stems characterized by gemination of the second radical comprise one of the most intriguing aspects of the verbal system in the Amarna letters from Canaan. This chapter will deal with the D stem and its derivatives, the Akkadian Dt and the WS Dp.

MORPHOLOGICAL PROBLEMS

The basic Akkadian patterns of the D stem were reasonably well understood by the Canaanite scribes. There were, nevertheless, a number of factors that led to complications in the morphology. Most of those features can be accounted for as pidgin developments. Only a limited degree of true WS influence can be detected.

CONTAMINATION OF G AND D STEM FORMS.

G PRESENT-FUTURES AS D STEM. Among the complicating phenomena in the analysis of the D stem is the fact that these scribes often seem to have looked upon the Akkadian present future forms as D (noted already by Ebeling 1910:52). It is not always possible, however, to be sure that a particular scribe chose an Akkadian G stem theme with gemination in order to express a D stem nuance. Individual cases will be dealt with in the ensuing discussion.

Ebeling (*loc. cit.*) pointed to the causative precative *li-ba-lu-uṭ-ni* "May he give me life" (EA 198:20) as evidence for confusion between G and D stems. The precative should take the same thematic vowel as the D preterite but here it has the G present-future as its theme. Another case in point would be *lu-ḫa-mu-uṭ* "May (the king) hasten (troops)" (EA 88:40, also to be completed in line 24; Rainey 1975b:415 n. 173). If they had been proper D stem forms, then both these precatives should have had the *-i-* theme vowel, of course.

Precative forms from outside the Canaanite dialectical sphere suggest that Western Peripheral may have recognized a D stem for *naṣāru* "to guard, keep." One of them is from an Amurru letter:

> ᴵ*A-zi-ri* ᴸᵁ́ÌR-*ka* / *i-na aš-ra-nu la tu-wa-aḫ-ḫe-er-šu* / *ar-ḫi-iš uš-še-ra-šu* / *ù* KUR.MEŠ *ša* LUGAL EN-*ni li-na-aṣ-ṣár* "Aziru is your servant. Do not delay him there. Send him quickly and let him protect the lands of the king, our lord" (EA 169:12-15; Izreʾel 1985:248).

The other is from Alalakh:

> DINGIR.MEŠ *ša* AN *u* KI / *li-bal-li-ṭú-ú-šu li-na-ṣa-ru-šu* "May the gods of heaven and the nether world keep him alive and protect him" (*Idrimi Stele,* lines 99-100; cf. *CAD* B:59a; *contra* Giacumakis 1970:91).

These examples provide the background for a phenomenon observed by Albright and Moran (1950:165-166). They noted the forms of *naṣāru* in EA 112, namely 3rd m.s. *yi-na-ṣa-ru-ni* (EA 112:17) versus *yi-na-ṣí-ru* (EA 112:14), *yi-na-ṣí-ru-ni* (EA 112:18), *yi-na-ṣí-ra-ni* (EA 112:13) and *yi-na-ṣí-ra-an-ni* (EA 112:20) and explained them as follows: "the Can. scribes treated the unfamiliar Acc. *iqattal* as a Can. *piʿel*" (*loc. cit.*). To those forms may be added the 1st c.s. *i-na-ṣí-ru* (EA 119:15; 130:49), *i-na-ṣí-ru-na* (EA 123:32), *i-na-ṣí-ra* (EA 123:27) and the 3rd m.pl. *ti-na-ṣí-ru* (EA 130:48). The unusual *-i-* theme in these examples is difficult to explain except as a contamination from the D stem.

Albright and Moran were themselves commenting (*loc. cit.*) on the 3rd m.s. *yi-ša-i-lu* (EA 89:15, 34, 45). If it were not for the 1st c.s. forms from *naṣāru* cited above, one would be tempted to transcribe *yu-ša-i-lu* and *yu-na-ṣí-ru,* etc.

PREFIX VOWEL *i*- ON D STEM FORMS. Another phenomenon related to the confusion between G present-futures and D stems verbs is the analogic carry-over of the prefix vowel *i*- to real D stem verbs: 3rd m.s. *i-ba-li-iṭ* (EA 147:9; Tyre), *i-bá-al-*⌜*li*⌝*-iṭ* (EA 152:53; Tyre); *i-ḫa-li-iq* (EA 287:37; Jerusalem), *i-ka-al* (EA 138:130), *yi-ša-i-lu* (EA 89:35, 45), *yi-* / [*i*]*š-ši-ra* (EA 139:30-31; cf. Knudtzon 1915:589 n. g), *yi-iš-ši-ru* (EA 139:34, 36, 38), 2nd m.s. *ti-pa-ṭe₆-er* (EA 138:11; or N stem? Cf. *supra*, p. 131), *ti-ša-i-lu* (EA 89:40); 1st c.s. *i-ba-lu* (EA 326:19), *i-ba-ú* (EA 362:58), *i-r*[*i*]*-du* (EA 186:7), *i-ru-du* (EA 250:51, 59), *i-ru-dam* (EA 300:20), *i-wa-ši-ir* (EA 137:8), 3rd m.pl. *ti₇-ba-ú-na* (EA 362:24), *ti-ba-ú-na* (EA 129:29; 362:45), *ti-ba-ú-na-ši* (EA 129:19), *ti-dáb-bi-ru* (EA 138:69), *ti-pa-li-ḫu-na* (EA 105:22), 1st c.pl. *ni-du-bu-ur* (EA 279:20), *ni-wa-aš-ši-ru-šu* (EA 197:18).

It was thought by Ebeling (1910:61-62) and Dhorme (1914:39-41 = 1951:434-436) that these vocalic variations between preformative *u* and *i* vowels reflected the existence of a Canaanite vowel like the vocal shewa in Hebrew. A much better explanation is that given above, namely that the *i* vowel of the Akkadian G stem 3rd m.s., whether *iparras* or *iprus* (also 1st c.pl. *niparras* and *niprus*), has been carried over analogically to some D stem verbs of various persons just as it has been carried over from the G 3rd m.s. to the 1st c.s., 2nd m.s. and 3rd m.pl. suffixes. In other words, this is more likely to have developed as an interlanguage phenomenon rather than as some kind of West Semitic trait.

Of particular interest are the forms of *turru* with *i*- as the preformative vowel. The contexts all require a transitive meaning and the forms are found, not in Canaanized texts, but in letters from Tyre or other non-WS sources: 1st c.s. present-future, *i-ta-ar-ra-aš-šu* (EA 59:20), 3rd m.s. past with *-t-* infix, *it-te-er* (EA 29:126; 148:38; 149:13, 31; Albright 1937:202 n. 3), same plus 1st c.pl. accusative suffix, *i-te-er-ni* (EA 149:12), 3rd m.pl. preterite, *i-it-te-ru-šu* (RS 4.449:12; Virolleaud 1936:23). Note also *i-na-ka-ru* for *ú-na-ka-ru* at Emar (Ikeda 1995:79). One can hardly explain the use of the *i*- prefix in these widely scattered texts as WS vocalization; they are simply confusion with G *iparras* forms.

A word is in order here about the synchronic evidence from Ugarit. A D stem 1st c.s. form such as *amid* (*KTU* 1.14:II,5), which must represent *ʾamaʾʾid-, indicates that the prefix vowel for first person, at least, was *a*. On the other hand, a PN based on the D participle is documented at Ugarit in the syllabic orthography: *mu-na-ḫi-mu* (for references, cf. Sivan 1984:253). The D participle must have been **munaḫḫimu,* with the normal *u* vowel. The question remains open concerning the Ugaritic prefix vowel for second and third persons and for the first plural. Did they have *a* like the 1st c.s. or did they have *u* like the participle? The most unlikely possibility in Ugaritic would be an *i* as the prefix vowel of the D (and Š) stems.

AMBIGUOUS ORTHOGRAPHY.

GEMINATED RADICALS. It must always be borne in mind that the ancient scribes who wrote Akkadian did not feel compelled to express gemination in the orthography. This fact had fooled scholars for many years with regard to the Akkadian G stem present-future; older textbooks represented gemination of the second radical of such forms as optional. The D stem forms should have given them a clue. In any case, the Canaanite scribes may express the gemination by use of syllabic signs but they often do not. Reconstruction of the forms (normalization) must always reckon with gemination of the second radical (of the last radical on Babylonian hollow roots, cf. *turru, infra,* pp. 154-157) as a morphological feature of D stem verb forms.

PREFIX VOWELS. When the prefix is *Øv-* or *tv-*, the cuneiform signs are pretty unambiguous. The 1st c.s. has the *ú* sign unless the form is one of those with *i-* discussed above. The *tv-* suffixes are almost always written with the *tu* sign; *tù* in this function is confined to the non-WS Aziru letters or the Mitanni correspondence (*tù-bal-la-ṭá-an-ni* (EA 169:7, *tù-ma-ra-aṣ*, EA 170:80; with Š stem EA 19:36, 38; 27:2, 4, 33). An exception is a text from Sidon which employs *tú-te-ra-am* (EA 145:26) and *tú-ti-ra-an-ni* (EA 145:10). The most glaring exceptions, however, are those with *ti-* or *ti*$_7$ mentioned in the preceding section above. There the TE has been rendered *ti*$_7$ because of the 1st c.s. forms with I signs, never with E (= i_{15}). The 1st c.pl. forms have the NU sign.

The 3rd m.s. forms present a different problem. Only in cases such as *yu-uš-ši-ra* (EA 271:18 *et al*) does the orthography confirm that the PI sign is to be read *yu*. Most D stem forms, however, do not have an initial closed syllable; therefore, the orthography cannot distinguish the vowel. Note, e.g. PI-*ba-li-iṭ* (EA 74:55; 85:18) where one can hardly deny that the proper reading is *yu-ba-li-iṭ* on the analogy of *nu-ba-li-iṭ* (EA 85:38), *nu-bal-li-iṭ* (EA 68:28) and *tu-ba-li-ṭú-na* (EA 114:56): the aberrant *i-ba-li-iṭ* (EA 147:9) and *i-bá-al-li-iṭ* (EA 152:53) are from Tyre. The overwhelming majority of D stem prefix forms with consonantal prefixes have a *u* vowel; this is exactly what would be expected on comparative grounds (Akkadian, Arabic). Therefore, it is with reasonable assurance that D forms are transcribed *yu-ra-du* (EA 193:17), *yu-wa-ši-ru* (EA 112:37), etc.

THEMATIC VOWEL. The preferred thematic vowels will be discussed under the individual verbs. One particular detail should be pointed out here, viz. the cases where the final radical is *r*. These often reveal a shift of *i* › *e* (*GAG*:12, §9h) when the *r* closes the syllable. The evidence in the Amarna texts is equivocal. Forms with a closed final syllable are relatively rare in the prefix conjugation. One finds a few instances like 1st c.s. preterite *ú-wa-ši-ir* (EA 333:24) which may be compared with 1st c.s. preterite with infixed *-t-* (or lexical Dt?) *ut-te-er* (EA 189:r. 15; note the 3rd m.s. S stem *yu-šu-te-er* EA 292:37). Among the imperatives with -Ø suffix, there is *uš-še-er* (EA 35:17, 41; 162:53; Alashia and Egypt only) but more often *uš-ši-ir* (EA 34:35; 82:28; 120:36; 121:42; Alashia but also Byblos). The forms with vocalic suffixes show the variants such as *yu-wa-še-ru* (EA 255:17) and *yu-wa-ši-ru* (EA 112:37). The variation between the *i* and the *e* is probably nothing but a "remembrance" of the Babylonian rule (*uwaššer* rather than *uwaššir*). What this seems to mean is that a few scribes had faithfully learned the correct Akkadian form, *uwaššer*, and had used it as their theme for verbal forms with Canaanite prefixes and suffixes. Other scribes, evidently working on the analogy with most D stem forms, which have an *i* theme, simply used syllabic signs having an *i* vowel, regardless of the final *r*.

A few cases such as *yu-šar-mi* (EA 131:32) where it might be a more accurate representation of the scribe's intention to read with *šir*$_9$ instead of *šar* because of the tense factor will be discussed in their proper place (e.g. the 3rd m.s. precative *li-wa-aš-šir*$_9$ EA 149:17, 76, from Tyre).

D STEM VERBS

The following discussion will cover the D stem verbs used by the Canaanite scribes according to three semantic categories: factitive, causative and intensive. Note will be taken of the themes chosen by the scribes upon which they imposed their West Semitic modal and tense morphemes. Of particular interest is their choice of thematic vowel. It will be seen that the *i* theme predominates for all tenses although some *a* theme forms do occur. All comparative evidence points to an *i* theme for the WS dialects. The correspondence between the Akkadian D preterite (and precative) theme and the basic D theme in WS did not escape the notice of the Canaanite authors.

The verbs will be cited according to the D infinitival form unless the D stem usage is rare; in such cases, the G stem infinitive will precede that of the D stem

FACTITIVE VERBS.

bulluṭu. With the exception of two prefix forms (3rd m.s. EA 105:83; 1st c.s. EA 123:26), and five precatives (3rd m.s. in oaths: EA 85:39, 86; 256:10, 11; 289:37), the overwhelming majority of G stem forms from this verb are in the stative (Ebeling 1915:1388). The G stem means "to be alive, to live, to have life, to have sustenance." The D stem forms express a factitive nuance, "to give life, to give sustenance." The most frequent D stem idiom in the Amarna texts is that of furnishing sustenance to someone in the form of food supplies (which are called *balāṭu*, *CAD* B:52a, a substantival use of the G infinitive):

> *li-ìš-mé šàr-ru a-wa-te* ÌR-*šu* / *ù ia-di-na ba-la-ṭá* ÌR-*šu* / *ù yu-ba-li-iṭ* ÌR-*šu* "May the king heed the words of his servant and may he grant the sustenance for his servant and may he supply his servant" (EA 74:53-55); *yi-ìš-mé šàr-ru* EN-*li a-wa-te* / ÌR *ki-ti-šu ù yu-wa-ši-ra* / ŠE.*IM*.ḪÁ *i-na lìb-bi* GIŠMÁ *ù yu-ba-li-iṭ* / ÌR-*šu* "May the king, my lord, heed the words of his faithful servant and may he send grain in a ship that he may sustain his servant" (EA 85:16-19).

Note the jussives with *i* theme vowel. The two documented forms with *a* theme happen to be written ideographically with the appropriate phonetic complements: 3rd m.s. *yu*-TIL.LA-*aṭ-šu-nu* (EA 94:66), TE.LA-*aṭ-šu-nu-ma* (EA 94:69; cf. *supra*, pp. 117-118).

In some contexts, namely those with 1st c.pl., the best rendering would be "to obtain supplies," although one might think of "to furnish supplies":

> *i-na* LÚMAŠÍM *šàr-ri* / *ša i-šu-ú i-na* URU*Ṣu-mu-ur* / *ba-la-ṭá-at* URU*Gub-la* / *a-nu-um-ma* I*Pa-ḫa-am*[-*n*]*a-ta* / LÚMAŠÍM LUGAL *ša i*[-*n*]*a* URU*Ṣu-mu-ur*KI *i-*[*d*]*e-mì* / *pu-uš-qa-am* \ *ma-gal*! / *ša* UGU URU*Gub-la* / *iš-tu* KUR*Ia-ri-im-mu-ta* / *nu-ba-li-iṭ* "By the commissioner whom he has in Ṣumur, Byblos is supplied. Now Paḫam[n]ata, the king's commissioner in Ṣumur, knows the great pressure on Byblos; from the land of Yarimmuta we get supplies" (EA 68:19-28; Moran 1950a:146; cf. 1987b:243 n. 3; 1992:138 n. 3); *li-*[*i*]*d-mì-iq i-na pa-ni* / *šàr-ri* EN-*ia ù yu-da-na*$_7$ / ŠE.*IM*.ḪÁ *mu-ú-ṣa* KUR*Ia-ri-mu-ta* / *ša-a yu-da-*⌈*nu*⌉ *pa-na-nu i-na* URU*Ṣu-mu-ra* / [*y*]*u-da-na*$_7$ [*i*]*-na-na i-na* URU*Gub-la* / [*ù*] *nu-ba-li-iṭ a-di ti-š*[*a*!*-i*!*-l*]*u*! / [*a-n*]*a* URU-*li-ka* "May it please the king, my lord, that grain be given, the produce of Yarimuta; that which was being supplied formerly in Ṣumur, may it be supplied [n]ow in Byblos [that] we may get supplies until you i[nvestiga]te(!) [concerni]ng your city" (EA 85:33-39; Moran 1950a:158; 1987b:271 n. 4; 1992:157 n. 6; *CAD* B:61; M/2:249b).

One scribe seems to have been confused by this idiom and almost produced a hybrid G/D form:

> *[š]a-ni-tam qí-ba-mi a-na* [LUGAL] / *ù yu-da-na a-n[a* ^{URU}*Gub-la]* / *mu-ú-ṣa ša* ^{KUR}*Ia-r[i!-mu-ta]* / *ki-ma na-da-ni-šu [pa-na-nu]* / *a-na* ^{URU}*Ṣu-mu-ra [ù]* / *ni-ub-lu-uṭ a-di y[i-ša-i-lu]* / *šàr-ru a-na* URU-*šu* "[Fu]rthermore, speak to [the king] that the produce of Yar[imuta] be given t[o Byblos] as it was given [formerly] to Ṣumur [that] we may be sustained until the king in[quires] concerning his city" (EA 86:31-37; Youngblood 1961:284, 291).

Note the same usage with the 3rd m.pl.:

> *mi-lik a-na* ÌR *ki-ti-k[a] p[a-n]a-nu* / *iš-tu* ^{KUR}*Ia-ri-mu-ta* / *tu-ba-li-ṭú-na* LÚ.MEŠ / *ḫu-up-ši-ia* "Take thought for yo[ur] faithful servant; f[orm]erly, from the land of Yarimuta my yeoman farmers got supplies" (EA 114:54-57; following Moran 1950a:44; 1987b:316-317; 1992:188-189).

Actually, the verb form, *tuballiṭūna,* could have an indefinite subject, "they," with the yeoman farmers as the object, i.e. "they were supplying my yeoman farmers".

The two Tyrian 3rd m.s. forms with *i* prefix (cf. *supra,* p. 137) seem to express a more abstract concept based on Egyptian royal ideology, viz. that of "infusing life." It is particularly clear in one of the poetic passages where pharaoh is described as:

> *ša i-ba-li-iṭ i-na še-ḫi-šu* DÙG.GA "who gives life by his sweet breath" (EA 147:9; Albright 1937:198 nn. 6, 12).

The second example, *i-bá-al[-l]i-iṭ* (EA 152:53), is in an obscure but apparently similar, context. One might debate whether this idiom should be viewed as factitive, or whether it actually should be classified in the category of causatives.

buʾʾû. The idea of "making a search" is the basic meaning of this verb, the meanings "to wish, to ask (also demand), to intend" being especially typical of peripheral Akkadian (*CAD* B:363-364). With only two exceptions (*ú-ba-ú* EA 88:22; *ú-ba-a-šu-nu* EA 96:21), the 3rd m.s. forms have consonantal *y-*

prefixes. The 3rd m.pl. forms usually have *tu-* as the prefix but one scribe, the author of EA 129 and EA 362, uses *ti-* or *ti*$_7$. One Jerusalem example follows the purely Akkadian pattern typical of that scribe, viz. *ú-ba-á*ʾ*-ú* (EA 287:35). The Jerusalem spelling is matched by three other texts in the use of a syllabic sign to represent the geminated second radical, namely 3rd m.s. *yu-ba-á*ʾ*-ú* (EA 244:43; 250:56) and 3rd m.pl. *tu-*⸢*bi*⸣*-*⸢ʾ*u*$_5$⸣*-na* (EA 250:10), which latter is unique in reflecting an *i/e* vowel in the second syllable. It is like an MB form (cf. 2nd m.s. *tu-bi-*ʾ*i-i-ma* EA 4:15, 1st c.s. *ú-bi-*ʾ*u-ú* BE 17 23:30). Elsewhere, the geminated second consonant is expressed graphically only as a syllable boundary between vowels. All of the Canaanized forms are in the imperfect tense.

The particular nuance or aspect of "seeking" is fairly broad. The thing being sought may be represented by an accusative pronominal suffix. The most basic semantic nuance (in more classical Akkadian also) is the simple process of looking for something:

> *a-šar i-ba-ša-at / ši-pí-ir-ti* LUGAL EN*-ia / ša-ri* TIL.LA*-ia ù ú-ba-[ú-n]a-ši / ù uš-ši-ru-na-ši / a-na* LUGAL EN*-ia ša-ri* TIL.LA*-ia* "Wherever the request of the king, my lord, the breath of my life, is located, then I wi[ll se]ek it and I will send it to the king, my lord, the breath of my life" (EA 143:13-17; cf, also EA 96:19-22).

One may also be seeking someone for the purpose of doing harm to him:

> DUMU.M[EŠ] / ${}^{\text{LÚ}}$*ša-ri šàr-ri / tu-ba-ú-na-nu* "The son[s] of the king's rebel are after us" (EA 100:15-17); *ù / a-na-ku* URU.MEŠ*-ia a-na* ${}^{\text{I}}$*A-zi-ri / ù ia-ti yu-ba-ú* "But as for me, Aziru has my towns and he is after me" (EA 125:36-38).

The object of the search may be expressed by a prepositional phrase as complement to the verb. Various semantic nuances are possible:

šu-nu ki-ma / UR.GI$_7$ *ù ia-nu* / *ša-a yu-ba-ú ar-ki-šu-nu* "They are like dog(s) but there is no one to investigate them" (EA 130:33-35; contrast Moran 1987b:348; 1992:212); *ù yi-de-mi šàr-ri* EN-*ia i-nu-ma* / *ma-ni* UD.KA[M.ME]Š *tu-*⌈*bé*⌉-⌈*ʾu$_5$*⌉*-na* UGU-*ia* / 2 DUMU *La-ab-a-ya* "May the king, my lord, be apprised that for many days the two sons of Labʾayu have been after me (pressuring me)" (EA 250:9-11).

Another nuance is that of making a demand for something:

yi-de LUGAL *be-li* / *ip-ši ša yi-pu-šu-ni* / [I]*Ia-an-ḫa-mu*/ *iš-tu a-ṣé-ia* / [*i*]*š-tu mu-ḫi* LUGAL EN-*ia* / [*i*]*-nu-ma yu-ba-*[*ú*] / *2 li-im* KÙ.BABBAR / *iš-tu qa-ti-ia* "May the king be apprised of the things which Yanḫamu is doing to me since my leaving the presence of the king, my lord, viz. that he is demanding two thousand (shekels of) silver from me" (EA 270:9-16).

On the other hand, one may be seeking in one's heart, i.e. desiring, something:

ša-ni-tam ú-ul ti-i-de / *at-ta* KUR *A-mur-ri ur-ra* / *mu-ša tu-ba-ú-na* / ERÍN.MEŠ *pí-ṭá-ti* "Furthermore, don't you know the land of Amurru? Day and night, they are longing for the regular army' (EA 82:47-49);

or some activity (i.e. to do some deed), which itself can be either of a positive or a negative nature, of which the following examples provide an interesting contrast:

[URU]*Ir-qa-ta tu-b*[*a-ú*] / *ki-ta a-na šàr-r*[*i*] "ᶜIrqata des[ires] loyalty to the king" (EA 100:18-19); *ù ú-ba-áʾ-ú ar-na kab-ta* GAL "And they sought (to commit) a very serious crime" (EA 287:35; Akkadian preterite from Jerusalem); *ù ar-na a*[*r-na-ma*] / [*t*]*u-ba-ú-na* "And they are seeking (to commit) crime upon cr[ime]" (EA 109:24-25; for the translation, cf. Moran 1987n:308; 1992:182).

Both positive and negative are contrasted in the following highly rhetorical passage:

> [*šum-m*]*a* LÚ *ša-a yu-ba-ú* / [*l*]*um-na a-n*[*a*] ⌈EN⌉[*-š*]*u šum-ma du-na du-na-ma* / ⌈*ú*⌉*-ba-ú a-na-ku* [*a-n*]*a* EN-*ia* "[Wheth]er (I am)a man who seeks evil for [hi]s lord, or whether it is strength upon strength that I seek [fo]r my lord" (EA 109:53-55).

This idiom is not confined to the Canaanized texts from Canaan. It is well known in official legal documents of the Hittite empire (*CAD* B:364):

> *ma-an-nu-me-e a-ma-ta* / *mi-im-ma ṣa-bur-ta ù le-mut-ta a-na muḫ-*[*ḫi* [I]*Pí-i*]*a-ši-il-lì la-a* ⌈*ú*⌉*-bá-ʾa-a* "Nobody will seek any malicious or evil thing agai[nst Piy]ashilli" (*KBo* 1 1:30-31); *šum-ma a-na* [I]ZAG.ŠEŠ-*na lu-ú a-na* DUMU-*šu* DUMU.DUMU-*šu ma-am-ma ma-ši-ik-ta ú-ba-ʾa-a a-na* LUGAL KUR URU *Ḫa-at-ti* / \ *ù a-na* DUMU.MEŠ KUR URU *Ḫa-at-ti* [LÚ]KÚR-*šu-nu šu-ú-ut* "If anyone plots evil against Pendeshena or against his son or his grandson, he is the enemy of the king of Khatti and of the people of Khatti" (*KBo* 1 8:32-33); *ša m*[*a-ši-i*]*k-ta ú-ba-ʾa-a* "who seeks evil" (NBC 3934: r. 5'; Goetze 1947:243; Cochavi-Rainey 1988:*48; from Egypt); *a-na muḫ-ḫi* [I]*A-mis-tam-ri* / *ma-ru-uṣ* SAG.DU-*šu ub-ta-ʾi-i* "she sought personal harm to ᶜAmistamru" (RS 17.159:6-7; Nougayrol 1956:126).

An important syntagma with *buʾʾû* is its government of an infinitive as direct object (cf. *infra*, pp. 391-393). Such constructions are apparently unique to the Amarna texts from Canaan although the government of a verb by means of a prepositional phrase as adverbial complement is known elsewhere in Akkadian dialects, especially from peripheral areas.

When the infinitive is serving as the direct object, it usually follows its governing verb directly and this most probably reflects WS syntax. There is, however, one instance in which it is fronted and is given special emphasis by the addition of enclitic *-ma:*

> *ù* LÚ.MEŠ / *ḫu-‹up›-ši-ia* / *pa-ṭá-ra-ma tu-ba-ú-na* "And as for my ye[om]en farmers, it is to desert that they desire" (EA 114:21-22).

Like the passage cited above, the following infinitives also have as their subject the subject of the governing verb, viz. "to go," and "to do":

> *ù yu-ba-ù* / *a-la-k*[a_{13}] *a-di* URU*Gub-la* "And he seeks to com[e] as far as Byblos" (EA 85:52-53).

> *ù ka-li* / LÚ.MEŠ *ḫa-za-nu-te tu-ba-ú-na* / *i-pé-eš an-nu-tu*$_4$ (sic!) *a-na* IÌR-*A-ši-ir-ta* "And all the city rulers desire to do this to ᶜAbdi-Ashirta" (EA 73:23-25; cf. also EA 79:23-25; 129:29).

Numerous texts employ a hybrid or WS infinitive form (probably modeled on the WS pattern) from *leqû*, which in turn takes an objective genitive:

> 2 URU.KI.MEŠ *ša ir-ti-ḫu a-na* [*ia-ši*] / *ù tu-ba-ú-na la-qa-šu*[*-nu*] / *íš-tu qa-at šàr-ri* "As for the two towns that remain to me, now they are seeking to take th[em]" (EA 79:27-29; 129:18-19; cf. also EA 76:10, 12-13, 15-16; 78:12; 81:10; 91:13, 22-23).

The object of the infinitive may also take the accusative case, in which instance it may be fronted, even preceding the main verb for emphasis:

> *a-nu-ma la-qú* URU*Ul-la-sà ù* / URU*Ṣu-mu-ra tu-ba-ù-na la-qa* "Now they have taken Ullasa and it is Ṣumur they're trying to take!" (EA 105:23-24)

In parallel semantic contexts, the verb *ṣabātu* may also fulfill this function:

> *ù a-nu-ma* / *ti*$_7$*-ba-ú-na ṣa-bat* URU.MEŠ *Gub-li* "And now they are seeking to seize the towns of Byblos" (EA 362:23-24).

The following context was probably meant to contain the same construction:

> *šum-ma-mí* / *i-ia-nu pa-ni-ma* / *ša-nu-ta*$_5$ *i-na* [I]*La-ab-a-ya* / *ṣa!*(A)-*ba-at* [URU]*Ma-gid*$_6$-*da*[[KI]] / *yu-ba-á*ʾ-*ú* "since Labʾayu has no other intention; it is the seizure of Megiddo that he's seeking" (EA 244:38-43; Moran 1987b:469 n. 6; 1992:469 n. 6).

By contrast, in the syntagmas with the verb (*w*)*aṣû* as object, the infinitives have a subject different from that of their governing verb:

> *ù gáb-bi* LÚ.MEŠ *ḫa-za-nu-ti*$_7$ / *la-a ra-i-mu i-nu-ma* / *tu-ṣú* ERÍN.MEŠ *pí-ṭá-tu* / *i-nu-ma pa-ši-iḫ a-na šu-nu* / *ù a-na-ku i-ba-ú a-ṣé-ši* / *i-nu-ma ma-ri-iṣ* ‹*a-na*› *ia-a-ši* "But all the city rulers are unhappy that the army might come out because it is tranquil for them, but I seek its coming forth because it is bitter ‹for› me" (EA 362:54-59); [*ù y*]*i-de* LUGAL EN-*ia* / [*i-nu-ma*] [KUR]*A-mur-ri ur-ra* / [*mu-ša*] *tu-ba*‹*-ú*› *a-ṣa pí-ṭá-ti* "[but] the king, my lord, should know [that] Amurru seek‹s› day and night the coming forth of the army" (EA 70:24-26; Rainey 1974:302; Moran 1987b:246 n. 4; 1992:140 n. 4).

The infinitive may be subordinated in an adverbial complement dependent on the preposition *ana* as in these two instances:

> *a-nu-ma gáb-bi* / ⌈LUGAL⌉.⌈ḪA⌉ *ša* LUGAL ERÍN.MEŠ *Ḫur-ri* / [*t*]*u-*[*b*]*a-ú-ni*$_7$ KUR.ḪÁ / *a-na ḫa-ba-lí iš-t*[*u*] / [Š]U-*ia ù* ŠU [L][ÚMAŠKÍM] / [*š*]*a* LUGAL EN-[*ia*] "Now, all the kings of the king of the Hurrian army [a]re [se]eking to snatch the territories from my [han]d and the hand [o]f the [commissioner] / [o]f the king, my lord" (EA 60:13-18; *contra* Moran 1987b:234 n. 5; 1992:132 n. 5); UD-*ma a*[*n*]*-nu-um a-na ḫal-li-iq* / KUR LUGAL EN-*ia yu-ba-á*ʾ-*ú* [I]⌈*Mil*⌉-⌈*ki*⌉-⌈*li*⌉ "Today, Milkilu is seeking to cause the loss of the territory of the king, my lord" (EA 250:55-56; Campbell 1965:204).

In the last example, the object of the desiring is expressed by an adverb that refers to the topic discussed in the previous lines, viz. that the writer of the letter be allowed to travel to pharaoh's court:

> *a-nu-ma ki-a-ma ú-ba-ú ur-ra / mu-*[*š*]*a* "Now, it is thus that I am longing for day and night" (EA 74:64-65).

dubbubu. The only D stem example is in the suffix conjugation (cf. *infra*, p. 309).

dubburu. Although OB spellings reflect *duppuru*, *CAD* D:186-188 recognizes the existence of *dubburu*, especially in EA; *AHw*:1380 wrongly assumes *ṭuppuru* (Moran 1981). All of the EA examples come from Canaan. The meaning must be "to expel, to exterminate." Rib-Haddi complains about his treacherous brother:

> *ù a-m*[*ur-mi*] / LÚ-*lu ar-nu a-*[*n*]*a na-*[*d*]*a-›na‹*[*-ni*] *a-n*[*a*] ∤ *›a-na‹* ^{I}*A-zi-ri y*[*i-p*]*u-*[*u*]*š ip-ša* G[AL] / *ù la-qí* ‹NÍG›.GA *ù y*[*u-*]*dab*[*-b*]*i-*[*r*]*a*[*-n*]*i* "And be[hold], as for (that) rebellious man, in order to pay Aziru, he committed a great crime and took the ‹trea›sure and expelled [m]e" (EA 138:103-106; Moran 1987b:364, 367 nn. 24-25; 1992:222, 224 nn. 24-25).

The form is 3rd m.s. preterite with 1st c.s. accusative suffix attached by means of the ventive. The 3rd f.s. in the next example could either be ventive or volitive (which are identical in the orthography); the context would call for a jussive or a volitive following the imperative:

> *i-na* UD.KAM.MEŠ / [*an-nu*]*-ti uš-ši-ra* ERÍN.MEŠ [*pí-ṭá-ti*] / [*ù tu-*]*da-bi-ra-šu i*[*š-tu*] / [^{KUR}*A-mur-*]*ri* "At [thi]s time, send [regular] troops [that they may] expel him f[rom Amur]ru" (EA 85:79-83; for the temporal adverbial expression, cf. Moran 1950a:158; 1987b:270; 1992:157; Greenberg 1955:37; Youngblood 1961:281).

A similar context lacks the *-a* suffix:

> *uš-ši-ra* ERÍN.MEŠ *pí-ṭá-ti* / *ra-ba ù tu-da-bi-ir* / *a-ia-bi* LUGAL *iš-tu* / *lìb-bi* KUR-*šu* "Send a large army and it will expel the king's enemies from his land" (EA 76:38-41).

The form is obviously the WS jussive built on the Akkadian preterite theme.

Again, in the following example, one cannot say whether the 1st c.s. form has the ventive or the WS volitive suffix . A jussive or volitive would be perfectly natural in the apodosis (Moran 1950a:73-74, 102-103), especially with an ideal, hypothetical case such as this:

> *i-nu-ma* 1 *ḫa-za-nu* / *lìb-bu-šu it-ti lìb-bi-ia* / *ù ú-dab-bi-ra* ᴵÌR-*A-ši-ir-ta* / *iš-tu* ᴷᵁᴿ*A-mur-ri* "If one city ruler were of the same mind with me, then I would expel ᶜAbdi-Ashirta from Amurru" (EA 85:66-69; Greenberg 1955:37; Moran 1950a:102).

The one real 3rd m.pl. form (*contra* Ebeling 1915:1394-1395) is a preterite. It requires the full context to be properly understood:

> *ù ti-mu-ru* URU.⌜KI⌝ ⌜*i*⌝-*nu-m*[*a*] ERÍN.MEŠ *ša-nu* \ *a-ša-bu* (sic!)/ *a-na* URU.KI *ù t*[*i-m*]*a-ga-r*[*u*] / ‹*a-na*› *i-re-bi*‹-*šu*› (sic!) *a-na* U[RU⌝.KI *ù t*[*i*-]*iq-bu* / *a-na ša-a-su a*[*l*]-*lu-ú-mi* BA.UG₅ / *be*(!)-*èl-nu ki-i ta-aq-bu mi-it* / ᴵ*Ri-ib-ad-di ki-ka-n*[*u*] *iš-tu* / ŠU.MEŠ*qa-ti*-*š*[*u*] *la-a-mi* [*ia-a*]*š-pu-ra* / *a-na* KUR.MEŠ *Mi-iṣ-ri ù yi-ì*[*l*]-*qa-nu* / *qa-du* DUMU.MEŠ-*nu ù ti*[-*da*]*b-bi-ru* / ERÍN.MEŠ ᴵ*A-zi-ri iš-t*[*u*] URU.KI "So the city saw that another army was situated (sic!) against the city and they agreed ‹to its› entering the city and they said to him, 'Behold, our lord is dead? How can you say, "Rib-Haddi is dead!" (Those) like us are free from his control? May he not [wr]ite to the lands of Egypt that he may capture us with ou[r] children!' So they expelled the army of Aziru from the city" (EA 138:60-70; Moran 1987b:363; 1992:222; Rainey 1989-90:63).

Two forms of the 1st c.pl. are attested. One of them, the jussive *nu-da-bir*$_5$, is cited *supra*, p. 125. The other is a strange hybrid; the scribe seems to have confused the Akkadian G present-future with the D but then he may have gotten flustered and hypercorrected when he tried to make up for his initial mistake:

> *ù l*[*u*]*-ú ni-zi*[*-i*]*z* / UGU-*šu-nu ù lu-*[*ú*] / *ni-du-bu-ur* / LÚ.MEŠ *ša-ru-ta* / *iš-tu* KUR *šàr-ri* / EN-*ia* "And let us oppose them and let us drive the rebellious men from the land of the king, my lord" (EA 279:18-23).

qubbulu. *CAD*, following an oral suggestion by A. Horowitz that was accepted by Moran (1975a:148), lists this D stem verb for EA 252:18 with the meaning "to fight" (*CAD* Q:292b). Albright's equation was with Hebrew *qibbēl*, "to accept, receive" (Albright 1943b:31 n. 16) but *qubbulu*, "to receive," is very late in Akkadian (only NB; *CAD* Q:191a-b). Though the text has been cited previously in this work (cf. *supra*, pp. 5, 65, 78), it will be unnessessary to repeat it here. It seems more appropriate to see here the verb *kapālu* (*qapālu*) "to curl up" (transitive and intransitive; *CAD* K:174-175; Rainey 1989-90:68b-69a).

urrudu. The verb *arādu*/*urrudu* "to serve," a denominative from (*w*)*ardu* "slave" (cf. *infra*, pp. 259, 378), is exclusive to the EA texts from Canaan (*CAD* A/2:220). In spite of six examples where the infinitive is formed in the G stem pattern, *a-ra-ad* LUGAL (EA 144:32; also EA 112:24; 118:40; 119:43), *a-ra-di-ka* (EA 89:17; 114:43), the finite forms are all evidently D stem. The theme vowel is *-a-* with four exceptions. The 1st c.s. forms such as the jussive ⌈*ur*⌉-⌈*ra*⌉-⌈*ad*⌉ (EA 84:30), the apparent volitive *ur-ra-da* (EA 294:33) and the imperfect *ú-ra-du-šu* (EA 257:18) are representative of the most common pattern. Thus 3rd f.s. [*t*]*u-ra-du-šu* (EA 257:20) and 3rd m.s. *yu-ra-ad* (EA 207:7), *yu-ra-du* (EA 193:7), *yu-ra-du-ka* (EA 114:66) and *ú-ra-ad-šu* (EA 147:42; from Tyre) follow the same pattern. Four variant forms show that this denominative was not a standard construction: *i-ru-du*

(EA 250:51, 59), *i-ru-da-am* (EA 300:20; cf. *infra*, p. 259) and *i-ri-du* (EA 186:7) plus the more widely documented *ur-ru-du* (EA 189:r. 21, 24; 197:22; 241:11; 264:24; 295:9). These latter are obviously imitations of the D infinitive, *ur-ru-ud* LUGAL (EA 191:10; 253:28; and EA 189: r. 17); note also *ur-ra-di* (EA 294:20).

CAUSATIVE VERBS.

This category includes verbs with an intransitive G stem. The D stem is employed in a transitive, or causative meaning.

ḫulluqu. Only four D stem prefix forms are attested for this verb although the G stem stative and prefix conjugations are fairly frequent (given the nature of the troubles described in so many of the letters). The object of all these forms is always a place or geographical/political entity and the meaning is not necessarily literally "to destroy," but "to cause to be lost (from effective Egyptian political control)" (Moran 1987b:289 n. 1; 1992:170 n. 1; Greenberg 1955:44; cf. also the remarks of Campbell 1965:203 n. 20).

The Jerusalem scribe uses the 3rd m.s. Akkadian G present future as a causative. Since he always uses the Akkadian present-future for present-future and the suffix forms for the past tense, it would seem that he is doing the same here. A present meaning suits this particular context admirably, though perhaps the past tense could not be entirely ruled out if we wish to take this verb as a hybrid D preterite:

> ^I^*I-li-mil-ku* / *i-ḫal-li-iq gáb-bi* KUR *šàr-ri* "Ilimilku (sic! = Milkilu) is destroying all the territory of the king" (EA 286:36-37; Rainey 1978c:142).

A real 3rd m.s. D stem preterite (without *y-* prefix) appears alongside a 2nd m.s. preterite:

> [*la*]-*a tu-ḫal-li-iq* / [KUR.MEŠ LUGAL] ⌜*ú*⌝-*ḫal-li-iq* / [KUR.MEŠ LUGAL] / [^I^ÌR-*A-ši-ir-ta*] "You did [no]t destroy [the territory

of the king]; [ᶜAbdi-Ashirta] destroyed [the territory of the king]" (EA 97:9-12; Moran 1987b:289 n. 1; 1992:170 n. 1).

The last form is 3rd m.s. WS imperfect built on the Akkadian D preterite theme. It represents a present tense contrast to a D stem prefix form in the previous clause (*contra* Gevirtz 1973a:100-101):

> *ù a-mur* ᴵ*I-ta-at-ka-ma* / *ḫu-li-iq* KUR *Qì-is-sà u an-nu-ú* / ᴵ*Ar-za-wu-ya qa-du* ᴵ*Bi-ri-da-aš-wa* / *yu-ḫa-li-qú* KUR *A-pí* "Behold, Itatama (sic! = Etakama) caused the loss of the land of Kedesh and lo, Arzawuya , with Biridashwa, is causing the loss of the land of Api" (EA 197:31-34; Rainey 1975b:418).

ḫummuṭu. The D stem of this verb is exclusive to the Amarna texts from Canaan. The MA passages cited by *CAD* Ḫ:63 have been shown by *AHw* :316b-317a to belong to the D stem of *ḫamāṭu* B, "to burn (trans.), to fire (vessels)." Three examples (including an imperative, EA 102:29) have an *-a* suffix which could be volitive or ventive. All of the attested forms are injunctives.

In three instances(including two precatives, EA 88:24, 40; Rainey 1975b:415), the verb takes as its direct object the infantry (and chariotry):

> *ù yu-ḫa-mi-ṭa be-li* / ERÍN.MEŠ *pí-ṭá-ṭa₅* "So may my lord hasten the regular army" (EA 362:40-41).

However, there are three other examples (including the one imperative) where this verb governs an infinitive as direct object:

> *yu-ḫa-mi-iṭ be-li* / *uš-šar* ERÍN.MEŠ *pí-ṭá-ṭi ki-ma* / *ar-ḫi-iš* "May the king hasten to send (or: hasten the sending of) the regular army quickly" (EA 362:7-8; also EA 129:78-79); *šá-ni-tam* / *ši-me-e ia-ši ḫu-mi-ṭa₅ ki-ma* / *ar-ḫi-iš ka-ša-da* "Furthermore, listen to me, hasten quickly to come" (EA 102:28-30; cf. *infra*, pp. 396-397).

kubbudu. The Mitanni letters use the D stem of this root numerous times, but there is only one occurrence of a prefix verbal form in the WS texts. It is a gloss on the Sumerian logogram DUGUD and certainly must reflect the cognate Canaanite verb (Böhl 1909:83, §37m; Sivan 1984:177). It is 3rd m.s. D preterite:

> *ša-ni-tam mi-na-am-mi ep-ša-ku-mì / a-na šàr-ri* EN-*ia / i-nu-ma* SIG-*ia* \ *ya-qí-il-li-ni / ù* DUGUD \ *yu-ka-bi-id* / ŠEŠ.ḪÁ-*ia ṣé-eḫ-ru-ta₅* "Furthermore, what have I done to the king, my lord, that he should have belittled me and honored my junior colleagues?" (EA 245:36-40)

kullu. One example of this verb is found in a Rib-Haddi letter from Beirut. Since the scribe was uncertain that his form would be properly understood, he glossed it with a Canaanite word:

> *a-na* URU-*ia* ŠE[.*IM*] / *i-ku-al* \ *ḫa-ṣí-ri* "For (= from?) the city, he is holding (gloss: detained) the grain" (EA 138:129-130).

This is evidently a misspelling of *ukāl,* which often has a timeless, or stative tense function (*GAG*:102, §78b). The gloss may be a stative participle, **ᶜaṣīrī,* with *hireq compaginis* (Moran 1961:60, 69 n. 52). Since there is no G stem for *kullu,* one must either posit that the scribe intended a D or else that he was constructing his own hypercorrected G form and using it as a stative. In fact, the gloss and the absence of a *y-* prefix on *i-ka-al* may support this view. Moran (1987b:364; 1992:223) renders "on retient," "is held back." The gloss also gives credence to the idea that a form without a consonantal prefix may actually be a calque on a Canaanite participle or stative of the suffix conjugation.

lamādu, lummudu. The G stem prefix forms of this verb with their "stative" meaning are well known. Only two D causatives are attested in the Amarna archive, one is in an epistle from Egypt (EA-162:30; Cochavi-Rainey 1988:175) and the other is in a difficult context from another letter that was written in Canaan:

> *ù yu-la-mi-dá* / LUGAL *be-li* ERÍN.MEŠ-*šu* G[IŠGIGIR]-*šu a-na ia-š*[*i-i*]*a* "And may the king, my lord, order his infantry (and) his c[hariotry] to me" (EA 272:23-25).

The awkwardness of all translations for this passage (*CAD* L:58a; Moran 1987b:496; 1992:317) shows that the nuance in this context is not easy to reconcile with the general usage of this verb in the D stem, viz. "to instruct." In fact, Bezold and Budge indicate that the *la* sign is damaged. Perhaps it is an error for *ḫa;* the resulting emendation would give *yu-ḫa-mi-dá,* which is exactly the form used elsewhere in similar contexts (cf. above)! It also would make better sense in the present context (Rainey 1989-90:70a).

magāru, mugguru. Only one instance of what may be a D stem (*CAD* M/1:42a):

> *mi-ia-mi yu-ma-gi-ir ur-ru-ba it-ti* I*šàr-ri* EN-*ia* "Who has achieved entrance to the king, my lord?" (EA 283:10-11).

muššuru. The semantic development of this verb discussed under *wuššuru* (cf. *infra,* pp. 157-168), viz. the shift whereby the original "to release," became "to send," affected the MB forms (with *m* › *w*) as well as the conservative forms that preserved the original *w*. The meaning, "to send," is not restricted to Canaanite epistles (*AHw*:1485); it appears in letters from pharaoh: *um-te-še-ra-ak-ku* "I have sent to you" (EA 369:5; 367:6; 370:7). The Jerusalem letters also have four attestations, two of which are 3rd m.s. preterites with the ventive:

> *am-mi-ni*₇ DUMU LÚKIN *k*[*i-ma ar-ḫi-i*]*š* / *la-a ú-ma-še-ra* ⌜*šàr*⌝[*-ru* EN-*ia*] / [*k*]*i-na-a*[*n-n*]*a ú-ma-š*[*e-ra*] / [I*E-en-ḫa-*]*mu e-m*[*u-qa*] "Why did the king not send an emissary q[uickly]? Thus [Yanḫa]mu has sent a fo[rce]" (EA 285:7-10; Naʾaman 1975:97; Moran 1987b:507 n. 3; 1992:325).

A reasonable hypothesis for the change in meaning from "releasing" to "sending" is that the latter nuance developed from the use of the ventive with *muššuru/wuššuru*. However, in the texts as we now have them, there are many examples without the ventive that carry the meaning "to send." Such is the case with the other attestations from Jerusalem:

> LÚ.MEŠ *ma-ṣar-ta*$_5$^{MEŠ} *ša tu-ma-še-er* / *i-na* ŠU ^{I}*Ḫa-ya* DUMU *Mi-ia-re-e* / *[l]a-qí-mi* ^{I}*Ad-da-yu ša-ka-an* / *i-na* É*-šu i-na* ^{URU}*Ḫa-za-ti* ^{KI} / *[ù* 2]0 ⸢LÚ⸣.MEŠ *a-na* ^{KUR}*Mi-iš-ri* ^{KI} / *ú-ma-še[-e]r* "The guardsmen whom you sent under the command of Ḫaya, son of Miya-Rēᶜ, Addayu has taken and placed in his house in Gaza, [and] he sent [twe]nty men to Egypt" (EA 289:30-35).

Note, incidentally, that the Jerusalem scribe reflects accurately the Akkadian shift *i* › *e* before syllable closing *r*.

puḫḫuru. The D preterite serves as theme for WS imperfect with present tense meaning:

> *a-nu-ma i-te*$_9$*-li* ERÍN.MEŠ *i-na* / ^{URU}*Gub-la ù la-qa-ši*$_{\text{x}}$(ŠE) / *i-na-na a-di yu-pa-ḫi-ru ka[-li]* / URU.MEŠ *ù yi-ìl-qú-ši*$_{\text{x}}$(ŠE) "Now, an army came up against Byblos and took it; now again he is assembling al[l] the cities and he will take it" (EA 124:12-15; contrast Moran 1987b:336; 1992:203);

and for a WS volitive:

> *ú-ul yu-pa-ḫi-ra ka-li* / LÚ.MEŠ GAZ.MEŠ *ù* / *ji-ìl-qa* ^{URU}*Ši-ga-t[a]* "Lest he assemble all the *ᶜapîrû* men and take Shigata" (EA 71:28-30; also EA 85:77-79).

ṣeḫēru, ṣuḫḫuru. There is only one attested prefix example of this verb and it has been interpreted variously as Akkadian G stem (but with past tense meaning! *CAD* Ṣ:123a) or as a D stem (*AHw*:1420b). It would appear from the context that the *CAD* rendering was on the right track as far as the general meaning of the passage was concerned, but the form in question is surely D stem:

> *šá-ni-tam ù in-du-um / yu-ṣa-ḫi-ra-am a-na ia-ši / ù im-lu-uk iš-tu / lìb-bi-ia* "Furthermore, and when he (i.e. Aziru) tightened up on me, I took counsel in my heart" (EA 136:24-26).

CAD has suggested comparison with Hebrew *qāṣēr* "short." However, the usage in this passage is probably a calque on WS **ṣrr*, "to be narrow," in the causative stem, cf. *uḇəᶜēṯ hāṣēr lô* (2 Chron. 28:22). Note that the Akkadian D preterite provides the theme. The use of the ventive is practically unique (cf. *CAD* Ṣ:123b for one NB example, YOS 9 80:27), especially in the earlier periods; its use here enhances the directional nature of the action.

turru. Because of the common epistolary expression, "to send back a word (reply)," it is not surprising that the causative of *târu* "to return" should appear in the Amarna letters. Some scribes in Canaan formed their own Š stem conjugation of *târu* (cf. *infra*, p. 182), apparently because the WS idiom contained the causative of the verbal root **ṯwb* (Youngblood 1961:244). However, most epistles in the EA archive use the D stem. There is an abundance of examples from the non-WS texts, but also quite a few from Canaan. Aside from the stock expression, "to send a reply," the D stem of this verb can also signify the return of people, political entities (towns) and other things. The Akkadian D preterite provides the basic theme; six out of the ten attestations in Canaanite letters have an *e* thematic vowel. Three have an *i* vowel, unless we should read the *ti* sign as te_9.

An epistle that does not use the *y-* prefix has a 3rd m.s. form with WS imperfect suffix with 1st c.s. dative pronominal suffix:

> *ù a-di-mi ú-ti-ru-ni₇!* / *šu-uṭ mu-ul-ka / ša ú-ša-aṭ mil-ka /* [ᴵ]*Pa-a-pu* "And he still replies to me, 'Denounce the government! He who denounces the king is Pāpu" (EA 333:19-22; cf. Albright 1942b:33-34 n. 8; Rainey 1989-90:72b).

One of the 3rd m.s. forms is WS imperfect in the protasis of a conditional sentence; it has a 1st c.s. accusative suffix:

> *šum-ma* LUGAL *be-li yi-iḫ-na-nu-ni ù / yu-te-ru-ni a-na* URU.KI *ù a-na-ṣár-š[i]* ⌜*ki*⌝-[*ma*] / ›*ki*‹ *pa-na* "If the king, my lord, will be gracious to me and return me to the city, then I will guard it as in the past" (EA 137:81-83; cf. Moran 1987b:361 n. 15; 1992:221 n. 15).

The other two 3rd m.s. forms are imperfect energic and one has the 1st c.s. suffix *-ni* as indirect object:

> *ù yu-te-ru-/na-ni šàr-ru be-lí-ia / a-wa-at yu-te-ru-na / ù a-na a-wa-at / šàr-ri iš-mu* "And the king may return to me whatever word that he may return and I will give heed to the word of the king" (EA 251:11-15).

All three 2nd m.s. forms are from Sidon. One appears to be a hybrid, possibly treated as third weak! The vowel after the first radical is *a* but there is an *i* vowel after the final root consonant:

> *ù yi-din-ni* / LUGAL *i-[n]a qa[-at]* LÚ-*lì ša yi-la-ak / i-na pa-ni* ERÍN.MEŠ *pí-ṭá-at* LUGAL / *i-na ša-al* URU.DIDLI.KI[.Ḫ]Á *ša in₄-né-ep-šu / a-na* LÚ.MEŠ SA.GAZ.MEŠ / *ù tú-ta-ar*!(RI)-*ši-na i-na / qa-ti-ia* "So may the king put me in the charge of the man who is coming at the head of the king's army to investigate the towns that have gone over to the *ᶜapîrû* men, and may you(!) return them to my control" (EA 144:26-32; Moran 1987b:375 n. 2; 1992:230-231 n. 3).

The actual spelling is *tú-ta-ri-ši-na;* perhaps the final, otiose, *i* vowel was meant to be the ventive but was assimilated to the *i* vowel of the 3rd f.s. accusative suffix, or it might be an overhanging vowel that occurs here and there in forms with -Ø suffix plus an accusative suffix pronoun (cf. e.g. *yi-ik-ki-mi-ni,* EA 283:16, cited by Kühne 1971:370 n. 4). Still, the possibility of a scribal error of RI in place of AR is equally probable. The prefix is expressed by the UD sign which almost never has the value *tú* in the EA and other peripheral letters. However, the other two 2nd m.s. examples from Sidon (below) have *tú* as their prefix;

therefore, Moran felt justified in adopting that reading here (Moran 1987b:375 n. 2; 1992:230-231 n. 3; von Soden and Röllig 1976:42 No. 221). The other attestations also carry the ventive suffix:

> [*lu-ú*] *ti-i-de i-nu-ma* / *šal-*[*m*]*a-ku ù at-ta iš-tu* / *šul-mi-k*[*a i*]*š-tu* / *ma-ḫar šàr-ri* [E]N-*ia* / *ša-a-ri* ^{UZU}KA \ *pí-ka* / *tú-ti-ra-an-ni* "[May] you be apprised that I am well and that (is because?) you, from your well being (or: blessing) from the presence of the king, my lord, the breath of your (his?) mouth, have returned to me" (EA 145:5-10; Moran 1987b:376 nn. 2-3; 1992:231 nn. 2-3); *a-na* KUR.ḪÁ *A-mur-ri a-wa-at-mi* / *ti-iš-te*$_9$*-mé iš-tu aš-ra-*[*n*]*u-u*[*m*] / *t*[*ú*]*-te-ra-am a-na ia-a-ti* "The word that you have heard from there concerning Amurru, send back to me" (EA 145:24-26).

There is one 1st c.s. form, this time with infixed *-t-* , in a text which employs the Akkadian prefix forms for present-future (and past continuous) alongside the Canaanized suffix forms for past tense, much like the Jerusalem letters. It is EA 189 from northern Canaan, perhaps from the same scribal tradition as the Jerusalem scribe. The temptation to see here the Akkadian past with infixed *-t-* as expressing the *result* of previous actions in the manner of OB is very appealing:

> *ù ka-aš-da-ti*$_7$ *ù il*$_5$*-la-ak* / DINGIR.MEŠ-*nu-ka ù* ^{d}UTU-*ka* / *a-na pa-ni-ia ù* URU.DIDLI.ḪÁ *ut-te-er* / *a-na* LUGAL EN-*ia iš-tu* / LÚ.MEŠ SA.GAZ.MEŠ *aš-šum ur-ru-di-šu* "But I arrived and your god(s) and your sun god were going before me so that I brought back the cities to the king, my lord, from the *apîru* men in order to serve you" (EA 189:13-17).

One of the two 3rd m.pl. forms has to do with carrying messages but in the immediate context the idiom "to reply" is expressed by the Š infinitive (*a-na šu-te-er* / *a-wa-ti* EA 108:49-50). Nevertheless, it is the D stem that is employed by the scribe of this letter when he wants to describe the activity of diplomatic couriers:

> *mu-ša / tu-ba-lu-na ù mu-ša / tu-te-ru-na* LÚ.MEŠ / DUMU *ši-ip-ri ša-a šàr-ri / iš-tu pa-ni* UR.GI$_7$ "By night the couriers of the king bring and by night they take back because of the dog" (EA 108:52-55).

The second passage apparently is defective; the subject of the verb has to be supplied (cf. Moran 1987b:371 n. 6; 1992:228 n. 5):

> *šá-ni-tam ù a!-mur* ‹ERÍN.MEŠ› *ša* LUGAL EN‹*-ia*› / ^{d}UTU*-ia* DINGIR.MEŠ*-ia ša-ri* TIL.LA*-ia / tu-ti-ru [g]i-mi-li* ÌR*-šu* "Furthermore, and behold, may ‹the army› of the king, ‹my› lord, avenge his servant" (EA 141:36-38; *CAD* G:74b).

wuššuru. The most frequent D stem verb in the EA corpus is this one. The more proper MB forms, used mainly by the Jerusalem scribe, have been treated under *muššuru* (cf. *supra*, pp. 152-153). The customary orthography in most of the other texts from Canaan preserves the first radical but does not represent the gemination of the second. Spellings with gemination are typical of some non-WS texts, e.g the later texts from Amurru: 3rd m.s. *ú-wa-aš-ši-ra-an-ni* (EA 171:13), 1st c.s. *ú-wa-aš-šar-šu* (EA 171:29) and also *ú-wa-aš-šar-ra-an-ni* (EA 165:36; 171:5; and Qatna EA 53:69); a borderline case is 1st c.pl. *ni-wa-aš-ši-ru-šu* (EA 197:18).

On the other hand, a few shortened forms without the first radical almost always have orthographic gemination. Note: 3rd m.s. *yu-uš-ši-ra* (EA 180:6; 182:8; 269:11, 14; 270:24; 271:18; 279:14); *yu-uš-ši-ir-mi* (EA 280:9); but also: 3rd m.s. *yu-ša-ru* (EA 362:10), *yu-ši-ru* (EA 126:22; 131:15; *yu-ši-ra* (EA 104:14; 131:12; 216:15; 281:11, 27; 366:30). Only four Byblos tablets employ the shortened forms. One Rib-Haddi letter written in Beirut has the 3rd m.s. hybrids *yi-iš-ši-ru* (EA 139:34, 36, 38), *yi-iš-ši-ra* (EA 139:30-31) while a non-Rib-Haddi letter from Byblos has 3rd m.s. *iš-ši-ir* (EA 140:8, 24, 28) for the suffix conjugation form usually written *uš-ši-ir* (EA 86:16; *et al.*). From Alashia comes 1st c.s. *uš-šar* (EA 35:45). An example of 1st c.s. *i-wa-ši-ra* (TT 2:23) comes from 15th century Taanach.

In sharp contrast to *muššuru*, the *wuššuru* forms show an overwhelming preference for an *-i-* thematic vowel rather than *-e-*. The few forms with an *-e-* theme are restricted to four texts. The two earliest were found at Taanach: 2nd m.s. *tu-wa-še-ru* (TT 6 :5), 2nd m.s. energic *tu-wa-še-ru-na* (TT 6:11); and 2nd m.s. imperative *uš-še-ra-šu-*⸢*nu*⸣ (TT 5:13). From Tyre comes 1st c.s. *uš-še-er* (EA 151:45) and in a Mut-Baᶜlu letter we find 3rd m.s. *yu-wa-še-ru* (EA 255:17), 1st c.s. *ú-wa-še-ru* (EA 255:13), and 3rd m.s. precative *li-wa-še-ra* (EA 255:22).

The normal meaning of the D stem of this verb in Akkadian is "to release, to permit," etc. (*AHw*:1484a-1487a). Such a meaning is attested, alongside the more recent semantic development, in the non-WS texts of the various peripheral areas, e.g even from an epistle in the Amurru correspondence:

> EN-*ia iš-tu pa-*⸢*na*⸣*-nu-um-ma* / *a-ra-a*ʾ*-a-am a-na* LÚ.ÌR.MEŠ / LUGAL EN-*ia ù* LÚ.MEŠ GAL-*bu-te*MEŠ / *ša* URU*Ṣu-mu-ri la-a ú-wa-aš-ša-ru-ni-ni* "My lord, for a long time I have wanted to be a servant of the king, my lord, but the officials at Ṣumur would not permit me" (EA 157:9-12; Izreʾel 1991a:II, 18-19).

Another text, the morphosyntax of which at least partially adheres to the WS patterns, has:

> *ù ti*$_{7}$*-iq-bu-na* / *al-ka-am-mi nu-du-uk* I*Bir*$_{5}$*-ia-wa-za* / *ù la-a ni-wa-aš-ši-ru-šu a-na* / [KUR*Ta*]*ḫ-še* "And they are saying, 'Come! Let us attack Biryawaza and not permit him (to go to) [the land of Takh]si!" (EA 197:16-19; Rainey 1989-90:67).

But the most important attestation of this meaning is EA 123. In the same letter, we find this verb also used in the meaning "to send." The release of three captured men is the subject of Rib-Haddi's petition:

> [*u*]*š-ši-ir* I*Pí-ḫu-ra* / [LÚ].MEŠ KUR *Su-te d*[*a-ku*] / [LÚ] *še-er-da-ni* [*ù*] / [*l*]*a-qú* 3 LÚ [*ù*] / [*š*]*u-ri-bu* ⸢*i*⸣?[*-na*] / KUR*Mi-iš-ri* [*šum-ma*] / [*l*]*a-a yu-wa*[*-ši-ru*] / *šu-nu šàr-ru* EN[*-li*] / [*a-*]*di ti-pu-šu*[*-na*] /

> *ar-na* UGU-*ia* / [*šum-*]*ma i-ra-am šà*[*r-ru*] / [E]N-*li* ÌR *ki-t*[*i-šu*] / [*ù*] *uš-ši-ra* / [3] LÚ *ù ib-lu-ṭá* . . . *3* LÚ *ša-a šu-ri-ib* / ^I^*Pí-ḫu-ra uš-š*[*i-*]*ra ù bal-ṭá-ti* / ^I^ÌR-*i-ra-ma* / ^I^SUM.^d^IŠKUR ^I⌈^ÌR⌉.LUGAL "Paḫura sent the Sutian [m]en; they s[lew] a Sherdanian [man and th]ey took three men [and] [s]ent (them) t[o] Egypt. [If] the king, [my] lor[d] does not re[lease] them, they will [ag]ain commit a crime against me. [I]f the k[ing], my [lo]rd, loves [his] faith[ful] servant, then release (or: send) the [three] men that I may live . . . . The three men whom Paḫura sent (to Egypt) send that I may live, (viz.) ᶜAbdi-rāma, Yattin-Haddu/Baᶜl, ᶜAbdi-milki" (EA 123:13-34).

Admittedly, one is hard pressed to distinguish the exact nuance of the imperatives and the imperfect *yu-wa*[*-ši-ru*]; *wuššuru* is juxtaposed to *šūrubu*. Nevertheless, it seems most likely that Rib-Haddi is pleading for the men's release, and what better verb to use than *wuššuru*? The imperatives here happen to have the ventive and a logical explanation for the semantic shift of this verb from "to release, to permit" to the direct nuance "to send" is that it developed as a lexical variant derived from the ventive.

With the meaning "to send," *wuššuru* is employed when referring to the sending of goods and gifts (EA 34:46-48; 85:17-18; 130:33-39; 296:14-17) but the majority of cases deal with the sending of people, either individuals (EA 64:10-13; 74:59-61; 77:21-23; 83:34-35; 89:54-55; 95:31-32; 100:11-12; 114:35-37; 116:30-33; 117:66, 76-77; 137:8-9, 79-80; 151:44-46; 280:9-10; 33:23-26) or military units (e.g. EA 71:13-14, 21-23, *et passim*). Of special interest is its use concerning the expediting of caravans (EA 255:8-11, 12-14, 14-20; 264:9-10) or the sending of ships (EA 143:18-21; cf. EA 245:28-30). It can even depict the sending forth of one's hand (EA 299:20). But the most vivid idiom is the sending of cities to the flames (EA 125:40-45; 185:18, 23, 31, 39). Imperatives, infinitives and the suffix conjugation forms are all employed throughout the corpus of Canaanite correspondence in these semantic nuances.

There can be no doubt that the ventive contributed something to the semantic development. Though it is not a mandatory addition in order to give the meaning "to send," it is present in numerous syntactic environments. Note the following Alashia example of the preterite with the ventive:

> *a-na mi-nim-mi la-a tu-wa-ši-ra* / LÚDUMU *ši-ip-ri-ka a-na maḫ-ri-ia* "Why didn't you send your emissary to me?" (EA 34:9-10).

Another preterite with the ventive ending is attested in a circumstantial clause employed in the strongly Canaanized epistle written by the leaders from ᶜIrqata:

> *i-nu-ma yu-wa-ši-r*[*a* LU]GAL / EN-*nu* ᴵD[UMU]-*Bi-ḫa-a* [*ù*] / *yi-iq-bi a-na ia*[*-ši-nu*] . . . "When the [ki]ng, our lord, sent D[UMU]-Biḫā [and] he said to u[s] . . . (EA 100:11-13).

A Byblos example of the preterite even has the *-a-* thematic vowel!

> [*ù*] *aš-ta-pár* / *a-na* É.GAL *ù yu-w*[*a-ša-*]*ra* / ›*ù yu-wa-ša-ra*‹ ⸢*šàr*⸣*-ru* ERÍN.MEŠ / *ra-ba* "[and] I wrote to the palace and he se[n]t ›and he sent‹ a large army" (EA 117:24-27).

Moran (1960:16-18; 1987b:323; 1992:193) translates the second clause as if it were a purpose clause but this is hardly suitable in the context. Rib-Haddi is simply recounting what happened in the past. There can be no doubt here that the *-a* suffix is the Akkadian ventive, not the WS volitive. On the other hand, the thematic vowel from the Akkadian present-future is fixed by the orthography as *-a-* but it has no influence on the tense of the clause.

Some other forms have the *šar* sign with -Ø suffix and one might feel constrained to argue that $\check{s}ir_9$ is the correct reading. One of these particular contexts actually requires the preterite form:

> [*ù*] / *yu-šir*$_9$*-mi* LUGAL *ab-b*[*u-ka*] / ERÍN.MEŠ *pí-ṭá-ta*$_5$ TUR *ù* ⸢*yi*⸣*-í*[*l-*]*q*[*é*] / *gáb-ba* "[But] the king, [your] fath[er], sent a small force and he to[ok] everything" (EA 131:31-34).

In line 6 of the same text we find [*yu-š*]*i*-[*r*]*u*, in line 12 *yu-ši-ra*, and in line 15 *yu-ši-ru*. So one should probably read *yu-šir*$_9$*-mi* in line 31 above. The other context with this same spelling calls for a jussive:

> *la-a yu-wa-šir*$_9$ LUGAL *be-li* MU \ *ša-ni-ta*$_5$ *a-ni-ta*$_5$ / *a-na* DUMU.MEŠ ^{I}ÌR-*A-ši-ir-ta ù ti-dí-šu-*⌜*na*⌝ DUMU!.‹MEŠ› / *gáb-bi-šu-nu a-na* KUR.MEŠ LUGAL *be-li-ia* "Should the king, my lord, not send this year against the sons of ᶜAbdi-Ashirta, the sons, all of them, will tread down the lands of the king, my lord" (EA 362:66-68; Rainey 1978b:22-23; *contra* Moran 1987b:557; 1992:360).

This is evidently a case of the negated jussive (i.e. the equivalent of a positive imperative) in the protasis of a conditional sentence without *šumma*. The next is an unquestionable jussive with *-a-* theme (in good Akkadian this would be a positive affirmation unsuitable to the present context, cf. Edzard 1973:129):

> [*u*] *lu*[*-ú*] ⌜*yu*⌝-⌜*wa*⌝-⌜*ša*⌝-*a*[*r*] / ERÍN.M[EŠ] ⌜*pí*⌝-⌜*ṭá*⌝-⌜*ta*⌝-[*š*]*u* "[so] ma[y] he send his regular troop[s]" (EA 300:15-16).

When an *-a-* theme form does have present-future reference, it is because of a WS modal suffix. Note the WS imperfect with final *-u:*

> *šum-ma* LUGAL *be-li* / *la-a yu-ša-ru* ERÍN.MEŠ *pí-ṭá-ta*$_5$ / *ù ni-nu-mi* BA.UG$_7$.MEŠ$^{ni\text{-}mu\text{-}ut}$ / *ù* URU.MEŠ *Gub*^{ub}*-li* / *tu-ul*$_{11}$*-qú* "If the king, my lord, does not send regular troops then we will die and the cities of Byblos will be taken" (EA 362:9-13).

The other documented example has the augmented suffix of the WS imperfect energic:

> [*šum-ma*] *la-a yu-wa-*⌜*ša*⌝*-ru-na* / [*a-na* $^{\mathrm{URU.KI}}$*Gub-l*]*a ù la-qú-ši* "[If] he does not send [to Bybl]os then they will take it" (EA 131:59-60; Moran 1987b:350; 1992:213).

There are a few genuine preterites with an *-i-* thematic vowel and -Ø modal suffix. Only one happens to be 3rd m.s.:

> LUGAL *b[e]-li yu-uš-ši-ir-ni* / *a-na* [*e*]*-pu-uš*(sic!) *nu-kúr-ti₇* / *i-na* [U]RU*Qí-il₅-ti₇* "The king, my lord, sent me to make war on Keilah" (EA 280:9-10).

The rest are 1st c.s., viz. a long form from Tell el-Ḥesī, a hybrid long form from Beirut and a short form from Tyre:

> *ù* / [*i-na-n*]*a* ⌈I⌉*Ra-pí*-DINGIR *ù-wa*-⌈*ši*⌉-⌈*ir*⌉ "So [no]w I have sent Rāpī-ʾIlu" (EA 333:23-24); *ù i-wa-ši-ir* LÚDUMU *š*[*ìp-ri-ia*] / *a-na* É*-ti* É.GAL "so I have sent [my] em[issary] to the palace" (EA 137:8-9); *a-nu-um-ma* / *uš-še-er* IDINGIR.LUGAL LÚKIN*-ri* / *a-na maḫ-ri* LUGAL *be-li-ia* "Now I have sent ʾIlimilku, my emissary, to the king, my lord" (EA 151:44-46).

The form *uš-ši-ru-ši-*(*mi*) (EA 185:18, 23, 31, 39) is most likely to be reckoned as suffix conjugation rather than prefix preterites.

Since it is obvious from all the examples treated above that the tense and mode of the prefix forms from *wuššuru* are not determined by the thematic *-a-* vowel, it remains to analyze the plethora of forms with *-i-* theme. It will be clear that the determining factor is the WS modal suffix and that numerous forms cannot be preterite in meaning as would be required by the Akkadian paradigm.

Forms with *-i-* theme vowel and WS imperfect suffix express the full spectrum of "present tense" nuances, e.g. in a general present:

> *mi-ia-ti a-na-ku ù la-a* / *ú-wa-še-ru* KASKAL*-ra-ni* ḪÁ / *šàr-ri* EN*-ia* "Who am I that I should not expedite the caravans of the king, my lord?" (EA 255:12-14); *mi-nu* UR.G[I₇.MEŠ] / IDUMU.MEŠ IÌR*-A-ši-ir-t*[*a*] / *ù* ›*ù*‹ *ti-pu-šu-na* / *ki-ma lìb-bi-šu-nu ù* / *tu-wa-ši-ru-na* URU.MEŠ / *šàr-ri i-na* dIZI "Who are the do[gs], the sons of ʿAbdi-Ashirta, that they do whatever they want and send the cities of the king up in flames?" (EA 125:40-45);

> *ša-ni-tam* / Ì.MEŠ *ù* GADA.MEŠ *a-na mi-ni*$_7$ *la-a* / *tu-wa-ši-ru-ni* "Furthermore, why do you not send me oils and garments?" (EA 34:46-48).

Also in the protasis of conditional sentences:

> *šum-ma* ŠE.MEŠ *qè-e-ṣí la-a yu-ši-ru* / LUGAL ERÍN.MEŠ ⸢*pí*⸣-⸢*ṭá*⸣-*ta*$_5$ *a-na* $^{URU.KI}$*Gub-l*[*a*] / *ù la-q*[*é*]-*m*[*i*] *ti-ìl-qú-na-ši* "If by the season of summer grain the king does not send regular troops to Byblos, they will surely take it" (EA 131:15-17; Moran 1950a:176; *contra* Moran 1987b:349, 350 nn. 2, 3; 1992:212, 213 nn. 2, 3; Rainey 1989-90:62a; cf. also EA 123:18-22, 50-52);

or in a purpose clause dependent on another imperfect (Moran 1950a:81; 1951:33-34):

> *a-di* [*y*]*i du šàr-ru* / *a-*[*n*]*a* KUR.MEŠ-*šu ù yu-wa-ši-ru* / ERÍN.MEŠ *pí-ṭá-ti-šu ù* / *yu-ša-ap-ši-ḫu* KUR.MEŠ-*šu* "Until the king takes cognizance of his territories that he may send regular troops and that he may pacify his territories" (EA 112:36-39)

Another well known function of the imperfect is to express continued or repeated action in the past. There are several attestations of *wuššuru* reflecting the various nuances of this specific WS meaning (indicatd by the Akkadian present in standard dialects):

> [*pa-n*]*a-nu-um Ba-az-ú-nu* / DUMU *Na-ar-sí tu-wa-še-ru* / *a-na ia-a-ši* "[For]merly you used to send Bazʾunu, son of Narsi, to me" (TT 6:4-6); [*m*]*a-ni* UD.KÁM.MEŠ *ù-wa-ši-ru-šu* / *ù la-a yi-le-ú* / *i-re-ba a-na* ^{URU}*Ṣu-mu-ra* "How often have I sent him and he was unable to enter Ṣumur?" (EA 114:35-37); *ù pa-na-nu* . . . *ù yu-ši-ru be-li* ERÍN.MEŠ / *a-na ša-a-šu-nu* "And formerly . . . and my lord was sending troops to them" (EA 126:18-23); *a-mur* / ^{I}[*La-a*]*b-a-ia a-bi-ia* / [*yu-ra-d*]*u šàr-ra* EN-*šu* / [*ù šu-ut*] *yu-wa-še-ru* / [*ka-li* KASKAL]-*ra-ni* ^{ḪÁ} / [*ša yu-wa-š*]*e-ru šàr-ru* / *a-na* ^{KUR}*Ḫa-na-gal-bat* / *a-na* ^{KUR}*Ka-ra-du-ni-ia-aš* "Behold,

> [Lab]ʾayu, my father, [was serv]ing the king, his lord, [and he] expedited [all the cara]vans [that] the king [would se]nd to Ḫanigalbat, to Babylonia" (EA 255:14-20); *‹la-›a ia-aš-ku-un* [L]UGAL ŠÀ-*šu* / *i-na mi-im-mi ša yi-iš-ši-ru* / ᴵ*A-zi-ru a-na ša-šu mi-im-mu* / *ša yi-iš-ši-ru a-wa-ti Ṣu-mu\-ru* / *ù mi-im-‹mu›* ᴵ*Ḫa-za-ni* LUGAL / *š[a d]a-ak yi-iš-ši-ru* / *a-na ka-ta* "May the [k]ing ‹no›t pay attention to the property which Aziru has been sending to him; the property which he has been sending is things of Ṣumur; and the proper‹ty› of the king's city ruler wh[ich he k]illed, he has been sending to you" (EA 130:33-39).

There is also a full spectrum of energic nuances. First, there is the simple emphasis on the verbal action:

> LUGAL EN-*ia ša-pár a-na mu-ḫi-[i]a* ᴵ*Ḫa-a-ia* / *a-na qa-bi* KASKAL-*ra-ni* ḪÁ / KUR*Ḫa-na-gal₉-bat an-nu-ú* / *ú-wa-še-ru-na ù uš-še-ru-ši* "The king, my lord, sent Ḫāya to [m]e to say 'This Khanigalbat caravan, I am sending, so expedite it!'" (EA 255:8-11); *an-nu-ú* LÚ.MEŠMAŠKÍM *šàr-ri* / *yu-wa-ši-ru-na* ⸢*šàr*⸣*-ru ù* / *ia-aq-bi šàr-ru a-na ša-šu-nu* / *ù tu-pa-ri-šu be-ri-ku-ni* "Behold, it is the king who actually sends the royal commissioners, so may the king speak to them that they should adjudicate between the two of you" (EA 116:30-33; with Moran 1973:52 *contra* Moran 1987b:320; 1992:191).

or to express an urgent commital to action on the part of the speaker:

> *a-šar i-ba-ša-at* / *ši-pí-ir-ti* LUGAL EN-*ia* / *ša-ri* TIL.LA-*ia ù ú-ba-[ú-n]a-ši* / *ù uš-ši-ru-na-ši* / *a-na* LUGAL EN-*ia ša-ri* TIL.LA-*ia*/ *[š]á-n[i-t]am a-nu-um-ma i-na i-re-bi* / [GI]ŠMÁ.ḪÁ *ša* LUGAL EN-*ia* / *[š]a sí-ki-pu* / *i-na* URUPÚ.ḪÁ *uš-si-ru-n[a-ši!]* "Wherever the king's consignment is, I will sea[rc]h for it and I will send it to the king, my lord, the breath of my life; ⸢Furthermore⸣, now, with the arrival of the king, my lord's, ships, [whi]ch have sailed into Beirut, I will send [it]" (EA 143:13-21; Moran 1987b:374 n.2; 1992:229 n. 2; *CAD* S:73b).

One of the most frequent uses of the energic is in questions. The earliest example is from Taanach:

> *ša-ni-tam a-na* ⸢*mi*⸣-[*ni*$_7$] / ⸢*la!*⸣-⸢*a*⸣ *tu-wa*-[⸢*ša*⸣-*ru*-⸢*na*⸣] / *šu-lum-ka a-na* ⸢*ia*⸣![-*ši!*] "Furthermore, wh[y] ⸢don't] you se[⸢nd⸣] your greeting to m[e]?" (TT 1:12-14; Rainey 1977:39).

And, where an imperfect is required in a purpose clause dependent on another imperfect or a stative (Moran 1950a:81-82; 1951:33), an energic imperfect may be used if the context is interrogative:

> *a-na mi-ni*$_7$ / *qa-la-ta ù la-a ti-iq-bu a-na šàr-ri* / *ù yu-wa-ši-ru-na* / ERÍN.MEŠ *pí-ṭá-ti ù* / *ti-ìl-te*$_9$*-qú-na* / ^{URU}*Ṣu-mu-ra* "Why are you silent and do not speak to the king that he may send regular troops that they may take Ṣumur?" (EA 71:10-16; cf. also EA 114:59-62); [*ú*]-*ul ta-aq*[-*bu a-n*]*a* EN-*ia ù* / *yu-wa-šı-ru-n*[*a-k*]*a i-na* / *pa-ni* ERÍN.MEŠ.*pí*[-*ṭá*]-*t*]*i ù* / *tu-ša-am-ri-ru* LÚ.MEŠ GAZ / *iš-tu* LÚ.MEŠ [*ḫ*]*a-za-nu-ti* "[W]on't you spea[k t]o your lord so that he may sen[d y]ou at the head of the regular army so that you may drive out the *ʿapîru* men from the city rulers?" (EA 77:21-25).

The greatest enigma surrounds the many forms with the *-a* suffix. It has been demonstrated above that *wuššuru* often takes the Akkadian ventive. Only two possible jussives with -Ø suffix have been noted (EA 300:15-16, *supra,* p. 161; EA 362:66-68, *supra,* p. 161). On the other hand, of the 2nd m.s. imperatives, six or seven have -Ø suffix as against nearly fifty with *-a;* furthermore, nearly all of the precatives also have *-a.* Admittedly, *wuššuru* can take the WS imperfect and imperfect energic suffixes at the expence of the ventive with no loss of meaning; the suffix conjugation forms also lack any ventive morpheme (cf. *infra,* p. 311). Moran's demonstration of the *yaqtula* volitive in the Byblos texts (Moran 1950a:89-104; 1960) rests on a broad spectrun of examples, many from verbs that do not ordinarily take the ventive in Akkadian (cf. discussion *infra,* pp. 254-264). But several of the verbs he cites do sometimes have a lexical ventive, including verbs of motion, speaking and giving. One of those verbs is *wuššuru.* With the few exceptions mentioned above, the overwhelming majority of injunctive forms from *wuššuru* have the *-a* suffix. There are, in fact, some twenty attestations of prefix forms from *wuššuru* plus *-a* in injunctive contexts! The same question must be posed for them as for the imperatives: Is the *-a* suffix Akkadian ventive or WS volitive? The Hebrew cohortative *-āh* was carried over sometimes to the 2nd m.s. imperative (Ps. 17:13; 74:22; 82:8; *et al.*) but are we justified in seeing the *-a* suffixes on the imperatives of *wuššuru* as carry overs from the volitive? The ensuing repertoire of examples all have injunctive force; they may be jussives with the Akkadian *-a* superseding the WS -Ø or they may be the WS volitive *-a.* One might be tempted to see here a convergence of the Akkadian and the WS elements. Since the verb *wuššuru* often took the ventive, perhaps the injunctive form with *-a* (the volitive) came to be preferred over that with -Ø (the jussive).

In light of the questions posed above, it is noteworthy that injunctives of *wuššuru* that depend on a preceding precative are usually accompanied by a chain of other injunctives, all of them in the jussive with -Ø suffix, which would make the *wuššuru* form the only *yaqtula* in the chain; note the following typical examples:

> *ù li-it-ru-uṣ / i-na pa-ni šàr-ri* EN-*ia ù / lu-ú yu-ši-ra* [I]*Ia-an-ḫa-ma / ù lu-ú ni-pa-aš gá-bu-ma / nu-kúr-ti ù lu-ú tu-te-er /* KUR.KI.ḪÁ ša *šàr-ri* EN-*ia / a-na* ZAG.ḪI.‹A›-*ši \ up-sí-ḫi* "May it be pleasing in the sight of the king, my lord, that he send Yanḥamu so that we can all make war and so that you will gain back the territories of the king, my lord, to their utmost extremity" (EA 366:28-34; similarly EA 74:59-61 and probably EA 182:6-13).

These injunctives of *wuššuru* may be dependent on a preceding jussive and are often followed by another jussive: In injunctive chains such as these, the *wuššuru* form is alone in having the *-a* suffix:

> *ù lu-ú* / *yi-de* LUGAL / *ip-ša an-na-am* / *ù lu-ú yu-uš-ši-ra* / LUGAL *be-li* / ^{GIŠ}GIGIR.MEŠ *ù lu-ú* / *yi-ìl-te-qé-ni* / *a-na mu-ḫi-šu la-a* / *iḫ-la-aq* "So may the king be apprised of this deed and may the king, my lord, send chariots that he may take me to himself lest I perish" (EA 270:21-28; cf. EA 64:10-13; 83:34; 85:17; 89:54; 121:47; 139:29-33).

The earliest attestation of this verb with *-a* suffix is in a confusing chain of injunctives:

> *ša-ni-tam li-ru-*⸢*ba*⸣*-*⸢*am*⸣ ^{I}DINGIR-*Ra-pí-i*ʾ / *a-na* ^{URU}*Ra-ḫa-bi ù lu-*[*ú*] / *i-wa-ši-ra* LÚ-*ia a-na maḫ-ri-ka* / *ù lu-ú i-pu-šu ḫa-at-nu-ta*$_5$ "Furthermore, let Ilu-Rāpiʾ enter into Raḥābu and le[t] me send my man to you and let me/them make a marriage arrangement" (TT 2:21-24; Rainey 1977:52, 54).

The third verb in this chain is problematic. Perhaps it is an error for *i-pu-uš!* or *i-pu-ša;* it is only remotely possible that it is 3rd m.pl.

The most frequent usage of injunctive *wuššuru* is as an independent jussive/volitive or as the first injunctive in a chain of purpose clauses. All of the examples have *-a* suffix, as do some of the ensuing verbs in the associated chains, e.g.

> *ù* LÚ-*ia* / *an-nu-ú yu-wa-ši-ra-šu šàr-ru* / *ki-ma ar-ḫi-is ù ia-di-na* / LÚ.MEŠ *ma-ṣa-ar-ta*!(RA) *a-na* / *na-ṣa-ar* ÌR *ki-ti-šu ù* URU-*šu* "And as for this man of mine, may the king send him quickly and may he grant garrison troops to protect his faithful servant and his city" (EA 117:76-80; cf. also EA 95:31, Youngblood 1961:31, Moran 1987b:287 n. 2; 1992:169 n. 2; EA 104:14-15; 116:72; 117:66, 92; 118:42; 123:41; 137:79-80; 180:6-9; 216:15-17; 269:11-13, 14-17; 279:14-15; 281:11-12, 27-28).

Finally, there are two instances of injunctive *wuššuru* in the apodosis of a conditional sentence. Since this is a common function for both the jussive and the volitive (Moran 1950a:74), these two examples cannot be used to decide the proper understanding of the injunctives with *-a*:

> *šum-ma lìb-bi* LUGAL *be-li-ia* / *a-na* URU.KI*Gub*ub*-la ù* / *yu-ši-ra be-li* 3 ME ERÍN.MEŠ 30 GIŠGIGIR.MEŠ / ME LÚ.MEŠ KUR.MEŠ *Ka-ši ù ti-na-ṣa-ru* / URU.[K]I*Gub* ub*-la* "If the king, my lord, is concerned about Byblos, then let my lord send three hundred (regular) troops, thirty chariots, one hundred men of the lands of Cush that they may protect Byblos" (EA 131:10-14); *šum-ma i-ia-nu* / *yu-uš-ši-ra* / LUGAL *be-li* GIŠGIGIR.MEŠ / *a-na la-qé-n*[*u l*]*a-a* / *ti*7*-ma-ḫa-ṣú-nu* ÌR.MEŠ-*nu* "If not, then may the king, my lord, send chariots to take u[s l]est our servants smite us" (EA 271:17-21).

"INTENSIVE" VERBS

In this category we have placed those D stem prefix forms which pertain to verbs for which the basic orientation of the G stem is not significantly altered by it use in the D. It is possible, of course, that a particular scribe really intended to express a more "intensive" action by his preference for the D stem, even without precedent from the parent language. In other instances, one might suspect that a Canaanite idiom, with a WS verb in the D stem, stands behind some unusual Akkadian D form. Allowance must also be made in a few particularly difficult forms for simple scribal confusion.

kalû, kullû. The D stem of this verb is rare in Akkadian (*CAD* K: 102b-103a). One example occurs in a Byblos text:

> *i-nu-ma uš-ši-ir-ti* 2 LÚ / DUMU *ši-ip-ri a-na* URU*Ṣu-mu-ra* / *ù ú-ka-li* LÚ*-lí* / *an-nu-ú a-na šu-te-er* / *a-wa-ti a-na šàr-ri* "When I sent two emissaries to Ṣumur, then I held back this man in order to send word back to the king" (EA 108:46-50).

kašādu, kuššudu. Several D stem attestations of this verb in the non-WS texts from Amarna carry causative meaning, "to send," i.e. "to cause (someone) to arrive," like the Š stem *šukšudu* (*CAD* K:281b). However, the lone attestation in a text from Canaan is only partially preserved, viz. [*yu*]*-kaš-si-id* (EA 293:22) and the context does not seem to have place for a direct object or a destination. Therefore, it is more likely that the meaning intended was closer, or identical with that of the G stem. Line 19 of the same text has [*y*x-*kaš*-]*ša-ad*, with an *-a* thematic vowel, which Knudtzon took as G stem.

maḫāṣu, muḫḫuṣu. The D stem of this verb seems to carry the same basic meanings as the G stem (*CAD* M/82a-83b). The one passage where the D stem might be found has an ambiguous orthography. It is equally possible that the form is built on the Akkadian 3rd m.s. G stem theme. It has an *-a-* thematic vowel but the context seems to call for a preterite. The relevant passage (EA 252:19) has been cited above (*supra*, pp. 5, 65, 78, 148-149). The form in question is to be read either *yi-ma-ḫa-aš-ši* or *yu-ma-ḫa-aš-ši*. As noted before, the Canaanite scribes seem to have confused the Akkadian G *iparras* forms with the D stem in many instances. This present context might also be just such a case, whether we choose to read the prefixed PI sign as *yi-* or *yu-*.

maqātu. The D stem of this verb is extremely rare in Akkadian (*CAD* M/1:248b) and its attested meanings do not suit the five passages to be discussed here. Furthermore, the orthography of the EA forms is clearly G stem. Nevertheless, given the scribes' tendency sometimes to equate the Akkadian G present-future with the D stem, these five examples are mentioned in this chapter because they express a common nuance apart from that evidence in the usual epistolary formula (*amqut*/*nimqut* "I/we have fallen "prostrated my-/ourselve[s]). All of the references are to making an attack, "falling upon" an enemy. To be sure, this is a valid G stem meaning (*CAD* M/1:247b-248b) in Akkadian but the fact that the WS modal nuances are based on the *iparras* theme suggest that the scribes thought of such action as properly D stem. Two of the forms are 3rd m.s. negative jussive:

> *ú-ul yi-ma-qú-ta* [UGU] / [URU-]*ia ù yi-il-qa-ni* "Let him not fall upon me in order to capture me" (EA 81:31-32; Moran 1987b:261; 1992:151); *ú-ul yi-ma-qú-ta* ERÍN.MEŠ *ka-ra*[-*š*]*i* /

UGU-*ia* "Let not an expeditionary force fall upon me" (EA 83:43-44; Moran 1987b:265; 1992:153).

One is 2nd m.s. imperfect in a purpose clause following a stative other WS imperfects:

> *a-na mi-ni*$_7$ / *qa-la-ta ù la-a taq-bu* / *a-na šàr-ri* EN-*li-ka* / *ù tu-ṣa-na qa-du* ERÍN.MEŠ / *pí-ṭá-ti ù ti-ma-qú-tu* / UGU ^{KUR}*A-mur-ri* "Why do you keep silent and do not speak to the king, your lord, in order that you should come forth with the regular army so that you can attack Amurru?" (EA 73:6-11).

A broken context seems to have a 1st c.s. (or 3rd m.s.?) preterite:

> [*ù* ^{GI}]^{Š}GIGIR-*t*[*i* UGU] / [^{KUR}]*Am-qí i-ma-qú-u*[*t*] "(with my troops?) [and chariots] I(?) fell [upon the land of] ᶜAmqi" (EA 173:1-2).

And finally, there is a 1st c.pl. injunctive (jussive or volitive):

> AŠ É.NINIB *pu-ḫu-ru-nim-mi ù* / *ni-ma-qú-ut* UGU ^{URU}*Gub-la* "Assemble in Bīt-NINIB and let us fall on Byblos" (EA 74:31-32).

naʾāṣu. This is a rare verb in Akkadian and the finite forms are G stem with *-a-* thematic vowel (*CAD* N/2:53). The two Amarna attestations are in one letter written in Beirut. One is definitely not D stem, viz. 3rd m.s. *ia-an-aṣ-ni* "(my brother) scorned me" (EA 137:23) but the other has an *-i-* theme and can most logically be reckoned as a hybrid 3rd m.pl. D stem preterite:

> *ù ti-mu-ru* L[Ú.MEŠ É]-*ia* / *i-nu-ma la-a na-di-in* KÙ.BABBAR *ti-iš-la-ḫu* / *a-na ia-ši ki-ma* LÚ.MEŠ *ḫa*^{MEŠ}*-za-ni* ŠEŠ-*ia* / *ù ti-na-i-ṣú-ni* "And the m[en of] my [house] saw that no silver was given (and) they ridiculed(?) me like the city rulers, my colleagues, and they scorned me" (EA 137:11-14; cf. Albright, Mendenhall and Moran 1955:483b; cf. Moran 1987b:359 n. 2; 1992:219 n. 2).

naṣāru, nuṣṣuru. Peripheral texts attest to the rare use of D stem with this verb (*CAD* N/2:46a; Rainey 1974:306; 1975b:417-418; 1978b:84). From the fifteenth century B.C.E. we have:

> DINGIR.MEŠ *ša* AN *u* KI / *li-bal-li-ṭú-ú-šu li-na-ṣa-ru-šu* "May the gods of heaven and earth keep him alive and protect him" (*Idrimi Stele*, lines 99-100; *cf. CAD* B:59a

Another such precative is found in an Amurru letter:

> I*A-zi-ri* LÚÌR-*ka* / *i-na aš-ra-nu la tu-wa-aḫ-ḫe-er-šu* / *ar-ḫi-iš uš-še-ra-aš-šu* / *ù* KUR.MEŠ *ša* LUGAL EN-*ni li-na-aṣ-ṣár* "ᶜAziru is your servant. Do not delay him there. Send him quickly and let him protect the lands of the king, our lord" (EA 169:12-15; cf. Izreᵓel 1985:170; 1991a:I, 165 §2.4.2.11).

But in a Canaanized letter a 1st c.s. D form is also attested:

> [*i*]*š-te-mé* MAŠ[KÍM] / LUGAL *a-na ia-ši* / *a-na na-ṣár* URU.DIDLI.KI.ḪI[.A *a-n*]*a* / I*šàr-ri* BE-*ia* [*ù*] / *ú-na-ṣár* ⌜*ma*⌝*-gal* "[I] have heeded the words of the commis[sioner] of the king to me to guard the citie[s fo]r the king, my lord, [and] I will guard (them) very diligently" (EA 327:1-5).

The absence of the suffix -*u* leaves two alternatives of modal interpretation. The usual form in this syntagma is the WS imperfect (for examples, cf. Rainey 1975b:404-405; Rainey 1971b:97-100). The -*Ø* suffix could mean that here we have a WS jussive or it could simply indicate that *ú-na-ṣár* is intended to be taken as a regular Akkadian D present-future. In any event, it seems obvious that the scribe recognized a D stem for *naṣāru*.

So there was ample justification for the suggestion of Albright and Moran (1950:165b-166a; cf. *supra*, p. 58) that the forms of *naṣāru* with geminated second radical and usually an -*i*- thematic vowel were considered to be D stem. There are eight such forms, limited to five Byblos letters. The 3rd m.s. examples are all in the WS imperfect, *yi-na-ṣí-ru* (EA 112:14), *yi-na-ṣí-ru-ni*

(EA 112:18), though two of them have accusative suffixes attached by means of the Akkadian ventive, viz. *yi-na-ṣí-ra-an-ni* (EA 112:13; 121:10), *yi-na-ṣí-ra-ni* (EA 130:20). The 1st c.s. attestations include the WS imperfect *i-na-ṣí-ru* (EA 119:15; 130:49), the imperfect energic *i-na-ṣí-ru-na* (EA 123:32), and the volitive *i-na-ṣí-ra* (EA 123:27). The 3rd m.pl. form is jussive/volitive *ti-na-ṣí-ru* (EA 130:48). Because of the 1st c.s. prefix *i-* and the 3rd m.pl. *ti-*, we have transcribed the 3rd m.s. prefixes by *yi-* rather than *yu-*.

In fact, those *-i-* theme formations alternate with *-a-* themes in identical syntagmas; compare, e.g. the following examples:

> *iš-tu ma-an-ni i-na-ṣa-ru-na / iš-tu na-ak-ri-ia / ù iš-tu* LÚ.MEŠ*ḫu-up-ši-ia / mi-nu yi-na-ṣí-ra-an-ni / šum-ma* LUGAL ⸢*yi*⸣-⸢*na*⸣-⸢*ṣí*⸣-*ru* / ÌR-*šu [ù ba-al-ṭá-]ti / [ù šum-m]a [šà]r-ru la-a / [yi-n]a-ṣa-ru-ni mi-nu / yi-na-ṣí-ru-ni* "From whom shall I guard? From my enemies? And from my yeomen farmers who will protect me? If the king will ⸢protect⸣ his servant, [then] I [will live,] [but i]f the [ki]ng does not [pro]tect me, who will protect me?" (EA 112:10-18).

As a consequence, it may follow that the preference among some Canaanite scribes for the Akkadian G present-future theme of *naṣāru* might reflect a calque on some Canaanite D stem verb. Neither Akkadian (apart from the Alalakh and Amurru references treated above) nor the WS dialects attest to a D stem for *naṣāru*.

palāḫu, pulluḫu. The D stem of this stative verb is relatively rare (*AHw*:813b); in normal Akkadian, the D stem is causative in meaning. However, this does not seem to be the case with the Amarna example(s), which can be rendered exactly like the G. The one certain passage is 2nd m.s.:

> *la tu-pal-la-a[ḫ]* "Do not fear" (EA 102:36; Moran 1987b:296; 1992:175).

One may view this verb as WS negative jussive but outwardly it is identical with the Akkadian prohibitive (*GAG*:106, §81h; Edzard 1973:131).

Another example, with an *-i-* theme, was most probably meant by the scribe to be taken as D stem. It is WS 3rd m.pl. imperfect:

> *i-na a-ṣí* ERÍN.MEŠ / *pí-ṭá-ti ka-*⸢*li*] ⸢*mi*⸣*-am* [I]ÌR-*A-ši-ir-ta* / *it-ti-šu-nu la-a la-qí ù* GIŠMÁ.MEŠ-*šu-nu* / *a-ṣa ki-ma iš-tu* KUR*Mi-iṣ-ri* / *ki-na-na la-a ti-pa-li-ḫu-na* "With the coming forth of the regular army, all the property of ᶜAbdi-Ashirta was not taken with them, and their ships sailed duly out of Egypt. Therefore, they do not fear" (EA 105:18-22; cf. Moran 1987b:300; 1992:178; *CAD* K:472a).

**rağāṣu* (*raḫāṣu*). There are four passages, two in Ugarit and two in Amarna, which attest to a verb probably from the root **rğṣ* (Sivan 1984:160 n. 13, and 264). The meaning is "to smash." The Hebrew and Aramaic reflexes are **rṣṣ* and **rᶜᶜ* respectively (Rainey 1979:158-161). What leads one to think of the D stem is the usage in texts found at Ugarit. Both examples are injunctives, one a true precative and the other a hybrid precative:

> *šum-ma ú-ra še-ra* / *a-na-ku* BA.UG$_7$ *mi-ta-ku* / *ù ša* MÍ*Ku-ba-ba* DUMU.MÍ *Ták-a-an* / DAM-*ia iš-tu* ŠEŠ-*ia* / ›*ša*‹ *i-ḫu-uz-ši* / dIŠKUR *li-ra-ḫi-iṣ-šu* / GIŠGU.ZA *la ú-ra-bi* / É.ḪÁ *la i-ši-ib* / dIŠKUR EN ḪUR.SAG *Ḫa-zi* / *li-ra-ḫi-iṣ-šu* "If in the future I die, then as for the one who has taken Kubaba, daughter of Takᵓan, my wife, from my brother, may Baal smash him, (may) he not magnify (his) throne, may (his) palace not flourish — may Baal, lord of Mount Khazi smash him!" (RS 16.144:4-13; Nougayrol 1955:76);

and also:

> *šum-ma i-na-an-din* DINGIR.MEŠ *a-na* ŠU-*ti-ni* / *ù lu-ú ni-ra-aḫ-ḫi-iṣ* UZUDUR-*šu i-na* KI-*ti*!(BAR) / *ù i-gám-me-ru-ni*$_7$

I-*en še-ra-ni-ia* "If the god gives (him) into our hand, then we will verily smash his *face*(?) in the earth(?), and my adversaries will be annihilated" (RS 20.33:30-32'; Nougayrol 1968:74).

In view of those passages, it may be tentatively suggested that the following example from Beirut be defined as a hybrid D stem form:

> *ù lu-ú ti-ra-ḫa-aṣ* ERÍN.ḪI.‹A› *pí-ṭá-‹ti›-šu* / *ša* LUGAL EN-*ia* dUTU-*ia* DINGIR.MEŠ-*ia* / UZUSAG.DU LÚ.MEŠ*a-ia-bi-šu* "and may the army of the king, my lord, my sun god, my deity, smash the head of his enemies" (EA 141:31-33).

The fourth example of this verb is from the suffix conjugation and will be discussed there (cf. *infra*, p. 306).

šaʾālu. The D stem of this verb is extremely rare (*AHw*:1152a). The first to identify D forms in an Amarna text were Albright and Moran (1950:165b). In the tablet that they were discussing (EA 89), it is most likely that the scribe considered all of his forms of this verb as D, with *-a-* as well as with *-i-* thematic vowel:

> *i-na-na la-a* ⸢*yi*⸣*-ša-a-lu šàr-ru* / *a-na ḫa-za-*⸢*ni*⸣*-šu a-na a-ḫi-ia yi‹-iš-me›* LUGAL *a-wa-te-ia* / *ú-ul* ⸢*ki*⸣-⸢*na*⸣ *a-wa!*(NA)*-ti-šu-nu* / *šum-ma šàr-ru yi-ša-i-lu* / *ù na-*⸢*ad*⸣*-na pa-ni-nu a-na a-ra-di-ka* "Now the king does not inquire concerning the city ruler, concerning my brother(-in-law). May the king h‹eed› my words. Their words are not true, 'If the king inquires, then we have set our faces to serve you" (EA 89:12-17); *šum-ma a-na a-ḫi-[ia]* / *yi-ša-i-lu šàr-ru . . . ù šum-ma a-na a-ḫi-ia* / *ti-ša-i-lu ù ta-aq-bu* / URU *an-nu-ú la-a ḫa-za-nu ša-al* / *šàr-ru* UGU-*šu . . . šum-ma a-na ḫa-za-ni* URU*Ṣur-ri* / *la-a yi-ša-i-lu šàr-ru* "If concerning [my] brother(-in-law) the king should inquire . . . and if concerning my brother(-in-law) you should inquire, then the city will say 'This is not the city ruler. Inquire, oh king, concerning him' . . . Will the king not inquire concerning the

> city ruler of Tyre?" (EA 89:33-34, 39-42, 44-45; Albright and Moran 1950:164).

It must be admitted, however, that the presence of a G imperative in line 41 weighs somewhat against the view that the prefix forms are D stem. The G imperative was undoubtedly a widely used form, in writing as well as in speech. Therefore, the thematic *-i-* on all the prefix forms but one can best be explained by assuming hybridization following the pattern of the D stem. All of the prefix forms in question here are WS imperfect, with the expected *-u* suffix. Syntactically, they are all found in the protases of conditional sentences.

šâṭu, šuṭṭu. The only D stem attestations for this verb are from EA 333 (cf. *AHw*:1205a) as discovered by Albright (Albright 1942b:33 n. 8, 35 n. 19). There is one 3rd m.pl. WS imperfect:

> *lu-ú ti-i-de i-nu-ma / tu-ša-ṭú-na* ^{I}DI.KUD.⸢^{d}⸣⸢IŠKUR⸣ / *ù* ^{I}*Zi-im-re-da / pu-uḫ-ri-iš* "May you be apprised that Shipṭi-Baal and Zimredda have behaved in a treasonous manner together" (EA 333:4-7).

Then we have a form that could either be Akkadian 3rd m.s. present-future or WS preterite (with -Ø prefix):

> *ša ú-ša-aṭ mil-ka* / [^{I}]*Pa-a-pu ù uš-ši-ir-*⸢*šu*⸣ / [*a-n*]*a pa-ni-ia* "The one who is/has been behaving/behaved treacherously is Pāpu, so send him to me" (EA 333:21-23).

AHw:1205a takes these forms as Gp but that is hardly likely since one of them clearly has an accusative, *mil-ka.*

The third form in this epistle, *šu-uṭ mu-ul-ka,* remains enigmatic. It could be a G imperative but Albright had proposed to see in it a gerund or "construct infinitive." The main drawback of Albright's suggestion is that *mulka* is in the accusative while the dependent case would be more proper for the object of a nominal form.

ṭarādu, ṭurrudu. While the G stem of this verb means "to send," the D means "to drive out, expel" (*AHw*:1381a). Unlike the OB letters, which employ *ṭarādu* as a standard word for sending, the Amarna archive has only two attestations. Obviously, *wuššuru* has taken the place of G stem *ṭarādu* while the D stem functions were more often fulfilled by *dubburu*. One of the Amarna examples is 1st c.s. G preterite (EA 62:38) while the other is 3rd m.s. D preterite:

> *i-nu-ma yi-mur* LÚŠEŠ-*ia i-nu-ma / a-ṣí* LÚDUMU *šìp‹-ri›-ia ri-qa-mi / i-ia-nu* ERÍN.MEŠ *ma-ṣa-ar-ta*$_5$ *it-ti-šu / ù ia-an-aṣ-ni ù ki-na-an-na / yi-pu-uš ar-na ù yu-ṭá-ri-id-ni / iš-tu* URU-*li*KI "When my brother saw that my ambassador came forth (from Egypt) empty-handed, no garrison troops being with him, then he scorned me and committed treason and expelled me from the city" (EA 137:20-25).

THE Dt STEM

Among the Amarna letters from Canaan, one does not find any examples of the Dt stem serving as the passive of the D stem. This remarkable departure from good Akkadian practice can be accounted for by the presence in West Semitic of a Dp conjugation (cf. *infra*, pp. 179-180). Even the number of D stem preterites with infixed *-t-* are extremely limited, mainly confined to a few possible forms from *turru* (cf. *supra*, pp. 154-157) and *wuššuru*. These latter will be dealt with here since they may reflect a special usage and not be preterites at all.

Some of the *wuššuru* forms with infixed *-t-* are clearly future in meaning and cannot, therefore, reflect the Akkadian *-t-* preterite. Some of the examples have a geminated infix, *-tt-*, possibly by analogy with the G stem where Ist waw verbs have forms like 3rd m.s. *it-tab-lu* (EA 29:23) and *it-ta-ša-ab* (EA 29:154). The most striking feature in some cases is the use of an *-a-* thematic vowel! This theme could only represent the present-future of the Akkadian Dt! The crucial passage for our discussion is the following:

ù yi-iq-bi a-na ia-a-[-ši] / i-na-mí SÀG [GIŠ]MÁ \ *a-na-yi / ú-ta-aš-ša-ru-uš-šu / a-na šàr-ri* "And he said to me, 'In a ship I will send him away to the king'" (EA 245:27-30).

This 1st c.s. form, *ú-ta-aš-ša-ru-uš-šu,* not only has the *-a-* theme, it also has the WS imperfect suffix, *-u,* and probably the imperfect energic *-n*(*a*) assimilated to the *š* of the accusative suffix (Rainey 1976b:338-339). The transitive meaning precludes any thought of the passive Dt. Therefore, if one can assign any meaning at all to the infix, it must be separative. Therefore, we have translated "send him *away.*"

The same epistle has three examples of *wuššuru* with infixed *-t-* that are clearly preterites. They are all written with the SAR sign, most naturally rendered *šar,* but admittedly, it could be transcribed $šir_9$ (von Soden and Röllig 1976:35, No. 184). The particular contexts are:

ù yi-íl-qé-šu / [I]šú-ra-ta ù yu-ta-šar-šu / iš-tu [URU]*Ḫi-na-tu-na*[KI] */ a-na* É*-šu . . . ù [I]šú-ra-ta yu-ta-šar / [I]La-ab-a-ia ù [I]šú-ra-ta / yu-ta-šar-mí* [I]IŠKUR*-me-ḫér / a-na* É*-šu-ni* "So Surata took him and he released him from Hannathon to his home . . . so Surata released Labʾayu and Surata released Baal-meher to their home" (EA 245:30-33, 41-45).

This is one of the few contexts where the original Akkadian meaning, "to release," is appropriate. It deals with a prisoner from whom a ransom was accepted in order to set him free. As mentioned above, one could transcribe the three verbs in question: *yu-ta-šir₉-šu, yu-ta-šir₉,* and *yu-ta-šir₉-mí* respectively. That would permit the assumption that the scribe was simply using the Akkadian D preterite with infix *-t-* as his theme.

The same could be said for the 1st c.s. preterites in one of the Alashia letters:

ù a-nu-ma ut-ta-šir₉ / [LÚ]DUMU *ši-ip-ri-ia a-na maḫ-ri-ka₄ / ù al-lu-ú ut-ta-šir₉-ka / i-na qa-ti* [LÚ]DUMU *ši-ip-‹ri-›ia a-na ka-ta₅ . . . ut-ta-šir₉ / [i-na qa-ti* [LÚ]DUMU *š]ip-ri-ia* "And now I have sent my ambassador to you and, behold, I have sent to you by the hand of my ambas‹sa›dor . . . I have sent [by the hand of] my [am]bassador" (EA 34:14-17, 30-31).

Furthermore, there are some 1st c.s. preterites with unmistakable *-i-* thematic vowels. One of them, *[ut-t]a-še-er* (EA 173:14), is in a broken context. However, the other, from Byblos, is clear:

LÚ-*ia ut-ta-ši-ir a-na ma*[*-ḫa*]*r* / EN-*ia* "I have sent my man to my lord" (EA 83:10).

Finally, there is a 1st c.s. form with *-e-* thematic vowel that has definite present-future meaning. It has the WS imperfect energic suffix plus a 3rd m.pl. accusative suffix pronoun. The context and the WS modal suffix eliminate any possibility of this form being preterite. Furthermore, there is no resemblance to the Akkadian function of the *-t-* preterite with *anumma* (*contra* Wilhelm 1982:124 n. 8, who cited Heimpel and Guidi 1969 for support).

ù / *ti₇-iq-ta-bi* / *a-nu-ma i-na* ŠU-⸢*ti*⸣/ LÚ*ṣú-ḫa-ri-ia* / *ut-ta-aš-še-ru-un-na-šu-nu* "And you said (each time), 'Now I am sending them by the hand of my servant'" (KL 72:600:4-8).

Although the preceding verb is probably iterative (Rainey 1976:338), the geminated infix in *ut-ta-aš-še-ru-un-na-šu-nu* cannot possibly have that meaning. Since the passive and the preterite are also ruled out, the only possible nuance for the infix would be the separative. This context is not as clear cut as EA 245:27-30 cited above because of the *-e-* theme. Nevertheless, the frequent use of the ventive with D stem forms of *wuššuru* is suggestive. If the scribes knew that *wuššuru* could have a special nuance with the ventive, then perhaps some of them also felt that the infixed *-t-* could have the separative function. This would create a situation similar to that of normal Akkadian verbs of motion. On them the ventive directs the action towards the speaker while the infixed *-t-* directs it away from some reference point.

THE Dp STEM

Some passive forms from *wuššuru* were recognized by the pioneer scholars in EA 126 (Böhl 1909:61; Ebeling 1910:59-60; Dhorme 1913:383 = 1951:420). However, they did not classify them as specifically D stem, probably because they were not sure that *wuššuru* did not function in the G. Furthermore, they may not have realized just how much of a departure from normal Akkadian this would be. The first of these two passages is as follows:

> *ù pa-na-nu / a-na* LÚ*a-bu-ti-ia yu-ša-ru / iš-tu* É.GAL.MEŠ KÙ.BABBAR / *ù mi-im-mu a-na ba-la-ṭì-šu-‹nu› / ù yu-ši-ru be-li* ERÍN.MEŠ / *a-na ša-a-šu-nu / ù a-nu-ma / a-na-ku aš-pu-ru a-na be-li-ia a-na* ERÍN.MEŠ *ù* ERÍN.MEŠ *ma-ṣa-ar-tu / la-a tu-[ša-ru] ù mi-im-mu [la-a-]mi / yu-da-nu [a-na]* ⌜*ia*⌝*-a-ši* "but formerly to my ancestors there were being sent money and material for the‹ir› sustenance and my lord was sending troops to them. But now I write to my lord for troops and a garrison is not s[ent] nor is material given to me" (EA 126:18-23).

The first verb, *yu-ša-ru,* is 3rd m.s. because *kaspū u mimmû* are treated as a hendiadys like *mimmâ u balāṭa* in line 15 (Moran 1950a:174); the imperfect mode (with *-u*) after *panānu* reflects continuous or iterative action in the past (Moran 1950a:43-47). The correct rendering of the 3rd f.s. *tu-[ša-ru]* was also seen my Moran (1950a:174).

The second context, in the same epistle, is also in the negative; the form is 3rd m.s. for the collective ERÍN.MEŠ (Moran 1950a:131 n. 163):

> ERÍN.MEŠ *la-a yu-ša-r[u] / ù* LÚDUMU *ši-ip-*⌜*ri*⌝*[-ia] / la-a tu-ša-ṣu-na* "A force is not give[n] and my ambassador you/they are not sending forth" (EA 129:40-43).

The second verb is considered either a plural of majesty or a 2nd m.s. imperfect energic (Moran 1950a:62-63). It would be especially interesting if it were 3rd m.pl. imperfect (active) with an impersonal subject. The latter would signify another means of expressing the passive.

Since these were passives of the short form of *wuššuru,* they could not be of much help in determining the vocalization of the Canaanite D passive in strong verbs. The *yuššaru* forms looked just like the Gp *yuppaš-* forms. The letter from Kâmid el-Lôz cited in the discussion of the Dt also provided the solution to the Dp vocalization:

> *ù ú-ul tu-wa-aš-ša-ru-na / ú-nu-tu*MEŠ*-šu / qi-bi ù lu-ú tu-wa-aš-ša-ru-na ú-nu-tu*MEŠ*-šu* "But his implements are not sent! Speak that his implements be sent!" (KL 72:600:9-13).

It was the nominative *ú-nu-tu*MEŠ*-šu* plus the exact parallel with a known Gp verb that clinched the interpretation of *tu-wa-aš-ša-ru-na* as Dp 3rd m.pl. imperfect. That parallel was:

> *ù qi-bi ù lu-ú tu-ud-da-nu-*⌈*na*⌉ "So speak that they be given" (KL 72:600:19-21).

These two constructions are remarkable for their use of the indicative to express purpose after an imperative. With active verbs, the jussive or the volitive would surely have been used (Moran 1950a:81-88, especially 87). The latter passage, with *lū tuddanūna,* brings to mind a similar use of the same verb after *lū* in a Taanach letter (TT 2:19-20; Rainey 1976:340).

Now, *tu-wa-aš-ša-ru-na* can be legitimately used as evidence for the original Canaanite D passive vocalization of the suffix conjugation. That form was *tuqaṭṭalūna.* The discovery of this isogloss with Classical Arabic marks another milestone in the comparative linguistics of the West Semitic dialects.

CHAPTER VIII

PREFIX CONJUGATION — Š AND H

In contrast to the many D stem verbs used by the Canaanite scribes, there is a relative paucity of Š stem forms. One underlying reason that comes to mind is that the Š stem was probably missing in Canaanite (like Phoenician, Hebrew, Moabite). Still, these scribes were using Akkadian as their base language, so it is not surprising that some Š stem forms do occur. For easy reference, the verbs discussed will be listed with by the G infinitive followed by that of the Š.

Š STEM CAUSATIVES

erēbu / šūrubu. Two examples come from the Jerusalem letters, where the prefix verbs are basically Akkadian, usually present-future. In this case, however, the Akkadian preterite is employed instead of a suffix conjugation form for the past tense, perhaps because of the "literary" nature of the passage, i.e. a translation of an Egyptian idiom:

> *zu-ru-uḫ šàr-ri* KAL.GA / *ú-še-ri-ba-an-ni a-na* É ^{LÚ}*a-bi-ia* "The mighty arm of the king has installed me in my father's house" (EA 286:12-13).

Another form (3rd m.pl.?), *ú-še-ru-bu* (EA 287:11), is in a broken context; it appears to be present-future with Assyrian vowel harmony (‹ *ušērabū;* Moran 1975b:153). From Tyre comes another broken passage, [*ú*]-*še-ri-ib-ka* (EA 149:33). Finally, one Canaanite text has a form that looks like a hybrid based on the Š infinitive (*šūrub-*):

> [*t*]*u-šu-r*[*u*]*-ba-ni* / *a-na* URU.DIDLI.KI-*ni*-[*i*]*a* "(May) [yo]u reinstall me in [m]y cities" (EA 300:18-19).

târu / **šutūru*. Only in the Amarna letters from Canaan do we find a few Š forms from this verb (*AHw:1336*a; Youngblood 1961:244). There are imperatives (EA 83:23; KL 74:300:15), a hybrid infinitive (EA 108:49), a 3rd f.s. suffix form (EA 280:14), and two prefix forms based on the theme of the hybrid infinitive, *šu-te-er* (EA 108:49). One of them is 3rd m.s. imperfect:

> *ù la-a* ›⌈*ep*⌉‹ / *ep-pu-šu mi-im-ma a-*⌈*di*⌉ / *yu-šu-*⌈*te*⌉*ru* LUGAL *a-wa-ta*$_5$ / *a-na* ÌR-*šu* "But I will not do anything until the king sends word back to his servant" (EA 280:37-39).

The second form is a jussive:

> *ù* NU-*id a-na* [I]*Re-a-na-ap* / [LÚ]MAŠKÍM *ù yu-šu-te-er* / URU.KI *i-na qa-te-ia ù* / *ú-še*$_{20}$*-šu-ru a-na pa-ni* / ERÍN.MEŠ *pí-ṭá-at* LUGAL EN-ia "So command Reᶜ-anap, my commissioner, that he may return my city to my charge; then I will make the preparations for the regular army of the king, my lord" (EA 292:36-40).

(*w*)*abālu* / *šūbulu*. The Š of this verb is known from the letters outside Canaan, e.g. from Egypt (EA 367:3; 369:3; 370:3), Alashia (EA 35:20; 40:15), but only appears twice in the Canaanite texts. One instance demonstrates how a scribe could use an Akkadianism that he had apparently learned in school. The form has the *š* › *l* shift and is in a clause dependent on a noun in construct:

> *a-wa-at ul-te-bi-la* / LUGAL EN-*ia* DINGIR.MEŠ-*ia* / [d]UTU-*ia a*[*-n*]*a ia-ši* / *a-nu-um-ma i-šu-ši-ru-šu* / *a-na* ⌈LUGAL⌉ EN-*ia* "As for the word which the king, my lord, has sent to me, now I am arranging it for the king, my lord" (EA 267:9-13).

The other passage is in a Rib-Haddi letter. The scribe employed the SI sign with the value *šé*, an unusual but not unknown value here (EA 77:8; 84:26; Youngblood 1961:318). That orthography misled Ebeling (1910:43) into thinking that this was an example of *št* › *ss*, i.e. *yussēbila* ‹ *yuštēbila*. Such a shift and such a spelling are unwarranted. The passage is not without difficulties but it is possible to suggest several improvements in the reading and the interpretation:

> *šá-ni-tam a-wi-* / *la yu-šé-bi-la be-li a-na* ÌR-*š*[*u!*] / *ki-ma ar-ḫi-iš a-na* MAŠKÍM! *ù na-*‹*ṣa*›*-ri* ›U[RU]‹ / URU.KI *a-na ša-šu ù bal-*‹*ṭá*›*-ti* "Furthermore, may my lord send a man to h[is] servant in a hurry as commissioner(!) and (to) guard the city for him so that I may l‹i›ve" (EA 88:34-39; cf. Moran 1950a:160; 1987b:276 n. 10; 1992:161 n. 12; Youngblood 1961:318).

(*w*)*aṣû* / *šūṣû*. Only one example comes from a Canaanite text. To understand the context, one should remember that in Egyptian, "to go in," means to enter Egypt (to visit the palace) while "to go out, to come forth," means "to leave Egypt." The form in question may be either 2nd m.s. imperfect energic, 2nd m.pl. (of "majesty"), or 3rd m.pl. imperfect:

> *ù a*[*l-lu uš-ši-ir*]*-~~ti~~* / LÚDUMU *ši-*‹*ip*›*-ri-ia a-n*[*a* LUGAL *b*]*e-li-ia* / ERÍN.MEŠ *la-a yu-ša-r*[*u*] / *ù* LÚDUMU *ši-ip-r*[*i-ia*] / *la-a tu-ša-ṣú-na* "And be[hold] I have [sent] my ambassador t[o the king] my [l]ord; an army is not being sent and [my] ambassador you/they are not sending forth" (EA 126:38-42).

Š STEM FACTITIVES

The three verbs treated in this section are stative in the G stem. The Š stem means to "cause (someone) to enter (the particular state of being)." All of them also have D stem causatives in Akkadian.

balāṭu / *šubluṭu*. The D stem is used extensively in the Amarna texts from Canaan, usually with the meaning, "to furnish supplies" (cf. *supra*, pp. 138-140). The Š stem is unique to the Amarna texts (*CAD* B:63a) and is only documented for this one passage:

at-tu-nu tu-ša-ab-li-ṭú-na-nu / *ù at-tu-nu* / \ *ti-mi-tu-na-nu* "You (pl.) give us life and you(pl.) give us death" (EA 238:31-33; Moran 1987b:464; 1992:95).

ḫalāqu / *šuḫluqu*. The regular causative for this verb is in the D stem. The Š stem is documented in the meaning "to help to escape," but only in NA and NB. The Š stem does not carry the meaning "to destroy," but that idea can be expressed by the ŠD stem. The Št stem means "to cause permanent damage" (*CAD* Ḫ:39b-40a; *AHw*:311a). The one Amarna example is in a letter from Kedesh on the Orontes which has typical WS features. Semantically, the Š stem form under discussion here expresses the same nuance as the D stem examples in other letters, viz. "to cause (lands, cities, etc.) to be lost to Egyptian control" (Moran 1987b:429 n. 2 and 289 n. 1; 1992:270 n. 2 and 170 n. 1). This explicit context makes that meaning perfectly clear:

ur-ru-du LUGAL EN-*ia ù gáb-bi* KUR.[MEŠ-*ka*] / *ú-ša-aḫ-li-iq* ^{I}*Bir*$_5$*-ia-wa-za* "I serve the king, my lord, but Biryawaza is causing all [your] land[s] to fall away" (EA 189:24-25).

Biryawaza was known as an important commissioner in the Lebanese Beqa^c Valley. In the preceding sections of the letter, he had been accused by Etakkama, ruler of Kedesh, of turning loyal city states over to the *^{c}apîru* men. These latter people were so designated precisely because they were reputedly not acknowledging Egyptian authority.

pašāḫu / *šupšuḫu*. The Š stem is widely used in Akkadian as well as the D (*AHw*:840-841). The Byblos letters make frequent use of the Š imperative (EA 74:59; 113:33; 121:50; 132:59). There are two 3rd m.s. prefix forms, both of them in purpose clauses. One is an imperfect virtually dependent on another imperfect to express purpose (Moran 1950a:81; 1951:33):

a-di [*y*]*i-du šàr-ru* / *a-*[*n*]*a* KUR.MEŠ-*šu ù yu-wa-ši-ru* / ERÍN.MEŠ *pí-ṭá-ti-šu ù* / *yu-ša-ap-ši-ḫu* KUR.MEŠ-*šu* "Until the king takes heed to his territories and sends his army in order to pacify his territories" (EA 112:34-39).

The other is a jussive virtually dependent on another injunctive (either volitive or jussive):

ù / yu-wa-ši-ra šàr-ru ⸢ERÍN⸣.MEŠ-*šu / pí-ṭá-ti*[-*š*]*u / ù yu-ša-ap-ši-iḫ* KUR-*šu* "So may the king send his troops, his regulars, that he may pacify his land" (EA 118:41-44).

**šḫḫn*. The verb forms appearing to have this root were evidently generated in Hurrian speaking areas from *šukēnu*, ""to prostrate oneself" (*GAG*:158, §109m; *AHw*:1263). The phenomenon appears, for example, at Nuzi. The examples with infixed *-t-*, which all have an *i-* prefix, were discussed in Chapter V on the Gt (cf. *supra*, pp. 109-110). All the forms in question (with and without *-t-*) are known in the Amarna archive only from texts written in Canaan. In addition, there are a few examples from Ugarit and Hattusas (*AHw*:1293). When there is no infixed *-t-*, the verb is treated as a quadriconsonantal of the Š class, hence their inclusion here. The ubiquitous parallels in the "obeisance formulae," usually with *amqut* "I have fallen down," etc., explain the selection of the root **šḫḫn* "to get low." The forms with the infixed *-t-* may have some reflexive nuance. The other attested forms are all 1st c.s. preterites in one of three orthographies: *uš-ḫé-ḫi-in* (EA 221:7; 232:9; 233:13; 234:9; 366:9), *uš-ḫé-ḫi-in*$_4$ (EA 223:6; 242:8; probably also EA 214:6), and *uš-ḫe-ḫi-in*$_4$ (EA 22:9); note also the defective *ḫé-ḫi-in*$_4$ (EA 235:9). Only one representative passage will be cited here; it is particularly noteworthy for its explicit description of the process of doing obeisance:

um-ma [I]*Sú-ra-ta* / LÚ [URU]*Ak-ka* ÌR *ša šàr-ri / ep-ru ša* GÌR.MEŠ-*šu ù qa-qa-ru ša ka-ba-ši-šu / a-na* GÌR.MEŠ LUGAL EN-*ia* / [d]UTU *iš-tu ša-me-e / 7-šu 7-ta-a-an / uš-ḫé-ḫi-in / i-na pa-an-te-e \ ba-aṭ-nu-ma / ù ṣi-ru-ma \ ṣú-ú*ʾ*-ru-ma* "Thus (said) Surata, ruler of Acco, the servant of the king, the dirt under his feet and the

> ground of his tread, 'At the feet of the king, my lord, the sun god from heaven, seven times (and) seven times I have gone low, on the stomach and on the back'" (EA 233:3-11).

SPECIAL LEXICAL MEANINGS

The two verbs discussed in this section have special lexical meanings attached to the Š stem. These are semantic functions known throughout the Akkadian dialects and evidently learned by the Canaanite scribes.

ešēru / šūšuru / šutēšuru. Ebeling (1915:1383-1384) had originally confused these Š forms with *(w)ašāru / wuššuru.* The special semantic nuance reflected in the Amarna tablets is common to OA and OB (*CAD* E:358) but it is not the only meaning for the Š of this verb. The fundamental idea, from the verb, *ešēru* "to be straight, is "to make (something / someone) go / be straight." The developed meaning is "to put in order, to prepare." The passages are usually replies to an order from pharaoh to make ready for the arrival of the Egyptian army by getting together supplies and men. When the writer wished to state that his preparations were completed, he used a hybrid form of the suffix conjugation (cf. *infra,* pp. 313-314). But when he meant to say that he was engaged in such preparations, he used a West Semitic imperfect of the prefix conjugation. In either case, the replies were 1st c.s. There is one example of an Assyrianized present-future theme, viz. *ú-še$_{20}$-šu-ru* ‹ **ušeššaru* (EA 292:39). The text was discussed above (cf. *supra,* p 182). Otherwise, the theme is usually from the Š preterite; typical examples of the "correct" orthography are these general statements:

> *gáb-bi mi-im-mi / ša yi-qa-bu / šàr-ru be-lí / ú-še-ši-ru-mi* "Everything that the king, my lord, says, I am preparing" (EA 223:7-10; probably also EA 233:18-20; 247:19).

But the following passage illustrates the contrast between the imperfect in present time and the preterite in past time:

LÚDUMU *ši-ip-ri* / *ša* LUGAL EN-*ia* / *ša iš-tap-r-an-n*[*i*] / *iš-te₉-me a-wa-te*M[EŠ-*š*]*u* / *ma-gal ma-gal* / *ù a-nu-ma* / *ú-še-ši-ru-mì* / *ki-ma ša qa-bi-šu* "As for the ambassador of the king, my lord, that he sent to me, I have heeded [h]is words very diligently and now I am making preparations according to what he said" (EA 329:13-20; cf. also EA 302:11-18).

Then we have several hybrid forms with *i-* prefix attached to a theme that resembles that used for the suffix conjugation, i.e. **šūšir* / **šūšer* (cf. Izreʾel 1978b:74-75 and *infra*, pp. 313-314):

a-wa-at iš-⌈*tap*⌉*-pár* / LUGAL EN-*ia* DINGIR.MEŠ-*ia* / dUTU-*ia* *a-na ia-ši* / *a-nu-ma i-šu-ši-ru-šu* / *a-na* LUGAL EN-*ia* "As for the thing that the king, my lord, my deity, my sun god, wrote to me, now I am preparing it for the king, my lord" (EA 277:8-12; also EA 267:12 [*supra*, p. 182]; 276:12; 278:12; and without accusative suffix: EA 216:10; 226:15; 316:23; 325:20); *a-wu-ut iq-ba*(sic!)*-bi* / [LU]GAL EN-*ia* / [DINGIR].MEŠ-*ia* dUTU-*ia* / [*a-n*]*a ia-ši i-šu-še-ru-šu* / [*a-na*] LUGAL EN-*ia* "As for the thing that the [ki]ng, my lord, my [dei]ty, my sun god, said [t]o me, I am preparing it [for] the king, my lord" (EA 275:9-14; Moran 1987b:499; 1992:319).

Finally, *CAD* E:359a assigns a special Amarna meaning to two forms with infixed *-t-*. These are subsumed under a unique category of *šūtešuru*, signifying "to dispatch." One of these examples is a precative in an Alashia letter which does not show WS grammatical features:

ù e-ni-in₄-na ŠEŠ-*ia* ⌈DUMU⌉? [*ši-ip-*]*r*[*i-i*]*a* / *ḫa-mu-ta li-iš-t*[*e-š*]*i-ra-a*[*m-m*]*a* / *šu-ul-ma-na ša* ⌈ŠEŠ⌉-[*i*]*a* / *lu-uš-a-al* "So now, may my brother dispatch my ⌈ambassador⌉ quickly that I may inquire about my brother's welfare" (EA 37:13-15; cf. Moran 1987b:205 nn. 5-6; 1992:110 nn. 5-6).

The other example is in an epistle from Beirut. In spite of the broken context, the meaning seems fairly certain:

> [*iš-te-m*]*e a-wa-te*^{MEŠ} DUB *ša uš-te*₉-⌈*šir*₄⌉-*šu* / [*a-na ia-ši*] LUGAL EN-*ia* "[I have hear]d the words of the tablet which the king, my lord, has dispatched [to me] (EA 142:6-7; compare the suggestion by Moran 1987b:373 n. 1; 1992:229 n. 2).

It is hard to say, on the basis of these two examples, but it would appear that the infix *-t-* here must have had separative force. If so, this is then the only lexical Št verb used in the Canaanite Amarna letters.

ezēbu / *šūzubu*. Besides the various causative nuances of the Š stem related to the G stem meaning of "to leave, to abandon," etc., this verb has a specialized Š stem semantic function. It is the meaning, "to deliver, to save" (*CAD* E:424-425; *AHw*:264b). The most prevalent verb expressing this meaning in the Canaanite Amarna letters is G stem *ekēmu*, but there are four prefix examples and three imperatives from *šūzubu*. The imperatives are all Assyrian in form (EA 62:30; 318:8, 14). Two of the prefix forms are in relative clauses from the same Byblos letter. Both of them are 3rd m.s. without the *y*- prefix, which suggests that they derive from a corpus of learned expressions (especially relative clauses); their orthographies do look, in fact, like Akkadianisms. The theme for both forms has been vocalized here as present-future (reading *ze* instead of *zi*):

> AŠ É.NIN.IB *pu-ḫu-ru-nim-mi ù* / *ni-ma-qú-ut* UGU ^{URU}*Gub-la šum-ma ia-*[*nu*] / LÚ-*LIM ša ú-še*₂₀*-ze-bu-ši*ₓ(ŠE) *iš-tu qa-ti-n*[*u*] "In Bīt-NINIB assemble ye that we may attack Byblos; behold, there is no man who can deliver it from our grasp" (EA 74:30-31; Moran 1953:78 n. 4; 1987b:252 nn. 9-11; 1992:144 nn. 9-11); *ù ki-na-na pa-al-ḫa-ti ma-gal ma-gal* ›*i-nu-ma*‹ / [*i*]*-nu-ma ia-nu* LÚ *ša ú-še-ze-ba-an-ni* / [*iš*]*-tu qa-ti-šu-nu* "So thus I am very much afraid since there is no one who can deliver me from their hand" (EA 74:43-45).

Note that the first form, *ušezzebuši*, could be Akkadian subjunctive in a relative clause introduced by *ša*, but that would be practically unique in these texts. Instead, we prefer to see the WS imperfect. The second form has its accusative suffix attached by means of the ventive morpheme.

The 2nd m.s. form is in a passage from a letter by Dagān-takala, whose texts are more N. Syrian in style than they are Canaanite (Artzi 1968). The same text has two of the Assyrian style imperatives; the finite form is vocalized here as present-future, though the context seems to require the WS jussive. Its accusative suffix is attached by means of the ventive, which is typical of the Š forms of this verb in the corpus of texts from this area:

> *ù at-*⌈*ta*⌉ LUGAL GAL / *be-li-ia* / *tu-še-ze-ba-an-ni* / *ù i-na-ba-a-a*[*t*] / *a-na* LUGAL GAL *be-li-ia* "So thou, (O) great king, my lord, deliver me that I may esca[pe] to the great king, my lord" (EA 318:18-22; Artzi 1968:170; contrast the rendering of Moran 1987b:542 and n. 4; 1992:350 n. 4).

The final example also comes from a text that is hardly West Semitic in its flavor. The context seems to require a preterite but the form has gemination of the second radical as if it were an Akkadian present-future. However, when we note that the imperative also has gemination it becomes obvious that this is merely an orthographic or phonetic feature and not a tense determinant.

> *ù iq-bu-ni*$_7$ *šu-nu a-na ia-ši* / *še-ez-zi-bá-an-na-ši-mi iš-tu* ŠU-*ti* / ERÍN.MEŠ URU*Še-eḫ-la-li*KI *ù ú-še-ez-zi-*[*bá-š*]*u-nu* / *iš-tu* ŠU-*ti* ERÍN.MEŠ URU*Še-eḫ-la-li*KI "So they said to me, 'Deliver us from the hand of the troops of Sheᶜlalu,' so I deliver[ed th]em from the hand of the troops of Sheᶜlalu" (EA 62:29-32; cf. the remarks of Izreᵓel, who does not deal with the gemination, 1985:76, 168, *8; 1991a:278, 309).

This is a narrative of a past event that began with a preterite verb, *iq-bu-ni*$_7$ "they said . . . ." The context thus demands that the form *ú-še-ez-zi-*[*bá-š*]*u-nu* be interpreted as a preterite. Since this is an

Amurru text, its use of the verb form in question must be judged in the light of the practices in that corpus.

CANAANITE H STEM FORMS

There are a few prefix forms that have been interpreted as Canaanite H stem causatives (Sivan 1984:174-176). Although some of them are surely Canaanite causative forms, they each reflect problems of orthography and morphology. It is, therefore, impossible to achieve a clear diachronic interpretation of the H stem in 14th century Canaanite.

ḫlq. This root is common to Akkadian and WS. The 3rd m.s. transitive *ya-aḫ-li-qú* "that he should lose" (EA 254:9) might be WS H stem (cf. *supra*, p. 53).

**mwt*. The example from this root is the most certain of all. The passage has already been cited above because of the parallelism with an Š stem formation of *balāṭu* (cf. *supra*, pp. p. 184). It will be useful to cite it again:

> *at-tu-nu tu-ša-ab-li-ṭú-na-nu* / *ù at-tu-nu* / \: *ti-mi-tu-na-nu* "You (pl.) give us life and you(pl.) give us death" (EA 238:31-33; Moran 1987b:464 n. 2; cf. Moran 1992:295 n. 2; Rainey 1989-90:68a).

The context and the orthography leave no room for doubt that we have here a 2nd m.pl. Canaanite H stem form, **timîtûnanû*. The one glaring "problem" is the initial prefix vowel. On comparative grounds (Akkadian and Arabic), we might have expected **tumîtûnanû*. Comparison with Hebrew would have suggested **tamîtûnanû* (‹ **tuhamîtûnanû*). It would appear that we have here a case of assimilation, the prefix vowel assimilating to the long thematic vowel. However, against that notion is the fact that the parallel verb is **tušabliṭūnanu*, with the normal *tu-* prefix. Vowel assimilation, **tuhamîtûnanû* › *timîtûnanû*, seems to be the most sensible solution.

*qll. The causative form from this root appears as a gloss in a Megiddo letter. The Sumerogram, SIG (plus Akkadian 1st c.s. possessive suffix!), corresponds to Akkadian *qatnu, qatānu* (*CAD* Q:163b-164a; 173b-175b) rather than to Akkadian *qalālu* (*CAD* Q:55a). Although the Akkadian D stem, *qullulu*, suits the present context, the orthography of the form in question cannot possibly represent an Akkadian D; there was no justification for classifying our passage under *qullulu* (*CAD* Q:57b). The form as written by the Megiddo scribe can only be that of a Canaanite causative verb (Böhl 1909:64, §32a; Ebeling 1915:1446); the G stem from this root is stative in meaning and built on the *yiqtal* pattern (Rainey 1978a:*9a, 11*a and n. 53). From the Sumerogram (written with the 1st c.s. Akkadian pronominal suffix!) and the context, its meaning is certain:

> *ša-ni-tam mi-na-am-mi ep-ša-ku-mì* / *a-na šàr-ri* EN-*ia* / *i-nu-ma* SIG-*ia* \ *ya-qí-ìl-li-ni* / *ù* DUGUD \ *yu-ka-bi-id* / ŠEŠ.ḪÁ-*ia* *ṣé-eḫ-ru-ta* 5 "Furthermore, what have I done to the king, my lord, that he has belittled me and honored my younger colleagues?" (EA 245:36-40).

A special problem arises from the fact that the prefix is written with the PI sign (wrongly given as *ia-* in *CAD* Q:57b). Under most circumstances, it is notable that scribes use the PI sign when the prefix vowel is either *u* or *i*, not *a*. Of course some *ya-* readings do occur (cf. *supra*, p. 35-36), but they are the rare exceptions. So, in the present case, the form may have been **yuqillini* or **yiqillini* although **yaqillini*, the usual assumption in the literature, is not impossible.

The connecting vowel before the accusative suffix is also something of an enigma. Comparison with the verb in antithetic parallelism, *yu-ka-bi-id*, proves that the tense of both verbs is preterite. Pharaoh had done something, apparently specific, to belittle Biridiya in relation to the other city rulers.

Therefore, **yaqillini*/**yiqillini*/**yuqillini* is based on the *yaqtul* zero form, i.e. the *e*/*i* vowel between the final root consonant and the accusative suffix is anaptyctic, to preserve the gemination of the last radical. Obviously, it could not be *-u* because that would change the tense to imperfect; it could not be *-a* since that would change the tense and mood to volitive. It must have the value of Ø to preresent the preterite.

**rym*. Sivan (1984:157 and n. 13, 164) has dealt with the attestations of this root in PN's from the West Semitic area, especially Ugarit. Because of the presence of so many examples in Ugarit, where Ugaritic does not seem to have an H causative, Sivan has suggested that the actual root was **rym* and not a causative from **rwm*. There is one isolated orthography in a broken context from northern Canaan, viz. *ia-ri-im* (EA 186:77).

**yṣʾ*. There is one gloss from this root which can hardly be anything other than an H causative (Sivan 1984:175):

> *yu-uš-ši-ra* ‹^{I}›^{I}*šàr-ri* / EN-*ia* ERÍN.MEŠ *pí-ṭá-ti* / *ma-aʾ-da ma-gal* / *ù yi-ki-im-ni* / \ *ia-ṣí-ni* "May the king, my lord, send a very large army that he may deliver me (gloss: that he may take me out)" (EA 282:10-14).

The problem here is that, in this form, the prefix syllable is written *ia-* so there is little doubt that the form has to be reconstructed **yaṣiʾnî*. The Hebrew form, *yôṣîʾēnî* (Micah 7:9), harks back to the original **wṣʾ*. If such a form were identical in ancient Canaanite, we would have expected to find a syllabic spelling such as **yu-ṣí-ni* (‹**yawṣiʾnî*). Perhaps we must assume that the Canaanite H causative was based on the biconsonantal root **ṣʾ* This would contrast with the other Semitic languages; even in Arabic, the causative stem of Ist waw verbs is treated as triconsonantal (Fischer 1972:115, §242).

There is one additional form that was at one time interpreted as an H stem from this root:

> *ù ta-aš-ta-ni a-wa-*ta_5 *a-na ia-ši* / *uš-ši-ir-mi* ^{GIŠ}MÁ *a-na* / ^{KUR}*Ia-ri-mu-ta ù ú-ṣa-ka* / KÙ.BABBAR.MEŠ *lu-bu-ši iš-tu ša-šu-nu* "And you have repeatedly said to me, 'Send a ship to

Yarimuta and silver for clothing will *be issued* for you'"
(EA 82:27-30).

Ebeling (1910:64) classed the form, *ú-ṣa-ka,* as a 1st c.s. Canaanite H form and he was followed by Albright and Moran (1948:247) and by Youngblood (1961:232-233), the latter of whom even posits a ventive ending for this Canaanite form! In the final analysis, there are too many anomalies required to make this a 1st c.s. H prefix form. In fact, Moran (1987b:263 and n. 3; 1992:152 n. 3) now favors an Akkadian G present-future.

The context is that of a purpose or result clause after an imperative. We should either have a jussive, a volitive or a suffix form (Moran 1950a:82-86, and 31-34 respectively). Since there is no consonantal prefix and the 1st c.s. seems unwarranted (Amanappa is most probably not in Yarimuta himself), the odds are in favor of a suffix form. Therefore, we propose to see here an Hp 3rd m.s. with KÙ.BABBAR.MEŠ as the subject (in construct with *lu-bu-ši*). In other words, one might reconstruct **(h)ûṣaʾka* ‹ **huwṣaʾka.* The 2nd m.s. suffix pronoun can have dative function, whatever the verb form may be.

Admittedly, an Hp suffix form in a reply from an Egyptian official may tax our credulity. Moran's resort to a simple Akkadian G present-future does have the advantage of simplicity.

CONCLUDING REMARKS

H STEM. Unfortunately, not much can be learned from these forms about the H stem prefix conjugation in Canaanite of the Amarna period.

The three verbs from which we have reconstructed Canaanite forms, viz. *timîtûnanû, *yaqillini / *yiqillini / *yuqillini* and **yaṣiʾnî,* seem to point in different directions. If all of these three verb forms are really H causative, then we have evidence for a prefix *Ci-* in hollow roots beside *Ca-* for Ist waw. From a diachronic point of view, it is difficult to see just where these forms would fit in to the overall WS pattern of causative stems.

The solution may be that an internal Canaanite phonetic tendancy has blurred the picture, e.g. the prefix vowel in *timîtûnanû* might be the result of vowel harmony.

The problems pertaining to the H stem suffix form will be dealt with in a later chapter (cf. *infra,* p. 315).

Š STEM. The question also arises as to whether there may be evidence here for the presence of a real Š stem in the WS mother tongue of the scribes. The Š stem verb forms treated above are all of truly Akkadian verbs. Some are from high-frequency expressions (e.g. the forms of *šūzubu*). An innovation, such as the Š of *târu,* is more likely a simple construction devised by local scribes rather than some hint of an underlying WS Š verb. Under the present circumstances, it seems unlikely that the S dialect spoken by the scribes of these letters possesed a Š stem like Ugaritic.

The Š stem suffix conjugation forms are discussed above (cf. *infra* pp. 312-315).

CHAPTER IX

PREFIX CONJUGATION — MOODS AND TENSES

Since the system of modes and tenses reflected in the Amarna letters from Canaan may reflect the true WS pattern of the Late Bronze Age, the question naturally arises: What of the normal Akkadian conjugation patterns which serve to signify various syntactic positions or semantic nuances? Since some of the morphological features identified by Moran as Canaanite are homophonous with verbal suffixes of classical Akkadian, viz. *-u* (like the Akkadian so-called subjunctive) and *-a*(*m*) (like the Akkadian ventive), it will be necessary to play the devil's advocate and to justify the use of such features as Canaanite morphemes rather than as Akkadian.

THE SO-CALLED "SUBJUNCTIVE"

True modality in Akkadian is expressed by various morphosyntactic constructions (Edzard 1973), some of which involve the use of the verbal marker of subordination, *-u* in Babylonian dialects, and (*-u*) + *-ni* in Assyrian (*GAG*:108-109, §83). However, this so-called "subjunctive" marker does not, in itself, express the *subjunctive* nuances of the European or other languages. It is purely a position marker indicating that the clause in which the verb so marked stands happens to be dependent on some element in a main clause. Such subordinated clauses may be dependent on: (1) the relative pronoun *ša;* (2) a subordinating conjunction such as *inūma, adi, ištu et al.;* (3) a substantive in the bound form (construct). Nominal phrases standing in these same syntactic positions are marked by the dependent case (genitive) on the substantive (*GAG:108*, §83a; Adler 1976:64, §48; Edzard 1973:124 n.7). However, there are some truly modal syntagmas in which the *-u* suffix is employed, viz. the positive and negative asseverations (Edzard 1973:129, 132). It will be seen in the ensuing discussion of the Canaanite modal system that other forms, viz. the jussive with -Ø and the volitive with *-a*, serve these same purposes.

PERIPHERAL DIALECTS. Among the various dialects of peripheral Akkadian during the Late Bronze Age, the use of the Akkadian subordination marker is not consistent. The Mitannian letters do show a remarkable degree of uniformity, using the *-u* suffix whenever the rules of Babylonian grammar require it, and not employing it erroneously where it would not belong (Adler 1976:64-66, §48). The chancellory scribes of the Mitannian empire had evidently learned their Babylonian fairly well. In one isolated case, the Assyrian *-ni* appears, viz. *ša i-ra-ʾa-ma-an-ni-ni* "the one who likes me" (EA 17:15). The private archives from Nuzi display some inconsistency in the use or non-use of the *-u* (Gordon 1938:219, §5.10), but the Assyrian *-ni* is almost non-existent (Wilhelm 1970:40, §9; with three examples). At the other end of the Mitannian empire, in Alalakh, the relative clauses (dependent on *ša*) regularly have the proper *-u* suffix (Giacumakis 1970:53, §8.*11*). Circumstantial clauses introduced by *inūma* do not show this consistency. Of course, one of Giacumakis' examples, viz. *ša* . . . *i-il-la-kam* (AT 108:8-10) is invalid because the verb has the ventive which precludes the use of the *-u*! Nevertheless, one may compare *i-nu-ma* . . . *i-ḫi-ir* (AT *409:45) with *i-nu-ma* . . . *i-ḫi-ru* (AT *35:8-12), both meaning "when . . . he chose" (cited Giacumakis 1970:53, §8.*11*, and 62, §10.6, respectively). Both of those examples are date formulae from Stratum VII, dating to the end of the OB period. The inscription on the Idrimi statue often uses the *-u* in main clauses where it should not be (Giacumakis 1970:53, §8.12 for examples). In this case, the explanation of Aro (1954-56:364), viz. that these are mistakes of barbaric Akkadian, seems the most likely.

The same inconsistency, use or misuse of the *-u* marker, is evident in the Akkadian texts from Hattusas (Labat 1932:79-80). The correspondence from Carchemish also shows the lack of *-u* in about half of the instances when it would be expected (Huehnergard 1979:60). It would appear that the grammatical level of the scribes in the Hittite empire was lower than that of their Mitanni predecessors.

The Akkadian texts written by Egyptian scribes, from both the 14th and the 13th centuries B.C.E., usually have the subjunctive when Akkadian grammar would demand it, but there are a few cases, both in the earlier texts (from EA) and the later Ramesside correspondence found at Boghazkoï, where the *-u* is missing (Cochavi-Rainey 1988:191-192, §2.4.9; 1990b:21-22).

The corpus of Amurru letters, which also spans the 14th and the 13th centuries B.C.E., shows no use of the Akkadian subjunctive marker whatever (Izre'el 1985:171, §2.4.4; also 1991a:166, §2.4.4). And note also from Cyprus: *i-nu-ma tu-ša-ab a-na* GIŠGU.ZA / *šàr-ra-⸢ta⸣-ka* "when you take your seat on the throne of your royalty" (EA 34:52-53).

Likewise, the native scribes of Ugarit do not use the subjunctive form in their everyday compositions (letters, economic and legal documents). Only one case of the proper use of the subjunctive is documented (Huehnergard:1979:242-243; 1989:169; cf. van Soldt 1991:440).

Therefore, one must take note of the fact that Levantine scribal traditions, Ugarit and Amurru, show a distinct aversion to the Akkadian marker of subordination. While other peripheral areas, e.g. Nuzi, Alalakh, Carchemish, Hattusas, Egypt, reveal that the scribes were familiar with the function of the Akkadian *-u* suffix, they were somewhat lax in employing it. With this background in mind, one may review the evidence from the texts originating in Canaan.

THE TEXTS FROM CANAAN. It can be stated categorically that the scribes writing Akkadian in Canaan do not use the subjunctive marker, either the Babylonian or the Assyrian. Such a sweeping statement will seem brash, if not impertinent, in view of the fact that one does find the *-u* ending on subordinated verbs, e.g. in relative clauses (rare indeed):

gáb-bi mi-im-mì / *ša yi-pu-šu* / LUGAL EN-*ia a-na* KUR-*šu* / *gáb-bu* SIG_5.GA / *ma-gal ma-gal* "As for everything that the king, my lord, is doing for his land, it is all very, very good" (EA 262:7-11); *gáb-bi mi-im-mì / ša yi-iq-bu* / LUGAL EN-*ia* "Everything that the king, my lord, says, I am obeying" (EA 261:7-10); *a-šar ti-la-ku* "wherever you go" (EA 296:4'); *a-di a-šar ti₇-la-ku* "to wherever you go" (EA 203:19; EA 204:19; 205:1);

and in "that" clauses:

i-nu-ma / ⸢*yu*⸣*-ba-ú la-qa* / KUR LUGAL *a-na ša-a-šu* "that he seeks to take the land of the king for himself" (EA 76:15-16); *i-nu-ma yi-iš-ta-pa-ru šàr-ru* / EN-*li* "Inasmuch as the king, my lord, keeps writing" (EA 119:8).

However, the contention that the *-u* suffix in such cases is not the Akkadian marker of subordination, but rather the WS marker of the indicative imperfect, can be validated in two ways. Under the appropriate section below (*infra*, pp. 222-244), the modal function of this WS *-u* suffix (and its concomitant plural marker, *-ūna*) will be demonstrated; it will be seen that the *-u*/*-ūna* suffix appears regularly in main clauses where no subordinating element exists. One can point to over thirty instances where Akkadian would employ the *-u* but where these texts from Canaan have *-Ø*.

(1) First of all, we have the preformative statives, for which one could argue that any peripheral scribe might treat them as something different from the prefix conjugation (in peripheral, the stative, even 3rd m.s., often lacks the subjunctive *-u*),

li-iš-al LUGAL LÚMAŠKÍM-*šu ša i-de₄* / KUR*Ki-na-aḫ-na* "May the king ask his commissioner who knows Canaan" (EA 148:46-47); *ù* SIG₅ / *e-nu-ma i-de₄* "And it is well that he know" (EA 147:70-71); LÚ-*lì ša i-ba-aš-ši i-na* URU*Gub-la* "the man who is in Byblos" (EA 74:12); *aš-šum* NA₄*me-ku ša i-bá-aš-ši* / *it-ti-ia* "concerning the raw glass that is with me" (EA 148:5-6).

Contrast the following construction in a text from Egypt:

^{LÚ}*pá-ma-ḫa-a ša ḫa-an-ni-pa i-de*$_4$*-e-i-ú* "the commissioner who knows villainy" (EA 162:74; Cochavi-Rainey 1988:192; 1990b:21).

(2) On the other hand, the following preterites and *t*- preterites cannot be explained away; the Canaanite scribe simply did not use the Akkadian marker of subordination even when he eschewed the WS 3rd m.s. *y*- prefix. This dictum applies to relative clauses:

[U]RU.KI.ḪÁ *ša ìl-qé* / ^{I}ÌR-*Aš-ra-ti* "the towns which ᶜAbdi-Ashirta has taken" (EA 92:17-18); *lu-ú i-de* LUGAL EN-*ia i-nu-ma* / *šal-ma-at* ^{URU}*Ṣí-du-na*^{KI} GEMÉ-*ti* / LUGAL EN-*ia ša i-din a-na qa-ti-ia* "May the king, my lord, be apprised that Sidon, the handmaiden of the king, my lord, which he has given into my charge, is at peace" (EA 144:10-12); URU LUGAL / *ša ip-qí-id i-na qa-ti-ia* "the king's city which he has entrusted to me" (EA 151:6-7); URU.DIDLI.ḪÁ *ša* NU-*id* ^{LÚ}GAL / EN *ia i-na qa-ti-ia* "the towns which the officer, my lord, entrusted to me" (EA 23:4-5)

which include some apparent translations of Egyptian royal epithets, clauses dependent on the determinative or the relative pronoun, some pertaining to pharaoh:

ša id-din ri-ig-ma-šu i-na sa-me ki-ma ^{d}IŠKUR "who gave his voice in the heavens like Baal" (EA 147:13-14); DUMU ^{d}[U]TU ⸢*ša*⸣ *ti-ra-am* / ^{d}UTU "son of the sun-god whom the sun-god loved" (EA 323:22-23).

and two describing a loyal or disloyal servant of the king:

ša iš-mé a-na LUGAL *be-li-šu ù* / *ú-ra-ad-šu i-na aš-ra-ni-šu* "who obeyed the king, his lord, and serves/served him in his place" (EA 147:41-42); *ù ša la iš-te-mé* "and as for the one who has not obeyed" (EA 153:12).

These may reflect Egyptian participles or relative forms.

There are also numerous "that" clauses and circumstantial clauses:

> *ù yi-de* LUGAL *be-li* / *i-nu-ma il*$_{5}$*-te-qé* / URU.KI-*ia* ^{I}ÌR-*Ḫe-ba* / *is-tu qa-ti-ia* "and may the king, my lord, be apprised that ᶜAbdi-Kheba took my town from me" (EA 280:21-24); *e-nu-ma* / *iq-bi* LUGAL *be-li-ia* "when the king, my lord said . . . " (EA 147:35-36; cf. also lines 33-34); SIG$_{5}$ *i-nu-ma iš-bat* ^{URU}*Gub-la* "Is it good that he take Byblos?" (EA 84:36); *ù i-nu-ma iš-te-mé a-wa-at* / LUGAL EN-*ia i-nu-ma iš-tap-pár a-na* ÌR-*šu* "and when I heard the word of the king, my lord, when he wrote to his servant" (EA 144:13-14).

Note also the following clause dependent on a noun in construct:

> *a-wa-at iš-tap-pár* / LUGAL EN-*ia* DINGIR.MEŠ-*ia* / [^{d}]UTU-*ia a-na ia-ši* "the word which the king, my lord, my deity, my sun-god, wrote to me" (EA 276:9-11).

Even the Jerusalem letters, which generally restrict the WS imperfect forms to quotations from direct speech, and use the Akkadian present (*iparras*) for the epistolary text, ignore the Akkadian subjunctive:

> *e-nu-ma à-qa-bi* "because I say" (EA 286:22; Moran 1975b:151).

(3) Therefore, it is not surprising that other forms having the WS prefix *y-* appear in subordinate clauses without the Akkadian subjunctive marker, e.g. relative clauses:

> *gáb-bi mi-im-mì* / *ša yi-id-din šàr-*[*r*]*u* / ⸢EN⸣-*ia a-*[*n*]*a* ÌR-[*šu*] "everything which the ki[n]g, my lord, gave to [his] servant" (EA 248:10-12); *ia-nu* / *ša* ‹*ya*›*-aq-bi mi-im-ma a-na* / ^{I}ÌR-*A-ši-ir-ta* "There is none who has said anything to ᶜAbdi-Ashirta" (EA 75:27-29); *ša ia-aš-tap-pár* LUGAL / *be-lí-ia a-na* ÌR-*šu* / *yi-iš-te*$_{9}$*-mu* "what the king, my lord has written to his servant, he is obeying" (EA 233:16-18);

and also circumstantial clauses:

> *i-nu-ma yi-iz-zi-iz* / UGU ^{URU}*Šu-na-ma ù* UGU ^{URU}*Bur-*⸢*qú*⸣*-na* / *ù* UGU ^{URU}*Ḫa-ra-bu* "when he attacked Shunem and Burquna and ᶜArrabu" (EA 250:42-44); *ša-ni-tam i-nu-ma yi-iq-bi* ^{I}*Ia-an-ḫa-mu* / [*na-a*]*d-na-ti-mi* ŠE.*IM*.ḪÁ *a-na* ^{I}*Ri-ib-* ^{d}IŠKUR "Furthermore, if Yanḫamu has said, 'I [have] given grain to Rib-Haddi'" (EA 5:23-24); *i-nu-ma yi-iš-ta-pár a-na* LÚ.MEŠ / ^{URU}*Am-mi-ia* "because he wrote to the men of Ammia" (EA 73:26-27).

To these we may add some 1st c.s. and 2nd m.s. examples:

> *i-nu-ma aq-bi a-na* ^{LÚ}GAL / ^{I}*Pu-ḫu-ri* "when I said to the officer Paḫurru" (EA 19:16-17); *u* i_{15}*-nu-ma iš-te-me a-wa-te*^{MEŠ}-ka / *an-nu-*ta_5 "and when I heard these words of yours" (EA 227:8-9); *ù qa-la-ta* / [*a-na ip-ši-š*]*u-nu i-nu-ma ti-iš-me* / [^{URU}*Ul-l*]*a-sà la-qú* "but you kept ignoring [th]eir [deed] when you heard that they had taken [Ull]asa" (EA 109:13-15).

In conclusion, it may prove useful to cite a passage in which the subordinated verbs do not have the Akkadian subjunctive marker but in which the verb of the main clause does have a *-u* suffix:

> *ù a-wa-ta ša-a i-de* / *ù ša-a eš-te-me aš-pu-*⸢*ru*⸣ / *a-na šàr-ri* EN*-ia* "and the word which I know or which I have heard, I write to the king, my lord" (EA 108:23-24; cf. also EA 233:16-18 cited *supra*, p. 200).

The passage speaks about the character of a faithful servant and the point is that such a servant always reports the facts to the king. Thus, the suffix *-u* on *ašpuru* signifies habitual behavior. Such forms with WS imperfect meaning will be treated below. It suffices here to point out that this text shows clearly that a Canaanite scribe ignored the Akkadian positional suffix *-u* but utilized the WS modal suffix *-u*. There can be no doubt that the

EA texts from Canaan have an entirely different system of verbal suffixes than that required by the rules of normative Akkadian.

THE AKKADIAN VENTIVE

The situation is different with regard to the Akkadian ventive. It will be demonstrated below that the Canaanite scribes were well aware of the function of that suffix. One finds both *-a* and *-am*, even in cases where there is no enclitic or personal suffix on the verb. The scribes are especially sensitive to the semantic nuances applied to verbs of motion and verbs of communication (speaking, writing) by the addition of the ventive, and they make good use of them. When the application of the *-a*(*m*) conflicted with the need for a WS verbal suffix, then the scribes had to make some kind of compromise or accomodation. Various solutions to that dilemma will be seen below (Rainey 1991-93).

STOCK EXPRESSIONS. The Canaanite scribes were familiar, of course, with the use of the ventive in letters which they received from outside of Canaan (mainly from Egypt). Recognition of such forms would have been part of their training. The letters from pharaoh to local Canaanite rulers have:

> *ṭup-pa an-na-a uš-te-bi-la-ku* . . . LUGAL *um-te-eš-še-ra-ku* / [I]*Ḫa-an-ni* "this tablet have I sent to you . . . the king has sent to you Ḫanni" (EA 367:3, 6-7; Rainey19788:37); *ṭup-pa an-*⸢*na*⸣*-*⸢*am*⸣ / *ul-te-bi-la-ak-ku* . . . *um-te-še-ra-ak-ku* [I]*Ḫa-an-ia* "this tablet have I sent to you . . . I have sent to you Ḫanya" (EA 369:3, 5; Rainey 1978b:41).

Therefore, it is not surprising to find the following Akkadianism in a text which is obviously a reply to just such a pharaonic message:

> *a-wa-at ul-te-bi-la* / LUGAL EN-*ia* DINGIR.MEŠ-*ia* / [d]UTU-*ia* *a*[*-n*]*a ia-ši* "As for the word which the king, my lord, my sun-god, sent to me" (EA 267:9-11).

WITH ACCUSATIVE SUFFIX. The Jerusalem letters, which use mainly Akkadian prefix forms, also apply the ventive plus accusative suffix:

> *zu-ru-uḫ šàr-ri* KALAG.GA / *⸢ù⸣-še-ri-ba-an-ni a-na* É LÚ*a-bi-ia* "The strong arm of the king installed me in my father's house" (EA 286:12-13; cf. EA 300:17-19).

The Byblos letters contain several examples of the ventive plus accusative 1st c.s. *-ni* in purely indicative contexts. The same tablet which has *mi-nu / yi-na-ṣí-ru-ni* "who will protect me?" (EA 112:17) also has *mi-nu yi-na-ṣí-ra-an-ni* (EA 112:13). Other examples of the same phenomenon are: *[m]i-nu yi-na-ṣa-ra-ni* (EA 119:10); *mi-nu yi-n[a-ṣí-]ra[-an-ni]* (EA 121:10); *ma-an-nu / yi-na-ṣí-ra-ni* (EA 130:19).

šapāru. Another standard usage is the ventive with *šaparu* "to send in writing," as in this Taanach letter:

> *at-ta ta-⸢aš⸣-pu-⸢ra⸣ / a-na ia-ši* "you have written to me" (TT 1:8-9; Rainey 1977:43).

And there are numerous stock expressions with this verb employed by the Canaanite scribes when replying to a message from pharaoh:

> *iš-te$_{9}$-né-me / a-wa-at* LUGAL EN-*ia / ša is-tap-pa-ra-ni* "I continually heed the word of the king, my lord, which he sent to me" (EA 305:15-17; also EA 145:11-13; 253:7-10; 254:6-7; 304:15-17; 329:13-15); LÚMAŠKÍM \ *ra-bi-iṣ / ša* LUGAL EN-*ia / ša iš-tap-ra-am /* LUGAL EN-*ia . . . a-na ia-a-ši* "As for the commissioner of the king, my lord, whom the king, my lord has sent to me" (EA 321:15-20; 32:17-20).

Within a more West Semitized context, the same verb can also be in the preterite with ventive, even with the WS 3rd m.s. suffix *y-*. Note the following "that" clauses:

i-nu-ma yi-iš-tap-pa-ra / *šàr-ru a-na ia-ši* "Inasmuch as the king has written to me" (EA 130:9-10, 14-16; also EA 77:6-8; 102:14).

wuššuru/*muššuru*. The most ubiquitous verb with the *-a* suffix in the corpus of Canaanite texts is *wuššuru*/*muššuru* (cf. *supra*, pp. 185-186, 191-205). The unique western meaning for this verb, "to send," may have developed from the original meaning, "to release," plus the ventive (*supra*, pp. 157-168). It may be impossible to prove that theory; in the texts one finds forms both with and without the ventive in the meaning "to send." Nevertheless, it is notable how many of the examples of this verb do carry an *-a* suffix. Many of these are in injunctive contexts and will be discussed below (*infra*, pp. 257-261). Here it is important to note the few instances when the *-a* is present, but the meaning is not injunctive.

[*ù*] *aš-ta-pár* / *a-na* É.GAL *ù yu-w*[*a-ša-*]*ra* / ›*ù yu-wa-ša-ra*‹ ⸢*šàr*⸣*-ru* ERÍN.MEŠ / *ra-ba* "[and] I wrote to the palace and he se[n]t ›and he sent‹ a large army" (EA 117:24-27).

Moran (1960:16-18; 1987b:323; 1992:193) translates the second clause as if it were a purpose clause but this is hardly suitable in the context. Rib-Haddi is simply recounting what happened in the past. In spite of the *-a-* theme vowel, there can be no doubt here that the *-a* suffix is the Akkadian ventive, not the WS volitive. The same holds true for the following, which is an interrogative sentence and cannot possibly be injunctive:

a-na mi-nim-mi la-a tu-wa-ši-ra / LÚDUMU *ši-ip-ri-ka a-na maḫ-ri-ia* "Why didn't you send your emissary to me?" (EA 34:9-10; Moran 1987b:198; 1992:105).

This Alashian text is paralleled by a similar question from Jerusalem:

am-mi-ni$_7$ DUMU LÚKIN *k*[*i-ma ar-ḫi-i*]*š* / *la-a ú-ma-še-ra* ⸢*šàr*⸣[*-ru* EN-*ia*] "Why did the king not send an emissary q[uickly]?"

(EA 285:7-10; cf. Na᾽aman 1975:97; Moran 1987b:507 n. 3; 1992:325 n. 3).

Another preterite with the ventive ending is attested in a circumstantial clause employed in the strongly Canaanized epistle written by the leaders from ᶜIrqata:

i-nu-ma yu-wa-ši-r[*a* LU]GAL / EN-*nu* ᴵD[UMU]-*Bi-ḫa-a* [*ù*] / *yi-iq-bi a-na ia*[*-ši-nu*] . . . "When the [ki]ng, our lord, sent D[UMU]-Biḫā [and] he said to u[s] . . . (EA 100:11-13).

These certain examples of the ventive raise the question of the *-a* suffix that appears with most of the imperative forms of *wuššuru*, viz. *uššira* (*passim*) and also on many examples of the precative. It seems logical to assume that these were also *ventives* in spite of the temptation to see them as *modus attraction* from a volitive *-a* used on regular prefix forms in injunctive contexts; cf. the similar phenomenon in Hebrew:

qûmāʰ ᵓᵉlôhîm šop̄ṭāʰ hāᵓāreṣ "Arise oh God, judge the earth" (Ps. 82:8).

Youngblood (1961:94-95) surveyed all the *uššira* imperatives and found that while the simple *uššir* means simply "send" (elsewhere), *uššira* always means "send (to me, the speaker)." One does not find *uššira . . . ana yâši* but a circumlocution may be used, *uš-ši-ra-mi . . . it-ti-ia* (EA 82:15; Youngblood 1961:230; cf. also *infra*, pp. 331-332, 335).

leqû. Besides the usual verbs of motion and of speaking, etc., it would appear that the Canaanite scribes had also learned some special nuances for particular verbs. One of the most important of these is *leqû* "to take." The scribes were fully aware that the ventive of this verb can express "to bring along (with)." They would have encountered this usage in epistles from other contemporary sources. Note, for example, this passage from a Mitanni letter:

ù ṭup-pa / ša il-qà-a al-ta-ta-as-sí-ma [ù a]-ma-t[i]-šu el-te-me "I have carefully read the tablet which he had brought along" (EA 19:11; *CAD* L:133b).

A Jerusalem text also has this nuance on a precative:

lu-ma-še-er / šàr-ru ^LÚ^MAŠKÍM *ù li-il-qé-a-ni / a-na ia-a-ši* (for *ka-ta*$_5$) *a-di* ŠEŠ.MEŠ *ù* BA.UG$_7$ / *ni-mu-tu*$_4$ *it-ti šàr-ru*(sic!) EN-*nu* "May the king send the commissioner and may he take me away to *you*(!) with (my) colleagues that we may die with the king our lord" (EA 288:58-61).

But the clearest example of this particular usage is found in a letter from Biryawaza:

ù yi-la-ak ^I^*Ar-za-wu-ya / a-na* ^URU^*Qì-i[s-sà] ù yi-il*$_5$*-qa* / ERÍN.MEŠ ^I^*A-zi-[ri u yi]-iṣ-ba-at* / ^URU^*Ša-ad-du u yi-di-in*$_4$*-ši a-na* / LÚ.MEŠ SA.GAZ *u la-a yi-di-in*$_4$*-ši / a-na* LUGAL EN-*ia* "and Arzawuya went to Ke[desh] and he *took along* the troops of Azi[ru and he] seized the town of Shaddu and he gave it to the *ᶜapîru* men and did not give it to the king, his lord" (EA 197:26-31)

izuzzu. Another verb which sometimes takes the ventive to express a particular nuance is the irregular *izuzzu* "to stand." With the ventive, it may signify something like "to take a stand," "to present oneself," much like the Hebrew *hiṯyaṣṣēḇ*. In OB we have:

PA.PA *ù* DUMU.É *ṭup-pa-a-ti / iz-zi-zu-ni-ma* "The PA.PA officer and the archivist presented themselves" (*VAS* 7, 198:14-15 = *VAB* 6, 254:14-15 = *AbB* 6, 215).

and OA:

A-šùr be-li / i-zi-za-⌈*ma*⌉ *iš-tù a-bu-ul ṣé-n[i]-im / a-dí a-bu-ul ni-ší-im qà-*⌈*qé*⌉*-re-e / a-na A-šùr be-[l]i-a e-zi-ib* "Asshur, my lord, stood by me, so I reserved the ground between the sheep gate and the people's gate for Asshur, my lord" (Landsberger and Balkan 1950:224, 8-11; 225 *CAD* E:420b; Q:119a).

and also in MB:

> *ù pa-*⸢*an*⸣ *be-li-šu ú-zu-uz-zu* / *i-na-an-na a-na pa-ni be-lí-ia-ma* / *ú-zu-uz-za* "And before his lord they stand; now it is before my lord that I present myself" (PBS 13, 6:16-18);

and in literary texts from Amarna itself:

> *i-lu iš-te-en i-na pí-i ba-a-bi iz-za-*⸢*za*⸣ "A god is standing at the gate" (EA 357:55); *ša ša iz-za-za qáb-la-šu li-pu-la* LUGAL "those (expenses) of the ones who help him in battle, let the king pay" (EA 359:19; Rainey 1978b:12-13).

There are some examples of *izuzzu* in the Canaanite letters where the *-a* suffix has to be ventive since the context requires an indicative, not an injunctive, e.g.

> *ša-ma-ma šu-nu* / ›*šu-nu*‹ *i-nu-ma i-te*$_9$*-ru-bu* / *i-na* ^{URU}*Ṣu-mu-ra* / URU.MEŠ *an-nu-tu* ^{GIŠ}⸢MÁ⸣.⸢MEŠ⸣ / *ù* DUMU.MEŠ ^{I}ÌR-*A-ši-i*[*r-*]\ *ta* / *i-na ṣé-ri ù* / [*i*]*z-*⸢*zi*⸣*-za* UGU‹*-šu-nu*› *ù* / *la-a i-le-ú* / *a-ṣa ù ep-ša-at* ^{URU}*Gub-la* / [*a*]*-na* LÚ.MEŠ GAZ.MEŠ "If they hear that I am entering into Ṣumur, these cities (will be in) ships and the sons of ᶜAbdi-Ashirta (will be) on land and I will be up against ‹them› and I will be unable to go forth lest Byblos go over to the *ᶜapîrû* men" (EA 104:43-52).

The entire string of clauses constitutes the protasis of a conditional sentence of which the protasis is a clause beginning with an absolute infinitive (Rainey 1989-90:59b-60a; *contra* Moran 1950a:164;1987b:300 n. 3; 1992:177 n. 3). The first clauses of the apodosis are non-verbal and the subsequent clause is indicative, viz. *la-a i-le-ú*. Therefore, [*i*]*z-*⸢*zi*⸣*-za* can hardly have any other WS modal stance than indicative. The scribe felt that he needed the lexical nuance of the ventive, "to take a stand," with UGU, "to stand up against." Therefore, he used *izzizza* as 1st c.s. indicative imperfect without any WS indicator of mood or tense!

The same conclusion seems unavoidable with regard to *yizzizza* in the next passage:

> *šum-ma i-na-na* / *qa-la-ta ù* I*Pí-ḫu-ra* / *la-a yi-zi-za i-na* / URU*Ku-mì-di u ka-li* LÚ.MEŠ / [*ḫ*]*a-za-ni-ka tù-da-ku*[*-n*]*a* " If now you keep silent and Paḫura does not take up position in Kômidi, then all of your [ci]ty rulers will be sla[i]n!" (EA 132:46-50; Rainey 1989-90:62).

Moran (1950a:98; 1960:14; 1987b:352; 1992:214) takes the clause *ù* I*Pí-ḫu-ra* / *la-a yi-zi-za i-na* / URU*Ku-mì-di* as the apodosis. But this leaves the next clause, *u ka-li* LÚ.MEŠ / [*ḫ*]*a-za-ni-ka tù-da-ku*[*-n*]*a*, dangling by itself. The latter is, in fact, the apodosis, the dreaded result of possible pharaonic negligence. So even if Piḫurra's failure to take/hold his position in Kômidi is part of the apodosis, then it must agree in mood with the verb in the next clause, *ù-da-ku*[*-n*]*a*. However, it seems more likely that Piḫurra's being posted in Kômidi is viewed here as a necessary condition to prevent the slaying of the city rulers. Therefore, this clause must be part of the protasis, which happens to have a suffix conjugation verb (the modal equivalent of a prefix conjugation indicative). Therefore, whether in the protasis or in the apodosis, *yi-zi-za* must be indicative; it follows, then, that the *-a* suffix is Akkadian ventive and not WS volitive.

(w)aṣû. Definite lexical force attaches to the ventive used with *(w)aṣû* "to go out," viz. "to come forth." Some of the contexts where this construction is employed require an indicative, not a volitive:

> [*i-d*]*e*9 *ki-i-ma* / [*l*]*a-mi-in šum-ka* / *a-na pa-ni* LUGAL *ù* / [*l*]*a-a ti-ta-ṣa-am* / [*i*]*š-tu* KUR*Mi-iṣ-ri* "[I kn]ow that your name is [vi]lified before the king so that you [can]not come forth [f]rom Egypt" (EA 97:4-8; cf. also *CAD* L:123b; Moran 1987b:289; 1992:170).

The form *ti-ta-ṣa-am* (for Akkadian *tattaṣ[ṣ]âm*) is either Gt present or preterite (less likely Gtn preterite), the infixed *-t-* expressing the separative nuance. The context expresses no injunctive nuance. The second clause is a result clause, not a purpose clause, and even if it were the latter, it would be dependent on a nominal clause (= indicative) which would require an indicative in the clause expressing purpose. Therefore, the only possible definition of *ti-ta-ṣa-am* is as an Akkadian ventive in an indicative syntagma.

The same holds true for the next example:

> [*ša-ni-tam a-na-k*]*u la uṣ-ṣa-am* "[Further, as for m]e, I cannot come out" (EA 88:51; Youngblood 1961:321).

Moran (1987b:275, 276 n. 12; 1992:160-161 n 9) took the verb *uṣ-ṣa-am* to be 3rd m.s. as a parallel to EA 87:17, but Youngblood (1961:321) compares EA 87:29 and adopts the reading above. The resulting 1st c.s. verb must be in an indicative context (even Moran's 3rd m.s. could hardly be injunctive here).

It is not possible to construe the following example as volitive; it is clearly parallel to a preceding preterite:

> *ù aš-pu-ur* / *ù tu-ṣa* ERÍN.MEŠ *pí-ṭá-tu* / *ù ti*$_{7}$*-ìl-qé* ^{I}*a-ba-šu-nu* "so I wrote and the army came forth and it captured their father" (EA 362:18-20; Moran 1960:4; 1987b:556; 1992:359-360; *contra* Moran 1950a:178); *ù aš-pu-ur* / *a-na* LUGAL *be-li-ia* .⌜*ù*⌝ *tu-ṣa* ERÍN.MEŠ / [*ù*] *ti-ìl-qé* ^{URU}*Ṣu*[*-m*]*u-ri ù* / [^{I}ÌR-*A-ši-*]*ir!-ti* "and I wrote to the king, my lord, and the army came forth [and] it took Ṣu[m]ur and [ᶜAbdi-Ash]irta" (EA 138:31-34).

The form *tu-ṣa* is obviously preterite in both passages..

A few passages reveal a special solution to the conflict between the need for an Akkadian ventive and for a WS indicative on the same form. The scribe simply adds the energic *-na* to the ventive! This could presumably stand for an energic volitive (cf. discussion *infra*, pp. 263-264), but the latter was so rare in the Canaanite Amarna texts as to cast doubt on its existence there at all. So the scribe(s) in question seem to have felt that ventive plus *-na* would solve their dilemma.

The first text is a purpose clause dependent on an indicative:

> *a-na mi-ni*$_7$ / *qa-la-ta ù la-a taq-bu* / *a-na šàr-ri* EN-*li-ka* / *ù tu-ṣa-na qa-du* ERÍN.MEŠ / *pí-ṭá-ti ù ti-ma-qú-tu* / UGU ^{KUR}*A-mur-ri* "Why do you keep silent and not speak to the king, your lord, so that you come forth with the army and so that you fall on Amurru?" (EA 73:6-11).

The other two passages are in the protasis of conditional sentences with *šumma*. In all of Moran's examples, he never found a volitive in a *šumma* clause.

> *šum-ma ap-pu-na-ma yu-ṣa-na šàr-ru* / *ù ka-li* KUR.KUR.KI *nu-kúr-tu*$_4$ *a-na ša-šu* / *ù mi-na yi-pu-šu a-na ia-ši-nu* "If the king comes forth and all the countries are against him, then what can he do to us?" (EA 74:39-41; Moran 1987b:250; 1992:)143; *šum-ma* MU.MEŠ *a*[*n*]-⌜*ni*⌝-*ta ú-ul* / *yu-ṣa-na* ERÍN.MEŠ [*pí-ṭ*]*á-ta* / *ù in-ni*[*-ip-ša-a*]*t ka-li* / KUR.KUR.KI.MEŠ *a*[*-na* LÚ.MEŠ GA]Z "If this year the army does not come forth, then all the countries will go [over] t[o the *ᶜapîru* me]n" (EA 77:26-29; Moran 1987b:257; 1992:148).

Finally, the same interpretation, ventive plus indicative energic *-na*, must apply to the following:

> *ša-ni-tam ú-ul aš-ta-pár a-na šàr-ri* / *a-nu-ma* 2 LÚ ^{KUR}*Mi-iš-ri šu-nu* / *tu-ṣa-na ša-ri a-na ia-ši* / *ù la-a a-ṣa* "Furthermore, did I not write to the king: 'Now, as for those two Egyptians, my breath will come forth to me'? But it did not come" (EA 117:53-56; contrast Moran 1987b:323, 325 n. 11; 1992:193, 195 n. 11).

turru. It remains to note that, in one instance, *tú-ti-ra-an-ni* (EA 145:10), Moran (1987b:375; 1992:231) renders this ventive of *turru* as a preterite although it is an injunctive; cf. *t[ú-te-ra-am* in the same text (EA 145:26; Moran 1987b:376 n. 6; 1992:232 n. 6).

CONCLUSION. The foregoing illustrations prove that the Akkadian ventive was used extensively in the EA letters from Canaan. Most of the examples are preterite, i.e. Akkadian verb formations plus the -Ø suffix of the past tense (applicable to both Akkadian and WS). The final passage has a chain of past events:

> [^{I}*Zi-ir*]*-dam-ia*[*-a*]*š-da* / *p*[*a-*]*ṭá-ar iš-t*[*u*] / [^{I}*B*]*ir*$_5$*-ia-wa-za i*[*-ba-ši*] / *it-ti* ^{I}*Šu-ta* Ì[R] / *šàr-ri i-na* URU ⌜UN⌝[*-ti*] / [*l*]*a-a yi-qa-bi mi-im*[*-m*]*i* / [*a-n*]*a ša-šu tu-uṣ-ṣa* / [E]RÍN.MEŠ LUGAL EN*-ia i-ba*[*-ši*] /*it-ti-ši i-na* ^{URU}*Ma-gíd-da*[^{KI}] / *la-a qa-bi mi-mu a-na ša-š*[*u*] / *ù yi-ip-ṭú-ra a-na mu-ḫi-ia* / *ù a-nu-ma* / *ia-aš-pu-ra* ^{I}*Šu-ta a-na ia-ši i-din-mì* / ^{I}*Zi-ir-dam-ia-aš-da* / *a-na* ^{I}*Bir*$_5$*-ia-wa-za* "[Zir]damyashda departed from [B]iryawaza; he wa[s] with Shuta, the servant of the king in the garrison town, he said nothing to him; the king's army came forth; he was with it in Megiddo; nothing was said to him; then he departed to me and now Shuta has written to me: 'Give Zirdamyashda to Biryawaza'" (EA 234:11-26; Rabiner 1981:99-100, §5.2.2.3; Moran 1987b:460, 461 n. 4; 1992:29 n 4).

THE PRECATIVE

Another verbal construction peculiar to Akkadian is the precative. It is used frequently by the Canaanite scribes in spite of the existence of a WS conjugation pattern which fulfills the same functions (the jussive; cf. *infra,* pp. 244-254; Rainey 1993). The precative is formed by combining the particle *lū* with the forms of the prefix conjugations used for the preterite (Edzard 1973:130-131). The particle may originally have been a marker for conditional, primarily unreal conditions (Huehnergard 1983:573b). It has been argued that Akkadian *liprus*(*ū* / *ā*) and *laprus* (in Assyrian) cannot have developed from *lū* + **yaprus* or *lū* + **ʾaprus* respectively (Huehnergard 1983:574-575; Edzard 1973:131). However, the argument from phonetic shifts alone is inadequate. The factor at work in the Akkadian precative paradigm is *differentiation of person* which is a semantic need that can override the usual phonetics if the latter would lead to obscurity. Third person *liprus* preserved an echo of the original *y*- which was needed as a 3rd m.s. person marker; in Babylonian the vowel class of the *lū* was admissible in first person *luprus* because there was no danger of confusion with the third person. In Assyrian, on the other hand, *laprus* kept an echo of the original ᵓ- by analogy with the third person's echoing its *y*-. That the precative constructions of the stative and the forms with preformative *t*- all have *lū* is sufficient proof that the original particle at play in the third and first persons was also *lū*; there is no need to posit the existence of a particle **la* (*contra* Huehnergard 1983:574b-575a).

MORPHOLOGY. The scribes generally use the correct forms for the precative with only a few divergences noted below. Nearly all of the documented examples are 3rd m.s. A selection of the principal constructions are as follows: *li-ib-lu-uṭ* (EA 85:39, 86; 256:10, 11; 289:37); *li-id-mì-iq* (EA 85:33); *li-ru-ub* (EA 149:78); *li-iḫ-šu-uš-mi* (EA 228:18); *li-il*$_5$*-ma-ad* (EA 75:35; 238:29; 282:8; 335:14); *li-il-qé et al.* (EA 285:18 *et al.*); *li-im-li-ik et al.* (EA 149:8, 54; 155:14, 70; 263:18 *et al.*); *li-din et al.* (EA 102:6; 286:53; 288:49 et al.); *li-iṣ-ṣur* (EA 84:28); *li-ṣú-ru* (EA 326:12); *li-ip-qí-id et al.* (EA 148:28; 253:32); *li-is-ki-in et al.* (EA 285:26; 290:29 *et al.*); *li-iš-al et al.* (EA 96:6; 97:3; 148:46; 151:21 *et al.*); *li-iš-me et al.* (EA 88:23; 290:19 *et al.*); *li-it-ri-iš et al.* (EA 92:46; 106:35 *et al.*); *li-iz-kur* (EA 289:41). There are two 3rd m.s. forms with -*u*- instead of -*i*- as the prefix vowel, viz.

> *ù lu-uḫ-di* LUGAL EN-*ia* / *a-na I-tag-ga*$_{14}$*-ma* ÌR-*šu* "So may the king, my lord, rejoice in Etaggama, his servant" (EA 189:19-20); *lu-uk-šu-da-am-mì* / ERÍN.MEŠ *pí-ṭá-at* LUGAL [EN-*ia*] / *ù* MAŠKÍM.MEŠ-*šu* "May the army of the king, [my lord] come hither" (EA 191:11-13).

Note also the correct Babylonian example from (*w*)*aṣû*: *li-ṣi-mi* (EA 286:51) alongside Assyrian *lu-ṣi-mi* (EA 286:56) in the same Jerusalem text (Moran 1975b:153).

For 1st c.s. there are three Assyrian forms from Jerusalem (Moran 1975b:153): *la-mu-ur* (EA 286:46); *la-mur-mi* (EA 286:40); and *le-lu-ub* (EA 286:46; for *lērub*). From Tyre one also finds 1st c.s. *le-ru-ub* (EA 148:16; 151:17) but in the same context the 1st c.s. *li-mur* (EA 148:17) which may be an indication that the Tyrian scribe has simply used 3rd m.s. forms for first person; if so, then read *li-ru-ub*.

For the D stem there are some instances where the scribes observed the correct Babylonian 3rd m.s. form: *li-ši-ra* (EA 94:71; *lū* + *uššera*); *li-wa-še-ra* (EA 255:22); *li-wa-aš-šir₄* (EA 149:17, 76); *li-te-ra-an-ni* (EA 96:32). On the other hand, there are some instances when the typical Assyrian 3rd m.s. form appears (particularly from Jerusalem): *lu-ma-še-er* (EA 288:58; 289:42); *lu-ma-šir₉* (EA 290:20); *lu-ma-še-ra* (EA 285:28; 287:18); *lu-li-ra* (EA 290:21). But from Byblos, there are also: *lu-wa-ši-ra-am* (EA 84:26; 106:26, 42); and elsewhere with suffixes: *lu-w*[*a-a*]*š-ši-ra-an-ni-mi* (EA 238:9); *lu-wa-ši-ra-ni* (EA 263:23).

It is a question whether 3rd m.s. *li-sà-ḫír* (EA 151:70) is D stem or N: most likely it is the latter (cf. *CAD* S:52b-53a).

The verb *idû* presents a unique picture. The OB and OA precative was *lū īde*, which is somewhat anomalous. It probably derived from the function of the preterite, *īde*, *tīde*, etc., as a syntactic stative (*GAG*:102, §78b). The precative *lū īde* corresponded to *lū paris*. The EA texts from Canaan often use *lū īde*, usually written *lu i-de* (EA 68:9; *et al.*), but some of the scribes created a more "conventional" injunctive, *li-de*-(*mi*) (EA 174:18; *et al.*). However, the fact that a WS jussive pattern was in use in these texts led to the adoption of forms such as *lu-ú yi-de* (EA 243:21; *et al.*; cf. *infra*, p. 249).

The apparent confusion on the part of the WS scribes between the Akkadian G present and the D stem may have led to the following examples in which a form other than the **yiprus* was joined to the *lū*: *li-*⌈*da*⌉*-gal* (EA 74:10); *lu-ḫa-mu-uṭ* (EA 88:40); ⌈*li*⌉*-mu-*⌈*ḫu*⌉?-[*ṣú*] (EA 209:10); *li-ma-lik* (EA 94:72; possibly N stem); *lì-pa-qa-ad* (EA 197:35); *li-qáb-bi-šu-nu* (EA 171:17; not Canaanite).

Some other stems are represented by the following: Possibly Gt — [*li-*]*iš-te-mé* (EA 63:11); Gtn according to *AHw*:702b — *li-it-ta-din* (EA 148:9, 13, 26; 151:37); Dt(?) — *li-it-te-er* (EA 149:84), unless this is simply a use of the Akkadian *-t-* preterite.

SYNTAX. The various syntagmas in which the precative appears are similar to those of standard Akkadian but they often show the influence of the local WS dialect. One striking difference is, of course, the fact that these precatives, like most verbs in the corpus under study, come at the head of their clauses rather than at the end (Finley 1979:60-61). One exception is the introductory formula used in three Tanaach letters:

> ^{d}IŠKUR ZI-*ta-ka li-iṣ-ṣur* "May Baal preserve your life!" (TT 5:3; 6:3); EN DINGIR.MEŠ-*nu* / ZI-*ka lí-iṣ-ṣur* "May Baal, the great god, preserve your life!" (TT 2:2-3; Rainey 1977:50).

This is a well known formula, documented in Mari:

> DINGIR-*lum na-*⸢*pí*⸣*-iš-ta-ka* / ⸢*aš*⸣*-šu-mi-ia li-iṣ-ṣú-ur* / ⸢*na*⸣*-pí-iš-ta-ni a-na da-ri-iš u*$_4$*-mi-im* / DINGIR-*lum* ⸢*li*⸣*-iṣ-ṣú-ur* "May god protect your life for my sake; may god protect our life forever!" (*ARM* 4, 59:6-8; *AHw*:738a);

and also in Cassite letters:

> ^{d}*Gu-la a-ši-ib-ti* ^{URU}*I-si-in nap-šá-ti-ka li-iṣ-ṣur* "May Gula, who dwells in Isin, protect your life!" (Lutz 1919:No. 30:4-5; Waschow 1936:10-11; Salonen 1967:60-61); BÀD.DINGIR.KI *ù* ⸢^{d}⸣KA.DI / *na-ap-ša-*⸢*at*⸣ *be-lí-ia li-iṣ-ṣu-ru* / DINGIR.MEŠ *ma-la be-lí* / *pa-al-ḫu-šu-nu-ti* / *na-ap-ša-a-ti ša be-lí-ia* / *li-iṣ-ṣu-ru* "May Dēr and Ištaran protect the life of of my lord! May all the gods that my lord worships protect the life of my lord!" (Radau 1908: No. 5:6-11; Waschow 1936:20; Salonen 1967:60).

The other Taanach letter has a different formulation. It is WS in flavor and in word order, but still uses the precative (Rainey 1977:51):

> DINGIR.MEŠ *li-iš-a-lu* / ⸢*šu*⸣*-lum-ka šu-lum* / ⸢É⸣*-ka* DUMU.MEŠ-*ka* "May the gods show concern for your welfare, the welfare of your household (and) of your children!" (TT 1:5-7).

The precative is in the plural in accordance with the subject. The same formula appears in an EA letter from an Egyptian official to Rib-Haddi, but here the precative is 3rd m.s., evidently taking the subject as a "plural of majesty":

> DINGIR.MEŠ-*nu* / *šu-lum-ka šu-lum* É-*ka* / *li-iš-al* "May the deity show concern for your welfare (and) the welfare of your household" (EA 96:4-6; Youngblood 1961:398; Moran 1987b:288: 1992:170).

Likewise, the same plural subject with 3rd m.s. precative is found in a text from Yapa^{c}-Haddi:

> [DINGIR.M]EŠ *šu-lum-ka li-[iš-a]l* "May [the dei]ty [show concern] for your welfare!" (EA 97:3).

Once a Byblos author uses the precative in an oft repeated formula where the Byblos scribes normally make use of the 3rd f.s. WS jussive, *tiddin*, instead (e.g. EA 73:4; 74:3) *et al.*). The lone example of the precative in this syntagma has the 3rd m.s. for the 3rd f.s. subject, which is, of course, in accordance with the standard Babylonian practice:

> ^{d}NIN *ša* ^{URU}*Gub-la* / DINGIR LUGAL BE-*ia li-din* / TÉS^{ba}*-ka a-na pa-ni* LUGAL *be-li-ku* (sic!) / ^{d}UTU KUR.DIDLI.MEŠ.KI "May the Lady of Byblos, the deity of the king, my lord, give you dignity in the presence of the king, your lord, the sun-god of the lands!" (EA 102:5-8).

Another familiar syntagma is the oath formula. Besides two broken passages from Byblos (EA 85:39-40, 86), there are two complete texts from Peḫel and Jerusalem respectively:

> *li-ib-lu-uṭ / šàr-ru* EN-*ia li-ib-lu-uṭ / šàr-ru* EN-*ia šum-ma i*$_{15}$*-ba-ši / *[I]*A-ia-ab i-na* [URU]*Pí-ḫi-lì* "May the king, my lord, live! May the king, my lord, live! If Ayyāb is in Peḫel" (EA 256:10-13; Moran 1987b:483, 484 n. 1; 1992:309 and n. 1); *li-ib-lu-uṭ šàr-ri / lu-ú ir-pí-šu* [I]*Pu-ú-ru / pa-ṭar i-na ma-aḫ-ri-ia / i-na* [URU]*Ḫa-za-ti i-ba-aš-ši* "As the king lives, his official Pawura has left me! He is in Gaza" (EA 289:37-40).

It is possible that the precative is intended by the Sumerogram TI in the following two texts:

> *ù /* DINGIR.MEŠ KUR-*k*[*a*] ⸢TI⸣ *ga-am-ru* DUMU.MEŠ-*nu* [MÍ]DUMU.MÍ.MEŠ‹-*nu*› / ⸢GIŠ⸣ É!-*nu i*[-*n*]*a na-da-ni*$_7$ *i-na* [KUR]*Ia-ri-mu-ta / i-na ba-l*[*a*]*-ṭá* "As the god(s) of your land ⸢live⸣, our sons, ‹our› daughters, the furniture of our house, are used up in payment in Yarimuta for our sustenance" (EA 74:14-17; Youngblood 1961:122, 133); *ù* TI DINGIR-*ka! /* [I]*Mi-ya* LÚ ⸢URU⸣*A-ra-aš-ni / iṣ-ṣa-bat* [URU]*Ar-*[*d*]*a-ta* "but as your god lives, Miya, the ruler of Arashni has seized Ar[d]ata" (EA 75:29-31; Youngblood 1961:163; Moran 1987b:253; 1992:145).

Though the second passage is now called in question (Moran 1987b:254 n. 6; 1992:146 n. 6), the first one is certain. Whether the scribe intended the precative or not is unprovable. He might have had the stative in mind, just as in the following:

> *i-nu-ma ba-al-ṭú /* LÚ.MEŠ MAŠKÍM *ù / a-da-bu-bu ka-li ip-ši-šu-nu* "As the commissioners live, I will report all their deeds" (EA 119:21-23; *CAD* B:57a; contrast Moran 1950a:134 n. 187); *e-nu-ma* LUGAL ⸢EN⸣[-*ia*] / TIL.LA *e-nu-ma it-ta-ṣu-ú* [LÚ]⸢MAŠKÍM⸣.M[EŠ] / *a-qa-bi ḫal-qa-at-mi* KUR.ḪÁ *šàr-ri / la ta-ša-mé-ú a-na ia-a-ši* "As the king, [my] lord, lives, whenever the commissio[ners] came forth, I have been saying 'The lands

of the king are lost!' (but) they have not been listening to me" (EA 286:47-50; Nitzán 1973:72).

The most frequent use of the precative in the Canaanite letters is as the first in a chain of injunctive clauses, the subsequent verb forms being either WS jussives or volitives (cf. *infra*, pp. 251-252), e.g.

> *li-iš-me šàr-ru a-wa-te* ÌR-*šu* / *ù ia-di-na ba-la-ṭá* ÌR-*šu* / *yu-ba-li-iṭ* / ÌR-*šu ù* / *a-na-ṣa-*⌜*ra*⌝ [URU] ⌜*ki*⌝-*it-ti-šu a-di* ⌜NIN⌝-*nu* / DINGIR.MEŠ-*nu a*[*-na ka-ta*$_5$] "May the king listen to the words of his servant so that he grant his servant's sustenance, and may he sustain his servant so that I may protect his loyal [city] with our Lady (and) our god(s) f[or you]!" (EA 74:53-57).

The precative itself may even be preceded by an independent particle *lū*:

> *ù lu-ú-mi* / *li-ik-ki-im-mi* / *šàr-ru* URU.KI-*šu la-a-mì* / *yi-iṣ-bat-ši* / [I]*La-ab-a-yu* / . . . *ù lu-ú* / *li-di-nam-mi šàr-ru* / 1 ME LÚ.MEŠ *ma-an-ṣa-ar-ta*$_5$ / *a-na na-ṣa-ri* URU.KI-*šu* / *la-a-mì yi-iṣ-bat-ši* / [I]*La-ab-a-yu* "May the king verily deliver his city lest Labʾayu seize it . . . so may the king provide one hundred guardsmen to protect the city lest Labʾayu seize it!" (EA 244:25-38; Campbell 1965:193; Albright, Mendenhall and Moran 1955:485a; Rabiner 1981:99, 110); *uš-ši-ra-am-mi* [LÚ]DUMU.KIN-*ka* / *it-ti-ia a-na ma-ḫar* / LUGAL BE-*ka ù lu-ú* / *li-di-na-ku* ERÍN.MEŠ *ù* [GIŠ]GIGIR.MEŠ / *i-zi-ir-ta*$_5$ *a-na ka-ta*$_5$ / *ù ti-ṣú-ru* URU "Send your ambassador to me, to the presence of the king, your lord, and he will verily grant you troops and chariots as help for you, that they may guard the city" (EA 87:9-14).

Since the Jerusalem scribe uses WS constructions for the suffix conjugation but not for the prefix conjugation (except for a few examples of direct speech), a considerable number of precatives are employed. They may even appear in a chain of injunctives:

> *ù li-it-ru-uṣ i-na pa-ni* LUGA[L *ù*] / *lu-ma-še-ra* LÚ.MEŠ *ma-ṣar-ta* / *ù le-lu*(sic!)*-ub ù la-mu-ur* 2 I[GI] / LUGAL EN-*ia* "May it be right in the king's sight [that] he send garrison troops, so that I may enter(!) and so that I may see the two e[yes] of the king, my lord" (EA 286:44-47; Nitzan 1973:62, 75); *li-din* LUGAL *pa-ni-šu a-na* LÚ.MEŠ *pi-ṭa-ti* / *ù lu-ṣi* LÚ.MEŠ ERÍN *pi-ṭa-ti* / LUGAL EN-*ia* "May the king give his attention to the army so that the army of the king may come forth" (EA 286:53-55); *ù li-is-kín šàr-ri a-na* ERÍN.MEŠ *pi-ṭa-tu ú* / *lu-ma-še-ra* ERÍN.MEŠ *pi-ṭa-ti a-na* LÚ.MEŠ / *ša ip-pu-šu ar-na a-na šàr-ri* EN-*ia* "May the king take thought for the army so that he may send the army against the men who are committing crime against the king, my lord" (EA 287:17-19; Moran 1987b:512 n. 6; 1992:329 n. 6; also EA 298:41-42; 290:19-21).

At the same time, the precative may be in a clause dependent on what appears to be a preceding WS jussive in a direct quote:

> *a-na-ku a-qa-bi e-ru-ub-mi* / *it-ti šàr-ri* EN-*ia ù la-mur-mi* / 2 IGI LUGAL EN-*ia* "I have been saying, 'May I enter in to the king, my lord, that I may see the two eyes of the king, my lord" (EA 286:39-41; Nitzan 1973:69)

The Tyrian scribe happens to share this use of the precative in injunctive chains:

> *li-it-ta-din* LUGAL *be-li-ia* / *pa-ni-šu a-na* ÌR-*šu* / *ù li-id-din* URU*Ú-sú*KI / *a-na* ÌR-*šu* DUG \ *a-ku-ni* \ *mi-ma* / *a-na ši-te-šu li-it-ta-din* / LUGAL *be-li-ia* 10 LÚGÌR / *a-na na-ṣa-ri* / URU-*šu ù le-ru-ub* / *ù li-mur pa-ni* LU[GAL] *be-li-ia* "May the king, may lord, take thought for his servant so that the town of Usû may give to your servant an amphora of water for him to drink; may the king, my lord, provide ten troopers to protect his city so that I may enter in and so that I may see the face of the ki[ng] my lord" (EA 148:9-17; contrast Moran 1987b:380; 1992:235).

Note that *AHw*:702b takes *li-it-ta-din* in these passages as Gtn. Perhaps rightly, but the scribe seems to distinguish royal "giving" from that of some other element, such as Usû, for which he used *li-id-din*.

CONCLUSION. The emphasis in this discussion has been on 3rd m.s. and 1st c.s. forms because the other persons have the uncontracted *lū* in the precative and they can just as well be WS jussives or volitives.

Such is the case when injunctive *lū* appears with the Canaanite 3rd m.pl. jussive/volitive which has a consonantal *t*-prefix:

> *ù lu-ú / ti-na-ṣa-ru* URU.KI "And may they protect the city!" (EA 136:19; Moran 1951:34 n. 11; 1950a:84); *ù lu-ú ti-mu-ru* 2 IGI.MEŠ ÌR-*ka* "And may your servant's two eyes behold . . . " (EA 141:34).

No Canaanite scribe uses the cohortative particle *i* with 1st c.pl. The one supposed instance of this particle (with an imperative) is obviously to be read DUMU!.‹MEŠ› (EA 138:137). Although the cohortative constructions with *i* are known in the non-WS texts (EA 9:21, 22; 20:79; 23:30; 41:22), the Canaanite scribes employ *lū*, viz.

> *ù* ⸢*lu*⸣*-ú ni-zi-*⸢*iz*⸣ / UGU-*šu-nu ù lu-*[*ú*] *ni-du-bu-ur* / LÚ.MEŠ *ša-ru-ta* "And let us take a stand against them and let us drive out the miscreants" (EA 279:18-21); *ù lu-ú ni-pa-aš gáb-bu-ma* / *nu-kúr-ti* "and let us all make war" (EA 366:31-32); *ù lu-ú ni-ip-ṭú-ur* URU*Ú-ru-sa-lim* KI "And let us desert Jerusalem" (EA 289:29; Albright, Mendenhall and Moran 1955:489a).

The latter example, from the Jerusalem letters, could have legitimately been classified by Moran (1975b:153) as an Assyrianism in view of the close adherence by the Jerusalem scribe to the Assyrian pattern in the precative. Whether the use of injunctive *lū* with 1st c.pl. verbs in the texts from other places than

Jerusalem should be classified as Assyrianisms is an open question. The usage is more likely a simple extension of the particle on the analogy of the other persons in the precative paradigm.

It is clear from the examples adduced that the Canaanite scribes were well versed in the morphology and the use of the precative. There are, nevertheless, a few minor deviations from the normal Akkadian paradigm forms.

The Canaanite scribes frequently incorporate the precative into their letters and often use it in parallel with forms based on the WS injunctive jussive and volitive. The gloss of a precative by a WS jussive (EA 228:18) will be discussed in the next chapter (*infra*, p. 254).

CHAPTER X

WEST SEMITIC MODES AND TENSES

The core of the peculiar jargon developed by the scribes of Canaan in the Amarna Age is the system of verbal modes and tenses. The Akkadian syntactic verb markers reflected in the EA texts from Canaan have been explored in the previous chapter. The next step is to demonstrate how the West Semitic system is employed and how it conflicts with the usual Akkadian norms.

It was Moran (1950a; 1951; 1960) who first deciphered the "code" by which the Akkadian verb forms of the Byblos dialect were made to express the nuances of the local Canaanite dialect of the scribes. Certain morphological features which have only been alluded to or taken for granted in the previous chapters will be seen to be temporal and modal indicators. It was these conjugational forms which Moran analyzed in their respective syntagmas to arrive at a system of modes and tenses that is both coherent within itself and commensurate with the known patterns of better attested dialects from a later period (particularly biblical Hebrew; Rainey 1986, 1988).

THE BASIC PATTERNS

It would appear that six basic patterns were originally in use in the NWS verbal system. They divide naturally into two modes, the former being concerned with tenses, the latter with volition. Each mode has three conjugations and a certain symmetry may be observed between their respective functions. Their arrangement and proposed nomenclature are (Rainey 1990):

INDICATIVE		INJUNCTIVE	
Preterite	*yaqtul, -û*	Jussive	*yaqtul, -û*
Imperfect	*yaqtulu, -ûna*	Volitive	*yaqtula, -û*
Energic	*yaqtulun(n)a*	Energic	*yaqtulan(n)a*

Besides the plural suffixes given above, it must be remembered that the 3rd m.pl. forms have the *t-* prefix (Ebeling 1910:48-49, 51-52; Herdner 1938; Izre'el 1987; cf. *supra,* pp. 43-45). Justification for our choice of nomenclature will be presented in the ensuing discussion of each pattern. One could say that Ebeling had successfully identified the indicative preterite (Ebeling 1910:46-50) and energic (*Ibid.*:69-73) although he failed to see that the many indicative imperfect plurals were not necessarily energics just because they had the *-ûna* suffix. He apparently did recognize the correct meaning of a few of the jussive *yaqtul* forms (e.g. the gloss *ia-az-ku-ur* in EA 228:19; Ebeling 1910:46) but did not draw the necessary conclusion that the jussive was the Canaanite counterpart to the Akkadian precative. He did, however, recognize that the Akkadian *iparras* was not paralleled by a Canaanite **yaqattal* (*ibid.*:51-52; Mendenhall 1947:5-7).

The function of the respective conjugation patterns can best be demonstrated by citing contexts in which the same verb appears in two different functions. Thus, the ensuing discussion will frequently deal with not one but two of the patterns posited above. The synchronic relationships with Ugaritic (Rainey 1987:397-400) may be touched upon when necessary.

THE INDICATIVE MODE

PRETERITE.

This conjugation pattern is distinguished morphologically by the use of the standard personal prefixes plus -Ø suffix on all the attested singulars (no 2nd f.s. forms are documented) and on 1st c.pl. The suffix for 3rd m.pl. and 2nd m.pl. is *-û* (in contrast to *-ûna* of the imperfect).

IN MAIN CLAUSES. The *yaqtul* preterite was relatively rare in the Byblos texts; the predominant form for expressing action in the past was the suffix conjugation (Moran 1950a:30-31, 51-52; cf. *infra,* pp. 348-352). Therefore, Moran was inclined to accept the *yaqtul* preterites as Akkadianisms (Moran 1950a:51). In the next section it will be shown that *yaqtul* preterite was often used as a contrast to *yaqtulu* present/future, especially outside of Byblos. However, there are many other examples of the *yaqtul* preterite, especially in 3rd m.s. with the Canaanite *y-* prefix, which surely indicate that the preterite was a living tense form in spoken WS of the time. Take, for example, the report from Biryawaza, commissioner of Kômidi about the misdeeds of some rulers in his district:

> *yi-mur-ma* ^{I}*Bi-ri-da-aš-wa ip-ša an-na* / *ù yi-nam*!(MAŠ.NA)*-mu-uš* ^{URU}*Ya-nu-am-ma* UGU*-ia* / *u yi-du-ul* KÀ.GAL *a-na* EGIR*-ia* / *ù yi-il*$_5$*-qé* ^{GIŠ}GIGIR.MEŠ *i-na* ^{URU}*Aš-tar-ti*$_7$ / *ù ya-di-in*$_4$*-šu-ni a-na* LÚ.MEŠ SA.GAZ / *ù la-a ya-di-in*$_4$*-šu-ni a-na* LUGAL EN*-ia* / *yi-mur-ma šàr* ^{URU}*Bu-uṣ-ru-na* / *ù šàr* ^{URU}*Ḫa-lu-un-ni u ti*$_7$*-pa-šu* / *nu-kúr-ta it-ti* ^{I}*Bi-ri-da-aš-wa* / *a-na mu-ḫi-ia . . . ù yi-la-ak* ^{I}*Ar-za-wi-ia* / *a-na* ^{URU}*Qì-i*[*s-sà*] *ù yi-il*$_5$*-qa* / ERÍN.MEŠ ^{I}*A-zi-*[*ri u yi*!]*-iṣ-ba-at* / ^{URU}*Ša-ad-du u ya-di-in*$_4$*-ši a-na* / LÚ.MEŠ SA.GAZ *u la-a ia-di-in*$_4$*-ši* / *a-na* LUGAL EN*-ia* "Biridashwa saw this deed and caused Yanûᶜammu to defect from me and locked the gate behind me and took chariots from Ashtaroth and turned both of them over to the *ᶜapîrû* and did not turn them over to the king, my lord. Then the king of Buṣrūna and the king of ᶜAlunni saw, and they began hostilities with Biridashwa against me . . . and Arzawiya went to Qi[ssa (= Kedesh)] and he took Azi[ru]'s troo[ps and sei]zed Shaddu. Then he gave it to the *ᶜapîru-* men and did not give it to the king, my lord" (EA 197:7-16, 26-32).

Note that all the verbs in the passage cited have to be past tense even though two of them, *yinammuš* and *yillak,* utilize the Akkadian present as their base form, or theme.

IN SUBORDINATE CLAUSES. Special note should be taken of certain preterite verb forms which appear in relative clauses. Three points are significant: (1) these forms are also paralleled by *qtl*'s; (2) the prefix verbs in this slot never have the Akkadian subjunctive marker; (3) only rarely do the verb forms have the WS

3rd m.s. prefix *y*-. Three examples of *išpur* appear in the Gezer letters and were discussed by Izre'el (1978b:61):

> *iš-te-mé* / *a-wa-te*^{MEŠ} *ša iš-pu-ur* / LUGAL EN-*ia a-na* ÌR-*šu* "I have heard the words which the king, my lord, sent to his servant" (EA 292:17-19; likewise EA 294:6-8); [*iš-*]*te-mé a-wa-at* / *ša iš-pu-ur* LUGAL EN-*ia* / *a-na* ÌR-*šu* "I have heard the word which the king, my lord, sent to his servant" (EA 293:8-10).

Compare these Akkadian preterites with the following, where a *qtl* verb is used instead:

> *a-nu-ma* / *iṣ-*[*ṣ*]*ú-ru a-wa-at ša* / *qa-*⸢*ba*⸣ LU[GAL] EN-*ia a-na ia-ši* "Now I am keeping the word that the ki[ng], my lord, spoke to me" (EA 294:11-13); *mi-im-ma ša qa-ba* / LUGAL EN-*ia a-na ia-ši* / *iš-te-mé-šu ma-gal* / SIG$_5$-*iš* "As for everything that the king, my lord, said to me, I have heeded it very well" (EA 297:8-11); *mi-im-ma ša qa-ba* LUGAL EN-*ia* / *a-nu-ma i-na-ṣa-ru* KÁM.UD / *u mu-ša a-wa-ta*$_5$ LUGAL EN-*ia* "Everything which the king, my lord, has said, now I am keeping the word of the king, my lord" (EA 315:10-12); *u mi-im-ma ša ša-pár* / L[UGAL] EN-*ia a-na ia-ši* / *iš-te*$_9$*-mu-uš-šu* / *ma-gal ma-gal* "And everything that the k[ing], my lord, has sent to me, I am heeding it very diligently" (EA 320:18-21).

In the next passage, one verb in a relative clause lacks the *y*- prefix (and has the Akkadian ventive) while a second verb in a subordinated clause does have it:

> [*ù*] ^{LÚ}[*ra-*]*bi-iṣ* / [*ša*] LUGAL ⸢EN⸣-*ia* / [*š*]*a iš-*⸢*pu*⸣*-ra-*⸢*am*⸣ / [L]UGAL EN-*i*[*a*] ⸢*a*⸣-⸢*na*⸣ *i*[*a-ši*] / *a-nu-ma iš-te*$_9$*-me* / *gáb-bi a-wa-te*^{M}[^{EŠ}] / *ša yi-iq-*⸢*bi*⸣ / ^{I}*Ma-ia* ^{LÚ}‹MA›ŠKÍM / *a-na ia-ši a-nu-ma i-pu-šu gáb-bi* "[And] as for the [com]missioner [of] the king, my lord, [wh]ich the [k]ing, m[y] lord, sent to me, now I have heard all of the words which Maya the ‹com›missioner spoke to me; now I am doing everything" (EA 328:17-26; Moran 1987b:548; 1992:354).

AKKADIAN *iparras* AS WS PRETERITE. Because the expressions cited above with *(y)aqtul*+Ø usually seem to relate to something specific which the king has said/sent, evidently in a letter just received, all the relative clauses are past tense, dealing with a single instance. Therefore, it may be surmised that the following, with an apparent Akkadian G present, is also preterite in meaning:

> *šá-ni-tam* / *gáb-bi* URU.KI.ḪÁ-*ia ša i-qa-bi a-na pa-ni* BE-*ia* / *i-de be-li šum-ma ta-ru i-na* UD.KÁM / *pa-ṭá-ar* ERÍN.MEŠ KI.KAL.KASKAL+x.BAD *be-li*[-*i*]*a* / *na-ak-ru gáb-bu* "Furthermore, as for all the towns of which I spoke in the presence of my lord, my lord knows whether (or not) they have returned; on the day that the expeditionary force departed, they all became hostile!" (EA 106:45-49; cf. Moran 1987b:303, 304 n. 9; 1992:179, 180 n 10).

In fact there are some very clear instances of Akkadian *iparras* forms with -Ø suffix that can only be preterite in function. Note, for example, the forms *yi-nam*!(MAŠ.NA)-*mu-uš* (EA 197:8) and *yi-la-ak* (EA 197:26) cited above (*supra*, p. 223). Additional examples are:

> *ù a*[*n-n*]*u-ú i-še*$_{20}$*-me a-na* / *a-wa-te*^{MEŠ}*-ka ù ú-wa-š*[*ir*$_4$*-šu*] / *ù uṣ-ṣa-am ri-qú-tám* / *ù i-še*$_{20}$*-me e-nu-ú ia-nu-um* ⸢ERÍN⸣.MEŠ / *it-ti-šu* "And b[eho]ld, I heeded your words and I sent [him] but he came back empty-handed and he heard that there were no troops with him" (EA 87:15-19; Rainey 1975b:424-426; Moran 1987b:273 n. 1; 1992:159cf. Youngblood 1961:298).

Probably *ú-ba-a*[*l*] (EA 327:9) also belongs here.

CONTRAST WITH IMPERFECT. There are a number of contexts, especially from outside Byblos, where prefix forms with -Ø suffix were directly contrasted with prefix forms having -*u*. The former expressed single instances in the past while the latter denoted present/future continuous (Rainey 1971c:96-102).

> *iš-te-mé* / *a-wa-te*MEŠ *ša iš-pu-ur* / LUGAL EN-*ia a-na* ÌR-*šu* / *ú-ṣur-mi* LÚMAŠKÍM-*ka* / *ù ú-ṣur* URU.DIDLI.ḪÁ *ša* / LUGAL EN-*ka a-nu-ma* / ⌈*iṣ*⌉-*ṣú-ru ú a-nu-ma* / ⌈*iš*⌉-*te-mu* UD.KÁM-*ma* / *ù mu-ša a-wa-te*MEŠ *ša* / LUGAL EN-*ia* "I have heeded the words which the king, my lord, sent to his servant, 'Guard your commissioner and guard the cities of the king, your lord.' Now I am guarding and now I am heeding day and night the words of the king, my lord" (EA 292:17-26; Rainey 1975b:406-407).

The zero form (*yaqtul*), *iš-te-mé,* refers to the single event of hearing the message sent by the king (i.e. having the tablet read aloud). The *yaqtulu* forms, ⌈*iṣ*⌉-*ṣú-ru* and ⌈*iš*⌉-*te-mu,* affirm the continuous compliance with the king's instructions, "day and night." Especially striking here is the contrast between *iš-te-mé* and ⌈*iš*⌉-*te-mu,* 1st c.s. forms of *šemû* "to hear" (with the preformative vowel of 3rd m.s., cf. *supra,* pp.40-43); It is the suffix -*u* on the latter that sets it apart as present/future. On the one hand, *išteme*/*ešteme* is used frequently in letters responding to a message from Pharaoh when the writer wishes to indicate that he has heard (i.e. had read to him) the message from the king (EA *141*:8, 23; 142:[6],8; 144:13; 145:*11*, 27(?); 178:13; 192:10; 196:5; 213:10; 216:6; 217:7; 220:9; 221:8; 227:7; 243:8; 246:8; 247:*11*; 253:7; 254:6; 269:8; 294:6; 297:10, 17; 299:12; 301:15; 302:14; 303:13, 19; 304:15; 319:15; 321:21; 326:13; 327:1; 328:21; 329:16; 330:*11*; 364:10). On the other hand, present and future compliance with the king's instructions is expressed by forms with the -*u* suffix as in EA 292:24 cited above. The force of *eštemû*/*ištemû* (*eštemu*/*ištemu*?) is further demonstrated by a context in which it is parallel to a real Akkadian Gtn present:

> *u a-nu-ma* [*é*]*l-t*[*e*9-*n*]*é-mé* / *a-na a-w*[*a-*]*t*[*e* ME]Š L[UGA]L EN-ia / ⌈*u*⌉ *iš-*[*t*]*e*9-*mu* [*a-n*]*a a-wa-te*MEŠ / I*Ma-i*[*a* LÚM]AŠ[KÍ]M [LU]GAL / EN-*ia* ⌈d⌉[UTU] *iš-tu* / AN*ša-ma* D[UMU] ⌈d⌉UTU "And now [I] a[m] heeding the words of the ki[ng], my lord, and I am heeding the words of Maya, [the co]mm[issio]ner of the [ki]ng, my lord, the [sun god] from heaven, the s[on of] the sun god" (EA 300:23-28; Rainey 1971b:97-98; *supra, pp.* 114-116).

In spite of the preponderance of *qtl* to express the past tense of transitive verbs at Byblos, there are still instances of the same *yaqtul-yaqtulu* contrast:

> *i-na-an-na* / *tu-ma-al ša-al-ša-mi* / *ti₇-iq-bu-ni ia-nu-mi* / ERÍN.MEŠ *pí-ṭá-ta₅ ù aš-pu-ur* / *ù tu-ṣa* ERÍN.MEŠ *pí-ṭá-tu* / *ù ti₇-ìl-qé* ˡ*a-ba-šu-nu* . . . *ù be-li i-de i-nu-ma* / *la-a aš-pu-ru a-wa-at* / *ka-az-bu-te a-na be-li-ia* "Now previously they said to me, 'There is no regular army force,' so I wrote and a regular army force came forth and it seized their father . . . . And my lord knows that I never write a word of falsehood to my lord" (EA 362:15-20, 51-53; cf. discussion by Rainey 1971c:102).

The contrast between *ašpur* and *ašpuru* is that between a past event and habitual practice.

IMPERFECT.

TERMINOLOGY. A word is in order about the choice of the term imperfect (Rainey 1986a:7). In his dissertation, Moran called the *yaqtulu* form "indicative" following the usual practice of Arabic grammars. In Arabic the zero form had lost its preterite function almost entirely (except for the negative *lam yaqtul, lammâ yaqtul,* Fischer 1972:96, §194), and the energic in *-un*(*n*)*a* had long before given some of its functions to the energic in *-an*(*n*)*a* (cf. *infra*, pp. 234-244), so there was no need to differentiate between various forms; the only prefix indicative was *yaqtulu*. Note, however, that Wright had mentioned the fact that the suffix conjugation in Arabic also functions in indicative contexts (Wright 1896:52, §79).

Presently, Moran and others, e.g. Huehnergard, prefer the term "durative" which they apply to WS *yaqtulu* and to Akkadian *iparras*. That these forms can, and frequently do, express durative action is certainly true, but they can also express punctiliar action in the future. In such cases as those treated below, the durative notion is hardly appropriate as Moran himself had acknowledged:

> . . . though in present contexts the form, as is natural, carries a durative force, still this is not true of its use in future contexts where it expresses the simple fact of the occurrence of an action in the future (Moran 1950a:48).

Huehnergard has objected that, if "durative" does not cover single actions in the future, neither does imperfect. However, one can only endorse the citation by Moran (1950a:49) of S. R. Driver's description of the imperfect's use for future actions:

> The same form [the imperfect] is further employed to describe events belonging to the *future:* for the future is emphatically τὸ μέλλον and this is just the attribute specially expressed by the imperfect. . . . that which is in the process of coming to pass is also that which is *destined* or *must* come to pass (τὸ μέλλον) . . . " (Driver 1892:28-29).

With these points in mind, one may also acknowledge Moran's assertion that *yaqtulu* is not primarily a tense (Moran 1950a:48). It will be seen herein that it can express present, future and past continuous actions. Its main semantic feature is expression of action not completed. That is not to say that the ancient Canaanite scribes had no sense of time. Quite the contrary, the ensuing discussion will show that they were perfectly aware of the time factor in their linguistic expression.

PRESENT. The function of *yaqtulu* as a present is clearly demonstrated in a gloss which also happens to strengthen the case for *yaqtulu* as the WS counterpart to the Akkadian *iparras* (cf. *supra,* p. 67; Rainey 1975b:423):

> *a-nu-um-ma a-na-ku-ma / er-ri-šu \ aḫ-ri-šu / i-na* ^{URU}*Šu-na-ma*^{KI}
> "Now, it is I who am cultivating in Shunem" (EA 365:10-12).

The hybrid form *errišu* is Akkadian 1st c.s. with gemination, plus the WS indicative imperfect suffix *-u.* The gloss, with exactly the same meaning, stands for the cognate WS form **ʾaḥrišu* (‹**ʾaḥriṯu*), a purely WS construction without gemination but with the same -*u* suffix. The particular context, with introductory *anumma* "now," is present tense.

Another firm context is this passage from Megiddo:

> *ù a-nu-ma i-na-ṣa-*⸢*ru*⸣ / ^{URU}*Ma-gi*$_5$*-da*^{KI} / URU.KI *šàr-ri* EN-*ia* / ⸢UD⸣/KÁM *ù* GI$_6$*-ša* \ *l*[*e-l*]*a* / UD.KÁM *i-na-ṣa-ru* / ⸢*iš*⸣*-tu* A.ŠÀ.MEŠ / *i-na* GIGIR.MEŠ *ù* G[I$_6$*-ša*] / *i-na-ṣa-ru* BÀD ⸢URU⸣.K[I] / *šàr-ri* EN-*ia* "And now I am guarding Megiddo, the city of the king, my lord, day and night; by day I am guarding from the open fields in chariots and by night I am guarding the wall of the city of the king, my lord" (EA 243:10-18; Rainey 1975b:404-405).

There is certainly no pretext here for deriving the present-future nuance from the Akkadian *iparras* theme upon which the verb forms are built. This is abundantly clear in the following excerpts from the same epistle, first:

> [*a*]*-*⸢*nu*⸣*-ma iṣ-ṣú-ru* / [UR]U.KI LUGAL EN-*ia* ^{d}U[TU]-*ia* / *a-di ka-ša-di* / ^{LÚ}MAŠKÍM *šàr-ri* EN-*ia* / ^{d}UTU-*ia* (EA 220:15-19);

but later on:

> *a-nu-ma i*$_{15}$*-na-ṣa-ru* / URU.KI *ša šàr-ri* EN-*ia* / ^{d}UTU-*ia ša it-ti-ia* / *a-di ka-ša-di* / ^{LÚ}MAŠKÍM *šàr-ri* EN-*ia* / ^{d}UTU-*ia* (EA 220:25-30);

and both passages are to be rendered:

> "Now I am guarding the city of the king, my lord (line 27: which is in my charge) until the arrival of the commissioner of the king, my lord (and) my sun-god" (Rainey 1975b:405).

The present tense is the natural vehicle to serve as an indicator of habitual action as illustrated by the following passage:

> *mi-ia-mì* LÚ*kal-bu* / *u la-a yi-iš-mu* / *a-na a-wa-te* LUGAL EN-*šu* "Who is the dog that he would not listen to the words of the king, his lord?" (EA 320:22-24; 322:17-19); *mi-nu* / IÌR-*A-ši-ir-ta* ÌR / UR.GI$_7$ *ù* [*y*]*i-ìl-qú* / KUR LUGAL *a-na ša-a-šu* "What is ᶜAbdi-Ashirta, a slave? a dog? that he should take the land of the king for himself?" (EA 71:16-19).

Again, one must observe that forms like *yi-iš-mu* and [*y*]*i-ìl-qú* prove that the Akkadian preterite theme acquires its present tense nuance by the addition of the -*u* suffix. Likewise, it is equally certain that the following *yi-iš-te*$_9$-*mu* and *iš-te*$_9$-*mu* forms are built on the Akkadian -*t*- preterite and not on the Gt present (*ištemme;* which is homophonous, of course, with the Gtn preterite):

> *mi-ia-mi* / LÚUR.KU$_8$ *u la-a* / *yi-iš-te*$_9$-*mu a-wa-ta*$_5$ / LUGAL EN-*ia* "Who is the dog that he would not obey the word of the king, my lord?" (EA 323:17-20; also EA 324:16-18; 325:12-14); *mi-ia-ti a-na-ku ù la* / *iš-te*$_9$-*mu a-na* MAŠKÍM LUGAL EN-‹*ia*› "Who am I that I should not listen to the commissioner of the king, ‹my› lord?" (EA 220:11-12).

FUTURE. The future tense is exemplified by various passages, e.g. conditional sentences, both protasis and apodosis (Moran 1950a:72, 74-75):

> *ù šum-ma ap-pu-na-ma yu-ṣa-na šàr-ru* / *ù ka-li* KUR.KUR.KI *nu-kúr-tu*$_4$ *a-na ša-šu* / *ù mi-na yi-pu-šu a-na ia-ši-nu* "But if, moreover, the king should come forth and all the lands are hostile to him, then what can he do to us?" (EA 74:39-41); *šum-ma a-wa-te-ia tu-uš-mu-*[*na*] / *a-di yu-ú-ul-qú* I*A-za-ru ki-ma a*[*-bi-š*]*u* "If my words be heeded, Aziru will yet be captured like his father" (EA 117:32-33).

Compare also the following dependent clauses where the -*u* suffix is WS imperfect and not Akkadian subjunctive as one might suppose at first glance; cf. *supra,* pp. 195-202, for the demonstration that the Akkadian subjunctive was not used by the Canaanite scribes.

> *i-na-ṣa-ru-šu* / *a-di yi-im-lu-ku* LUGAL "I am guarding him until the king takes counsel (concerning his servant)" (EA 142:16-17); *a-nu-ma* / *a-na-ṣa-ru* / URU *šàr-ri* EN-*ia a-di ti-ik-šu-du* / *a-wa-at šàr-ri* / EN‹-*ia*› *a-na ia-ši* "Now I am guarding the city of the king, my lord, until the word of the king, ‹my› lord, reaches me" (EA 221:11-16); *a-di yi-du* "until he takes cognizance" (EA 12:36; 182:14); *a-di yu-šu-te-ru* "until he responds" (EA 280:38-39); *a-nu-ma ki-ia-am* / *qa-la-ta a-di-mi* / *yi-ìl-ma-du šàr-ru* / *be-lí-ia a-wa-ta*$_5$ / *an-ni-ta*$_5$ "And thus you keep silent, (saying) 'Until the king, my lord, looks into this matter'" (EA 251:7-11).

It must be noted that all the verbs in clauses dependent upon *adi* cited above are built on the theme of the Akkadian preterite, viz. *yi-im-lu-ku, ti-ik-šu-du, yi-du, yu-šu-te-ru, yi-ìl-ma-du*. Their future tense is determined by the clear indications of their contexts. Therefore, it is obvious that the *-u* suffix on the verbs is the WS indicator of indicative imperfect and not the Akkadian subjunctive marker. Therefore, in the following examples, one may state with confidence that the future meaning is signified by the suffix *-u* and not because the verb forms happen to be constructed on the Akkadian present theme:

> *a-šar ti-la-ku* "wherever you go" (EA 296:4'); *a-di a-šar ti*$_7$*-la-ku* "to wherever you go" (EA 203:19; 204:19; 205:18); *a-di a-šar yi-qa-bu* "to wherever you say" (EA 195:31; 201:21); *ia-nu a-šar er-ru-bu* "There is nowhere I can enter" (EA 76:21: also EA 71:34).

Another important syntagma requiring the *yaqtulu* is the purpose clause when it is dependent on a verbal clause having either the indicative or a suffix conjugation form of the verb. This was one of Moan's most significant discoveries concerning the syntax of the Byblos letters (Moran 1950a:81-82; 1951:33-34; 1960:9-12):

i-na-na a-di yu-pa-ḫi-ru ka[*-li*] / URU.MEŠ *ù yi-ìl-qú-ši*ₓ(ŠE) "Now he is again assembling all the towns in order that he seize it (Byblos)" (EA 124:14-15); *a-na mi-ni₇* / *qa-la-ta ù la-a* / *ti-iq-bu a-na šàr-ri* / *ù yu-wa-ši-ru-na* / ERÍN.MEŠ *pí-ṭá-ti ù ti-ìl-te₉-qú-na* / URU*Ṣu-mu-ra* "Why do you keep silent and not speak to the king that he should send the regular troops in order that they occupy Ṣumur?" (EA 71:10-16); LUGAL / KUR*Ka-aš-ši ù* LUGAL KUR*Mi-ta-ni šu-nu* / *ù ti-ìl-qú-na* / KUR *šàr-ri a-na* / *ša-šu-nu* "Are they the king of the Cassites and the king of Mitanni that they take the land of the king for themselves?" (EA 104:19-24).

All of the verb forms in the purpose clauses, viz. *yi-ìl-qú-ši*ₓ(ŠE), *yu-wa-ši-ru-na, ti-ìl-te₉-qú-na,* are all built on Akkadian preterite or *-t-* preterite themes. Their future nuance is due to the *-u* suffix.

PAST CONTINUOUS. One of Moran's most important discoveries was the function of the indicative imperfect to express repeated or continuous action in the past (Moran 1950a:43-47):

pa-na-nu / [LU]GAL KUR*Mi-ta-na nu-*KÚR *a-na a-bu-tu-ka* / ⌈*ù*⌉ *la-a ti*!(PI)*-na-mu-šu-*⌈*na*⌉ / [*a*]*-bu-tu-ka iš-tu a-*⌈*bu*⌉*-t*[*i-ia*] "Formerly, the king of Mitanni was hostile with your fathers but your [fa]thers never abandoned [my] fathers" (EA 109:5-8; cf. Moran 1950a:124a n. 104; cf. Izre'el 1987:87);

or, when a nominal (non-verbal) sentence is coupled with an imperfect verbal clause:

pa-na-nu LÚ.MEŠ *ma-ṣa-ar-ti* / *šàr-ri it-ti-ia ù* / *šàr-ru ia-di-nu* ŠE.*IM*.ḪÁ / *iš-tu* KUR*Ia-ri-mu-ta* / *a-na a-ka-li-šu-nu* "Formerly, the king's garrison troops were with me and the king was furnishing grain from Yarimuta for their sustenance" (EA 125:14-18; Moran 1950a:44, 96).

Thus, one finds many examples with the WS imperfect to express past continuous action (EA 114:54-57; 117:43-44; 118:50-53; 126:18-23; 138:94-95). Moran (1950a:45; 1961:63) has seen fit to cite the following passage in its entirety because it demonstrates so clearly the refinements of tense nuance achieved by the alternation between *yaqtulu* and *qatal* verb forms:

> *mi-ia-mi* / DUMU.MEŠ ^{I}ÌR-*A-ši-ir-ta* / ÌR UR.GI$_7$ LUGAL / ^{KUR}*Ka-aš-ši ù* LUGAL ^{KUR}*Mi-ta-ni šu-nu* / *ù ti-ìl-qú-na* / KUR *šàr-ri a-na* / *ša-šu-nu pa-na-nu* / *ti-ì[l-q]ú[-n]a* URU.MEŠ / *ḫa-za-ni-ka ù qa-la-ta* / *an-nu-ú i-na-na du-bi-r[u]* / ^{LÚ}MAŠKÍM-*ka ù la-qú* / URU.MEŠ-*šu a-na ša-šu-nu a-nu-ma la-qú* ^{URU}*Ul-la-sà* / *šum-ma ki-a-ma qa-la-ta* / *a-di ti-ìl-qú-na* / ^{URU}*Ṣu-mu-ra ù* / ›*ù*‹ *ti-du-ku-na* ^{LÚ}MAŠKÍM / *ù* ERÍN.MEŠ *til*!(BI)-*la-ti* / *ša i-na Ṣu-mu-ra* "Who are the sons of ᶜAbdi-Ashirta, the slave, the dog? Are they the king of the Cassites and the king of Mitanni that they take the land of the king for themselves? Previously, they were taking over the towns of the city rulers, and you kept silent. Behold, now they have expelled your commissioner and have taken your towns for themselves. Behold, they have taken Ullasa. If you thus remain silent, they will take Ṣumur in addition and they will kill the commissioner and the auxiliary troops who are in Ṣumur" (EA 104:17-36; Moran 1987b:299 n. 1; 1992:177 n. 1).

Each of the three occurrences of *tilqûna* has a different temporal nuance; that following *panānu* describes a series of actions conducted in the past. The suffix verb, *qâlāta,* defines responses in the past and then in the present in the conditional sentence).

Normally, *pānānu*(*m*) comes at the head of such clauses of repeated, or continuous action in the past. Nevertheless, other factors, such as the subordination of the clause, may change the order so that *pānānu* may come later in the clause. Note the following relativized clause in which past continuous is contrasted symmetrically with a volitive expressing a wish for the present:

> *ša-a yu-da-*⸢*nu*⸣ *pa-na-nu i-na* ^{URU}*Ṣu-mu-ra* / [*y*]*u-da-na*$_7$ ⸢*i*⸣*-na-na i-na* ^{URU}*Gub-la* "What used to be sold formerly in Ṣumur, let it be sold now in Byblos" (EA 85:36-37; cf. Moran 1950a:43, 95).

CIRCUMSTANTIAL. Finally, Moran (1950a:47) also noted some illustrations of the circumstantial function of *yaqtulu*. One of them, dependent on *kīma*, was cited *supra*, pp. 85-86, where a suggested correction of Knudtzon's reading provides two *yaqtulu* past continuous verbs instead of one:

> *a-nu-ma / ki-ma iš-[tap-]ru a-na ka-ta*$_5$ UGU / ^{URU}*Ṣu-mu-ra a-nu-ma i-te*$_9$*-lu*! / *ù a[ḫ-]ta-ni* ERÍN.M[EŠ] *a-na / [na-ṣa-ri-]ši ù a-nu-‹ma› i-te*$_9$*-zi-ib-ši / [ù pa-aṭ-ru* LÚ.MEŠ] UN-*tù ù / [ki-na-na iš-tap-]ru* "Now, as (*contra* Moran 1987b:317 n. 4; 1992:189 n. 4) I was wr[iti]ng to you concerning Ṣumur, now I was going up (there) and I ex[ho]rted the troops to [guard i]t, but now I have abandoned it [and] the garrison [troops have departed (Moran 1987b:318 n. 6; 1992:190 n. 7)] and [thus I have been writ]ing (Moran 1987b:318 n. 7; 1992:190 n. 8)" (EA 114:26-32).

In the other passage, the circumstantial clause does not have a subordinating conjunction; it is followed by a negative existential clause, also referring to past time:

> *ša-ni-tam šàr* ^{KUR}*‹Mi›-ta-[n]a a-ṣí / a-di* ^{URU}*Ṣu-mu-ra ù yu-ba-ú / a-la-⸢ka*$_{13}$⸣ *a-di* ^{URU}*Gub-la ù i[a]-nu* / A.MEŠ(!) *a-na ⸢ša⸣-te-šu ù ta-ra / a-na* KUR-*šu* "Furthermore, the king of ‹Mi›tanni came out as far as Ṣumur and when he was seeking to come to Byblos, there was no water for him to drink so he returned to his land" (EA 85:51-55).

It is also possible to translate: "and he was seeking to come to Byblos but there was no water for him to drink." The nature of *yubaʾʾû*, as a past continuous is obvious by its place between two *qtl* verbs.

ENERGIC.

Ebeling did recognize the energic forms in the EA texts and collected all the references in a section of his study (Ebeling 1910:69-73). The sufformative is *-una*, perhaps *-unna*. The clearest example of the gemination of the *nûn* is from Kāmed el-Lôz: *ut-ta-aš-še-ru-un-na-šu-nu* "I am most assuredly sending them" (KL 72:600:8; Rainey 1976b:338-339; Wilhelm 1982:124). Another apparent indication of gemination is *ti-il*$_5$*-la-ku-un*!(EN)*-na* (TT 6:9; Rainey 1977:37, 40; 1976b:338-339; Sachs *apud* Albright 1944b:24 n. 88). Orthographically unexpressed gemination might also be a factor in the presence or absence of a vowel before suffixes attached to the energic (cf. KL 72:600:8 cited above). Forms having such a vowel are: *yu-te-ru-/na-ni* (EA 251:11-12; with dative suffix); *yu-wa-ši-ru-n[a-k]a* (EA 77:22; acc. suff.); *ti[l]-la-[k]u-na-mì* (EA 250:26); *ú-ba-[ú-n]a-ši* (EA 143:15); *uš-ši-ru-na-ši* (EA 143:16); cf. also the apparent injunctive volitive energic *ti-ma-ḫa-ṣa-na-n[i]* (EA 77:37; *infra*, pp. 263-264). Examples of what may be the energic with the loss of the final *-a* and the assimilation of the ungeminated *-n-* are: *i-na-ṣa-ru-um-mi* (EA 228:14); *ni-ik-šu-du-um-mi* (EA 245:5); *ú-ta-aš-ša-ru-uš-šu* (EA 245:29); *nu-ub-ba-lu-uš-šu* (EA 245:7); note that *yi-na-ṣí-ra-an-ni* (EA 112:13; 121:10) is evidently a ventive plus suffix.

The energic is a strengthening of the imperfect (with one injunctive exception discussed below (cf. *infra*, pp. 263-264). It does not seem to be compulsory in any syntagma, but rather serves as an optional means for strengthening the force of the verb (cf. e.g. EA 121:7-10 with EA 123:29-32; Zewi 1987:183). Since Ebeling's day, various studies have contributed to further refinement of our understanding of these energic forms. Moran's discoveries concerning the nature and function of the imperfect, especially the proof that the 3rd m.s. plural was *taqtulūna*, corrected Ebeling's classification of the forms by eliminating the plurals from consideration (Moran 1950a:53-56; 1951). In fact, there is no way to distinguish in the script between the indicative imperfect plural and the indicative energic plural. The main focus must be on the singulars, for only with them can a satisfactory classification of syntagmas be achieved. Aistleitner (1957:263-269, 280-286) adduced the EA energic forms in his discussion of the energic in Ugaritic. He seemingly was unaware of Moran's work and commits some basic errors in his classification. The main fault lies in his unawareness that the EA texts can use either the Akkadian preterite theme, *iprus*, or the present, *iparras*, for building imperfect forms (cf. discussion, *supra*, pp. 50-61). So he sought to distinguish between the energics on Akkadian preterites and those on the Akkadian present. This and also his comparison (negative) with the Assyrian subjunctive *-uni* were irrelevant. Williams (1972:80-81) made reference to Moran's study of the EA energic in his study of the energic in biblical Hebrew; again, a confusion of the singulars and the plurals (in Hebrew especially) vitiated somewhat the validity of the argument (cf. the remarks by Rainey 1975d:185-187). Blau (1978:127) deduced, like Rainey (1975d:186), that the indicative energic with *-una* must be the ancestor of the energic survivals in Hebrew (imperfect with accusative suffixes *-enhû, -ennû,* etc.) and Aramaic (with -[*i*]*nn*- preceding accusative suffixes on the imperfect). The most recent, and most thorough, discussion of the energic in the EA texts is by T. Zewi (1987:172-188). The ensuing discussion is based largely on her classification and analysis of the texts (energic suffixes on plural imperatives will be discussed *infra*, pp. 271-272).

INTERROGATIVE SENTENCES. The majority of the passages in which this energic suffix is added to the imperfect verb are questions. In clauses having an interrogative particle or phrase, such as *ana mīni* "why?" there may have been felt a need to give additional emphasis to the verbal action as the focus (the logical predicate) of the question. Without such emphasis, the interrogative particle or phrase is itself the logical predicate.

Several examples reflect the writer's rhetorical question "what can I *do*?" The point is, of course, that he feels powerless in a given circumstance. Often the idea is that he is helpless because he is by himself:

> *mi-na i-pu-šu-na a-na-ku i-na* / [*i*]*-de-ni-ia* "What can I do by myself?" (EA 74:63-64; 81:50-51; 90:22-23; 91:25-26; 134:15-16);

or sometimes the emphasis may be on the writer himself as a particular individual:

mi-na i-pu-šu-na a-na-ku "What can *I* do?" (EA 115:10; 117:92; 119:14; 122:48-49; 130:30-31; 249:10-11); *šum-ma mi-ta-ti mi-na i-pu-‹šu›-na* "If I am dead, what can I ‹d›o?" (EA 119:17-18).

Once, we have a plural energic in the same syntagma:

u mi-na-am-mi ni-pu-šu-na / ni-nu "and what are we to do?" (EA 98:21-22).

Sometimes another attendant circumstance is proffered as justification:

mi-na i-pu-šu-na / a-na-ku ša-a aš-ba-ti / i-na lìb-bi LÚ.MEŠ GAZ.MEŠ "What shall I do who is located among the *ᶜapîrû* men?" (EA 134:15-16); *mi-na / i-pu-šu-na ù a-na-ku / la i-le-ù a-la-*⌈*ka*$_{13}$⌉ */ a-na Ṣu-mu-ra* "What can I do since I am unable to go to Ṣumur?" (EA 104:36-39); *ù mi-na ip-p[u-š]u-[na*⌉ */ ù aš-tap-pár* LÚ KIN-*ia a-na* LUGAL ⌈BE⌉-*ia* "What can I do since I have (already) sent my emissary to the king, my lord?" (EA 92:15-16).

Other verbs also take the energic in similar rhetorical questions:

ia-nu ŠE.*IM*.ḪÁ *a-na / a-ka-li a-na ia-ši-nu mi-na a-*⌈*qa*⌉*-bu-na / a-na* LÚ.MEŠ *ḫu-up-ši-ia* "There is no grain for us to eat (so) what can I say to my yeoman farmers?" (EA 85:10-12); *mi-na a-qa-bu-na / ap-pu-na-ma* "What more can I say?" (EA 119:53); *a-ia[-mi] / i-zi-zu-na a-na-ku* "Where can *I* stay?" (EA 124:15-16);

and especially the following:

iš-tu ma-an-ni i-na-ṣa-ru-na / iš-tu na-ak-ri-ia / ù iš-tu LÚ.MEŠ *ḫu-up-ši-ia / mi-nu yi-na-ṣí-na-an-ni* "From whom should I be on guard? From my enemies? And from my yeoman farmers, who will protect me?" (EA 112:10-13; contrast Moran 1950a:169; 1987b:312; 1992:186; Rainey 1975b:416 nn. 185, 190); *i-nu-ma*

> *i-ša-pa-ru* / *šàr-ru ù-ṣur-mi* / *ra-ma-an-ka iš-tu ma-ni* / *i-na-ṣí-ru-na* "Inasmuch as the king has written, 'Protect yourself!' from whom shall I be on guard?" (EA 123:29-32); *iš-t[u] ma-ni* / *i-na-ṣa-ru-na ra-ma-ni-ia ù* URU [LUGAL] "From whom shall I protect myself and the city of [the king]" (EA 125:11-13).

The following compound sentence probably contains a question, depending on how one interprets the particle *ki-i:*

> *i-nu-ma šap-ra-ta* / *a-na ia-a-ši ù!-ṣur-mì* / LÚ.MEŠ *ša ṣa-ab-tu* URU / *ki-i uš-šur-ru-na* LÚ.MEŠ "Inasmuch as you have written to me, 'Keep watch on the men who have seized the town,' how can I keep watch over the men?" (EA 252:5-8).

There are also a number of 2nd m.s. energics in interrogative clauses:

> *ša-ni-tam a-na* ⸢*mi*⸣-[*ni*$_7$] / ⸢*la*⸣!-⸢*a*⸣! *tu-wa*-⸢*ša*⸣-[*ru*]-⸢*na*⸣! / *šu-lum-ka a-na* ⸢*ia*⸣![-*ši*!] "Furthermore, why do you not send to me regarding your welfare?" (TT 1:12-14); *a*[*l-lu-*]*mì* / *ia-aq-bu šàr-ru* EN-*li a*[-*n*]*a* / *mi-ni at-ta-ma ti-iš-tap-ru-na* / *a-na ia-ši* "Behold, the king, my lord, says, 'Why do you continually write to me?'" (EA 117:6-9); *a-na mi-ni la-a tu-te-ru-*[*n*]*a* / *a-wa-ta*$_5$ *a-na ia-a-ši* "Why do you not send word back to me? (EA 83:7-8); *a-na mi-ni ti-iš-mu-na* / LÚ.MEŠ *ša-nu-tu* "Why do you listen to other men?" (EA 108:51-52); *aq-ta-bi ù aš-ta-ni* / *a-na ka-ta*$_5$ *ú-ul ti-le-ú-na* / *la-qa-ia iš-tu qa-at* / ^{I}ÌR-*A-ši-ir-ta* "I have said repeatedly to you: 'Are you unable to rescue me from the power of ^{c}Abdi-Ashirta?'" (EA 82:5-8).

One 3rd m.s. form occurs in a context that lends itself to translation as a question (for an alternative view, cf. *infra*, p. 244):

> [*a-nu*]-*ma ki-a-ma-am iš-tap-ru a-na šàr-ri* EN-*ia* / *ù la-a yi-iš-mu-na a-wa-te-ia* "[No]w thus have I been writing to the king, my lord, but doesn't he even listen to my words?" (EA 85:6-7).

ASSOCIATED WITH QUESTIONS. The next category includes clauses that are either consecutive after a question or else juxtaposed to an interrogative "that"-clause. The interrogative nuance has evidently been carried over to the associated clause. This is especially true of purpose clauses in which an indicative imperfect is required after a question:

> *a-na mi-ni$_7$ / qa-ta-ta ù la-a / ti-iq-bu a-na šàr-ri / ù yu-wa-ši-ru-na* / ERÍN.MEŠ *pí-ṭá-ti ù / ti-ìl-te$_9$-qú-na* / URU *Ṣu-mu-ra* "Why do you keep silent and not speak to the king that he send the regular troops in order that they may occupy Ṣumur?" (EA 71:10-16; also EA 77:18-25; 114:61-63).

In the next example, the energic also serves to convert a verb with the ventive *-a* suffix into an indicative:

> *a-na mi-ni$_7$ / qa-la-ta ù la-a táq-bu / a-na šàr-ri* EN-*li-ka / ù tu-ṣa-na qa-du* ERÍN.MEŠ / *pí-ṭá-ti ù ti-ma-qú-tu* / UGU KUR*A-mur-ri* "Why have you kept silent and do not speak to the king, your lord, so that you can come forth with the army and attack Amurru?" (EA 73:6-11; Rainey 1990:418-419).

A "that"-clause in juxtaposition to a question also contains an energic:

> *i-nu-ma yi-iš-tap-ru-na / šàr-ru* EN-*ia a-na ia-*[*š*]*i / ù-ṣur-mi* [*r*]*a-m*[*a-a*]*n-k*[*a*] *mi-nu yi-n*[*a-ṣí*]*-ra*[*-an-ni*] "Inasmuch as the king. my lord, has written to me, 'Protect ⌜yourself,' who will prote[ct me]?" (EA 121:7-10).

CONDITIONAL SENTENCES. There are numerous instances when an energic is used in the protasis of a conditional sentence:

> *šum-ma-mi a-na-ku / uṣ-ṣú-na* UGU KUR / *ša* LUGAL *ù a-na ia-ši / in$_4$-né-ep-ša-ta* "If I go forth against the land of the king, then you will be on my side" (EA 333:15-18; cf. Moran 1987b:551, 552 n. 8; 1992:356, 357 n. 8).

Moran (1953; 1987b:551, 552 n. 7; 1992:356, 357 n. 7) claims that *šumma* here is not the conditional particle but rather a presentation particle, "Look." On the other hand, one wonders if this clause may not, in fact, be a question: "If I go forth against the land of the king, then will you be on my side?" The next examples are much clearer:

> *šum-ma / la-a* ERÍN.MEŠ *pí-ṭá-‹ta› la-a / tu-wa-‹ši›-ru-na ù ia-nu* URU *ša-a ti-ir-te$_9$-ḫu / a-na ka-ta$_5$ ù šum-ma* ERÍN.MEŠ *pí-ṭ[á-tu] / i-ba-ša-at ka-li* KUR.MEŠ / *ni-ìl-qú a-na šàr-ri* "If you do not send regular troops, then there is no town that will remain to you; but if there will be regular troops, then we will take all the lands for the king" (EA 103:51-57); *šum-ma la-a / tu-te-ru-na a-wa-ta$_5$ a-na ia-ši / ù i-te$_9$-zi-ib* URU *ù / pa-aṭ-ra-ti qa-du* LÚ.MEŠ */ ša i-ra-a-mu-ni* "If you do not send word to me, then I will abandon the city and I will go away with the men who are devoted to me" (EA 83:47-51); *šum-ma / šàr-ru yu-wa-ši-ru-na* LÚ.MEŠ / ^{KUR}*Mi-iṣ-ri ù* ^{KUR}*Mi-lu-ḫa / ù* ANŠE.KUR.RA.MEŠ *a-na qa-at /* LÚ-*ia an-nu-ú ki-ma / ar-ḫi-iš ù bal-ṭá-ti / a-na a-ra-ad šàr-ri* EN-*ia* "If the king sends men of the land of Egypt and of the land of Nubia and horses in the charge of this man of mine quickly, then I will live to serve the king, my lord" (EA 112:18-24); *[ù šum-ma] la-a yu-wa-[š]a-ru-na / [a-na* $^{\mathrm{URU.KI}}$*Gub-l]a ù la-qú-ši* "[But if] he (the king) does not send (troops) [to Gubl]a, then they will seize it" (EA 131:15-18; Moran 1987b:349; 1992:212).

The next two examples reflect the conversion of an Akkadian ventive with *-a* suffix to an indicative by means of the energic *-na* (Rainey 1990b:418-419):

> *ù šum-ma ap-pu-na-ma yu-ṣa-na šàr-ru / ù ka-li* KUR.KUR.KI *nu-kúr-tu$_4$ a-na ša-šu / ù mi-na yi-pu-šu a-na ia-ši-nu* "And, moreover, if the king comes forth and all the lands will be hostile to him, then what can he do to us?" (EA 74:39-41); *šum-ma* MU.MEŠ *a[n]-ni-ta ú-ul / yu-ṣa-na* ERÍN.ME[Š *pí-ṭ]á-ti / ù in-né-[ep-ša-a]t ka-li /* KUR.KUR.KI.MEŠ [*a-na* LÚ.MEŠ GA]Z

"If this year the reg[ular ar]my does not come forth, then all the lands will join the [*ʿapî*]*ru* men" (EA 77:26-29).

Assuming that the two verb forms with *-u* + gemination do represent the energic, i. e. **-unmi* › *-ummi* and **-unšu* › *-uššu* (cf. *supra*, p. 235), then we have an example of the energic in both the protasis and the apodosis, the latter also serving to express a promise or an asseveration:

šum-ma-mi yi-pu-šu-mi / DINGIR.MEŠ-*nu ša šàr-ri* EN-*nu* / *ù ni-ik-šu-du-um-mi* / [I]*La-ab-a-ia ù* TIL.LA-*nu-um-ma* \ *ḫa-ia-ma* / *nu-ub-ba-lu-uš-šu a-na šàr-ri* EN-*nu* "If the deity of the king, our lord, grants that we catch Labʾayu, then it is *alive* that we must send him to the king, our lord" (EA 245:3-7).

The following is a conditional sentence without *šumma:*

ù yu-te-ru-/ *na-ni šàr-ru be-lí-ia* / *a-wa-at yu-te-ru-na* / *ù a-na a-wa-at šàr-ri iš-mu* "So let the king return to me whatever word that he would return, and I will heed the word of the king" (EA 251:11-15)

There are a few cases where the energic is used in the apodosis of a conditional sentence. In one of these, the apodosis is itself a question (EA 119:17-18; cf. *supra*, p 237). In two other passages, there is special stress on the carrying out of some action, cf. below.

ASSEVERATIONS. Like the rhetorical questions, first person examples predominate in the asseverative use of the energic. The two texts mentioned above as being in the apodosis of conditional clauses reflect intense feeling or strong asseveration. One example is in the apodosis of a temporal conditional sentence:

ù an-nu-[*ú*] / *ka-ši-id a-na* [URU]*Pí-ḫi-lì* / *ù is-te-mu-na a-w*[*a-*]*t*[*e-ka*] "And behold, as soon as he arrives in Peḥel, I will surely obey [your] orders" (EA 256:33-35).

The second, a well known letter from Labᵓayu, is charged with emotional content. The precise nuance of the verb in question has long been a subject of discussion:

> *ša-ni-tam šum-ma ti-qa-bu / ap-pu-na-ma / nu-pu-ul-mì / ta-aḫ-ta-mu ù / ti-ma-ḫa-ṣú-ka / i-bi ú-ṣur-ru-na* "Furthermore, if you should say, moreover, 'Fall down beneath them that they may smite you,' my enemy (or: the enemies) I will most certainly watch out for!" (EA 252:23-30; cf. Rainey 1989-90:68b-69a).

And the ensuing sentence reiterates the asseveration:

> LÚ.MEŠ *ša ṣa-ab-tu*$_4$ URU ‹*ù*› / *i-li šu-sú-mì a-bi-ia / ù ú-ṣur-ru-šu-nu* "The men who seized the town ‹and› my god are the plunderers of my father, and I will certainly watch out for them" (EA 252:29-31).

Promises and assurances to send something characterize the following examples:

> *a-šar i-ba-ša-at / ši-pi-ir-ti* LUGAL EN-*ia / ša-ri* TIL.LA-*ia ù ù-ba-*[*ú-n*]*a-ši / ù uš-ši-ru-na-ši / a-na* LUGAL EN-*ia ša-ri* TIL.LA!-*ia* "Wherever the request of the king, my lord, may be, then I will surely look for it and I will send it to the king, my lord, the breath of my life" (EA 143:10-17); *ù / ti*$_7$*-iq-ta-bi / a-nu-ma i-na* ŠU-*t*[*i*] / ^{LÚ}*ṣú-ḫa-ri-ia / ut-ta-aš-še-ru-un-na-šu-nu* "And you said (each time), 'By the hand of my servant I will verily send them'" (KL 72:600:4-8; Rainey 1976:338-339; cf. Wilhelm 1982:124); LUGAL EN-*ia ša-pár a-na mu-ḫi-*[*i*]*a* ^{I}*Ḫa-a-ia / a-na qa-bi* KASKAL-*ra-ni*^{ḪÁ} / ^{KUR}*Ḫa-na-gal*$_9$*-bat an-nu-ú / ú-wa-še-ru-na ù uš-ši-ru-ši* "The king, my lord, sent to me Ḫāya to say 'Behold, I am surely sending Ḫanigalbat caravans, so expedite them!'" (EA 255:8-11).

If the form is really energic, i.e. **-unšu* › *-ššu* (cf. *infra*, p. 235), then this passage also belongs in the same category:

> *ù* ^{I}*Sú-ra-t*[*a*] / *yi-il*$_5$*-qé-mì* ^{I}*La-*[*ab-a-ia*] / *iš-tu* ^{URU}*Ma-gid*$_6$*-da*[^{KI}] / *ù yi-iq-bi a-na ia-a*[*-ši*] / *i-na-mì* ŠÀ ^{GIŠ}MÀ \ *a-na-yi* / *ú-ta-aš-ša-ru-uš-šu* / *a-na šàr-ri* "But Surata took Labʾayu from Megiddo and he said to me, 'By ship will I send him to the king'" (EA 245:24-30).

Such an energic asseveration may also be applied concerning a third person:

> *i-nu-ma yi-iš-tap-pa-ra* / *šàr-ru a-na ia-ši a-nu-ma* / ^{I}*I-ri-ma-ia-aš-ša* / *ia-ak-šu-du-na a-na* / *mu-ḫi-ka ú-ul ka-ši-id* / *a-na mu-ḫi-ia* "Inasmuch as the king has written to me, 'Now Irimayassa will surely come to you,' he has not come to me" (EA 130:9-14).

ARGUMENTATIVE. Finally, there are a few passages where the force of the energic seems to be mainly charged with emotion. This usage is perhaps an extension of the asseverative discussed above, which also reflects deep feelings. Especially noteworthy is the use of the energic in a Taanach letter where a senior official is chiding a local ruler:

> *ša-ni-tam la-a-mi* / ˹*i*˺*-na ma-an-ṣa-ar-*˹*ti*˺ *i-*˹*ba*˺*-*[*šu*] / ˹*ḫa*˺*-na-ku-u-ka ù la-a-mi* / *ti-il*$_5$*-la-ku-un*!(EN)*-na at-t*[*a*] / *a-na maḫ-ri-ia ù šum-ma-mi* / *tu-wa-še-ru-na* ŠEŠ*-ka* / *ša-ni-tam i-na* ^{URU}*Ḫa-za-ti* / *i-ba-ša-ti ù la-a-mi* / ˹*ti*˺*-*˹*il*$_5$˺*-la-ku-*˹*na*˺ *a-na* ˹*maḫ*˺*-*[*r*]*i-ia* "Your *warriors* are not in the garrison and you do not come yourself to me nor do you send your brother; furthermore, I am in Gaza and you do not come to me!" (ṪT 6:6-14)

The verb in line 5 may also have been energic, viz. *tu-wa-še-ru*[*-na*(?)]. In any case these 2nd m.s. forms, all in negative clauses, express the anger of the sender.

The same use of the energic may be seen in the following:

> ERÍN.MEŠ *la-a yu-ša-*[*ru*] / *ù* ^{LÚ}DUMU *ši-ip-*[*ri*]*-*[*ia*] / *la-a tu-ša-ṣú-na* "The army is not being sent and you are not sending

forth my ambassador" (EA 126:40-43); *aš-tap-pár aš-ta-ni la-a / ia-tu-ru-na a-wa-tu / a-na ia-a-ši* "I have been writing repeatedly (but) word does not come back to me" (EA 126:53-55).

Two other passages may also belong to this category:

[*a-nu*]*-ma ki-a-ma-am iš-tap-ru a-na šàr-ri* EN-*ia / ù la-a yi-iš-mu-na a-wa-te-ia* "[No]w thus have I been writing to the king, my lord, but he doesn't even listen to my words!" (EA 85:6-7; cf. *supra*, p. 238); *an-nu-ú*. LÚ.MEŠ MAŠKÍM *šàr-ri / yu-wa-ši-ru-na šàr-ru* "Behold, the king is sending royal commissioners" (EA 116:30-31; cf. *infra*, pp. 247-247)

SUBORDINATE CLAUSES. Two examples in subordinate clauses may also belong, in fact, to the previous section. Their contexts appear to be charged with emotion. One of them has to do with a painful dispute over property:

ù y[*u*]*-wa-ši-ra* LUGAL ⌜LÚ⌝⌜MAŠKÍM⌝ / [*ù*] *y*[*u-p*]*a-r*[*i-ì*]*š* [*b*]*e-ri-nu ka-li / mi-im-me ša-a yu-ú-ul-qú-na / ìš-tu ša-a-šu-nu a-na šàr-ri ú-ul / yi-ìl-qé-šu* LÚ *ša-nu a-na ša-šu* "So may the king send a commissioner that he may decide between us; all the property that was taken from them belongs to the king; let not another man take it for himself!" (EA 117:66-70).

The other was cited above (*supra*, p. 241). One energic form is subordinated to a noun in construct: *a-wa-at yu-te-ru-na* "whatever word that he would return" (EA 251:13). Again, it may have been the emotion involved which dictated the use of the energic.

THE INJUNCTIVE

Three other conjugation patterns are posited for the injunctive mode. Inasmuch as the proof for the existence of one pattern may derive from contrasts with syntagmas using one of the indicative patterns (especially the imperfect), examples will be brought of such contextual parallels employing two different forms and expressing two different nuances.

JUSSIVE

The jussive was not clearly defined by Ebeling or any of the other early grammarians of EA, though many translators rendered it correctly in context. Furthermore, Ebeling (1910:46) did recognize the correct meaning of a gloss from Hazor containing the jussive, which in fact proves its existence in the native language of the scribes:

> [*ù*] *li-iḫ-šu-uš-mi* / \ *ia-az-ku-ur-mi* / [I]*šàr-ri* EN-*ia* / *mi-im-ma ša* / *in₄-né-pu-uš-mi* / UGU [URU]*Ḫa-ṣú-ra*[KI] / URU.KI-*ka ù* / UGU ÌR-*ka* "[So] may the king, my lord, take thought for everything that has been done against Hazor, your city, and against your servant" (EA 228:18-25).

The very fact that the gloss, *ia-az-ku-ur*, defines an Akkadian precative, is adequate witness to the presence of real jussive forms in Canaanite. Of course, this assumption has behind it the comparative material from Hebrew (Driver 1892:51-55) and Arabic (Fischer 1972:96-97, § 195) and now also Ugaritic (Rainey 1987a:397-398). However, one of Moran's most important achievements was the delineation of the syntactic functions of the jussive in the Byblos dialect (Moran 1950a:49-51; 1951).

MORPHOLOGY. The prefix jussive forms have -*Ø* suffix on the 3rd m.s., 2nd f.s., 2nd m.s., 1st c.s. and 1st c.pl., and -*ū* on the 3rd m.pl. and 2nd m.pl. The third weak verbs are characterized by their bare thematic vowel in final position on the singulars and on 1st c.pl., e.g. jussive *ia-aq-bi* (EA 83:34) and *yi-iq-bi* (EA 85:32) as against imperfect *yi-iq-bu* (EA 129:84), jussive *yi-iš-me* (EA 79:13) in contrast to imperfect *yi-iš-mu* (EA 320:23). The plurals are also easy to distinguish by their suffixes, imperfect -*ūna* but jussive -*ū*. It is obvious that the jussive conjugation pattern is identical with that of the preterite.

WISH, REQUEST, COMMAND. This is the most common function of the jussive in the texts just as it is the most prevalent usage in the West Semitic languages in general. Many translators have recognized the jussive nuance of the various examples. Perhaps the most discussed syntagma is the wish or blessing formula used in Rib-Haddi's letters (cf. Youngblood 1961:11-13). There are two formulations, in fact, one addressed to high officials and the other addressed directly to pharaoh. First the idiom applied in letters to officials:

> ^{d}NIN *ša* ^{URU}*Gub-la ti-din* / *ba-aš-ta-*⸢*ka*⸣ *i-na pa-ni* / *šàr-ri* EN-*ka* "May the Lady of Byblos grant your dignity in the presence of the king, your lord!" (EA 73:4-6; also EA 69:5-8; 70:3-5; 77:3-6; for EA 71:4-6 and EA 95:3-6 cf. *infra*).

And for the king, the blessing is:

> [^{d}]NIN *ša* ^{URU}*Gub-la* / *ti-id-di-in*$_4$ *du-na* / *a-na* LUGAL *be-li-ia* "May the Lady of Byblos grant strength to the king, my lord" (EA 68:4-6; also EA 74:2-4 *et passim* in the Rib-Haddi letters).

The verb form employed is 3rd f.s. *tiddin*. When two deities are invoked, the jussive form is 3rd m.pl. *tiddinū*:

> ^{d}*A-ma-na ù* / ›*ù*‹ ^{d}NIN *ša* ^{URU}*Gub-la* / *ti-di-nu* TÉŠ-*ka i-na pa-ni* / *šàr-ri* EN-*li-ka-ma* "May Amon and the Lady of Byblos grant your dignity in the presence of the king, your lord!" (EA 95:3-6).

From this it becomes obvious that in the following passages either the name of the second deity has been inadvertently omitted or else the scribe was using a "plural of majesty":

> ^{d}*A-ma-na* DINGIR *ša* ⸢LUGAL⸣ [*be-li-k*]*a* / *ti-di-nu* TÉS-*ka i-na* / *pa-ni* LUGAL *be-li-ka* "May Amon, the deity of the king, [yo]ur [lord], grant your dignity in the presence of the king, your lord!" (EA 71:4-6 and EA 86:3-5; Albright 1946:12; Moran 1950a:62, 63; 1951:35 n. 14; 1964:80-81; Youngblood 1961:84).

Lest there should be any doubts that *tiddin/tiddinū* in these contexts is jussive, one must not forget the one instance when the same formula is employed using the Akkadian precative, *liddin*, viz. EA 102:5-8 (cf. *supra*, p. 215).

As a third person command, the jussive may also be a verb which governs an infinitive in the accusative:

> *yu-ḫa-mi-it be-li* / *uš-šar* ERÍN.MEŠ *pí-ṭá-ti₇ ki-ma* / *ar-ḫi-iš* "May my lord hasten to send regular troops in a hurry!" (EA 362:7-9).

The jussive can be followed by imperatives. In this example the jussive is a stative verb with impersonal subject; it is then followed by a direct imperative:

> *ù* / *yi-it-ru-uṣ i-[n]a p[a-n]i* / EN ^{d}UTU KUR.ḪÁ *ù* / *id-na-ni* 20 *ta-pal* / ANŠE.KUR.RA.MEŠ *a-na ia-ši* / *ù uš-ši-ra til-la-ta* / *ki-ma ar-ḫi-iš* / *a-na* ^{URU}*Ṣu-mu-ra a-na* / *na-ṣa-ri-ši$_x$*(ŠE) "And may it be pleasing in the sight of the lord, the sun-god of the lands, so give me twenty spans of horses and send an auxiliary force quickly to Ṣumur to protect it" (EA 103:39-47).

Or the jussive may introduce a chain of volitives in clauses of purpose or intended result; these latter can have the same subject as the initial jussive or they can have another subject:

> *yi-iš-mé šàr-ru* EN-*nu* / *a-wa-te* ÌR.MEŠ *ki-ti-šu* / *ù ia-di-na* NÍG.BA / *a-na* ÌR-*šu ù ti-da-ga-lu* / LÚ.MEŠ *a-ia-bu-nu ù* / *ti-ka-lu ep-ra* "May the king, our lord, listen to the words of his loyal servants and may he give a present to his servant so that our enemies may see and eat dirt!" (EA 100:31-36).

These examples are sufficient to illustrate the general usage in this syntagma. The next example is deceptive at first sight, viz. EA 116:30-33. The jussive has been thought to be dependent on an indicative energic which Moran (1950a:50) originally took to be a "virtual command." Since then, he has recognized that it is indicative; we have categorized it as an expression of strong, argumentative force (*supra*, p. 244). The ensuing jussives are logically related but not syntactically subordinated to the indicative energic:

> *an-nu-ú* LÚ.MEŠ MAŠKÍM *šàr-ri* / *yu-wa-ši-ru-na šàr-ru ù* / *ia-aq-bi šàr-ru a-na ša-šu-nu* / *ù tu-pa-pa-ri-šu be-ri-ku-ni* "Behold, the king is sending royal commissioners so may the king speak to them so that they may decide between the two of you" (EA 116:30-33; Moran 1973:52).

Naturally, the jussive also serves to express negative wishes. It is a peculiar feature of the EA texts from Canaan that the Akkadian negative particles, *ul* and *lā*, have each encroached on the semantic spheres of the other. This can be seen by comparing negative jussives from the same verbs, one example with *lā* and the other with *ul*.

> *la-a yi-iš-mé* LUGAL *be-li* / *a-wa-te*^{MEŠ} LÚ.MEŠ *ša-nu-ti* "May the king, my lord, not listen to the words of other men!" (EA 362:48-49; 126:62-63); [*ú*]-*ul yi-iš-me* LUGAL *kar*$_5$-*ṣí* / ⸢ÌR⸣ *ki-ti-šu* "May the king not listen to the slander of his loyal servant!" (EA 119:26-27).

Note the use of *lā* and *ul* in the same letter:

> *ù la-a* ‹*i*›*a*-⸢*qúl*⸣-*mì* / LUGAL EN-*ia iš-tu* / ⸢URU⸣*Ṣu-mu-ur*^{KI} "And may the king, my lord, not keep silent concerning Ṣumur!" (EA 68:14-16; also EA 139:5-6, 10); *ù ú-ul* / [*ia*]-*qúl-mì* LUGAL *iš*-[*tu*] / [UR]U.DIDLI.KI.-*šu* "And may the king not keep silent concer[ning] his [ci]ties" (EA 68:30-32; also EA 132:43-45; 76:44-46; 90:57).

On occasion the jussive may be reinforced by the optative particle *lū*. Forms with a *t*- prefix, i.e. 3rd f.s., 2nd m.s., 3rd m.pl. and 2nd m.pl. would thus be identical in form with the Akkadian precative. However, forms of 3rd m.s., with prefixed *y*-, represent an obvious substitute for the precative. This is particularly clear with regard to the verb *idû* "to know." Instead of the standard OB construction, *lū īde*, or the new hybrid precative *līde* (cf. *supra*, p. 213), we find examples such as:

> *ù lu-ú yi-de / šàr-ru* EN-*ia a-na* KUR.KI-*šu* "So may the king, my lord, take cognizance of his territory!" (EA 243:21-22; also EA 60:30; 245:46; 307:6).

Other 3rd m.s. jussives with the injunctive *lū* are the following:

> [*l*]*u-ú yi-ìl-ma-ad šàr-ru* / EN-*ia* ⌜*i*⌝*-nu-ma iz-zi-bu-ni / gáb-bi* ŠEŠ.ḪÁ-*ia* "May the king, my lord, be apprised that all my colleagues have abandoned me!" (EA 366:17-19); *lu-ú yi-iš-me* LUGAL EN-*ia* / *a-wa-te* ÌR-*šu* "May the king, my lord, give heed to the words of his servant!" (EA 136:6-7); *u lu-ú / yi-it-ra-ni*! EN-*ia / is-tu qa-at* / LÚSA.GAZ.MEŠ "So may he deliver me!" (EA 299:21-22; Izreᵓel apud Naᵓaman 1979:679 n. 29; cf. Izreᵓel 1977:165);

Usually the jussive stands at the head of its clause but note the following striking exception:

> *a-nu-ma ṭup-pí ša-nu / ù ka-li ú-nu-tu-ia / ša it-ti* ᴵ*Ia-pa-*ᵈIŠKUR / *šu-ut yi-ša-kan / i-na pa-ni šàr-ri* "Now (here is) another tablet and all my implements that are with Yapaᶜ-Haddi; let it be placed before the king" (EA 119:55-59).

PURPOSE CLAUSES. Another widespread use of the jussive is in clauses of purpose or intended result. As Moran has noted, due to the paratactic sentence structure in these epistles, it is often difficult, not to say impossible, to distinguish between wishes, requests and commands on the one hand, and clauses of purpose on the other (Moran 1950a:88; 1960:6 n. 1). Though there may be logical subordination between clauses in these injunctive chains, it is not realized by the use of subordinating conjunctions. Instead, the clauses are joined by the coordinating conjunction *u* or joined asyndetically. The choice of mood, injunctive or indicative, operates according to what Moran has called "modal congruence (Moran 1950a:81-88; 1951:33; 1960:9). If the initial clause contains an indicative (including *qtl* forms), then the purpose clause will also contain indicatives. Conversely, if the initial clause contains an injunctive (including imperatives), then the verbs of the purpose clauses will also be injunctives. First, some examples following an imperative:

> *qa-bi*$_4$*-ti*$_7$ *a-na* LUGAL *be-lí-[i]a uš-ši-ra-mi* / ⸢ERÍN⸣.⸢MEŠ⸣ *pí-ṭá-ti ù ti-il*$_5$*-*⸢*qé*⸣ ^{I}ÌR-*Aš-ra-ta* "I said to the king, my lord, 'Send the army that it may capture ᶜAbdi-Ashirta" (EA 94:10-11; Moran 1950a:84; 1960:12 n. 1; Youngblood 1961:384); *ù uš-ši-ra* ERÍN.MEŠ / *pí-ṭá-ti ù ti-ìl-qé-šu* / *ù ta-ap-šu-uḫ* KUR LUGAL "So send the army that it may capture him so that the land of the king may become tranquil" (EA 107:29-31; Moran 1950a:82); *uš-ši-ra* ERÍN.MEŠ *pí-ṭá-ti* / *ra-ba ù tu-da-bi-ir* / *a-ia-bi* LUGAL *iš-tu* / *líb-bi* KUR-*šu ù* / *ti-né-ep-šu ka-li* / KUR.KUR.MEŠ *a-na šàr-ri* "Send a large army that it may drive out the enemies of the king from the midst of his land and so that all the lands may side with the king" (EA 76:38-43).

Note that *ti-né-ep-šu* is 3rd m.pl. jussive.

The jussive in a purpose clause may also be reinforced by the optative particle *lū*. The ensuing passages have jussives in 1st c.pl. The construction is foreign to Babylonian, but evidently was correct in Assyrian, although the evidence is restricted to OA and very scanty. *ÇAD* L:225a and *GAG:106, §81*g, both cite the same text, viz. *lu ni-iš-me-ma* / *lu né-pu-uš* "As soon as we hear, we will do" (BIN 4 106:17-18 = EL 244:17-18). Hecker (1968:129-129, §71) does not cite this text, and has no attestations for 1st c.pl. The *lū niprus* pattern appears in a small number of contexts in the EA letters from Canaan, but, with the exception of one Jerusalem passage, can hardly be ascribed to Assyrian influence. It is more likely a simple use of the *lū yiprus* construction with the 1st c.pl.

> *[yi-i]š-[me* LUGAL] / [LÚ.]MEŠ *ḫa-za-nu-[ti-šu]* / *ù* ⸢*lu*⸣*-ú ni-zi-*⸢*iz*⸣ / UGU-*šu-nu ù lu-[ú] ni-du-bu-ur* / LÚ.MEŠ *ša-ru-ta*

"[Ma]y [the king] [he]e[d his] city rulers so that we may take a stand against them and so that we may drive out the miscreants" (EA 279:18-21); *ù lu-ú ni-pa-aš gáb-bu-ma / nu-kúr-ti* "and let us all make war" (EA 366:31-32; cf. *infra*, pp. 251-252 for the full citation); *id-nu-mi gáb-bi e-ri-iš-ti-šu-nu / a-na* LÚ.MEŠ URU*Qí-il-ti / ù lu-ú ni-ip-ṭú-ur* URU*Ú-ru-sa-lim* KI "And let us desert Jerusalem" (EA 289:29; Albright, Mendenhall and Moran 1955:489a).

The purpose clause may be dependent upon a volitive without itself taking the *-a* suffix:

yu-ḫa-mi-ṭá uš-šar ERÍN.MEŠ *pí-ṭá-ti* / LUGAL *ù yi-il-qé-šu-nu ù / ti-né-pu-uš* KUR.MEŠ *a-na* LUGAL BE-*i*[*a*] "May he hasten to send the king's army so that he may capture them and so that the lands may go over to the king, my lord" (EA 129:78-80); [*yu-wa*]-*ši-ra šàr-ru* LÚMAŠKÍM-*šu* / [*ù yu*]-*pa-ra-aš be-ri-ku-*[*n*]*i* "May the king send his commissioner [so that he] may decide between the two of you" (EA 113:17-18; Moran 1950a:82-83; 1973:52); *ù y*[*u*]-*wa-ši-ra* LUGAL ⌈LÚ⌉⌈MAŠKÍM⌉ / [*ù*] *y*[*u-p*]*a-r*[*i-i*]*š* [*b*]*e-ri-nu* "So may the king send the commissioner [so that] he may decide between us" (EA 117:66-67).

There are also injunctive chains that begin with an Akkadian precative (cf. *supra*, p. 217):

ù li-di-na LUGAL EN-*ia* / ERÍN.MEŠ *pí-ṭá-ta / ù ni-pu-uš* / URU.DIDLI.ḪÁ LUGAL EN-*ia* / *ù ni-ša-ab / a-na* URU.DIDLI.ḪÁ / LUGAL EN-*ia* DINGIR-*ia* / dUTU-*ia* "So may the king, my lord, furnish troops that we may rebuild(?) the cities of the king, my lord, and so that we may settle in the cities of the king, my lord, my deity" (EA 363:17-23); *ù li-it-ru-uṣ / i-na pa-ni šàr-ri* EN-*ia ù / lu-ú yu-ši-ra* I*la-an-ḫa-ma / ù lu-ú ni-pa-aš gáb-bu-ma / nu-kúr-ti ù lu-ú tu-te-er* / KUR.KI.ḪÁ *ša šàr-ri* EN-*ia / a-na* ZAG.ḪI.‹A›-*ši* \ *up-sí-ḫi* "So may it be pleasing in the sight of the king, my lord, so that he may send

Yanḫamu and so that we may all make war and so that you may restore the lands of the king, my lord, to its farthest extent" (EA 366:28-34; Finklestein 1969:33).

Purpose clauses may also express a negative wish or purpose:

> *ia-aq-bi* LUGAL *a-na* 3 URU.MEŠ / *ù* ^{GIŠ}MÁ LÚ.MEŠ *mi-ši* / *ù la-a ti-la-ku a-na* / ^{KUR}*A-mur-ri* "May the king speak to the three cities and the ship of the expeditionary force so that they go not to Amurru" (EA 101:32-35); *ù lu-ù-mi* / *li-ik-ki-im-mi* / *šàr-ru* URU.KI-*šu la-a-mì* / *yi-iṣ-bat-ši* / ^{I}*La-ab-a-yu* "So may the king deliver his city lest Labʾayu capture it" (EA 244:25-29); *ù lu-ú* / *li-di-nam-mi šàr-ru* / 1 ME LÚ.MEŠ *ma-an-ṣa-ar-ta*$_5$ / *a-na na-ṣa-ri* URU.KI-*šu* / *la-a-mì yi-iṣ-bat-ši* / ^{I}*La-ab-a-yu* "So may the king furnish one hundred garrison troops to guard his city so that Labʾayu may not capture it" (EA 244:33-38); *yi-ki-im* LUGAL / *be-li* KUR-*šu* / *iš-tu qa-te* / LÚ.MEŠ SA.GAZ.MEŠ / *la-a ti*$_7$*-iḫ-la-aq* / *la-qí-ta* / ^{URU}*Ṣa-bu-ma*^{KI} "May the king deliver his city from the hands of the *ʿapîrû* men lest Ṣabuma be lost (captured)" (EA 274:10-16; Albright 1943a:17 n. 60); *ù lu-ú yu-uš-ši-ra* / LUGAL *be-li* / ^{GIŠ}GIGIR.MEŠ *ù lu-ù* / *yi-ìl-te-qé-ni* / *a-na mu-ḫi-šu la-a* / *iḫ-la-aq* "So may the king, my lord, send chariots so that they may take me lest I perish" (EA 270:24-29; Rainey 1978a:11*).

CONDITIONAL SENTENCES. There are also many instances where the apodosis of a conditional sentence has a verb in the jussive. One of the clearest illustrations of the form is the following where the apodosis is introduced by the coordinating conjunction:

> *šum-ma* LUGAL *be-li* / *la-a yu-ša-ru* ERÍN.MEŠ *pí-ṭá-ta*$_5$ / *ù ni-nu-mi* BA.UG$_7$$^{\text{ni-mu-ut}}$ / *ù* URU.MEŠ *Gub*^{ub}*-li* / *tu-ul*$_{11}$*-qú* "If the king, my lord, does not send the army then we will die and the towns of Byblos will be taken" (EA 362:9-13; Rainey 1978b:18-19; Moran 1987b:556; 1992:359-360).

The apodosis may, however, be introduced asyndetically as so often in standard Akkadian:

> *šum-ma lìb-bi* LUGAL *ba-li uš-ša-[ar]* / ERÍN.MEŠ *pí-ṭá-ti ia-aš-pu-ur a-na* / ^{I}*Ia-an-ḫa-mì ù a-na* ^{I}*Pí-ḫu-ra* / *al-ku-mi qa-du* LÚ.MEŠ *ḫa-za-ni-ku-nu* / *le-qú-na* ^{KUR}*A-mur-ri* "If the king does not intend to send the army, let him write to Yanḫamu and to Piḫura, 'Go with your city rulers, take Amurru'" (EA 117:59-63; Moran 1987b:324; 1992:194).

The apodosis may also consist of several clauses:

> *šum-ma ia-[nu]* / LÚ-*LIM ša ú-še*$_{20}$*-ze-bu-*⸢*ši*$_{x}$⸣(⸢ŠE⸣) *iš-tu qa-ti-n[u]* / *ù nu-da-bir*$_{5}$ LÚ.MEŠ *ḫa-za-nu-ta is-tu* / *lìb-bi* KUR.KUR.KI *ù ti-né-pu-uš ka-li* KUR.KUR.MEŠ.KI / *a-na* LÚ.MEŠ ⸢GAZ⸣ *ù* ⸢*ki*⸣*-tu ti-in-‹né-pu-uš›-ma* / *a-na ka-li* KUR.KUR.KI *ù pa-aš-ḫu* DUMU.MEŠ / *ù* ^{MÍ}DUMU.MÍ.MEŠ *a-‹na› da-ri-ti* UD.KÁM.MEŠ "If there is no man who can deliver it from [o]ur hand, then let us expel the city rulers from the lands and all the lands will side with the *ᶜapîru* men and a treaty may ‹be made› for all the lands and the sons and daughters will be at peace for ever more" (EA 74:32-38; Mendenhall 1947a:123-124).

Finally, there is one possible instance of a jussive in the protasis of a conditional sentence. Moran (1950a:73) had signaled the use of the volitive in the protasis and had noted the evidence of similar usages in Hebrew (*GKC*:494, §159*d-e;* cited by Moran 1950a:134 n. 190). In biblical Hebrew both jussives and cohortatives can serve in the protasis. Note that in the ensuing passage, the protasis seems to consist simply of a jussive clause but the apodosis apparently begins with a verb in the indicative imperfect (though its interpretation is disputed):

> *la-a yu-wa-šar* LUGAL *be-li* MU*ša-ni-ta an-ni-ta*$_{5}$ / *a-na* DUMU.MEŠ ^{I}ÌR-*A-ši-ir-ti u ti-dì-šu-*⸢*nu*⸣ DUMU.‹MEŠ› / *gáb-bi-šu-nu a-na* KUR.MEŠ LUGAL *be-li-ia* "(If) the king, my

lord, does not send (troops) this year against the sons of ᶜAbdi-Ashirta, then the son‹s› (of ᶜAbdi-Ashirta) will all trample(?) the lands of the king, my lord" (EA 362:66-68).

COMPLEX SENTENCES. The following example might be looked upon as a conditional sentence but it is more likely a complex sentence made up of two juxtaposed clauses, the first being the topic, the second being the comment (Rainey 1992a:186-191). In fact, the "comment" may consist of three clauses, the first one containing a negative jussive:

> *i-nu-ma yi-iq-bu a-na pa-ni* LUGAL / BA.UG$_7$ \ *mu-tu-mi a-na* KUR.MEŠ / *la-a yi-iš-mé* LUGAL *be-li* / *a-wa-te*^{MEŠ} LÚ.MEŠ *ša-nu-te ia-nu-mi* / *mu-ta-na a-na* KUR.MEŠ *ša-lim iš-tu pa-na-‹nu›-⸢um⸣* "Inasmuch as he says in the king's presence, 'There is death in the lands,' may the king, my lord, not listen to the words of other men! There is no epidemic in the land; it is healthier than before" (EA 362:46-50; *CAD* M/2:296a).

VOLITIVE

TERMINOLOGY. The term "volitive" has been borrowed from Moran (1950a: *passim*), who applied it to all injunctives. Moran, in turn, had adopted the term "volitive" from Joüon (1923:307-312, §114; Joüon and Muraoka 1991:373-379, §114). The *yaqtula* conjugation pattern was called "subjunctive" by Moran, following the convention of Arabic grammar (Moran 1950a:89-104). When Moran presented the evidence gathered in his dissertation to a wider audience, he called the conjugation pattern simply the ""Early Canaanite *yaqtula"* (Moran 1960). That article had considerable impact on Semitic linguistics (Moscati *et al.* 1964:135; Fleisch 1968; Blau 1971; cf. now Rainey 1991-93).

"Volitive" has been arbitrarily chosen as the title for the *yaqtula* conjugation pattern to distinguish it from the jussive and the imperative. However, that distinction is one of convenience only since volitive and injunctive would both be valid definitions for all conjugation patterns in this non-indicative mood.

MORPHOLOGY. The characteristic feature of this conjugation pattern is assumed to be the following (using Arabic as a model): the 3rd m.s., 3rd f.s., 2nd m.s., 1st c.s. and 1st c.pl. are marked by an *-a* suffix; the 3rd m.pl. and the 2nd m.pl. are identical with those of the preterite and the jussive, i.e. they lack the *-na* suffix of the imperfect. This means that all injunctive 2nd and 3rd plurals except energics, which are virtually unattested, are the same. If the *yaqtula* conjugation pattern is to be identified in the EA texts from Canaan, then it is only on the singulars and the 1st c.pl. No injunctive glosses of purely Canaanite verbs are known with the volitive *-a* suffix, except for the apparent Canaanite imperative *ku-na* (EA 147:36; cf. *infra*, pp. 265-266).

The greatest obstacle to distinguishing volitive forms in these texts is the fact, as recognized by Moran (1950a:91-92; 1960:2), that they are written in Akkadian and Akkadian has the homophonous morpheme known as the ventive, i.e. the suffix (on singulars) *-a*(*m*). For that reason, an intensive survey of all the texts in question was made in search of evidence for the Akkadian ventive (cf. *supra*, pp. 202-211). It was seen that ventives are prevalent throughout the corpus. Izreʾel (1978b:80-82) had made a similar study, with special reference to the Gezer letters but against the background of the corpus as a whole, and had come to similar conclusions. Many verbs with *-a* suffix are those which naturally took the ventive in Akkadian. Rabiner (1981:99-100) also noted that forms with *-a* in EA 234 (from Acco) appear on preterites; they seem to function like the forms with *-Ø* both as preterites and injunctives. Therefore, the use of the ventive is evidently more widespread than one might deduce just from reading Moran's presentation. As the ventive occurs on truly preterite verb forms in this corpus, those which appear in injunctive contexts could just as well be ventives in the WS jussive mode. Moran did prove beyond all doubt that those forms were injunctive and not indicative. He provided numerous contrasts between verbs with *-u*, which are indicative (our imperfect), and those with *-a*, which are injunctive. But he also demonstrated that the jussives and the injunctives with *-a* all can serve in the same syntagmas! Who is to say that the *-a* forms are not simply jussives with Akkadian ventive? The ensuing discussion will be limited to those examples where an Akkadian ventive might not be required. It will be seen that in most cases, there is a possible ventive on some other verb in the immediate context, so that modus attraction could also have been at work.

The examples will be cited according the same syntactic constructions as those described for the jussive.

WISH, REQUEST, COMMAND. The plethora of texts in which a request and a chain of further injunctive clauses begin with a form of *wuššuru* will not be adduced here since there is too strong a possibility that the *-a* suffix really is the ventive. On the other hand, there are other verbs with similar meanings, such as *ḫummuṭu* "to hasten":

> *ki-n[a-na]* / *yu-ḫa-mi-ṭá uš-šar* ERÍN.MEŠ *p[í-ṭá]-t[i]* / LUGAL *ù yi-ìl-qé-šu-nu ù* / *ti-né-pu-uš* KUR.MEŠ *a-na* LUGAL ⸢BE⸣-*i[a]* "The[refore] may he hasten to send the army in order that it may capture them and that the lands be si[de] with the king, my lord!" (EA 129:77-80);

and from the same scribe:

> *ù yu-ḫa-mi-ṭá be-li* / ERÍN.MEŠ *pí-ṭá-ta*₅ *ù ni*-UG₇.BA "So may my lord send the army or we will die" (EA 362:40-41; Rainey 1978b:2-21).

The D stem of this verb is rare in any case, but it must be noted that the use of the ventive with the G stem *ḫamāṭu* is widespread (*CAD* Ḫ:62b-63a). A unique construction is the verb form derived from the adverb *arḫiš* (as noted by S. Izreʾel; cf. *supra*, p. 69; *contra AHw*:943b). In light of the two passages with *ḫummuṭu*, it is logical to assume that this *hapax* also has the ventive:

> *ù ya-ar-ḫi-ša* LUGAL *be-li-[ia]* / ERÍN.MEŠ *pí-ṭá[-t]a*₅ *ù ti-iṣ-ba-tu* / URU *ki-ma ar-ḫi-iš* "So may the king, [my] lord, hasten the troops that they may seize the city quickly!" (EA 137:97-99).

Another verb appearing in a negative wish is *puḫḫuru* "to assemble," which is also used generally with the ventive (*AHw*:810b-811b):

> *ú-ul yu-pa-ḫi-ra ka-li* / LÚ.MEŠ GAZ.MEŠ *ù* / *yi-ìl-qa* URU*Ši-ga-t*[*a*] / *ù* URU*Am-pí* "Let him not assemble the ᶜ*apîru* men that he may take Shigata and Ampi" (EA 71:28-31; also EA 85:77-79).

PURPOSE CLAUSES. When dependent upon another injunctive clause, purpose clauses take a jussive or volitive verb. The following negative result clause employs *šemû* "to hear," which does not characteristically take the ventive (*AHw*:1211a-1213b):

> *aq-bi a-na ka-ta₅ la-a* / *i-le-ù uš-šar-*[*šu*] / *ù-ul yi-iš-ma* ᴵÌR-*A-ši-i*[*r-ta*] / *ù ma-an-nu ìl-te₉-qa-n*[*i*] / *i*[*š-*]*tu qa-ti-šu* "I said to you, 'I am unable to send [him] lest ᶜAbdi-Ashirta hear, and who will deliver me from his hand?" (EA 82:21-25; Moran 1960:4; Albright and Moran 1948:246 n. 17).

Another verb which does not normally take the ventive is *naṣāru* "to protect, guard." However, in the following passage, the purpose clause is dependent upon an injunctive of *wuššuru*, which, as we have seen, probably developed extensive use of the ventive. Therefore, one could argue that the ventive on the second verb is due to modus attraction from the first:

> *ša-ni-tam* / *yu-wa-ši-ra šàr-ru* ANŠE.KUR.RA.‹MEŠ› *a-na* / ›*a-*⌈*na*⌉‹ ÌR-*šu u a-na-ṣa-ra* URU.KI "Furthermore, may the king send horse‹s› to his servant so that I may protect the city" (EA 117:71-73; Rainey 1975b:414).

Modus attraction is a bit more difficult to maintain for the next passage though one might argue that the scribe wished to alternate between verbs with -Ø and verbs with -*a*, for whatever reasons.

> *li-iš-mé šàr-ru a-wa-te* ÌR-*šu* / *ù ia-di-na ba-la-ṭá* ÌR-*šu ù* / *a-na-ṣa-*⌈*ra*⌉ [URU] ⌈*ki*⌉*-it-ti-šu a-di* ⌈NIN⌉*-nu* / DINGIR.MEŠ-*nu a*[*-na ka-ta*$_5$] *ù yi-da-ga*[*l* LUGAL] / [KUR]-*šu ù* [URU-*šu*] "May the king heed the words of his servant and may he provide his servant's sustenance that his servant may live and so that I may protect his loyal [city] with our Lady, our deity, fo[r you] and to that [the king] may see his [land] and [his city]" (EA 74:53-58; Youngblood 1961:152; Rainey 1965b:414; Moran 1987b:253 n. 15; 1992:145 n. 15).

Another verb which does not usually take the ventive is *epēšu* (but note that in the idiom *alākam epēšum*, this verb usually does have the ventive! *CAD* E:201b). But again, the preceding imperative certainly has the ventive and modus attraction may have been at play:

> *šu-te-ra a-wa-ta*$_5$ / *a-na ia-ši ù i-pu-ša a-na-ku* / *ki-ta it-ti* [I]ÌR-*A-ši-ir-ta* / *ki-ma* [I]*Ia-pa-* [d]IŠKUR *ù* [I]*Zi-im-re-*[*d*]*a* / *ù bal-ṭá-ti* "Send word back to me or I will make an alliance with ᶜAbdi-Ashirta like Yapaᶜ-Haddi and Zimredda that I may live" (EA 83:23-25; Moran 1950a:100; 1987b:264; 1992:153).

Perhaps a better case might be made for the next passage. The verb in question, *maḫāṣu* "to smite," does not customarily take the ventive. Still, it occurs in a negative result clause (*contrast* Izreᵓel 1978b:63) after an imperative with the ventive:

> *ù yi-iq-bu* / *a-na ia-ši id-na-*⌈*ni*⌉ / DAM-*ka ù* / DUMU.MEŠ-*ka ù lu-ú* / *i-ma-ḫa-ṣa* "And he is saying to me, 'Give me your wife and your children or else I will attack!'" (EA 270:17-21; Moran 1987b:494-495; 1992:316-317).

It spite of what one might expect, *dubburu/duppuru* "to go away, to expel" (intransitive and transitive of the D stem) does not seem to take the ventive in classical Akkadian (*CAD* D:186-188; *AHw*:177). Like the examples above, this one has an imperative with the ventive:

> *ù i-na* UD.MEŠ / [*an-nu-*]*ti uš-še-ra* ERÍN.MEŠ [GAL] / [*ù tu-*]*du-bi-ra-šu i*[*š-tu*] / [KUR*A-mur-*]*ri* "So in [the]se days, send a [large] army [that it may] expel him f[rom Amur]ru" (EA 85:79-82; Youngblood 1961:281; Moran 1950a:158; 1987b:271 n. 10; 1992:158 n. 12; cf. EA 76:38-41 without *-a*).

The verb *arādu*/*urrudu* "to serve," a denominative from (*w*)*ardu* "slave" (cf. *supra*, pp. 148-149, *infra*, p. 378), is unique to the EA texts from Canaan (*CAD* A/2:220). It seldom takes the *-a,* and its semantic range is hardly commensurate with the ventive. Nevertheless, it does happen to be more or less homophonous with MB (*w*)*arādu* "to go down," a verb of motion that would naturally take the ventive on many occasions. Furthermore, the contexts where *urrudu* does have an *-a* suffix are in tandem with another form having *-a* which is most likely a ventive:

> [*u*]*lu*[*-ú*] ⌜*yu*⌝*-*⌜*wu*⌝*-*⌜*šu*⌝*-u*[*r*] / ⌜ERÍN⌝.⌜MEŠ⌝ ⌜*pí*⌝*-*⌜*ṭú*⌝*-*⌜*tu*⌝*-š*[*u*] / *šu-nu* / [*t*]*u-šu-r*[*u*]*-ba-ni* / *a-na* URU.DIDLI.KI*-ni-ia* / *u l*[*u*]*-ú i-ru-da-am* / LUGAL EN*-ia* "[So] may he send h[is] troops; it is they who can install me in my towns that I may truly serve the king, my lord" (EA 300:15-21; Izreʾel 1978b:14; Moran 1987b:530; 1992:341).

The syntagma is difficult to define because of the possible lacuna in the latter part of line 17, but there may not be anything missing there. Assuming the interpretation given above, the clause *šu-nu* / [*t*]*u-šu-r*[*u*]*-ba-ni* is not necessarily injunctive; in fact, it is more likely indicative. So the status of the clause with *i-ru-da-am* may not be injunctive either. It would appear, then, that the suffix *-am* on the latter verb is truly a ventive, the result of modus attraction from the preceding Š form from *šūrubu,* which would by nature be appropriate for the ventive.

The final passage to be discussed here has several special features. The imperative on which the subsequent purpose clause depends is in the plural, apparently with the energic *-na;* the verb in the purpose clause, *izuzzu,* is used frequently with the ventive in good Akkadian (*supra,* pp. 206-208).

> *ù* / *uš-ši-ru-na-ni* 50 *ta-pal* / ANŠE.KUR.RA *ù* 2 ME ERÍN.MEŠ GÌR.MEŠ / *ù i-zi-za i-na* URU*Ši-ga-ta* / *i-na pa-ni-šu a-di* / *a-ṣí* ERÍN.MEŠ *pí-ṭá-ti* "So send to me fifty spans of horses and two hundred foot troops so that I may take up a position in Shigata facing him until the coming forth of the army" (EA 71:22-27).

AFTER A VERB OF FEARING. Moran (1950a:100;1960:14) noted that, in Arabic, the subjunctive *yaqtula* follows verbs of fearing (Wright 1898:25). It so happens that, in this regard, there is one lone example in the EA texts from Canaan. Furthermore, the verb, a G passive of *dâku*, is one which does not take the ventive in Akkadian. There is no contextual reason to suppose modus attraction to explain the *-a* suffix on the verb in question. Although the final sign is somewhat defaced on the tablet, it is most probably *k*[*a*] (Moran 1987b:351 n. 7).

> *pa*[*l-ḫ*]*a-ti a-n*[*a-k*]*u* / *la-a-mi ú-da-a-k*[*a*] "I am afraid lest I be killed" (EA 131:27-28).

CONDITIONAL SENTENCES. Note the following example in the protasis of a conditional sentence:

> *i-nu-ma* / [*a*]*-mu-ta mi-nu* / ⌜*yi*⌝*-na-ṣa-ru-ši*$_x$(ŠE) "If I die, who will protect it?" (EA 130:50-52; Moran 1960:14; 1950a:73).

Now the verb *mâtu* "to die" does sometimes take the ventive in literary Akkadian (*CAD* M/1:424a):

> *mūt bubāti u ṣummi limūta* "let him die the death of hunger and thirst" (Langdon 1931:Pl. 5:9; cited *CAD* B:302a); [*i*]*na šuttati amâtama* "Shall I die in the pit?" (*Ibid.*, Pl. 3:26); *qarrādān šina imuttānim* "two heroes will die" (*YOS* 10, 31:ix, 27).

It should be remembered that the Semitic root **mwt/mūt* belongs to a class that defines the transition from one state to another (Landsberger 1926:362; 1976:9). Therefore, the ventive was not felt by the ancient Mesopotamians to be out of place on this verb.

The ensuing cases of the *-a* suffix come in a chain of injunctives which comprise the apodosis of a conditional sentence. The first verb in the injunctive chain is an imperative (Moran 1950a:74) with the ventive suffix:

> [*šum-*]*ma i-ra-am* ⸢*šàr*⸣-[*ru*] / [E]N-*li* ÌR *ki-t*[*i-šu*] / [*ù*] *uš-ši-ra* / [3] LÚ *ù ib-lu-ṭá* / *ù i-na-ṣí-ra* / URU *a-na šàr-ri* "[I]f the ki[ng], my [lo]rd, cares for [his] faithf[ul] servant, [then] send the [three] men that I may survive and that I may protect the city for the king" (EA 123:23-28; Rainey 1975b:414).

It was observed above that *dubburu/duppuru* does not seem to normally take the ventive (*supra*, p. 258). So in the apodosis of this conditional sentence there is no reason to assume modus attraction:

> *i-nu-ma* 1 *ḫa-za-nu* / *lìb-bu-šu it-ti lìb-bi-ia* / *ù ú-da-bi-ra* ÌR-*A-ši-ir-ta* / *iš-tu* KUR*A-mur-ri* "If there were one governor of the same mind as I, then I would drive out ᶜAbdi-Ashirta from Amurru" (EA 85:66-69; Moran 1960:15).

COMPLEX SENTENCES. The following passage is very complex indeed. It begins with an *inūma* clause as topic and continues with an oath as comment. The oath itself is in the form of a conditional sentence introduced by *inūma*, the apodosis is what appears to be an injunctive clause the verb of which has the *-a* suffix. Although this latter verb is a verb of speaking, it is not one that generally appears with the ventive suffix (*CAD* D:186b-188b) like some other verbs of speaking.

> *i-nu-ma qa-bi a-na* / *pa-ni šàr-ri* I*Ri-ib-*dIŠKUR / *šu-mi-it* ERÍN.MEŠ *pí-ṭá-at šàr-ri i-nu-ma ba-al-ṭú* / LÚ.MEŠ MAŠKÍM.MEŠ *ù* / *a-da-bu-ba ka-li ip-ši*[*-š*]*u-nu* "Inasmuch as it is said in the king's presence, 'Rib-Haddi has caused the death of the king's army,' as the commissioners live, I shall report all their deeds" (EA 119:18-23; Moran 1960:15; 1950a:100; 1987b:329 n. 2; *CAD* D:7a).

EVALUATION. It is abundantly clear that the EA texts have not given us any conclusive evidence for the existence of a Canaanite *yaqtula* pattern. In spite of Moran's brilliant mustering of the evidence, it is still possible to argue that the *-a* suffix is merely the Akkadian ventive. Moran was not unaware of the problem. His main argument was the injunctive nature of all the various contexts in which he found this *-a* suffix in the Byblos letters. However, the *-a* suffix almost always was attached to verbs which tend to be employed with the ventive and in many of the examples cited, especially the purpose clauses, there were other, parallel verbs with the same syntactic function but with the -Ø suffix of the jussive. There are no glosses or strictly Canaanite verbal forms with the *-a* suffix (unlike the evidence for the WS imperfect and jussive). Furthermore, even in the Byblos corpus, there were some instances where the *-a* suffix appeared in past narrative and in some *inūma* clauses (topic clauses in complex sentences); those contexts were completely unsuitable for an injunctive and leave little doubt that the *-a*(*m*) suffix is the Akkadian ventive (Moran 1960:16-17). Outside of the Byblos corpus, there are many more preterites and other passages where the ventive was employed.

The synchronic and diachronic evidence was also adduced by Moran but he refused to base his case on it (Moran 1960:11-13). He did point out the more than theoretical possibility that *yaqtula* had survived in the Hebrew cohortative (Moran 1961:64 = 1965:73-74). And he stressed the similarity in function between the Arabic subjunctive and *yaqtula* in the Byblos texts (Moran 1950a:102-104). In fact, *yaqtula* finds an unequivocal witness in Ugaritic, in spite of the limited nature of the orthography. The following cohortative context is indisputable:

> *iqra . ilm n*[*ᶜmm*] = **ʾiqraʾa ʾilî,a na*[*ᶜîmîma*] "I herewith invoke the g[oodly] deities" (*KTU* 1.23:1; Gordon 1965:72; Rainey 1985b; 1987a:398-399).

The diachronic witness of the Hebrew cohortative and the Arabic subjunctive also strengthens the case for an early NWS *yaqtula* pattern. The contrast between *yaqtulu* and *yaqtula,* the latter being employed in a syntactically subordinate manner, was not lost on Arab grammarians, who observed that *yaqtula* bears the accusative, or subordinate, suffix, while *yaqtulu* has the nominative, or independent ending.

As far as the EA evidence goes, Moran was probably on the right track when he suggested that the Canaanite scribes probably employed Akkadian ventives in injunctive contexts *because it was homophonous* with a *yaqtula* in their native tongue. The present review of the EA examples seems to suggest that such was the case. However, the almost complete parallelism between the use of the jussives and the forms with -*a*(*m*) suffix indicates that, if there was a *yaqtula* in Amarna Age Canaanite, it was hardly distinguishable in its nuances from the jussive. It might be assumed that the original, fullblown *yaqtula* was a more emphatic injunctive than the simple jussive. This is certainly not true in the EA letters.

Are these injunctive forms with -*a*(*m*) suffix Akkadian ventives recruited to serve as Canaanite *yaqtula*'s? Or were they simply true Akkadian ventives standing in as Canaanite jussives having an additional lexical (not modal) indicator of direction (ventive)? The answer to these questions cannot be given on the basis of the materials at hand. The comparative evidence from Ugaritic, Hebrew and Arabic suggests that the Canaanite scribes had a *yaqtula* in their native repertoire which made them partial to Akkadian ventives (cf. the remarks of Izreʾel 1978b:82).

ENERGIC

Finally, there is one Byblos occurrence of an injunctive energic. It is in a negative purpose clause after a verb of fearing. Moran (1950a:60, 100-101) construed the form as 3rd f.s. with a collective 3rd m.pl. subject.

> *pal-ḫa-ti* LÚ.MEŠ *ḫu*!-⌜*up*⌝[-*ši-ia*] / *ul ti-ma-ḫa-ṣa-na-n*[*i*] "I am afraid of [my] tenant [farmers] lest they smite m[e]" (EA 77:36-37).

The injunctive nature of the verb form seems assured by its role in a negative purpose clause. Moran had noted that injunctives can appear after verbs of fearing (cf. *supra,* p. 260 regarding EA 131:27-28). Other explanations could be suggested, however. The *-a* suffix could be the Akkadian ventive even though *maḫāṣu* does not normally take the ventive (cf. *supra,* p. 258 regarding EA 270:17-21). A less likely possibility is that the suffix is the missing 3rd f.pl., i.e. *-āna,* but the subject is a plural masculine noun; such a masculine plural can take a 3rd f.s. verb (Moran 1950a:60, 131-132 n. 163). Therefore, the best solution at present seems to be that we do have here a true injunctive energic.

The injunctive energic is also documented in Ugaritic, in the same text from which was cited the 1st c.s. volitive.

> *iqran . ilm nᶜmm* = **ʾiqraʾan(n)a ʾilîma naᶜîmîma* "I will invoke the goodly deities" (*KTU* 1.23:23; Gordon 1965:72; Rainey 1985b; 1987a:398-399).

The strongest motivation for positing an ancient *yaqtulan(n)a* is the presence of just such an energic in Arabic. While the Canaanite EA texts have indicative energics in *-un(n)a,* this one, lone example (EA 77:36-37) is the only injunctive energic. Forms like *yi-na-ṣí-ra-an-ni* (EA 112:13), *yi-na-ṣí-ra-ni* (EA 130:20), and *yi-na-ṣa-ra-ni* (EA 119:10) are all in questions; the accusative suffix is attached by means of the ventive; they are paralleled by *yi-na-ṣí-ru-ni* (EA 112:18) in the same syntagma.

Diachronically, the indicative energic survived in Hebrew in the accusative suffixes *-enhû, -ennû, -enhā,* and perhaps also *-ekkā* (Rainey 1975b:186b; Blau 1978; Rainey 1986:10-12). It is possible that the injunctive energic survived in the same accusative suffixes when they appear on the cohortative (Huehnergard 1988:23; Rainey 1988a:36). As for the Arabic energic, T. Zewi has demonstrated that it functions in many injunctive syntagmas but also in some indicative constructions, such as the interrogative sentence (Zewi 1987:6-74).

CHAPTER XI

THE IMPERATIVE

The imperative cannot be divorced from the prefix conjugation injunctives. Formally, the imperative usually represents the basic stem form to which the personal markers of the prefix conjugation pattern can be attached. Such is the case with Akkadian and WS. In the older grammatical studies of the EA texts, the imperative was almost completely ignored. Böhl did not discuss it. Ebeling (1910:58-59, §8) wrongly thought that it displayed no unusual features. Dhorme (1913:371-376 = 1951:407-412) did try to deal with it but deduced all the wrong diachronic conclusions.

MORPHOLOGY

CANAANITE. Only two true Canaanite imperatives are attested. The clearest is from a verb which does not exist in Akkadian (the two homophonous verbs, *napālu* A and B have entirely different meanings and semantic ranges, *CAD* N/1:272b-277a). Furthermore, the imperative in question, from a I[st] *Nun* root, preserved the first radical, unlike Akkadian in which the initial consonant is dropped in the imperative. The example in question is, in fact, in a very West Semitized context:

> *nu-pu-ul-mì* / *ta-aḫ-ta-mu ù* / *ti-ma-ḫa-ṣú-ka* "Fall beneath them that they may smite you!" (EA 252:25-26; Knudtzon 1915:1601; Albright 1943b:32 n. 23).

There is another possible Canaanite form which appears with a gloss sign in a letter from Tyre:

> *i*$_{15}$*-nu-ma* / *iq-bi* LUGAL *be-li-ia* \\ *ku-na* / *a-na pa-ni* ERÍN.MEŠ GAL *ù iq-bi* / ÌR-*du a-na be-li-šu* \\ *ia-a-ia-ia* "When the king, my lord, said 'Be ready for (the coming of) the great army,' the

servant answers 'Yes, yes, yes!" (EA 147:35-38; *CAD* K:171b; Albright 1937:197).

Unless the form is a unique example of the Akkadian plural suffix -*ā*, or the Akkadian ventive suffix -*a*(*m*), both of which are highly unlikely on a Canaanite verb form, this imperative of **kwn*/*kūn* must have an injunctive -*a*. The injunctive -*ā* of ancient Hebrew is often attached to the imperative .

qûmāʰ ʾᵉlôhîm šop̄ṭāʰ hāʾāreṣ "Arise, oh God, judge the earth" (Ps. 82:8).

This possibility might have bearing on the many imperatives of *wuššuru*, viz. *uššira* (*passim*) and also on many examples of the precative. On the one hand, it seems logical to assume that those were simply ventives in spite of the temptation to see them as *modus attraction* from a volitive -*a* (cf. *supra*, pp. 204-206). Nevertheless, the -*a* suffix on what appears to be a purely Canaanite verb, *ku-na*, argues for some injunctive significance, at least by homophony, for the many -*a* suffixes on imperatives (and perhaps on precatives and other prefix verbs). In turn, that might strengthen the argument in favor of positing a true WS *yaqtula* rather than the Akkadian ventive in the EA texts (cf. discussion *supra*, pp. 254-264).

AKKADIAN. As for the Akkadian imperative forms, the standard vocalic patterns are attested (departures from the norm will be treated below).

For the G stem of the strong verb, one finds:

qutul

bu-lu-uṭ "live!" (TT 1:4); *du-gu-la* "look!" (EA 283:9; for *dugla* with ventive); *ku-uš-da* "come!" (EA 82:52; 86:6; 95:34; *ku-uš-di* in broken context, EA 95:15, unexplained); *qú-ru-ud-mi* "call out, entreat!" (EA 69:38; 87:25; Moran 1987b:274 n.4; 1992:160 n. 4; Civil 1984:294-295 and n. 21; CAD Q:126); *šu-pur* (EA 38:17;

149:56; 151:51); *šu-pu-ur-mì* "send!" (EA 98:22); *šu-up!-ra-am* "send hither!" (TT 1:15-18).

qitil

mi-li-ik (EA 132:8); *mi-lik* (EA 114:54, 67; *et al.*); *mi-lik-mi* "take thought!" (EA 90:11); *pí-qí-id* "command!" (TT 2:13);

qital

li-ma-ad "learn, be apprised!" (EA 34:3; 58:4; 70:11; *et al.*); also ⌜*li*⌝*-ma-ad* (EA 284:6).

From a verb IInd *Aleph*:

ša-al (EA 89:41; 256:16, 17, 19; 264:11); *ša-a-la* "ask!" (EA 113:4; Moran 1987b:314, cf. 315 n. 2; 1992:187 and n. 4).

From Ist *Aleph* verbs:

a-mur (*passim*); *a-mu-ur-mi* "behold, look!" (EA 185:42, 64; *et al.*); especially as a presentation particle (Rainey 1989b); *i-pu-uš-mi* "make (war)!" (EA 250:16, 41); cf. from Egypt *e-pu-uš* (EA 38:22; 162:39; 367:13); *a-li-ik-mi* (EA 136:11, 27); *a-lik-mi* "go!" (EA 102:15); *al-ka-am-mi* "come!" (EA 197:17).

From Ist *Nun* verbs:

(q)utul

ú-ṣur (EA 126:32; *et al.*); *ù-ṣur-mi* (EA 112:9; *et al.*); *ù-ṣur-mì* "guard, protect!" (EA 117:84; *et al.*); cf. from Egypt *uṣ-*⌜*ṣur*⌝ (EA 117:84); *uṣ-ṣur* (EA 367:4, 14; 370:4; Rainey 1978b:84)

(q)itil

i-di-in$_4$ (EA 116:35); *i-din-mì* "give!" (EA 234:24).

From IIIrd *Aleph* verbs:

> *li-qé* "take!" (EA 107:16); *li-qá* (EA 120:25); *li-qa-mi* "take away!" (EA 60:11; 95:35; 37-39); *ši-me* (EA 79:20); *ši-me-e* (EA 102:29); *ši-mé* (EA 83:14; *et al.*); *ši-mé-ma* (EA 317:21); *ši-mé-mi* "listen!" (EA 294:8).

From a IIIrd weak verb:

> *qí-bi* (EA 73:43; *et al.*); *qí-bi-ma* (EA 286:1; 287:65; 290:2); *qí-bí-ma* (EA 363:2; 365:2; 366:2; 367:2; 370:2); *qí-bi-mi* (EA 362:1); *qí-ba-mi* "speak!" (EA 73:33; *et al.*).

From the irregular verb *izuzzu*: *i-zi-iz* "stand, stay" (EA 102:15).

Moran (1987b:283 n. 5; 1992:166 n. 5) reads a Gt plural imperative, ⸢*at*⸣-[*la*]-*ku* "go forth!" (EA 92:37). It is an alleged quotation from a message by pharaoh.

An imperative, also plural, from the N stem is from the irregularly conjugated verb *nēnpušu* (cf. *supra*, pp. 123-126; Rainey 1973c:250-254), viz. *in*$_4$-*né*-[*ep-šu*] (EA 81:12), unless the broken text (at the right hand edge) could be completed *in*$_4$-*né*-[*ep-ša-tu-nu*] (2nd m.pl. suffix conjugation), which seems a bit too long for the available space.

Imperatives are naturally attested for the D stem as well. From the strong verb: *bu-li-iṭ* "grant life!" (EA 215:16) and the MB forms from *wuššuru* typical of the Jerusalem letters: *mu-še-ra* "send!" (EA 287:52; 289:45). The most prevalent form, however, is the short imperative. Although this latter form is known from MA (Mayer 1971:77, §78), it had already begun to appear in OB, e.g. *ú-še-er* (*CT* 29, Pl. 4c:6; *AbB* 2, 126:6). There can be no doubt that the Canaanite scribes inherited it from later OB and not from Assyrian. This is the most widely attested imperative in the entire EA corpus, with close to fifty occurrences. Besides *uš-ši-ir-mi* "send!" (EA 82:28; 120:36; 121:42), there are nearly forty examples with an *-a* suffix. e.g. *uš-ši-ra* (EA 75:43; *et passim*); *uš-ši-ra-am-mi* (EA 96:28); *uš-ši-ra-mi* (EA 82:15; *et al.*). Youngblood (1961:94-95) surveyed all the *uššira* imperatives and found that while the simple *uššir* means simply "send!" (elsewhere), *uššira* always means "send (to me)!" One does not find *uššira . . . ana yâši* but a circumlocution may be used, *uš-ši-ra-mi . . . it-ti-ia* (EA 82:15; Youngblood 1961:230; cf. *supra,* p. 205, *infra,* p. 271-272).

The D stem imperative from *turru* "to return," appears twice: *te-ra-ni* "send back to me!" (EA 114:25); *ti-ir-nu-mi* "return to us (our cities)!" (EA 138:138).

One example from *buʾʾû* "to seek" is also known; it is singular with an *-a* suffix: *bu-a-mi* "seek!" (EA 92:24). Judging from the context, it looks as though it is 2nd m.s. with ventive suffix rather than Akkadian 2nd c.pl. Since that epistle comes from an Egyptian official, an Akkadian 2nd c.pl. is not impossible.

Imperatives from the Š stem are rare. There is the Akkadian *še-zi-ba-an-ni* "deliver me!" (EA 318:8, 14) and another with erroneous gemination of the second radical, *še-ez-zi-bá-an-na-ši-mi* "deliver us!" (EA 62:30). From the Š of *târu,* exclusively in EA Canaanite (*AHw*:1336a): *šu-te-ra* "send back!" (EA 83:23; Youngblood 1961:244); *šu-te₉-ra-ni-mi* "send to me!" (KL 74:300:15; Edzard 1976:64).

ANOMALOUS FORMS. It is hard to define the following examples accept as aberrations from the norm:

(1) *ur-ru-ba* "enter!" (EA 283:8) — it could be analogous to the D infinitive in line 11, also written *ur-ru-ba* "to enter" (*CAD* E:269a), i.e. it should have been **urriba.*

(2) *iz-zi-ib-mi* "abandon!" (EA 294:29; Rainey 1974:298; Izreʾel 1978b:79) — gemination of the second radical, probably by analogy with the subsequent *iz-zi-ba* "I will (verily) abandon" (EA 294:31).

(3) *uṣ-*⌈*ṣur*⌉ (EA 117:84); *uṣ-ṣur* (EA 367:4, 14; 370:4; Rainey 1978b:84) — all the examples except the first are in letters sent from Egypt, and the Byblos spelling is a quotation from pharaoh's letter; the gemination is evidently an analogy with the preterite (Cochavi-Rainey 1988:144, §2.4.2.3). The plural form,

⌜*ú*⌝-*ṣa-ru-m*[*i*] (EA 100:14) with preservation of the (wrong) thematic vowel seems to be an analogous construction derived from the Akkadian present; so here, too, the second radical is probably geminated, i.e. *uṣṣarūmi.*

(4) *da-gal-šu* "examine him!" (EA 107:18) — the imperative is built on the Akkadian G present (Rainey 1978b:68), possibly for D stem. Ebeling (1910:58) had cited this form as if it were the proper *qatal* Akkadian imperative. Even the imperative with proper thematic vowel, *du-gu-la* (EA 283:9), is evidently built on the analogy of *ur-ru-*⌜*ba*⌝ in the same context (EA 283:8; cf. *supra,* p. 269). The correct form, with the *-a* suffix, should have elided the theme vowel, i.e. **dugla;* cf. *kušda* (EA 82:52; *et al.*). So the scribes may have intended **daggalšu* and **duggula* respectively.

(5) *pu-ḫu-ru-nim-mi* "assemble!" (EA 74:31) — the form in Akkadian would be *puḫrānimmi* for 2nd c.pl. (Youngblood 1961:142) assuming that G stem is intended. The presence of the thematic vowel, even if incorrect, could indicate that the scribe had the D stem in mind, in which case the proper Akkadian form would have been *puḫḫirānimmi.* It is impossible to determine what the original intention was. Either the transitive D or the intransitive G would suit the context.

(6) *pa-aṭ-ra-an-ni* "he has left me" (EA 287:50) — This form had been taken for an imperative (Albright, Mendenhall and Moran 1955:488b) but it clearly is not as Moran has noted (1987b:511, 513 n. 14; 1992:328, 330 n. 14).

PLURAL. It is amazing that Ebeling and Böhl did not notice the striking difference between the 2nd c.pl. forms in the EA texts and the standard forms of Akkadian. Whereas Akkadian uses the *-ā* plural suffix for masculine and feminine, the EA texts from Canaan always employ *-ū* (cf. *supra,* pp. 45-46). Besides the apparent Canaanite form *ku-na* (EA 147:36; *supra,* pp.265-266) discussed above, which seems more likely to be singular, there is one instance of a plural imperative where the proper Akkadian ending is employed. The context is important for the correct understanding of the form:

> UGU *ma-an-ni* / *iš-tap-pár* ᴵÌR-*Ḫe-ba* / *a-na* LÚ.MEŠ ᵁᴿᵁ*Qí-il*$_5$*-ti*$_7$ / [*l*]*e-qa-mi* KÙ.BABBAR.MEŠ *ù* / [*a*]*l-ku-ni a-na ar-ki-ia* "Why did ᶜAbdi-Kheba write to the men of Keilah, 'Take money and follow me!" (EA 280:16-20).

The other attested plural imperatives have -*ū* as the plural person marker:

> *al-ku-mi* "go!" (EA 117:62); ˹*at*˺-[*la*]-*ku* "go forth!" (EA 92:37; Moran 1987b:283 n. 5; 1992:166 n. 5); *du-ku-mi* "kill!" (EA 73:27; 74:25; 81:12); *i-zi-bu-šu* "desert him!" (EA 138:44); ˹*ú*˺-*ṣa-ru-m*[*i*] "guard!" (EA 100:14); *in*$_4$*-né-ep-šu* "become allied/aligned!" (EA 81:12; Moran 1987a); *uš-ši-ru* "send!" (EA 90:45; 134:26); *uš-še-ru-ši* "expedite it!" (EA 255:11; Rainey 1989-90:69b; cf. Moran 1987b:483 n. 1; 1992:308 n. 1).

Especially noteworthy are two examples with the ventive suffix: [*a*]*l-ku-ni* (EA 280:20; cited above); and *pu-ḫu-ru-nim-mi* (EA 74:31) discussed above with regard to its basic form (*supra*, p. 270). These plurals have some bearing on the question of the -*a* suffix applied to so many singular imperatives. They strengthen the impression that the -*a*, like the -*ūni*(*m*), must also have been intended for the ventive, not the WS volitive (cf. *supra*, pp. 205, 268-269).

The picture is different with regard to two instances where the energic is applied to the imperative. The contexts are important:

> *šum-ma lìb-bi* LUGAL *ba-li uš-ša-*[*ar*] / ERÍN.MEŠ *pí-ṭá-ti ia-aš-pu-ur a-na* / ᴵ*Ia-an-ḫa-mì ù a-na* ᴵ*Pí-ḫu-ra* / *al-ku-mi qa-du* LÚ.MEŠ *ḫa-za-ni-ku-nu* / *le-qú-na* ᴷᵁᴿ*A-mur-ri* "If the king does not intend to send the army, let him write to Yanḫamu and to Piḫura, 'Go with your city rulers, take Amurru'" (EA 117:59-63; Moran 1987b:323; 1992:193).

The first imperative, *al-ku-mi*, has the simple plural suffix. The second has *-ūn(n)a*. The other passage is:

> *ù* / *uš-ši-ru-na-ni* 50 *ta-pal* / ANŠE.KUR.RA *ù* 2 ME ERÍN.MEŠ GÌR.MEŠ / *ù i-zi-za i-na* URU*Ši-ga-ta* / *i-na pa-ni-šu a-di* / *a-ṣí* ERÍN.MEŠ *pí-ṭá-ti* "So send to me fifty spans of horses and two hundred foot troops so that I may take up a position in Shigata in front of him until the regular army comes forth" (EA 71:22-27).

The form *uš-ši-ru-na-ni* is a "plural of majesty" applied to pharaoh and the *-na* suffix has to be the energic (Youngblood 1961:94-95; cf. *supra*, pp. 205, 268-269). There is evidently no way of distinguishing the energic injunctive plural from the indicative energic plural due to the orthography.

WITH PRONOMINAL SUFFIXES. The accusative suffix is usually attached to the bare imperative form:

> *da-gal-šu* "examine him!" (EA 107:18); *ša-al-šu* "interrogate him!" (EA 74:51; *et al.*); *ša-al-šu-nu* "interrogate them!" (EA 230:18); *uš-ši-ir-šu* "send him!" (EA 333:22); and pl. *uš-še-ru-ši* "expedite it!" (EA 255:11); *i-zi-bu-šu* "desert him!" (EA 138:44).

Occasionally, the accusative suffix is attached to the ventive: *uš-ši-ra-aš-ši* "send it!" (TT 2:11); *uš-ši-ra-šu* "send him!" (EA 84:41; 126:43). The verb *šūzubu* "to save, deliver, rescue," often takes the object being saved in the accusative attached by means of the ventive (*CAD* E:424a-425b). Such is the case with the two documented imperatives: *še-zi-ba-an-ni* "deliver me!" (EA 318:14); *še-ez-zi-bá-an-na-ši-im* "deliver us!" (EA 62:30; note the dative 1st c.pl. suffix pronoun which is evidently being used accusatively).

Conversely, the 1st c.s. dative is expressed by the accusative suffix attached to the ventive, a practice not uncommon in the peripheral dialects generally, namely: *id-na-ni* "give to me!" (EA 103:42; 270:18; 333:12); *te-ra-ni* "return to me!" (EA 114:25);

uš-še-er-an-ni (EA 35:25), *uš-še-ra-an-ni* (EA 35:26), *uš-ši-ra-ni* "send to me!" (EA 70:17; 76:24; 108:66).

These suffixed forms tend to confirm what other lines of argument suggest, viz. that the *-a* suffix attached to the imperative really is in fact the Akkadian ventive, at least in nearly all instances. The ventive on other injunctive forms, e.g. the jussive and the Akkadian precative, should not be surprising.

SYNTAGMAS

It remains to survey the uses of the imperative in the EA texts from Canaan. One important syntactical feature that almost goes without saying is the fact that the imperative almost always comes at the head of its clause. Such is not always the case in letters from neighboring areas, e.g. Amurru (cf. e.g. EA 158:11-13; Izreʾel 1985:245, §3.4.1.4). A glaring exception in the Canaanite epistles is the introductory formulae which generally follow established patterns accepted in international scribal circles (Salonen 1967:62-63; Knudtzon 1913).

INTRODUCTORY FORMULAE. One Rib-Haddi letter opens with an imperative, and that in a syntagma that is usually filled in the earlier Byblos letters by a finite preterite verb, *iqbi* (cf. e.g. EA 74:1-2; *et al.*):

> ^{I}*Ri-ib-*^{d}IŠKUR*-di qí-bi-mi* / *a-na* LUGAL *be-li-ia* "Rib-Haddi (says) 'Speak to the king, my lord!'" (EA 362:1-2).

Many other letters follow the common international pattern; note that the imperative is written with the *bí* sign, which is otherwise quite rare in these texts, thus showing the ancient, learned nature of this formula:

> *a-na* LUGAL EN*-ia* DINGIR*-ia* ^{d}UTU*-ia* / *qí-bí-ma* / *um-ma* ÌR*-re-ša* ÌR*-ka* "To the king, my lord, my god, my sungod, speak! Thus (says) ᶜAbdi-rēša, your servant" (EA 363:1-3; further examples: EA 365:1-3; 366:1-3).

The Jerusalem letters employ the same formula, but with the common *bi* sign:

> [*a*]-*na* ILUGAL EN-*ia qí-bi-ma* / *um-ma* IÌR-*Ḫe-ba* ÌR-*ka-ma* " [T]o the king, my lord, speak! Thus (says) ᶜAbdi-Ḫeba, your servant" (EA 286:1-2; also EA 285:1-2; 287:1-2; 288:1-2; 289:1-2; 290:1-2; and to the scribe EA 287:64-65).

A diluted tradition is reflected in those letters where the enclitic -*ma* is not attached to the imperative:

> *a-na* ILUGAL dBE-*ia qí-bi* / *um-ma* I*Ia-ma* ÌR-*ka* "To the king, my lord, speak! Thus (says) Yamma, your servant" (EA 230:1-2).

BLESSING. An unusual blessing formula comes from the 15th century B.C.E. in a Taanach letter: *bu-lu-uṭ dam-qí-*[*iš*] "Live well!" (TT 1:4; Rainey 1977:43). Two instances of the same greeting occur in Alalakh, where the correct reading is: *bu-lu-uṭ* SIG_5!-*qí-iš* (AT 109:3; 116:15; correctly understood *AHw*:157a; the entry for **dumqiš* in *CAD* D:180a is to be deleted).

PRESENTATION PARTICLE. The imperative of *amāru* "to see," is used as a presentation particle. This function is unknown in classical Babylonian but its distribution in the peripheral dialects is of the utmost interest. One finds it numerous times in the texts from Canaan and it also appears in the Egyptian correspondence (EA 1:28; 162:30, 67) including texts from the 13th century B.C.E. which were sent from Egypt to Hattusas (Cochavi-Rainey 1988:228). The example recorded from Ugarit (*CAD* A/2:19) is actually in a letter sent from Amurru (RS 17.116:9', 21'; Nougayrol 1956:132, 133; Izre'el 1985:2471991a:154). The scribes of Ugarit do not seem to have used it (Huehnergard 1989:193-201). Some examples are cited for Hattusas, but with the exception of a letter from Hattusili III to Kadashman-Ellil II (*KBo* 1, 10:50), all the texts using *amur* as a presentation particle were written by Egyptian scribes (Cochavi-Rainey 1988:228), including the treaty between Ramesses II and Hattusili III (*KBo* 1, 7:*passim*). The Egyptian version of that same treaty confirms that the use of the corresponding imperative from the Egyptian verb "to see," viz. *ptr*, was being used in the same function (Rainey 1989a). It would appear that this is a calque within the sphere of Egyptian control over the Canaanite population. The same function in rare instances reflects sporadic influence on the scribes at Hattusas following the extensive correspondence with the scribes of Ramesses II).

The original nature of *amur* as an imperative was not really lost. The earliest documented example, in a Taanach letter from the 15th century B.C.E., carries the 1st c.sg. acc. pronominal suffix:

> ⸢*i*⸣-⸢*na*⸣-*an-na a-mur-ni i-nu-ma* / *i-pu*-⸢*šu*⸣ ⸢DÙG⸣.⸢GA⸣ *it-ti-ka* "Now, behold me, that I will do good for you!" (TT 2:17-18; Rainey 1977:46).

On occasion, the imperative *amur* governs a nominal direct object:

> *a-mur i-pí-iš* / ⸢URU⸣ *Ṣur-ri* "Behold the deed of Tyre!" EA 89:10-11; Youngblood 1961:329); *a-mur ip-ša an-ni-ú ip-ši* ^{I}*Mil-ki*-DINGIR / *ù ip-ši* DUMU.MEŠ *La-ab-a-ya* "Behold this deed, the deeds of Milkilu and the deeds of the sons of Labʾayu!" (EA 287:29-30; also apparently EA 288:7-8 where ‹*a-mur*› must be supplied); *ša-ni*-⸢*tam*⸣ *a-mur ar-na* ⸢*ša*⸣! / [*yi*]-*pu-iš* ^{I}*A-zi-ru* "Furthermore, behold the crime which(!) Aziru has [co]mmitted!" (EA 140:20-21; and possibly also EA 106:4 and 140:18-19).

This happens even when the direct object is in extraposition to the clause that follows:

> *a-mur* / ÌR-*da ša iš-me a-na* ›*a-na*‹ *be-li-šu* / *šul-mu* URU-*šu šul-mu* É-*šu* / *šum-šu a-na da-ri-ti* "Behold, the servant who has obeyed his lord: his city is at peace, his house is at peace, his name endures forever" (EA 147:48-51).

In the following Jerusalem passage, the awkward context seems to require that the particle *amur* or something comparable should probably be supplied:

> ‹*a-mur*› *ḫa-an-pa* / *ša iḫ-nu-pu a-na mu-ḫi-ia* "‹Behold,› the audacity that they have exercised against me" (EA 288:7-8; contrast Moran 1987b:515; 1992:331).

An optional addition to *amur* is the enclitic *-mi.* Whether this is to mark the ensuing clause as direct speech, or whether it is the Canaanite enclitic for emphasis is open to question. Enclitic *-ma* is never used with *amur.* The optional nature of the enclitic with *amur* may be seen from the two passages in the same epistle, one with an enclitic and one without it:

> *a-mur-mi a-na-ku* ÌR *ša* ^{I}*šàr-ri* "Behold, I am a servant of the king" (EA 264:5); *ša-ni-tam a-mur ni-nu a-na mu-ḫi-ka*$_4$ / 2 IGI-*ia* "Furthermore, behold (as for) us, my(*sic!*) eyes are towards you" (EA 264:14-15).

This is not the place to discuss the many other aspects of this function from the point of view of a presentation particle. Those are treated elsewhere (cf. *CAT* 3:202-210).

EXHORTATION. Once the imperative from *alāku* "to go" is used as an exhortation:

> *ù im-lu-uk iš-tu* / ŠÀ-*ia a-li-ik-mi a-na-ku* / *i-pu-ša!*(MA)-*am* DÙG.GA \ tu-ka / *it-ti-šu ša* ^{I}*Am-mu-ni-ra* "then I took counsel in my heart,'Come, I will make an alliance with ^{c}Ammunīra'" (EA 136:26-29; *CAD* E:223a; Moran 1987b:356 n. 5; 1992:217 n. 5; 1963:173-174)

The 1st c.s. independent pronoun, *anāku,* might suggest that the verb *a-li-ik-mi* is 1st c.s. Akkadian preterite serving as a jussive, i.e. *allikmi* instead of the imperative *alikmi.* Against such an interpretation, it must be remembered that the texts from Canaan never use the Akkadian preterite as their theme for hybrid verb forms; they invariably use *-llak* (cf. *supra*, p. 51). But note also that the imperative *a-li-ik-mi* occurs earlier in the same letter (EA 136:11). Compare the following example taken from biblical Hebrew:

> *lᵊḵāʰ niṯrāʾeʰ pānîm* "Come! Let us confront one another!" (2 Ki. 14:8).

COMMANDS. Naturally, the imperative is to be found expressing direct orders, especially from the king, e.g. in this quote from a royal message recently received:

> *a-na mi-ni yi-ìš-ta-pa-ru / šàr-ru* EN-*li a-na ia-ši / ú-ṣur-mi lu-ú na-ṣir-ta* "Why does the king write to me, 'Guard! May you be on guard'?" (EA 112:7-9);

or from his officials,

> *šum-ma / šàr-ru* EN-*lì* ANŠE.MEŠ / *bu-a-mi* ANŠE.MEŠ / LUGAL "If the king is owner of the asses, look for the asses of the king" (EA 96:22-25); *ù a-nu-ma / ia-aš-pu-ra* ᴵ*Šu-ta / a-na ia-ši i-din-mì /* ᴵ*Zi-ir-dam-ia-aš-da / a-na* ᴵ*Bir₅-ia-wa-za* "But now Shuta has written to me, 'Hand over Zirdamyashda to Biryawaza!'" (EA 234:22-26).

Such a royal command might even be construed as an invitation:

> *ù [š]a-ap-r[a]* ᴵ*šàr-ri* E[N-*i*]*a / a-na ia-ši ur-ru-*⌈*ba*⌉ [*it-ti*] \ ᴵ*šàr-ri* EN-*ia / du-gu-la lí-qé* "And the king, [m]y lo[rd], wrote to me, 'Enter in [to], the king, my(sic!) lord, behold, take!'" (EA 283:7-9; cf. Moran 1987b:505 nn. 2-3; 1992:324 nn. 3, 5).

But on the other hand, it may also embody a threat,

> *ù yi-iq-bu / a-na ia-ši id-na-*⌈*ni*⌉ / DAM-*ka ù* / DUMU.MEŠ-*ka ù lu-ú / i-ma-ḫa-ṣa* "And he is saying to me, 'Give me your wife

and your children or else I will attack!'" (EA 270:17-21; Moran 1987b:495; 1992:317).

REQUESTS. A vassal may use the imperative in addressing the king, obviously not from a position of seniority. Given the subservient status of the vassal rulers in Canaan, one should view such imperatives as requests or even entreaties, but there is no breach of etiquette involved when using the imperative. In such cases, the imperative seems to be an expression of desire directed to the second person, e.g.

ša-ni-tam mi-li-ik / URU*Gub-la* URU *ki-ti-ka* "Furthermore, take care of Byblos, your loyal city" (EA 132:8-9; *CAD* M/1:156b).

ADVICE. Sometimes an appeal to the king may be construed as a form of advice. That was certainly the intention of Rib-Haddi in the following:

uš-ši-ra ERÍN.MEŠ *pí-ṭá-ti* / *ra-ba ù tu-da-bi-ir* / *a-ia-bi* LUGAL *iš-tu* / *lìb-bi* KUR-*šu ù* / *ti-né-ep-šu ka-li* / KUR.KUR.MEŠ *a-na šàr-ri* "Send a large army and you can drive the enemies of the king from the midst of his land and all the lands will become loyal to the king" (EA 76:38-43).

ADJURATIONS. Some vassal ruler may pressure one or several of his peers by means of the imperative:

ù ki-i-am ṭi-iq-bu-na / 2 DUMU *La-ab-a-ya a-na ia-ši i-pu-uš-mì* / *nu-kúr-ta*$_5$ *i-na* LÚ.MEŠ KUR*Gi-na* "So thus the two sons of Labʾayu are saying to me, 'Make war against the men of Gina!'" (EA 250:15-17; and cf. also Shuwardata's EA 280:16-20 cited *supra*, p. 271).

APODOSES. One of the options for the apodosis of a conditional sentence is the imperative (Moran 1950a:74). A Taanach letter has the earliest documented example in a letter with WS syntax:

ù / šum-ma ga-am-ra-at GIŠBAN / *i-pé-ša-am ù uš-ši-ra-aš-ši / i-na* ŠU I*Pu-ur-da-ya* "And if the bow is finished being made, then send it by the hand of Purdaya" (TT 2:9-12; Rainey 1977:45, 61).

There are several good illustrations from Byblos, e.g.

šum-ma lìb-bi šàr-ri [a-n]a / na-ṣa-ar URU-*šu ù* / ÌR-*šu uš-ši-ra* / LÚ.MEŠ *ma-ṣa-ar-ta / ù ti-na-ṣí-ru* URU "If it is the king's desire [t]o protect his city and his servant, send garrison troops that they may guard the city" (EA 130:44-48; cf. also EA 107:20-22; 112:30-39; 114:44-46; 116:34-35; 123:23-26; 129:49-50).

PURPOSE CLAUSES. Like other injunctives, the imperative can also appear in clauses of intended result after another injunctive. Strangely enough, this function of the imperative is ignored by Moran (1950a:83-86). The number of examples is admitedly small. Two of them come from the same epistle.

ša-ni-tam yi-iš-mé / šàr-ru EN *a-wa-te* ÌR-*šu / ù uš-ši-‹ra›* LÚ.MEŠ *ma-ṣa-ar-ta / a-na* URU*Ṣu-mu-ra ù / a-na* URU*[I]r-qa-ta* "Furthermore, may the king heed the words of his servant and send garrison troops to Ṣumur and to ᶜIrqata" (EA 103:32-36); *ù / yi-it-ru-uṣ i-[n]a p[a-n]i* / EN dUTU KUR.ḪÁ *ù / id-na-ni* 20 *ta-pal* / ANŠE.KUR.RA.MEŠ *a-na ia-ši / ù uš-ši-ra til-la-ta / ki-ma ar-ḫi-iš / a-na* URU*Ṣu-mu-ra a-na / na-ṣa-ri-ši*x(ŠE) "So may it be pleasing in the sight of the lord, the sungod of the lands, and give me twenty spans of horses and send auxiliary troops quickly to Ṣumur to protect it" (EA 103:40-47; Moran 1987b:298; 1992:176).

The other-clear cut passage is also probably from the same scribe; at least it stems from the same chronological period in the Byblos correspondence:

ù yi-i[š-me] / [šà]r-ru a-wa-te ÌR-*šu ù uš-ši-ra-ni* / [2]0 LÚ.MEŠ KUR*Mi-li-ḫa* 20 LÚ.MEŠ KUR*Mi-iṣ-ri / a-na na-ṣa-ar* URU *a-na šà[r-r]i* / dUTU EN-*ia* "So may the [ki]ng he[ed] the words of his

> servant, and send to me twenty men of Miluḫḫa and twenty men of Egypt to guard the city for the k[in]g!" (EA 108:65-69).

Finally there is the broken passage, EA 133:10-14, where the crucial verb has to be supplied at the end of a broken line.

CHAPTER XII

THE SUFFIX CONJUGATION — MORPHOLOGY

At the beginning of Amarna research, scholars were struck by the unusual morphology of the suffix conjugation. The close resemblance to forms known from biblical Hebrew, mainly the 1st c.s. suffix *-ti*, indicated that WS influences were at work (Zimmern 1890a). After a century of study in the language of the EA tablets, it may be possible to summarize the accumulated evidence and present a more comprehensive picture of the suffix conjugation as it functions in the texts from Canaan. It should be remarked, incidentally, that even the Jerusalem (Nitzán 1973:56, §4.32) and the Tyrian (Finkle 1977:105-107) letters, which generally go their own way in the use of the prefix conjugation patterns, employ the WS suffix forms extensively, especially for past tense.

Knudtzon (1892), evidently followed by Bergsträsser (1929:11) and independently Moran (1950a:34-39), concluded that the suffix conjugation, both the Akkadian stative and the WS so-called "perfect," had developed from the nominal sentence. More recently, Buccellati has developed this theme with regard to the Akkadian suffix conjugation (1968). There has been of late some disagreement as to whether the suffix conjugation forms of Akkadian should be classed as verbs (Kraus 1984:10-13) or not (Huehnergard 1986, 1987). From the standpoint of surface morphology, the suffix conjugation forms do share certain features with the prefix conjugation, e.g. they can take the Akkadian positional subjunctive (marker of subordination) and the Akkadian ventive suffix. Although the suffix conjugation in Akkadian is generally applied to the verbal adjectives from the respective root and stems to express a stative for intransitive verbs or a passive of transitive verbs, there are some verbs whose suffix conjugation forms express transitive meaning (a large collection of examples was assembled by Rowton 1962). On the other hand, the suffix conjugation was, perhaps as a later development, applied to nouns to express the permansive. Huehnergard (1987b:229-232) would now prefer to distinguish the two main classes of suffix forms: from the verbal adjective and from nouns, and transitives related to transitive verbs. The former, he would call "predicative forms" and include their clauses in the non-verbal category. For the latter, the transitives of the suffix conjugation, he would call "pseudo verbal." This proposal is attractive from a descriptive point of view. The term "stative," which is often applied to the suffix conjugation of Akkadian and also of Egyptian (e.g. Callendar 1975:22-23, §3.5.2.2), would best be reserved to verb classes and not to a conjugation pattern (Landsberger 1967:142 n. 15; cited by Huehnergard 1987b:229 n. 50 and Reiner 1970:292) but it has become so commonplace in discussion of the suffix forms that it can hardly be avoided today. The term "pseudo-verbal" for the suffix conjugation forms from transitive verbs in Akkadian has some justification but will be avoided here since it is not particularly relevant to the WS languages. At least one may note that the use of suffix forms from transitive verbs for transitive meaning demonstrates the potential of the suffix pattern, even in Akkadian where passive, permansive and stative meanings predominate. The truly verbal, transitive, function is realized more fully in the WS dialects. On the other hand, the traditional term, "perfect," applied to the suffix conjugation pattern in Hebrew, Arabic, Aramaic, Phoenician, etc., will be strictly avoided here because it is definitely a misnomer. The syntactic discussion (Ch. 14) that will follow the description of the morphological features in the Canaanite EA texts will demonstrate that there is nothing, inherent or developed, in the basic construction of the suffix conjugation to associate it with "completed action." The western tradition, beginning with Ewald (1831-33:II, 112) and fostered and made popular by Driver (1892:13-26), of supposing that the suffix conjugation was primarily expressing completed action is thoroughly misguided. For this reason the term "perfect" should be abandoned once and for all. It should be stricken from our gramar books.

For convenience, the term "suffix conjugation" will often be supplanted in our ensuing discussion by the noncommittal theme, *qtl* (cf. Gordon 1965:68, §9.4). That latter term has gained wide acceptance in practical discussions and it is hoped that its use here will make for a more readable text.

MORPHOLOGY

For all practical purposes, the Canaanite scribes used the suffix forms as calques on their own native conjugation patterns. As a result, the same process of hybridization came into play, thus producing morphological constructions which have no precedents or parallels in the cuneiform world, even among the peripheral dialects. There are also a number of glosses and other constructions that represent true Canaanite *qtl* verb forms. These are useful for demonstrating the original Canaanite forms (Sivan 1984:136-145) and for comparison with the Akkadian and hybrid creations that comprise the majority of the forms in this category.

PERSON MARKERS

AKKADIAN FIRST COMMON SINGULAR. The most striking morphological divergence of WS from the Hamito-Semitic pattern is the abandonment of the *-k-* element for first person singular. However, the Canaanite scribes knew this older element from their study of Akkadian where they encountered the standard *-āku* suffix. Of the nearly 120 examples of 1st c.s. *qtl* forms, twenty-eight have the regular Akkadian form with *-āku*. They represent about sixteen different verbs and include the G, D and Š stems. The G forms of this type with stative or passive meaning are:

> *ar-ba-ku* "I have entered" (TT 2:6; Rainey 1977:60 *contra* Glock 1983:60), *ar-na-ku* (EA 253:16; 254:11), *aš-ba-ku* (EA 62:16, 18), *ḫa-ad-ia-ku* (EA 154:10), *ḫa-ṭá-ku* (EA 253:17; 254:12); *ma-*⌜*ṣa*⌝*-ku* (EA 127:34), *mar-ṣa-ku* (EA 106:23; 306:22), *na-aṣ-ra-ku* (EA 142:11), *pal-ḫa-ku* (EA 102:28; 155:33), *šal-ma-ku* (EA 34:3; 145:6).

The Megiddo letters employ two such forms as transitive verbs:

> *ša-ni-tam mi-na-am-mi ep-ša-ku-mì* / *a-na šàr-ri* EN-*ia* "Furthermore, what have I done to the king, my lord?" (EA 245:36), *al-lu-ú-mì na-ad-na-ku* / ⌜ŠU⌝.KAM *šàr-ri* "Behold, I have furnished the request of the king" (EA 242:9-10; Moran 1979; Rabiner 1981:95, §5.2.1.1.1).

A broken context contains another example on a verb of speaking:

> [*g*]*áb-bi mi-im-mì* / [*ša iš-m*]*e qa-ba-ku* / [*a-na* LUGAL E]N-*ia* "[E]verything [that I have hea]rd, I have reported [to the king], my [lo]rd" (EA 259:7),

which matches a D stem form used in a Megiddo letter:

> *ša-ni-tam du-ub-bu-ba-ku-mì* / UGU ŠEŠ.MEŠ-*ia* "Furthermore, I exhorted my colleagues" (EA 245:1-2; cf. Rabiner 1981:68, §4.5.1.1).

Furthermore, the Š stem forms, which would be passives in normative Akkadian, are transitive in these texts: *šu-še-ra-ku* (EA 144:19), *šu-ši-ra-ku* (EA 141:24; 142:25; 144:21; 191:14), "I have prepared."

Finally, the hybrid forms developed from the so-called preformative stative, *ibašši* (*GAG*:102, §78b; Youngblood 1961:120-121), can also take the Akkadian 1st c.s. suffix, *-āku*: *i-ba-aš-ša-ku* (EA 248:20); i_{15}*-ba-ša-ku* (EA 143:29); i_{15}*-ba-ša-ku-mì* (EA 193:6).

CANAANITE FIRST COMMON SINGULAR. Over eighty percent of 1st c.s. *qtl* forms in the EA texts from Canaan have a personal suffix *-ti*. An Akkadian stative with *-āku* is glossed by a Canaanite form with *-ti*:

> ⌜*la*⌝(!) *ma-ṣa-ku* \ *ṣí-ir-ti* "I am not adequate (I am hard pressed)" (EA 127:25).

Three problematic instances of *pal-ḫa-tu* (EA 129:82; 137:68; 138:120) in the late Rib-Haddi correspondence are hardly evidence for 1st c.s. (Böhl 1909:46, §27 l;Ebeling 1910:56); they represent either the feminine stative participle (Moran 1987b:361 n. 13, 367 n. 28; 1992:220 n. 13, 225 n. 29) or a corrupt text (Moran 1987b:347 n. 29; 1992:211 n. 28).

Of the nearly one hundred forms with the WS *-ti* suffix, about eighty percent have the suffix attached to the Akkadian form with its connective *-ā-* vowel. In other words, the *-ti* simply displaced the *-ku* on the Akkadian stem form; except for a few special constructions to be discussed below, the principal G stem examples are:

> *al-ka-ti* (EA 107:48; *et al.*); *aš-ba-ti* (EA 81:20; *et al.*); *bal-ṭá-ti* (EA 83:27; *et al.*); *da-ag-la-ti* (EA 266:9, 10, 13; 296:11, 12, 14), *da-ag-la-ti*$_7$ (EA 292:8, 9, 11); *di*$_{12}$*-ka-ti* (EA 287:73); *ep-ša-ti* (EA 89:17; *et al.*); *ep-ša-ti*$_7$ (EA 249:6); *ḫa-ad-ia-ti* (EA 147:27); *ḫa-dì-ia-ti* (EA 147:29); *ka-aš-da-ti* (EA 93:7); *ka-aš-da-ti-šu* (EA 138:80); *ka-aš-da-ti*$_7$ (EA 189: r. 13); *lem-né-ti* (EA 180:19); *ma-ka*$_4$*-ti* (EA 116:11; *AHw*:591a); *ma-aq-ta-ti* (EA 63:6; *et al.*); *ma-aq-ta-ti*$_7$ (EA 138:4); *mi-ta-ti* (EA 119:17); *mi-ta-ti*!(UD) (EA 138:137); *na-ad-na-ti* (EA 73:38; *et al.*); *na-ad-na-ti-šu* (EA 108:65); *na-ad-na-ti*$_7$*-šu* (EA 254:36); *na-aṣ-ra-ti* (EA 227:5); *na-aṣ-ra-ti*$_7$*-ši* (EA 237:15); *pa-al-ḫa-ti* (EA 116:50); *pa-aṭ-ra-ti* (EA 82:44; *et al.*); *qa-la-ti* (EA 81:20); *ra-aṣ-pa-ti*$_7$ (EA 292:29); *ša-ak-na-ti* (EA 266:16; EA 288:32); *ša-ak-na-ti*$_7$ (EA 257:13); *ša-ap-ra-ti* (EA 117:13, 15, 21; EA 284:13); *šap-ra-ti* (EA 96:30; EA 139:16); *šap-ra-ti*$_7$ (KL 72:600:1; Rainey 1976b:338; Wilhelm 1982:184).

In other stems we have N *in*$_4$*-né-ep-ša-ti*$_7$ (EA 297:12) and Š *šu-ši-ra-ti*$_7$ (EA 193:21).

There is no warrant, however, for assuming that the *-āti* suffix is in any way related to WS constructions: it is simply a carry over from the Akkadian form (Ebeling 1910:57-58). Although certain patterns with a connective *-ā-* exist in Arabic (e.g. *maddâta*; Wright 1898:69 D) and in Hebrew (*sabbôṯā*;

GKC:176-177, 203), there is no reason to associate them with the attested form in the EA texts.

The true WS verb forms (including glosses) show that the native suffix was actually *-ti* without any connecting *-ā-* vowel. Two strong verbs are attested:

> *ia-pa-aq-ti* "I have issued" (EA 64:23; Krahmalkov 1971:140-143);
> [*na*]*-aq-ṣa-ap-ti* "I was [di]stressed" (EA 93:5; *CAD* Q:146a);

as are four middle weak verbs:

> *nu-uḫ-ti* "I am at rest" (EA 147:56); *ma-at-ti* "I (would) die" (EA 287:70; 289:50; Finkelstein 1969:33b-34; Moran disagrees; 1987b:514 n. 20, 1992:330 n. 20); *ṣí-ir-ti* "I am hard pressed" (EA 127:34; Moran 1987b:343 n. 9; 1992:208 n. 9); *ši-ir-ti* "I am maligned" (EA 252:14).

One certain third weak verb also shows the *-ti* suffix: ⸢*ba*⸣-⸢*ni*⸣-⸢*ti*⸣ "I have built" (EA 292:29) = **banîtî* ‹ **baniytî* (Sivan 1984:142, §1.2.1). Two forms which may represent roots with gutturals in the third position are *ba-ṭì-i-ti* "I am at rest" (EA 147:56), possibly = **baṭiḥtî* (Albright 1937:192 n. 2), and *ša-mi-ti*$_7$ "I have heard" (EA 362:5), which was at least probably inspired by WS **šami*^{c}*tî* (Rainey 1973c:238; Sivan 1984:141, §1.2.1). By the same token, one finds *la-qí-ti* (EA 109:30) and *la-qí-ti*$_7$ (EA 251:1) which might be echoes of WS **laqiḥtî*.

Therefore, it is not so surprising to find hybrid forms without the characteristic *-ā-* of Akkadian. In fact, there are nearly twenty instances of hybrids with only the *-ti*. The G stem examples are:

> *a-ṣí-ti* (EA 227:9); [*da-ak*]*-ti-šu* (EA 81:16); *i-re-eb-ti* (EA 263:8); *ka-ša-ad-ti-šu* (EA 138:80); *qa-bi-ti* (EA 119:46; 132:31, 37; 263:20); *qa-bi*$_4$*-ti*$_7$ (EA 94:10); *qí-bi*$_4$*-ti* (EA 137:72); *ša-pár-ti* (EA 126:34; 256:31).

The *-ti* suffix is favored with D stem verbs:

> *bu-i-ti*$_7$ (EA 264:6, 20); *ur-ra-ad-ti* (EA 296:27); *uš-ši-ir-ti* (EA 70:12; *et al.*); *uš-ši-ir-ti-šu* (EA 82:17; 114:34, 35) *uš-ši-ir-ti*$_7$*-šu* (EA 180:4; 208:9); *uš-še-er-ti* (EA 151:26); *uš-še-er-ti*$_7$ (EA 265:4); *uš-‹ši›-ir-ti* (EA 105:14; Ebeling 1910:63); *mu-še-er-ti* (EA 287:53; Ebeling 1910:63; Böhl 1909:47);

and also with the Š stem:

> *šu!-ḫi-iz-ti* (EA 153:9); *šu-ri-ib-ti* (EA 116:24); *šu-ši-ir-ti* (EA 324:12; 325:15, 19); *šu-ši-ir-ti*$_7$ (EA 337:19); *šu-še-er-ti* (EA 213:13).

SECOND MASCULINE SINGULAR. There are no attested forms for 2nd f.s. The 2nd m.s. examples all have *-āta* except for *na-ṣir-ta* (EA 112:9) and D stem *uš-ši-ir-ta* (EA 194:22). The G stem examples are:

> *aš-ba-ta* (EA 91:3; 116:65); *er-ba-ta* (EA 102:37); *lam-da-ta* (EA 102:9); *lum-da-ta* (EA 98:26); *mi-[t]a-t[a]* (EA 87:30); *na-ṣa-ra-ta* (EA 99:8; 117:84); *qa-la-ta* (EA 71:11; *et al.*); *ša-ak-na-ta* (EA 211:22); *ša-ak-na-ta-ni* (EA 149:47); *ša-ap-ra-ta* (EA 201:11; *et al.*); *ša-ap-ra-‹ta›* (EA 206:10); *šap-ra-ta* (EA 252:5);

while there are also N stem *in*$_4$*-né-ep-ša-ta* and Š *šu-šu-ra-tá* (EA 367:15; from Egypt, Cochavi-Rainey 1988:166, §2.4.5.1).

THIRD MASCULINE SINGULAR. Because classical Arabic shows an *-a* vowel on 3rd m.s. forms of the *qtl* conjugation pattern, viz. *qatala, qattala, 'aqtala*, etc., which also shows up in Hebrew before suffix pronouns, e.g *š*^{ə}*māranî* (Gen. 25:20), it is interesting that a few *qtl* forms in the EA texts also had such a final vowel (Ebeling 1910:57). Furthermore, there is evidence that the vowel existed in Ugaritic; note forms such as: *yṣa, šna, mla* (Gordon 1965:69, §9.6; cf. Sivan 1984:136-138). There is also the Ugaritic term in syllabic texts which appears once as *ṣa-ma-t[a]* "It is transferred" (RS 15.86:16; Nougayrol 1955:52; Boyd 1975:205-206). The morpheme is known on WS PN's from the Ur III period as well (Buccellati 1966:219-220). Gelb (1965:79) suggested that this *-a* suffix was originally a marker of predication. The relevant forms from the Canaanite EA corpus are as follows:

> *dam-qá* (EA 326:18); SIG$_5$-*qá* (EA 258:9; 262:10; 315:15); *da-an-qa* (EA 84:27); *da-a-kà* (EA 154:19); *di-ka* (EA 132:42); *di*$_{12}$-*ka* (EA 288:41, 45); *ḫa-⌜ba⌝-ta* (EA 113:14); *la-qa-a* (EA 125:23; 134:34); *ša-pa-ra* (EA 65:7); *ša-ap-ra* (EA 283:7); *ša-ar-ra* (EA 151:53); *ta-ra* (EA 85:54: 124:53); also *i-ba-aš-ša* (EA 141:28); *i*$_{15}$-*ba-aš-ša* (EA 142:15, 19, 29).

These few examples from among dozens of 3rd m.s. verb forms can only be taken as possible hints to the existence of the short *-a* vowel on the native Canaanite of that day. Most 3rd m.s. forms have -Ø suffix.

THIRD FEMININE SINGULAR. A Jerusalem gloss, *a-ba-da-at* "it is lost" (EA 288:52) suggests that with the addition of the 3rd f.s. suffix *-at,* the thematic vowel did not elide. In the same epistles, a hybrid Akkadian form, *pa-ṭa-ra-at* "it has defected" (EA 286:35; 289:44; 290:12, 17, 23), also preserved the thematic vowel contrary to the standard Akkadian form, *pa-aṭ-ra-at* (EA 272:14). Another hybrid Canaanite form, *ia-ṣa-at* "(it) went forth" (EA 227:11), is equivocal; it ought to represent **yaṣa'at* (cf. Ug. *yṣat* Gordon 1965:70, §9.8). Another example with the thematic vowel preserved is *n*[*a*]-*ki-ra-at* "(It) became hostile" (EA 335:16). The spelling NA.KAR$_5$-*ra-at* (EA 137:67) is evidently logographic (Moran 1987b:361 n. 13; 1992:220-221 n. 13). One other enigmatic form is *iz-zi-la-at* (EA 140:17), often taken as an Akkadian form with assimilated infixed *-t-*. It might be a WS verb from the root **ʾzl* "to go out, to be depleted," in which case it might be D stem. The hybrid *i-pu-ša-at* "(It) has become" (EA 273:10) may in fact be built on the Akkadian present theme, *ippuš,* like the 1st c.s. *ip-pu-uš-ti* (EA 280:12).

Here and there, the final syllable sign may have been lost or inadvertently skipped, e.g *mar-ṣa-‹at›* (EA 103:49; Rainey 1973c:256; Moran 1987b:298 n. 3; 1992:176 n. 3) and *ṣa-ab-ta-‹at›*

(EA 179:24). In a broken context, we find *a-ṣí-it* (EA 250:35), the significance of which is enigmatic.

Apart from the above mentioned instances, the usual formation of the 3rd f.s. is by the addition of the suffix *-at* to the appropriate Akkadian form after elision of the thematic vowel. In other words, the forms are normal Akkadian. A selection of examples are:

> *ga-am-ra-at* (EA 273:11; *et al.*); *ḫal-qa-at* (EA 288:24; *et al.*); *kà-aš-dá-at* (EA 149:64); *na-ad-na-at* (EA 138:98); *na-aṣ-ra-at* (EA 255:25; *et al.*); *pal-ḫa-at* (EA 147:32; *et al.*); *pa-aš-ḫa-at* (EA 127:41; *et al.*); *ṣa-ab-ta-at* (EA 252:9, 12, 22); *šal-ma-at* (EA 280:13; *et passim*).

From *danānu* one finds *dan-na-at* (EA 137:102); *da-an-na-at* (EA 145:14; 243:19); *da-na-at* (EA 63:13; *et passim*). Hollow roots provide *da-kà-at-šu-nu* (EA 149:65) and *ta-ra-at* (EA 137:51). Verbs Ist Waw: *aš-ba-at* (EA 69:9); *a-ṣa-at* (EA 92:22; *et al.*); and Ist Aleph: *a-ba-da-at* (EA 288:52; Canaanite gloss cited *supra*); *ep-ša-at* (EA 104:5').

FIRST COMMON PLURAL. Only one example is attested of the 1st c.pl. in the *qtl* conjugation pattern and that one has a peculiar spelling, evidently influenced by an equally unusual spelling for the independent 1st c.pl. pronoun:

> *ù a-nu-ma* / *ti*$_7$*-ba-ú-na ṣa-bat* URU.MEŠ *Gub-li* / *ù ti*$_7$*-iq-bu-ni ṣa-bat-mi* / *ni-nu-u*$_{16}$ URU.MEŠ *Gub*^{ub}*-li* / *ù da-na-nu-u*$_{16}$ *a-mur-mi* / ⸢*ṣa*⸣*-bat-mi šu-nu* URU.‹MEŠ›.KI *Gub-li* / *ù da-an-nu*
> "And now they seek to capture the towns of Byblos and they said to me, 'If we seize the towns of Byblos, then we will be strong'; behold, they have seized the town‹s› of Byblos and they are strong" (EA 362:23-29).

The context is cited in full to demonstrate that there can be no doubt about the 1st c.pl. form. The parallel spellings of the 1st c.pl. independent pronoun, *ni-nu-u*$_{16}$, and the 1st c.pl. *qtl*, *da-na-nu-u*$_{16}$, prove the intention of the scribe. That it uses the UM sign in both vocables is without any logical explanation. Therefore, we have transcribed the *um* signs in the two contexts as u_{16} to make the verbal meaning clear.

SECOND MASCULINE PLURAL. The 2nd m.pl. is documented only twice (in the same Byblos text): *pa-aš-ḫa-tu-nu* (EA 74:27) and on the hybrid *i-ba-ša-tu-nu* (EA 74:26). The suffixes are standard Akkadian. Nothing can be learned about the contemporary Canaanite suffixes.

THIRD MASCULINE PLURAL. Three clear Canaanite forms show that in the G stem the thematic vowel did not elide with the addition of the 3rd m.pl. suffix, *-ū*. The first of these contexts, with **ḫasilū*, is:

> *la-qí-i* / *gáb-bi iš-tu* É-*ti* ÌR-*ka* / *la-qí-i* KÙ.BABBAR.MEŠ *la-qí-i* / LÚ.MEŠ *la-qí-i* UDU.UDU.MEŠ \ *ṣú-ú-nu* / \ *ḫa-sí-lu* URU.MEŠ-*nu be-li-ia* "Everything has been taken from the house of your servant; the silver has been taken; the personnel have been taken; the flock has been taken; the towns of my lord have been demolished" (EA 263:9-13; Held 1965:398-401; Moran 1987b:489 n. 3; 1992:313 n. 3).

A Jerusalem letter has two more WS forms, one an active and the other a passive from the very same root (**lqḥ*). Both of these examples also reveal the preservation of the thematic vowel:

> [*la*]-*qa-ḫu ú-nu-ta*$_5$-*šu-nu* "They took their tools/weapons" (EA 287:36); *mu-še-er-ti a-na šàr-ri* ⸢EN⸣[-*ia*] / [x]⸢LÚ⸣.MEŠ *a-ší-ru* 5 *li-im* [y] / [*ù*] ⸢8⸣ LÚ.MEŠ *ú-bi-li-mi* KASKAL.ḪÁ LUGA[L] / *la-qí-*⸢*ḫu*⸣ *i-na* ⸢*ú*⸣-⸢*ga*⸣-⸢*ri*⸣ \ *ša-de*$_4$-*e* [*a-na*] / ^{URU}*Ia-lu-na*^{KI} "I sent to the king, [my] lord, *x* foot troops, five thousand [. . . and] eight porters of the caravans of the king; they were taken in the open territory of Ayalon" (EA 287:53-57; cf. Moran 1987b:514 nn. 17-18; 1992:330 nn. 17-18).

In the same letter, we are justified in viewing another form as reflecting the WS form of a 3rd m.pl. *qtl* with the thematic vowel preserved:

> *li-de*$_4$ *[šàr]-ri* / *gáb-bi* KUR.ḪÁ ⸢*ša*⸣*-li-mu a-na ia-a-ši nu-kúr-tú* "May my [ki]ng be apprised: all the lands are at peace; against me there is hostility" (EA 287:11-12).

So these constructions evidently bear witness to three genuine WS verbal forms: **ḥasilū, laqaḥū, laqiḥū,* and *šalimū.*

A fifth example of this particular type seems to be used in an oath:

> *ù i-de-mi* / LUGAL *be-li i-nu-ma* DINGIR.MEŠ URU*Gub-la* / *qa-di-šu ù mur-ṣú-ú ma-gal* / *ù ḫi-i*$_{15}$*-ṭí ep-‹ša›-ti a-na* DINGIR.MEŠ / *ki-na-an-na la-a i-re-bu* / *a-na ma-ḫar* LUGAL *be-li-iu* "So may the king know, as the gods of Byblos are holy, that the illness is serious and I have com‹mit›ted my sin against the gods, thus I cannot enter into the presence of the king, my lord" (EA 137:30-35; Moran 1987b:357-358, 359-360 nn. 3-4; 1992:218, 219 nn. 3-4).

The 3rd m.pl. *qa-di-šu* in this syntagma may be compared with *balṭū* in the following oath:

> *i-nu-ma ba-al-ṭu* / LÚ.MEŠ MAŠKÍM.MEŠ *ù* / *a-da-bu-ba ka-li ip-ši-[š]u-nu* "As the commissioners live, I will continue to report their deeds" (EA 119:21-23; cf. *CAD* B:57a, D:7a; Moran 1960:15).

A Ugaritic term used in syllabic cuneiform texts dealing with transfers of real property (cf. above concerning the 3rd m.s.) happens to appear once in the 3rd m.pl., viz.

> *an-nu-tù a-na pa-ni* LUGAL / ŠÀM.TIL.LA.BI.ŠÈ \ *ṣa-ma-tù* / *a-na* I*A-ri-ra-di* / [*ù*] *a-na* DUMU.MEŠ*-šu a-na da-ri-ti* "These have devolved for their full price to Ariradu [and] to his sons

forever" (RS 16.147:12-15; Nougayrol 1955:90; Huehnergard 1989:68 n. 142, 165).

The preservation of the thematic vowel in the 3rd m.pl. might reflect an original feature of Ugaritic (Sivan 1984:139).

Another Canaanite gloss shows the elision of the thematic vowel, but for a very good reason:

ù ir-ka-ab-mi / it-it [I]*Ya-aš-da-ta / ù a-di ka-ša-di-ia / ù da-ku-šu* \ *ma-aḫ-ṣú-ú* "So I mounted up with Yashdata but by the time I arrived, they had slain him" (EA 245:11-14).

There can be no doubt about the meaning of the gloss. It is certain that the final *-ú* sign represents the 3rd m.s. accusative pronominal suffix (Borger 1967:239; Rainey 1969a:108). Therefore, the reconstructed form would be **maḫṣūhu* and the elision of the thematic vowel is probably due to the addition of the accusative suffix. Compare, however, *mì-iḫ-⸢ṣú⸣-mì*, passive from the same verb (EA 313:4; collation 31.1.80), albeit in a text that does not show definite features of a Canaanite scribal tradition.

There are a few examples of Akkadian verbs which, nevertheless, have not elided the thematic vowel, perhaps in some measure due to the morphology of the corresponding Canaanite word:

a-ṣa-ú (EA 105:17); *a-ša-bu* (EA 138:62; *contra* Moran 1987b:366 n. 15; 1992:224 n. 15); *sé-ki-pu* "(which) have been sailed" (EA 143:20; *CAD* S:73b).

The forms *i-zi-bu* (EA 73:13) and *iz-zi-bu-ni* (EA 366:18) are evidently based on the Akkadian present as theme. Thus, preservation of the thematic vowel is a function of the gemination of the second radical.

There are approximately 130 other G stem examples of 3rd m.pl. *qtl* forms attested in the EA texts from Canaan. All of them that are from strong roots show the expected elision of the thematic vowel.

THIRD FEMININE PLURAL? Ebeling listed a few *qtl* forms as 3rd f.pl. The presence of such forms would be a major exception to the general picture whereby feminine plural subjects usually have either a 3rd m.pl. or 3rd f.s. verb (Moran 1950a:61). Of course, standard Akkadian does have the *-ā* suffix for 3rd f.pl. and it is not impossible that a true Akkadian form of this nature was employed. This would seem to be the case in the following example:

> *ú-ul ⸢ki⸣-⸢na⸣ a-wa!*(NA)*-ti-šu-nu* "Their words are not true" (EA 89:14; Albright and Moran 1950:164; Moran 1950a:29; 1950c:170-171 n. 18).

With this text may be compared a passage from an epistle written in Egypt:

> *ù ú-ul ki-i-na / gáb-bi a-wa-te*MEŠ *ša tàš-pur* UGU-*ši-na* "And all the words concerning which you wrote are untrue" (EA 162:19-20; Cochavi-Rainey 1988:156).

Therefore, it is likely that the scribe was intentionally using an Akkadianism. Perhaps he had learned this paticular phrase in school.

Another passage with a verb listed by Ebeling as 3rd f.pl. is the following:

> *ša-ni-tam šum-ma / ap-pu-na-ma a-nu-ma pa-aṭ-ra /* URUṢ*[u-]mu-ra ù* URUÉ-*Ar-[ḫ]a* "Furthermore, if, moreover, now Ṣumur and Bīt-Arkha have defected" (EA 83:27-29).

However, Moran (1950a:60) adduced another example in which the subject is plural masculine while the verb has the *-a* suffix:

> *ù* LÚ.MEŠ / *[ḫ]a-za-nu-tu ú-u[l] tar-ṣa it-ti-ia* "And the city rulers are not just to me" (EA 109:60-61; cf. also Moran 1987b:308-309; 1992:183).

So the passage in EA 83:27-29, with two towns as the subject (i.e. two feminines in Canaanite), may be following the same rule as EA 109:60-61), viz. with a 3rd m.s. verb.

There are five instances of *a-ṣa* which have plural subjects. In one case the subjects are feminine:

> *ù* GIŠMÁ.MEŠ-*šu-nu* / *a-ṣa ki-ma ki-ti iš-tu* KUR*Mi-iṣ-ri* "And their ships duly went forth from Egypt" (EA 105:20-21; *CAD* K:472a).

Moran (1950a:61) agreed that the verb might be 3rd f.pl. However, in the same epistle we have:

> ⌈LÚ⌉.MEŠ KUR*Mi-iṣ-ri* / [*š*]*a a-ṣa iš-tu* URU*Ul-la-sà* [*a*]-*nu-ma it-ti-ia šu-nu* "As for the Egyptians who came forth from Ullasa, [n]ow they are with me" (EA 105:83-84).

Here Moran (1950a:60) cites the passage as an example of the singular verb form with a masculine plural subject!

Three more instances of *a-ṣa* occur in another Byblos letter. On the surface, it appears that in all three cases, the subject is two Egyptians whom Rib-Haddi had sent to Egypt but who had not returned.

> *ù* 2 LÚ / KUR*Mi-iṣ-ri ša-a ša-ap-ra-ti* / *a-na* É.GAL *ú-ul a-ṣa* "But the two Egyptians whom I sent to the palace have not come forth" (EA 117:12-14); *a-nu-ma* 2 LÚ *an-nu-tu* / *tu-ba-lu-na ṭup-pí a-na šàr-ri* / *ù an-na ú-ul a-ṣa* "Now these two men were bringing a tablet to the king but, behold, they have not come forth" (EA 117:17-19); *ša-ni-tam ú-ul aš-ta-pár a-na šàr-ri* / *a-nu-ma* 2 LÚ KUR*Mi-iṣ-ri šu-nu* / *tu-ṣa-na ša-ri a-na ia-ši* / *ù la-a a-ṣa* "Furthermore, did I not write to the king, 'Now these two are Egyptians, the breath of the king will come forth to me?' But they did not come forth" (EA 117:53-56).

With regard to these passages, Moran (1950a:62) said that the verbs might be dual or singular but that the evidence was not decisive. It so happens that the normal singular of the *qtl* conjugation was *a-ṣí* (EA 85:51; 109:63; 116:61; 137:21). The three passages in EA 117 cited above all pertain to "coming forth" from Egypt. Therefore, it is quite logical to suggest that all three verb forms are, in fact, 3rd m.s. *aṣi* + ventive *-a*. In the last passage, the writer added the ventive to *tūṣi*, thus producing *tūṣâ*; but to avoid the impression of a volitive, he added the energic *-na* (cf. discussion *supra*, pp. 209-211). That the *qtl* forms of (*w*)*aṣû* should also have the ventive makes excellent sense.

A final passage is one where Albright and Moran (1950:166) posited a 1st c.pl. verb with *na-* prefix (cf. *supra*, p. 46, *infra*, p. 405). Actually the verb form could have 3rd f.pl. stative *nadnā* though the subject would have properly been *pānūnu* rather than accusative *pānīnu*:

> *ù na-[a]d-na pa-ni-nu a-na / a-ra-di-ka* "Our faces are set to serve you" or: "We have set our faces to serve you" (EA 89:16-17; Albright and Moran 1950:166).

From the discussion above, it does not seem probable that there are any genuine 3rd f.pl. verb forms in the *qtl* conjugation pattern with the ancient Semitic *-ā* suffix except with the expression, *ul kīnā* (EA 89:14). This particular form is an Akkadianism appearing in what was probably a learned phrase. Therefore, it seems likely that Canaanite preferred either the 3rd m.pl. or the 3rd f.s. with plural feminine subjects.

THEMATIC FORMS

The choice of thematic structures in the *qtl* conjugation pattern as employed in the Canaanite EA letters has been of considerable interest. Note that by thematic form we mean a vocalic pattern which carries meaning; this is in contrast to what we have termed the theme, which is an Akkadian thematic form used primarily for its lexical significance only. In the *qtl*, as against the prefix conjugation pattern, the scribes usually employ a vocalic pattern which carries semantic as well as lexical meaning, even when they are using an Akkadian verb. As is well known, the basic patterns in the Semitic languages for the G stem of this conjugation are *qatal, qatil* and *qatul*. Even in the late 19th century, Assyriologists had become aware that Akkadian favored the *qatil* above the others. The contrast with the WS languages was clearly discerned. WS normally used *qatal* for transitives and verbs of motion, *qatil* and *qatul* for statives and sometimes for the passive. In Akkadian, on the other hand, the suffix conjugation pattern was almost completely devoted to expressing the stative and passive; thus the strong preference in the G stem for *qatil* or occasionally *qatul*, although *qatal*'s with stative meaning are also known (e.g. *rapaš* "wide"). Nevertheless, a transitive function for certain verbs in the suffix conjugation did develop (even in *qatil*). There is considerable evidence for this phenomenon in "classic Babylonian" (Rowton 1962). But examples can also be cited from the MB letters in the EA archive:

> DUMU.MÍ LUGAL GAL *i-na* 5 ^{GIŠ}⸢GIGIR⸣ [*a-n*]*a* KUR⸢*Mi*⸣-⸢*iṣ*⸣-⸢*ri*⸣-⸢*i*⸣ ⸢*na*⸣-⸢*šu*⸣-⸢*ú*⸣-⸢*ši*⸣ "As for the daughter of the great king, they brought her in five chariots to Egypt" (EA 11:22); 40 ⸢*ma*⸣-*na* GUŠKIN *ša na-šu-ni* "the forty minas which they brought to me" (EA 7:71); 20 *ma-na* GUŠKIN *ša na-ša-a ul ma-li* "The twenty minas of gold which he brought were not complete" (EA 10:19; *CAD* M/1:179b); *a-ma-ta ba-ni-ta ša ul-tu pa-na i-na qá-at šar-ra-ni / ma-aḫ-ra-nu-ma* "the state of friendly relations which we have taken over from earlier kings" (EA 7:37-38; Oppenheim 1967:114; *CAD* B:82b); *du-ul-la ṣa-ab-ta-ku-ma* "I am engaged in a project" (EA 7:63; *loc. cit.*).

Because the EA letters from Canaan represent such a unique symbiosis of Akkadian and WS, it should be no surprise that use of the three forms, *qatal, qatil* and perhaps *qatul*, reflects mainly the WS system, but with some interference from the Akkadian usages.

qatal. The normal WS use of *qatal* as transitive is illustrated by the Canaanite forms *ia-pa-aq-ti* (EA 64:23) and [*la*]-*qa-ḫu* (EA 287:36). There are, nevertheless, a few attestations of intransitive meaning for *qatal* forms. For instance, there is an ubiquitous verb, *qâlu* "to keep silent" (*CAD* Q:72b-73a):

> *šum-ma qa-al* LUGAL *a-na* URU.KI / *gáb-bi* DIDLI.URU.KI ^{KUR}*Ki-na-aḫ-ni ia-nu a-*⸢*na*⸣ *ša-šu* "If the king keeps silent concerning the city, none of the towns of Canaan will be his" (EA 137:75-76).

The ensuing passage includes a *qatal* stative, *na-ka-ar*, and a *qatal* transitive, *na-da-an*. The *i-ru-ub* form is probably also to be considered as *qtl* (Izre'el 1978b:53); it will be treated under special constructions (cf. *infra*, pp. 341-342).

> *li-il-ma-ad* LUGAL / EN-*ia i-nu-ma* / ^{LÚ}ŠEŠ-*ia* TUR.[TU]R / *na-ka-ar iš-tu* / *ia-ši u i-ru-ub* / *a-na* ^{URU}*Mu-*⸢*ú'*⸣*-ḫa-zi* / *u na-da-an* 2 *qa-‹te›-šu* / *a-na* ^{LÚ}[S]A.GAZ.KI "May the king, my lord, be apprised that my younger brother has become hostile to me and he has entered into Môḫazu and he has proffered his two ha‹nd›s to the '*apîru*" (EA 298:20-27).

This use of *nakar* should be compared with *nakirat* in the following:

> *li-il*$_5$[*-m*]*a-ad* / ^{I}*šàr-ri* EN-*ia ki-ma* / *n*[*a*]*-ki-ra-at* ^{URU}*La-ki-ši* / *ù ṣa-a*[*b-t*]*a-at* ^{URU}*Mu-ú'-ra-aš-ti* "May my king, my lord, be apprised that Lachish has become hostile and Môʾrashti has been taken" (EA 335:14-17).

Concerning the passive *ṣabtat*, cf. below.

The verb of motion, *kašādu* "to reach, arrive at, come," normally appears in *qatil* (*CAD* K:271b) but takes the *qatal* form in a Jerusalem letter:

> [. . .] / [*k*]*a-ša-ad a-na mu-ḫi-ia* [. . .] / *na-ad-na-ti* 10 ^{LÚ}ÌR.MEŠ [*a-na qa-*]⸢*ti*⸣[*-šu*] / ^{I}*Šu-ú-ta* ^{LÚ}MAŠKÍM *šàr-ri ka-š*[*a-ad*] / [*a*]*-na mu-ḫi-ia* 21 ^{MÍ}DUMU.MÍ.MEŠ / [8]0 LÚ.MEŠ *a-ší-ri na-ad-na-ti* / [*a-*]*na qa-ti* ^{I}*Šu-ú-ta* NÍG.BA LUGAL EN-*ia* "[PN c]ame to me

> [. . .]; I handed over ten slaves [to his char[ge]; Shuta, the commissioner of the king, ca[me t]o me; twenty-one servant girls, [eig]hty troopers (or: prisoners), I handed over [t]o the charge of Shuta, a gift to the king, my lord" (EA 288:16-22; Albright, Mendenhall and Moran 1955:488b; Rainey 1967a; Moran 1987b:515. 516 n. 4; 1992:331, 332 n. 4).

Another verb of motion, *paṭāru* "to depart, defect," also takes *qatal* as its suffix conjugation form although its standard form in Akkadian is *paṭer* (*AHw*:849-851 *passim*).

> *ki-na-an-na li-ib-lu-uṭ šàr-ri / lu-ú ir-pí-šu* [I]*Pu-ú-ru / pa-ṭa-ar i-na ma-aḫ-ri-ia / i-na* [URU]*Ḫa-za-ti i-ba-aš-ši* "Thus, as my king lives, his nobleman, Puwuru, has verily departed; he is in Gaza" (EA 289:37-40); *i-ka-lu ka-ar-ṣi-ia \ ú-ša-a-ru / i-na pa-ni* LUGAL EN-*ri* (!) [I]ÌR-*ḫé-ba / pa-ṭa-ar-mi a-na šàr-ri* EN-*šu* "They are slandering me (I am being slandered) in the presence of the king, my(!) lord, 'ᶜAbdi-Kheba has defected from the king, his lord" (EA 286:6-8).

For the transitive function of *qatal*, a WS 3rd m.pl. in a Jerusalem letter confirms the usage in contemporary Canaanite:

> [*la*]-*qa-ḫu ú-nu-ta*$_5$-*šu-nu* "They took their tools/weapons" (EA 287:36; cf. *supra*, p. 290).

A widely used verb with transitive meaning in the suffix conjugation *ṣabātu* "to seize" appears in one of the Shechem letters four times, twice in a transitive and twice in a passive meaning:

> *ú*!-*ṣur*!-*mì* / LÚ.MEŠ *ša ṣa-ab-tu* URU "Keep watch on the men who seized the town!" (EA 252:6-7; Rainey cited by Moran 1987b:479 n. 1; 1992:306 n. 1); *ṣa-ab-ta-at-mì* URU "the town was taken" (EA 252:12); *ù / ṣa-ab-ta-at-mì* 2 URU-*ia* "And my two towns are seized" (EA 252:21-22); LÚ.MEŠ *ša ṣa-ab-tu*$_4$ URU ‹*ù*› / *i-li* "the men who seized my town ‹and› my god" (EA 252:29-30).

These forms, 3rd m.pl. and 3rd f.s., do not reveal the thematic form, which in Akkadian should be *ṣabit* (*CAD* Ṣ:5b).

The following passage provides the 3rd m.s. with the WS thematic vowel *-a-* characteristic of transitive verbs:

> *lu-ú i-de* LUGAL EN-*ia* / *i-nu-ma nu-* KÚR [I]*A-zi-ru* ⌜*it*⌝!-‹*ti*›-*ia* / *ù ṣa-bat* 12 LÚ.MEŠ-*ia ù ša-ka-an* / *ip-tì-ra be-ri-nu* 50 KÙ.BABBAR.MEŠ *ù* / LÚ.MEŠ *ša-a* [*u*]*š-ši-ir-ti a-na* / [URU]*Ṣu-mu-ra ṣa-›ab‹-bat i-na* / ⌜URU⌝*Ya-aḫ-li-ia* "May the king, my lord, be apprised that Aziru is hostile to me and he has seized twelve of my men and fixed a ransom between us, fifty silver (shekels), and the men whom I sent to Ṣumur he seized in Yaᶜlia" (EA 114:6-12; contrast Moran 1987b:316, 317 n. 2; 1992:188. 189 n. 2).

Further on, the writer used the transitive *sa-bat* once again (EA 114:17). Note also the transitive use of *ša-ka-an* "he placed, fixed." This verb appears frequently in the Canaanite letters in the *qatal* (EA 98:13; 138:60; 174:15; 175:12; 176:12; 286:26; 287:60; 288:5; 289:32; 292:34; 326:16), thus signaling one of the foremost departures from standard Akkadian usage. The suffix conjugation theme for this verb in Akkadian is the well known *šakin* (*AHw*:1135); for a possible transitive *šakin* in this corpus, cf. *infra*, p. 370; for passives cf. *infra*, pp. 303-306.

Another important *qatal* transitive is *šapāru* "to send." Theinstances of *šapar* cannot be taken as examples of the infinitive because the subject either precedes the verb or else is in the nominative after it. Note the following:

> LUGAL EN-*li ša-pár a-na mu-ḫi-*[*i*]*a* [I]*Ḫa-a-ia* "The king, my lord, has sent Ḫaʾya to [m]e" (EA 255:8); [I]*Ḫa-an-ia ša-pár* / *šàr-ru* EN-*ia* [d]UTU / *iš-tu* AN[*ša-me*] *a-na ia-ši* "The king, my lord, the sun god from heaven, sent to me Ḫanya" (EA 301:12-14).

An additional verb which has passive *qatil* in Akkadian but transitive *qatal* in the EA texts from Canaan is *ḫabātu* "to rob, plunder" (*CAD* Ḫ:10; *AHw*:303b).

LÚ.MEŠ *ḫa-pí-ru ḫa-bat gáb-bi* KUR.ḪÁ LUGAL "The *'apîrû* men have stolen/plundered all the king's lands" (EA 286:56).

Likewise, the transitive *dâku* "to kill" has passive *qatil* in the suffix conjugation while the transitive *qatal* is frequent in our corpus, e.g.

a-mur [I]*A-zi-ru* [I]*A-du-na šàr* [KUR]*Ir-qà-ta* / *da-ak šàr* [KUR]*Am-mi-ia* / *ù šàr* [KUR]*Ar-da-ta* / *ù* [LÚ]GAL *da-ak ù la-qa* / URU.MEŠ-*šu-nu* "Look, Aziru has killed Adôna, king of ᶜIrqat; he killed the king of Ammiya and the king of Ardat and he has killed the official, and he has taken their towns" (EA 140:10-14).

The suffix theme for *epēšu* "to do, make" is the passive *epiš*, but in the Canaanite EA texts, special transitive forms in *qatal* were developed. The best known is the active hybrid form *a-pa-aš* as illustrated in the following:

a-mur ar-na ša / *a-*⸢*pa*⸣!*-aš* [I]*A-zi-ru i-na šàr-ri* "Behold the crime which Aziru has committed against the king" (EA 139:12-13; contrast Moran 1950a:178; 1987b:368 and n. 3; 1992:225, 226 n. 4).

One text from the Beqaᶜ Valley adopts *i-pa-aš* as the transitive form:

la-a i-pa-aš ep-‹ša› an-na LÚ *iš-tu* / *da-ri-ti*$_7$ "A man has never committed this deed" (EA 196:32-33); *ù la-a* / [*ia*]*-qù-ul* LUGAL EN-*ia* / [*iš*]*-tu ep-ši an-ni ša* / [*i*]*-pa-aš* [I]*Bi-ri-da-aš-wa* "And may the king, my lord, not keep silent concerning this deed which Biridashwa has committed!" (EA 196:38-41; Rainey 1973c:239).

A Byblos epistle employs both the active *apaš* and the passive *apiš*:

ù [I]*Pa-ḫu-ra* / *a-pa-aš ep-ša ra-ba* / *a-na ia-ši* "And Paḫura has committed a great (mis)deed against me" (EA 122:31-33); *ù al-le-e* / *ta-aq-bu* URU *ep-šu* / *ša la a-pí-iš iš-tu* / *da-ri-ti a-pí-iš* /

> *a-na ia-ši-nu* "And behold the city is saying 'A deed that has never been done before has been done to us'" (EA 122:40-44; Rainey 1973c:238-239).

The ubiquitous verb of speaking, *qabû*, appears frequently in the Canaanite letters in the *qtl*. The active (transitive) is written *qa-ba*:

> *mi-nu qa-ba mi-im-ma / a-na ša-a-šu* "Who said anything to him?" (EA 134:35-36; cf. also EA 63:7; 263:26; 294:13; 297:8; 315:10, 14; 323:13; 325:18; 331:16).

Examples will be given below of the passive, which is written *qa-bi*.

qatil. The most prevalent, and probably the most original, thematic form for the suffix conjugation is *qatil*. Naturally, some *qatil*'s expressing a stative are found in these texts. Even the gloss *ba-ṭì-ti* ‹ **baṭiḫtî* "I am secure, at rest" (EA 147:56) confirms the stative function of *qatil* for the Canaanite of that period. Some typical examples are:

> *da-mi-iq it-ti-ka / a-na ia-ši* "It is good for me (to be) with you" (EA 74:62-63); *ia-nu mi-im-mu a-na ia-ši / ga-mi-ir gáb-bu i-na na-da-ni / i-na ba-la-aṭ* ZI-*ia* "I have no property, it is all used up in payment for my sustenance" (EA 117:74-76); *ù ḫa-di lìb* ÌR-*ka* "and the heart of your servant rejoiced" (EA 141:11); *ḫal-qá-at* URU-[*š*]*u ḫa-li-iq* É-*šu* "his city is destroyed, his house is perished" (EA 147:46).

Verbs of motion also appear in *qatil*. In contrast to Hebrew *hālaḵ*, the Canaanite scribes used *alik* (note that they also preferred *illak* as the theme for the prefix conjugation, *supra*, p. 51).

> *a-ya-mi* LÚ-*lu / ša a-lik iš-tu* KUR.MEŠ *Mi-iṣ-ri a-na maḫ-‹ri›-šu* "Where is the man who has come to him from Egypt?" (EA 138:91-92; *CAD* A/1:220b).

Note the following passage from Tyre where *alāku* apparently has the well attested Akkadian idiomatic connotation, "to render service" (cf. *CAD* A/1:309a-310b):

> *a-mur* LÚ ^{URU}P[Ú]*-ru-ti i-na* / [1] ^{GIŠ}MÁ *a-li-ik ù* LÚ ^{URU}*Ṣí-du-*[*n*]*a i-na* 2 ^{GIŠ}M[Á] / [*i*]*-la-ak ù a-na-ku i-la-ak qa-du gáb-bi* ^{GIŠ}MÁ-⸢*ka*⸣ "Behold, the ruler of Beirut served in one ship and the ruler of Sidon serves in two ships while I will serve with all your ships" (EA 155:67-69; Moran 1987b:391; 1992:242).

Another verb of motion popular in the EA texts is *kašādu* "to reach, arrive, come," and it can appear in either *qatal*: as in the Jerusalem letter EA 288:16-22 (*supra*, pp. 297-298) or *qatil* (the standard Akkadian usage; *CAD* K: 271b):

> *ù la-a ka-ši-id* / *i-re-šu ù uš-ši-ir-ti-šu* "As soon as the request arrives, I will send it" (EA 82:16-17; Moran 1950a:53; 1987b:263; 1992:152).

Since even in standard Akkadian, *qatil* can express a transitive action, it is not surprising that some examples appear in the EA texts from Canaan. The WS forms, ⸢*ba*⸣-⸢*ni*⸣-⸢*ti*⸣ "I have built" (EA 292:29) ‹**banîtî* and *ša-mi-ti*$_7$ "I have heard" ‹**šami'tî* (EA 362:5), reveal the transitive use of *qatil*. However, each of these verbs is vocalized in accordance with phonetic and thematic considerations prevailing in certain of the NWS languages, viz. the Barth-Ginsberg law (cf. *supra*, pp. 61-75). Verbs with a guttural as second or third radical take *yiqtal* in the G prefix conjugation pattern and either *qatil* or *qatul* in the suffix conjugation pattern (Barth 1894:1-2).

It was noted that the Canaanite EA texts prefer *šakan* as the transitive of *šakānu* (cf. *supra*, p. 299). However, there is also an apparent transitive of *šakin* in the following passage:

> *ù i-še*$_{20}$*-me e-nu!-ú ia-nu-um* ⸢ERÍN⸣.MEŠ / *it-ti-šu ù te!-né-pu-*[*u*]*š* / ^{URU}*Bat-ru-na a-na ša-šu* / *ù* ERÍN.MEŠ SA.GAZ.MEŠ *ù* ^{GIŠ}GIGIR.MEŠ / *ša-ki-in*$_4$ *i-na lìb-bi-*‹*ši*› / *ù la!*

> *i-nam-mu-šu-ni₇* / [*i*]*š-tu pí* KÁ.GAL ^{uru}*Gub*‹*-la*›^{KI} "And he (ᶜAbdi-Ashirta) heard that there were no troops with him; then Baṭruna went over to him and he placed ᵓ*apîrû* troops and chariotry in ‹its› midst and they do not depart from the entrance of the city gate of Byblos" (EA 87:18-24; Rainey 1975b:424-425; Youngblood 1961:300; Moran 1950a:159; 1987b:273 nn. 1-3; 1992:159-160 nn. 1-3).

Admittedly, one might take ERÍN.MEŠ SA.GAZ.MEŠ *ù* ^{GIŠ}GIGIR.MEŠ as the collective subject of *šakin*, but it is more likely that the verb would then be 3rd f.s. (Moran 1950a:61). The larger context has been cited here to make it clear why it is more fitting to take *šakin* as a transitive.

In spite of the evidence for Canaanite **laqaḫū* (cf. *supra*, p. 298), one still finds examples of transitive *qatil* from *leqû*:

> ^{I}*Sú-ra-ta* / *la-qí-mi* KÙ.BABBAR.ḪÁ *ip-ṭì-ri-šu* / *i-na* ŠU-*ti-šu* \ *ba-di-ú* "Surata took his ransom money from his hand" (EA 245:33-35); *la-a la-qí-šu-nu* "he did not capture them" (EA 129:83).

There is also the following difficult passage where (*w*)*abālu* "to bring" (*CAD* A/1:20b) is perhaps more likely than *apālu* "to pay":

> *ia-nu mi-i*[*m-ma*] *a-na* / *ša-šu-nu ša-a* 2 *ša-a* 3 *a-bi-*⌜*il*⌝ / KÙ.BABBAR.MEŠ *ip-ṭì-ri* "They have no property, one brought two, another three (shekels of) silver as ransom money" (EA 116:42-44; cf. Moran 1987b:322 n. 7; 1992:192 n. 7).

The most significant feature of *qatil* in these texts from Canaan is its function as the passive (Moran 1950a:116-117 n. 70). Of course, *qatil* is the standard passive of transitive verbs in Akkadian. Nevertheless, there is no trace whatever of a Canaanite passive *qutil*(*a*) like the Arabic. Instead, there are Canaanite glosses and other forms which confirm *qatil* as the theme form for the passive.

qa-bi / *qa-ar-ṣí-ia* \ *ši-ir-ti* / *i-na pa-ni* ᴵLUGAL-*ma be-li-ia* "I have been slandered" (EA 252:13-15).

Note that this particular scribe mixed up the Akkadian idiom, which should have been like the Jerusalem version:

i-ka-lu ka-ar-ṣi-ya \ *ú-ša-a-ru* "They are eating a chunk of my flesh \ I am being slandered" (EA 286:6; Nitzán 1973:62, §4.36, 89, §6.2)

Here the Akkadian idiom (which goes back to OB, *CAD* K:222b-223a) is couched in the 3rd m.pl. present but is glossed by the indicative imperfect 1st c.s. of the same WS verb. The Shechem scribe is dealing with a past event and thus prefers the *qtl* for both the Akkadian and the Canaanite verb; *qa-bi* is to be reckoned as passive (in contrast to active *qa-ba*, cf. *supra*, p. 301). The Aramaic parallel cited by Held 1961:12b, viz. *krṣy ʾyš lʾ ʾmrt* "you did not slander anyone" (*KAI* 269:2) is 4th century B.C.E. and may be nothing more than a mix-up of the metaphor just like the Shechem passage under discussion here. In any case, the most important point is that *ši-ir-ti* is 1st c.s. passive on a Canaanite verb.

The Canaanite active form [*la*]-*qa-ḫu* (EA 287:36) has its passive counterpart in the same text (cf. *supra*, p. 290):

la-qí-⸢*ḫu*⸣ *i-na* ⸢*ú*⸣-⸢*ga*⸣-⸢*ri*⸣ \ *ša-de*$_4$*-e* [*a-na*] / ᵁᴿᵁ*Ia-lu-na*ᴷᴵ "They were taken in the open territory of Ayalon" (EA 287:56-57; cf. Moran 1987b:514 nn. 17-18).

Many examples could be cited of passive *qatil*'s corresponding to active *qatal*'s. A representative selection will suffice to illustrate the point. First, passive *a-pí-iš* for active *a-pa-aš*:

ù al-le-e / *taq-bu* URU *ep-šu* / *ša la a-pí-iš iš-tu* / *da-ri-ti a-pí-iš* / *a-na ia-ši-nu* "And behold, the city is saying, 'A deed which has never been done has been committed against us" (EA 122:40-44).

Passive *di-ka* for active *da-ak*:

> *ú-ul* / *ia-qú-ul* LUGAL *a-na i-[p]é-ši* / *an-nu-ú i-nu-ma di-ka* / LÚMAŠKÍM "May the king not keep silent concerning this deed, that the commissioner has been killed!" (EA 132:43-46).

Passive *la-qí-i* for active *la-qa, la-qa-a*:

> *i-[r]i-[i]b-ti a-na* É-*ti* / *be-[l]i-ia la-qí-i* / *gáb-bu iš-tu* É-*ti* ÌR-*ka* / *la-qí-i* KÙ.BABBAR *la-qí-i* / LÚ.MEŠ *la-qí-i* UDU.UDU.MEŠ \ *ṣú-ú-nu* / \ *ḫa-sí-lu* URU.MEŠ-*nu be-li-ia* / *ù mi-im-mu ša na-da-an* / *be-li-ia a-na* ÌR-*šu ù šu-ut* / *la-qí-i* "I have entered into the house of my lord; everything has been taken from the house of your servant; the silver has been taken; the personnel have been taken; the cattle have been taken; the cities of my lord have been demolished and the property which my lord gave to his servant has been taken" (EA 263:8-17; Held 1965:398; Moran 1987b:489 n. 3; 1992:313 n. 3).

The active *na-da-an* in the passage cited above is matched by passive *na-di-in*:

> *ù ti-mu-ru* ⸢LÚ⸣.⸢MEŠ⸣ [É]-*ia* / *i-nu-ma la-a na-di-in* KÙ.BABBAR *ti-iš-la-ḫu* / *a-na ia-ši ki-ma* LÚ.MEŠ *ḫa*MEŠ-*za-ni* ŠEŠ-*ia* "And the men of my house saw that the money that you used to send to me was not given like (to) the city rulers, my colleagues" (EA 137:11-13).

Finally, alongside the active *šakan*, one finds many passives from the same verb. Note, for example, the 3rd f.s. form in the following passage, which surely has been derived from the passive *šakin*:

> *ki-ma* MUŠEN.MEŠ *ša* / *i-na lìb-bi ḫu-ḫa-ri* \ *ki-lu-bi* / *ša-ak-na-at ki-šu-ma a-na-ku i-na* / URU*Gu[b-l]a* "Like birds placed in a cage, thus am I in By[bl]os" (EA 74:46-49 = EA 78:13-16; 79:35-38; 81:34-36; 90:39-42; 105:8-10; 116:18-20).

qitil / qetil. Two verbs reveal suffix forms with this pattern instead of *qatal*. Both have ṣ and a guttural (*ḫ* or *ǵ*) in the root, so they might be the cause of the special vocalization. One verb, *maḫāṣu*, uses this theme for the passive: 3rd m.s. *mi-iḫ-iš* (EA 220:24), *me-ḫi-iṣ* (EA 264:8, 12); 3rd m.pl. *mi-ḫi-ṣú* (EA 273:23), *me-eḫ-*˹*ṣú*˺*-mì* (EA 313:4); and *mi-ḫi-ṣa* (EA 335:8, dual?). The other verb, **raǵāṣu / raḫāṣu*, has one apparent form that could be 3rd m.s. active or passive (with plural subject), viz. 3rd m.s. *ri-ḫi-iṣ-mi* (EA 127:33; Rainey 1989-90:61b; cf, *supra*, pp. 173-174).

qatul. There is one example that appears most likely to be in the *qatul* pattern though other interpretations are possible. It is in a Jerusalem letter and the context is:

> *a-mur* LUGAL EN-*ia ša-du-uq a-na ia-a-ši* / *aš-šum* LÚ.MEŠ *Ka-ši-yi* "Behold, (o) king, my lord, I have a just case with regard to the Cushites" (EA 287:32-33; cf. Moran 1987b:513 n. 8).

The form *ṣa-du-uq* (*CAD* Ṣ:59b) is evidently predicative as signaled by the -Ø suffix. It appears to be the same element as *šaduq / ṣaduqa* in Amorite PN's, e.g *Aḫiṣaduq*, *'Ammiṣaduqa* (Huffmon 1965:257). As such a predicating element, it is unlikely that the thematic form might be that of the G absolute infinitive like Hebrew *ṣāḏôq* (Böhl 1909:25, §13g; Sivan 1984:144, §1.3.1). The syntagma, with an impersonal 3rd m.s. subject, is like *ma-ri-iš ma-gal a-na ia-ši* "It is most excruciating for me" (EA 114:50) and *da-mi-iq a-na ia-ši* "It is good for me" (EA 116:48). Incidentally, there is no way to justify taking *šarru bēliya* as the subject (*contra* Cazelles 1973:76, who does not understand that *amur* begins a new topic!).

Note that, in Babylonian, *marāṣu* normally takes the form *maruṣ* in the suffix conjugation, though *maraṣ* and *mariṣ* are also known in Assyrian (*CAD* M/1:269a). The EA texts know only *mariṣ*. For *i-ru-ub*, cf. *infra*, p. 342).

qittul = *pitrus*. The suffix conjugation hybrids with infix *-t-* for a few verbs will be discussed in the next chapter (*infra*, pp.

339-342). There is, however one obscure passage where a Gt stative may be intended:

> *ù a-na-ku a-tu-ur a-na* É-*ia* / *ù id-du-ul* É *iš-tu* / *pa-ni-ia* "And I returned to my house (palace) but the house was locked in my face" (EA 136:33-35)

Rather than assuming that the form *id-du-ul* is active with Rib-Haddi's brother as the subject (Moran 1987b:356 n. 6), it is more suitable to the context (the brother is not mentioned explicitly in the letter) to take the form in question as a passive (*CAD* E:26b). However, it is not necessary to posit an N stem as does *CAD*. For N one would expect *innedil*. *CAD* does list Gt as an attested stem for this verb, but it does not devote a special paragraph to that stem. *AHw* does not list any Gt for *edēlu*. What seems a most likely possibility is that the form is really the Gt suffix conjugation form, perhaps *iddul* ‹ **itdul*.

naqtal. Four glosses provide confirmation of the Canaanite N stem theme form for the suffix conjugation pattern. The vocalization is just what one would have expected on diachronic grounds, e.g. the *-a-* vowel of the stem prefix is not attenuated as it is in Hebrew *nip̄ᶜal*. Other special N stem hybrids will be dealt with in the next chapter (*infra*, pp. 333-337). One of the glosses has been assumed to be 3rd m.pl. In spite of considerable disagreement about the Akkadian verb being glossed, the general meaning is fairly clear:

> *ša-ni-tam ú-ul ti-i-de* / *at-ta* ^{KUR}*A-mur-ri ur-ra* / *mu-sa tu-ba-ú-na* / ERÍN.MEŠ *pí-ṭá-ti ú-ul ta-ša-aš* / \ *na-aq-ṣa-pu* "Furthermore, don't you know Amurru? Day (and) night they are asking for the army. Don't be angry!" (EA 82:47-51; Albright and Moran 1948:242, 244 n. 6; Youngblood 1961:235-236; *CAD* B:363a; Moran 1987b:264 n. 6; 1992:152 n. 6; *contra CAD* A/2:424b).

The form *ú-ul ta-ša-aš* must be 2nd m.s. negative jussive. Amurru was treated as 3rd m.pl. with the verb *tu-ba-ú-na*, and many scholars have assumed that it is subsequently treated as a collective (Albright and Moran 1948:242, 244 n. 6; Youngblood 1961:235-236; *CAD* B:363a; Moran 1987b:264 n. 6). They thus assumed that the gloss is 3rd m.pl., *qtl* as the translation of a 3rd f.s. preterite. The negation by *ú-ul* could then be a rhetorical question. However, it may be a negative jussive (used here instead of *lā*, as is sometimes the case). The gloss may then be an N infinitive added to confirm the meaning of the Akkadian verb.

The second gloss from the same N stem is 1st c.s., translating the same Akkadian verb:

> [*a-mur a*]*-ta-ša-aš a-na-ku* / [\ *na-*]*aq-ṣa-ap-ti* / [*i-n*]*a a-wa-te-ka* "[Behold] I was angered [a]t your words" (EA 93:4-6; Youngblood 1961:375; Moran 1987b:285 n. 1; *contra CAD* A/2:424b; cf. also *CAD* Q:14a).

Another 3rd m.pl. gloss translates an irregular Akkadian verb, which the scribe probably felt should be explained.

> *ù* ^{I}*Sú-ra-ta* LÚ ^{URU}*Ak-ka*^{KI} / *ù* ^{I}*In*$_4$*-tá!-*˹*ru*˺*?-ta* LÚ ^{uru}*Ak-ša-pa* / *šu-ni-ma in*$_4$*-né-ri-ru* \ *na-az-a-qú* / *i-na* 50 ^{GIŠ}GIGIR.ḪÁ / *a-na mu-ḫi-ia* "And Surata, the ruler of Acco, and Intaruta, the ruler of Achshaph, the two of them, hastened to help with fifty chariots to me" (EA 366:22-26; Finklestein 1969:33a; *CAD* N/1:7b; Moran 1973:51; 1987b:562 nn. 2-3; 1992:364 nn. 2-3; *contra* Albright 1975:114-115).

From the same letter comes another gloss which up to now has not been considered as an example of the N stem (cf. *supra*, pp. 130-131).

> *li-il-ma-ad šàr-ru* EN*-ia* / *i-nu-ma* LÚ SA.GAZ ˹*ša*˺ / *yi-na-aš-ši* \ *na-aš-ša-a* / *i-na* KUR.KI.ḪÁ *na-da-an* / DINGIR*-lu*$_4$ *ša šàr-ri* EN*-ia a-na ia-ši* / *ù i-du-uk-šu* "May the king, my lord, be apprised that as for the *ᶜapîru* who rose up (has risen up) in the territories, the god of the king, my lord, has delivered to me and I have smitten him!" (EA 366:11-16; Naʾaman 1975:120;

Rainey 1978b:32-33; Moran 1987b:561-562 and n. 1; 1992:363 and n. 1).

It is possible, of course, that the gemination of the *š* in both or either of these forms is purely graphic. However, it is most likely that the scribe intended as the gloss, **naśśa'a* ‹ **nanśa'a*, 3rd m.s. N stem suffix conjugation. If that be the case, then the verb form being glossed might also be intended for N stem, **yinnašši* 3rd m.s. based on the Akkadian N present-future theme with WS *y-* and -Ø for the past tense. Such a meaning as required by this context is consistent with the N stem of **nś'* in Hebrew. That verb in both Akkadian and WS is transitive in the G stem. Although *CAD* (N/2:103a) places this passage under the intransitive G, they also record an instance of the meaning "to rise up against" for the N stem (*CAD* N/2:112a). Therefore, we apparently have the 3rd m.s. N stem suffix form here.

quttul. This standard theme for the Akkadian D stem has only three examples in the texts under discussion. As the stative of the D stem, they should be passive in nature but this is not the case. One is from a verb of speaking for which the D stative *du-ub-bu-ba-a-ku-ma* means "I am being pestered" (*YOS* 2 70:8; cited *CAD*: D:12b). The same form in a Megiddo letter is transitive:

ša-ni-tam du-ub-bu-ba-ku-mì / UGU ŠEŠ.ḪÁ-*ia* "Furthermore, I spoke before my colleagues" (EA 245:1)

The other verb, *dubburu*, is also normally passive in the stative, e.g *ina qaṣêmma dubburū* "They (the cattle) have been removed to the steppe" (*ARM* 5 37:9; cited *CAD* D:187b). But one of the Canaanite scribes uses even the correct D stative theme in transitive meaning:

[*u*] *na-ak-šu-mì* / GU_4.MEŠ *ù* / *du-ub-bu-ru-ni* "[and] they (the men of Taanach) have slaughtered my oxen and expelled me" (EA 248:15-17).

The third example is *uḫ-ḫu-ra-ta a-ṣa* "you have delayed coming forth" (EA 102:9), from *uḫḫuru* " to be late, to delay," here with an infinitive as direct accusative.

quttil. The standard theme for D stem *qtl*'s is *quttil*, as demonstrated by Izreᵓel (1978b:74-78). The crucial question with regard to this D theme is its diachronic significance. Akkadian has *quttul*; the ancient dialect from which Hebrew developed evidently had *qittil* (Blau 1971:152-158). The assumption of Ebeling (1910:63) and Dhorme (1914:37-38 = 1951:432-433) that EA *quttil* was due to the influence of WS *qôtil* (Heb. *pôlēl*, Arabic *fâᶜala*) really has nothing to commend it. The lengthened vowel of WS *qôtil* ‹ *qâtil* is a lengthening of the first vowel in place of lengthening of the second radical, e.g. *qa:til* instead of *qat:il*. The EA forms usually have orthographic gemination. It is certainly unreasonable to assume forms with *qo:t:il*. Although there are no glosses to prove the contemporary Canaanite form, there is a pair of verbs which were native to Canaanite as well as Akkadian, viz. *ḫu-li-iq* (EA 197:32) and *ḫu-lí-iq* (EA 250:8, 39) "he destroyed." and *du-bi-ru* "they expelled" (EA 104:27). Furthermore, there is the evidence of the D infinitive forms from Ugarit, viz. *ḫu-wa-ú* for **ḥuwwayu*, "to give life" (*Ug* 5, 137:II, 17') and *pu-la-ṭu* for **pullaṭu*, "to rescue, deliver" (*Ug* 5, 137:II, 20'; Rainey 1969a:108). The *-u-* vowel in the first syllable is highly suggestive for the EA forms since the D infinitive of *wuššuru* in the Canaanite EA texts is *uš-ša-ar* (EA 82:22) as noted by Youngblood (1961:231; he realized that the theme vowel should be short *a* because otherwise a Byblian scribe would have written *uš-šu-ur*, which would resemble the later Akkadian form of this verb's infinitive).

Therefore, *quttil* as the theme form for the D stem suffix conjugation in these texts might reflect the true D stem theme in contemporary Canaanite. But how does it relate to Hebrew *qittēl?* It seems impossible to explain the relationship as diachronic, i.e. that *qittil* developed from *quttil*. But then, there is no reason to assume that Hebrew is a direct, linear descendant from the Canaanite spoken by the EA scribes. When dealing with the causative stem, one is faced with certain evidence in favor of rival patterns, *u-i* and *i-i*. Furthermore, it seems highly probable that the D stem form borrowed from Canaanite into Egyptian was *qittal*, apparently a development from an original *qittil*. For example, the loan word, "to bless" in Egyptian inscriptions of the late New Kingdom has the form (in Egyptian "syllabic" writing) *bí-ra-kú* (Sivan and Cochavi-Rainey 1992:57-58) and this vocalic pattern is characteristic of several verbs. Of course, there is always the possibility that the Egyptians borrowed the D infinitive. In that case, their borrowed **qittal*(*u*) could easily be comprehended as a counterpart to the *quttalu* of Ugaritic.

From a purely descriptive point of view, *quttil* seems to be built on the active *-i-* thematic vowel of the secondary stems plus the *-u-* vowel of the prefixes in the secondary stems (person markers in the prefix conjugation and the nominalizing prefix, *mu-*, of the participle). One distinct possibility is that the suffix conjugation theme is nothing but the 2nd m.s. imperative, i.e. *quttil*! If that suggestion should turn out to be correct, then all the speculations about synchronic and diachronic developments are a waste of time.

The various attestations pertain to only eight verbs, one of which, *wuššuru*, is of very high frequency. All the others are known from one or two, or perhaps four examples. There are over a dozen spellings for *wuššuru*, the principal ones being: 3rd m.s. *uš-ši-ir* (EA 86:16; *et passim*); 3rd f.s. *uš-ši-ra-at* (EA 117:50; 138:125); 2nd m.s. *uš-ši-ir-ta* (EA 194:22); 1st c.s. *uš-ši-ir-ti* (EA 34:52; *et passim*); *uš-še-er-ti* (EA 151:26); *uš-šir$_4$-ti$_7$* (EA 265:4) *et al*.; also *mu-še-er-ti* (EA 287:53; Jerusalem). The other verbs are: *buʾʾû* — 1st c.s. *bu-i-ti$_7$* (EA 264:6, 20); 3rd m.pl. ⸢*bu*⸣*-ú* (EA 104:53; Rainey 1989-90:59b); *dubburu* — 3rd m.pl. *du-bi-ru* (EA 104:27); *ḫulluqu* — 3rd m.s. *ḫu-li-iq* (EA 197:32), *ḫu-lí-iq* (EA 250:8, 39); *muššuru* — cf. *wuššuru* above; *nuddû* — 3rd m.s. *nu-di-ni* "he has cast me aside" (EA 283:23; *AHw*:709; *CAD* N/2:309; Moran 1987b:505 n. 4); *puḫḫuru* — 3rd m.s. *pu-ḫi-ir* (EA 76:17; 129:91; 132:20); 3rd m.pl. *pu-ḫi-*[*ru*] (EA 295:21) and almost certainly *pu*!(MU)*-ḫi-ru* (EA 290:8; Zimmern 1891c:141 n. 5; Greenberg 1955:49; Rainey 1978c:149; *contra* Moran 1975b:151, 162 n. 42; 1987b:520 n. 2; 1992:334 n. 2); *turruṣu* — *tu-ur-ri-ṣú-mì* (EA 250:5).

qattul. The possibility that a D stative in this pattern, typical only of Assyrian, has been posited for one passage by Moran. If he is correct, then the form is expressing the passive in accordance with standard Akadian usage:

> *ù ra-⌜bi⌝-ṣú* LÚ *e[m-qú šu-ut]* / *ša ka-bu-ut ma-⌜gal⌝* "and the commissioner [was] a wi[se] man, who was highly respected" (EA 129:15-16; cf. Moran 1987b:344, 346 nn. 7-8; 1992:209, 210 n. 7).

quttal. Only one D stem *qtl* takes this form and it is an anomaly. The verb is denominative from *(w)ardu* "slave," and is based on an infinitive **urrudu* / **urradu* (only bound forms are attested) as well as a G infinitive *arādu* (again only bound forms attested). The one D stem *qtl* is 1st c.s.:

> *i-nu-ma* TUR *a-na-ku ù šu-ri-ba-ni a-na* KUR*Mi-iṣ-ri* / *ù ur-ra-ad-ti* LUGAL / *be-li-ia ù iz-zi-iz-ti* / *i-na* KÁ.GAL LUGAL *be-li-ia* "When I was young, he (Yanḫamu) installed me in Egypt and I served the king, my lord, and I stood in the gate of the king, my lord" (EA 296:25-29).

Note that *urradti* stands between a Š stem *qtl*, *šūribani*, and a G stem hybrid of *izzuzu* (cf. *infra*, pp. 321-323), built on the Akkadian 3rd m.s. present plus 1st c.s. suffix. Therefore, it seems obvious that *urradti* is also a hybrid, based on the infinitive or, more probably, on the 3rd m.s. Akkadian present (if such existed) plus 1st c.s. suffix.

šuqtil. Izreʾel (1978b:74-75) observed that *šuqtil*, the theme form for Š stem *qtl*'s, reflects the same *u-i* vocalization as the D stem *quttil*. A major problem arises here, however, in that an original Canaanite Š stem is not very likely for the contemporary Canaanite. The likelihood that the theme is simply taken from the 2nd m.s. imperative is thus increased. Forms from three verbs are attested: *šūšuru*, *šūrubu*, and *šutūru* (restricted to the EA texts from Canaan, *AHw*:1336a).

All of the examples from *šūšuru* "to prepare" (*CAD* E:358a; Rainey 1978b:70) are responses to an order from pharaoh to prepare supplies and manpower in view of the impending arrival of an Egyptian expeditionary force (Schulman 1964:63-64 n. 99; Reviv 1966b). Thus, most of the forms are 1st c.s. as the rulers report their compliance. The initial order from Egypt is found in EA 367, a letter sent by pharaoh to Indaruta, the ruler of Achshaph:

> *ù lu-ú šu-šu-ra-tá a-na pa-ni* / ERÍN.MEŠ *pí-ṭa-ti* LUGAL NINDA *ma-a-ad* / GEŠTIN *gáb-bu mi-im-ma ma-a-ad* "and may you be prepared in anticipation of the king's troops, food being plentiful, wine (and) everything else being plentiful" (EA 367:15-17; Cochavi-Rainey 1988:*32, *34).

The precative , *lū šūšurāta*, is here translated as a stative though it has been taken as transitive (Albright, Mendenhall and Moran 1955:484b; Moran 1987b:563; 1992:365). However, it would appear that the supplies being mentioned are not the direct object of the verb but rather the subjects of circumstantial clauses with the statives, *ma-a-ad* as their predicates. This is typical of Egyptian syntax and may reflect the linguistic background of the Egyptian scribe (Cochavi-Rainey 1990:62-63).

The replies to this command from Beirut and from Rôġiṣu in the northern Beqaᶜ Valley employ the proper Akkadian 1st c.s. suffix although they attach it to the hybrid *šūšir-* rather than to the proper *šūšur-* of the Egyptian text. In three of the Beirut passages, the verb is stative in meaning; one lengthy citation will suffice to show the semantic context:

> *šá-ni-tam i-nu-ma ša-pa-ar šàr-ru* / EN-*ia* ᵈUTU-*ia a-na* ÌR-*šu* / *ù i-pí-ri ša* GÌR.MEŠ-*šu* / *šu-ši-ir-mi a-na* [*p*]*a-ni* / ERÍN.ḪÁ *pí-ṭá-at ša* LUGAL EN-*ka*₄ / *iš-te-mé ma-gal ma-gal* / *ù a-›na‹-nu-um-ma šu-ši-ra-ku* / *qa-du* ANŠE.KUR.RA.ḪÁ-*ia ù qa-du* / *gáb-bi mi-im-mi-ia*ᴴᴬ́ / *ša i-ba-aš-ša it-ti* / ÌR *ša* LUGAL EN-*ia a-na* / *pa-ni* ERÍN.ḪÁ *pí-ṭá-at ša* LUGAL EN-*ia* "Furthermore, when the king, my lord, my sun god, wrote to his servant and the dust of

> his feet, 'Prepare in anticipation of the troops of the king, your lord', I heeded very diligently and now I am prepared with my horses and with everything of mine that there is with the servant of the king, my lord, in anticipation of the troops of the king, my lord" (EA 141:18-30; cf. also EA 142:25-31).

In another letter an intransitive and a transitive appear together:

> *ù i-de* / LUGAL *i-nu-ma šu-še-ra-ku i-na pa-ni* ERÍN.MEŠ *pí-ṭá-ti* LUGAL EN-*ia* / *šu-ši-ra-ku gáb-ba ki-ma qa-bi* LUGAL EN-*ia* "And may the king be apprised that I am prepared in anticipation of the troops of the king, my lord; I have prepared everything in accordance with the command of the king, my lord" (EA 144:18-21).

Compare the following transitive as well:

> *lu-uk-šu-da-am-mì* / ERÍN.MEŠ *pí-ṭá-at* LUGAL / *ù* MAŠKÍM.MEŠ-*šu ù a-na-[k]u* / *šu-ši-ra-ku gáb-bá* "Let the army of the king and his commissioners arrive and I (will) have (already) prepared everything" (EA 191:11-15; cf. Moran 1987b:430; 1992:271).

The other six examples of 1st c.s. have the *-āti* suffix (EA 193:21; 227:13) or plain *-ti*. The contexts are all transitive, e.g.

> *a-nu-ma šu-ši-ir-ti* NINDA.MEŠ / KAŠ.MEŠ Ì.MEŠ ŠE.MEŠ GU_4.MEŠ / ÙZ.MEŠ *a-na pa-ni* ERÍN.MEŠ LUGAL EN-*ia* "Now I have prepared food, beer, oil, grain, oxen, goats, in anticipation of the troops of the king, my lord" (EA 324:12-14; Naʾaman 1975:54* n. 47; Moran 1987b:546 n. 2; 1992:352 n. 1; also EA 325:15-19).

The other spellings are: *šu-še-er-ti* (EA 213:13); *šu-ši-ir-ti*$_7$ (EA 337:19); *šu-ši-ra-ti* (EA 227:13); *šu-uš-ši-ra-ti*$_7$ (EA 193:21).

The one truly passive example is from the Š stem of *târu*, which is a special creation by some of the Canaanite EA scribes.

> *ip-pu-uš-ti nu-kúr-ta / šal-ma-at a-na ia-ti-ia / šu-te-ra-at* URU.KI-*ia / a-na ia-ti-ia* "I make war; it is well with me; my town has been returned to me" (EA 280:12-15).

This is also the only Š 3rd f.s. *qtl*.

The last verb in this group, *šūrubu*, is represented by 1st c.s. *šu-ri-ib-ti-šu-nu* (EA 123:17), 3rd m.s. *šu-ri-ib* (EA 112:49, also 46; 122:37; 123:33 and 3rd m.pl. [*š*]*u-ri-bu* (EA 123:17). All of the examples are transitive. For 3rd m.s. with an accusative 1st c.s. suffix, *šu-ri-ba-ni*, cf. *supra*, p. 312 (EA 296:25-29).

hiqtil. One lone example of a Canaanite verb, introduced by the gloss sign, bears witness to the H stem suffix form. The context is:

> *ki-i qa-bi-mì / i-na pa-ni-ka* ᴵ*Mu-ut-*ᵈIŠKUR-*mì / in-né-bi-it* ᴵ*A-ia-ab / \ ḫi-iḫ-bi-e ki-i in₄-né-bi-tu / šàr* ᵁᴿᵁ*Pí-ḫi-lì iš-tu / pa-ni* LÚ.MEŠ *ra-bi-ṣí \ sú-ki-ni / šàr-ri* EN-*ia* "How is it said in your presence, 'Mut-Baal has deserted, he has hidden Ayyâb'? How could the king of Peḥel desert from the presence of the commissioners?" (EA 256:4-10; Albright 1943a:10-11; Albright, Mendenhall and Moran 1955:486; Moran 1987b:483; 1992:309).

Albright (1943a:11) felt that the scribe had forgotten the proper Akkadian term, *puzzuru* "to hide," so he inserted a Canaanite word with the gloss sign; so the scribe used his native verb from the root **ḥb'*. This form is evidence for the H stem prefix vowel *-i-*, which is thought to have developed from an original *-u-* (Blau 1971:152-158), this in spite of synchronic evidence in Hebrew pointing to an original *-a-*, e.g. the Ist Waw verbs, *hôrîḏ* ‹ **hawrid*. On the other hand, Heb. *hēqîm* indicates an *-i-* vowel, the diachronic significance of which has been much debated (Moran 1961:62 = 1965:71). The orthography of the form under discussion is also problematic. The main possibilities are: *ḫi-iḫ-bi-i*₁₅, *ḫi-iḫ-bé-e*. What was the exact form that the scribe was trying to represent? Was it **hiḥbî*, **hiḥbi'* or **hiḥbē(')*? It is likely that the third radical, *aleph*, was quiescent.

SUMMARY. It can be seen from the above that four trends are at work in the scribal choice of thematic form in the suffix conjugation pattern. On occasion, they employ a purely Canaanite verb form, represented as best they can in syllabic cuneiform script. Sometimes they use an Akkadian verb in its original thematic form. This practice is most clearly discerned in the transitive use of *qatil*, forms like *šakin*, etc., or the D stem examples in *quttul*, even when the verb is expressing transitive meaning contrary to normal Akkadian grammar. The third trend, and the most illuminating, is the employment of thematic forms in accordance with the principles of West Semitic. Such a practice is represented by the contrasts between transitive *qatal* and passive *qatil* with particular verbs such as *leqû, dâku, epēšu*, etc. It is when such a process can be properly isolated and identified that we have the best evidence for the semantic categories of the contemporary Canaanite. Finally, there are some instances when the scribes simply followed their usual practice for the active prefix conjugation, viz. to adopt a theme from the Akkadian lexical stock and to inflect it with the WS suffixes. It is an open question whether the *quttil* and *šuqtil* patterns are the result of such a process, i.e. use of the D and Š imperative forms as themes, or whether *quttil* and *šuqtil* reflect an original Canaanite pattern. A final possibility, which would be a fifth trend, is that thematic forms like *quttil* and *šuqtil* may have been special developments within the mixed language, the so-called jargon of these texts. With the material presently at hand, it is impossible to give a satisfactory answer to those questions.

CHAPTER XIII

SUFFIX CONJUGATION — SPECIAL HYBRIDS

Besides the routine aspects of morphology in the suffix conjugation, there are a number of special hybrid features in the EA texts from Canaan which caught the attention of scholars from the very beginning. After a century of research, in classical Akkadian, in the peripheral dialects, and in NWS languages, it is possible to place these special phenomena in proper perspective. This chapter will attempt to trace the processes at work in the EA texts from Canaan which produced these unusual formations.

THE PREFORMATIVE STATIVES

One of the special features of Akkadian syntax that was unknown to the pioneer students of the EA tablets is the existence of a group of verbs, some defective, that generally lack a real stative conjugation but whose prefix forms function syntactically as statives (*GAG*:102, §78b; Hecker 1968:122, §74a). Of the eight verbs in this category, *ukāl,* the present-future of *kullu,* meaning "to hold," does not occur in the WS texts from EA, and neither does *išqallal,* the present-future of *šuqallulu* "to hang." Though *uqa''a,* the present-future of *quʾʾû* "to expect," can have this function (Hecker *loc. cit.*), it appears in the Canaanite texts only in the WS indicative imperfect: 1st c.s. *ú-qa-mu* "I am awaiting" (EA 136:38); 3rd m.pl. *tu-qa-ú-na* "(they) are awaiting" (EA 195:20; in EA 73:20 and EA 129:54, the reading is *tu-ba!-ú-na,* Rainey 1973c:262). That such indicatives are specifically differentiated from the tenseless stative function will become obvious in the treatment of other verbs in this group.

išû. One of the defective verbs included here is *išû,* which is nevertheless transitive in Akkadian and means "to have." Such standard usage can be found in the non-WS letters from EA, e.g.

> *ù* GUŠKIN *ša-nu-ú ma-ʾ-du ša pa-ṭá la i-šu-ú* "and much other gold that had no limit" (EA 27:28).

However, Ebeling (1915:1430) and Moran (1950a:9; 1987b:242; 1992:138) suggested that the two occurrences of this verb in Byblos expressed a meaning and a syntactic function identical to the existential particles of Hebrew (*yēš*) and Ugaritic (*iṯ* = **ʾiṯ, ʾêṯ*).

> *i-na* ^LÚ^MAŠKÍM *šàr-ri / ša i-šu-ú i-na* ^URU^*Ṣu-mu-ur / ba-al-ṭá-at* ^URU^*Gub-la* "Byblos is sustained by the king's commissioner whom he (the king) has in Ṣumur" (EA 68:19-21).

Ebeling and Moran render here, "the king's commissioner who is in Ṣumur." However, this interpretation is not very attractive because the very next sentence achieves their meaning without the use of *išû*:

> *a-nu-ma* ^I^*Pa-ḫa-am-[na]-ta* / ^LÚ^MAŠKÍM LUGAL *ša i-⸢na⸣* / ^URU^*Ṣu-mu-ur*^KI^ "Now, Paḫamnata, the king's commissioner who is in Ṣumur" (EA 68:22-24).

The second passage which Ebeling and Moran adduce looks on the surface as if it might support their view. If *išû* were transitive here, then there would be no need for the dative complement, *ana yâši*.

> [*ti*]-⸢*i*⸣-*de* ^d^NIN / *ša* ^URU^*Gub-⸢la⸣ šum-ma ⸢i⸣?-šu* / URUDU.MEŠ *ù* ⸢*ši*⸣-⸢*in*$_4$⸣-*ni* [*a*]-⸢*na*⸣ / ›*a-na*‹ *ia-ši* "The Lady of Byblos knows if I have copper and ivory" (EA 77:8-11; Youngblood 1961:183; Moran 1987b:257, nn. 2-3; 1992:148 nn. 2-3; cf. Rainey 1973c:243).

The word ⸢*i*⸣?-*šu* is written on the edge of the tablet and Schroeder's copy shows the beginning of the *i* sign. Even though he does not show much space after the first part of the *i*, it is not impossible that the original reading was ⸢*i*⸣-[*ba*]-*šu*, or else we should read ⸢*i*⸣-‹*ba*›-*šu*. In the Byblos correspondence and elsewhere in Canaan, the commonly used syntagma for the expression of possession would be *ibaššû ana yâši* (Rainey 1990a:174).

The example from Sidon seems to make better sense if *išu* is understood to mean "he has."

> *ù la-a ti-ik-šu-du-na* / *ša-a-ri pí-i-šu* / *a-na ma-ḫar* ÌR.MEŠ-*šu ša i-šu*[-*ú?*] / *i-na* KUR.ḪÁ *Ṣú-uḫ-ri* "and his utterances do not reach his servants whom he has in the lands of Ṣuḫri" (EA 145:19-22; Rainey 1973c:243 n. 50; contrast. Moran 1987b:376 n. 5; 1992:231 n. 5).

In short, the evidence for an atypical usage of *išû* to express existence instead of possession is most tenuous. In view of the abundance of forms of *bašû* to express existence (cf. *infra*), it would be wise to reserve judgement.

ibašši. A crucial verb in the discussion of the suffix conjugation is *bašû*. As noted above, the Akkadian present, *ibašši*, functions as a stative (usually in imperfect tense meaning) in standard Akkadian (*GAG*:102, §78b). This is true of OA, OB and literary Akkadian as well as MB and the peripheral dialects (*CAD* B:145b-155a); preterites and precatives do occur when a past tense or injunctive nuance is required, but G present *ibašši* is the dominant form. In *CH*, *ibašši* serves as the present while N stem *ibbašši* and *ittabši* express the future and the past respectively (cf. examples *CAD* B:158b, 160a).

The texts from Canaanite scribes (Ebeling 1915:1390; Rainey 1978b:67) including the Taanach letters (Rainey 1977:58-59) present an interesting conjugation table, unique in the cuneiform world. There are no 3rd m.s. forms with the Canaanite *y*- prefix typical of most prefix verbs. All the 3rd m.s. texts do have final -*i* (including EA 179:15 where the final *še* sign surely is to be read $\check{s}i_x$), except two epistles from Beirut where the forms end in -*a*. This latter can hardly be the ventive or the Canaanite volitive. Instead, it is to be compared to the final -*a* that appears occasionally on *qtl* verbs (cf. *supra*, p. 287-288).

All instances of 3rd f.s. have *i-ba-ša-at* (EA 84:38; *et al.*). The Akkadian present thus serves as the theme to which the Canaanite (and Akkadian) 3rd f.s. suffix *-at* is appended! The 2nd m.s. forms have the suffix *-āta*, i.e. *i-ba-ša-ta* (EA 73:40; TT 6:17). The 2nd m.pl. is likewise *i-ba-ša-tu-nu* (EA 74:26) and *i-ba-aš-ša-tu*[*-nu?*] (EA 246:r. 3). But most significant of all, the 1st c.s. forms have in three cases the Akkadian suffix, *-āku*, viz. *i-ba-aš-ša*$_{10}$*-ku* (EA 248:20), *i*$_{15}$*-ba-ša-ku* (EA 143:29; 193:6) while the others have the hybrid suffix *-āti*, *i-ba-ša-ti* (EA 78:19; *et al.*), *i-ba-ša-ti*$_{7}$ (EA 230:3, 6), except for one obvious scribal confusion, *i-ba-šu-ti* (EA 284:8). The 1st c.pl. forms, all from one scribe, are *i*$_{15}$*-ba-ša-nu* (EA 174:8; *et al.*) and *i*$_{15}$*-ba-ša-‹nu›* (EA 363:7).

Therefore, there is no reason not to include all the 3rd m.pl. forms among the suffix conjugation verbs as well. Like the 3rd m.s. *ibašši*, the 3rd m.pl. *ibaššû* are identical with the standard Akkadian forms. They never have the *y-* prefix or the *t-* prefix typical of 3rd m.pl. in these texts. The attested 3rd m.pl. forms are *i-ba-aš-šu* (EA 74:21, 28; 81:49; 366:27), *i-ba-šu* (EA 89:19; 101:17; 107:42; 134:17), *i-ba-šu-ú* (EA 285:23), *i*$_{15}$*-ba-šu-mi* (EA 185:50). Two of the forms which Ebeling interpreted as 3rd m.s. are actually the 3rd m.pl.:

> *a-nu-ma* ^{I}*A-zi-ru* DUMU / ^{I}ÌR-*A-ši-ir-ta qa-du* / ŠEŠ.MEŠ-*šu i-na* ^{URU}*Du-ma-aš-qa* / *ù uš-ši-ra* ERÍN.MEŠ / *pí-ṭá-ti ù ti-ìl-qé-šu* / *ù ta-ap-šu-uḫ* KUR LUGAL / *ù šum-ma ki-a-ma i-ba-šu* / *ù* ⸢*la*⸣*-a ti-zi-za* / ^{URU}*Ṣu-mu-ra* "Now Aziru, son of ᶜAbdi-Ashirta, with his brothers are in Damascus, so send the army that it may capture him and the land of the king may become peaceful; but if thus they be (here), then Ṣumur will not stand (against them)" (EA 107:26-34; Rainey 1973c:249; cf. Moran 1950a:98; 1987b:304; 1992:181); *šá-ni-tam yi-il*$_{5}$*-ma-ad* LUGAL EN-*ia* / *i*$_{15}$*-pí-iš* ŠEŠ-*šu ša i*$_{15}$*-ba-aš-*⸢*ša*⸣ / *i-na* ^{URU}*Gub-la i-nu-ma na-*⸢*da*⸣*-*[*an*] / DUMU.DUMU.MEŠ *ša* ^{I}*Ri-*⸢*ib*⸣*-*⸢^{d}⸣⸢IŠKUR⸣ / ⸢*ša*⸣! *i*$_{15}$*-ba-aṣ-šu it-ti-*⸢*šu*⸣! / *a-na* LÚ.MEŠ *ar-nu-*⸢*ti*⸣! ⸢*ša*⸣ / *šàr-ri ša i-na* ^{KUR}*A-*⸢*mur*⸣*-r*[*i*] "Furthermore, may the king, my lord, learn the deed of his brother who is in Byblos, that he has handed over the sons of Rib-Haddi who were with him(!) to the traitors to

the king who are in the land of Amurru!" (EA 142:18-24; Rainey 1973c:249 n. 68, 262).

It was Youngblood (1961:120-121) who first recognized that the EA scribes from Canaan used *ibašši* as the theme for their hybrid suffix conjugation verb "to be" because they knew about its status as a prefix stative in Akkadian. Syntactically, all the inflected forms of *bašû* in these texts (including those from Taanach) function as *qtl*'s.

The invention of *ibaššâku, ibaššâti, ibaššâta, ibaššât, ibaššânu* and *ibaššâtunu* generated other hybrids including some from *izzuzu* and others from verbs not originally belonging to the "prefix statives." The description of the additional hybrids on this pattern will be given below.

izuzzu. Treatment of the irregular verb *izuzzu* by the Canaanite scribes is mixed. There are over a dozen instances of prefix forms, in the various modes: e.g. 3rd m.s. indicative imperfect *yi-zi-zu* (EA 362:65), and probably with ventive *yi-zi-za* (EA 132:48; cf. *supra*, pp. 53, 206-208), jussive *yi-zi-iz* (EA 74:61; 89:55; probably also EA 113:37, 44); and preterite *yi-iz-zi-iz* (EA 250:42), *yi-zi-iz* (EA 132:10), ; 3rd f.s. volitive (?) *ti-zi-za* (EA 107:33); 1st c.s. preterite *iz-zi-iz* (EA 197:20; 245:9); indicative energic *i-zi-zu-na* (EA 124:16); volitive *i-zi-za* (EA 71:25; 104:49!); 1st c.pl. jussive *ni-zi-iz* (EA 279:18).

On the other hand, there are 1st c.s. statives to which the suffix has been appended on the model of the *ibaššâti* forms. One of them expresses the present:

ù a-nu-ma i-na / URU*Ṣu-mu-ra i-zi-za-ti* "and now I am stationed in Ṣumur" (EA 103:14-15).

Another is in past tense:

i-nu-ma TUR *a-na-ku ù* / *šu-ri-ba-ni a-na* KUR*Mi-iṣ-ri* / *ù ur-ra-ad-ti* LUGAL / *be-li-ia ù iz-zi-iz-ti* / *i-na* KÁ.GAL LUGAL *be-li-ia* "When I was you, then he sent me down to Egypt and I served the king, my lord, and I stood (was stationed) in the city gate of the king, my lord" (EA 296:25-29).

It can even be in the future:

a-di ma-ti i-zi-[za]-ti$_7$ it-ti-šu "How long shall I stay with him?" (EA 138:133).

A question arises about the 3rd m.s. forms which lack the *y-* prefix. Many of the contexts are obscure but they all seem to be past tense.

a-nu-ma 3-ta-an i-zi-iz UGU-*ia* MU.KÁM.MEŠ/ *a-ni-ta* "Now three times he has attacked me this year" (EA 85:8-9); *ù iq-bi a-na* LÚ *ù iz-zi-iz* / GÍR ZABAR UGU-*ia* "and he spoke to a man and he attacked me with a bronze dagger" (EA 82:37-38; Albright and Moran 1948:247-248 n. 24; Moran 1987b:264 n. 5; 1992:152 n. 5).

There are also three forms which are written in the theme of the Akkadian G present, *izzazzu*, which could be 3rd m.s. imperfect or 3rd m.pl. *izzazzū*. The parallel verb forms are *il$_5$-te$_9$-qú-ú*: (EA 237:2; 238:27) and *il$_5$-te$_9$-qú* (EA 237:5), which could be 3rd m.pl. if one assumes a purely Akkadian form (Moran 1987b:463, 464; 1992:294, 295), *ilteqû*. However, one of the two texts in question has *i$_{15}$-ba-aš-š[a-]ti* (EA 237:13), a clearly Canaanite hybrid; therefore, it seems logical to assume that the scribe would have used the *t-* prefix if he were intending to represent the prefix conjugation. Of course, it is possible that the absence of either the *y-* or the *t-* prefix may indicate that the scribe was using the prefixless verb forms as equivalent of his own *qtl* conjugation pattern. In that case, *ilteqû* and *izzazzū* would simply be 3rd m.pl.

[i]l$_5$-te$_9$-qú-ú [I]*La-a[b-a-ya]* / *ù iz-za-az-zu* UGU URU.DI[DLI.ḪÁ] / *ša* [I]*šàr-ri* EN-*ia* / *ù il$_5$-te$_9$-qú* URU.DIDLI.ḪÁ / *ša* [I]LUGAL EN-*ia* "They have taken La[bʾaya] and they have attacked the cit[ies] of the king, my lord, and they have taken the cities of

> the king, my lord" (EA 237:2-6); *a-nu-um-ma* / *iš-tu u*$_4$*-mi* *uš-ši-*⸢*ir*⸣[*-ti*] / *ṭup-pa an-na-am* / *i-na* É.GAL [*ù*] / *iz-za-zu* U[GU-*ia*] "Now, from the day [I] sent this tablet to the palace, they have attacked [me]" (EA 237:18-22); *ù il*$_5$*-te*$_9$*-qú* [. . .] / *ù* *iz-za--zu* UGU[*-ia*] / *ù il*$_5$ *-te*$_9$ *-qú* URU.DIDLI[.ḪÁ] / *ša* ^{LÚ}GAL EN-*ia* "and they took [. . .] and they attacked [me] and they took the citie[s] of the official, my lord" (EA 238:25-28).

In any case, the forms of *izzuzu*, with their *-a-* thematic vowel, must be viewed as past tense. The *ilteqû* forms could all be Gtn preterite; the plural accusatives, "cities," could imply iterative action, one attack after another. Then the *izzazzu* forms could be for Akkadian *iparras* form in past continuous.

idû. Perhaps the most high frequency verb from among the Akkadian "preformative statives" is *idû* "to know" (*GAG*:102, §78b). The Akkadian preterite, *īde*, *tīde*, etc., was the basic conjugated form in this stative function; 1st c.s. was *īde* like the 3rd m.s. This usage is also known in the other peripheral dialects, e.g. from Egypt:

> *ù im-ma-ti ta-aš-pu-ra* LÚ-*ka* DUGUD / *ša i-de*$_4$ *a-ḫa-at-ka* "but when have you sent one of your important men who knows/knew your sister?" (EA 1:15-16; Pintore 1972a; Moran 1975a:156 n. 1; 1987b:62 n. 4; 1992:3 n. 4; Cochavi-Rainey 1990b:21).

The texts from Canaan do not show any 1st c.s. forms with the *-(ā)ti* suffix or any other persons with suffixes from the *qtl* pattern. On the other hand, personal prefixes, *y-*, *t-* and *n-* are common. There are two examples of Canaanite imperfect as future:

> *a-di* ⸢*yi*⸣*-du šàr-ru* / *a-*⸢*na*⸣ KUR.MEŠ-*šu ù yu-wa-ši-ru* / ERÍN.MEŠ *pí-ṭá-ti-šu ù* / *yu-ša-ap-ši-ḫu* KUR.MEŠ-*šu* "until the king is apprised concerning his lands and sends his army and pacifies his lands" (EA 112:36-39; also EA 182:14-15).

And there are two others as present:

> *[ia-]nu* ⌈LÚ⌉ *ša yi-iq-b[i]* / *ki-ti-ia a-na pa-ni šàr-ri* / EN-*ia ki-ti-ia yi-du* ‹LUGAL› / *yi-du* LUGAL *ma-ni* UD.KÁM.MEŠ / *yi-pu-šu du-um-qa* / *a-na ia-ši i-nu-ma* / *ia-nu lìb-bi ša-na a-*⌈*na*⌉ *ia-ši* / *pa-nu-ia-ma a-na a-ra-ad* / *šàr-ri* EN-*ia* "There was [n]o man who tol[d] the king of my loyalty; ‹the king› knows my loyalty; the king knows how long a time he has done good to me because I have no other intention; it is my purpose to serve the king, my lord" (EA 119:36-44).

All the other instances of this verb lack any prefix modal suffixes except -Ø. The majority of occurrences are injunctive, with or without a personal prefix. The definition and categorization of these many injunctives is a special challenge. The OB and OA precative was *lū īde,* which is somewhat anomalous (cf. *supra,* p. 213). It probably derived from the function of the preterite, *īde, tīde,* etc., as a syntactic stative. The precative *lū īde* evidently corresponded to *lū paris*. Such injunctives are plentiful, mainly in the Byblos texts. Contrary to a former suggestion (Rainey 1973c:245-246), those particular constructions may not be understood as affirmations. They must be interpreted as real injunctives.

> *lu-ú i-de šàr-ru* / EN *i-nu-ma šal-ma-at* URU*Gub-la* GEMÉ / *ki-it-ti ša šàr-ri iš-tu* UD.KÁM.MEŠ / *ša ab-bu-ti-šu ù* ⌈*an*⌉*-nu-uš i-na-an-na* / *i-te-zi-ib šàr-ru* URU *ki-it-ti-šu* / *iš-tu qa-ti-šu* "May the king, the lord, be apprised that Byblos, the faithful handmaiden of the king, has been at peace since the days of his fathers, but now the king has abandoned his faithful city!" (EA 74:5-10).

Numerous other passages of this type may be cited (EA 68:9; 76:7; 78:7; 81:6; 116:6; 144:10; *et al.*).

Some of the scribes in Canaan created a more "conventional" injunctive, conforming to the precative pattern, viz. *li-de-*(*mi*) (EA 174:18; *et al.*).

> *li-de-mi* / *šàr-ru* EN-*ia i-nu-ma* / *iš-tu i-re-bi* ERÍN.MEŠ *pí-ṭá-ti* / *i-te*$_9$ *-pu-uš-mì* [I]*La-ab-a-yu* / *nu-kúr-ta i-na mu-uḫ-ḫi-ia* "May the king, my lord, be apprised that, since the army has gone home, Labʾayu has made war against me!" (EA 244:8-12; Rainey 1973c:244).

However, the WS jussive pattern led to the adoption of forms such as *lu-ú yi-de*. For example, another Megiddo letter has the parallel text to that cited just above:

> *ù a-nu-um-ma d*[*a*]*-a*[*n-na-a*]*t* / *nu-kúr-ti*$_7$ LÚ.MEŠ ⸢SA⸣.GAZ *i-na* KUR-*ti ù lu-ú yi-de* / *šàr-ru* EN-*ia a-na* KUR.KI-*šu* "And now the hostility of the ᶜ*apîrû* men is in[tensi]ve in the land, so may the king take cognizance of his land" (EA 243:19-22).

As jussives the prefix forms with -Ø suffix can be used without the particle *lū*, for example:

> *yi-de šàr-ru* EN-*li* / *i-nu-ma* [I]*Pu-ba-á'-la* / [I]DUMU ÌR-*A-ši-ir-ta* / *i-te*$_9$ *-ru-ub a-na* [URU]*Ul-la-sà* "May the king, my lord, be apprised that Pu-Baᶜla, the son of ᶜAbdi-Ashirta, has entered into Ullasa!" (EA 104:6-9).

In the same manner, forms without the *y-* prefix can also serve as injunctives:

> *i-de lìb-bi* / LUGAL EN *i-nu-ma ni-na-ṣa-ru* / [URU]*Ir-qa-ta a-na sa*[*-š*]*u* "May the heart of the king know that we are protecting the town of ᶜIrqata for him!" (EA 100:8-10; Moran 1987b:293 n. 2; 1992:173; cf. also e.g. EA 106:47; 137:30-31; 144:19, 22; 260:12-13; 304:22-23; 305:23-24).

The practical understanding of such forms is clear from their contexts but the theoretical classification is another matter. Were they, in the eyes of the scribes, simply jussives without the *y*-prefix, or were they considered to be statives in the optative mode? Two similar passages, both with 1st c.s. *īde*, but with an essential difference, may shed some light on this question. The first example is that of a purpose clause which is dependent upon an imperative:

> *ù / te-ra-ni a-wa-ta*$_5$ *ù i-de / ip-ša ša i-pu-šu* "So send back word to me that I may know the thing that I must do" (EA 114:24-26).

The second is a purpose clause dependent upon an indicative question:

> *a-na mi-ni la-a tu-te-ru-[n]a / a-wa-ta a-na ia-a-ši ù / i-de ip-ša ša i-pu-[šu]* "Why do you not send word back to me so that I may know the thing that I must d[o]?" (EA 83:7-9; the context of EA 85:59-60 is unclear).

In accordance with the rule of modal congruence for purpose clauses (Moran 1950a:81-89), *īde* in EA 114:24-26 ought to be an injunctive, viz. a jussive. By the same rule, *īde* in EA 83:7-9 ought to be an indicative, i.e. the equivalent of an imperfect since the preceding clause also contained an imperfect energic, 2nd m.s. *tuterrūna*. However, there is another possible common denominator which might have been the factor behind this usage, viz. the status of *īde* as a stative. The stative, like the suffix conjugation in all its nuances, is syntactically the equivalent of the indicative imperfect; on the other hand, the suffix conjugation, including statives, can express succession after injunctives, especially the imperative (Moran 1950a:139 n. 228). This future tense function of *qtl* will be discussed at length in the next chapter (cf. *infra*, pp. 358-365). The conclusion seems to be that the Canaanite scribes did have a feel for the stative function of the verb *idû* and that they employed it as such within the modal framework of their epistolary language (in spite of the obvious inflectional differences).

Of further interest are the many passages where *īde, tīde* and *nīde* express the indicative past, present or future. In the preterite no modal suffix other than the normal -Ø would be expected:

> *a-na-ku* ÌR *ki-ti-ka* / *ù a-wa-ta ša-a i-de* / *ù ša-a eš-te-me aš-pu-r*[*u*] / *a-na šàr-ri* "I am your faithful servant and the thing which I have learned and the thing which I have heard, I write to the king" (EA 108:22-25); *i-nu-ma ni-de ù* KAL.GA / *ni-iq-‹bi› a-na* LUGAL KAL.GA "When we became aware that they were strong, we sai‹d› to the king, 'They are strong'" (EA 108:43-44; Moran 1987b:306, 307 n. 7; 1992:182 n. 8).

The parallels in each case to another preterite assures the tense value of 1st c.s. *īde* and 1st c.pl. *nīde* respectively.

The context shows that the next example also has to be interpreted as a preterite:

> *ša-ni-tam* / *a-na* ^{I}DUMU.MU-*ia ša-pár šàr-ru* / *ú-ul* i_{15}*-de i-nu-ma* / ^{I}DUMU.MU-*ia it-ti* / LÚ.MEŠ SA.GAZ / *it-ta-na-la-ku* "Furthermore, the king has written concerning my son; I did not know that my son was associating with the *ʾapîrû* men" (EA 254:30-35).

The present tense examples, of which there are almost twenty, do not have the imperfect *-u* suffix. Rib-Haddi said to his commissioner:

> *ú-ul* / *ti-i-de* ^{KUR}*A-mur-ri i-nu-ma* / *a-šar da-an-ni ti-la-ku-na* "Don't you know Amurru, that they will follow the strong one?" (EA 73:14-16); *ti-i-de pa-ar-ṣa-ia* / *i-nu-ma i-ba-ša-ta i-na* / $^{\mathrm{⸢URU⸣}}$⸢*Ṣu*⸣*-mu-ra i-nu-ma* / ⸢ÌR⸣ ⸢*ki*⸣*-it-ti-ka a-na-ku* "You know my behavior when you were in Ṣumur, that I am/was your loyal servant" (EA 73:39-42).

In a letter to Pharaoh he says:

> *a-nu-um-ma* ^{I}*Pa-ḫa-am*[*-n*]*a-ta* / ^{LÚ}MAŠKÍM LUGAL *ša i*[*-n*]*a* / ^{URU}*Ṣu-mu-ra*^{KI} *i-*[*d*]*e-mì* / *pu-uš-qám* \ *ma-gal* / *ša* UGU ^{URU}*Gub-la* "Now Paḫamnata, the king's commissioner, who is in Ṣumur, knows the great pressure that is on Byblos" (EA 68:22-26)

The Tyrian letters do not use *īde* injunctively but only as an indicative present (or future, cf. *infra*, pp. 352-358) , e.g.

> *li-iš-al* LUGAL / [LÚ]MAŠKÍM-*šu ša i-de*$_4$ [KUR]*Ki-na-aḫ-na* "May the king ask his commissioner who knows Canaan!" (EA 148:46); LUGAL *i-de*$_4$ *šu-u*[*m*]-*ma ša-ak-na-ta-ni* / *i-na* [LÚ]MAŠKÍM *i-na* [KUR]*Ṣur-ri* "The king knows whether he appointed me as commissioner in Tyre" (EA 149:47-48; cf. also EA 149:81-82; 152:53-55; 155:58-59).

The ruler of Shechem also says:

> *i*$_{15}$-*de ip-še-et* / [I]*Mil-ki-li* UGU-*ia* "I know the deed of Milkili against me" (EA 254:28-29).

Note that in the same epistle, *īde* is also used in a preterite sense (EA 254:30-35; *supra*, p. 326-327).

The 3rd m.pl. *īdû* is also used with present meaning:

> *i-nu-ma ša-ṭe*$_6$-*er be-li* / *a-na maḫ-ri-ia ù a-nu-mi* / *ù i-du i-nu-ma ta-mu-tu-na* "Since my lord has written to me, now they know that they will die" (EA 362:42-44).

The examples with future tense significance are rare, two or three at best. One from Byblos (EA 83:9) has already been compared with an injunctive (cf. *supra*, p. 326). An additional passage, from Tyre, reads as follows:

> *a-nu-um-ma iš-pu-ra a-na be-li-ia ù* SIG$_5$ *e-nu-ma i-de*$_4$ "Now I have written to my lord and it is good that he know" (EA 147:70).

leʾû. The other prefix stative that is treated according to the prefix conjugation pattern is *leʾû* "to be able." Injunctives do not seem to be attested, probably due to the special semantic nuance of this verb. Most of the forms are inflected as indicative imperfects expressing present tense. The Jerusalem letters avoid

WS inflections and employ acceptable Akkadian forms, just as they do for other prefix verbal constructions (cf. below). One Jerusalem form is a Babylonian construction:

> *ù la-a i-le-é*ʾ*-e e-za-bi-ša* / KUR.ḪÁ [URU]*Ú-ru-ša*$_{10}$*-lim* [KI] "And I am unable to abandon it, (namely) the territory of Jerusalem" (EA 287:62-63);

Two other instances are Assyrian in form:

> *ù la a-la-á*ʾ*-e* / *e-ra-ba iš-tu*(sic!) LUGAL EN-*ia* "And I am unable to come before(!) the king, my lord" (EA 286:41-43; Moran 1975b:154); *la-a a-la-á*ʾ*-e* / *mu-še-ra* KASKAL.MEŠ / *a-na šàr-ri* EN-*ia* "I am unable to send caravans to the king, my lord" (EA 287:57-59; Moran *loc. cit.*).

There are a few instances in the Byblos and other texts where *le*ʾ*û* appears without any prefix conjugation modal suffix (other than the original -Ø). Comparison between forms with WS imperfect suffixes and those with none reveals that they all express the same meaning. For 3rd m.s. with *y*- and imperfect -*u* note:

> *a-nu-ma* / [PN] DUMU *ši-ip-ri-*[*ia*] / [*uš*]*-ši-ir-ti-šu ù aš-ta-ni* / [*m*]*a-ni* UD.KÁM.MEŠ *ú-wa-ši-ru-šu* / *ù la-a yi-le-ú* / *i-re-ba a-na* [URU]*Ṣu-mu-ra* "Now, as for [PN,] my ambassador, I have sent him repeatedly; how long have I been sending him and he has been unable to enter Ṣumur!" (EA 114:35-37);

where the context indicates repeated action in the past. To express that nuance the scribe felt compelled to use an imperfect form of *le*ʾ*û*. On the other hand, for the protasis of a conditional sentence, the bare form, with Ø suffix, is used:

> [*šum-m*]*a la-a i-le-e* / [*šàr-r*]*u la-qa-ia iš-tu* / [*qa-at*] *na-ak-ri-šu* / [*ù i*]*n*$_4$*-né-ep-ša-at* / [*ka-l*]*i* KUR.KI.MEŠ / [*a-na* [I]Ì]R-*A-ši-ir-ta* "[If the kin]g is unable to rescue me from his enemies, [then al]l the

> lands will be joined to ᶜAbdi-Ashirta" (EA 79:39-44; also EA 92:51);

However, other Byblos scribes use the WS imperfect in the same syntagma:

> *šum-ma la-a ti-le-ú la-qa-*⌈*ia*⌉ / *iš-tu qa-at na-ak-ri-ia ù* / *te-ra-ni a-wa-ta*$_5$ "If you are unable to deliver me from my enemies, then send me word" (EA 114:23-25).

When a question was involved, the imperfect energic was used:

> *aq-ta-bi ù aš-ta-ni* / *a-na ka-ta*$_5$ *ú-ul ti-le-ú-na* / *la-qa-ia iš-tu qa-at* / ᴵÌR-*A-ši-ir-ta* "I have said to you repeatedly, 'Are you unable to deliver me from ᶜAbdi-Ashirta?'" (EA 82:5-8).

The 1st c.s. imperfect forms, written *i-le-ú*, are almost all present in meaning:

> *mi-na* / *i-pu-šu-na ù a-na-ku* / *la-a i-le-ú a-la-*⌈*ka*$_{13}$⌉ / *a-na Ṣu-mu-ra* "What can I do since I am unable to go to Ṣumur?" (EA 104:36-39; also EA 82:22; 102:24; 105:29, 87; 109:56; 113:29; 116:52; 126:7; 264:9).

The same letter employs the future tense in the apodosis of a conditional sentence:

> *ša-ma-ma šu-nu* / ›*šu-nu*‹ *i-nu-ma i-te*$_9$*-ru-bu* / *i-na* ᵁᴿᵁ*Ṣu-mu-ra* / URU.MEŠ *an-nu-tu* ‹*i-na*› ᴳᴵŠMÀ.MEŠ / *ù* DUMU.MEŠ ᴵÌR-*A-ši-i*[*r-*]*ta* / *i-na ṣé-ri ù* / [*i*]*z-*[*z*]*i-za* UGU-‹*šu-nu*› *ù* / *la-a i-le-ú* / *a-ṣa ù ep-ša-at* ᵁᴿᵁ*Gub-la* / [*a*]*-na* LÚ.MEŠ GAZ.MEŠ *a-na* ᵁᴿᵁ*I-bir*$_5$*-ta* / *al-ka-*‹*ti*› *ù* ⌈*bu*⌉*-ú in*$_4$*-né-ep-ša* / *a-na* LÚ.MEŠ GAZ.MEŠ "If they hear that I am entering into Ṣumur, these cities (will be in) ships and the sons of ᶜAbdi-Ashirta (will be) on land and I will be up against ‹them› and I will be unable to go forth lest Byblos go over to the *ᶜapîrû* men." (EA 104:43-52; Rainey 1989-90:59b).

In one letter, there might be a distinction between present with *-u* and past with -Ø:

> *šá-ni-tam / i-nu-ma ta-aš-pu-ra a-na ia-ši / a-lik-mi i-zi-iz a-na* URU*Ṣu-mu-ur / a-di ka-ša-di-ia / [t]i-de i-nu-ma nu-kúr-tu*$_4$MEŠ / KAL.GA *ma-gal* UGU-*ia / ù ú-ul i-le-*⌈*ḫé*⌉ *a-la[-k]a*$_{13}$ "Furthermore, inasmuch as you have written to me, 'Go, take up a position in Ṣumur until my arrival,' you should know that hostilities are very intense against me and I was unable to go" (EA 102:13-19; Moran 1987b:296; 1992:175).

This passage may be compared with another further on:

> *ù ki-na-an-na la i-le-ú / a-la-ka*$_{13}$ "and thus I am unable to go" (EA 102:24-25).

In fact, *i-le-ú* in line 24 strongly suggests that the unique spelling in line 19, *i-le-*⌈*ḫé*⌉ is nothing but an illusion; the disputed form is much more likely to be read *i-le-ú*!

The usual nuance of the 1st c.s. forms with -Ø suffix is, as with most of the other persons, present tense:

> *a-nu-ma / [ki-a]-ma aš-ba-ti ù qa-la-ti i-na / [lìb-bi* URU-]*ia la-a i-le-e a-ṣa / [a-na* EDIN.MEŠ] "Now, [th]us I sit and I keep quiet [with]in my [town]; I am unable to go forth [to the open field]" (EA 81:19-22; Moran 1987b:262 n. 5; 1992:151); *ù* URU.KI *ša i*$_{15}$*-ba-aš-ša-ti / i-na lìb-bi-ši la-a e-le-é*ʾ*-e / na-ṣa-ar-ši* "And as for the city within which I am, I am unable to protect it" (EA 238:7-9).

Nearly all of the sentences containing a form of *le'û* are in the negative. One exception to this rule also happens to have future connotation; the text is from Sidon:

> *ù yi-din-ni /* LUGAL *i-[n]a qa[-a]t* LÚ-*lì ša yi-la-ak / i-na pa-ni* ERÍN.MEŠ *pí-ṭá-at* LUGAL / *a-na ša-al* URU.DIDLI.KI.[Ḫ]Á *ša in*$_4$*-né-ep-šu / a-na* LÚ.MEŠ SA.GAZ.MEŠ / *ù tú-ta-ri-ši-na i-na /*

> *qa-ti-ia ù i-lé-i a-ra-ad* / LUGAL EN-*ia ki-i-ma* LÚ.MEŠ *a-bu-ti-nu* / *pa-na-nu-um* "May the king assign me to the man who is coming at the head of the king's army to attack the citie[s] which have gone over to the *ᶜapîrû* men so that it may return them to my authority and I will be able to serve the king, my lord like my fathers before!" (EA 144:26-34 Moran 1987b:375 n. 2; 1992:230-231 n. 3).

An example of the positive and the negative in the same context also illustrates the 3rd m.pl. without a WS prefix or a WS imperfect *-na* suffix:

> *ù a-nu-ma i-na-an-na ši-iḫ-ṭá-at* / URU*Ṣu-mu-ra a-di a-bu-li-ši* / *ša-ḫa-aṭ-ši i-le-ú ù ṣa-bat-ši la i-le-ú* "And now Ṣumur is hard pressed (plundered) up to its gate; to press it hard (to plunder it) they are able, but to conquer it they are not able" (EA 106:10-13; *CAD* A/1:84b; Moran 1950a:29; 1987b:302; 1992:179).

Finally, it should be noted that all forms of *leʾû* employed in these texts govern some infinitive in the accusative, *alāka*, *uššar(a)*, *naṣār(a)*, *erāba*, etc. In effect, the constructions with *le'û* can be called "verbal compounds." One apparent exception to the rule that *le'û* governs an infinitive is the following passage from Tyre where the infinitival accusatives are unexpressed but implied from the context:

> *pa-nu-ia a-na a-la-ki* / *a-na a-ma-ri pa-ni* LUGAL *be-li-[i]a* / *ù la-a i-lé-e iš-tu* / *qa-ti* I*Zi-im-re-da* URU*Ṣí-du-na*KI "My intention is to come and to see the face of the king, my lord, but I am unable because of Zimredda (of) Sidon" (EA 151:8-11; contrast Moran 1987b:385; 1992:238).

In summary, one can say that the Canaanite scribes do use forms of *leʾû* as "prefix statives" on some occasions but they never append the personal suffixes of the *qtl* conjugation pattern. On the other hand, they most often inflect *leʾû* as a prefix verb, using the

WS person markers and modal suffixes of the imperfect and the imperfect energic.

OTHER SUFFIX CONJUGATION HYBRIDS

If the conjugation of *ibašši* with personal suffixes of the WS *qtl* pattern, which evidently fostered the similar application of such constructions to *izzuzu*, did not bear fruit with regard to *idû* and *le'û*, it was productive with regard to other verbs, mainly those of a reflexive or particularly stative nature.

REFLEXIVE STEMS.

nenpušu. Since the forms of *bašû* in these texts were all based on the Akkadian present 3rd m.s. *ibašši*, the N stem of that verb was ignored (except for the lone example of Ntn preterite, *ittabšû* in TT 2:26). So the Canaanite scribes evidently sought another means to express "to become." Their choice fell on the N stem of *epēšu*. The majority of passages, however, cannot be precisely rendered "become"; they pertain to those groups or persons who transferred their allegiance to one political factor or the other, usually the *ᶜapîru* ([SA.]GAZ) or, conversely, the king of Egypt. The best rendering is "to align oneself with, to join" (Moran 1987a). An example of this special idiom also illustrates the contrast between *bašû* and *nenpušu*:

> *gáb-‹bi›* URU.MEŠ-*ia ša i-na* ḪUR.SAG \ *ḫa-ar-ri ù i-na aḫi a-ia-ab* / *i-ba-aš-šu in-né-ep-šu a-na* ERÍN.MEŠ GAZ "All of my towns that are in the mountains and on the sea coast have committed themselves to the *ᶜapîrû*" (EA 74:19-21).

Moran (1950a:62) had recognized that both verbs were 3rd m.pl. (and not 3rd m.s. plus Akkadian subjunctive) and Youngblood (1961:138) remarked that they reflect the use of 3rd m.pl. for a feminine plural subject (*ālāniya* in Byblos is always treated as feminine! Albright 1943a:17; Moran 1950a:129 n. 149) in the Canaanite *qtl* conjugation pattern.

However, unlike *ibašši*, *nenpušu* is inflected both according to the prefix and the suffix conjugation patterns. The theme adopted for both patterns is, nevertheless, the same; it is the 3rd m.s. N stem preterite, *innepuš*. The initial syllable sign is *in* or EN, which latter has been uniformly transcribed *in*$_4$ in all our transliterations; ample justification for this practice is furnished by the spellings in EA 77:28 and EA 362:63; cf. below). Likewise, the second syllable sign is invariably NI, which has been transcribed here as *né*; the sign NE (Labat No. 173) is never used in the EA texts with the value *ne* (it often does appear with the old value *bí*), so there is no sound reason not to transcribe NI by *né* when grammar is in favor of it.

The majority of the attested forms from *nenpušu* show elision of the thematic vowel when vocalic suffixes are added, viz. 1st c.s. *in*$_4$*-né-ep-ša-ti*$_7$ (EA 297:12), 2nd m.s. *in*$_4$*-né-ep-ša-ta* (EA 333:18), 3rd f.s. *in-né-ep-ša-at* (EA 77:28), 3rd m.pl. *in-né-ep-šu* (EA 74:21), and *in*$_4$*-né-ep-šu* (EA 79:19; 81:41; *et al.*). On the other hand, there is 3rd f.s. *i-né-pu-ša-at* (EA 362:63), where the thematic vowel is not elided. Some prefix forms also drop the thematic vowel, e.g. 3rd f.s. *ti-né-ep-šu* (EA 8:33), 3rd m.pl. *ti-né-ep-šu* (EA 74:27; 76:42), while others do not: 3rd m.s. *yi-né-pu-ša* (EA 234:32), 3rd m.pl. *ti-né-pu-šu* (EA 73:32), and *te-né-pu-šu-na* (EA 138:83). It is hardly likely that those latter forms reflect the Akkadian present theme (*inneppuš-*); some scribes simply did not obey the rules of Akkadian phonology. The supposed preterite 3rd m.s. *yi-in*$_4$*-na-pí-iš* (EA 250:33) has been corrected by Moran (1987b:476 n. 4; 1992:304 n. 4) to *yi-in*$_4$-⸢*na*⸣-⸢*pí*⸣-⸢*il*⸣! Note also the use of the same theme for the 2nd m.pl. imperative *in-né-ep-šu* (EA 73:28; 81:12; Moran 1950a:150) and for a form which can hardly be anything else but an infinitive, *in*$_4$*-né-ep-ša* (EA 104:53; cf. *infra*, p. 377). The syntactic functions of the prefix forms have already been discussed (*supra*, pp. 123-126).

The most striking morphological feature of *nenpušu* is the use of hybrid forms from the suffix conjugation. Their semantic nuances and their syntactic contexts are illustrative of the role of the N stem from *epēšu* in the EA texts from Canaan. It is not surprising that one function is as the passive of the G stem, this in spite of the fact that G passives from *epēšu* do occur (cf. *supra*, pp. 77, 300-301, 304). Three passages with what must be taken as *qtl* forms illustrate this function, one from Hazor:

> [*ù*] *li-iḫ-šu-uš-mi* / \ *ia-az-ku-ur-mi* / ^{I}*šàr-ri* EN-*ia* / *mi-im-ma ša* / *in*$_4$*-né-pu-uš-mi* UGU ^{URU}*Ḫa-ṣú-ra*^{KI} / URU.KI-*ka ù* / UGU ÌR-*ka* "[So] may my king, my lord, remember everything that has been done against Hazor your city and against your servant" (EA 228:18-25; Rainey 1973c:252-253).

Another is in a somewhat broken context from Byblos:

> *i-na-an-na* / KÚR-*kùr-tu*$_4$^{MEŠ} ⸢*maš*⸣-*ši-ik-tu*$_4$ *it-ti-*[*ia*] ⸢*in*$_4$⸣-*né-pu-uš* "Now a vicious aggression has been perpetrated against [me]" (EA 92:11; Moran 1950a:161; Youngblood 1961:367; Rainey 1973c:252).

The third selection requires an obvious emendation:

> *al-lu-mi* ^{I}*Ri-ib-* ^{d}IŠKUR / *i-na qa-ti-ka ù mi-im-mu* / *ša* ‹*in*$_4$›*-né-ep-šu a-na ša-šu* UGU-⸢*ka*⸣ "Behold, Rib-Haddi is in your charge and everything that is/has been done to him is your responsibility" (EA 83:40-42; Moran 1950a:31; 1987b:265,266 n. 6; 1992:153, 154 n. 6; Youngblood 1961:317; cf. also Rainey 1973c:252).

The forms in EA 106:30-34 were evidently intended to be taken as prefix verbs (cf. *supra*, p. 124).

The meaning "to become" is actually rare. Two passages with that nuance evidently reflect what must have been a popular proverbial saying. The first example provides the only instance of the 1st c.s. suffix with this verb:

> *ša-ni-tam ù in*$_4$*-né-ep-ša-ti*$_7$ / *ki-ma ri-qí* URUDU \ *sí-ri* / *ḫu-bu-ul-li* / ⸢*iš*⸣-*tu qa-at* / LÚ.MEŠ ⸢*Su*⸣-*te*^{MEŠ} "Furthermore, so I have become like a damaged copper pot due to the Sutû" (EA 297:12-16; Rainey 1973c:251; 1989-90:71b-72a; contrast

Moran 1987b:522 n. 4, 527 n. 1; 1992:335 n. 4; Albright, Mendenhall and Moran 1955:490a);

The second example is in the 3rd f.s.:

> *a-mur ip-ši* / ^{I}*Pé-e-ia* DUMU ^{MÍ}*Gu-la-t*[*i*$_7$] / *a-na* ^{URU}*Gaz-ri* ^{MÍ}GEMÉ-*ti*$_7$ / *ša* LUGAL EN-*ia ma-ni* / UD.KÁM.MEŠ *yi-šal-la-l*[*u*]*-š*[*i*] / *ù in*$_4$*-né-ep-ša-at* [*ki-ma*] / *ri-qí ḫu-bu-l*[*i*] / *a-na ša-šu* "Behold the deed of Peʾya, son of Gulati, against Gaza, the handmaiden of the king, my lord; how long will he plunder it so that she becomes [like] a damaged pot because of him?" (EA 292:41-49; contra Moran 1987b:522 n. 4; 1992:335 n. 4).

A third example is from Byblos:

> *ù iq-bi a-na* LÚ.MEŠ [^{URU}*Baṭ-ru-n*]*a* / [*du-*]*ku-mi* EN-*ku-nu ù in*$_4$*-né-*[*ep-šu*] / [*a-na*] LÚ.MEŠ GAZ *ki-ma* ^{URU}*Am-m*[*i-ia*] / [*ù*] *in*$_4$*-né-ep-šu ar-‹nu› a-na* [*ia-ši*] "And he said to the men of [Baṭrun]a, 'Kill your lord and jo[in] the *ʿapîrû* men like Amm[iya]' [and] they became trai‹tors› to [me]" (EA 81:11-14; Rainey 1973c:252; Moran 1987b:261-262 n. 2; 1992:151 n. 2).

The 2nd m.pl. imperative *in*$_4$*-né-*[*ep-šu*] cited above reflects the third nuance for which *nenpušu* is best known in the EA texts from Canaan, viz. "to become (allied) with, to join." With this meaning there are nearly twenty examples of the suffix conjugation and ten examples of the prefix conjugation. Over a dozen of these verb forms reflect the defection of people or towns, i.e. political bodies, to the (SA.)GAZ = '*apîru*. That had led to the assumption that *nenpušu* in such contexts meant "to become (*ʿapîrû*)" (Liverani 1979). However, the other passages refer to defection to someone, including the speaker:

> *šum-ma-mi a-na-ku* / *uṣ-ṣú-na* UGU KUR / *ša* LUGAL *ù a-na ia-ši* / *in*$_4$*-né-ep-ša-ta* "If (when) I go forth against the land of the king, then will you be with me?" (EA 333:15-18; cf. Moran 1987b:551, 552 n. 7; 1992:356, 357 n. 7).

or to another person, such as ^{c}Abdi-Ashirta (cf. EA 79:18-26, 38-44 cited below) or his son Aziru (EA 138:93) or conversely, the king of Egypt:

> ˹*a*˺-˹*mur*˺-*mi a-na ú-mi tu-ṣú* / *ù i-né-pu-ša-at gáb-bi* / KUR.MEŠ *a-na* LUGAL *be-li-ia* "Behold, on the day that you come forth, then all the lands will become aligned with the king, my lord" (EA 362:62-64).

Moran (1987a) has pointed out that these latter prove conclusively that "to become" is impossible; the town or people cannot "become" ^{c}Abdi-Ashirta, Aziru or the king! Moran explains the nuance "to become (allied with)" as a corollary to the active use of *epēšu* with "city" as the object, with the meaning "to take over" (Moran 1987a:211; *CAD* E:202a, citing EA 174:22; 176:17; 179:17; 363:19 [all from the same scribe] plus Mari references]).

EA 148:45 and EA 79:24 are cited by Moran as additional examples of this idiom with G stem *epēšu*. The latter passage seems to reflect both the G and the N stem usages:

> [*šum-m*]*a ia-nu* ERÍN.MEŠ *pí-›pí‹*[*-ṭá-ti*] / *ù in*$_4$*-né-*˹*ep*˺*-šu ka-*[*li*] / [KUR.]MEŠ *a-na* LÚ.˹MEŠ˺ ˹GAZ˺.MEŠ *ši-me* / [*iš*]*-tu ṣa-ba-at* ^{URU}É-*A*[*r-ḫa*] / [*a-na*] *pí-i* ^{I}ÌR-*A-ši-ir-ta* / [*ù*] *ki-na-na tu-ba-ú-na* / [*i-p*]*é-ša* ^{URU}*Gub-la ù* / ^{URU}*Baṭ-ru-na*^{KI} *ù in*$_4$*-*[*né-ep-šu*] / *ka-li* KUR.KUR.MEŠ *a-na* LÚ.MEŠ GAZ.MEŠ . . . *ša-ni-tam* / [*šum-m*]*a la-a i-le-e* / [*šàr-r*]*u la-qa-ia ìš-tu* / [*qa-at*] *na-ak-ri-šu* / [*ù i*]*n*$_4$*-né-ep-ša-at* / [*ka-l*]*i* KUR.KI.MEŠ / [*a-na* ^{I}ÌR]-*A-ši-ir-ta* "[I]f there are no troops then al[l] the lands will become aligned with the ^{c}*apîrû* men. Listen! [Si]nce the capture of Bīt-A[rḫa] at the command of ^{c}Abdi-Ashirta, [then] thus they have been seeking [the take]over of Byblos and Baṭruna so that all the lands will [become aligned] with the ^{c}*apîrû* men . . . Furthermore, [if] the [kin]g is unable to rescue me from [the hand of] his enemies, [then] [al]l the lands will become aligned [with] ^{c}Abdi-Ashirta" (EA 79:18-26, 38-44; Moran 1987a:258; 1987b:259; 1992:149).

etpušu. Although there are some prefix examples of this verb with identical meaning to *nenpušu* (cf. *supra*, pp. 111-113), none of the examples can be assigned with certainly to the suffix conjugation pattern.

ḫatû. This verb, meaning "to smite" (*CAD* Ḫ:151a-152b; *AHw*:336b) seems to be represented once in what may be a conflation of a *ti-* prefix and a *-ti* suffix. The strange form appears in a Byblos letter:

> *ù an-nu-ú i-na-an-na ti-ir-bu* / *a-na* É*-ti ri-qí ga-mi-ir gáb-bu* / *ti-iḫ-ta-ti gáb-ba* "And now, you will enter an empty house, everything is used up, I am despoiled of everything" (EA 102:11-13; Albright 1941:48; Moran 1987b:296; 1992:175).

Support for the interpretation of *ti-iḫ-ta-ti* as a 1st c.s. suffix form comes from a similar construction, *ta-šap-pár-ta* in the previous line (EA 102:10; cf. *supra*, p. 60, *infra*, pp. 345-346).

riāḫu. With one exception, the forms of this verb in the Canaanite Amarna texts are hybrids of the suffix conjugation (Rainey 1971b:93-94; 1973c:255-256; cf. *supra*, p. 101).

It may be that the G preterite with infixed *-t-* was chosen as the theme for all forms in accordance with a known tendency among peripheral scribes to prefer *-t-* augmented forms for weak verbs (cf. Gordon 1938:215). Nevertheless, one cannot escape the impression that the Canaanite scribes associated some reflexive nuance, expressed by a Gt, with the stative concept, "to remain, to be left over."

That the forms in the Canaanite texts which do not have a consonantal prefix are to be reckoned as *qtl*'s is demonstrated by the 3rd f.s.:

> *ù ìl-qe* / [*ka*]*-li* URU.MEŠ*-ia* URU*Gub-la* / [*i*]*-na i-de-ni-ši ir-ti-ḫa-at* / [*a*]*-na ia-ši ù yu-ba-ú* [erasure] / *la-qa-ši* "and he has taken all of my towns; Byblos alone remains to me and he is seeking to take it" (EA 91:19-23; also EA 124:9-10).

Another example which has been taken for a dual because two towns are involved, might also be a defectively written 3rd f.s. since the normal rule with a feminine plural subject is either masculine plural or feminine singular (Moran 1950a:61). So the following rendering may be suggested:

> URU*Gub-la ù* ⌜URU⌝*Baṭ-ru*[*-na*] / [*ir-t*]*i-ḫa-‹at› a-na ia-ši ù* 2 ⌜URU⌝ ⌜*yu*⌝*-*[*ba*]*-ù* / [*la*]*-*⌜*qa*⌝*-a* "Byblos and Baṭruna remain to me and (these) two towns he is seeking to take " (EA 81:9-11).

The similar contexts with 3rd m.pl. forms must also be reckoned as *qtl*'s:

> URU*Gub-‹la› qa-du* 2 URU.MEŠ *ir-ti-ḫu a-na ia-ši* "Byblos with two towns remain to me" (EA 74:22); *a-nu-*⌜*ma*⌝ 2 URU *ša ir-ti-ḫu* / [*a*]-[*na*] *ia-ši yu-ba-ú la-qa* "Now he is seeking to take the two towns that remain to me" (EA 76:9-10); URU*Ṣu-mu-ru* / *ù* URU*Ir-qa-ta ir-ti-ḫu* / *a-na* LÚGAL "Ṣumur and ʿIrqata remain to the officer" (EA 103:11-13); *ka-li* / LÚ.MEŠ *ma-ṣa-ar-ti* / *ša-a ir-ti-ḫu mar-ṣa‹-at›* "All of the garrison troops that remain are ill (EA 103:47-49; Rainey 1973c:256 n. 101).

VERBS OF MOTION

(*w*)*aṣû*. Gt forms of this verb have been treated in an earlier chapter (cf. *supra*, pp. 82-83). There is one 3rd f.s. hybrid suffix form:

> *ù a-nu-ma iš-te-m*[*é*] / *ša*$_{10}$*-ri ša* LUGAL DÙG*-ta* / *ù it-ta-ṣa-at* / *a-na ia-ši ù pa-ši-iḫ* / *lìb-bi-ia ma-gal* "And now I have heard the sweet breath of the king, and it has come forth to me so that my heart is greatly relieved" (EA 297:16-21; Rainey 1971b:90; 1973c:256).

elû. For Gt forms of this verb within the prefix conjugation pattern, cf. *supra*, pp. 83-86. Some of those examples have a consonantal prefix but a few are characterized as prefix conjugation only by the indicative imperfect *-u* (EA 92:23; *114*:27; 127:31). However, there are a few others, all 3rd m.s., without any consonantal *y-* and with either *-Ø* or the Akkadian ventive, which seem to fill syntactic slots normally occupied by a *qtl*. One of these passages, with two examples, is a simple past narrative:

> [*šá-ni-t*]*am aš-tap-pár* LÚDUMU.KIN-*ia i-nu-ma* / [*ìl-q*]*é* URU.KI.ḪÁ-*ia ù i-te₉-la!-a*[*m*] / [*a-n*]*a ṣe-ri-ia ù a-nu-um-ma* / [*i-n*]*a-an-na ìl-qé* URU*Baṭ-ru-na* / ⌈*ù*⌉ *i-te-la-am a-na ṣe-ri-ia* / [*ma?*]-*ḫar* URU UGU! *pí* KÁ.GAL / [URU]*Gub-la* "[Furtherm]ore I have sent my emissary when he took my cities and came [aga]inst me and even now he has taken Baṭruna and he has come against me, [be]fore(?) the city, at the entrance of the city gate of Byblos" (EA 88:13-19; cf. Rainey 1975b:425 and nn. 253-258; Youngblood 1961:312-313; Moran 1987b:274, 275 nn. 2-3; 1992:160, 161 nn. 2-3).

The forms in question combine infixed *-t-* with the Akkadian ventive, both natural additions to this verb of motion; *ītelâm* and *ilqe* may be taken as purely Akkadian forms and *aštappar* is most probably Gtn preterite. Still, it would seem likely that the 3rd m.s. verbs are at least calques on Canaanite suffix forms.

In the next passages Moran (1987b:336; 1992:203) assumes that we have a conditional sentence. There is no conditional particle unless *a-nu-ma* is considered at error for *i-nu-ma*. Taken at face value, the passage and the following sentence would seem to represent straight narrative reporting. But if that should prove to be the case, then the "taking" of Byblos in the first clause would be an event not easy to identify in the course of Rib-Haddi's troubled career. However, the use of *a-di* "still, again" (= Heb. *'ôḏ*) in the next sentence does seem to suggest that we have here a series of events, not a hypothetical, conditional clause followed by a report:

> *a-nu-ma i-te₉-li* ERÍN.MEŠ *i-na* / URU*Gub-la ù la-qa-šiₓ*(ŠE) / *i-na-na a-di yu-pa-ḫi-ru ka-*[*li*] / URU.MEŠ *ù yi-ìl-qú-šiₓ*(ŠE)"Now,

the army came up against Byblos and took it; now he is again mustering al[l] the cities and he will take it" (EA 124:12-15).

Here *i-te*$_9$*-li* is in tandem with *la-qa-ši*$_x$(ŠE), a *qtl* verb. The next clause is in the WS indicative imperfect. Therefore, it is quite probable that *īteli*, in the mind of the scribe, is filling the syntactic slot of a *qtl*.

In the third passage, *ītela* and *ilteqe* are in the apodosis of a conditional sentence.

⌜*šum*⌝*-ma* 2 ITI.MEŠ *la-a tu*[*-ṣa-na*] / [ERÍN].MEŠ *pí-ṭá-ti ù i-te*$_9$*-la-*[*am!*] / [^{I}Ì]R-*A-ši-ir-ta ù il-te*$_9$*-qé* 2 U[RU] "If in two months the army does not come forth, then ᶜAbdi-Ashirta will come up and he will take the two to[wns]" (EA 81:45-47; Rainey 1973c:259).

The fact that the second verb can only be the Akkadian *-t-* preterite in form, precludes taking *i-te*$_9$*-la-*[*am*] as a defective writing for *ītellam*, the Akkadian Gt present. From the standpoint of Canaanite syntax, such Akkadian preterite forms can hardly be considered as anything else but calques for underlying WS *qtl* verbs.

erēbu. For this verb there are two 1st c.s. hybrids built on the Akkadian present as theme. They are in parallel passages from two of the Shechem letters (contrast the view expressed by Rainey 1973c:258):

an-nu-ú ar-nu-ia / *ù an-nu-ú* / ⌜*ḫi*⌝*-ṭú-ia i-nu-ma* / *ir-ru-ba-ti i-na* ^{URU}*Gaz-ri*^{KI} "Behold my crime and behold my sin, that I entered into Gezer" (EA 253:18-22); *ša-ni-tam* / *i*$_{15}$*-ba-aš-ši ar-ni-ia* / *i-nu-ma ir-ru-ba-ti* / *a-na* ^{URU}*Gaz-ri* "Furthermore, my crime is that I entered into Gezer" (EA 254:19-22)

In the light of these 1st c.s. hybrids, one must also consider the following example of what appears to be a simple Akkadian G preterite (cf. *supra*, p. 297):

> *li-il-ma-ad* LUGAL / EN-*ia i-nu-ma* / LÚŠEŠ-*ia* TUR.[TU]R / *na-ka-ar iš-tu* / *ia-ši u i-ru-ub* / *a-na* URU*Mu-*⌈*ú*ʾ⌉*-ḫa-zi* / *u na-da-an* 2 *qa-‹te›-šu* / *a-na* LÚ[S]A.GAZ.KI "May the king, my lord be apprised that my younger brother has become hostile to me and he has entered into Môḫazu and he has proffered his two ha‹nd›s to the ᶜ*apîrû*!" (EA 298:20-27).

Izreʾel (1978b:53) had noted that *i-ru-ub* was sandwiched between *na-ka-ar* and *na-da-an* and therefore, in the mind of the Gezer scribe it must have had the force of a *qtl*.

Of the forms with infixed *-t-* (cf. *supra*, pp. 86-87), only one may be suggested as a calque on the *qtl*. It is 3rd m.s. and lacks the consonantal prefix:

> *yi-de šàr-ru* EN-*li* / *i-nu-ma* I*Pu-ba-á*ʾ*-la* / IDUMU ÌR-*A-ši-ir-ta* / *i-te₉-ru-ub a-na* URU*Ul-la-sà* "May the king, my lord, be apprised that Pu-Baᶜla, the son of ᶜAbdi-Ashirta, has entered into Ullasa!" (EA 104:6-9).

OTHER VERBS

epēšu. Several forms from this verb have already been discussed (*supra*, p. 368). Here it remains to deal with a special 1st c.s. hybrid based on the Akkadian present rather than on the usual Akkadian stative theme:

> *ip-pu-uš-ti nu-kúr-ta* / *šal-ma-at a-na ia-ti-ia* / *šu-te-ra-at* URU.KI-*ia* / *a-na ia-ti-ia* "I made war, all is well with me, my town has been returned to me" (EA 280:12-15).

ezēbu. The remarkable point about the hybrids of this verb is that they also seem to be based on the Akkadian present rather than on the preterite. Shuwardata reported to Pharaoh that only he and three other rulers were still fighting on the king's side (EA 366:20-28), but as for his immediate colleagues, those who were supposed to be closely linked with him, they had all deserted his cause:

> *[l]u yi-ìl-ma-ad šàr-ru* / EN-*ia* ⌜*i*⌝*-nu-ma iz-zi-bu-ni* / *gáb-bi* ŠEŠ.ḪÁ-*ia* "[M]ay the king, my lord, be apprised that all my colleagues have abandoned me!" (EA 366:17-19; Rainey 1973c:260).

The form *izzibūni* with its geminated second radical is clearly expressing an action that has already taken place. Thus, it is on a par with *ibaššâti, izzizāti, irrubāti* and *ippušāti,* a calque on WS *qtl* built on the Akkadian present form. Therefore, it is probably justified to view the next form of *ezēbu* in the same light.

> *šum-ma* / *ti-iš-mu-na a-ṣí-mi* ERÍN.MEŠ / *pí-ṭá-ti ù i-zi-bu* URU.MEŠ-*šu-nu* / *ù pa-aṭ-ru* "If they hear 'The army has come forth,' they will leave their cities and depart" (EA 73:11-14; Rainey 1973c:259; Moran 1950a:149; Rainey 1989-90:58b; cf. *infra*, pp. 36, 370, 384).

The status and function of *paṭrū* is perfectly obvious. Syntactically it is WS *qtl* expressing a future action in the apodosis of a conditional sentence (Moran 1950a:74). The verb of the protasis is indicative imperfect, which imposes a future meaning on what follows (Moran 1950a:32-33). The parallelism between *i-zi-bu* and *pa-aṭ-ru* implies that the former is a calque on the WS *qtl.*

raʾāmu. This verb, "to love," reflects the stative nuance of personal commitment. Two forms in the EA texts from Canaan have been taken by *AHw*:952a as participles. It may be that the participle was chosen as the theme for some of the *qtl* forms. On the other hand, the tendency to preserve the *qatil* pattern must have been a factor. Note the singular:

> *a-nu-ma* URU.KI *mi-ši-i*[*l*]*-ši ra-im* / *a-na* DUMU.MEŠ ÌR-*A-ši-*⌜*ir*⌝*-ti ù mi-ši-il-ši* / *a-na be-li-ia* "Now, as for the city, half of it favors the sons of ᶜAbdi-Ashirta and half it (favors) my lord" (EA 138:71-73; Rainey 1973c:260).

There is also a plural:

> *ù gáb-bi* LÚ.MEŠ *ḫa-za-nu-te / la-a ra-i-mu i-nu-ma / tu-ṣú* ERÍN.MEŠ *pí-ṭá-tu / i-nu-ma pa-ši-iḫ a-na šu-nu / ù a-na-ku i-ba-ù a-ṣé-ši / i-nu-ma ma-ri-iṣ ia-a-ši* "But all the city rulers do not want that the army should come forth because it is well with them; I desire its coming forth because it is grievous for me" (EA 362:54-56; Rainey 1973c:260; 1978b:21).

The contrast between the *qtl* form *ra-i-mu* and the imperfect *i-ba-ú*, one governing a clause and the other an infinitive, serves to underscore the semantic nuance of *ra'āmu*, viz. "to want, desire."

Another shade of meaning is "to be loyal, to support." This is demonstrated by the nominal use of the participle in the following:

> *a-mur ma-á'-du /* LÚ.MEŠ *ra-i-mu-ia a-na lìb-bi* URU.KI / TUR LÚ.MEŠ *ša-ru-tu a-na lìb-bi-ši* "Behold, many are my supporters within the city (while) few are the wicked men within her" (EA 137:46-48; Rainey 1973c:260 n. 123).

Although there are some prefix hybrids of this verb such as the WS imperfects, 2nd m.s. *ta-ra-ia-mu* (EA 286:18), 3rd m.s. *i-ra-mu*, and the preterite 3rd f.s. *ti-ra-am* (EA 323:23), there is also one 3rd m.pl. Akkadian present form without a WS consonantal prefix that certainly would seem to be used as a calque on the stative *qtl*:

> *at-ta ú-ul / ti-i-de* KUR*A-mur-ri i-nu-ma / a-šar da-an-ni ti-la-ku-na / ù an-nu-uš i-na-an-na / [ú]-ul i-ra-a-mu a-na* IÌR-*A-ši-ir-ta* "Don't you know Amurru, that they always follow the strong one? But now, they don't favor ᶜAbdi-Ashirta!" (EA 73:14-18; Rainey 1973c:261).

With the above-cited passage in mind, it is worth considering some other Akkadian prefix forms which probably are functioning within the framework of WS syntax as calques on the *qtl* pattern.

The clearest context with 3rd m.s. is:

> [*šum-*]*ma i-ra-am šà*[*r-ru*] / [E]N-*li* ÌR *ki-t*[*i-šu*] / [*ù*] *uš-ši-ra* / [3] LÚ *ù ib-lu-ṭa* / *ù i-na-ṣí-ra* / URU *a-na šàr-ri* "[I]f the ki[ng,] my lord, cares for [his] loy[al] servant, [then] send [three] men that I may live and that I will protect the city for the king" (EA 123:22-28; cf. also EA 89:63; 121:61).

The form could represent the Akkadian G present (or preterite for that matter). In the protasis of a conditional sentence, the texts from Canaan usually have either the WS imperfect, *yaqtulu*, or a stative of the suffix conjugation. This particular context, with the verb *ra'āmu* "to love," would be quite appropriate for the use of the suffix stative form.

Other 3rd m.pl. examples of this verb, based on the Akkadian present theme, are:

> *ù* / *pa-aṭ-ra-ti qa-du* LÚ.MEŠ / *ša i-ra-a-mu-ni* "and I will depart with the men who support me" (EA 83:49-51); *ù gáb-bi* LÚ.MEŠ *i-ra-'a*$_4$*-mu-šu* "and all the men like him" (EA 106:40; cf. EA 110:3).

If one must reckon these verbs forms as Akkadianisms, at least one may presume that they are most likely fulfilling the syntactic function of an underlying Canaanite verb which operated something like Hebrew *ʾāhôḇ*, which exhibits both stative *ʾāhēḇ*, and transitive *ʾôhēḇ* as well as other related finite forms (Young 1952-1953).

šapāru. There is the unusual passive form, *a-na mi-ni*$_7$ *ta-šap-pár-ta* "Why were you sent?" (EA 102:10; Moran 1950a:163). And in addition, one also finds instances of stock expressions such as *ša iš-pu-ur* / LUGAL EN-*ia* "that the king, my lord sent" (EA 292:18-19) where the Akkadian preterite is most likely a calque on the WS *qt*. Parallel passages can also have a suffix form in place of the preterite: *ša ša-pár* / L[UGAL] EN-*ia* (EA 320:18-19; 211:10-11). In the mind of the Canaanite scribe, the verbal form represented a single, specific instance in the past (Izre'el 1978b:55, §7.1.1, 61, §7.2.3.1).

CONCLUDING OBSERVATIONS

It has been noted above that the Cananite scribes demonstrate a surprising knowledge of the function and use of the Akkadian preformative statives, especially *ibašši* and its various conjugation forms for other persons. One might even cite the evidence for forms like *ibaššāti*, etc., as further corroboration of the view that the preformative statives were truly recognized as a special case by the original Mesopotamian grammatical tradition. The opposite side of the coin is that the scribes of Assyria and Babylonia in the previous and contemporary periods did not use a stative, *baši*, *bašâku*, etc.

The underlying question that recurs with every discussion of a peculiarity like this one in the Canaanites' Akkadian interlanguage is that of origins. When and where did the scribes of Canaan learn to write Akkadian? Obviously, their original teachers had brought to them a very sophisticated knowledge of the finer nuances of Akkadian grammar and syntax.

These hybrid forms, which caught the eye of the earlier grammarians from the very beginning of Amarna studies, can be seen today as a tantalizing indication, not only of the Canaanite scribes' comprehension of their originally acquired Akkadian (i.e. Old Babylonian) but also as a testimony to their productivity in the generation of analogous forms for verbs other than *ibašši* and *izuzzu*. Throughout this and previous chapters, the question has arisen concerning Akkadian 3rd m.s. and 3rd m.pl. prefix forms from various verbs and stems to which the WS prefixes, *y*- and *t*-, have not been added. Frequently, it has been sugested that such forms were calques for WS suffix verbs (Izre'el 1978b:55, §7.1.1, 61, §7.2.3.1).

CHAPTER XIV

SUFFIX CONJUGATION — SYNTAX

With all the attention given to the morphology of the suffix conjugation in the EA letters, a syntactical analysis was not attempted until the work of Moran (1950a:28-34; 1961:64-65 = 1965:74-75). Though he restricted himself to the Byblos letters, his observations hold true for the other EA texts from Canaanite scribes.

It will become clear in the following discussion that the *qtl* conjugation pattern did not serve primarily to express completed action. The suffix conjugation will be seen to fulfill various functions, some of them past, some present, some future. Many of the syntagmas are indicative but others are modal, injunctive or optative.

The picture that emerges from this fourteenth century B.C.E. corpus of texts is that *qtl* is in the process of taking over various functions that originally had been fulfilled by the prefix conjugation patterns. The seeming parity, or polarity, between a prefix conjugation, and a suffix conjugation is illusory. Each developed from different origins and different linguistic needs. Only gradually did the NWS dialects arrive at the stage reflected in biblical Hebrew, ancient Phoenician and Moabite. Ugaritic and the EA texts from Canaan reflect a somewhat earlier stage.

As with all other facets of these documents, the symbiosis of east Semitic and west Semitic must be taken into account. The scribes were aware of the accepted Akkadian functions of the suffix conjugation and the differences between that and their native Canaanite was never far from their thinking. The degree that they played on one wavelength or the other is what makes the linguistic study of these letters so fascinating.

The various syntagmas in which suffix forms are employed in these texts will be dealt with in terms of their tense nuances, past, present or future.

PAST TENSE

Moran's survey of the Byblos evidence did reveal a preference for *qṭl* in past tense declarations (Moran 1950a:30). There are, to be sure, a certain number of prefix preterites in the Byblos letters (cf. *supra*, pp. 222-227). However, there are many more *qtl*'s in this preterite function, and in a few crucial expressions the Byblos scribe prefers *qtl* where other scribes use the *yqtl* preterite.

TRANSITIVES. A typical example is the ubiquitous context in which a vassal acknowledges a message from the king. Most Canaanite examples have a prefix form with infixed *-t-* from *šemû* "to hear, to heed," e.g from Beirut:

> *šá-ni-tam iš-te-me a-wa-te*^{MEŠ} ⸢DUB⸣ *ša šàr-ri* EN-*ia* "Furthermore, I have heard the words of the tablet of the king, my lord" (EA 141:8-9; also EA 234:8; 254:6; 292:17-19; 302:14; 328:21; 364:10; *et al.*; cf. *supra*, pp. 225-226; Rainey 1971c:97-101).

By contrast, the same stereotyped response in a letter from Byblos is formulated thus:

> *a-nu-ma ša-mi-ti*$_7$ *a-wa-te*^{MEŠ} / LUGAL EN-*ia* "Now I have heard the words of the king, my lord" (EA 362:5-6; cf. *supra*, p. 302).

The great majority of past tense narrative forms of *qtl* are, as in the syntagmas discussed above, transitives. The contrast between a past action and a current action is illustrated by the following:

> *ù a-mur* ^{I}*I-ta-ak*!(AT)*-ka-ma* / *ḫu-li-iq* ^{KUR}*Qì-is-sà u an-nu-ú* / ^{I}*Ar-za-wi-ya qa-du* ^{I}*Bi-ri-da-aš-wa* / *yu-ḫa-li-qú* ^{KUR}*A-pí* "And behold, Etakkama has caused the loss of Kedesh and behold, Arzawiya, with Biridashwa, is causing the loss of the land of Api" (EA 197:31-34; Rainey 1975b:418; cf. Moran 1987b:289 n. 1,

436 n. 6; 1992:170-171 n. 1, 275 n. 6; Greenberg 1955:44; contra Gevirtz 1973a:100-101).

Likewise, a passage from a Byblos letter:

> *ù an-nu-ú i-na-na* / *nu*-KÚR [I]*Ia-pa*- [d]IŠKUR *it-ti* [I]*A-zi-ri* / *a-na ia-ši ù al-lu-ú ṣa-bat* [GIŠ]MÁ-*ia* / *ù al-lu-ú ki-na-na-ma yi-te$_9$-lu* / *i-na* ⸢*lìb*⸣-*bi a-ia-ba aš-šum ṣa-ba-at* / [GIŠ]MÁ.MEŠ-*ia* "And behold now, Yapa^c-Haddi is hostile with Aziru against me and, behold, he seized my ship and, behold, likewise, he is going out to sea in order to seize my ships" (EA 114:15-20).

There one finds the stative *nu*-KÚR (or: *nu-kúr*) in present tense, the transitive *ṣa-bat* for single instance in the past (seizing only one ship) and the imperfect *yi-te$_9$-lu* to express the present continuous action.

VERBS OF MOTION. Another familiar context is the obeisance formula so prevalent in the introduction to epistles throughout the peripheral area, viz.

> *a-na* KI.TA / GÌR.MEŠ BE-*ia 7 u 7 am-qut* [ut] "At the feet of my lord seven times and seven times I have fallen" (EA 126:2-3; Salonen 1967:66-71).

A small handful of texts, one or perhaps two from Beirut and five or six from somewhere in southern Canaan (Na$^{\supset}$aman 1979:676-677), substitute a suffix form for the almost universally attested Akkadian preterite *amqut* "I have/am fallen." The documented *qtl* examples are:

> *a-na* GÌR.MEŠ [I]*šàr-ri* EN-*ia am-qut* / 7 *ù* 7 *mi-la-an-na* / *ma-aq-ta-ti a-na* GÌR.MEŠ *šàr-ri* EN-*ia* "At the feet of the king, my lord, I have fallen, seven times and seven times have I fallen at the feet of the king, my lord" (EA 283:4-6; also EA 63:6, 65:5; 282:4; 336:5); *a-na* KI.TA GÌR.MEŠ LUGAL EN-*li-i*[*a*] / *7-tam ù* 7 ⸢*ma*⸣-*aq-ta-ti$_7$* "Beneath the feet of the king, my lord, seven times

and seven times have I fallen" (EA 138:3-4; probably also EA 137:3-4).

Two texts employ the unusual form *ma-aq-ti-ti* (EA 64:5; 284:4, 5, 22). The Ugaritic translations of this formula also use a *qtl* conjugation with forms from **qyl* "to fall" (probably cognate to Akkadian *qiʾālu*, von Soden 1967:295-296, cf. *CAD* Q:75b-76a), viz. *qlt* = **qilti(?)* "I have fallen" (*KTU* 2.12:11; *et al.*), *qlny* "we have fallen" (*KTU* 2.11:7; *et.al.*).

Note the following verbs of motion in past narration, the first in *qtl*, the second in *yqtl* preterite:

> *ù al-ka-ti / a-na* É-*šu aš-šum / e-pu-uš* DÙG.GA *bi-ri-‹nu› / ù a-na-ku a-tu-ur a-na* É-*ia* "So I went to his place in order to make a friendship treaty with him, then I returned to my place" (EA 136:30-33; Moran 1987b:356 n. 5; 1992:217 n. 5).

STATIVE. Stative and passive *qtl*'s can also be in past tense, of course. An example of *ibašši* has been noted:

> *šá-ni-tam yi-il*$_{5}$*-ma-ad* LUGAL EN-*ia* / *i*$_{15}$*-pí-iš* ŠEŠ-*šu ša* *i*$_{15}$*-ba-aš-*⸢*ša*⸣ / *i-na* ^{URU}*Gub-la i-nu-ma na-*⸢*da*⸣*-[an]* / DUMU.DUMU.MEŠ *ša* ^{I}*Ri-*⸢*ib*⸣*-*⸢^{d}⸣⸢IŠKUR⸣ / ⸢*ša*⸣! *i*$_{15}$*-ba-aš-šu it-ti-*⸢*šu*⸣! / *a-na* LÚ.MEŠ *ar-nu-*⸢*ti*⸣! ⸢*ša*⸣ / *šàr-ri ša i-na* ^{KUR}*A-*⸢*mur*⸣*-r[i]* "Furthermore, may the king, my lord, learn the deed of his brother who is in Byblos, that he has handed over the sons of Rib-Haddi who were with him(!) to the traitors to the king who are in the land of Amurru" (EA 142:18-24; Rainey 1973c:249 n. 68, 262; cf. *supra*, pp. 320-321).

The 3rd m.s. *i*$_{15}$*-ba-aš-*⸢*ša*⸣ is present tense, but in the object clause, past tense transitive *na-*⸢*da*⸣*-[an]* is paralleled by past tense (actually past perfect!) 3rd m.pl. *i*$_{15}$*-ba-aš-šu*. The following example is also in a subordinate clause:

> *ti-i-de pa-ar-ṣa-ia / i-nu-ma i-ba-ša-ta i-na /* ⸢^{URU}⸣⸢*Ṣu*⸣*-mu-ra* "You know my behavior when you were in Ṣumur" (EA 73:39-41).

The intransitive *ḫadû* "to rejoice" can appear in the same syntagma as a prefix or as a suffix conjugation verb. Compare the parallel passages from identical contexts as formulated in two different epistles, both written in Beirut:

> *ù en-du-um* / [*iš*]-*te-me a-wa-te*MEŠ DUB LUGAL EN-*ia* / *ù yi-iḫ-di* ŠÀ-*ia ù* / [*i*]*n*₄-*nam-mu-ru* 2 IGI.MEŠ *ma-gal* "And when [I] heard the words of the tablets of the king, my lord, then my heart rejoiced and my eyes brightened greatly" (EA 142:7-10; also EA 144:15); *šá-ni-tam iš-te-me* / *a-wa-te*MEŠ ⌜DUB⌝ *ša šàr-ri* EN-*ia* . . . *ù ḫa-di* ŠÀ ÌR-*ka* "Furthermore, I heard the words of the tablet of the king, my lord, . . . and the heart of your servant rejoiced" (EA 141:8-11; also EA 209:7).

A Tyrian letter uses 1st c.s. *ḫa-ad-ia-ti* in the same context (EA 147:25-27).

The stative *qtl* is especially functional in expressing a state of affairs which prevailed for some time in the past. This is especially clear when the clause in question is introduced by *pānānu* "Formerly." Note the following:

> [*a*]-*mur pa-na-nu* LÚ.MEŠ *a-bu-ti-ia* / ⌜*da*⌝-*nu nu*-KÚR *a-na ša-šu*-⌜*nu*⌝ / [*ù*] *ma-ṣa-ar-ti* / [LUGAL] *it*-‹*ti*›-*šu-nu ba-l*[*a-aṭ*] / [LUGAL] UGU-*šu-nu* "Behold, formerly, as regards my fathers, hostilities were strong against them, [but] the [king's] garrison was with them, [the king's] pro[visions] were (provided) for them" (EA 130:21-25; Moran 1950a:124a n. 104); [*pa*]-*na-nu* URUṢ*u-mu-ra ù* LÚ.MEŠ[-*ši*] / [*da*]*n-nu*-⌜*tu*₄⌝ ⌜*i*⌝-*ba-aš-šu ù* LÚ.[MEŠ] / [*ma*-]⌜*ṣa*⌝-*ar*-⌜*tu*⌝ *it-ti-nu* "Formerly, Ṣumur and [its] men were strong and garrison troops were with us" (EA 81:48-50; *CAD* D:99b-100a; Moran 1987b:261; 1992:151; in 1950a:124a, Moran still classed *ibašši* as a present; cf. also EA 112:50-53; 121:11-15).

A stative can also express a situation which, while perhaps obtaining at the present, was the result or continuation of what had prevailed for a considerable time:

> *[lu-ú]* / ⸢*i*⸣*-de* LUGAL EN-*li i-nu-[ma]* / *šal-ma-at* URU*Gub-la* GE[MÉ-*ka*] / ⸢*iš*⸣*-tu*!(IŠ) *da-ri-it* UD.[KÁM.]MEŠ "May the king, my lord, be apprised that Byblos, [your] hand[maiden], has been at peace since of old" (EA 75:7-9; cf. Youngblood 1961:160; Rainey 1973c:241; Moran 1987b:254 n. 1; 1992:146 n. 1).

From these passages it may be seen that even something that had taken place in the past was not necessarily viewed as punctiliar.

One final text will illustrate the nuances possible with transitive *qtl*, passive *qtl* and stative *qtl* (in circumstantial function) interwoven with the imperfect for repeated action in the past:

> *a-nu-ma* / [PN] DUMU *ši-ip-ri-[ia]* / *[uš]-ši-ir-ti-šu ù aš-ta-ni* / *[m]a-ni* / UD.KÁM.MEŠ *ú-wa-ši-ru-šu* / *ù la-a yi-le-ú* / *i-re-ba a-na* URU*Ṣu-mu-ra ša-ab-tu* / *ka-li* KASKAL.MEŠ *a-na ša-a-šu* / *a-na nu-*KÚR *ša-a* UGU-*ia ù* UGU / URU*Ṣu-mu-ra šu-ut i-da-gal* / 2 ITU *a-ši-ib it-ti-ia* "Now, as for [PN], [my] emissary, I [s]ent him repeatedly—how many times did I send him and he was unable to enter Ṣumur? All the routes to it have been seized through the hostilities against me and against Ṣumur. He has seen two months while sitting with me" (EA 114:32-41; contrast Moran 1987b:316; 1992:188-189).

PRESENT TENSE

In view of the function of the stative suffix conjugation in classical Akkadian and also in ancient Egyptian, it should not be surprising that the present tense should be represented in the texts from Canaan written under the influence of West Semitic. Practically all of the *qtl* forms expressing present tense are statives or passives. In fact, Moran (1950a:30) only found one active verb in present tense:

> *ka-li* / LÚ.MEŠ GAZ.MEŠ *it-ti-šu* / *ù* LÚ.MEŠ *ḫa-za-nu-tu ú-ul* / *ti-iš-mu-na mi-im-ma* / *ù šap-ru a-na ša-a-šu* "All the ᶜ*apîrû* men are with him and the city rulers don't hear anything but what they write to him" (EA 82:8-12).

Some glosses are stative presents, e.g. *ṣí-ir-ti* "I am pressed" (EA 127:34); *ši-ir-ti* "I am slandered" (EA 252"14). Typical present tense statives in declarative sentences are:

> *ti-de i‹-nu-ma›* / LÚGAL *ù* LÚ.MEŠ *be-li* URU-*lì* / *šal-mu it-ti* ⌈DUMU⌉.MEŠ ÌR-*Aš-ra-ta* "May you be apprised t‹hat› the officer and the nobles of the city are at peace with the sons of ᶜAbdi-Ashirta!" (EA 102:21-23); *yi-de-mi šàr-ru* EN-*ia* / *i-nu-ma šal-ma-at* URU.KI-⌈*šu*⌉ "May the king, my lord, know that his city is at peace!" (EA 226:67; cf. EA 68:10; 144:11; 257:10; 268:9).

The contrast between stative *qtl* and transitive *yaqtulu* imperfect is clearly illustrated in the following:

> *ù gáb-bi* LÚ.MEŠ *ḫa-za-nu-te* / *la-a ra-i-mu i-nu-ma* / *tu-ṣú* ERÍN.MEŠ *pí-ṭá-tu* / *i-nu-ma pa-ši-iḫ a-na šu-nu* / *ù a-na-ku i-ba-ù a-ṣé-ši* / *i-nu-ma ma-ri-iṣ ia-a-ši* "But all the city rulers do not want that the army should come forth because it is tranquil for them; I desire its coming forth because it is grievous for me" (EA 362:54-56; Rainey 1973c:260; 1978b:21).

An even more striking contrast concerns essentially the same verb form, a *qtl* of the Š stem; *šūšerāku*/*šūširāku* can have stative/passive meaning, "I am prepared" (EA 141:24; 142:25), or it can be transitive with past tense reference, "I have prepared" (EA 191:14). And in one context it appears in both nuances:

> *ù i-de* / LUGAL *i-nu-ma šu-še-ra-ku i-na* / *pa-ni* ERÍN.MEŠ *pí-ṭá-ti* LUGAL EN-*ia* / *šu-ši-ra-ku gáb-ba ki-ma qa-bi* LUGAL EN-*ia* "So may the king be apprised that I am prepared in anticipation of the army of the king, my lord! I have prepared everything according to what the king, my lord, commanded" (EA 144:18-21).

Here one must note the numerous impersonal statives (Moran 1950a:64-65). Two are cited in the passage above, *pa-ši-iḫ a-na šu-nu* "it is tranquil for them" (EA 362:57; cf. EA 297:20), and *ma-ri-iṣ ia-a-ši* "it is grievous for me" (EA 362:59; cf. EA 84:24-25; 103:7-8; 114:50; 116:54-55; 131:26). Another is *damiq;* one such example underscores the difference between stative verbs in *qtl* and transitives in *yaqtulu*:

> *ša-ni-tam da-mi-iq i-na pa-ni / šàr-ri ša ki-ma* ^{d}⌜IŠKUR⌝ / *ù* ^{d}UTU *i-na ša-me i-ba-ši / ù ti-pu-šu-na* DUMU.MEŠ / ^{I}ÌR-*A-ši-ir-ta ki-ma / lìb-bi-šu-nu* "Furthermore, is it pleasing to the king, who is like Baal and Shamash in heaven, that the sons of ᶜAbdi-Ashirta are doing as they please?" (EA 108:8-13).

A present state may be the result of a process that has been going on in the past:

> *a-nu-ma a-na-ku la-a e-la-ú-mi / i-re-ba a-na* KUR.MEŠ *Mi-iṣ-re-e / ši-ba-ti ù mur-ṣú dan-nu / a-na* UZU *ra-ma-ni-ia* "I am unable to enter into Egypt; I am old and my own flesh has a grievous sickness" (EA 137:27-30).

The hybrid stative *ši-ba-ti* could be rendered "I have become old." Moran (1950a:29) noted a number of other clear examples of this type:

> *ù an-nu-ú i-na-an-na ti-ir-bu / a-na* É-*ti ri-qí ga-mi-ir gáb-bu / ti-iḫ-ta-ti gáb-bu* "Behold, now, you will enter an empty house; everything is used up, I am wholly ruined" (EA 102:11-13); *ù a-nu-ma i-na-an-na ši-iḫ-ṭá-at /* ^{URU}*Ṣu-mu-ur a-di a-bu-li-ši* "And even now, Ṣumur is ravaged up to its city gate" (EA 106:10-11; cf. *CAD* A/1:84).

It should be clear that the stative nuance of *qtl* in the EA texts from Canaan correlates positively with the norm for the suffix conjugation in Akkadian and, from the standpoint of tense, with the function of the same conjugation pattern in classical Egyptian. Stative verbs generally appear in the suffix conjugation pattern to express a present situation. They can, of course, serve to express a state that prevailed in the past. Transitives and verbs of motion, on the other hand, do not normally express present tense by means of the suffix forms.

FUTURE TENSE

The most fascinating usage of the suffix conjugation is for actions or states to be accomplished in the future. There are several specific syntagmas in which a *qtl* verb has future reference. Moran (1950a:30-34) had defined these syntactic functions for the Byblos texts and his categories hold true for the rest of the corpus.

PROTASES. There are over a dozen instances in which *qtl* conjugation forms (including Akkadian prefix statives) appear in the protasis of a conditional sentence. Nearly all of them are stative in nuance and refer to present-future.

There are three examples of *ibašši*:

> *ù šum-ma* ERÍN.MEŠ *pí-ṭ[á-ti]* / *i-ba-ša-at ka-li* KUR.MEŠ / *ni-ìl-qú a-na šàr-ri* "But if there will be regular troops, we will take all the lands" (EA 103:55-57); *šum-ma i-ba-aš-ši* LÚERÍN.MEŠ *pi-ṭa-ti* / *i-na* MU *an-ni-ti i-ba-as-ši* KUR.ḪÁ / LUGAL EN‹*-ia*› "But if there will be regular troops this year, the lands of the king will remain (his)" (EA 286:57-59; cf. also EA 289:15-17).

One passage has the impersonal *damiq*:

> *ù šum[-ma] da-mi[-iq]* / *i-na pa-ni-ka ù* / *š[u]-ku-un i-na* / LÚMAŠKÍM*-ši* DUGUD *i-n[a]* / *pa-ni* LÚ.MEŠ *ḫa-za-nu-ti* LU[GAL] "And if it be amenable to you, then appoint as commissioner one who is respected by the king's city rulers" (EA 107:20-24; Moran 1975a:155; 1987b:304, 305 n. 2; 1992:181 and n. 2).

Two conditional sentences have prefix stative forms of *leʾû* (cf. *supra*, pp. 331-332). These are in contrast to the usual WS imperfect forms of this verb:

> *[šum-m]a la-a i-le-e* / *[šàr-r]u la-qa-ia ì-š-tu* / *[qa-at] na-ak-ri-šu* / *[ù i]n$_4$-né-ep-ša-at* / *[ka-l]i* KUR.KI.MEŠ / *[a-na* ^{I}ÌR]-*A-ši-ir-ta* "[I]f [the kin]g is unable to deliver me from his enemies, [then al]l the lands will [j]oin ʿAbdi-Ashirta" (EA 79:39-44; also EA 92:51).

Likewise, there is what appears to be a calque on the *qtl* from the WS verb that corresponds to *raʾāmu* "to love, prefer, like" (cf. *supra*, pp. 343-345):

> *[šum-]ma i-ra-am* ⌜*šàr*⌝-*[ru]* / [E]N-*li* ÌR *ki-t[i-šu]* / *[ù] uš-ši-ra* / [3] LÚ *ù ib-lu-ṭá* / *ù i-na-ṣí-ra* / URU *a-na šàr-ri* "[I]f the ki[ng], my [l]ord, loves [his] faithful servant, [then] send [three] men and that I may live and that I may protect the city for the king" (EA 123:23-28).

Two other passages deal with someone's possible death, obviously a reference to something in the future:

> *[šum-ma] at-ta mi-[t]a-t[a ù]* / *[a-na-ku]* BA.UG$_7$-*at* "[If] you ⌜die⌝, [then I] will die" (EA 87:30-31); *šum-ma mi-ta-ti mi-na* / *i-pu-‹šu›-na* "If I should die, then what could I do?" (EA 119:17-18).

Another pair of contexts contain the 2nd m.s. of *qâlu* "to keep silent":

> *šum-ma ki-a-ma qa-la-ta* / *a-di ti-ìl-qú-na* / ^{URU}*Ṣu-mu-ra ù* / ›*ù*‹ *ti-du-ku-na* ^{LÚ}MAŠKÍM / *ù* ERÍN.MEŠ *til!*(BI)-*la-ti* / *ša i-na Ṣu-mu-ra* "If thus you keep silent until they take Ṣumur, then they will slay the commissioner and the auxiliary troops that are in Ṣumur" (EA 104:31-36); *šum-ma i-na-na* / *qa-la-ta ù* ^{I}*Pi-ḫu-ra* / *la-a yi-zi-za i-na* / ^{URU}*Ku-mì-di u ka-li* LÚ.MEŠ / *[ḫ]a-za-ni-ka tù-da-ku[-na]* "If now you keep silent and Paḫura does not take up a position in Kômidi, then all the city rulers will be killed" (EA 132:46-50; Rainey 1989-90:62).

Especially noteworthy is the *qtl* of *zêru* "to hate," since it is a transitive verb. The time reference is present-future:

> *šum-ma* LUGAL / *za-ir* URU.K[I]-*šu ù i-zi-ba-ši* "If the king should hate his city, then I would abandon it" (EA 126:44-45; Rainey 1989-90:61a; *contra* Moran 1987b:340, 341 n. 7; 1992:206, 206-207 n. 7).

There are two passages which could have past tense reference in the protasis. One has a verb of motion, *paṭāru* "to depart (fall away)."

> *ša-ni-tam šum-ma / ap-pu-na-ma a-nu-ma pa-aṭ-ra* / URUṢ[*u*-]*mu-ra ù* URUÉ-*Ar*-[*ḫ̮*]*a* / ⌜*yi*⌝!(UT)-*din-ni i-na qa-at* / I*a-an-ḫ̮a-mi ù ia-ti-na* / ŠE.*IM*.ḪÁ *a-na a-ka-li ia-ši* "Furthermore, if, moreover, now Ṣumur and Bit-Arkha have defected, let him assign me to the charge of Yanḫamu that he may issue grain for me to eat" (EA 83:27-32; cf. Moran 1987b:265 n.2; 1992:154 n. 2; Youngblood 1961:248).

And finally, there is one example of a transitive verb which can most easily be rendered as a past tense, thus making an unreal condition. Nevertheless, it could also be interpreted as a future:

> *ša-ni-tam ki-i*15 *šum*[-*m*]*a* / *a-na* DAM-*ia ša-pár šàr-ru* / *ki-i*15 *a-kal-lu-ši ki-i*15 / *šum-ma a-na ia-ši* / *ša-pár šàr-ru* / *šu-ku-un* GÍR ZABAR / *i-na lìb-bi-ka ù* / BA.UG7 *ki-i*15 *la-a* / *ip-pu-šu ši-pí-ir-ti šàr-ri* "Furthermore, how, if for my wife the king had written, how could I withhold her? Because if the king had written to me 'Put a bronze dagger into your heart and die,' how could I not carry out the directive of the king?" (EA 254:38-46; cf. Rabiner 1981:95).

The same problem with regard to the determination of tense pertains to the following conditional sentence which is not introduced by *šumma*:

> *ma-an-nu* LÚ-*lu*$_4$ / *ù ša-pár* LUGAL / EN-*šu a-na ša-*[*šu*] / *ù la-a yi-iš-*⌜*mu*⌝*-mi* "Who is the man, (who) if the king has written/should write to him, who would not heed?" (EA 232:12-15; Rabiner 1981:95)

APODOSES. There are over twenty examples of suffix conjugation verb forms in the apodosis of a conditional sentence (for Byblos, cf. Moran 1950a:74; for elsewhere cf. Albright 1942b:34 n. 16 who cites *GKC* 496, §159q for Hebrew). In such contexts as these there can be no question that the reference is to the future. Moran (1950a:75) has noted that the conditional sentence in West Semitic is essentially two independent clauses which explains why, unlike Akkadian, the apodosis is so frequently joined by the conjunction. When the conjunction is missing, the apodosis is usually injunctive (e.g. EA 112:30-39) or interrogative (e.g. EA 112:16-18). The conjunction is normal, however, when the verb of the apodosis is from the suffix conjugation.

Exceptions to this latter rule are known from the Jerusalem letters. Note that the employment of a gloss in the first example cited below is especially worthy of note; it confirms that a suffix conjugation form in the apodosis is an original feature of the native WS dialect of the scribe:

> [*ù*] *šum-ma ia-a-nu-mi* ERÍN.MEŠ *pi-ṭa-tu*$_4$ / *i-na* MU *an-ni-ti ḫal-qa-at a-ba-da-at* / \ *gáb-bi* KUR.ḪÁ *šàr-ri* EN-*ia* "[But] if there are no regular troops this year, all the lands of the king, my lord, are lost" (EA 288:51-53); *ù šum-ma ia-a-nu* ERÍN.MEŠ *pi-ṭa-tu*$_4$ / *pa-ṭa-ra-at* KUR *šàr-ri a-na* LÚ.MEŠ / \ *ḫa-pí-ri* "But if there are no regular troops, the land of the king will defect to the *ʿapîrû* men" (EA 290:22-24); *šum-ma i-ba-aš-ši* LÚ.ERÍN.MEŠ *pi-ṭa-ti* / *i-na* MU *an-ni-ti i-ba-aš-ši* KUR.ḪÁ / LUGAL EN-‹*ia*› *ù šum-ma ia-a-nu-mi* LÚ.ERÍN *pi-ṭa-ti* / [*ḫ*]*al-qa-at* KUR.ḪÁ LUGAL EN-*ia* "If there are regular troops in this year, the lands of the king, ‹my› lord, will still be (his), but if there are no regular troops, the lands of the king, my lord, will be lost" (EA 286:57-60).

The use of the conjunction to introduce the apodosis is the general rule. This function is also known elsewhere in some other Akkadian dialects (OA — Hecker 1968:235-236, §138a; OB Mari — Finet 1956:225-226 §§82c-f), especially the peripheral (Nuzi — Gordon 1938:229; Mitanni — Adler 1976:79; Alalakh — Giacumakis 1970:63; Carchemish — Huehnergard 1979:124-125; Egypt — Cochavi-Rainey 1988:232-233, §2.10.1; Amurru — Izre'el 1985:334-335, §4.6.1; 1991a:326, §4.6.1; Ugarit — Huehnergard 1979:330-331 and n. 580; 1989:242). The following passage is unusual in that the verb of the protasis is a preterite and thus shows that the condition is not referable to the future. The apodosis, with a stative of *idû*, may also be viewed as present-future:

> *šum-ma la-a / iš-mé a-na* LÚ*ḫa-za-ni / ú šu-ut i-de$_4$-ma* "If I have not heeded the commissioner, then he surely knows/will know" (EA 317:23-25; cf. Moran 1987b:541; 1992:349).

The majority of examples with the conjunction are from Byblos. The use of a *qtl* in the apodosis of conditional clauses introduced by *šumma* usually accompanies either a verbless clause or an imperfect (energic) in the protasis:

> *šum-ma / šàr-ru yu-wa-ši-ru-na* LÚ.MEŠ / KUR*Mi-iṣ-ri ù* KUR*Mi-lu-ḫa / ù* ANŠE.KUR.RA.MEŠ *a-na qa-at* / LÚ-*ia an-nu-ú ki-ma / ar-ḫi-iš ù bal-ṭá-ti / a-na a-ra-ad šàr-ri* EN-*ia* "If the king will send Egyptians and Nubians and horses in the charge of this, my man, with haste, then I will survive to serve the king, my lord" (EA 112:18-24); *šum-ma* MU.MEŠ *a*[*n*]-⌜*ni*⌝-*ta ú-ul / yu-ṣa-na* ERÍN.MEŠ [*pí-ṭ*]*á-ti / ù in-né*[*-ep-ša-a*]*t ka-li* / KUR.KUR.MEŠ *a*[*-na* LÚ.MEŠ GA]Z "If this year the regular army does not come forth, then all the lands will be[come aligned] w[ith the *ʿapî*]*ru* [men]" (EA 77:26-29; also EA 79:39-44, *supra*, p. 356; EA 93:25-28).

In the following example, the apodosis apparently consists of two suffix conjugation verbs even though the first is apparently built on the Akkadian present (in spite of the lack of orthographic gemination) as theme (cf. *supra*, p. 343):

> *šum-ma / ti-iš-mu-na a-ṣí-mi* ERÍN.MEŠ / *pí-ṭá-ti ù i-zi-bu* URU.MEŠ-*šu-nu / ù pa-aṭ-ru* "If they hear 'The regular army has gone forth,' then they will abandon their towns and depart" (EA 73:11-14; Rainey 1989090:58b; cf. *infra*, pp. 370, 384).

However, this 3rd m.pl. passage must be compared with the following 1st c.s. where the first verb in the apodosis is a jussive, also from *ezēbu*:

> *šum-ma ki-a-ma la-a ti-iq-*⌈*bu*⌉(?) / *ù i-te₉-zi-ib* UR[U] *ù / pa-aṭ-ra-ti ša-ni-tam šum-ma la-a / tu-te-ru-na a-wa-ta₅ a-na ia-ši / ù i-te₉-zi-ib* URU *ù / pa-aṭ-ra-ti qa-du* LÚ.MEŠ / *ša i-ra-a-mu-ni* "If thus you do not speak, then I will abandon the ci[ty] and depart; moreover, if you don't send word back to me, then I will abandon the city and depart" (EA 83:45-51).

In fact, in the above example, one might argue that the suffix form, *paṭrāti*, is dependent on the jussive, *ītezib*, rather than being an independent part of the apodosis. On the other hand, the following two clause apodosis has a 3rd f.s. *qtl* (Rainey 1973c:252) in tandem with a prefix form, evidently the jussive 3rd m.pl. (Moran 1950a:62):

> *ù šu[m-ma la yi-iš-mu]* / [L]UGAL BE-*ia a-na a-wa-te* Ì[R-*šu*] / *ù in₄-né-ep-ša-‹at›* URU*Gub[-la] / a-na ša-šu ù gáb-bi* KUR.ḪÁ L[UGAL] / *a-di* KUR*Mi-iṣ-ri ti-né-ep-šu / a-na* LÚ.MEŠ SA.GAZ.MEŠ "But i[f] the king, my lord, [does not heed] the words of [his] ser[vant], then Byblos will become aligned with him (ᶜAbdi-Ashirta) and all the lands of the k[ing] as far as Egypt will become aligned with the ᶜ*apîrû* men" (EA 88:29-39; cf. Moran 1987a:210 and n. 8; 1987b:275; 1992:160).

It may not be coincidental that in the first apodosis clause, the verb is *qtl* and stands at the head of the clause while in the second clause, the verb comes in second position and is in the prefix jussive. One must admit, however, that instead of a 3rd m.pl. jussive, it could be 3rd f.s. imperfect.

Furthermore, a stative can also come in second position in the apodosis:

> *šum-ma-mi a-na-ku* / *uṣ-ṣú-na* UGU KUR / *ša* LUGAL *ù a-na ia-ši* / *in*$_4$*-né-ep-ša-ta* "If I go forth against the land of the king, then will you be aligned with me?" (EA 333:15-18).

Suffix forms also appear in the apodoses of conditional sentences which had a protasis introduced by an infinitive without *šumma*:

> *ṣa-bat-mi* / *ni-nu-u*$_{16}$ URU.MEŠ *Gub*^{ub}*-li* / *ù da-na-nu-u*$_{16}$ "If we seize the towns of Gubla, then we will be strong" (EA 362:25-27; Moran 1950a:57; 1950c:170).

It is in such a syntagma that we find four examples of transitive suffix conjugation forms:

> *al-lu* / *pa-ṭá-ri-ma* LÚ.MEŠ *ḫu-ub-ši ù* / *ṣa-ab-tu* LÚ.MEŠ GAZ.MEŠ / URU "Behold, if the yeomen farmers depart, then the *ᶜapîru* men will seize the city" (EA 118:36-39; Moran 1950a:57; 1950c:169b-170a); *a-pa-ši-m*[*ì*] / *at-ta ki-ta it-*[*ti* DUMU.M]EŠ / ᴵÌR-*A-ši-ir-ta ù* / *la-qú-ka* "If you make a treaty wi[th the son]s of ᶜAbdi-Ashirta, then they will capture you" (EA 132:32-35; Ebeling 1910:77; Moran 1950a:176-177; 1950c:70; 1960:10 n. 1; 1987b:352 n. 4; 1992:215 n. 4); *ba-li a-ṣí* ERÍN.MEŠ *pi-ṭ*[*á-tu*] / [*i-na* MU]$^{ša\text{-}an\text{-}ti}$ *an-ni-ti* / [*ù la*]*-qú-mi* URU.[K]I.[MEŠ] *Gub*^{ub}*-li* "If the regular tro[ops] do not come forth this year, [then] they will [take] the citi[es] of Byblos" (EA 132:32-35; Moran 1950a:170a); *a-ṣí-mi* ERÍN.MEŠ *pí-ṭá-tu ù ša-mu* / *a-na ú-mi ka-ša-di-ši ù* / *ta-ra-at* URU.KI *a-na* LUGAL *be-li-ia* "If the regular troops come forth they will hear of the day of its arrival and the city will return to the king, my lord" (EA 137:49-51; Moran 1950c:170a).

Like one passage cited above (EA 83:45-51), there are several others in which the first clause of the compound apodosis has an injunctive while the second has a suffix form. The latter could possibly be interpreted as representing a purpose clause dependent on the injunctive rather than a parallel member of the apodosis:

> ⸢*šum*⸣*-ma lìb-bi* LUGAL *be-li-ia* / *a-*⸢*na*⸣ *na-ṣa-*⸢*ar*⸣ URU-*šu ù ya-*[*d*]*i-*⸢*na*$_7$⸣ / BE-*ia* ⸢LÚ⸣.MEŠ *ma-ṣa-ar-‹ti›* ⸢*a*⸣-[*n*]*a* ⸢URU⸣ / ⸢*ù*⸣ *na-aṣ-ra-at* "If the king, my lord, is of a mind to protect his city, then let my lord give garrison troops for the city that it may be protected" (EA 127:26-29); *šum-ma* / 2 ITU *ia-nu* ERÍN.MEŠ *pí-ṭá-ti* / *ù i-te*$_9$*-zi-ib* URU.KI / *ù pa-aṭ-ra-ti ù* / *bal-ṭá-at* ZI-*ia a-di* / *i-pé-šu i-pí-iš lìb-bi-ia* "If in two months there are no regular troops, then I will abandon the city and I will depart so that my soul shall live until I can do whatever I wish" (EA 82:41-46; Moran 1987b:263; 1992:152).

Likewise, the much discussed passage, EA 74:29-38 (cf. *supra*, p. 125), has a *qtl* stative which is evidently dependent upon a preceding jussive (partly restored):

> *šum-ma ia-*[*nu*] / LÚ-*LIM ša ú-še*$_{20}$*-ze-bu-*⸢*ši*$_x$⸣(⸢ŠE⸣) *iš-tu qa-ti-n*[*u*] / *ù nu-da-bir*$_5$ $^{\text{LÚ.MEŠ}}$*ḫa-za-nu-ta iš-tu* / *lìb-bi* KUR.KUR.KI *ù ti-né-pu-uš ka-li* KUR.KUR.MEŠ.KI / *a-na* LÚ.MEŠ ⸢GAZ⸣ *ù* [*k*]*i-t*[*u*] *ti-in‹-né-pu-uš›-ma* / *a-na ka-li* KUR.KUR.KI *ù pa-aš-ḫu* DUMU.MEŠ / *ù* DUMU.MÍ.MEŠ *a-‹na› da-ri-ti* UD.KÁM.MEŠ "Since/if there is no man who can rescue it from our grasp, and we will exterminate the city rulers from within the territories and all of the territories will be aligned with the *ᶜapîrû* men; so let a ⸢treaty⸣ be ‹made› for all the territories so that the sons and daughters will be at peace forever more'" (EA 74:29-38; Mendenhall 1947a; Moran 1953:78 n. 4; 1987b:250, 252 nn. 10-13; 1992:143, 144 nn. 10-12, 145 n. 13).

All these contexts show that the apodosis with *qtl* is closely related to the intended result clauses after an injunctive.

PURPOSE CLAUSES. The logical nexus between the purpose clause and the apodosis of a conditional sentence is clearly seen in the following passage from Tyre:

> *ma-an-nu ba-la-aṭ* LÚ.GÍR / *e-nu-ma la-a it-ta-ṣí* / *ša-a-ru iš-tu* ^{UZU}*pí* LUGAL *be-li-šu* / *ù ba-li-iṭ šum-ma* LUGAL *iš-ta-pár* / [*a*]-*na* ÌR-*šu ù ba-li-iṭ* / [*a-na*] *da-ri-ti* "What is the life of foot soldier when/if the breath from the mouth of his lord has not come forth? If the king has written to his servant, then he lives [for]ever" (EA 149:21-26)

As with the two examples in the passage cited above, the following statives express intended results. Here they are predicated on the fulfillment of an imperative:

> 3 LÚ *ša-a šu-ri-ib* / ^{I}*Pí-ḫu-ra uš-š*[*i-*]*ra* / *ù bal-ṭá-ti* "Send the three men whom Piḫura had sent (to Egypt) in order that I may survive!" (EA 123:33-35); *du-ku* / [E]N!-*la-ku-nu ù i-ba-ša-tu-nu ki-ma ia-ti-nu* / *ù pa-aš-ḫa-tu-nu* "Slay your lord(!) so that you may be like us and so that you may be at peace!" (EA 74:25-27; cf. EA 73:27; 81:12; Moran 1987b:252 n. 7; 1992:144 n. 7; Youngblood 1961:139).

The latter passage may be compared with EA 107:29-31 where the intransitive prefix form, *ta-ap-šu-uḫ*, is employed instead of a suffix form.

The key verb in the next citation is also most likely an imperative, but since it has a nominal subject, it may just as well be meant for a 3rd m.s. jussive (without a *y-* prefix):

> *ù i*$_{15}$!(A)-*na-an-na* / *i*$_{15}$-*din il* LUGAL EN-*ia* DINGIR-*ia* ^{d}UTU-*ia* / *ù ṣa-ab-ta‹-at›* ^{URU}*Ṭú-bi-ḫi* / *ù i*$_{15}$-*ra-ar* ŠEŠ-*ia* / *ù i*$_{15}$-*na-ṣa-ar* ^{URU}*Ṭú-bi-ḫi* / *a-na* LUGAL EN-*ia* DINGIR-*ia* ⸢^{d}⸣[UTU-*ia*] "But now, may the god of the king, my lord, my god, my sun god, grant that Ṭôbiḫi be conquered, and I will disavow my brother and I will protect Ṭôbiḫi for the king, my lord, my god, [my sun] god!" (Rainey 1975b:413; *CAD* A/2:236a).

Finally, the *qtl* stative in this text is clearly linked to the 1st c.s. volitive in the preceding clause:

> *šu-te-ra a-wa-ta*$_5$ / *a-na ia-ši ù i-pu-ša a-na-ku* / *ki-ta it-ti* ^{I}ÌR-*A-ši-ir-ta* / *ki-ma* ^{I}*Ia-pa-* ^{d}IŠKUR *ù* ^{I}*Zi-im-re-*[*da*] / *ù bal-ṭá-ti* "Send back word to me and I will make a treaty with ᶜAbdi-Ashirta like Yapaᶜ-Haddi and Zimre[dda] so that I may live" (EA 83:23-27; cf. also EA 88:39; Moran 1987b:276 n. 10; 1992:161 n. 12).

The function of these suffix conjugation verbs in clauses of intended result is a frequent usage in biblical Hebrew (*GKC*:333, §112*q*, *r*). It is one of the many obvious contradictions to the erroneous concept that *qtl* was basically an expression of completed action.

OPTATIVE. Two passages interpreted by Finkelstein (1969:33b-34) demonstrate the optative function of the *qtl*, in spite of Moran's reservations (Moran 1987b:514 n. 20; 1992:330 n. 20). The expression in question is a Canaanite rendering of an expression well known in MB (also in Mari), *ana dinān bēliya lullik* "I would readily serve as a substitute (sacrifice) for my lord" (*CAD* D:148b-149a; Salonen 1967:59-60). The Canaanite examples, from Jerusalem, are as follows:

> ^{LÚ}*ú-e-é*ᵓ ⸢*šàr*⸣-*ri a-nu-ki* / *ma-at-ti a-na ka-ta*$_5$!(WA) "A soldier of the king am I, I would die for you!" (EA 287:69-70); *ma-at-ti ma-gal* / *a-na ka-ta*$_5$ ÌR-*ka a-na-ku* "I would readily die for you, your servant am I" (EA 289:50-51).

The following example of a verb of motion would appear to be an asseveration. Certainly [*ka*]-*aš-da-ti* is an expression of assurance to Rib-Haddi, to whom it was allegedly addressed:

> [*a-mur a-*]*ta-ša-aš a-na-ku* / [\ *na-*]*aq-ša-ap-ti* / [*i-n*]*a a-wa-te-ka a-nu-*⸢*ma*⸣ / [*ka*]-*aš-da-ti a-na ka-*⸢*ta*$_5$⸣ / [*ki-*]*a-ma ti-ša-pa-ru* / *a-na ia-ši* "[Behold, I] was distressed ([a]ngry) [a]t your words, 'Now

I am [co]ming to you', [th]us you keep writing to me" (EA 93:4-9).

The same passage contains a past tense stative, [*na-*]*aq-ša-ap-ti* which glosses a prefix conjugation preterite from a rarely used verb (Youngblood 1961:375; supported by Moran 1987b:285 n. 1; 1992:167 n. 1; *contra CAD* A/2:424).

SUMMARY

From the evidence presented above, it can be readily seen that Moran (1950a:34-39; 1961:64-65 = 1965:74-75) was not exaggerating the diachronic importance of the EA texts from Canaan for the study of the suffix conjugation pattern in the NWS dialects. The subject is of such importance that it merits a summary at this point. In the ensuing remarks, the synchronic relationship between the suffix conjugation functions and those of the prefix conjugation patterns will be pointed out.

The three basic time frames for the *qtl*—past, present and future—reflect the adaptation of this originally timeless conjugation pattern. The past tense function, which became widespread in Ugaritic prose and in later Phoenician, was prominent in Byblos and present elsewhere. It represents an encroachment on the natural territory of the prefix *yaqtul* preterite. The predominating nuance is transitive or intransitive verbs of motion though statives and passives are also found.

The present tense function of *qtl* is more typical of statives and passives and is consistent with the original usage of the suffix conjugation (as found in classical Akkadian). The present tense forms fill the same syntactic slots as non-verbal clauses and clauses with an indicative imperative *yaqtulu*, the latter being more widely preferred for transitive expression. Here one may single out the force of the *qtl* in the initial clauses for which modal congruence requires indicative imperfect verbs in the following purpose clauses.

Those syntagmas with future reference, namely the protasis and apodosis of conditional sentences, the purpose clauses predicated on an injunctive, and the optative, all represent the adoption of *qtl* as a substitute or a surrogate for the injunctives of the prefix conjugation pattern. The *qtl*'s are often employed in parallel with an injunctive, viz. the jussive or the volitive. In such cases, the *qtl* is generally employed for stative nuances while the prefix forms express motion or the transitive. There are naturally occasional exceptions; transitive *qtl*'s were noted in this syntactic function.

Such a wide spectrum of usages, paralleled by practically all of the main suffix forms, surely points to the suffix conjugation in many of these functions as something of a late comer in the Semitic languages. This is not to deny its prehistoric origin. But diachronically, one gets the impression that in the second millennium B.C.E., *qtl* was still in the process of expanding its field of employment in the NWS dialects.

Hopefully, this wide spectrum of usages and nuances in three time frames will finally convince one and all that the *qtl* conjugation pattern did not originate in an expression of completed action. On the contrary, the stative nuance, which certainly reflects the continuous and not the punctiliar, seems to be more ancient and original. The adaptation of *qtl* forms for transitive verbs apparently led to the past tense usage. The optative usage, probably originally frequent in wishes and affirmations, led to the various injunctive functions. The suffix conjugation pattern deserves to be treated in terms of its actual functions and not in terms of an outdated and unrealistic theory. A more inappropriate term than "perfect" could hardly be imagined!

CHAPTER XV

THE INFINITIVE — MORPHOLOGY

Previous studies have noted some of the salient features of morphology pertaining to the infinitive (Böhl 1909:63, §31; Ebeling 1910:59, §10) and Moran has dealt with the most striking syntactical usages (Moran 1950a:57-59; 1950c; 1951). On the other hand, because there are so many infinitive forms throughout the corpus, no one study has ever summarized all the evidence from the Cananite EA texts.

THEME FORMS

The following are the various theme forms employed in these texts. Most of them are the standard forms of classical Akkadian but a few of them represent deviations that are of special interest.

G STEM

qatāl. Over two hundred examples of infinitive forms are derived from this theme including those from weak verbs. The same theme form is employed in all the various syntagmas. The picture, then, is that of normal Akkadian usage, one basic infinitival form for all functions, unlike Hebrew, which developed special forms for construct situations while reserving the *qāṭôl* ‹ *qaṭâl* for certain "absolute" usages. The evidence for Ugaritic is mixed (Rainey 1971b:166-167, §9.25-9.27), but generally favor *qatāl* as the predominant form. The strong verbs the infinitive of which takes the *qatāl* in the letters from Canaanite scribes are: *balāṭu, baqāmu, dabābu, dagālu, kabāsu/kabāšu, kašādu, lamādu, maqātu, nadānu, namāšu, naṣāru, pašāḫu, paṭāru, ṣabātu, šapāru.*

To those may be added the I[st] Waw verbs (which have lost their initial consonant in line with all peripheral dialects), *(w)arādu* "to descend," and *(w)ašābu* "to sit, dwell, reside." I[st] Aleph verbs without vowel coloring are: *abātu, akālu, alāku, amāru,* including the denominative verb (from *ardu* ‹ *wardu* "slave"), *arādu* "to serve."

The I[st] Aleph verbs with vowel coloring do not present a uniform picture. To be sure, there are a few instances of standard Babylonian forms e.g.

> ⸢*ù*⸣ / *la-a ni-la-ú* / *e-ze-eb a-ba!-at!* / *šàr-ri* EN-*ia* "And we cannot abandon the word of the king, my lord" (EA 211:17-20),

where the Babylonian infinitive governs a typically Assyrian form of the noun. A letter written by an Egyptian official to the ruler of Byblos, which has WS features, also employs a Babylonian form:

> *la-a-mi* / *an-ti-in*$_4$*-nu e-re-eb* / LÚ.ME[Š] *ša* URU*Ṣu-mu-ri* KI / [*a*]-*n*[*a*] URU.KI-*ia* "I will not permit the men of Ṣumur to enter my city" (EA 96:7-10; Youngblood 1961:399-400; 1962:26).

On the other hand, the Jerusalem letters have Assyrian *e-ra-ba* (EA 286:43) and *e-za-bi-ša* (EA 287:62; Moran 1975b:153); cf. the I[st] Aleph with original $^{\supset}{}_1$, *e-re-š*[*i*] "to seek" (EA 289:7). Scribal negligence evidently is to blame for the following from Beirut:

> *aš-šum* / *e-pu-uš* DÙG.GA *bi-ri-‹nu›* "in order to establish a treaty between us" (EA 136:31-32; probably also [*e*]-*pu-uš* in EA 280:10).

The form *e-pu-uš* is evidently nothing but a slip whereby the thematic vowel of the G preterite and imperative was inserted.

Special deviations in the Byblos letters for I[st] $^{\supset}{}_3$ and $^{\supset}{}_4$ verbs are discussed below under *qitāl*/*qitīl* forms.

The IInd Aleph verb *šaʾālu* may have had *šâlu* as exemplified in *a-na ša-al* URU.DIDLI.KI.[Ḫ]Á (EA 144:29; cf. also the broken context EA 92:40), but a marginally Canaanized text also seems to have *b[a-]lu ša!-a-al* PN (EA 185:68; correction according to Moran 1987b:423 n. 8; 1992:267 n. 9).

The IInd Waw/Ū (middle weak) verbs attested are *dâku, da-k[i]* (EA 134:12) and *târu, ta-ri* (EA 85:70). One example is attested from *rêṣu* "to assist," *re-ṣí-ia* (EA 92:45).

For IIIrd Aleph verbs the situation is more complex. In many instances, an inflectional case vowel is expected and its relationship to the thematic *-ā-* vowel is hard to determine, particularly when the syllabic sign can be transcribed as *Ce* or *Ci*.

The one IIIrd $ʾ_1$ verb with infinitives attested in this corpus is *(w)aṣû* "to go out." One letter from Biryawaza treats the infinitive of this verb as having a strong aleph in the third position:

> *ù / ki-ma a-ṣa-i* dUTU.MEŠ */ iš-tu ša-me ki-na-an-na / tu-qa-ú-na* ÌR.MEŠ */ a-ṣa-i a-wa-te*MEŠ */ iš-tu* UZUKA / \ *pí-i be-li-šu-nu* "And like the coming(s) forth of the sun god from heaven, thus the servants are looking forward to the coming(s) forth of the words from the mouth of their lord" (EA 195:17-23).

The fact that these forms, *a-ṣa-i*, are in construct with their subject and the second form is an accusative, suggests that the scribe intended both of them to indicate the plural. Therefore, we have rendered "coming(s) forth." The fact that the subjects of both infinitives have the MEŠ determinative might even be a strengthening of the plural meaning here. Other accusative forms, which are not in construct, have a final *a* vowel, evidently meant to be long:

> *ù ú-ul ni-le-ú / a-ṣa-am a-na* EDIN.MEŠ "and we are unable to go forth to the open fields" (EA 88:20-21; Moran 1975a:156-157); *la-a i-le-e a-ṣa / [a-na* EDIN.MEŠ] "I am unable to go forth [to the open fields]" (EA 81:21-22; Moran *loc. cit.*); *ù / la-a i-le-ú / a-ṣa* "and I am unable to go out" (EA 104:49-51); *uḫ-ḫu-ra-ta / a-ṣa* "You were late coming" (EA 102:9-10).

The same orthography may also stand for the construct:

[. . .] *tu-ba-‹ú-na›* *a-ṣa pí-ṭá-ti* "they are see‹king› the coming forth of the army" (EA 70:26).

But surprisingly enough, accusatives in construct can also be written like genitives:

[*ù*] *tu-ba!-ú-na ur-ra* / [*ù*] *mu-ša-am a-ṣé* ERÍN.MEŠ / *pí-ṭá-ti* "[And] they are seeking day [and] night the coming forth of the army" (EA 73:20-22); *ù la-a-mì ni-le-ú* / *a-ṣé* KÁ*a-bu-ul-li* / *ša-aḫ-ri* / *iš-tu pa-ni* I*La-ab-a-ya* "And we are unable to go out the city gate because of Labʾayu" (EA 244:15-17).

The same holds true when there is a suffix pronoun as the subject of the infinitive:

ù a-na-ku i-ba-ú a-ṣé-ši "But I seek its coming forth" (EA 362:58).

A similar form may serve in the finite function of the infinitive, this time with an enclitic:

šum-ma / *ti-iš-mu-na a-ṣé-mi* ERÍN.MEŠ / *pí-ṭá-ti ù i-zi-bu* URU.MEŠ-*šu-nu* / *ù pa-aṭ-ru* "If they hear 'The army has come forth,' then they will leave their towns and depart" (EA 73:11-14; Rainey 1989-90:58b; cf. *supra*, pp. 343, 360; *infra*, p. 384).

Admittedly, the infinitive in this passage might simply be the object of *tišmûna*, in which case it would be a *nomen regens* plus the enclitic (thus Youngblood 1961:112). But comparison with the following passage tends to provide support for the rendering we have preferred above (cf. *infra*, pp. 385-386):

a-ṣé-mi ERÍN.MEŠ *pí-ṭá-tu ù ša-mu* / *a-na ú-mi ka-ša-di-ši ù ta-ra-at* URU.KI *a-na* LUGAL *be-li-ia* "As soon as the army comes forth and they hear about the day of its arrival, then the city will return to the king, my lord" (EA 137:49-51; cf. Moran 1950c:170a; 1987b:358 and 360 n. 9; 1992:218, 220 n. 9).

Likewise for the following, where the infinitive in a conditional sentence, in construct with its subject, is negated by *bali*:

> *[a-mur-m]i ba-li a-ṣé* ERÍN.MEŠ *pí-ṭ[á-ti]* / *[i-na* MU^{š}]$^{a\text{-}an\text{-}ti}$ *a-ni-ti* "[Behold], if there is no coming forth of the army [in] this [y]ear" (EA 129:40-41; Moran 1987b:347 n. 20; 1992:211 n. 19).

Such forms are expected, of course, when the infinitive is dependent upon a preposition, as constructs and with pronominal suffixes:

> *a-di* / *a-ṣé* ERÍN.MEŠ *pí-ṭá-ti* "until the coming forth of the army" (EA 71:26-27; also EA 70:23; 79:31; 82:19; 105:18-19; 127:38-39; cf. also EA 334:8); *iš-tu a-ṣé-ia* "after I came forth" (EA 270:12).

In all of these cases where the ZI sign has been used, we have transcribed *a-ṣé* on the assumption that the intended form is **(w)aṣāʾi › aṣê*.

One verb with IIIrd ʾ$_3$ is widely documented, viz. *leqû* "to take (to capture, to rescue)." All the Byblos occurrences of this verb have an *a* vowel in the first syllable, thus conforming to the Assyrian rather than the Babylonian pattern. There is reason to believe, however, that this pattern is due to a Canaanite or peripheral tendency, although Assyrian influence cannot be entirely ruled out. The other peripheral dialects do not present a uniform picture; some of them have forms with first syllable *le-* (e.g. Mitanni, EA 20:9) while ohers have *la-* (Hattusas, Labat 1932:155) or both (Ugarit, Huehnergard 1989:182).

More problematic is the second, or theme, vowel. Even the Assyrian form preserved the *ā* vowel, e.g. *a-na ṭup-pí-im ša kà-ri-im* / *lá-qá-im* "to bring a tablet of the Kārum" (*KTH* 16 A:9-11; cited by Hecker 1968:215, §127g). Therefore, it should not be surprising to find the suffixless accusative form with an *a* class vowel, apparently representing long *â*:

> ^{URU}*Ṣu-mu-ra tu-ba-ú-na la-qa* "Ṣumur they are seeking to take" (EA 105:23); *a-nu-⸢ma⸣* 2 URU *ša ir-ti-ḫu* / *a[-n]a ia-ši ⸢yu⸣-ba-ú*

> *la-qa* / [*a-na ša-a-šu*] "Now, the two towns which remain to me, he is seeking to take [for himself]" (EA 76:9-11; Youngblood 1961:172).

The latter of those passages can be compared with the continuation of the same letter where the same infinitive is in construct with its direct object:

> *ù yu-ba-ú* / [*la*]-*qa ka-li* URU.MEŠ *šàr-ru*(sic!) ᵈUTU / [*a-n*]*a ša-a-šu* / . . . *i-nu-ma* / ⸢*yu*⸣-*ba-ú la-qa* KUR LUGAL *a-na ša-a-šu* "And he is seeking [to ta]ke all the towns of the king, the sun god, [fo]r himself . . . that he is seeking to take the land of the king for himself" (EA 76:12-16; also EA 91:13).

To these may be added the various broken passages where lengthening of the final vowel of the infinite is represented graphically:

> *ù šu-nu y*[*u-ba-ú*] / [*la-*]*qa-a* "And these he [is seeking] [to ta]ke" (EA 73:12-13); *ù* 2 ⸢URU⸣ *y*[*u-ba-*]*ú* / [*la-q*]*a-a* "And the two towns he is seeking to [ta]ke" (EA 81:10-11).

It would seem that the scribes knew the independent accusative form of *leqû* as **laqâ* and the construct form as **laqā*. But the situation is not so simple. Accusatives in construct with its object are also attested with an *e* class vowel:

> *šum-ma la-a ti-le-ú la-qé* ÌR-*k*[*a*] "If you are unable to rescue yo[ur] servant" (EA 114:44); *mi-ia-mi yi-ma-gi-ir* / *ur-ru-ba it-ti* ᴵ*šàr-ri* EN-*ia* / *le-qé-ma* GUŠKIN! *ù* GUŠKIN.GUN / ᴵ*šàr-ri* EN-*ia* "Who would agree to entering in to the king, my lord, to take gold and red gold?" (EA 283:10-13; Rainey 1989-90:71).

Perhaps these scribes were making a hypercorrection, assuming **laqē*/**leqē*. Note that the latter form is the only instance in the texts from Canaan with first syllable *le-* (possibly influenced by the imperative *lé-qé* in line 11)

Accusative forms with suffix pronouns as their direct object invariably have an *a* vowel, for an assumed **laqā-*:

> *la-qa-ia* (EA 79:40; 82:7); *la-qa-ši* (EA 83:20; 91:23); *la-qa-šu*[*-nu*] (EA 79:28); *la-qa-*[*ši-na*] (EA 124:53).

For the "absolute" use of the infinitive to strengthen a finite verb, the evidence is mixed. All examples are from Byblos:

> [*ù*] *la-qa-ma* ^{URU}*Gub*[*-la*] / [*iš-t*]*u qa-ti-ka la-a-*[*mì*] / [*yi-il-qu*]*-ši*$_{x}$(ŠE) *a-di da-r*[*i-ti*] "[But] to take Byblos from your hand, [he will] never [take] it" (EA 124:54-56; cf. Moran 1987b:337,338 n. 10; 1992:203, 204 n. 10).

The final *a* vowel is consistent with other examples of this verbal usage (Moran 1950a:57). But note the following:

> *ù la-*⸢*qé*⸣*-*⸢*mi*⸣ *ti-il-qú-na-ši* "then they will surely capture it" (EA 131:17; cf. Moran 1950a:176).

The scribe may have been thinking of an original **laqēʾa › *laqê*.

When the infinitive is in the dependent case, after a preposition, it is also in construct with its object. The Megiddo scribe has a unique construction:

> *a-na la-qé-i* / ^{URU}*Ma-gi-id-da*^{KI} "to capture Megiddo" (EA 244:23-24; Rabiner 1981:82 §4.5.4).

It is possible that the scribe intended his form to be read **laqî*, but he may have meant **laqēʾi*. Other scribes, from Byblos and Tyre, make use of a shorter form:

> *a-na la-qé* / ANŠE.KUR.RA.MEŠ "to get horses" (EA 112:26-27; likewise EA 124:52; 362:36; from Tyre: EA 148:32-33; 154:16-17).

The same bound form is used with suffix pronouns as the object:

> *a-na la-qé-ši* "to take it" (EA 137:46); *a-na la-qé-ši-m*[*a*] "to take it" (EA 120:33); *a-na la-qé-n*[*u*] "to rescue u[s]" (EA 20).

These forms could also be read *la-qí, la-qí-ši* etc. It is impossible to know whether the scribe was thinking of *laqî, laqē-*, or whether he was simply constructing a form with the necessary case ending.

Another attested weak verb, with IIIrd ʾ4, is *šemû*. Once it appears in the well known adverbial function as reinforcement of a finite verb (for discussion, cf. *infra*, pp. 389-390), in this instance a G passive present-future:

> *ù ša-ma ú-ul* / [*tu-u*]*š-mu-na* "but they are really not heeded" (EA 89:9-10).

Comparison with *a-ša-b*[*a l*]*a a-ši-ib* "he is really not located" (EA 92:10) shows that the form in this function must be in the accusative, thus **šamâ*. However, in another syntagma, where strong verbs have either zero or the mysterious *-ī* (cf. *infra*, pp. 383-384), viz. as a finite verb, the same orthography is found:

> *ša-ma-ma šu-nu* "If they should hear" (EA 104:43; cf. Rainey 1989-90:59b).

In the two instances of dependent forms the orthography is *i-na ša-me* (EA 120:38; 144:17), reflecting the same problem as the comparable forms of *leqû*. Should these two examples perhaps be read *ša-mì* ? Both of them are bound forms followed by their direct object.

Two verbs which are IIIrd *Y*/*Ī* are attested. One of these, *qabû* "to speak," appears in a particular syntagma, after *kīma* in construct with its subject:

> *ki-ma qa-bi* LUGAL EN-*ia* "as the king, my lord, said" (EA 114:21;also EA 155:12; 216:11; 220:13-14; 323:11-12; 325:21-22).

Also with suffixes as the subject:

> *ki-ma qa-bi-ia* (EA 117:28); *[ki-m]a qa-bi-ka* (EA 193:22); *ki-ma ša qa-bi-šu* (EA 329:20; also EA 302:18).

The bound form is followed by its direct object, in the form of a direct citation:

> LUGAL EN-*li ša-pár a-na mu-ḫi-[i]a* ^I^*Ḫa-a-ia / a-na qa-bi* KASKAL-*ra-ni*ḪÁ / KUR*Ḫa-na-gal*$_9$*-bat an-nu-ú / ú-wa-še-ru-na ù uš-še-ru-ši* "The king, my lord, sent to me Ḫāya to say 'This Ḫanagalbat caravan I am sending, so expedite it!'" (EA 255:8-11).

The other verb is *šatû* "to drink." One Byblos example has a suffix as subject:

> *ù i[a-nu* / A.MEŠ! *a-na š[a]-te-šu* "but there was no water for him to drink" (EA 85:53-54).

However, the Tyrian scribe adopted a special unique form to be discussed below.

qitīl / qitāl. The Byblos letters have a particularly remarkable deviation from the norm for I^st^ Aleph verbs with $^{\text{ʾ}}{}_3$-$^{\text{ʾ}}{}_4$. Infinitive forms from this verb class are only attested with initial *i-* instead of the expected *e-*. Because of the ambiguity of the syllabary in this period, it is impossible to say for certain whether the Byblos scribes preserved the thematic *ē* vowel. Giving them the benefit of the doubt on that point, one may transcribe two forms by *i-pé-eš* (EA 73:25; 89:43) because of the final *eš* sign. This would also permit the renderings *i-pé-ša* (EA 129:27; also *[i-p]é-ša* EA 79:24) and *i-[p]é-ši*. (EA 132:44) as well as *i-re-ši* (EA 81:38; also *i-re-ši[-i]m* EA 74:19 and *[i-r]e-š[i]* (EA 90:44). But there are several attestations to *i-pí-iš*, which could be rendered *i-pé-eš*$_{15}$ (EA 69:17; 129:29; 362:45; and outside of Byblos, EA 250:21; 364:22). The source of these forms is most likely contamination with the noun *ipšu / epšu*, which has the meaning "act, deed," only in the western peripheral texts from Amarna, Taanach and Ugarit (*CAD* E:168b-169a); its construct form is written syllabically *i-pí-iš*

(EA 84:7 *et al.*). The question arises concerning a form in EA 179, a letter which consistently uses the *e* sign with the value i_{15}; should the transcription be *e-pé-šu* or i_{15}-*pé-šu* (EA 179:17)? The earliest attestation to the initial *i* vowel is from Tanaach: *i-pé-ša-am* (TT 2:11); the same letter happens to have the noun *ip-ša-šu-nu* "their work" (TT 2:14). A similar form, from *erēbu*, is attested in a Beirut letter, *i-re-bi* (EA 143:18).

Strangely enough, the Boghazköi IZI =*išatu* (*KBo* 1, 31) has two entries with *i-pé-šu* (lines r. 13', 14'; *CAD* E:192b) and a fragmentary epistle has *i-re-bi* (*KUB* 3, 82:11).

For the verb *šatû*, the texts from Tyre have a form not known elsewhere. All of the examples are dependent on *ana;* the bound form is followed by a nominal subject:

> *e-nu-ma it*[*-t*]*a-din* / LUGAL *be-li-ia* A.MEŠ *a-na ši-ti* / ÌR MÍ*Ma-ya-a-ti* "When the king, my lord, gave water for the servant of Mayāti to drink" (EA 155:24-26).

In two other similar contexts the form in question governs a suffix pronoun as subject:

> *a-na ši-ti-ya* "for me to drink" (EA 151:39); *a-na ši-te-šu* "for him to drink" (EA 148:13; 155:10).

The one infinitival form, hitherto unrecognized, from *izzuzu* is constructed like the preterite with accusative ending:

> *mi-ia-mi yi-ma-lik i-zi-za* [*i*]*-na pa-ni* / ERÍN.MEŠ *pí-ṭá-at* LUGAL *be-lí-ia* "Who would consider standing up to the army of the king, my lord?" (EA 94:12-13).

N STEM

One of the glosses has been assumed to be 3rd m.pl. It may very well be an infinitive in the nominative, used absolutely only to explain the basic meaning of the verb being glossed. If it really is an infinitive, then it testifies to *naqtal* as the N stem infinitive form. In spite of considerable disagreement about the Akkadian verb being glossed, the general meaning is fairly clear:

> *ša-ni-tam ú-ul ti-i-de* / *at-ta* KUR*A-mur-ri ur-ra* / *mu-sa tu-ba-ú-na* / ERÍN.MEŠ *pí-ṭá-ti ú-ul ta-ša-aš* / \ *na-aq-ṣa-pu* "Furthermore, don't you know Amurru? Day (and) night they are asking for the army. Don't be angry!" (EA 82:47-51; Albright and Moran 1948:242, 244 n. 6; Youngblood 1961:235-236; *CAD* B:363a; Moran 1987b:264 n. 6; 1992:152 n. 6; *contra CAD* A/2:424b).

The form *ú-ul ta-ša-aš* must be 2nd m.s. negative jussive. Amurru was treated as 3rd m.pl. with the verb *tu-ba-ú-na*, and many scholars have assumed that it is subsequently treated as a collective (Albright and Moran 1948:242, 244 n. 6; Youngblood 1961:235-236; *CAD* B:363a; Moran 1987b:264 n. 6 ; 1992:152; *CAD* Q:146a). They thus assumed that the gloss is 3rd m.pl., *qtl* as the translation of a 3rd f.s. preterite. The negation by *ú-ul* could then be a rhetorical question. However, it may be a negative jussive (used here instead of *lā*, as is sometimes the case). The gloss may then be an N infinitive added only to confirm the meaning.

The only N stem hybrid infinitive attested is also a preterite form with the accusative case ending added:

> *a-na* URU*I-*⸢*bir*$_5$⸣*-ta* / *al-ka ù b*[*u*]*-ú in*$_4$*-né-ep-ša* / *a-na* LÚ.MEŠ GAZ.MEŠ "I went to ᶜIbirta but they sought to join the *ᶜapîrû* men" (EA 104:52-54; Rainey 1989-90:59b).

D STEM

Few are the D stem infinitives on the standard Akkadian pattern. The deviations from the Akkadian theme form adopted by the scribes in Canaan have a special interest for WS linguistics.

quttul. Surprisingly, this is not the usual D stem theme for the infinitive in these texts from Canaan. The one strong verb appearing in the normal Akkadian theme form is in the following Tyrian passage:

> *ù* GIŠ.MEŠ *a-na šu-ḫu-ni-ia* "and wood to warm me" (EA 147:66; for the full context, cf. *infra*, p. 403).

Three examples of the denominative from MB *ardu* "servant," also conform to the *quttul* pattern.

> *ù i-ma-la-ku ba-li-mì / ur-ru-ud* LUGAL EN-*ia* "And would I consider not serving the king, my lord?" (EA 191:9-10); *ia-nu / pa-ni ša-nu-ta*$_5$ *iš-tu / ur-ru-ud šàr-ri* "There is no other intention other than to serve the king" (EA 253:26-28); *ù ut-te-er / a-na* LUGAL EN-*ia iš-tu* / LÚ.MEŠ SA.GAZ.MEŠ *aš-šum ur-ru-di-šu* "And I brought back (the towns) to the king, my lord, from the *ᶜapîrû* men in order to serve him" (EA 189:15-17).

quttal/*quttāl*. It is now clear that this was the standard D stem infinitival theme form in Ugaritic. The quadralingual dictionary has *pu-la-ṭu* for **pullaṭu* "to rescue, deliver" (*Ug* 5, 137:II, 20') and *ḫu-wa-ú* probably for **ḥuwwayu* "to give life" (*Ug* 5, 137:II, 17'; Rainey 1969a:108). Three verbs are attested in the Amarna letters from Canaan with this same theme form. One example is from the denominative of *ardu* which has been discussed above:

> [*a-m*]*ur ip-ši* ᴵ*Pí-i-ia* / ⸢DUMU⸣ ᴸᵁ́*Gu-la-ti*$_7$ / [*a-na*] *ia-ši* LÚ.MEŠ-*ia* / *š*[*a*] *uš-ši-ir-ti a-na / ur-ra-di i-na* ᵁᴿᵁ*Ia-pu / ù a-na na-ṣa-ri* / É-*ti* \ *šu-nu-ti* LUGAL EN-*ia / ù al-lu-ú il*$_5$*-qé-šu-nu* / ᴵ*Pí-i-ia* DUMU *Gu-la-ti* "[Beh]old the deed(s) of Pīya son of Gulati [against] me; as for my men whom I sent to serve in Joppa and to guard the granary of the king, my lord, then behold Pīya son of Gulati took them" (EA 294:16-24).

The Tyrian scribe probably had this form in mind, but confused it with the 1st c.s. suffix form:

> *ù id-din pa-ni-ia / a-na ur-da-ti-šu* [*ù*] / ᴵᴹᴵ́*Ma-ia-a-ti* BE-*ti-ia* "And I will set my face to serve him [and] Mayāti, my mistress" (EA 155:27-29).

The most frequent verb in this theme is from *wuššuru*, which, as mentioned previously (*supra*, pp. 157-168), has the special meaning "to send" in western peripheral texts, especially EA. Youngblood (1961:231-232) has observed that if this pattern represents a true Canaanite vocalization, then the thematic *a* vowel must have been short; otherwise it would have shifted to *ô* and in the cuneiform script it would have been written *uš-šu-ur*.

All the attested forms are direct objects governed by other verbs, e.g.

> *la-a-mi i-le-ú uš-šar* / ^{GIŠ}MÁ.MEŠ-*ia a-na aš-ra-nu* "I am unable to send my ships there" (EA 126:7-8; also EA 82:21-22; 105:86-87; 113:28-30; 117:43-44; 129:77-79).

In addition to the various *ši-ti* forms from *šatû* in the Tyre correspondence (*supra*, p. 376), there is also one apparent D stem form of the infinitive:

> *a-na na-da-an me-e a-na šu-ta-ia* "to give water for me to drink (or: for watering me)" (EA 147:65; for context cf. *infra*, p. 403).

qattil. A letter from Gath-padalla has two infinitives in the *qattil* theme from a root attested in Ugaritic. Since this is also the D infinitive form of Hebrew, it may have been preferred in the dialect of some EA scribes:

> *yi-de-mì šàr-ru* EN-*ia* [*i*]-*n*[*u*]-*ma* / *tu-ur-ri-ṣú-m*[*ì*] 2 DUMU ^{LÚ}*ar-ni* ⸢LUGAL⸣ [*b*]*e-lí-ia* / 2 DUMU ^{I}*La-ab-a*[*-y*]*a pa-ni-šu-ni* / *a-na ḫa-lí-iq* KUR ⸢*šàr*⸣-*ri* EN-*ia* "May the king, my lord, be apprised that the two sons of the traitor to the king, my lord, the two sons of Lab᾽ayu, have set their faces to destroy the land of the king, my lord" (EA 250:4-7); *a-na ḫal-lí-iq* / KUR LUGAL EN-*ia yu-ba-á᾽-ú* ^{I}⸢*Mil*⸣-⸢*ki*⸣-*l*[*ì*] "Milkilu seeks to destroy the land of the king, my lord" (EA 250:55-56).

Tagu of Gath-carmel has three other infinitives with this theme:

ù bu-i-ti$_7$ *pu-ḫi-ir* / KASKAL.ḪÁ *i-na qa-at* ŠEŠ-*ia* "And I sought to organize a caravan under the charge of my brother" (EA 264:6-7); *la-a i-le-ú uš-šir*$_4$ / KASKAL.ḪÁ-*ia a-na* [I]*šàr-ri* EN-*ia* "I am unable to send the caravan to the king, my lord" (*Ibid.*, lines 9-10); *i-na-an-na bu-i-ti*$_7$ *uš-šir*$_4$ / KASKAL.ḪÁ-*ia a-na* [I]*šàr-ri* / \ EN-*ia* "Now, I sought to send my caravan to the king, my lord" (*Ibid.*, lines 20-22).

The use of both *puḫḫir* and *uššir* show that *qattil* was the scribe's real understanding of the proper theme for the D stem infinitive.

The Jerusalem scribe has only one D stem infinitive and it conforms to the *qattil* pattern even though it has the characteristic initial *m-* which the Jerusalem scribe prefers for *wuššuru*:

la-a a-la-á'-e \ *mu-še-ra* KASKAL / *a-na šàr-ri* EN-*ia* "I am unable to send a caravan to the king, my lord" (EA 287:27-29).

Š STEM

The few Š stem infinitives attested all have a *šuqtil* theme rather than the appropriate Akkadian *šuqtul*. This is not surprising for the Š from *târu*, a stem usage exclusive to the Amarna texts from Canaan (*AHw*:1336a):

ù ú-ka-li LÚ-*LIM* / *an-nu-ú a-na šu-te-er* / *a-wa-ti a-na šàr-ri* "But I kept this man back in order to send back word to the king" (EA 108:48-50).

This non-standard pattern also prevails with the Š of *ešēru*, a verb frequently used in the correspondence about making preparations for the arrival of the Egyptian army. Over and over again one finds:

a-na šu-ši-ri a-na pa-ni ERÍN.MEŠ *pí-ṭá-at* LUGAL EN-*ia* "to prepare for the arrival of the army of the king, my lord" (EA 191:4-6; also EA 201:12-13; 203:11; 204:12; 205:10; 206:11; 216:8; 292:31-32).

The synchronic significance of this form is hard to determine. It is not typical of any other peripheral dialect. Is it influenced by a Canaanite pattern? After all, there is no clear evidence that Canaanite had a real Š stem. But it could be the influence of a corresponding Canaanite H stem infinitive. Evidence for the vocalization of the Ugaritic Š stem infinitive is lacking. The suffix conjugation pattern for this Š verb in the Amarna letters from Canaan, which is also on the *šuqtil* theme (cf. *supra*, pp. 312-315), comes immediately to mind.

Št STEM

One example is attested of Št stem. It is from *šutēšuru* "to dispatch" (*CAD* E:359a):

> *al-lu-ú uš-ši-i[r-]t[i]* / ÌR LUGAL *ša-n[a-a]m* / *a-na šu-*⌈*ta*⌉*-ši-r[i]* / *ù a-na da-ga-al* / *[pa-ni]* LUGAL dUTU *i[š-tu* AN*sa-mi-i*] "Behold, I have sent another royal servant in order to dispatch (messages) and in order to have an ⌈audience⌉ with the king, the sun god f[rom heaven]" (EA 306:22-27).

INFLECTION

Since the infinitives are nominal forms, it is to be expected that they will be inflected as substantives. On the whole, this is the situation with only a few striking exceptions. In the following two chapters, the syntagmas in which the infinitives are to be found will be discussed at length. It may, nevertheless, prove useful to bring together here some of the salient features of infinitival inflection with special reference to departures from the usual norms.

DEPENDENT. The majority of infinitive forms are dependent upon prepositions. The normal case ending is naturally *-i*. There is one instance of an erroneous accusative ending in which the infinitive form is actually in construct with a following substantive:

> *ga-am-ru* DUMU.MEŠ-*nu* MÍDUMU.MÍ.MEŠ-‹*nu*› / GIŠ! É-*nu* *i*[-*n*]*a na-da-ni₇ i-na* KUR*Ia-ri-mu-ta* / *i-na ba-l*[*a*]-*ṭá* ZI-*nu* "Our sons and our daughters (ànd) the implements of our houses are all used up to pay in Yarimuta for the sustenance for our lives" (EA 74:15-17; Youngblood 1961:122, 133; contrast Moran 1987b:251 n. 5; 1992:144 n. 5).

As Youngblood (1961:134) has observed, the proper form would be *ina balāṭ napištinu* with zero case ending.

ACCUSATIVE. In the same text cited above, there is an accusative: *ba-la-ṭá* ÌR-*šu* "the sustenance of his servant" (EA 74:54). Infinitives governed by finite verbs normally take the accusaive unless they are in construct, e.g.

> *la-a-mi i-le-ú uš-šar* / GIŠMÁ.MEŠ-*ia* "I am unable to send my ships" (EA 126:7-8).

FINITE. The example of an apparent nominative, *a-ša-bu* (EA 138:62) is probably 3rd m.pl.of the suffix conjugation (Rainey 1989-90:63). Infinitives standing in the function of finite verbs either have zero suffix or else an *-i*, which Moran (1961:60 = 1965:67-68) has compared to the *hireq compaginis* known from a number of examples in biblical Hebrew.

CHAPTER XVI

THE INFINITIVE — MORPHOSYNTAX

Discussion of the various syntagmas in which the infinitive is used will also entail explication of certain morphological variations, mainly inflectional suffixes, which accompany certain syntactic functions. The categories defined for the Canaanite EA texts are similar to those for Akkadian in general (Aro 1961), but in most syntagmas there are some unusual or distinguishing features of the Canaanite usages.

AS A FINITE VERB

One striking use of the infinitive, which does not have parallels in Akkadian, is its function as a finite verb in an independent clause. To Ebeling (1915:1491) goes the credit for this discovery. Practically all of the relevant passages were noted by Moran at one time or another (Moran 1950a:57-59; 1950c; 1952; 1961:61-62 = 1965:69-70). The construction is so unique in cuneiform texts (while documented for Ugaritic, Phoenician and Hebrew) that it seems appropriate to discuss every one of them here.

The examples cited below will be seen to have either -Ø (e.g. *ṣa-bat-mi* EA 129:32; 362:25) or an *-i* vowel (e.g. *pa-ṭá-ri-ma* EA 118:37; *ma-ti-ma* EA 89:38) as suffix. They also appear frequently with enclitic *-ma* or *-mi*. The -Ø tends to underline the "absolute" nature of these infinitival forms, except, of course, when the infinitive is in construct with a dependent subject or object. It would be interesting to know if the -Ø represents a West Semitic development. The *-i* vowel has been compared by Moran to the *hireq compaginis* known from a few forms in biblical Hebrew (Moran 1961:60 = 1965:67-68). A problem arises with regard to infinitives IIIrd Aleph or IIIrd Weak. Herein, transcriptions have been adopted such as *a-ṣé-mi* (EA 73:12) on the assumption that the scribe intended to express **aṣêmi* ‹ **(w)aṣāʾīmi*, i.e. with the *-i* suffix. It also seems likely that the preservation of this suffix indicates a long vowel, hence *-ī*. The variations between -Ø and *-i* with infinitives dependent on prepositions is a matter to be treated separately (cf. *infra*, pp. 402-403).

With one exception (EA 287:46; where the text is broken at the end of the line), all these infinitives are followed by an enclitic, either *-ma* to mark it as the logical predicate, or *-mi* signifying direct speech and/or to mark the logical predicate. Also, with few exceptions, all these infinitives are followed by their subject, either a substantive or an independent pronoun in the nominative. However, if the subject of the infinitive is identical to the subject of the finite verb in the following clause (which is logically linked to the infinitival clause), then the subject of the infinitive being used finitely need not be explicitly represented (EA 109:44-46; Moran 1950c:170 n. 16; EA 129:20-21; Moran 1987b:344, 346 n. 12; 1992:209, 210 n. 11; EA 116:10-12; Moran 1952:77 n. 11; 1987b:321 n. 1; 1992:192 n. 1),

PAST NARRATIVE. There are fewer examples of this usage than might be expected from synchronic comparison with Ugaritic (Gordon 1965:80, §9.29) and diachronic comparisons with later dialects such as Phoenician and Hebrew (Moran 1950c:169, 171). The key Amarna passage is in a Jerusalem letter:

> *pa-ṭa-a!-ri!* / [ᴵ*A*]*d-da-ya a-di* LÚ.MEŠ *ma-šar-ti* ᴸᵁ́*ú-e-e* / [*ša i*]*-din šàr-ri* "[A]ddaya departed with the garrison troops [which] my king [had] given" (EA 287:46-48; Moran 1952:77a; 1987b:513 n. 13; 1992:330 n. 13).

The next example was not recognized by Moran but seems to be explained best as an example of the infinitive in finite usage:

> *šum-ma* / *ti-iš-mu-na a-ṣé-mi* ERÍN.MEŠ / *pí-ṭá-ti ù i-zi-bu* URU.MEŠ-*šu-nu* / *ù pa-aṭ-ru* "If they hear 'The army has come forth,' then they will abandon their towns and they will depart" (EA 73:11-14; Rainey 1989-90:58; cf. *supra*, pp. 342-343, 360, 370).

The clause with **aṣêmi* is the object of the verb *tišmûna*. Another infinitive in a broken context has also gone unrecognized:

> *ù [a]-la-ak-mi a-na-‹ku› a-na* ^{URU}A.PÚ[^{KI}] / *a-na da[-ba-b]i a-na ma-ḫar* ^{I}*Ḫa-mu-ni[-ri]* "So ⸢I⸣! [w]ent to Beirut in order to plead before ᶜAmmuni[ra]" (EA 138:51-52).

The verb here is usually interpreted as a finite form; *allakmi* with zero suffix could be a preterite in these texts. However, it seems more commensurate with Canaanite scribal practice to posit an infinitive here alongside a defective writing of the 1st c.s. independent pronoun (certainly not a shortened **ʾana*!).

The last passage in this category was observed by Moran after the completion of his initial studies on the finite use of the infinitive. His subsequent analysis of the context involves some major improvements to the text:

> *yi-de* / [LU]GAL *i-nu-ma ma-qa-ti-ma a‹-na›* UN-*nu* / *ù ṣa-ab-tu-ši*$_{x}$(ŠE) DUMU.MEŠ ^{I}ÌR-*A-ši-ir[-t]a* "May the king be apprised that there was an attack ag[ainst] our garrison(!) and the sons of ᶜAbdi-Ashirta have captured it!" (EA 116:10-12; Moran 1952:77 n. 11; 1987b:321 n. 1; 1992:192 n. 1).

"AS SOON AS." Three passages reflect a temporal relationship between the clause with the infinitive and the following clause. The best of these is from *(w)aṣû* (cf. *supra*, p. 370) and has a 3rd f.s. subject; its clause is linked with a following clause having a 3rd m.pl. suffix verb:

> *a-ṣé-mi* ERÍN.MEŠ *pí-ṭá-tu ù ša-mu* / *a-na ú-mi ka-ša-di-ši ù ta-ra-at* URU.KI *a-na* LUGAL *be-li-ia* "As soon as the army comes forth and they hear about the day of its arrival, then the city will return to the king, my lord" (EA 137:49-51; cf. Moran 1950c:170a; 1987b:358 and 360 n. 9; 1992:218 and 220 n. 9).

Admittedly, this complex could be rendered as a conditional sentence, "If the army comes forth . . . ." However, the insertion of the clause about the Byblians' hearing "of the estimated time of arrival" of the Egyptian army strengthens the impression that the temporal relationship is being stressed.

Another such complex sentence with a temporal clause is the following:

> *ù ma-ti-ma šu-ut a-nu-‹ki›? / i-de-šu* "And as soon as he died, I learned of it" (EA 89:38-39; Moran 1950c:170a; 1987b:277; 1992:162; Youngblood 1961:333-334).

The reference is to someone whose death had already taken place. Another past event with similar temporal relationship has to do with a man sent by Rib-Haddi to a neighboring ruler:

> *ka-š[a-d]i-ma* LÚ*-ia ù / ra-ak-[š]a-šu* "As soon as my man arrived, he bound him" (EA 116:27-28; Moran 1950a:57; 1950c:169; 1952:77 n. 11).

CONDITIONAL SENTENCES. Seven or more passages where the infinitive is employed finitely have conditional connotation. The infinitive form in question introduced the protasis (Moran 1950a:74) and corresponds to the suffix conjugation in similar contexts. Two of these were recognized already by Ebeling (1915:1491):

> *pa-ṭá-ri-ma šu-ut [ù] / ia-nu ša-a yu-ba-lu [ṭup-pí-ia] / a-na mu-ḫi-ka* "If he departs, [then] there is no one who can deliver [my letter(s)] to you" (EA 113:40-42; Moran 1950a:57-58; 1950c:170); *al-lu / pa-ṭá-ri-ma* LÚ.MEŠ *ḫu-up-ši ù / ṣa-ab-tu* LÚ.MEŠ GAZ.MEŠ / URU "Behold, if the yeomen farmers desert, then the *ʿapîru* men will seize the city" (EA 118:37-39; Moran 1950a:57; 1950c:169-170; *contra CAD* A/1:358b).

Two other passages, from texts that were written by the same scribe (cf. Moran 1987b:341 n. 1; 1992:206 n. 1), serve to elucidate each other and also to confirm their interpretation (Moran 1950c:170):

ù ti-[i]q-bu-na ṣa-bat-mi n[i-nu] / URU.KI.MEŠ *Gub^{ub}-li ù mi[-na]* / ⸢*ti*⸣-⸢*pu*⸣-*šu* ERÍN.MEŠ *pí-ṭá-tu* "And they are saying, 'If w[e] capture the town(s) of Byblos, then wh[at] can the army do?'" (EA 129:32-34; Moran 1987b:346 n. 16; 1992:210 n. 15); *ù ti$_7$-iq-bu-ni ṣa-bat-mi* / *ni-nu-u$_{16}$* URU.MEŠ *Gub^{ub}-li* / *ù da-na-nu-u$_{16}$* "And they are saying, 'If we capture the town(s) of Byblos, then we will be strong'" (EA 362:25-27).

The next passage requires some corrections to Knudtzon's readings (Ebeling 1910:77); but nevertheless, it provides an excellent example of the infinitive in the protasis of a conditional sentence:

ù š[a-al-šu] / *šum-ma la-a qa-bi-ti* / *a-na ša-a-šu a-pa-ši-m[ì]* / *at-ta ki-ta it-[ti]* DUMU.MEŠ / ^{I}ÌR-*A-ši-ir-ta* [*ù*] / *la-qú-ka* "But a[sk him] if I didn't say to him, 'If you make a treaty wi[th] the sons of ᶜAbdi-Ashirta, then they will seize you'" (EA 132:30-35; Moran 1950c:170b).

The following has a hitherto unrecognized infinitive. Moran had taken the form in question to be a dual suffix form, **šamâ-ma* "they heard" (Moran 1987b:300 n. 3; 1992:177 n. 3), but such a dual form is otherwise unattested in this corpus and in fact is completely uncalled for. The full context is:

ša-ma-ma šu-nu / ›*šu-nu*‹ *i-nu-ma i-te$_9$-ru-bu* / *i-na* ^{URU}*Ṣu-mu-ra* / URU.MEŠ *an-nu-tu* ‹*i-na*› ^{GIŠ}MÁ.MEŠ / *ù* DUMU.MEŠ ^{I}ÌR-*A-ši-i[r-]ta* / *i-na ṣé-ri ù* / [*i*]*z-*[*z*]*i-za* UGU-‹*šu-nu*› *ù* / *la-a i-le-ú* / *a-ṣa ù ep-ša-at* ^{URU}*Gub-la* / [*a*]*-na* LÚ.MEŠ GAZ.MEŠ "If they hear that I am entering into Ṣumur, these cities (will be in) ships and the sons of ᶜAbdi-Ashirta (will be) on land and I will be up against ‹them› and I will be unable to go forth lest Byblos go over to the ᶜ*apîrû* men" (EA 104:43-53; Rainey:1989-90:59a; *contra* Moran 1987b:300 n. 3; 1992:177 n. 3).

Two more passages have transitive infinitives without an immediately expressed subject. Instead of its subject, each infinitive is followed by its direct object. One of the contexts in question would appear to be relatively free of exegetical complications:

> *pa-na-nu da-ga-li-ma* / ⸢LÚ⸣ KUR*Mi-iṣ-ri ù in*$_4$-‹*na*›-*ab-tu* / [LU]GAL.MEŠ KUR*Ki-na-a*[*ḫ*]-*ni iš-tu pa-n*[*i-šu*] "Formerly, if they saw a man from Egypt, then the [ki]ngs of Canaan would flee from be[fore him]" (EA 109:44-46; Moran 1950a:57; 1950c:170 n. 16).

The second passage is somewhat broken but the meaning is reasonably certain:

> [*la*]-*qé-mi ši-a-ti* [*ù* URU.KI*Gub*^{ub}-*la*] / [*ti*-]*ìl-q*[*ú*]-*na* "If they capture it (Baṭrôna), [then] they will take [Byblos]" (EA 129:20-21; Moran 1987b:344, 346 n. 12; 1992:209, 210 n. 11).

The infinitive is transcribed here as if it derives from **laqāʾī* › **laqê*. The direct object is expressed by the independent 3rd f.s. accusative pronoun, a true rarity in these texts. The restoration at the end of line 20 is problematic; the width of the tablet does not seem to permit all the signs proposed in the restoration. Perhaps the scribe finished his line by turning upwards along the edge, a not uncommon custom.

Finally, there exists one example of a negated infinitive in the protasis of a conditional sentence. The negation is accomplished by dependence on the negative particle *bali*. Although the syntax is different, viz. an adverbial phrase introduced by this negative preposition, it would appear that this was the accepted means of negating the infinitive in a conditional protasis:

> [a-*mur-m*]*i ba-li a-ṣé* ERÍN.MEŠ *pí-ṭ*[*á-ti*] / [*i-na* MU^{š}]$^{a-an-ti}$ *an-ni-ti* / [*ù la-*]*qú-mi* ⸢URU.⸣.⸢MEŠ⸣ ⸢*Gub*⸣$^{⸢ub⸣}$-*la* "[Behold], without the coming forth of the arm[y in] this [y]ear, [then] they [will ta]ke the town(s) of Byblos" (EA 129:40-42; Moran 1987b:347 n. 20; 1992:211 n. 19).

PARANOMASTIC USAGE

The syntagma of strengthening a finite verb by the adverbial use of the absolute infinitive is widely attested in OA and in OB, where the pattern is *qatālumma iqattal / iqtul*, etc. (*GAG*:202-203, §150a; Aro 1961:112-115). However, it is extremely rare in MB; only one example is cited by the grammars, *šá-a-lu ú-ul i-šá-a-la-an-ni* "He certainly didn't ask me" (BE 17/1 42:15; Aro 1955:122; 1961:114; *GAG*:203). An Egyptian epistle from the Ramesside period has: *ù la-qú-ú ul il-qa-aš-š*[*u-nu?*] "He verily did not take th[em?]" (*KUB* 3, 27:r. 19; Cochavi-Rainey 1988:183, §2.4.4). Otherwise, this construction seems to be unattested in the peripheral dialects. The infinitive is presumed to be in the locative-adverbial case (*GAG*:202). There are some instances in Assyrian when the infinitive stands in the accusative (*GAG*:203), including the MA examples (*CAD* N/1:290): *nu-pu-ša na-ap-pí-*[*ša*] (*KAV* 109:12) and *nu-pu-ša na-pí-ša* "air out (the garments)" (*KAV* 99:14).

Ugaritic employs the locative-adverbial with *-u* (not the nominative as Moran 1950a:127 n. 133, had assumed), as in the following:

> *rǵb . rǵbt* [...] *hm . ǵmu . ǵmit* = **raǵābu raǵibti . . . humma ǵamāʾu ǵamiʾti* "Are you verily hungry? . . . Or are you verily thirsty?" (*KTU* 1.4:33-34); *bu . tbu* = **bāʾu tubāʾu* "She verily came" (*KTU* 1.16:VI 3); *šṣu . ašṣu* = **šôṣiʾu ʾašôṣiʾu* "I will verily bring out" (*KTU* 2.34:up.ed. 2).

This is remarkable because the four examples from the Byblos texts have the infinitive in the accusative!

None of the four Byblos passages is satisfactory; all are broken or problematic. The case ending is certain, however, as in the following:

> *ù ša-ma ú-ul* / [*tu-u*]*š-mu-na* "But they were verily not [he]eded" (EA 89:9-10); *a-na* [*lì*]*b-bi-ši-na a-ša-b*[*a l*]*a a-ši-*[*i*]*b* "In their midst he is verily not located" (EA 92:10); [*ù*] *la-qa-ma* URU*Gub*[*-la*] /

> [*iš-t*]*u qa-ti-ka la-a-*[*mì*] / [*yi-ìl-qú*]-*ši*$_x$(ŠE) *a-di da-r*[*i-ti*] "[And] taking Byb[los] from your hand [he will] not [take] it forev[er]" (EA 124:54-56).

The final example is more difficult to interpret morphologically though the syntagma is clear:

> *ù la-*⸢*qé*⸣*-*⸢*mi*⸣ *ti-ìl-qú-na-ši* "then verily they will capture it" (EA 131:17; Moran 1950a:57, 176).

Perhaps the orthography was meant by the scribe to represent *laqē-mi,* with vowel coloring in proximity to the missing guttural.

DIRECT OBJECT OF ANOTHER VERB

One of the most frequent usages of the infinitive is as the object of a governing verb (Aro 1961:74-108). By such combinations, various modal nuances were expressed. It should be noted that the infinitive in this position takes the accusative case. This is usually signified by the *-a* suffix but if the infinitive governed its own object as a dependent noun or suffix, then it may take the bound form with -*Ø* suffix, cf. *i-pé-eš*$_{15}$ *ar-ni* "to commit a crime" (EA 362:45) with [*i-p*]*é-ša* URU*Gub-la* "to conquer Byblos" (EA 79:24; Moran 1987a:212). When the infinitive is third weak, the accusative *-a* may be expressed, e.g. *la-qa* URU*Gub-la* "to take Byblos" (EA 91:13), or may lead to a contracted form, e.g. *a-ṣé* KÁ*a-bu-ul-lí* \ *ša-aḫ-ri* "to go out the city gate" (EA 244:16). An enclitic, such as *-mi,* may intervene between the construct and its dependent subject or object, e.g. *a-ba-at-mì* URU*Ma-gid*$_6$*-da*[KI] "to destroy Meġiddo" (EA 244:42-43).

The ensuing catalogue of examples is arranged according to the governing verbs. In each case at least one example of every infinitive governed by the particular verb will be given and special features of the syntax will be highlighted. The majority of cases have the infinitive after the governing verb; only rarely does the infinitive precede its governing verb as in the standard Akkadian dialects (*GAG*:203, §150e). One may note that, in Mari, among the verbs governing an infinitive, only *raṭābu* "to continue," has its infinitive after the finite form; this construction is considered a West Semitism (Finet 268, §93d; *GAG*:183, §130d).

*bu*ʾʾ*û*. This is the second most frequently used verb to govern the infinitive (ca. 23 attestations). Its special meaning, "to seek, desire," is definitely of western peripheral provenance, mainly in the EA texts from Canaan but also in Ugarit and Hattusas (*CAD* B:363-364; cf. *infra*, pp. 140-146); only rarely does it appear in Nuzi or in NA contexts. The idiom is obviously a calque on some WS verb; roots such as the cognate to *bu*ʾʾ*û*, Ugaritic **bǵy*, or others such as **bqṯ* or Heb. **drš*, come to mind. One Ugaritic passage does employ the imperative *bqṯ* to translate *bu*ʾʾ*û* in a well known idiom (*KTU* 2.39:34; Rainey 1971b:162), but it is unattested with an infinitive as object.

The range of infinitives used with *bu*ʾʾ*û* is as follows; first two examples in which the infinitive precedes the finite verb:

> *a-ba-at-mì* URU*Ma-gid*$_6$*-da*[KI] / *yu-ba-á*ʾ*-ú* "He is seeking to destroy Megiddo" (EA 244:42-43); *ù* LÚ.MEŠ / *ḫu-‹ub›-ši-ia pa-ṭá-ra-ma tu-ba-ú-na* "But my yeoman farmers are seeking to desert" (EA 114:21-22).

As mentioned above, the infinitive usually comes after its governing finite verb. One verb of motion happens to have the same subject as the governing verb:

> *ù yu-ba-ú* / *a-la-k*[*a*$_{13}$] *a-di* URU*Gub-la* "And he was seeking to come as far as Byblos" (EA 85:52-53).

But another verb of motion has a subject different from that of the governing verb:

> [*ù*] *tu-ba!-ú-na ur-ra* / [*ù*] *mu-ša-am a-ṣé* ERÍN.MEŠ / *pí-ṭá-ti* "[And] they are seeking day and night the coming forth of the army" (EA 73:20-22; also EA 70:20); *ù a-na-ku i-ba-ú a-ṣé-ši* "But I am seeking its (the army's) coming forth" (EA 362:58).

A transitive infinitive, on the other hand, has the same subject as the governing verb and may express its own object as a dependent noun or pronoun:

> [*ù*] *ki-na-na tu-ba-ú-na* / [*i-p*]*é-ša* ^{URU}*Gub-la ù* / ^{URU}*Baṭ-ru-na*^{KI} "[And] thus they are seeking [to con]quer Byblos and Baṭrôna" (EA 79:23-25; for this meaning of *epēšu*, cf. Moran 1987a:212).

One might argue that, because of the final *-a* on the infinitive, the following GN's are not in the dependent case but rather in the accusative. However, the preservation of a case vowel on a nominal form in the construct, i.e. [*i-p*]*é-ša*, is not unknown in Akkadian written by WS scribes (Huehnergard 1989:150-151). Nevertheless, the usual bound form in the infinitive has -Ø suffix:

> *ù ka-li* / LÚ.MEŠ *ḫa-za-nu-te tu-ba-ú-na* / *i-pé-eš an-nu-tu*$_4$(sic!) *a-na* ^{I}ÌR-*A-ši-ir-ta* "And all the city rulers are seeking to do this to ᶜAbdi-Ashirta" (EA 73:23-25); *ù ti-ba-ú-na i-pé-eš*$_{15}$ *ar-ni* "But they are seeking to commit treason" (EA 362:45; also EA 129:29).

A contrived N stem infinitive of *epēšu* also has the same subject as its governing verb:

> *a-na* ^{URU}*I-˹bir*$_5$*˺-ta* / *al-ka ù ˹bu˺-ú in*$_4$*-né-ep-ša* / *a-na* LÚ.MEŠ GAZ.MEŠ "I went to ᶜIbirta but they sought to join the *ᶜapîrû* men" (EA 104:52-54; Rainey 1989-90:59a; *contra* Moran 1987b:300 n. 5; 1992:177 n. 3).

Infinitives of the transitive *leqû* also have the same subject as their governing verb and usually govern their own object as a dependent noun (EA 91:13) or pronoun (EA 79:28; 91:22-23). But for emphasis, the object of the infinitive may be placed at the head of the clause, before the governing verb:

> ^{URU}*Ṣu-mu-ra tu-ba-ú-na la-qa* "And Ṣumur (itself) they are seeking to take" (EA 105:23-24; also EA 73:1-13).

The same epistle may employ both constructions:

> *a-nu-*⸢*ma*⸣ 2 URU *ša ir-ti-ḫu* / *a*[*-n*]*a ia-ši* ⸢*yu*⸣*-ba-ú la-qa* / [*a-na ša-a-šu*] "Now, the two towns that remain to me he is seeking to take [for himself]" (EA 76:9-11); *ù yu-ba-ú* / [*la*]*-qa ka-li* URU.MEŠ *šàr-ru*(sic!) ^{d}UTU / [*a-n*]*a ša-a-šu* / . . . *i-nu-ma* / ⸢*yu*⸣*-ba-ú la-qa* KUR LUGAL *a-na ša-a-šu* "And he is seeking [to ta]ke all the towns of the king, the sun god, for himself . . . that he is seeking to take the king's land for himself" (EA 76:12-16).

Once the object of the infinitive appears as an accusative pronoun attached to the governing verb!

> [. . . *ù*] / $^{URU.KI}$*Baṭ-ru-na ir-ti-ḫ*[*a-at a-na ia-ši*] / *ù ti-ba-ú-na-ši la-q*[*a-a* (?)] "[And] Baṭrôna rema[ins to me] and they are seeking to ta[ke] it" (EA 129:17-19).

Various other transitive infinitives governed by finite forms of *bu*$^{\supset\supset}$*û* show the same constructions; the object of the infinitive is usually dependent upon it:

> *ù bu-i-ti*$_{7}$ *pu-ḫi-ir* / KASKAL.ḪÁ *i-na qa-at* ŠEŠ-*ia* "And I sought to assemble caravans in the charge of my brother" (EA 264:6-7); *i-na-an-na bu-i-ti*$_{7}$ *uš-šir*$_{4}$ / KASKAL.ḪÁ-*ia a-na* ^{I}*šàr-ri* / \ EN-*ia* "Now, I sought to send caravans to the king, my lord" (EA 264:20-22; also EA 117:43-44).

But for emphasis, the object may precede the finite verb:

> *šá-ni-tam šum-*[*ma*] / $^{⸢URU⸣}$*Gub-la ú-ba-ú ṣa-ba-ta* "Furthermore, if he seeks to take (even) Byblos" (EA 88:21-22).

le$^{\supset}$*û*. This is the verb used most frequently with an infinitive as object, some thirty-three times. In this manner the nuance "to be able" is realized; however, in the texts at hand, all the examples of *le*$^{\supset}$*û* are negated — in order to express the idea "to be unable"! As with *bu*$^{\supset\supset}$*û*, the overwhelming majority of examples place the infinitive immediately after its governing finite verbal form. There are intransitive verbs of motion, such as *alāku*:

> *ù a-na-ku la-a i-le-ú / a-la-ka*$_{13}$ *a-na til-la-ti / a-na* URU*Ṣu-mu-ra* "And I am unable to go the help of Ṣumur" (EA 105:29-31; also EA 102:17-19, 24-25; 104:36-39).

Similar intransitive examples are also attested with the motion verb, (*w*)*aṣû*,

> *ù ú-ul ni-le-ú / a-ṣa-am a-na* EDIN.MEŠ "And we are unable to go forth to the open fields" (EA 88:20-21; Moran 1975a:156-157; also EA 81:21-22; 104:49-51).

But this verb can also be transitive. In the following example it is followed by its object as dependent genitive:

> *ù la-a-mì ni-le-ú / a-ṣé* KÁ*a-bu-ul-lí* \ *ša-aḫ-ri* "And we are unable to go out the city gate" (EA 244:15-17).

The infinitive of the verb of motion *erēbu* is only attested with adverbial complements, not with direct objects:

> *ù la-a ni-le-ú / e-re-ba a-na* URU*Ṣu-mu-ri* "And we are unable to enter in to Ṣumur" (EA 98:19-20; 114:36-37); *ù la a-la-á*ʾ*-e / e-ra-ba iš-tu* (sic!) LUGAL EN-*ia* "And I am unable to enter in to(!) the king, my lord" (EA 286:42-43; for the Assyrian form, cf. Moran 1975b:153).

On the other hand, a transitive infinitive of an action verb may appear without an object:

> *ù la-a-mi ni-le-ú /* ZÚ.SI.GA *ba-qa-ni* \ *ka-*⸢*ṣí*⸣*-ra* "And we are unable to do the plucking (and) harvesting" (EA 244:13-14); *ù / [la-m]ì te-lé-ú-na* LÚ.MEŠ-*tu*$_4$ / *[da-g]a-la i-na mu-ḫi-i[a?]* "And the men are [no]t able [to se]rve you" (EA 249:12-14; cf. Moran 1987b:474; 1992:302).

A variety of infinitives from transitive action verbs can be found governed by a finite form of *leʾû*, normally with the object dependent upon the infinitive, e.g.

> *ù i-lé-i a-ra-ad* / LUGAL EN-*ia ki-i-ma* LÚ.MEŠ *a-bu-ti-nu* / *pa-na-nu-um* "that I may be able to serve the king, my lord, like my fathers in the past" (EA 144:32-34); *ú-ul ni-le-ú* / *i-pé-eš mi-im-mi* "We are unable to do anything" (EA 89:42-43; also EA 116:52-53; 69:17-18).

The object of the infinitive can be multiple:

> ⸢*ù*⸣ / *la-a ni-la-ú* / *e-ze-eb a-ba!-at!* / *šàr-ri* EN-*ia* / *ù* LÚ.MAŠKÍM / *ša-a ša-ak-na-t*[*a*] / UGU-*ia* "And we are unable to abandon the word of the king, my lord, and the commissioner whom you have appointed over me" (EA 211:17-23).

It can also be comprised of a dependent suffix with its own explicatory apposition:

> *ù la-a i-le-éʾ-e e-za-bi-ša* / KUR.ḪÁ URU*Ú-ru-sa-lim* KI "And I am unable to abandon it, viz. the land of Jerusalem" (EA 287:62-63).

The infinitive of *leqû* distinguishes two forms, one with a dependent noun, viz.

> *šum-ma la-a ti-le-ú la-qé* ÌR-*k*[*a*] "If you are unable to take yo[ur] servant" (EA 114:44),

and the other with suffix pronouns:

> *ú-ul ti-le-ú-na* / *la-qa-ia iš-tu qa-at* / IÌR-*A-ši-ir-ta* "Are you unable to deliver me from the hand of ᶜAbdi-Ashirta?" (EA 82:6-8; also EA 79:39-41; 83:20; 124:53).

Other transitive action infinitives governed by forms of *leʾû* are: *mu-še-ra* KASKAL "to send a caravan" (EA 287:27-29);

na-ṣa-ar-ši "to guard it" (EA 238:9); [*ṣa-*]*ba-at* URU*Baṭ-ru-n*[*a*] "[to ta]ke Baṭrôna" (EA 93:20); *uš-šir*$_4$ / KASKAL.ḪÁ-*ia a-na* I*šàr-ri* EN-*ia* "to send my caravans to the king" (EA 264:9-10); *uš-šar* / GIŠMÁ.MEŠ-*ia a-na aš-ra-nu* "to send my ships there" (EA 126:7-8; also EA 82:222; 113:29).

For emphasis, the infinitive as object may be placed at the head of the clause:

> *ša-ḫa-at-ši i-le-ú ù ṣa-bat-ši* / *la i-le-ú* "To besiege it they are able but to capture it they are not able" (EA 106:12-13); ⌜*ù*⌝ *uš-šar-šu-nu a-na* URU*Ṣu-mu-ra* / [*l*]*a-a i-le-*[*ú aš-š*]*um* ⌜GIŠ⌝MÁ.[MEŠ] ⌜URU⌝*Ar-wa-da* "But to send them to Ṣumur I am unab[le bec]ause of the ships of Arvad" (EA 105:86-87).

These must be compared with a unique instance in which the object begins the clause but the governed verb of which it is the object is expressed by an adverbial complement of purpose which itself appears at the end of the clause:

> URU*Ṣur-ri* / *la-a i-lé-ú-ni*$_7$ *a-na ṣa-bat* "Tyre they are unable to capture" (EA 149:65-66).

amāru. One very difficult passage has a transitive infinitive governed by a verb form of *amāru* that has caused many problems of interpretation (cf. Moran 1987b:560 n. 3; 1992:362 n. 3). It is possible even to take the governing form as an infinitive but that would create a syntagma for which there is no precedent. The following rendering takes it as an imperfect expressing continuous action in past time with the meaning "to muster (troops)" (*contra* Rainey 1978b:26-27, 63).

> *i-na* UD *aš-me ù* ⌜*a*⌝*-ma-*⌜*ru*⌝ / i-pé-*eš*$_{15}$ *nu-kúr-ti* / *i-na ša-a-šu* "From the day when I heard I have been mustering to make war with him" (EA 364:21-23).

ḫummuṭu. Of the lesser documented verbs, this one appears twice, both in injunctive contexts. In one instance it is itself in the imperative and in the other case it is a volitive (or jussive with ventive ending):

> *šá-ni-tam* / *ši-me-e ia-ši ḫu-mi-ṭa₅ ki-ma* / *ar-ḫi-iš ka-ša-da* "Furthermore, listen to me! Make haste to arrive quickly!" (EA 102:29-31); *ki-n[a-na]* / *yu-ḫa-mi-ṭá uš-šar* ERÍN.MEŠ *p[í-ṭá]-t[i]* "Th[us], may he make haste to send the army: (EA 129:77-79; cf. *supra*, p. 150).

magāru. This verb governs the infinitive of *nadānu* in two passages:

> *ù la-a* / *i-ma-gur na-da-an-šu* "But I did not agree to surrender him" (EA 234:26-27; also EA 185:61-62, 64).

namguru. Likewise, the N stem of the above also governs, or is complemented by, two accusative infinitives in a passage fraught with difficulties:

> *mi-ia-mi yi-ma-gi-ir* / *ur-ru-ba it-ti* ^I*šàr-ri* EN-*ia* / *le-qé-ma* GUŠKIN! *ù* GUŠKIN.GUN / ^I*šàr-ri* EN-*ia* "Who would agree (dare?) to enter into the (presence of) the king, my lord, to take the gold and the red gold of the king, my lord?" (EA 283:10-13; Rainey 1989-90:71; *contra* Moran 1987b:505 n. 3; 1992:324 n. 5).

malāku. Two contexts occur in which this verb governs a negated infinitive:

> *ù i-ma-la-ku ba-li-mì* / *ur-ru-ud* LUGAL EN-*ia* "But would I consider not serving the king, my lord?" (EA 191:9-10; *contra CAD* B:71b); *mi-ia-mi yi-ma-lik i-zi-za [i]-na pa-ni* / ERÍN.MEŠ *pí-ṭá-at* LUGAL *be-lí-ia* "Who would dare to stand before the army of the king, my lord?" (EA 94:12-13).

Actually, the latter example and possibly also the former may be from the N stem. The fact that they have different theme vowels may be a matter of geographical provenances.

nadānu. For expressing the idea of "permission" this verb is used. The subject of the infinitive is always different from that of the governing verb:

> *la-a-mi* / *an-ti-in₄-nu e-re-eb* / LÚ.ME[Š] *ša* URU*Ṣu-mu-ri* KI / [*a*]-*n*[*a*] URU.KI-*ia* "I will not permit the men of Ṣumur to enter my city" (EA 96:7-10; Youngblood 1962).

Once the subject of the infinitive appears as an accusative suffix on the governing verb:

> *ú-ul na-a*[*d-*]*nu-n*[*i i-r*]*e-ba* "They didn't permit me to enter" (EA 138:58).

qâlu. The one case where this verb seems to govern an infinitive happens to have the negative *balu*.

> *la-a i-qa-al* I*šàr-ru* / EN-*ia b*[*a-*]*lu ša!-a-al* I*A-*[*m*]*a-an-ḫa-at-pí* "May the king, my lord not keep silent without investigating Amanḫatpi" (EA 185:67-68; Moran 1987b:423 n. 8; 1992:267 n. 9).

quʾʾû. A lone instance of this verb with an unusually formed infinitive is attested. The morphological peculiarities of *a-ṣa-i*, a construct in the accusative, are discussed in the preceding chapter (cf. *supra*, p. 369).

> *ki-na-an-na* / *tu-qa-ú-na* ÌR.MEŠ / *a-ṣa-i a-wa-te*MEŠ / *iš-tu* UZUKA / \ *pí-i be-li-šu-nu* "Thus, the servants await the coming forth of the words from the mouth of their lord" (EA 195:19-23; Moran 1987b:432; 1992:273).

ṣabû "to desire." If the following broken context is properly restored, the object appears to come after the governing verb and before the infinitive:

> *a-di ti-iṣ-bu* [*ar-na*] / GAL *i-pé-ša* "Still they were determined to commit a great [crime]" (EA 129:26-27; cf. an alternative

interpretation by Moran 1987b:346 nn. 13, 15; 1992:210 nn. 13, 15).

uḫḫuru. Finally, this verb serves to add a temporal dimension to the action of its governed infinitive, which in each case is a verb of motion having the same subject as the finite form which governs it:

> *uḫ-ḫu-ra-ta* / *a-ṣa* "You were late coming forth" (EA 102:9-10); *šá-ni-tam la-mi* / [*tu-uḫ-ḫ*]*i-ra ka-ša-da* "Furthermore, don't [be la]te arriving" (EA 102:32-33).

ATTRIBUTIVE

Although the function of the infinitive as the direct object of a finite verb is substantival in nature, it is also verbal in that the infinitive itself nearly always governs either a dependent noun or pronoun as its subject or as its own direct object. Instances when an infinitive is viewed strictly as a noun are confined to an attributive function in which the infinitive is nominalized by the relative pronoun *ša* (Aro 1961:58-67). Examples are confined to two verbs, (*w*)*ašābu* "to sit" (1x) and *kabāsu* / *kabāšu* (13x).

The attested examples are all in introductory formulae of obeisance. The writer describes himself as a humble object designated for pharaoh's use:

> *um-ma* [I]*Bir*$_5$*-ia-wa-za* / ÌR-*ka* SAḪAR.MEŠ \ *ep-ri* / *ša* GÌR.MEŠ-*ka* *ù* / KI.MEŠ *ša ka-bá-sí-ka* / GIŠ.GU.ZA *ša a-ša-bi-ka* / *ù* GIŠ.GÌR.GUB \ *gi-iš-tap-pí* / *ša* GÌR.MEŠ-*ka* "Thus (says) Biryawaza, your servant, the dust of your feet, the ground of your treading, the chair of your sitting, and the footstool of your feet" (EA 195:4-10).

This is the only example with two infinitives. Elsewhere, only one is used: *ṭi*$_4$*-iṭ ša ka-bá-ši-ka* "the clay of your treading" (EA 213:5; 220:6; 241:6; 255:5); *qa-qa-ru ša ka-ba-ši-šu* "the ground of his treading" (EA 232:5; also EA 185:6; 231:8; 366:6; with KI.MEŠ

EA 233:8; 234:6); *i[p-ru]* / [*ša*] *ka-bá-š[e-ka]* "the dust of your treading" EA 253:3-4). One example consists of a construct relationship instead of employing the more customary syntax with the relative *ša*, viz. *qa-qa-ri* ka_4*-bá-sí!-*ka_4. "the ground of your treading" (EA 198:7).

In such cases as these, the dictionaries (*CAD* K:8a; *AHw*:415b) classify the relevant forms as verbal, i.e. as infinitives and not as substantives on the *qatālu* pattern. All of the examples cited also have a subject expressed by the suffix pronoun.

CHAPTER XVII

THE INFINITIVE — MORPHOSYNTAX (CONT.)

It remains to survey the functions of the infinitive in adverbial expressions, viz. in constructions with a preposition. These formations are the most ubiquitous of all the usages of the infinitive and might be considered such a commonplace as to warrant little special attention. However, it will be seen that these adverbial phrases form an essential part of the message in many verbal and even some non-verbal clauses in the EA letters. The WS word order that generally prevails in the EA texts from Canaan affects the place assigned to the adverbial vis à vis the governing verb. Examples gleaned from the EA texts in question will be discussed below under their respective semantic headings and according to the governing preposition. Of the 160 or so instances of prepositional phrases with infinitives, only a representative selection can be cited here. Emphasis will be on especially clear examples illustrating the main categories of usage, plus certain passages exhibiting unusual word order and/or semantic nuance

EXPRESSIONS OF PURPOSE

Over 100 examples, nearly two thirds of the entire collection, serve to express purpose. Except for a very few cases, the preposition involved is *ana* (Aro 1961:119-214)

ana. Moran (1950a:81) had observed that prepositional phrases with *ana* governing the infinitive were widely used in the Byblos texts, but he also noted that such was typical Akkadian usage anyway (*GAG*:202, §150h). The distinguishing feature of the EA texts from Canaan is that these adverbial complements generally follow the verb which governs them. Some typical examples are:

> *ù yu-wa-ši-ra* / 1 ^{LÚ}GAL *a-na na-ṣa-ri-ia* "So may he send one official to protect me!" (EA 64:12-13); *li-di-nam-mi šàr-ru* 1 ME LÚ.MEŠ *ma-an-ṣa-ar-ta*$_5$ / *a-na na-ṣa-ri* URU.KI.-*šu* "May the king send one hundred garrison troops to guard his city!" (EA 244:34-36); *ki-i-me e-nu-ma* / *ip-qí-id-ni* LUGAL *be-li-ia* / *a-na na-ṣa-ri* URU-*šu* "As when the king, my lord, appointed me to guard his city" (EA 148:20-22; cf. also EA 155:49-50); *ù ip-ḫu-ru-ni*$_7$ ^{GIŠ}MÁ.MEŠ-*šu-nu* / ^{GIŠ}GIGIR.MEŠ-*šu-nu* ERÍN.MEŠ GÌR-*šu-nu* / *a-na ṣa-ba-ti* ^{URU}*Ṣur-ri* GEMÉ LUGAL "And they have assembled their ships, their chariots, (and) the foot soldiers in order to capture Tyre, the handmaiden of the king" (EA 149:61-63).

In all of these particular passages, the direct object of the governing verb is the subject of the infinitive. The direct object of the infinitive is dependent upon it, either as a suffix pronoun or as a noun in the dependent case.

For emphasis, the adverbial may be placed at the head of its clause, before the governing verb:

> *a-na ḫal-li-iq* / KUR LUGAL EN-*ia yu-ba-á*ʾ*-ú* ^{I}⸢*Mil*⸣-⸢*ki*⸣-*l*[*ì*] "It is to subvert the land of the king that Milkili is seeking" (EA 250:55-56).

In this passage, as in many others, the subject of the governing verb is also the subject of the infinitive of purpose, e.g.

> *ù* ŠEŠ-*ia* TUR *iš-tu ia-ti* / *i-na-kar*$_5$*-mi* ^{URU}*Gub-la*^{KI} / *a-na na-da-ni* URU.KI-*li* / *a-na* DUMU.MEŠ ÌR-^{I}*A-ši-ir-ti* "And my younger brother has alienated the city of Byblos from me in order to give the city to the sons of ᶜAbdi-Ashirta" (EA 137:16-19).

It should be noted in this example that, though the infinitive is in construct with its direct object, it carries an *-i* suffix rather than the customary -Ø. As mentioned previously (*supra*, pp. 383-384), there is no way of knowing for sure whether this is just a reflection of the prevailing situation in Canaanite (i.e. case endings still preserved on constructs), or whether the *-i* is the enigmatic suffix *-i* found on infinitives in other syntactic positions. Many examples of this possible dependent case ending on the infinitive in construct could be cited (e.g. EA 60:12-13; 148:15-16; 150:6-7; 151:15-16; 196:35-36; 220:30-31; 253:35).

A different arrangement is for the object of the infinitive of purpose to precede it while the subject follows it as a dependent genitive suffix or substantive. Note the following text where the objects of the respective infinitives are themselves the dependent objects of a preceding infinitive of purpose:

> *ù a-nu-um-ma a-na-an-ṣár* / URUṢ*ur-ri* URU *ra-bi-tu* / *a-na* LUGAL *be-li-ia a-di* / *i-wa-ṣí* ZAG LUGAL *da-na-tu i-na muḫ-ḫi-ia* / *a-na na-da-an me-e a-na šu-ta-ia* / *ù* GIŠ.MEŠ *a-na šu-ḫu-ni-ia* "And now I am guarding Tyre, the great city, for the king, my lord, until the mighty arm of the king shall come forth to(sic!) me in order to give water for my drinking and wood for my warming" (EA 147:61-66).

Admittedly, the suffixes on the two D stem infinitives, *šuttāya* and *šuḫḫuniya*, may also be construed as objects (cf. *supra*, pp. 378, 379), "for watering me," and "for warming me." However the next example clearly seems to have a suffix pronoun as the subject of the G stem infinitive:

> *ù li-id-din* URUÚ-*sú*KI / *a-na* ÌR-*šu* DUG \ *a-ku-ni* \ *mi-ma* / *a-na ši-te-šu* "So may Usu give to his servant a jar of water for him to drink!" (EA 148:11-13; contrast Moran 1987b:380; 1992:235; likewise EA 151:37-40; 155:7-10, 24-26; also EA 79:32-33; 125:16-18).

The preceding object of the infinitive of purpose may also be the subject of an existential clause, either negative:

> *ù i[a-]nu* / A.MEŠ! *a-na š[a]-te-šu* "But there is no water for him to drink" (EA 85:53-54; also EA 85:10-11; 101:6-10; 107:37-38; 125:25-26);

or positive:

> *ù* LÚ.MEŠ [*ḫu-*]*ub-ši* / *pa-aṭ-ru a-na* URU.ME[Š] / *a-šar i-ba-ši* ŠE.*IM*.⸢ḪÁ⸣ / *a-na a-ka-li-šu-nu* "And the yeomen farmers have departed to towns where there is grain for them to eat" (EA 125:r. 27-30).

In one exceptional case the object of the infinitive of purpose is first of all the object of the main verb while the infinitive is in a relative clause; the scribe has neglected to employ a resumptive pronoun in the relative clause:

> *ù il*$_5$*-te*$_9$*-qú* URU.DIDLI.[Ḫ]Á / *ša* ^{I}LUGAL EN-*ia ša* [NU]-*i*[*d*] / ^{I}*šàr-ru* EN-*ia i-na qà-t*[*i-ia*] / *a-na na-ṣa-ar* "They have captured the cities of the king, my lord, which the king, my lord [intru]sted to [me] to guard" (EA 237:5-8).

Instead of taking a direct object, an infinitive of purpose may itself have an adverbial complement:

> *a-nu-ma eš-me pu-ḫi-ir-mi* / ⸢*ka*⸣*-li* LÚ.MEŠ GAZ.MEŠ / [*a-n*]*a ma-qa-ti* UGU-*ia* "Now I have heard, 'He has assembled all the *ʿapîrû* men [t]o fall on me'" (EA 91:23-25; cf. EA 94:74-76).

Clear examples of these adverbials expressing purpose are non-verbal clauses with *libbu*, "desire, intention" (*CAD* L:170b-171b).

> *šum-*[*ma*] / *lìb-bi šàr-ri a-na* / *ba-la-aṭ* ÌR-*šu ù* / URU-*li-šu uš-ši-ra* ‹LÚ.MEŠ› / [*m*]*a-ṣa-ar-ta ù* / *ti-na-ṣa-ru* URU-*ka ù* / ÌR-*ka* "If it is the king's desire that his servant and his city should live, send garrison troops that they may protect your city and your servant!" (EA 112:30-36).

There the subjects of the infinitive were not identical with the person whose desire was being queried, namely the king. In other texts, the king is also the subject of the infinitive:

⌜*šum*⌝-*ma lìb*-⌜*bi*⌝ LUGAL *be-li-ia* / *a*-[*n*]*a na-ṣa*-[*a*]*r* URU-*šu* "If it is the king's desire to protect his city" (EA 127:26-27; also EA 130:44-45).

A similar nominal expression with *pānū* expressing the meaning, "intention," also contains a subject identical to that of the infinitive of purpose:

pa-nu-ia-ma a-na a-ra-ad / *šàr-ri* EN-*ia* "It is *my* intention to serve the king, my lord" (EA 119:43-44; also EA 118:39-41; 129:31; 151:8-9; 295:r. 9-10; and 149:28-29, Moran 1987b:383 n. 3; 1992:237 n. 2).

Verbal clauses with a similar meaning confirm this relationship; the subject of the governing verb is identical to that of the infinitive of purpose:

ù na-[*a*]*d-na pa-ni-nu a-na* / *a-ra-di-ka* "We have set our faces to serve you" = "We have committed ourselves to serve you" (EA 89:16-17; Albright and Moran 1950:166), or "Our faces are seṭ to serve you" (cf. *supra*, pp. 46, 295); *ù a-nu-u*[*m-m*]*a* / [*t*]*a*!-*ri-iṣ pa-ni*[-*šu*] / *a-na la-qé-i* / URU*Ma-gi-id-da*KI "And now he has set [his] face to take Megiddo" (EA 244:21-24); *yi-de-mì šàr-ru* EN-*ia* [*i*]-*n*[*u*]-*ma* / *tu-ur-ri-ṣú-m*[*ì*] 2 DUMU LÚ*ar-ni* ⌜LUGAL⌝ [*b*]*e-lí-ia* / 2 DUMU I*La-ab-a*[-*y*]*a pa-ni-šu-ni* / *a-na ḫa-lí-iq* KUR ⌜*šàr*⌝-*ri* EN-*ia* "May the king, my lord, be apprised [t]hat the two sons of the traitor to the king, my lord, the two sons of Labʾayu, have set their faces to subvert the land of the king, my lord!" (EA 250:4-7).

Finally, there are a few instances where the prepositional phrase is employed in place of an injunctive (precative or jussive) in a widely used syntagma — expressing the desire that the king be apprised or take cognizance of the situation at hand.

ù a-na la-ma-di / ⌜LUGAL⌝ EN-*ia* "So for the king's information" (EA 274:17-18; 265:14-15).

aššum. There are also two passages like those just cited in which the preposition *aššum* is used instead of *ana*.

> *ù aš-šum la-ma-ad* / LUGAL EN-*ia* ^{d}UTU / *ša is-tu* [AN^{sa}]$^{-me}$ "So in order that the king, my lord, the sun god from [hea]ven, may be informed" (EA 301:21-23; apparently also EA 308:r. 2-8; 309:25-28); *aš-šum la-ma-de$_4$-ka* "For your information" (EA 287:59).

Infinitives of purpose dependent on *aššum* may also complement verbal clauses (Moran 1950a:81). First, examples where the subject of the infinitive is identical with that of the governing verb:

> *ù al-lu-ú ki-na-na-ma yite$_9$-lu* / *ina lì*[*b*]*-bi a-ia-ba aš-šum ṣa-ba-at* / ^{GIŠ}MÁ.MEŠ.-*ia* "And behold, thus he is going out to sea in order to seize my ships" (EA 114:18-19); *ù al-ka-ti* / *a-na* É-*šu aš-šum* / *e-pu-uš* DÙG.GA *bi-ri-‹nu›* "So I went to his house in order to make a treaty between us" (EA 136:30-32; cf. Moran 1987b:356; 1992:217).

The subject of the infinitive may also be the object of the governing verb as in the following:

> *ù ut-te-er* / *a-na* LUGAL EN-*ia iš-tu* / LÚ.MEŠ SA.GAZ.MEŠ *aš-šum ur-ru-di-šu* "And I restored the cities to the king, my lord, from the *ᶜapîrû* men in order to serve him" (EA 189:r. 15-17)

The infinitive of purpose may also be a component in a non-verbal clause. Here the whole context is cited to place the example in proper perspective:

> *šá-ni-tam li-it-‹ri›-iṣ a-na be*-EN-*ia* / *ù lu-wa-ši-ra* 20 *ta-pal ša* SIG$_5$-*qú* / ANŠE.KUR.RA *a-na* ÌR-*šu ma-du* LÚ.MEŠ / *it-ti-ia aš-šum-ma a-la-ki-ia* / *a-na nu-kúr-ti*^{MEŠ} LUGAL BE-*ia* "Furthermore, may it please my lord that he may send twenty

teams of the best horses to his servant; many are the men with me for my participation in the king's wars" (EA 106:41-45; contrast Moran 1987b:303; 1992:179).

The addition of enclitic *-ma* to the preposition suggests that its phrase is the logical predicate (Rainey 1976a). The writer may have wanted to stress that it was to fulfill his military obligations to the king that he had to, or would have to, assemble so many men: "It is for fighting the king's battles that so many men are needed."

The ensuing passage with *aššum* seems a bit awkward. This is the kind of expression where one might have expected *ištu* instead:

yi-ki-im-ni DINGIR-*LIM ša* LUGAL ⌜EN⌝-[*i*]*a* / *aš-šum i-pé-eš*$_{15}$ *nu-kúr-ti i-na* ⌜LÚ⌝.MEŠ ^{K}[^{UR}*G*]*i-na* / ÌR.MEŠ LUGAL EN-*ia* "May the god of the king, my lord, deliver me *concerning* making war with the men of [G]ina, servants of the king, my lord!" (EA 250:20-21).

ina. The following passage might be taken as concurrence, i.e. "while seizing . . . ," but it is far more likely that this is simply an error of *ina* in place of *ana*:

ù i-na-na iš-ši-ir / LÚ.MEŠ-*šu i-na ṣa-ba-at* KUR.KUR.MEŠ / *Am-qí ù* KI.KI "And now he has sent his men in order to seize the states of ᶜAmqu and the places" (EA 140:28-30; contrast Moran 1987b:369; 1992:226).

ištu. The following protestation of loyalty on the part of a vassal was formulated by the use of a negative assertion of purpose. Here the preposition *ištu* has the meaning "apart from" = "except":

ia-nu / *pa-ni ša-nu-ta*$_5$ *iš-tu* / *ur-ru-ud šàr-ri* "There is no other intention except to serve the king" (EA 253:26-28; Moran 1987b:408; 1992:306).

CIRCUMSTANTIAL

Certain prepositions combine with the infinitive to express action or state circumstantial to the main clause.

CONCURRENT

The preposition used to express concurrence is *ina* (Aro 1961:215-251). Some nine or ten examples are found in this corpus. One passage from Tyre reflects a clear translation, or calque, on the Egyptian circumstantial phrase, *m ḥtp* "at peace," viz.

> *ša it-ta-ṣa-ab gáb-bi* KUR-*ti* / *i-na pa-ša-ḫi i-na du-ni* ZAG \ *ḫa-ap-ši* "He of whom all the lands have become stable being at peace by the might of (his) arm" (EA 147:11-12)

Two striking passages use this syntagma to compare the present situation, exemplified by the imperfect verb forms, with that which will prevail in the future:

> *i-na ba-la-ṭì-ia i-na-ṣí-ru* / URU *šàr-ri a-na ša-a-šu ù* / *šum-ma mi-ta-ti mi-na* / *i-pu-‹šu›-na* "While I'm alive, I am guarding the king's city for him, but if I am dead, what can I do?" (EA 119:15-18); [*i*]-*na-ṣí-ru i-na* / [*b*]*a-la-ṭì-ia i-nu-ma* [*a*]-*mu-ta mi-nu* / ⸢*yi*⸣-*na-ṣa-ru-*$\check{s}i_x$(ŠE) "I am guarding while I'm alive; when I die, who will guard it?" (EA 130:49-52).

An obscure and broken passage (at the bottom of the tablet) seems to be using the adverbial phrase to express "as soon as," viz.

> [*š*]*á-n*[*i-t*]*am a-nu-um-ma i-na i-re-bi* / ⸢GIŠ⸣MÁ.ḪÁ *ša* LUGAL EN-*ia* / [*š*]*a sí-ki-pu* / *i-na* URUPÚ.ḪÁ *uš-ši-ru-n*[*a*] / MÍGEMÉ *ša* LUGAL EN-*ia* "⸢Furthermore,⸣ now with the entry of the ships of the king, my lord, that sailed into Beirut, the handmaiden of the king, my lord, I began sending . . . " (EA 143:18-22; *CAD* S:73b; contrast Moran 1987b:373; 1992:229).

A time frame relative to a past event is also reflected in the following:

> *ù yi-iḫ-di lìb-bi-ia ù* / *yi-*[*š*]*a-qí* SAG-*ia ù in$_4$-nam-ru* / 2 IGI-*ia* \ *ḫi-na-ia i-na ša-me* / *a-wa-at* LUGAL EN-*ia* "And my heart rejoiced and my head was lifted up and my eyes became bright upon hearing the word of the king, my lord" (EA 144:15-18; cf. EA 120:38).

The past event may be expressed by the stative:

> *da-mi-iq ki-a-ma pa-*⌜*ni*⌝ LUGAL / *i-na ša-pa-ri-ka a-na* [Í]R-[*ka*] / *šu-ri-ib-mi* ᴵ*Ḫa-ia a-na* / ᵁᴿᵁ*Ṣu-mu-ra* "It was pleasing to the king when you sent to [your] servant, 'Cause Ḫaya to enter Ṣumur!'" (EA 112:40-43).

Note in the passage just cited that the circumstantial infinitive has an adverbial complement ("to [your] servant") and a direct object, namely the quotation.

Instances of *gamāru* in the stative governing a circumstantial adverbial infinitival phrase reflect a present situation that is the culmination of a process that had been going on for a considerable length of time:

> *ga-am-ru* / DUMU.MEŠ-*šu-nu* DUMU.MÍ-*šu-nu* GIŠ.MEŠ É.MEŠ-*šu-nu* / *i-na na-da-ni i-na* ᴷᵁᴿ‹*Ia*›*-ri-mu-ta* / *i-na bá-la-aṭ* [Z]I-*nu* "Their sons, their daughters (and) their houshold goods are used up in paying to ‹Ya›rimuta to keep ourselves alive" (EA 85:12-15; Youngblood 1961:133-134; also EA 74:16; 75:11-14; 81:38-41; 9:36-39; 112:28; 117:75); *ù ga-am-ra-at* / KUR LUGAL EN-*ia* / *i-na pa-ṭá-ri i-na* LÚ.MEŠ SA.GAZ.MEŠ "The land of the king, my lord, has finished going over to the *ʿapîrû* men" (EA 273:11-14; cf. EA 272:11-17; Naʾaman 1979:680; Moran 1992:318 n. 5; cf. also the broken context, EA 313:5-6).

A negative existential clause uses the circumstantial phrase with the meaning of "since," viz.

> *[i]-ia-nu mi-im-ma / i-na* ⌜É⌝*-ia i-n[a] / [i-]re[-bi-]ia a-na ša-šu* "There is nothing in my house since my entering into it" (EA 316:18-20).

And the same appears to hold true for a positive existential clause:

> *ša-ni-tam / i-na ka-‹ša›-ad* [I]*Ap-pí-ḫa a-na maḫ-ri-ia / ši-si-tu*₄ UGU-*ia* "Furthermore, since Appaḫa ca‹m›e before me, there has been an outcry against me" (EA 69:24-26).

In these two passages, the preposition *ina* may have the nuance "from," but need not be translated "since." Since it may be rendered "when," they must be distinguished from those with *ištu* (cf. *infra,* pp. 412-413).

PROSPECTIVE

Adverbial phrases with infinitives may also express action to take place in the future.

ana ūmī . . . / ina ūmī. . . . One means of placing an action in the future is the construction with *ana ūmi* + the infinitive as a dependent.

> *a-ṣé-mi* ERÍN.MEŠ *pí-ṭá-tu ù ša-mu / a-na ú-mi ka-ša-di-ši ù / ta-ra-at* URU.KI *a-na* LUGAL *be-li-ia* "If the regular army comes forth and they hear about the time of its arrival, then the city will return to the king, my lord" (EA 137:49-51).

On the other hand, *ina* is most likely to have been the preposition used in the following passage:

> [KUR]*A-mur-ri ur-ra / [mu-ša] tu-ba-‹ú› a-ṣa pí-ṭá-ti / [i-na* UD].KÁM.MEŠ *ka-š[a-a]d* / [ERÍN.MEŠ *pí-*]*ṭá-ti* [KUR]*A-m[ur-ri] / [. . . in*₄*]-né-ep-ša-[at] / [gáb-bu a-n]a šàr-r[i* EN*-ia]* "Amurru is seek‹ing› day and night the coming forth of the army; [at the

ti]me of [the ar]my's ar[riv]al, Am[urru . . . wi]ll go ove[r entirely t]o the kin[g, my lord]" (EA 70:25-30).

When comparing the two passages, the [UD].KÁM.MEŠ in the second suggests that the final vowel on *ú-mi* in the first could represent the plural. For that reason the translation "time," has been preferred. However, in both instances, the singular may really be intended, the logogram in the second passage being only a convention.

adi. Infinitives dependent on *adi* pertain to an action expected in the future, i.e. "until" (Aro 1961:254-257). All of the documented examples are with one of two verbs, *kašādu* (9x) and (*w*)*aṣû* (11x). Only representative passages will be cited:

ù la-a ka-ši-id / i-re-šu ù uš-ši-ir-ti-šu / qa-du ERÍN.MEŠ *til-la-ti a-na ka-ta₅ / u-di u-ṣé* ERÍN.MEŠ *pí-ṭá-ti / a-na na-ṣa-ar* ZI *ka* "And as soon as the request arrives, I will send him with auxiliary troops for you until the regular army's coming forth, to protect your life" (EA 82:16-20; also EA 70:23; 71:26-27;79:31; 79:16-17; 105:18-19; 127:38-39; 334:8).

Practically all the instances with *kašādu* also have to do with the anticipated arrival of the army or the king at the head of the army. Similarly, a commissioner wrote to Rib-Haddi of Byblos:

a-lik-mi i-zi-iz a-na URUṢ*u-mu-ur / a-di ka-ša-di-ia* "Go, take up a position at Ṣumur until my arrival!" (EA 102:13-16).

Several texts are affirmations that a ruler is guarding his assigned city until the arrival of the Egyptian army:

ù uṣ-ṣú-ru URU.KIPÚ.ḪÁ */ a-na* LUGAL EN-*ia a-di ka-ša-di /* ERÍN.MEŠ *pí-ṭá-ti* LUGAL EN-*ia* "And I am guarding Beirut for the king, my lord,until the arrival of the army of the king, my lord" (EA 142:12-14; also EA 100:39-41; 103:25-29; 178:6-8; 220:15-19; 227:5-7).

Two other passages have different semantic contexts. One deals, like the above mentioned examples, with a future event:

> *ša-pár-ti a-na ša-šu / a-di ka-ša-di-ka / iš-tu* KASKAL-*ra-ni-ka* "I have written to him (to come) by the time you arrive from your mission" (EA 256:31-33; cf. an alternative below).

RETROSPECTIVE

adi. The last passage with *adi* deals with something that happened in the past:

> *ù a-di ka-ša-di-ia / ù da-ku-šu \ maḫ-ṣú-ú* "But before my arrival, they had smitten him" (EA 245:13-14).

ištu. There are eight examples of the infinitive with *ištu* signifying "since" (cf. Aro 1961:258-259). Five of them refer to past events after which there took place another event in the past. Two of the latter instances were simple, one time acts:

> *i-nu-ma iš-tu* / 10 ŠE-*ti ka-ša-di*[*-i*]*a a-na* URUA.PÚ.MEŠ / *uš-ši-ir-ti* DUMU-*ia a-na* É.GAL NUN "because ten seconds after my arrival in Beirut, I sent my son to the great palace" (EA 138:75-77; Moran 1987b:366 n. 17; 1992:224 n. 17); *ša-ni-tam an-nu-ú iš-tu / ša-pa-ri-ka ṭup-pa a-na mu-ḫi-ia / ša-pár-ti a-na ša-šu / a-di ka-ša-di-ka / iš-tu* KASKAL-*ra-ni-ka* "Furthermore, behold, after your sending a tablet to me, I wrote to him before your arrival from your journey" (EA 256:29-33).

Note that the former is an intransitive verb with dependent suffix as subject; the second is transitive, also with a suffix as subject followed by its object in the accusative.

The other three past events actually are acts, the effects of which have continued up to the time of the writing of the letter:

> *ša-ni-tam iš-tu / ta-ri a-bi-ka iš-tu /* URU*Ṣí-du-na iš-tu* UD.KÁM.MEŠ / *šu-wa-at* in_4*-ne-ep-ša-at* / KUR.MEŠ *a-na*

LÚ.MEŠ GAZ.MEŠ "Furthermore, after your father returned from Sidon, from that very time, the lands have joined the *ᶜapîrû* men" (EA 85:69-73); *li-de-mì* / *šàr-ru* EN-*ia i-nu-ma* / *iš-tu i-re-bi* ERÍN.MEŠ *pí-ṭá-ti* / *i-te*$_9$*-pu-uš-mì* ^{I}*La-ab-a-yu* / *nu-kúr-ta*$_5$ *i-na mu-uḫ-ḫi-ia* "May the king, my lord, be apprised that, since the army went back (to Egypt), Labᵓayu has made (been making?) war against me!" (EA 244:8-12); *li-ma-ad* / *i-nu-ma iš-tu ka-ša-ad* / ^{I}*A-ma-an-ap-pa a-na mu-ḫi-ia* / *ka-li* LÚ.MEŠ GAZ.MEŠ *na-ad-nu* / *pa-ni-šu-nu a-na ia-ši a-na* / KA*pí-i* ^{I}ÌR-*A-ši-ir*[*-ta*] "Be apprised that, since the coming of Aman-appa to me, all the *ᶜapîrû* men have set their faces against me at the command of ᶜAbdi-Ashirta!" (EA 79:7-12).

Three texts refer to past events that led up to actions being carried out in the present:

[*iš*]*-tu ṣu-ba-at* ^{URU}É-*A*[*r-ḫa*] / [*a-na*] *pí-i* ^{I}ÌR-*A-ši-ir-ta* / [*ù*] *ki-na-na tu-ba-ú-na* / [*i-p*]*é-ša* ^{URU}*Gub-la ù* / ^{URU}*Baṭ-ru-na*^{KI} "Since the seizure of Bīt-A[rḫa] at the command of ᶜAbdi-Ashirta, thus they are seeking to capture Byblos and Baṭrôna" (EA 79:21-25); *ša-ni-tam iš-tu pa-ṭá-ri* / ERÍN.MEŠ LUGAL EN-*li-ia* / *muḫ-ḫi-ia la-a i-na-an-din-ni* / LÚ ^{URU}*Ṣí-du-na* / LÚ.MEŠ-*ia a-ra-da* / *a-na er-ṣé-ti* / *a-na la-qé* GIŠ.MEŠ / *la-qé* A.MEŠ *a-na ši-t*[*i*] "Furthermore, since departure of the troops of the king, my lord, from me, the ruler of Sidon has not been permitting me (and) my men to go down to the land to take wood (and to) take water to drink" (EA 154:11-17); *yi-de* LUGAL *be-li* / *ip-ši ša yi-pu-šu-ni* / ^{I}*Ia-an-ḫa-mu* / *iš-tu a-ṣí-ia* / [*i*]*š-tu mu-ḫi* LUGAL EN-*ia* "May the king, my lord, be apprised of the deeds which Yanḫamu is committing against me since I came forth from the king, my lord!" (EA 270:9-13).

CORRESPONDENT

When the action of the main clause is said to conform or to correspond to some other action, the infinitive dependent on *kīma* is used for the latter (cf. Aro 1961:285-289). For example,

Rib-Haddi of Byblos wants a military contingent like that assigned to Surata of Acco:

> *ù ia-di-na* / 4 ME LÚ.MEŠ 30 *ta-pa[l* A]NŠE.KUR.RA.MEŠ / *ki-ma na-da-ni a-na* [I]*Sú-*⌜*ra*⌝*-*⌜*ta*⌝ "So may he grant four hundred men (and) thirty team[s of h]orses as were given to Surata" (EA 85:19-21; Moran 1987b:269, 270 n. 3)

Note that the subject of the infinitive is not overtly expressed. Thus, one may translate the infinitive as a passive (cf.Moran 1987b:269; 1992:156) or one may assume (correctly in this case) that the subject of the infinitive is identical with that of the main verb. It would, of course, be pharaoh who would make such an assignment of troops, i.e. "just as (he) gave to Surata."

The infinitive may have a different subject from that of the main verb, in which case it may be expressed by a dependent suffix as in the following rhetorical question:

> *ú-ul la-qí* [I]ÌR-*A-ši-ir-ta* / *qa-du mi-im-mi-šu ki-ma qa-bi-ia* "Was not ᶜAbdi-Ashirta captured along with his property, just as I had said?" (EA 117:27-28).

Six passages make reference to the compliance (or non-compliance) with pharaoh's orders. The sender of the letter wishes to affirm that he has obeyed a specific command from the king, e.g.

> *šu-ši-ra-ku gáb-ba ki-ma qa-bi* LUGAL EN-*ia* "I have prepared everything just as the king, my lord, has commanded" (EA 144:21; also EA 193:21-24; 216:10-11; 220:11-14; 323:9-13; 325:20-22).

The ruler of Tyre complained that pharaoh's orders concerning the welfare of his servant have not been carried out. The infinitive employed here, viz. *qabi*, harks back to a finite preterite, *iqbi*, in the previous sentence. The passage in question is as follows:

> LUGAL *iq-bi a-na* ÌR-*šu* [*ù*] / *a-na* ÌR ^{MÍ}*Ma-ia-a-ti* / *a-na na-da-ni še-ḫu ù a-n*[*a*] ‹*na-da-ni*› / A.MEŠ \ *mi-ma a-na ši-te-šu* / *ù la-a i-pu-uš-šu-ni*$_7$ *ki-ma qa-bi* LUGAL *be-li-ia* / *la-a i-na-an-din-nu-ni*$_7$ "The king commanded concerning his servant [and] the servant of Mayati that the breath (of life) be given and that water be given for him to drink; but they have not acted in accordance with the command of the king, my lord; they are not giving to me" (EA 155:7-13; Moran 1987b:390; also EA 155:39).

One or two passages employ *kīma ša* plus the infinitive in the same syntagma:

> *ù a-nu-ma* / *u-še-ši-ru-mì* / *ki-ma ša qa-bi-šu* "And now I am preparing in accordance with what he commanded" (EA 329:18-20; cf. also EA 302:16-18).

www.ingramcontent.com/pod-product-compliance
Lightning Source LLC
Chambersburg PA
CBHW020728160426
43192CB00006B/155